EXCLUSION AND ENGAGEMENT:
SOCIAL POLICY IN LATIN AMERICA

DATE DUE

D0554961

BRODART   Cat. No. 23-221

Exclusion and Engagement: Social Policy in Latin America

Edited by
Christopher Abel and Colin M. Lewis

Institute of Latin American Studies
31 Tavistock Square, London WC1H 9HA
http://www.sas.ac.uk/ilas/publicat.htm

This book has been produced with the financial assistance of the European Community. The views expressed herein are those of the authors and can therefore in no way be taken to reflect the official opinion of the European Community.

Institute of Latin American Studies
School of Advanced Study
University of London

British Library Cataloguing-in-Publication Data
A catalogue record for this book is available
from the British Library

ISBN   1900039 50 8

CONTENTS

vi

Notes on Contributors

Christopher Abel is Senior Lecturer in Latin American History at University College, London, and Associate Fellow of the Institute of Latin American Studies, University of London. His main research interests are in Colombia and the Hispanic Caribbean, together with comparative social policy and the contemporary history of healthcare in Latin America and the Caribbean. He has published two research papers on the history of healthcare with ILAS, London, has co-edited (with Colin M. Lewis) the book *Welfare, Poverty and Development in Latin America*, has authored a chapter on social policy in Latin America for the forthcoming final volume of the UNESCO *General History of Latin America* (ed. M. Palacios), and has contributed a co-authored chapter (with Peter Lloyd-Sherlock) to P. Lloyd-Sherlock (ed.), *Healthcare Reform and Poverty in Latin America* (London, 2000) and a chapter to a volume on social policy edited at FLACSO (Mexico City) by A. Puyana (forthcoming)

Marcial Bóo is Head of Strategy at the British Ministry for Education and Skills, Adult Basic Skills Strategy Unit, established in 2000 to reduce the number of adults in England with poor literacy and numeracy skills. Previously he worked as private secretary to a British Education Minister, and in educational institutions including private sector training providers, universities, teacher training colleges, business schools and, for two years, with the British Council in Ecuador. He is a qualified teacher of literacy and numeracy. His research background is in literacy and linguistics; and he read for the MA Area Studies (Latin America) at ILAS, University of London. He has published, in addition to a work of children's fiction, articles in the *Teacher Trainer*, the *International Journal of Comparative Education* and the *Journal of Latin American Studies*.

Anita Brumer is Professor of Sociology at the Federal University of Rio Grande do Sul (UFRGS), Porto Alegre, Brazil. She holds a first degree in Sociology, an MA in Rural Sociology from the UFRGS and a PhD in Sociology from the Hebrew University of Jerusalem. Her principal recent works include: *Identidade em mudança: pesquisa sociológica sobre os judeus no Rio Grande do Sul* (1994); *Estudos agrários no Brasil: modernização, violência e lutas sociais (desenvolvimento e limites da Sociologia Rural no final do século XX)*, in D.E. Piñeiro (ed.), *30 años de Sociologia Rural en América Latina* (2000); (with J. V. Tavares dos Santos) *Gênero e agricultura: a situação da mulher na agricultura do Rio Grande do Sul* (2000). She was founding editor of *Sociologias* and produced the first two special issues of the journal devoted to *Cidadania e Democracia* (1999) and *Sociedade Civil e Estado Social* (2000).

Claes Brundenius holds a PhD in Development Economics. His research focuses on Latin America (in particular Cuba and the Andean Region) and East Asia (China and Vietnam). At present he is employed as Senior Research Fellow at the Centre for Development Research, Copenhagen, Denmark. He has had a long career in international organisations (OECD and the United Nations) and has taught at Universities in Scandinavia, primarily Lund University, Sweden, and Roskilde University, Denmark. He is currently working on the political economy of globalisation, notably with regard to socialist Third World countries. He has authored and edited several books, the latest of which (edited with J. Weeks) is *Globalization and Third-World Socialism: Cuba and Vietnam* (2001). Earlier books on Cuba include *Revolutionary Cuba: The Challenge of Economic Growth with Equity* (1984) and (edited with A. Zimbalist) *The Cuban Economy: Measurement and Analysis of Socialist Performance* (1989).

Sylvia Chant is Professor in Geography at the London School of Economics and Associate Fellow of the Institute of Latin American Studies, University of London. She has worked in Costa Rica, Mexico and the Philippines on a range of issues relating to gender and development, including migration, poverty, employment, household survival strategies, lone parenthood and men and masculinities. Recent publications include *Women-Headed Households: Diversity and Dynamics in the Developing World* (1997), (with C. McIlwaine) *Three Generations, Two Genders, One World: Women and Men in a Changing Century* (1998) and (with M. Gutmann) *Mainstreaming Men into Gender and Development: Debates, Reflections and Experiences* (2000). She is currently writing up the results of a research project on Costa Rica entitled *Youth, Gender and 'Family Crisis'* and is working on a book on gender in Latin America with N. Craske.

Pascual Gerstenfeld is Director of the Uruguayan Office of the UN-Economic Commission for Latin America and the Caribbean and Co-ordinator and co-author of ECLAC´s annual publication *Social Panorama of Latin America*. He has published extensively on social policy and social conditions. A former Principal Expert of the Social Development Division at ECLAC headquarters, in Santiago de Chile, he is Professor of the Universidad Internacional de Andalucía, Spain, where he teaches on the Master's Programme. He has previously taught at universities in Chile, Uruguay and elsewhere in Latin America, offering postgraduate degree courses on social and economic policy and economic development. He is also a former advisor to the presidency of the Central Bank of Uruguay, and a consultant to several international organizations.

Alan Gilbert is Professor of Geography at University College London, currently working on housing subsidies in Chile, Colombia and South Africa, on the influence of Washington on the diffusion of knowledge about development policy, on secondary housing markets in Colombia and South Africa, on residential segregation in Rio de Janeiro and on the impact of globalisation on urban life in Latin America. He has published extensively on these and related topics in numerous learned journals and co-edited collections. His most recent books are *In Search of a Home* (1993) and *The Latin American City* (1998). In the last ten years, he has received major research grants from the Department for International Development, the Economic and Social Research Council and the United Nations University, and has acted as an adviser to several international institutions, including the Inter-American Development Bank, the United Nations Centre for Human Settlements (HABITAT), the United Nations University, UNESCO, United Nations Population Fund, the Woodrow Wilson Center and the World Bank.

John Gledhill is Max Gluckman Professor of Social Anthropology at the University of Manchester and taught previously at University College, London. He is co-managing editor of the journal *Critique of Anthropology*. He has carried out ethnographic research on both indigenous and non-indigenous communities in Mexico, in the states of Michoacán and Chiapas, with a focus on social movements, local politics, political economy and transnational migration, and also published extensively on broader historical, comparative and theoretical issues in anthropology. He is the author of *Power and its Disguises: Anthropological Perspectives on Politics* (1994), *Neoliberalism, Transnationalization and Rural Poverty: a Case Study of Michoacán, Mexico* (1995) and *Casi Nada: Agrarian Reform in the Homeland of Cardenismo* (2001). He has recently contributed articles to *Anthropology Today*, *Anthropology in Action* and *Identities: Global Studies in Culture and Power*.

Maria Cristina Gomes da Conceição studied at the Faculty of Medicine, Federal University at Rio de Janeiro (UFRJ) and took a Masters at FLACSO, Mexico. Most recently she has received a PhD in Population Studies from El Colegio de México. Her areas of research include ageing and social security, the economics of family life-cycles, and international migration, variously sponsored by the Oswaldo Cruz Foundation, Brazil, the Central Workers Union (CUT), Brazil, and the Population Council, Mexico. She has co-edited *Social Processes, Population and Domestic Space – Theoretical and Empirical Alternatives in Family Research* (2001) and has contributed chapters and articles to various books and journals in Portuguese and Spanish, for example *Revista da ABEP* and *Científica Nacional*.

Merilee S. Grindle is the Edward S. Mason Professor of International Development at the Kennedy School of Government at Harvard University. A political scientist with a PhD from MIT, she specialises in the comparative analysis of policymaking, implementation and public management in developing countries, focusing especially on the politics of policy and institutional reform. Although she has also done research in East Africa, her particular area of interest is Latin America. She is the author of many books, including *State and Countryside: Development Policy and Agrarian Politics in Latin America* (1986), *Searching for Rural Development: Labour Migration and Employment in Mexico* (1988), *Challenging the State: Crisis and Innovation in Latin America and Africa* (1996) and numerous articles about policy and politics. Among other collaborative works, she is editor of *Getting Good Government: Capacity-Building in the Public Sectors of Developing Countries* (1997) and co-author (with J. Thomas) of *Public Choices and Policy Change: the Political Economy of ReformiIn Developing Countries* (1991). Her most recent book is *Audacious Reforms: Institutional Invention and Democracy in Latin America* (2001). Currently, she is working on the politics of education policy reform in Latin America.

Nuria Homedes is a medical doctor and holds a PhD in public health. She is an Associate Professor at the School of Public Health, University of Texas-Houston. Previously she worked for the Rural Health Office at the University of Arizona, School of Medicine, and the World Bank. She is the co-editor of *Boletín Farmacos*, an electronic journal promoting the adequate use of pharmaceuticals. Her fields of interest are health and pharmaceutical policies and compliance with medical regimens. She has done extensive research in Mexico, Peru, Bolivia, Dominican Republic, Colombia, Guyana, Panama, Honduras and Costa Rica, as well as working in Mozambique, Chad and Papua New Guinea. She is currently studying health reform in Latin America.

Colin M. Lewis is Senior Lecturer in Latin American Economic History at the London School of Economics and Political Science and Associate Fellow of the Institute of Latin American Studies, University of London. He has undertaken research on British investment in Latin America, patterns of industrial growth and industrialisation and Latin American business history. Currently, he is working on issues related to social policy (particularly social insurance) and state-formation in the Argentine. His most recent co-edited publications include *Welfare, Poverty and Development in Latin America* (with C. Abel, 1993) and *Argentina in the Crisis Years (1983–1990)* (with N. Torrents, 1993). He has contributed 'The Economics of the Latin American State: Ideology, Policy and Performance, 1820–1945' to D.A.

Smith, D.J. Solinger and S.C. Topik (eds.), *States and Sovereignty in the Global Economy* (1999) and 'Argentina' to J. Buxton and N. Phillips (eds.), *Case Studies in Latin American Political Economy* (1999).

Peter Lloyd-Sherlock is a Lecturer in Social Development at the School of Development Studies, University of East Anglia. He has previously held lectureships at the London School of Hygiene and Tropical Medicine and the University of Glasgow. He has published the following books: *Old Age and Poverty in the Developing World: the Shanty Towns of Buenos Aires* (1997); (ed.) *Healthcare Reform and Poverty in Latin America* (2000); and (with P. Johnson, eds.) *Ageing and Social Policy: Global Comparisons* (1996). His main research interests are social policy in Latin America, health sector reform and policy responses to population ageing. He has carried out research projects in Argentina, Brazil, Thailand and South Africa. With C.M. Lewis he has written a review of social insurance systems in the Argentine and Brazil.

Rubén M. Lo Vuolo was trained as an Economist in the Argentine (Universidad Nacional del Litoral) and the USA (University of Pittsburgh). He is Senior Research Officer at the Interdisciplinary Centre for the Study of Public Policy (CIEPP), Buenos Aires, teaches at various universities in the Argentine and is an advisor to ECLAC, IDB, UNICEF and other international agencies. He has been a Visiting Professor at the University of Notre Dame (USA) and at the Institut des Hautes Études de L'Amérique Latine, Université de la Sorbonne Nouvelle – PARIS III. His co-authored books include: *El estado de bienestar: un paradigma en crisis* (1991); *La modernización excluyente: transformación económica y estado de bienestar en Argentina* (1992); *Contra la exclusión: la propuesta del ingreso ciudadano* (1995); *La nueva oscuridad de la política social: del estado populista al neoconservador* (1998); *La pobreza ... de la política contra la pobreza* (1999). He has also published extensively on poverty, social policy and state models in learned journals.

Andrew Nickson is Reader in Public Management and Latin American Development at the International Development Department of the School of Public Policy, University of Birmingham. His recent research in Latin America has focused on the policy transfer of New Public Management and private sector participation in urban water supply. His publications include: *The New Public Management in Latin America* (2001); *Local Government in Latin America* (1995); *Paraguay: an Annotated Bibliography* (1999); and (co-edited with P. Lambert) *The Transition to Democracy in Paraguay* (1997). Amongst his recent articles and research papers are 'Contratos de concesión en América Latina y su paralelo explicativo en

Gran Bretaña', in F. Delgadino (ed.), *Gestión, regulación y control de servicios públicos* (2000); 'Does the NPM Work in Less Developed Countries? The Case of the Urban Water Supply Sector', *Journal of International Development* (1999); and 'Building Municipal Capacity for Private Sector Participation Series' (Working paper no. 442 03. DFID). He is an advisor to the Department for International Development (London), the European Union, the World Bank and various UN agencies. From 1992–98 he directed a European Union training programme for senior public administrators in Latin America, and from 1999–2000 he was seconded to the post of Director of a European Union Project for State Reform in Paraguay.

Alicia Puyana was educated in Bogotá and Prague before taking a DPhil in Economics at the University of Oxford. She is currently professor in Economics at the Facultad Latinoamericana de Ciencias Sociales (FLAC-SO), Mexico. Her most recent publications include (with R. Thorp) *Colombia: la economía política de las explotaciones petrolíferas* (2000); (with J. Boltvinik) *Reformas macroeconómicas en América Latina y sus efectos sobre los niveles de pobreza* (1995); and 'The Campaign Against Absolute Poverty in Colombia: an Evaluation of Liberal Social Policy' in C. Abel and C.M. Lewis (eds.), *Welfare, Poverty and Development in Latin America* (1993). She has also published on comparative questions of oil and development and employment in Latin America. She has conducted research at, and on behalf of, various non-profit-making foundations, the Andean Pact and other international bodies, and served as an advisor on domestic and international issues to the Mexican and Colombian governments

Bryan R. Roberts is C.B. Smith Sr. Centennial Chair in US–Mexico Relations and Professor of Sociology at the University of Texas–Austin. He obtained a PhD at the University of Chicago and has previously taught at the University of Manchester. His many books include: *Organising Strangers: Poor Families in Guatemala City* (1973); *The Making of Citizens: Cities of Peasants Revisited* (1995); (with N. Long) *Miners, Peasants and Entrepreneurs: Regional Development in the Central Highlands of Peru* (1984); and (co-edited with R.G. Cushing and C. Wood) *The Sociology of Development in Latin America* (1995). In addition, he has edited and co-edited special issues of the *American Journal of Sociology* and other learned journals. His varied research interests, conducted in Mexico, Central America and the Andes, embrace: urbanisation, migration development; peasants and agrarian structures; urban welfare and changing work patterns; and informal employment.

Ernesto Schiefelbein holds a doctorate in Education from Harvard University and is currently President of Universidad Santo Tomás, Santiago de Chile. A former Chilean Minister of Education, he was sometime Director of the UNESCO Regional Office of Education for Latin America and the Caribbean, head of the UNESCO Regional Information System in Latin America and the Caribbean and Educational Economist in the World Bank. He was also Co-ordinator of the Red Latinoamericana de Documentación en Educación, Senior Researcher in the Centro de Investigación y Desarrollo de la Educación, Educational Planner for the Programa Regional del Empleo, ILO-PREALC, and a visiting professor at Harvard. Among his many books are: *Development of Educational Planning Models* (1974); *The Determinants of School Achievement*, (1979); *Education Costs and Financing Policies in Latin America* (1987); *Education in the Americas* (1998); and *Cost-effectiveness of Educational Policies in Latin America* (1998).

Paulina Schiefelbein is a Researcher at the Centro de Investigación y Desarrollo de la Educación (CIDE). Previously, she was Assistant Researcher in the Corporación de Promoción Universitaria (CPU). Having obtained a Licenciatura in Education, she studied vocational education in Berufsakademie, Karlsruhe, Germany. For CIDE, she is currently evaluating the Mentes Activas project on the teaching of mathematics in Chilean high schools. She has co-authored and contributed to: *Education in the Americas: Quality, Equity and Citizenship* (1997); *Formadores de profesores en siete países de América Latina* (1998); *Cost-Effectiveness of Education Policies in Latin América* (1998); *Slow Learning in Development Co-operation to Latin American Education* (2000); *El costo-efectividad de las políticas de educación primaria en América Central, Panamá y República Dominicana* (2000); and *Three Decentralisation Strategies in Two Decades: Chile 1981–2000* (2000). She has been a consultant for UNESCO, OAS, OEI and UNDP.

Antonio Ugalde is Professor of Sociology at the University of Texas–Austin and holds an adjunct professorship at the School of Public Health, University of Texas–Houston. His interests are in the area of health policies, North–South relations and social change. His principal recent publications include: (co-edited with A. Zwi) *Violencia, salud y política en América Latina* (1994); (with J.T. Jackson) 'The World Bank and International Health Policy: a Critical Review', *Journal of International Development* (1995); and 'Un acercamiento teórico a la participación comunitaria en la atención de la salud', in E.L. Menéndez (ed.), *Participación social: metodología, problemas y expectativas – el caso de Nicaragua, 1978–89* (1999). He is co-editor of the electronic journal, *Boletín Farmacos*, member of the advisory board of *Social Science and Medicine, Cuadernos Médico-Sociales* (Argentina) and *Medical Science Monitor.* He has been a visiting professor at the Universidad del Valle (Cali), UCA (San Salvador), the Escuela Andaluza de Salud Pública (Granada) and the University of Pittsburgh. He has been a consultant for WHO, UNDP, USAID, the World Bank and other international organisations.

Miguel Urrutia was educated at Harvard University and the University of California at Berkeley and has taught at the Universidad de los Andes and at the Universidad Nacional, both in Bogotá. He has served on the Board of Directors of the Banco de la República, Bogotá, and has been its Governor since 1993. A former Minister of Mines and Energy and Director of the National Planning Department, he was twice Executive Director of FEDESARROLLO, Bogotá, and was Manager of the Economic and Social Development Department of the Inter-American Bank. His publications include: *The Development of the Colombian Labor Movement* (1969); *Winners and Losers in Colombia's Economic Growth of the 1970s,* (1985); and co-edited (with A. Berry) *Income Distribution in Colombia* (1975); (with S. Yukawa) *Development Planning in Mixed Economics* (1988); (with S.Yukawa) *Economic Development Policies in Resource-Rich Countries,* (1988); and (with S. Ichimura and S. Yukawa) *The Political Economy of Fiscal Policy* (1989). He also edited *Financial Liberalization and the Internal Structure of Capital Markets in Asia and Latin America* (1988).

Anthony Zwi obtained his PhD in South Africa before training in epidemiology, public health and international health at the London School of Hygiene and Tropical Medicine (LSHTM). He co-edited (with J. Macrae) *War and Hunger: Rethinking International Responses to Complex Emergencies* (1994). He has also co-edited special issues of various journals: on health policy and developing countries (with A. Mills) for *Journal of International Development,* on political violence and health in the Third World (with A. Ugalde) for *Social Science and Medicine* and on health, apartheid and the frontline states (with N. Anderson and S. Marks) for *Social Science and Medicine.* He has contributed 'Injuries, Inequalities and Health: from Policy Vacuum to Policy Action' to D.A. Leon and G. Walt (eds.), *Poverty, Inequality, and Health: an International Perspective* (2001). Between 1995 and 2001, he was senior editor of *Health Policy, Social Science and Medicine.* He has long-standing interests in the impact of conflict upon health and health systems. Recently he has studied public health and health systems during humanitarian crises and periods of instability, the links between globalisation and policy transfer in health, and interactions between communities, policy-makers, academics and NGOs.

List of Tables

List of Figures

Acknowledgements

This book is the product of a Conference of the same title held by the Institute of Latin American Studies, University of London, in March 2001. The Conference followed a successful series of Study Groups under ILAS auspices which met informally over several years. The aim of both Conference and Study Groups was to investigate social policy debates and practices in Latin America.

The editors have numerous debts not all of which can be recorded here. Members of the Study Groups, notably Maxine Molyneux and Jim Thomas, played an important part in shaping the content and direction of the project. The Study Groups established the conceptual and intellectual framework for the Conference. Both examined definitions of social policy, explored connexions between theoretical and empirical issues and stressed the salience of ideas in policy formulation, execution and appraisal. The Study Groups and Conference underscored the importance of comparative analysis, embracing local, national and international dimensions.

The editors are grateful to chairs and discussants for their substantial intellectual contributions and their active part in the evolution of the project.[1] The role of academic and administrative staff at the Institute was indispensable. James Dunkerley gave warm encouragement throughout and, with Tony Bell, was instrumental in securing funding from the European Commission. Olga Jiménez displayed a consistent commitment to the success of the Conference (and book), and was responsible for its smooth organisation. John Maher has been most helpful in preparing the manuscript and artwork, and has demonstrated considerable forbearance in handling the idiosyncrasies of the editors. Without the generous assistance of the European Commission, the ambitious scope of the Conference and book could not have been realised.

CA & CML

---

[1] The chairs and discussants were: Armando Barrientos, James Dunkerley, Anthony Hall, David Howard, Gareth A. Jones, Barbara McPake, Shula Marks, Donny Meertens, Nicola Miller, Maxine Molyneux, Sheila Page, Francisco Panizza, Wil G. Pansters, Allyson Pollock and Leslie Sklair.

Preface

Why has social reform come to the fore? How far is the reform agenda being driven by 'globalised' expectations? And how far by over-generalised cross-country analyses and off-the-peg prescriptions advanced by near-hegemonic Washington agencies? It is a truism, though not one that can be avoided, that Latin America is the continent of greatest inequality. Three brutal questions arise. First, is social policy no more than a tool for managing the endemic crisis caused by sharp inequalities rather than a means of resolving and removing them? Secondly, can significant changes be achieved without a root-and-branch reform of the state at all levels? Thirdly, given the widespread, utopian assumption that political will alone can resolve fundamental problems, is the construction of powerful coalitions necessary to the transformation of ponderous, often patronage-ridden, structures?

The scale of the challenges confronting Latin America presents opportunities for a long overdue reappraisal of social policy. What are its functions and what are the prospects of it performing a new and more dynamic role? To what extent is asset redistribution a prerequisite for the construction of a progressive social policy; and how far is structural reform a precondition of broad-based support for the policy agenda of the progressive state? It has to be acknowledged that the meaning of 'social policy' has shifted over time: from an aspiration to an applied strategy, and then to embrace notions of social trust and social reciprocity and, most recently, social capital. Social policies have not been able to remove inequity; nor, until recently, have they addressed the problems of poverty and informality directly. As applied strategy, social policy has come to involve education, health, social security and housing. This does not exclude pressing issues of justice and crime, which, though conventionally excluded from definitions of social policy, are salient where questions of law and legality impinge upon everyday experience of social policy delivery. Nor does it overlook the urgency of environmental and ecological issues.

How dynamic is social policy, and how stable? To what extent are 'transitional' arrangements and temporary expedients acquiring an unstable permanence? Growth and the outcome of growth require the formulation of flexible social strategies that take account of mobility and shifting constituencies. For too long social policy has been treated as adjunct to political organisation and strategies of economic development. Examining social policy in its own right, from several disciplinary perspectives, this book starts from the premise that health, education, housing and social security connect with debates about poverty, equity, informality and distribution. These areas also intersect with discussions about policy over-extension, about rhetoric versus delivery and about state outreach, features that have often been advanced to explain past policy failures. Various issues arise: were social policies capable of reducing or removing inequity, or even designed to do so? Does the sequence of social programmes suggest a false linear progression from measures setting out to alleviate poverty and inequity to projects designed to reduce them, and then to strategies intended to abolish them?

The current debate about policy hinges on state competence and the machinery of government. Concerns about democratisation converge with discussion about which layer of the state is most suited to social policy provision – the centre, the province or the municipality. Reflecting shifts in ideology, this debate interacts, in turn, with other considerations about the appropriateness of the public and the private sectors for policy implementation and their efficiency. Should the state exercise a monopoly in the provision of social public goods; or is the private sector equally – or – more competent? The 'easy stage' of social policy expansion between the 1950s and 1970s was left behind as rising expectations, external pressures and costly technological change combined to require more complex and sophisticated approaches to policy delivery. Three examples illustrate essential changes in the parameters of social policy: transitions from a focus on public sanitation and hygiene and preventive campaigns against contagious diseases to the provision of well-equipped tertiary hospitals and networks of public health posts; from an emphasis on basic primary education to concerns about the availability of secondary schools and universities; and from a stress on Bismarckian social insurance to more comprehensive systems of assistance.

Projects for state reform, in part associated with a perceived need for institutional upgrading in order to cope with the complexity of social provision, appear contradictory. Reform can involve simultaneous tendencies to decentralisation and centralisation, which need not be mutually exclusive. Decentralising spending and delivery necessitate monitoring and target-setting, raising the question of which part of the bureaucracy is charged with which process and function. An additional complication is a legacy of the 1960s and 1970s, namely, high levels of turnover of ministers and officials in social policy administration, and a propensity to create new agencies whose functions duplicated and overlapped those of unreformed existing bodies. Many proponents of devolving power to provinces and municipalities have underestimated endemic weaknesses of local government in Latin America, notably, low municipal tax bases, pervasive clientelism and scarcity of well-trained personnel. These problems have been compounded by recent decisions of resource-starved central states to push further responsibilities onto the localities without a corresponding increase in funding. Moreover, the central state has retreated in some areas, but not in those it considers most important. Effective decentralisation implies budgetary 'deconcentration' with accountability. It also requires a well-motivated civil service and local officials open to, but not colonised by, society and responsive to goals and priorities that are democratically formulated. Market-style social policy reform has largely benefited the middle class, contrary to stated goals of universality. New arrangements for private healthcare, private education and private pensions are beyond the reach of the very poor, as corporate providers have come to accept. Despite the traumatic impact of dogmatic anti-statism in the era of adjustment, new thinking postulates that the state remains imperative to the task of poverty alleviation.

Although the literature on state reform has stressed democratisation as a goal, the main thrust of state reform in many instances has been allocative and productive efficiency, rather than an attempt to address the 'democratic deficit'. At the local level, young professionals and other citizens politicised by neighbourhood experiences of authoritarianism, recession, and the appearance of a state overwhelmed by the process of reform, have boldly challenged bureaucratic inertia and incompetence and demanded change. An open recognition of past state failure constitutes a substantial advance. Yet a 'failed' public sector is now being expected to implement and monitor reform, and also to extend and improve the regulatory framework needed to supervise an enlarged private sector. Such changes are consistent with a new public management structure that is charged with overseeing transitions from economic reactivation to 'social regeneration', moves from the state as direct provider to the state as strategic conductor, and shifts from appraising input data to assessing outcomes. Currently too little is expected of the public sector.

The nature of the relationship between economic strategy and social policy has been under constant re-evaluation over the past two decades. How is this to be explained? How far is it driven from below, in particular, and how far by social configurations created and recreated by successive economic crises since the early 1970s? How far was re-evaluation the upshot of an internationalisation of policy prescriptions emanating from Washington, elements of which were 'captured' by the domestic policy-making establishment committed to market reform? And how far was reappraisal consequent upon the reciprocal engagement of national and foreign interests? Explanations of policy change as either a top-down or bottom-up process, or as either externally imposed or domestically conceived often fail to take into account the difficulty of disentangling both causality and process. Such explanations also neglect the recent globalisation of aspiration associated with the empowerment of many poor communities.

The contention that social policy has been employed to legitimise the state may be reversed. Political and ideological aspects of state legitimacy can strengthen social policy and social action, even during periods of economic crisis. This raises the question of whether social policy practitioners see themselves as managers of economic strategy. Whereas, in the early 1990s, debate revolved around rolling back the state, some ten years later issues of welfare and equity are back on the agenda. What vision of 'the good society' prevails, and how is it to be realised? Recognising the vigour and vitality of social capital, what balance should be struck between competitive individualism and a new collectivism?

How is the social policy agenda set, and by whom shaped? How much significance should be attached to both social movements and pressure groups, especially non-governmental organisations (NGOs) and community-based organisations (CBOs), and how much to institutional structures, notably executive power and political parties? Who sustains the policy agenda: policy-makers or policy beneficiaries, the included or the excluded, or alliances of them? Processes of democratisation have demonstrated the importance of building 'reform constituencies' and persuading elites to accept reformist projects in the public interest. Social policy is too often discussed as if it were a neutral, technocratic activity. Effective social policy can be achieved only by 'bringing politics back into the frame', acknowledging that many initiatives are highly contentious and the arena of policy-making adversarial. Popular mobilisation is indispensable: no mobilisation, no action. Agenda-setting constitutes only a part of the process. A culture of accountability, the empowerment of policy consumers and an ethos of efficiency are vital to sustaining agenda delivery. This can be done by formalising the decision-making process and making it more accessible to reform constituencies and society at large. At each stage, from policy design via policy implementation to monitoring policy outcome, civil society must assume a role in extending and embedding the process.

Social policies have neither removed inequity nor substantially reduced poverty. Was poverty eradication ever a firm objective of policy? In the 1960s and the 1970s ambitious packages of 'modernisation and social progress' encountered systematic obstruction in legislatures, courts and the media, and in several countries met with violent resistance and count-er-mobilisation. Reforms were diluted by bureaucratic inertia, incompe-tence and under-funding, and were hijacked by professionals acting in sec-tional and individual interests. Outcomes were limited by an intrusive, top-down approach that took little cognisance of priorities on the ground. Can a similar pattern of opposition and obstruction be identified in the current conjuncture? The new social policy model (NSM) presumes two crucial transitions: from a narrow concern about cost reduction to the creation of a culture promoting quality enhancement, and from an emphasis on the better use of resources to a substantial increase in funding. Are these key transitions being accomplished, frustrated or aborted?

The urgency of a new social contract between state and citizen is appar-ent. Consolidating a reform alliance should raise expectations, increase social revenue, improve delivery and make regulation more effective. Latin American societies are under-taxed, and the burden of taxation notoriously inequitable. Gloomy expectations of social policy derive from the view that macroeconomic stability can be achieved only by reducing expenditure, low-ering the quality of services and better resource management. Why not solve the fiscal deficit by increased, progressive taxation? The optimal solution posited by neoliberals is that tax policy should be neutral. Neutral taxation during periods of growth and recession simply perpetuates – or exacerbates – social inequalities, nullifying any hope of social transformation.

Will a progressive social policy bring about asset redistribution, or is asset redistribution necessary for social reform? Can a progressive policy deliver social equity, or is progressive taxation a prerequisite of social progress? Perhaps an unstated assumption prevails in some quarters that a transition from neo-populism to social democracy is necessary. Multilateral agencies, which are technically not committed to any particular regime type, are pre-vented from making the case for such a transition explicit, and acknowledge that the main impetus for change must come from democratic forces with-in Latin America. Yet, it is unlikely that such changes can be achieved with-out both a reduction in the power of the Washington agencies and anti-reform elements, along with the restoration of the influence of internation-al and domestic organisations committed to an explicitly social agenda.

Current debate has been more concerned with prescribing how citi-zenship should be understood than with analysing how it has been conceived and articulated. Over time, citizenship rights and obligations have been invested with different meanings and practices, and distinct models of citizenship have competed for acceptance. Recently, questions of social rights and the social empowerment of the individual and communities have acquired prominence. Much of the literature fails to recognise that exclusion implies social membership and presupposes the existence of a society. How far have the cultural politics of nation building and market formation in Latin America served to create unity, incorporating indigenous peoples and immigrants in the nation-state? Has citizenship become more inclusive? For whom does social membership remain an issue, and of which society – the nation as a whole, the ethnic or religious community, or neighbourhood groups? Overlooking the likelihood of diverse political outcomes, the multilateral agencies advocate strategies of grass-roots democratisation, which, they contend, will promote participation, accountability and containment. To what extent is this position at odds with an insistence on market economics – a 'one-size-fits-all' approach? The debates and concepts outlined here are not mere abstractions, embodying, as they do, deep-rooted traditions of citizenship and evolving forms of civic action.

Conflicting assumptions and processes are at work. A rhetoric of liberating society from the state is often being expounded in circumstances where a state barely exists, save in juridical form. Additional demands are being placed on the 'reformed', decentralised state as a consequence of the public debate about citizenship rights and resultant rising expectations. Implicit in struggles for modernity and modernisation is the view that state and society are distinct and in conflict. Yet it can be argued that the exercise of citizenship connects society and state. States have a role in the formation of communities and social solidarity configures the state.

PART A:
CONCEPTS, MODELS AND PRACTICE

CHAPTER 1

Exclusion and Engagement:
A Diagnosis of Social Policy in Latin America in the Long Run

Christopher Abel and Colin M. Lewis

The New Social Policy is critical for sustaining consensus about economic strategy and political democracy. The aims of this chapter are to place contemporary social policy in a long-term historical perspective, to consider the connection between growth and welfare and to scrutinise debates about the efficacy of the state in the social sphere from both macro and micro perspectives. The chapter opens with an exploration of citizenship — its meaning, practice and significance — and raises contentious questions about inclusion and exclusion. The concept of active citizenship pervades argument about political, civil, social and economic rights and underscores processes of democratic consolidation in a remodelled state. The next section establishes the institutional and ideological framework in which social policy is formulated and applied. The administrative fabric and economic resources at the disposal of the state condition policy implementation and outcome. The state in Latin America has played a powerful role in shaping and strengthening markets and ordering society. This section contends that the emergence and growth of markets, the nature of state intervention and private-public relationships have — and have had — a profound impact on welfare and levels of access to social goods. The third section analyses the significance of economic activity and the administration of social expenditure for patterns of distribution and the dimensions of poverty. The section also charts the expansion, retrenchment and allocation of social spending, and assesses the efficiency of resource delivery by evaluating the competence of public and private management. The fourth section investigates equity and its interactions with education and employment. It stresses the role of education as the key to equitable development and empowerment, inquires into the impact of ideology upon education and welfare strategy, and emphasises the relationship between sustainable social expenditure and a robust fiscal policy. The section goes on to appraise the positive and negative connotations of measures to foster labour market integration and deregulation, notably their impact upon the informal sector. Defining equity has proved as problematic as defining poverty — both absolute and relative. The penultimate section looks at anti-poverty measures from 'above' and survival and self-defence strategies from 'within'; that is, policy devised by the state and action shaped by the community and the household, both rural and urban, to achieve solidarity in the face of indifference, discrimination and violence. The section considers too the role of Non-Governmental Organisations (NGOs) and their links with grassroots mobilisations, social movements and Community Based Organisations (CBOs). Communities and households have changed significantly over time, as have their interactions with the state — not least in areas of housing, health and social goods. The evolution of social capital networks is critical to the promotion of equity and intergenerational justice. The concluding section reflects upon the importance of constructing a durable model of social liberalism and a framework that departs from treating social policy as an adjunct to economic strategy and as a political expedient. Throughout, the chapter argues strongly for a pragmatic openness to experimentation in the formulation and execution of social policy that involves the entire citizenry.

Citizenship

Much current debate revolves around citizenship and the role of the state in giving effect to universal principles and abstract ideas of rights. A Weberian consensus prevails amongst scholars who stress the centrality of a vigorous urban society to the evolution of citizenship involving rights but conformed by power. Most commentators question how far citizenship is a universal concept and how far the product of a specific conjuncture of structural conditions peculiar to the industrialised West. The stage-model of T.H. Marshall, much criticised for its Whiggishness but widely admired for its clarity, outlined in the mid-twentieth century the evolution of British citizen rights and placed a valuable stress on a notion of social citizenship whose main ingredient was the welfare state.[1] For Marshall social citizenship was a means of redistributing resources to protect the needy in hard times against the vagaries of markets and the inequalities of the class system. But, while collectivist in principle, citizenship was founded upon individual obligations to contribute taxes that funded welfare provision, and thus shored up individual obligations and rights.

---

[1]   Marshall (1950).

The political culture of the USA has been rich in discourse on political and civil citizenship, but has contributed little to debate on social citizenship.[2] The civil rights movement was never complemented by a social rights movement. Kenneth L. Karst has sought to resolve the liberal conundrum that citizenship is founded upon equality in the law and the manifest reality of a society characterised by massive inequalities that influence access to law and give rise to variations in the quality of justice. Concerned that the ideal of equal citizenship should foster national consciousness and national community, Karst has, in a context where welfare dependence erodes self-respect because individualistic expectations of self-provision by families are normative, promoted the notion of a principle of equal citizenship. This, he argues, should focus upon inequalities likely to stigmatise, demoralise and impair effective participation in society. He pleads for serious judicial inquiry when inequalities undermine the foundations for assuming the responsibilities of citizenship and the legislative and executive branches of government turn a blind eye.[3] The writings of Karst prefigured a renewed interest in De Tocqueville, whose appeals to decentralisation, community and civic engagement have a wide resonance. De Tocqueville's warnings against 'big government' attract the right; and his concern about the sacrifice of national wellbeing to 'commercial passions' and 'industrial interests' commands the attention of the left.

The origins of citizenship in Hispanic America can perhaps be located in traditions of municipal resistance and immunities observed in the late colonial period, and, in a reassuringly Weberian manner, in the urban militias that proliferated during struggles for independence in the early nineteenth century.[4] Simón Bolívar acknowledged concepts of liberty, virtue, public opinion and moral power while lamenting the weight of absolutism and the 'dismemberments' of the new republics.[5] Citizenship was hotly debated between the 1820s and 1920s in numerous constituent assemblies and constitutional texts and in clashes between executive, legislature and judiciary. The wide diffusion of notions of citizenship was evident in the formation, from the mid-nineteenth century, of enduring political parties in some countries, together with political clubs and *tertulias*. It can also be seen in national guards and conscript armies which integrated peasants

2   Fraser and Gordon (1994).

3   Karst (1989), pp. 140–1.

4   Mallon (1995); McFarlane and Posada-Carbó (1998).

5   McFarlane (1998).

into political life and volunteer groups of colonist-farmers fighting for particular causes.[6] Notions of citizenship were further manifest in federalist resistance to centralising projects, in voting patterns and recurrent discussion about the composition of the franchise, and in resort to the courts by people of humble origins.[7] Unlike large parts of central and eastern Europe, concepts of citizenship were deeply embedded in the public celebrations, the cult of patriotic heroes and the popular cultures of several Latin American countries.

How narrowly construed was citizenship? Can sequences of openings and closures of access to citizenship be identified? Conservatives and Liberals debated who were the better patriots, the link between security of property and citizenship, and the compatibility of citizenship and privilege.[8] Argument about who and what make a 'good citizen' was a standard theme in the discourse on education, criminology and prison reform conducted by such intellectuals as Bello, Santander, Sarmiento, Martí and Vasconcelos.[9] Numerous public protests, demonstrations and tumults, market place oratory and 'signature campaigns', the circulation of newspapers and tracts, and intense electoral competition attested to the existence of a vitality of political life although the formal electorate was small.[10] Sporadic debate about accommodating indigenous peoples, ex-slaves, and immigrants from Europe and Asia within the polity (or their exclusion from it) further testifies to the vigour of civic culture. However, a stress on the virtues and responsibilities of citizenship obscured class and racial differences, and masked a reticence in moving towards universal male suffrage in countries with large indigenous and black populations. Powerful negative official images of blacks and Amerindians, that were rooted in the Iberian invasion and rationalised by the Enlightenment, were reinvigorated by the 'scientific' weight attributed to them during the positivist ascendancy.[11] Yet, even within regimes of 'democratic fiction', growing numbers of men adhered to, and argued for, an 'individual-citizen model' of public freedoms.[12] Gloomy reflections on presidential autocra-

---

6   Safford (2000).

7   Posada-Carbó (1995); Peloso and Tenenbaum (1996); Zimmermann (1999).

8   Ivereigh (2000).

9   Salvatore and Aguirre (1996); N. Miller (1999).

10   Annino (1995); Posada-Carbó (1996); Pineo and Baer (1998); Sabato (1999).

11   Solberg (1970); R. Graham (1989); Cooper, Holt and Scott (2000).

12   Guerra (1994).

cy and parliamentary oligarchy sustained by local caciques, regular armies and ballot rigging during formal elections are qualified by cautious optimism regarding the public ritual and civic liturgy of classical republicanism. These ideas and processes suggest an assumption that civic and civil rights could exist in the absence of formal political rights and that participation in politics was possible even for those lacking the franchise.

The acquisition — and uninterrupted exercise of — formal citizenship rights is of recent origin across Latin America. So too is the assumption that all people are to be treated as bearers of rights. Whereas a wide range of individuals and groups aspired to citizenship in the early decades of the twentieth century, and some achieved it, at mid-century formal citizenship rights remained discretionary in many countries and suspended in others. Assumptions from the era of export-led growth of a steady progress towards broader political citizenship had proved unjustified, while the boundaries of citizenship were demonstrably permeable. Women, for example, might be granted the franchise by a regime that never held elections. Liberal democracy and active citizenship were challenged in the 1930s and 1940s by a revival of Catholic corporatism and early manifestations of populism that placed the state above society and the group before the individual. Perhaps the crisis of philanthropy funding during the World Depression provided an opening for the state and advocates of a more active social role for government. Later, efforts to forge and strengthen representative democracy were thwarted by 'proto-plebiscitary' populism that offered the promise of economic development and a welfare state, along with conditional social rights and selective incorporation in place of open political contest.[13] Concepts of political citizenship were undermined and its exercise brutally curtailed during the neo-authoritarian cycle of the 1960s and 1970s. Paradoxically, notions of social rights (influenced both by Bismarckian pragmatism and Beveridgian idealism) gathered impetus during populist and authoritarian regimes, and evolved into a 'model' of social citizenship that was included in the bundle of civic rights central to re-democratisation.[14] 'Delegative democracy' of the 1990s, epitomised by the governments of Menem in the Argentine and Fujimori in Peru, echoed features of the proto-plebiscitary populism of half a century before. Electorates, it is argued, were prepared to acquiesce to 'rule by decree' and the curtailment of congressional scrutiny of the executive

---

[13]   Malloy (1979); Sikkink (1991).

[14]   O'Donnell (1973 and 1994); Malloy (1979); Abel and Lewis (1993).

because the NEM delivered macroeconomic stability and welfare gains. Subject to the realisation of these goals, citizens surrendered much power to an executive with a providential mission, whose authority was virtually untrammelled between elections. [15]

These issues raise questions about the validity and utility of concepts of citizenship in contemporary Latin America. Are there risks in imposing Eurocentric or US-centred notions of citizenship upon the region? To what extent are circumstances observed in Europe and the USA comparable with those in Latin America? Latin America since the 1980s has confronted issues of 'democratic consolidation' in a context very different from that of Western and Northern Europe in the late 1940s, where comprehensive welfare systems were assembled to promote social cohesion, political stability and economic growth.[16] How far did the construction of active social programmes serve a similar purpose, and foster solidarity, in late twentieth-century urban Latin America? In post-war Western Europe, social citizenship and the welfare state were important in generating political consensus. Can they perform similar functions in Latin America in the processes of re-democratisation and 'democratic consolidation'? Even today, the administrative framework of Latin American states, especially in the countryside, is more defective than that in much of war-torn Europe.[17] Contrary to neo-conservative arguments that all-pervasive welfare bureaucracies have a history of suffocating household, neighbourhood and community ties and voluntary associations, the welfare state is noted for its absence from much of Latin America. A deficit in formal provision is conspicuous precisely in those areas where the market economy lacks the buoyancy and dynamism to support an extension of choice and a network of private initiatives in social welfare that are designed to empower the consumer. [18]

One salient question is how valuable citizenship rights are where a growing gap exists between formalisation and informal practice, and between tolerance of political freedoms and attacks on civil liberties, as has occurred during the electoral *apertura* in Mexico and the aftermath of the Colombian Constitution of 1991. Both exemplify the problem inherent in Latin American liberalism of fluctuations between advances and retreats from citizenship rights, ' ... the intermittent, fragmentary and unequal appearance

[15]   O'Donnell (1996); Smith and Korzeniewicz (1997).
[16]   Hills et al. (1994); Midgley (1997 and 1998).
[17]   Baldwin (1990); Esping-Andersen (1990 and 1996); Nickson (1995).
[18]   Conaghan and Malloy (1994).

— and disappearance — of citizenship rights …'[19] and the constraints con-fronted by collective action in negotiating, achieving and defending them. Where citizenship rights entrenched in rational legal codes were designed by the exponents of a classical republicanism to enhance freedom for citizens, to liberate them from tyranny and to extend the rule of law as essential to the equality of citizens, this normative goal has seldom been fully achieved.

Social rights are distinguished from civil rights in that a commitment to the universalisation of social rights is widely questioned. Furthermore, social rights are provided by the administrative apparatus of the state but have to be claimed by the citizen. According to Habermas, invoking these rights can reduce an active citizenry to passivity and introduce an element of clientelism that debilitates citizenship.[20] This occurs particularly in Latin America where selective delivery of benefits is used as an instrument of political control and division, private interests and the state interpenetrate each other, and access to redress financed by legal aid seldom exists. Thus a progress to social citizenship is deferred as the substance of social rights is acted upon unequally or is denied, rights are subverted by fraud, and regimes pay lip service to forms of citizenship for the sake of international recognition, aid or loans. A yawning gap between rights-in-principle and rights-in-practice is perpetuated, along with variations within nations like Brazil between locations of patrimonialism and clientelism and enclaves of pluralistic tolerance.[21] Heterogeneous group identities of gender, race, community and workplace (or 'social movements') may militate against a homogeneous citizenship. Yet, while many social movements are initially motivated by immediate, particularist objectives, these are frequently transformed into claims for civil and political rights as movements collaborate forcefully to define, to demand and to disseminate rights.[22] Illustrative of these processes are the clauses in the Argentinian Constitution of 1994 and the Brazilian of 1998 that declare social rights to be an integral element of citizenship. Only in Cuba, however, is an enduring commitment to the universalisation of social rights unchallenged. Despite endemic fiscal crisis, the post-1959 regime has legitimised itself by sustaining an egalitarian revolution founded on lifelong entitlements, notwithstanding the long-standing problem of accommodating active social citizenship to the incontestable primacy of *el comandante* Fidel Castro.[23]

---

[19] Whitehead (1994), p. 84.

[20] Habermas (1994).

[21] Panizza (1993); Foweraker and Landman (1997), esp. pp. 20–1.

[22] Turner (1986); Mead (1986); Walzer (1989); Bellamy (1993).

[23] Eckstein (1994 and 1998); Whitehead (1998); Dilla Alfonso (2000).

Constraints upon the exercise of citizenship have varied considerably. National identification is often weak because it competes with other foci of individual and group loyalty: enterprises, regions, communities, ethnicity, class, patrons and family. Historians have underlined that, although from the early constitutional period Latin American governments viewed primary education as essential to citizenship, a broad inculcation of notions of citizenship was impeded by under-funding and maladministration in ministries of public instruction and a failure to take new ideas to the classroom.[24] Sociologists have stressed that the rights attached to citizenship have been of little practical value to Latin Americans as elites established them in order to rally support for particular projects while curtailing participation in policy-making.[25] Political scientists have emphasised the difficulties that popular actors have confronted during democratic openings in forging strong links of any kind — social pacts, 'democratic class compromises' — with democratising movements.[26] Economic and social crises precipitated by policy failure and external currency shocks may impede the arduous tasks of democratic institutionalisation and of rendering administrations accountable to citizens.[27] In 'delegative democracies' presidents have reduced the rotation of incumbents and have insulated technocrats from day-to-day pressure, making the executive less accountable.[28] Preventing regressions to autocracy, eliminating disproportionate rewards for office holders and perpetuating democratic rule necessitate effective social policy and routinised patterns of political co-operation and competition.[29] At local level, the inert structure of municipal government has further limited the exercise of citizenship.[30]

Until recently, citizenship in Ecuador was thwarted by little cumulative experience of popular democracy and by weaknesses of policy initiative stemming from both a political leadership devoid of an ideology of social partnership and the absence of a collective imperative to modernise.[31] In Mexico the exercise of citizenship rights has been inhibited by the discretionary and casuistic content of the law, which has frequently been applied

[24]   Newland (1996).

[25]   Roberts (1995).

[26]   Chalmers et al. (1997).

[27]   O'Donnell (1996); Domínguez and Lowenthal (1996).

[28]   O'Donnell (1996).

[29]   Schmitter (1996).

[30]   Nickson (1995).

[31]   de Janvry et al. (1994).

only if and when the political authorities, especially the federal executive, ordain it. Indeed, the victory of an opposition party in the recent presidential elections for the first time in 70 years has aroused widespread expectations of enforceable civil and political rights and a new system of resource allocation. Meanwhile, a regional struggle in Chiapas to construct citizenship out of confrontations with caciques, landowners and officials has become a national and international issue, given the success of the Zapatistas in promoting their cause through messages over the worldwide web, national consultations, street protests and caravans of aid.[32]

Citizenship has been constrained by lack of accountability for past abuses, in particular procrastination in prosecuting those who have committed human rights offences, not least in cases where the perpetrators of kidnapping and 'disappearances' were involved in a 'negotiated' return to civilian rule. This is exemplified by the slow road to democratisation in Brazil between 1980 and 1985.[33] Meanwhile, in Chile the military imposed an authoritarian constitution that placed the officer corps above the law, and in Uruguay the judiciary was institutionally weak and slow in prosecuting human rights abuses.[34] Similarly the return of the democratically elected President Jean-Bertrand Aristide in Haiti was conditional upon an amnesty for violators of human rights.[35]

Citizenship rights are in continuous flux, constantly being refurbished and refashioned, combining an awareness of membership in a bounded society and a shared conception of justice. Hence the contradictory character of citizenship, by which in Mexico, Colombia and elsewhere, institutional improvements may occur in the open electoral arena, in constitutional terms or in the monitoring of human rights violations, while the incidence of abuses of civil rights — extra-judicial executions, kidnappings and disappearances — grow, and rights-in-practice contract. Hence too the paradox by which the denial of basic civil liberties for the poorest groups in Brazil persists while popular access to decision-making over small town governance, environmental issues and sectoral industrial policy has expanded.[36] Moreover, states confront new challenges. As international diasporas multiply, and migrants, refugees and stateless persons demand

32   Harvey (1998).
33   Bacha and Klein (1986); Skidmore (1989); Sola (1996).
34   Barahona de Brito (1997).
35   Girault (1991); Andreu (1994).
36   Human Rights Watch (2000).

their rights, the practice of one citizenship blends with, and transcends, another.[37] In particular, trans-border migrants to the USA, active in campaigns for better wages and working conditions and political and civil rights, often transmit to their country of origin an ethos of activism and a self-confidence that comes from rights gained. Are national allegiances being weakened by the formation of regional entities like the MERCO-SUR/L and the revived Andean Group?

Diverse perceptions of citizenship compete for attention. A liberal stress on civil and civic citizenship prevails by which freedom for the individual citizen and control of his/her destiny are achieved through capitalist growth and liberation from political despotism, politicised religion and a hierarchical social order. And optimism surrounds the record number of citizens in terms of formal voting rights. This has been reformulated as an assumption that, after exposure to populist demagoguery and failure to deliver on promises of sustainable welfare, the citizenry of Latin American nations acknowledges the inherent virtue of a market economy and the folly and evil of state intervention. Roxborough has analysed the weakening of the labour movement during the crises of the 1980s and has demonstrated its incapacity to influence policies that aimed to resolve conflicts over growth, distribution, inflation and even wages. He has argued that a neoliberal transformation occurred in which the locus of political concern shifted from civil society to economic decision-making. The disarticulation of civil society resulted and new social cleavages appeared: some social movements were reinvigorated, while confusion was sown among political parties, and the influence of organised labour fell further.[38] Waisman goes further, arguing that the preoccupation of the state with macroeconomic policy and the maintenance of law and order to the detriment of social policy threatens to broaden the gap between the 'civic' and the 'disorganised segments' of society.[39] This view is refined by Caldeira who argues that the expansion of political citizenship resulting from an improved electoral democracy has been off-set by a brutal and biased system of criminal justice that negates civil citizenship.[40]

Argued from the premise that growth derives from market rules, and that it is the responsibility of the state to embed those rules, rational choice the-

[37]   N. Harris (1995).

[38]   Roxborough (1989 and 1997).

[39]   Waisman (1999).

[40]   Caldeira (2001).

orists appraise the extent to which states secured property rights and thereby the smooth functioning of the market. Extending this approach to citizenship and social policy, the role of the state can be presented as promoting stability by guaranteeing the supply of public social goods such as education, social security and health. The provision of public goods promotes the consent of the governed and empowers the state.[41] Social policy 'rights' emerged as a badge of citizenship before full political rights were enjoyed by many individuals; and states deployed conditional access to social goods as a mechanism of political control after the Second World War.[42] In most Latin American countries, access to social services was physically limited and politically rationed. Only since the 1980s has the tenor of the debate embraced both a market and citizenship dimension in which social goods are explicitly presented as an unconditional right of citizenship, even where supply is financially restricted. Hence, consumption of — and access to — a broad range of public goods is the benchmark of full citizenship. This view of citizenship as consumption enhances the position of the state as a supplier of public goods. It implies that, in part, state survival depends on an efficient delivery of social goods. Hence, too, the 'civilising' role of the market — the market as a force for social peace, political harmony and material abundance.[43] Other authors press for a more collective view of citizenship rooted in the strength of the community and in social solidarity. Rejecting what they see as an over-reliance on neoliberal equations of free markets and free politics, Jelin and her colleagues argue for more analysis of citizenship as the contingent outcome of struggles for dignity, voice and autonomy. They appeal too for more attention to sociopolitical processes and ethnographic detail.[44] Although their identity is problematical, social movements have constituted visible signs of gradualist and nonconformist struggles to re-evaluate democracy. Social movements have also defined and redefined the contours of citizenship within a frozen sphere and in unhopeful locations, like the periphery of large cities where there was no alternative effective representation for social interests. And 'associative networks' have in places flourished, characterised by flexible adaptation, day-to-day pragmatism, non-hierarchical structures and a 'purposeful interconnectedness' aiming to shape public policy. [45]

---

[41] Grindle (2000b).

[42] Malloy and Parodi (1993).

[43] Weiner (1999).

[44] Jelin (1996).

[45] Foweraker and Craig (1990); Fox (1994); Chalmers et al. (1997).

NGOs have played an important part in social movements that have fought for active citizenship and the effective exercise of civic rights. The term NGO is a convenient and, perhaps, misleading shorthand for organisations ranging from the international, such as OXFAM and Human Rights Watch, via the national, like the federation of indigenous communities in Colombia, to the local, for example, neighbourhood groups in the city of Rio de Janeiro. In addition, official attitudes to NGOs have changed. During the 1970s and 1980s, they were often accused by Latin American governments of fomenting agitation and subversion, and were suspected by the Bretton Woods agencies of disrupting the implementation of development projects by meddling irresponsibly on the ground. Today, ample evidence exists of a 'philosophy of partnership' in which host governments and the Washington agencies delegate to NGOs project management, which, with local engagement, can strengthen participatory citizenship.[46] By the late 1990s organisational diversity characterised NGOs: some were bureaucratised and highly professional; others were pluralistic, ephemeral and rooted in local communities and their issues. However, all organisations professed a concern about engaging citizens. The National Association of Brazilian NGOs, for example, argued that its members should press municipal government to create a social delivery framework that made possible a fuller realisation of citizenship rights. Nevertheless, many disenchanted professionals view the 'philosophy of partnership' as a second best for a comprehensive welfare state. Encouraged by the provision in the 1988 Constitution that proclaimed a single, universal and equitable health system, health professionals in the Brazilian NGOs tackling the resurgence of malaria, were discouraged when the state reneged on its responsibilities in the sector.[47]

CEPAL/ECLAC urges active, reflective citizenship in the light of problems of violence and ungovernability across Latin America that are linked to questions of citizen confidence in the judicial and security systems and, in particular, the protection of single female-headed households and the prevention of narcotics sales.[48] Similarly, the World Bank sees the strengthening of active citizenship as essential to promoting social cohesion and identification with collective goals, and has come to acknowledge that both private and public sector institutions were weakened by the debt crises.

---

[46]   Meyer (1999).

[47]   Cohn (1995).

[48]   CEPAL (1997)

Underlining the problem of state legitimacy caused by corruption and injustice, the Bank presses governments to be more alert to 'republican values' and to create 'more society'. By this is meant the creation of a broader awareness of individual and group rights and responsibilities in order to counter a decline of 'old defences' — family, community and Church. For the Bank, the disruption of traditional communities means a disruption of informal channels of exchange of information, to be resolved by a two-way flow of information and knowledge, which is essential to build trust among the poor.[49] These arguments overlook three problems. First, policy should not be predicated upon flawed historical assumptions about the universal existence and effectiveness of 'old defences'. Secondly, greater awareness among the poor of the degree of income inequality is likely to promote distrust of the rich, and a sense of betrayal by the state. Thirdly, the scale of tax evasion (in countries where direct tax rates are often low) by the upper class and private sector causes particular antagonism among public sector workers and employees whose taxes are deducted at source. Seldom do the international institutions remind the upper classes that they are under-taxed and that they have responsibilities as active citizens.

From this examination, it will be clear that debate on citizenship goes beyond narrow juridical definitions as a bundle of rights and obligations, and locates the concept explicitly within other discussions — of power differences, social justice, ethnicity and unequal access to assets and resources. Analyses, past and present, raise questions as to how far citizenship is active and how far passive, and how far developed from below and how far regulated from above. Moreover, the content, theory and practice of citizenship have changed over time — full citizenship has come to mean the exercise of social as well as political and civil rights. Will these notions of effective, universal citizenship remain unassailable, making previous exchanges about the nature — whether collectivist or individualist — redundant? Will debate about the quality of citizenship — whether a 'first-class' citizenship should be distinguished from a 'second-class', and whether 'low intensity' citizenship from full, mediated by law — prove superfluous? And will empowering asset-based citizenship deliver rights for all?

Ideology, States and Markets

Globalisation, monetarism and a stress on the hegemony of markets challenge several of Marshall's assumptions. How autonomous is the nation-

---

[49]   World Bank (2000).

state? How far has the capitalist world been reshaped since 1945 around the transnational corporations, whose managers and administrators — Latin American and Asian as well as North American — owe an allegiance to the enterprise that has come to supersede that to the state? To what extent has world capitalism been re-configured since the 1990s by the process of 'state retreat', the thorough globalisation of capital markets and the ascendancy of the Washington consensus? How far are these processes eroding notions of citizenship and social solidarity and challenging the authority of the nation-state?[50] How far has a determination to reverse abject market failures and to promote market stability fomented social instability?

The role and 'position' of the state has come to dominate much scholarship on economic development and social policy. Three questions head the research agenda: in what respects was the state active and in what passive; in what ways did the state inhibit or promote growth; what factors conditioned state action? This discussion tends to periodise the Latin American experience since the mid-nineteenth century in terms of alternative phases of growth and development or growth and crisis. According to much current thinking, each of these periods was characterised by specific, stylised 'state' and 'market' configurations. The oligarchic state between c.1870 and the world depression was responsible for the formation of markets and delegated much social provision to the charitable sector. The populist state of the middle third of the twentieth century promoted 'stabilising development' (*desarrollo estabilizador*) by intervening in markets and adopting an energetic programme of welfare and social progress.[51] The 'market-friendly state' of recent decades has, or so it is claimed, restored market mechanisms, by re-appraising social welfare legislation, by promoting the private supply of social services and by encouraging the citizen/consumer to engage with social policy provision.[52]

During the late nineteenth and early twentieth centuries, effective integration into the international economy transformed much of Latin America, promoting institutional change, offering opportunities and posing challenges to the state. The gains from international insertion were neither shared equitably by all sectors nor by all countries. How far was this a consequence of imperfect integration into the world economy, and how far of positivist strategies, associated with export-led expansion, that promoted growth at the expense of equity? Reflecting on the failure of liber-

[50]   Sunkel (1993).
[51]   Pazos (1983); FitzGerald (1994).
[52]   Thorp (1998); Tulchin and Garland (2000).

al 'projects' of the aftermath of Independence to foster viable markets, positivist policy-makers began from assumptions that an educated leadership, with a systematic mastery of modern science, should preside over the social regeneration of a 'sick continent'.[53] Historians debate the welfare and institutional gains deriving from the 'positivist project'. Did the promotion of European immigration result in rising incomes and the consolidation of a money economy, or depress wages for all and restrict access to the labour market for non-immigrants?[54] Esteemed by positivist *pensadores* for their skills, literacy and 'industriousness', migrants from Europe founded cultural associations, professional clubs, mutual societies and trade unions — expressions of social capital — that discriminated against 'nationals', further limiting social mobility for liberated slaves and itinerant rural and urban labourers.[55] Recent historiography has dispelled myths of racial democracy, but pointed to the use of constitutional provisions and progressive legal codes by blacks and people of mixed ancestry to achieve civic inclusion and citizens' rights.[56] What were the consequences of strategies that forced dispossessed peasants into the labour market? Positivist regimes presided over a massive transfer of land. First, a renewed attack on communal landholding occurred in such countries as Mexico and Guatemala in the late nineteenth century and the opening decade of the twentieth. Secondly, campaigns against nomadic indians culminated in brutal land clearing, most conspicuously during the so-called 'Desert Campaign' in Patagonia. Thirdly, the sale of public land to large landowners and foreign land companies and corporations often obstructed the consolidation of a yeoman farming class envisaged by earlier liberals.[57] Most scholars agree that immigration-labour policies were premised on assumptions of racial superiority and that the mechanisms of public and communal land disposal aggravated social inequalities and perpetuated inflexibilities in land tenure systems. Indeed, the 'positivist project' rarely reduced imperfections in either labour or land markets.

There was a greater congruence between concept and outcome in strategies to consolidate the national market. 'Occupying the national space' was both a political and an economic project. Considerable efforts

---

[53] Hale (1986).

[54] Holloway (1980); Leff (1982); Slatta (1983).

[55] Solberg (1971); Malaquer de Motes (1992).

[56] De la Fuente (1999 and 2001).

[57] Safford and Huber (1995).

were devoted to the construction of railways and public utilities, and the development of telegraph and postal services. These facilities were sometimes provided directly by the state, sometimes by private companies enjoying state subsidies. For positivist regimes, the modernisation of transport and communications was regarded as essential for state-building and market formation. Improvements in transport and communication enhanced the power of the central state, often at the expense of local communities, and complemented state action in other areas of public goods provision, notably education, policing and justice. Although intervening with the intention of promoting the formation of markets and of influencing them, and acknowledging that these interventions had social outcomes, Latin American states assumed a passive stance in much of social policy. Where the state adopted a more active role, it was mainly to promote orderly change in the cities demanded by national and provincial elites anxious about the 'social question', notably policing and labour discipline, which became a perennial theme. Additional concerns ranged from elementary schooling for new occupations like telegraphists, to special courses for sanitary engineers, to a regulatory framework for higher education in medicine and engineering. Often social policy — notoriously in the case of vaccination campaigns — strengthened the coercive power of the state, rather than generating class and community consensus.[58]

What were the implications for incipient social policy of the unorthodox economic 'liberalism' practised in early twentieth century Latin America and the evolving political economy of policy-making and private-public relations?[59] An incipient recognition of the limits of voluntarism and attempts to place it on a more systematic and effective basis were complemented by a growth of state action, which became co-optive rather than simply repressive, at least in the city. Yet it is doubtful that government intervention tackled effectively the serious drawbacks of voluntarism: uneven resource distribution, the perpetuation of paternalistic concepts of charity, activities whose main beneficiaries were status-hungry sponsors, and the stigmatising ethos of 'cringe or starve'. A parallel growth in state and private provision was accompanied by increased scope for autonomous action by associations of European immigrants, as well as organised urban and plantation workers and miners. Medical professionals, often prominent members of incipient left-wing parties allied to trade union leaders, identi-

[58]   Albert (1988).

[59]   Cárdenas, Ocampo and Thorp (2000a).

fied and plotted the incidence of diseases of poverty — both urban and rural — and campaigned against poor housing conditions — slum tenements in cities, plantation *barracones* and the dismal living quarters of miners and oil workers.[60] Coalitions of progressive professionals and labour activists demanded the regulation of insalubrious workplaces — particularly those employing women and children. Pro-natalist and social Darwinian ideologies aiming to 'improve the stock' gave rise in the 1910s and 1920s to debate about the health of women and infants, and the provision of maternity benefits.[61] The regulation of the length of the working day and safety and hygiene in the workplace were subjects of concern for social reformers and public officials. Although only catering to a very small proportion of working population, state agencies, private companies and mutual associations were increasingly active in areas such as social insurance. Social policy initiatives were influenced from outside Latin America by, for example, Bismarckian and social-democratic models in Germany and paternalistic Rockefeller health campaigns directed at poor black communities in the US South. The Russian Revolution, and a surge in urban social protest, aroused upper and middle class interest in preemptive, pro-active social policy initiatives to forestall class warfare.[62] The 'advanced' social content of the Mexican Constitution of 1917 created a new framework of debate beyond liberal and Catholic concerns with social palliatives.[63] 'Rights', such as free, universal primary education, trade union recognition, community resources, maternity benefits, minimum wage protection, that were enshrined in the constitution, resonated as far as Peru.

The inter-war depression had a profound impact on state structure, market and society. It was inevitable that the crash and the abrupt regime changes that followed would influence the economic and social policy debate and its ideological underpinning. The duration and intensity of the welfare crisis of the 1930s differed by country, sector and region; and the poor integration of national markets signified considerable variations in the cycle of contraction and recovery by city and region. The welfare consequences of the crisis differed according to the scale and flexibility of the subsistence sector — and of the state itself. In areas with histories of internal migrations, peasant communities absorbed returning first-generation

60   Abel (1996).
61   N. Stepan (1991).
62   Albert (1988).
63   Knight (1986 and 1991).

emigrants escaping urban unemployment. Later in the decade, particularly in those countries where commodity boards and price support schemes were set up, rural job opportunities expanded as production recovered. Continuing instability in the export sector and the growth of public spending in the cities contributed to rural-urban migration, a phenomenon that was to become more pronounced. In the early 1930s, hunger, unemployment and social deprivation had been most observed by commentators — and acted upon by government — in major cities and ports: export-related activities contracted and public spending fell as governments pursued largely orthodox fiscal and monetary policies. The balance of public-private relationships altered fundamentally as philanthropic organisations, overwhelmed by the depression, clamoured for state assistance or intervention. With a crisis of cash and confidence in the voluntary sector, the social stance of the state became more pro-active, influenced both by exponents of Catholic Social Action, who argued for a 'family wage' that would re-invigorate values of hierarchy and respect, and by ideologues of secular nationalism, who pressed for 'fair wages' and 'decent housing' to raise the dignity of workers. In Mexico, radicals demanding the implementation of constitutional social provisions agitated for the emancipation of peasants and their full integration into the nation.[64] By the late 1930s, economic policy regimes became increasingly counter-cyclical, designed either to promote aggregate domestic demand growth or to prevent further demand contraction. Public works, protection and unorthodox monetary and banking strategies helped to reactivate the economy and create employment. Spending on schools and hospitals (as on highways and railways) performed a pump-priming role. Social initiatives — state universities, factory supervisor training programmes, work inspectorates and other measures — that had been debated in the 1920s, or earlier, were re-appraised and often implemented. Social insurance coverage was extended in Brazil, Mexico and Uruguay; maternity benefits provided in the Argentine; and labour and then health ministries founded in several republics.[65]

Depression reactivated social movements and involved a restructuring of the class hierarchy — proletarianisation of peasants, decline and de-skilling of artisans and craftsmen, downward social mobility among the middle class. By the mid-1930s, social policy was reflecting both processes of adaptation by a

[64] Meyer, Segovia and Lajous (1979); Vaughan (1997); Ivereigh (2000).

[65] Malloy (1979); Hamilton (1982); Mesa-Lago and Cruz Saco (1998); Lewis and Lloyd-Sherlock (2001).

re-configured upper class to new challenges, and efforts to defuse conflict in specific locations and sectors. Parts of the private sector were more sympathetic than before to ameliorative action that averted unrest so long as it imposed few costs and 'improved' the workforce. Social policy met demands for public sector employment from the middle class, especially new graduates. In addition, official social interventions were claimed as victories by trade union federations struggling to prevent wages from falling below survival levels and to defend living conditions. Secular improvements in health and education indicators were observed from the late 1930s; and a new social awareness was evident in modest schemes to train teachers and social visitors and early cost-of-living analyses and nutrition surveys that prefigured moves towards the construction of a welfare state. However, social policy was unavoidably haphazard and inconsistent in content and patchy in implementation, owing to the coalition of incompatibles involved in its formulation and execution and a dearth of qualified personnel.

Between the late 1940s and late 1960s, import-substitution industrialisation (ISI) was the main economic aim of government.[66] Its implementation involved the distortion of the domestic terms of trade in favour of manufacturing, an overvalued (unstable) exchange rate, negative or low real rates of interest (in most cases) and protectionism. It is possible that ISI-related public expenditure crowded out social spending; yet there is little evidence to support the view that a reduction in expenditure targeting manufacturing would have resulted in more public social investment. An active social policy, which was consistent with prevailing Keynesian and Beveridgian thinking, was gradually grafted onto the ISI programme, challenging corporate social initiatives by progressive entrepreneurs rooted in Fordist and Taylorist notions of scientific management and ideas of 'welfare capitalism'.[67] Social policy also owed much to a recognition that the promotion of Hirschman-style unbalanced development tended to generate sectoral and sociopolitical tensions, that were aggravated by demographic growth and rapid urbanisation.[68] This vision of a journey towards progress in the *cepalista* decades overstates departures from earlier concepts of liberalism. For most countries, the main outcomes of ISI were fairly rapid growth and absolute welfare gains, notwithstanding macroeconomic instability and a sharp reduction in equity.[69] Yet capable economic man-

---

[66]   Pazos (1983); FitzGerald (1994); Cárdenas, Ocampo and Thorp (2000b).

[67]   Scott (1993); Weinstein (1996).

[68]   Teitel (1992).

[69]   Urrutia (1991).

agement did not equal good social outcomes. Comparing Peru and Colombia at the end of the 1980s, Thorp stressed how more effective short-term economic management in Colombia was not translated into a better performance in terms of welfare, distribution and basic needs.[70]

Increasing volatility in the external and fiscal accounts and rising inflation underwrote the lurch towards neo-structuralism and neoliberalism in the late 1960s and early 1970s. The exhaustion of the 'easy phase' of ISI was accompanied by the perception that 'stabilising development' was giving way to destabilising protest, exemplified by urban terrorism in the Argentine and Uruguay, political breakdown in Chile in 1973, and agrarian struggles in Central America and elsewhere. Remedial populist social policy was seen by neo-authoritarians to be costly, corrupt and ineffective in mitigating tensions, while eroding an ethos of voluntarism, pluralism and self-help.[71] When conservatives and neoliberals mounted assaults on state welfarism, welfare ministries and agencies that had been diverted from service provision to acting as sources of middle-class feather-bedding and instruments of power for trade union leaders had few defenders. Domestic pressures and the interest initiated a decade and more before by agencies like the Alliance for Progress contributed to feverish debate about demography and development. This was most clearly observed in the connection made between education, population control and economic progress. In this respect, demographic growth generated a demand for greater educational provision, while education was also seen as an important part of the solution to the population explosion. Issues of education, health, housing and equity (not least within the family) became linked and incorporated within the 'development debate'.[72]

The dominance of the neoliberal, new economic model (NEM) in the 1990s derived from the failure of heterodoxy — neo-structural solutions to the problem of loss of dynamism of the forced industrialisation model — and the debt/loan crises that conditioned and consolidated international re-insertion.[73] Hyperinflation and the institutionalised terrorism of the armed forces in the 1970s had destroyed the technocratic-authoritarian alliances that had administered the post-Second World War developmentalist and neo-developmentalist projects and the social policies associ-

---

[70]   Thorp (1991).

[71]   O'Donnell (1973); Collier (1979).

[72]   Gilbert (1998); Torres and Puiggros (1999); Lloyd-Sherlock (2000).

[73]   Meller (1991); Buxton and Phillips (1999a & b).

ated with them.[74] Yet, by the mid-1990s, the Washington agencies and their allies came to recognise what CEPAL and critics of neoliberal policies had been arguing for several years: for the NEM to survive, a 'new social policy model' had to be devised and new coalitions formed for its propagation and defence. A vigorous debate crystallised, initially addressing poverty reduction, and later embracing survival strategies and the concept of social exclusion. Nevertheless, the view of social policy as adjunct remained, namely that social interventions derived from a desire to expand the market by curbing poverty and counteracting immiseration. Only very recently has discussion of equity entered the frame, and then cast in terms of economic efficiency.[75] Even today there is insufficient emphasis on outcomes and the impact of process on total income and levels of poverty.

In the latter part of the nineteenth and early twentieth centuries, Latin American states attempted to 'embed enterprise' through external economic opening and pragmatic action in domestic markets. Most social interventions by the state were minimalist; many were repressive and reactive. From the 1930s, and more especially after the 1940s, government intervention became more explicit and domestic markets were progressively (but only partially) de-linked from the world economy. Useful in forging reform constituencies, social policy was given a higher priority, at times approaching economic policy in status.[76] The growth of the public sector assumed an economic and social dimension, represented in the provision of a wide range of products and services. Since the 1980s a growing rejection of economic interventionism has been accompanied by an increasing demand for greater transparency and accountability in politics and economics. During the 1990s market 'reforms', especially a trend towards privatisation, continued apace. How far a genuinely participative democracy, characterised by social 'inclusion' and distributive justice was intended by the reformers of the 1980s and 1990s, remains hotly disputed. Ideology — the creation of a system of beliefs in the morality or desirability of a particular kind of social order — enhances state survival.[77] Social policy — and the effective delivery of social goods — can be critical to the construction of ideology and legitimacy. This was acknowledged

---

74   Teitel (1992); Sunkel (1993).

75   Linz and Stepan (1996); Carpio, Klein and Novacovsky (1999); Carpio and Novacovsky (1999); Lievesley (1999).

76   Hirschman (1963); Teitel (1992).

77   Grindle (1996); Bin Wong (1997).

40 or so years ago, and is now being re-learnt, as the need for well-functioning states — not minimal states — is increasingly acknowledged, along with the importance of good government, capable of designing appropriate policies and strengthening the capacity of organisation.[78]

Distribution and Poverty: Social Policy Rhetoric and Delivery

Seldom outside post-1959 Cuba has social policy been concerned with issues of (re-)distribution. Poverty came to command the attention of policy-makers and NGOs across the continent in the 1960s, and was sometimes addressed explicitly and systematically. Governments of different ideological persuasions undertook anti-poverty programmes in the 1970s and early 1980s: for example, Chile under Allende, Mexico during the López Portillo *sexenio* and Colombia in the Barco presidency. But their impact was shallow and debated.[79] Initially distribution was considered largely as a growth-related variable. Only after 'targeting' and 'safety net' had crystallised as concept and strategy[80] did distribution in the late 1990s become a dominant issue of policy. Social strategy developed its own momentum and coherence as an area of state activity and as complementary to institutional stability. As Grindle has observed, 'The social agenda in Latin America in the mid-1990s was defined by renewed concern about poverty and inequality and their consequences for *sustained growth* and the *consolidation of democratic political regimes*.'[81] Disparities of affluence and gross asymmetries of power were reinforced by the unequal distribution of the benefits of international relationships — trade agreements, patent laws, medical initiatives and educational exchanges.

Following Mesa-Lago and Midgley, it can be argued with confidence that the effects of social policy have been regressive — or at best neutral. This was especially manifest in Bismarckian social insurance systems, the growth of which tended to confer additional benefits on relatively privileged groups rather than to extend coverage or promote equity. The first groups to be incorporated in contributory social insurance schemes, dating from the 1910s and 1920s in 'pioneer' countries, were professionals (civil servants, teachers,and employees of state enterprises). Subsequently, systems were expanded piecemeal to include strategically located sections

[78]   Grindle (1997).

[79]   Thorp (1991); Maddison (1992); Altimir (1997).

[80]   C. Graham (1994); Lustig (1995).

[81]   Grindle (2000b), p. 20, stress added.

of the skilled (usually urban) working classes.[82] The contributory nature of these arrangements and their close supervision by (or dependence on) the state when political participation was restricted, meant that the needs of the poorest sections of society were hardly considered. As the range of public social goods expanded to include non-basic education and health-care, the regressive impacts of different strands of social policy were repli-cated. The children of higher income groups were over-represented in ris-ing secondary school enrolments; and tertiary education until late in the twentieth century remained exclusive.[83] Similarly, access to health services was socially, sectorally and spatially restricted, even when technically free, and their quality and range were variable.[84] Social policy seldom challenged patronage practices; it generally re-fashioned them. And service delivery was streamlined at times in order to defeat challenges by opposition move-ments and parties in marginal constituencies. Whatever the intention, the outcome of policy was to perpetuate inequality.

Negative distributional consequences of social policy prevailed across Latin America. Data on access (or lack of it) may be presented as a proxy for the poor distributional effects of social policy. Sharp national divergences in coverage existed: whereas in 1960 almost all the Uruguayan workforce was enrolled in social insurance schemes, in Mexico the figure hardly exceeded 16 per cent.[85] However, official figures on coverage can be misleading. Argentinian official data show that over one half of the economically active population (EAP) was enrolled in state insurance schemes in 1960 and that enrolment rates reached 69 per cent by 1980. The same statistics also confirm that only 58 per cent of the population of retirement age was in receipt of a pension in 1980.[86] Given that a significant proportion of the retired held more than one pension, the real percentage of the elderly receiving a state pension was substantially less than the data indicate. These trends suggest a generational lag in both the diffusion of welfare provision and the distribu-tional gains that resulted from enlarging the social policy network.

Most evidence indicates that the piecemeal growth of social policy pro-vision in the past half century — including a proliferation of agencies and widening range of services — had little impact on the social geography of

82   Mesa-Lago (1978); Midgley and Tracy (1996); Midgley (1997 and 1998).

83   Maddison (1992); Torres and Puiggros (1999).

84   Mesa-Lago (1992); Mesa-Lago and Cruz Saco (1998).

85   Mesa-Lago (1991), p. 186.

86   Lewis and Lloyd-Sherlock (2001).

poverty. Patterns of income distribution are notoriously unequal in Latin America, particularly in Brazil. Distribution worsened in many countries during the 1980s, though inequality and poverty declined in Colombia, Costa Rica, Paraguay and Uruguay.[87] Similarly, some absolute setbacks experienced in the 'lost decade' were reversed in the 1990s. While levels of poverty (which were higher in 1990 than in 1970) decreased during the 1990s in several countries, equity indicators did not improve.[88] In their study of nine countries in the late 1990s, Stallings and Peres examine the impact of social spending, concluding that it had a strong distributive impact. However, they warn against inefficiencies in the allocation of social spending, caused by the influence of entrenched interest groups, institutional fragmentation, and defective administration.[89] Taking a longer view, Thorp shows that, having registered substantial gains in mid-twentieth century, the distribution of household income remained relatively steady over its last third, if subject to volatile short-term change.[90] In Colombia and Mexico especially, Gini coefficients continued to improve in the final decades of the century. Some argue that these changes indicated greater access to social services in the second half of the twentieth century, others that progress was driven by growth. Recent research queries whether, in line with the Kuznets hypothesis, an active social policy will deliver a narrowing of inequalities in the later phases of development.[91]

In the 1980s, the picture was less bleak than often suggested. The broad trend was for expenditure on health and education to follow the economic cycle. In most countries, funding contracted early in the decade and recovered towards its end, though in only a few cases was expenditure around 1990 higher than in 1980. And delivery of services to the most needy was achieved in a number of countries and policy areas only by strengthening institutions that circumvented existing control structures — admittedly at the risk of creating future problems of funding, staffing and agency duplication.[92] Adjustment-driven appraisals of social policy displayed positive features, notably a commitment to rectify gaps in coverage, to raise the quality of benefits and to remedy defects in delivery systems. Recovery at mid-decade was particularly observed in those countries applying neo-

---

[87]   Maddison (1992); Psacharopoulos et al. (1997).

[88]   Dornbusch and Edwards (1991); Maddison (1992); Ocampo (1998).

[89]   Stallings and Peres (2000).

[90]   Thorp (1998).

[91]   Gwatkin (2001).

[92]   Grindle (1991 and 1996).

structuralist, heterodox programmes of macroeconomic reactivation. Undeniably, the impact of public spending cuts was felt disproportionately by the poor, although the scale, intensity and content of crisis varied considerably, approximately the same solution was applied everywhere, even to the desperate problems confronted by rudimentary social schemes in the poorest countries. There was a continuing reluctance to ask who were the poor, to define what they wanted and to assure that consultation between provider agencies and recipients and diversity of provision generated the efficient delivery of services.

Demographics as much as politics also explain welfare (and distributional) changes. The post-1930s witnessed a demographic explosion and massive internal and cross-border migration. Initially, rural-urban migration consolidated the position of primate cities, which, from the 1980s, continued to expand on the basis of natural growth rather than inward migration. Now the most rapid rates of urbanisation are associated with intermediate cities. Some are mushrooming townships in the interior where public services are deplorable. Others are established cities prospering from the growth of new industries and the re-location of existing firms. The expansion of further intermediate cities is caused by urban-urban migration, both national and international. Since the 1970s it has been contended that, despite acute pressures placed on public services and social policy delivery, the urban poor have generally had easier access to basic education and healthcare than rural labourers.[93] Population growth rates fell from near-catastrophic indices in the mid and late 1960s to manageable levels in the late 1980s and 1990s. Only now is it argued by scholars like Altimir that the incidence of poverty and inequality is greater in the city than in the countryside.[94]

Since the 1940s, significant increases in the coverage and availability of social provision, aimed mainly at urban groups, were instigated above all by populist regimes, which conceived of social programmes as integral components of development. Many such programmes were founded on ideas transmitted by international bodies like the ILO, ECLA/CEPAL, UNESCO and PAHO/WHO, which synthesised theories imported from Europe and generalised policy instruments devised in specific republics from the 1930s onwards. Coined in Mexico, the slogan *desarrollo estabilizador* had a larger reach, implying social peace as well as macroeconomic stability. Yet it remains unclear how far social policy delivery conformed to the phases of 'populist economics' identified by Dornbusch and Edwards; and whether

---

[93]   Roberts (1978); Mesa-Lago (1992); Gilbert (1992 and 1998).

[94]   Altimir (1997).

neo-populist and post-populist regimes learnt from earlier experiences.[95] A daunting challenge confronting champions of an active social policy in the new century is to ensure that the distributional consequences of social policy are progressive, contribute to sustained growth and are consonant with the application and absorption of 'good practice'. Policy-makers need to avoid repeating the past 'bad' practice of funding social interventions through inflation. They have also to be careful not to clash with professionals like junior doctors, nurses and teachers who have responsibility for delivery and can mobilise public opinion, and whose expression of genuine grievances has too often been interpreted as obdurate, self-interested resistance to enlightened change. Moreover, if programmes of development assistance from external agencies like the European Union and the Inter-American Development Bank (IDB) are to have their desired effect and reach their intended beneficiaries, they require accountable managers on the ground and should be designed in such a way as to be comprehensible to, and engage the commitment of, local technicians. Because the final outcome of externally-funded projects is as good (or as bad) as available management skills, care in staff selection and training is imperative in, for example, those parts of Central America where a dearth of sound and efficient institutions exists.[96]

Policy-makers have to be alert to the limitations of public management reform. Too much may be claimed for public management changes that appear to be strategic and comprehensive but are no more than piecemeal and incremental. There is cause to question the current international lexicon and practice of privatisation, agencification, contractualisation, activity-costing and performance management, and whether these give rise to the flow of continuous quality improvements and efficiency gains that are claimed for them. Marketisation and agencification of government may yield unanticipated benefits while destroying direct lines of accountability.[97] A false impression of uniformity can also obscure the different meanings that policy changes carry in different places. Pollitt and Bouckaert argue that in a managerialist 'thought world' only a limited consciousness exists of the flimsiness of current 'principles' of good public management. Some gains in productivity, service quality, transparency and fairness may occur where public servants are given the opportunity to make local sense of reform rhetoric: but this is unlikely to add up to the transformation asserted by

---

[95]   Dornbusch and Edwards (1991).

[96]   Tussie (1995).

[97]   Massey (1997); Pollitt and Bouckaert (2001).

ideologues of the public reform culture.[98] Meanwhile social policy-makers have still to resolve the conundrum that, while the efficiency of economic policy can be measured in terms of productivity and competitiveness, criteria for measuring the efficacy of social policy are seldom comparable, let alone persuasive. Even sceptics about the 'new public management' admit that professionalisation of policy administration must occur both in the ministries and at the point of delivery if key reforms like budgetary deconcentration and decentralisation are to be effective. And an incipient consensus is emerging that, once established, an audit culture must not degenerate into a 'scientific' veneer for clientelism, and that, where it exists, a chasm between the expectations raised by project rhetoric and personalism in internal management practices must be bridged.

The NEM has curbed inflation: but will targeting and the new public management yield more equitable social policy outcomes? Over the past decade distributional outcomes have been influenced by a range of variance during transitions to the NEM, diverse patterns of income and asset distribution, inherited structural heterogeneity and relatively open competition for public office.[99] In the next decade much will depend on state capacity and competence, the introduction of a service ethos and a culture of disinterested professionalism. However Solimano argues that market-friendly social policies rely on growth-led poverty reduction, targeting and private sector participation in the delivery of social services.[100] As he shows, this strategy is flawed: growth rates are unpredictable; segmented administration is inefficient; policy delivery may not reach targeted groups. In the future, social policy objectives need to look beyond poverty reduction: pro-active programmes should replace passive and reactive measures. The state should be prepared to offend the private sector, and external agencies must stop condoning secretiveness and corruption in management.

Equity: Education and Employment

Equity concerns came to the fore in the late 1990s. Defining equity proves elusive, and the degree of priority to be attached to equity programmes is controversial. Alert to the risks of an economistic definition based on income inequality, CEPAL defines equity as the 'reduction of social inequality in its multiple manifestations'.[101] Le Grand appraises the impact

---

98 *Ibid.*
99 Whitehead (1996).
100 Solimano (1998).
101 Wood (1994); CEPAL (2000).

of assertions of a trade-off between equity and efficiency on the theory
and practice of public social policy provision. While arguing that equity
and equality are quite distinct, he distinguishes various layers of equality:
equality of expenditure; equality of cost; equality of delivery; equality of
use; equality of choice; equality of outcome.[102] Referring to health, Hills
speaks of equity as 'equal treatment for equal need'.[103] A political consensus from socialists to conservatives around the desirability of equity
reflects the lack of precision of the concept. Are liberals justified in claiming that equity concerns in social policy should be subordinate to the efficiency priorities of economic policy because market mechanisms are superior to non-market in achieving distributive justice and in allocating
resources? Dissenters from liberal orthodoxies need to explain why active
state intervention is required to rectify the social *brecha*.

A decline in equity raised anxieties about an 'exclusionary style of
development' that would prompt political instability and damage economic performance. Between the mid-1980s and mid-1990s the incidence of
poverty grew exponentially: the rate of growth in the number of poor was
twice that of the population as a whole.[104] The NEM brought about a fall
in real wages, rising unemployment and an enlargement of the informal
sector, resulting directly in further income concentration and deeper and
more widespread poverty. The poor were compelled to take informal
measures in response to a brusque contraction and casualisation of
employment and plummeting real wages, a significant fall in the real value
of welfare benefits and the removal of subsidies from deteriorating public services. Consequential factors, such as changes in the education structure had an even more significant, adverse impact.[105] Conversely, fiscal
reform had the progressive effect of pushing inflation rates down.[106]
Additionally, privatisation and deregulation reduced the discretion of the
state.[107] This does not mean that the state cannot reconcile equity and
prosperity in the interests of social cohesion. Modulated tax reforms
involving sumptuary taxes on luxury consumption, broadly-based value-
added taxes and tariff structures that move gradually towards uniformity

[102]   Le Grand (1982 and 1991).
[103]   Hills (1997), p. 59.
[104]   Vuskovic (1993); Tulchin and Garland (2000).
[105]   Tokman (1992); Thomas (1992 and 1995); Portes and Schaeffer (1993); Morley (2000).
[106]   Bulmer-Thomas (1996).
[107]   Dornbusch (1993).

can resolve the conundrum, while avoiding the progressive taxation of businesses that may threaten output, productivity and employment. [108]

Expressing alarm about the equity and employment consequences of social policy, Stallings and Peres observe considerable variations across the continent.[109] Their work confirms predictions of a sharpening inequality between the richer and the poorer countries. This is observed in a failure to expand social policy coverage in poorer republics and renewed moves towards universal coverage in the richer.[110] Divergences within countries are reflected in variations of earnings between workers in the public and private sectors, and self-employed professionals and non-professionals.[111]

Increasingly scholars argue that the key to equitable development — and, indeed, empowerment — is an educational policy that reduces inequalities in stratified systems like segmented Latin American labour markets. Morley draws particular attention to wide gaps in educational attainments between unskilled and skilled workers and between workers and graduates.[112] Likewise, Urrutia and Berry attribute a dual wage structure, characterised by income differentials between highly skilled workers in the 'modern sector' and other workers, especially in agriculture, to educational inequities.[113] While the dominant pattern in East Asia is to concentrate resources in universalising primary and secondary education, the majority of children in Latin America does not even attend secondary school. Over-generous provision for the tertiary sector at the expense of the secondary was rooted in responses to the University Reform Movement commencing in 1918, and was reinforced following student revolts in the 1960s and 1970s.[114] Birdsall draws lessons from East Asia, where virtuous circles of equity and growth have been created: education promotes growth, which in turn makes possible more investment in education; education spending reduces inequality, engendering growth, which further stimulates investment in education.[115] In Latin America education policy has been generally regressive and largely reactive. Pressure to extend

---

[108] Harberger (1993).

[109] Stallings and Peres (2000).

[110] Altimir (1997).

[111] Altimir and Piñera (1982); Altimir (1998).

[112] Morley (2000).

[113] Urrutia and Berry (1970); Urrutia (1991).

[114] Walter (1968).

[115] Birdsall et al. (1998).

the provision of schooling follows the demographic curve. Greater numbers of children compel governments to increase primary school places, and the ageing of generational cohorts increases demand for more secondary education.[116] If often neglected in contemporary Latin America (though recognised in the 1930s), counter-cyclical education expenditure can reactivate the economy while anticipating future demand and can influence the capacity of the poor to withstand economic shocks. A strong case exists for promoting public education during recession, even if positive results are not immediately apparent.

Several ideological currents shape thinking on education. Christian democrats maintain that education dignifies labour and humanises capital; socialists emphasise that education empowers workers and communities; developmentalists correlate education and structural change; and neoliberals contend that basic skills are critical for efficiency and competitiveness. CEPAL argues for widespread educational reform as a route to remedying the distributive failures of adjustment policies: a better qualified teaching force with more permanency, new incentives and compensation for merit, and an active role for the teaching unions.[117] To these should be added curriculum and administrative reorganisation embodied in the *escola nova/escuela nueva* experiments in Brazil and Colombia that attempt to break with traditions of preparing children for submissiveness and passivity rather than developing critical skills. For all the debate about education and equity, many schools function in such a way as to sustain the *status quo*, reproducing and legitimising inequality. Education objectives continue to be distorted by states that persist in projecting schools as instruments dispensing privileges granted by a benevolent government, not as institutions to which future citizens have rights of access, and by clientelistic networks that have turned teachers' rights into favours. Politicians are unlikely to surrender such a powerful source of patronage as the schooling system without demanding compensatory concessions. The bureaucratic diversion of resources away from the needs of pupils is a pronounced feature of education spending. Is the selection of teachers on the basis of political allegiance rather than competence an issue of management, misallocation of resources or structure? Adjustment policies have exacerbated the problem. Some teachers are less effective, because, with salary reductions they opt to teach double-shifts and resort to moonlighting; and spending on

---

[116]   Bóo (1996).

[117]   CEPAL (2000).

non-salary items and non-recurrent expenditure (from books and laboratory equipment to maintenance of buildings) remains conspicuously low. Claims from some neoliberals that the only major problems requiring attention are poor investment decisions and inadequacies of resource allocation are not convincing.[118]

More equity in education (and health) spending will be achieved only by expanding the tax base within the framework of a robust fiscal policy.[119] Urrutia and Berry have gone even further and argue in a series of publications since 1970 that the uneven distribution of education explains a large part of income differentials.[120] Persistent under-investment in education (and basic health) from about 1960 also marred economic performance even before adjustment policies were applied.[121] CEPAL confirms views that greater equity can be brought about only through a combination of economic and social policy. It points to an uneven performance: more equity in primary and secondary schooling, and health and nutrition; less in social security and university education; with housing in an intermediate position. Also urgent are more equitable and efficient labour relations with more justice and transparency for unionists, together with access to collective bargaining for small business and non-unionised workers.[122] Denial of political participation and lack of access to the law create further disparities of opportunities, labour instability, low incomes, obstacles to social mobility especially for women, ignorance of ethnic and cultural diversity and poor defences for the victims of disasters and other misfortunes.[123] Educational investment increases the 'property of human capital' in the population.[124]

Proponents of labour market flexibilisation argue that liberalising labour codes facilitates participation in the labour market as well as market integration, and results in job creation and greater efficiency — both for the macroeconomy and the individual firm. This approach chimes with the 'work as welfare' approach of the World Bank, that the principal causes of poverty are inflation and a lack of employment.[125] Hence, labour market

---

[118] Morales-Gómez and Torres (1992); Grindle (2000b).

[119] CEPAL (2000).

[120] Urrutia and Berry (1970); Urrutia (1991); Berry (1998).

[121] Urrutia (1991).

[122] Márquez (1995); CEPAL (2000).

[123] *Ibid.*

[124] Morley (2000).

[125] World Bank (1993).

flexibilisation will generate employment and income — in the long run, though it is acknowledged that sacrifices in equity in the short term may follow, and the poor could benefit from minimum wages.[126] Locational factors may, where migrations do not occur, continue to explain shortages and mis-matching of skills. Yet the terms 'flexibility' and 'deregulation' may suggest an illusory simplicity that conceals a range of histories and contexts of labour relations. And, the growth of informality indicates that 'flexibilisation' occurred in most economies in the 1980s and 1990s. Entrepreneurs often complain of vexatious labour standards without complying with them. They subcontract work to the unprotected informal sector in order to avoid fiscal and social obligations — payroll taxes, redundancy payments and accountancy costs — and obviate labour conflict. Fewer regulations are unlikely to lead to rises in output, wages and productivity. What is needed is a more effective regulatory regime that encroaches less on the freedom of action of entrepreneurs, while relying more on rules that are clear to both workers and employers, and less on an undefined authority of the state to intervene arbitrarily in conflicts. Furthermore, deregulation can mean, where poorly applied, the reassertion of informal linkages and identities and the streamlining of clientelism.[127] Edwards and Lustig argue for three priorities: the phasing out of unwarranted labour regulation in order to reduce labour costs, without compromising social protection; the conversion of severance payments schemes into deferred compensation plans; and the reform of payroll taxes so as to reduce non-wage labour costs. They call for converting a publicly managed, pay-as-you-go defined benefits system into one with a smaller public component, that co-exists with another system with a mandatory, privately managed, fully-funded component.[128]

Labour code reform is politically problematic, can be socially divisive and may destabilise labour markets as the employment record of Latin America in the 1990s demonstrates. Processes of labour reforms were often over-complex and apparently contradictory, aiming to reconcile simplicity in collective contracts, labour flexibility and mobility with a minimum wage and a modicum of social protection. In 1995 the real minimum wage in 13 of 17 countries studied was below that in 1980.[129] It has

---

[126]   Beccaria and Galín (1998), p. 82.

[127]   Márquez (1995); Thomas (1995).

[128]   Edwards and Lustig (1997).

[129]   CEPAL (1997).

become obvious that increasing access to employment in the formal sector means more than reducing institutional barriers to entry or promoting employer optimism by lowering the opportunity cost of labour recruitment. Orthodoxy in macroeconomic strategy can be complemented by a more interventionist micro-level policy, especially state support for small firms that aim to be efficient players in the market.[130] Targeted state assistance for these enterprises can be justified on grounds of economic efficiency and socially beneficial sustained employment. If large-scale corporations can position themselves to maximise opportunities created by state retreat and globalisation, small (often domestically-owned) firms, which have a better record of job creation than capital-intensive enterprises, require state encouragement to seize new commercial initiatives. Market mechanisms alone can guarantee neither the participation nor the survival of these firms. They have to be provided with the necessary information and incentives to enter the market. Are social programmes today more efficient than ten years ago, so that the individual and societal costs of frictional (if not structural) unemployment can be eased?

Why were labour markets fragmented and patterns of inequity so entrenched? The main explanation may lie with social reforms of the 1920s–1970s. Only selected groups benefited from state regulation of working conditions, social insurance, technical training and recognition of the right to organise that were influenced by Catholic social action, reformist socialism and Keynesian developmentalism. These measures intensified labour market divisions — between the formal and informal sector, between 'incorporated' and 'non-incorporated' groups, as well as historic divisions in labour movements between skilled/craft associations (the 'labour aristocracy') and mass unions.[131] Further segmentation that inhibited collective action resulted from gender and age prejudice, ethnic antagonism and ideological conflict involving migrant, seasonal and other categories of workers, that were exacerbated by structural change in the labour market. Co-optive state policy promoted imperfection: segmentation and segregation immobilised bodies of workers. Labour policy needs to connect with debate about education and human capital, in particular removing obstacles to investment in training.[132] Welfare reformers need also to ask if their schemes merely turn the absolute poor into the relative poor and the welfare poor into the working poor.

---

[130] Coutinho and Ferraz (1994); Suzigan and Villela (1997); Kosacoff (2000).

[131] Bergquist (1986); Roxborough (1994).

[132] Márquez (1995).

Intergenerational justice also plays an important part in discussions about equity. Johnson and others demonstrate how demographic change and ageing have a significant impact on the labour force, pay, productivity, mobility and international competitiveness — and on the household life-cycle of ascent from, and descent into, poverty. As life expectancy in Latin America comes to resemble that in Southern Europe one or two genera-tions ago, an incipient crisis of ageing arises. The 'third age' is entering the political discourse: the elderly press governments to 'respect' pension arrangements and to provide accessible and affordable housing and health-care, especially where family networks have been eroded by market eco-nomics, and by decline in family size and intergenerational solidarity.[133] Paradoxically, while the state is retreating — or encouraging private provi-sion — in fields such as education and general healthcare, it is being com-pelled to consider action regarding special care for the elderly. In order to implement inter-generational justice, the state must avoid clashes between the wage demands of workers and the pension requirements of the retired, and take account of the needs of enterprises to finance wages and invest-ments, while raising sufficient taxes to finance social interventions. Justice requires that the state assures recurrent training through life, promotes flexible responses to labour market volatility, counteracts gender differ-ences and educational deficits and redistributes wealth to the disabled. By assuring a generationally balanced fiscal policy, the state can also play a valuable role in smoothing out levels of income over the life cycle.[134]

Poverty, Community and Household

Latin America continues to be influenced by both European and US assumptions of poverty. Where US policy-makers apply strategies based on the assumption that help should be denied to the undeserving poor even when this unintentionally penalises the deserving poor, Europeans tend to prefer giving assistance to the undeserving for fear of overlooking the deserving. Anti-poverty strategies are influenced by several factors: primari-ly by the problem of reaching a definition of poverty that can be applied across time and space. Strategy is also shaped by a set of over-lapping alter-natives. Is the object to tackle absolute or relative poverty? Is the aim of pol-icy to handle structural or frictional poverty? How far are policy-makers

---

[133] Johnson and Lloyd-Sherlock (1996); Lloyd-Sherlock (1997).

[134] Johnson, Conrad and Thomson (1989); Johnson and Zimmermann (1993); Hills (1997).

seeking to eradicate causes of poverty, and how far symptoms? Outcomes can be confused and strategies derailed by uncertainty and inconsistency of objectives. For example, an intention to confront causes of relative poverty in general can be disrupted by dramatic changes in absolute levels of poverty.

Technical difficulties abound. For too long, definitions were overly focused on income levels (in order to determine the poverty line) and items to be included in the basket of essential goods, the consumption of which determined whether or not households were considered poor. Changes in the composition of the basket and culturally determined patterns of consumption tended to frustrate comparison. Hence the emergence of concepts and indicators like basic needs, entitlements, resources and purchasing power parity. Yet debate continues, about causes of poverty, consequences of policy and constructions to be placed on absolute and relative poverty, the one concerned largely with indigence and the other with equity.[135] Has absolute poverty become a policy concern only because its dimensions are so great that it poses an obstacle to growth? Has Latin America evolved its own assumptions about poverty and strategies to overcome it? Poverty policy today enjoys a priority that it has seldom had before. However, the efficacy of policy application is at times frustrated by competing agencies, with over-lapping jurisdictions, and by technical solutions to symptoms that do not tackle structural problems like mal-distribution of wealth or assets. An effective government can assist the poor through sensitive anti-cyclical macroeconomic policies and through the correction of distortions that have a particularly adverse affect on the poor. Perhaps Latin American states — and the poor — have been ill served by international agencies. In the early 1990s, the Asian and African counterparts of the IDB were much more successful in assisting governments to reach the poor. The Inter-American Development Bank could have been more pro-active and more interventionist.[136]

To what extent is poverty rooted in community? Scholarly analyses of the 1930s–1950s saw community in largely static terms and had limited policy impact outside Mexico. They popularised models of corporate community — isolated, village societies in equilibrium — and simple typologies that failed adequately to differentiate categories of 'primitive', 'peasant' and rural labourer.[137] Mainly anthropological, this work stressed issues

135   Altimir (1982); Sen (1997).

136   Tussie (1995).

137   Wolf and Mintz (1957); Wolf (1966); Duncan and Rutledge (1977), p. 3.

of kinship, land tenure and ownership, exchange and reciprocity, local administration, religion and the production of a surplus for ceremonial uses, paying special attention to 'moral economy' — which 'equalised' poverty by levelling down resource availability.[138] Unsatisfactory because they overlooked diversity, treated simplistically external forces (notably government, the market economy and migrations) and underplayed the role in rural communities of climatic cycles and natural calamities, these models were superseded by more dynamic analyses in the 1960s and 1970s.[139] Combining socio-historical investigations and geographical surveys with evolving anthropological methods, scholars forged innovative inter-disciplinary approaches to 'peasant studies' and analyses of haciendas and plantations, that produced subtle pictures which underlined diversity of agrarian enterprise and mapped out the complex and hierarchical features of social relations in the countryside. Academic research cross-fertilised with analyses of 'agrarian problems' carried out by international organisations and state agencies.[140] From intense debate about the scope and content of agrarian reform emerged less radical measures of frontier development and rural colonisation, plus a preoccupation with investment in agricultural productivity.[141] Implicit in these discussions were competing assumptions about, on the one hand, the vitality and flexibility of rural society, and, on the other, the urgency of capitalist rationalisation in the countryside. Breaking with liberal orthodoxies that depicted both landlords and peasants as hopelessly rigid, archaic and precapitalist, both assumptions implied significant transitions. The first envisaged a redistributive agrarian reform that promoted social justice and rural democracy, empowered 'peasant' proprietors to produce for the market and strengthened community. The second ascribed a central role to agribusinesses which, often assisted by state subsidies, gave a new impetus to large-scale production that tended to atomise community and equate solidarity with subversion.[142] Recent social science studies have interacted with a revisionist historiography that has re-appraised the history of landlord power, and peasant and indigenous insurrection and protest since the late colonial period. Much new writing has identified community rather than class as

138   Wolf (1957); Foster (1965).
139   Shanin (1971); Pearse (1975); Duncan and Rutledge (1977).
140   ECLA (1969b).
141   Lehmann (1974); Foweraker (1981); Sanderson (1985).
142   *Ibid.*; Scott (1991); de la Peña (1994).

the main vehicle of popular mobilisation, while stressing the importance of endogenous societal organisation and participation in the market.[143]

New analyses of rural community had a profound impact upon the study of community (and anonymity) in the city. In the 1950s and 1960s, the study of urban society was largely a preserve of historians, sociologists and political scientists scrutinising themes like political protest, the assimilation of European immigrants, labour activism and militancy and the social origins of populism.[144] How far, as has been claimed, did immigrant clubs, trade unions and, above all, populist movements re-create bonds of community in the primate cities of mid twentieth century Latin America? And, how far were the virtues of rural community replicated in shanty towns in the survival networks that confronted problems of poverty and adjustment? Meanwhile, geographers and anthropologists fiercely contested distinct conceptual approaches stressing a 'culture of poverty' and 'urban marginality'.[145] They debated whether, segregated from the capitalist mainstream of the city, the poor in squatter settlements evolved self-perpetuating mechanisms that transmitted misery across generations. Was it reasonable to contend that the poor were responsible for their own continuing poverty, from which only enlightened, modernising planners could rescue them? 'Urban reform', it should be stressed, never commanded the same attention as agrarian reform. The premises behind urban reform were more modest, because the orthodoxy prevailed that, complemented by limited government intervention to assure basic public services, autonomous market forces would supply affordable accommodation and assure employment. From the 1970s, social scientists broadened the discussion. Research into the dynamics of urban community and, more recently, of community and household complemented analyses of 'cities of peasants'.[146] Optimistic explorations of informality and self-help housing pointed to the vitality of urban economic networks and the potential strength of community when enabled by the state.[147] Pro-active policies were required to secure and distribute title and upgrade the urban infrastructure. This, or so it was argued, would promote a sequence of positive changes: first, owner occupation; secondly, housing improvement and investment; and, finally, the formation of

---

[143] Stern (1987); Katz (1988); Joseph and Nugent (1994); Huber and Safford (1995); Nugent (1998).
[144] Germani (1968); Weffort (1978).
[145] O. Lewis (1969); Roberts (1973 and 1978); Perlman (1976).
[146] Roberts (1978 and 1995).
[147] Gilbert and Ward (1985); Portes (1995).

social capital. The study of particular *barrios* was complemented by micro investigations of household and family, as gender studies focussed attention on domestic divisions of labour and their projection into community relations. Yet an anachronistic predominance of rural studies over urban persisted until the present, with adverse consequences for urban policy. Whereas in the 1930s, over two-thirds of Latin American lived in the countryside, by 2000 over three-quarters inhabited the cities. Even today, the study of urban community lags behind that of rural, and the study of community behind that of citizenship.

Programmes of community action in much of Latin America began as defensive responses, articulated by the Alliance for Progress, to challenges of rural insurgency and class struggle posed by the Cuban Revolution of 1959.[148] The first projects were reformist and sociopolitical in thrust. Directed at the countryside, and reaffirming the 'social function' of property, they confronted questions of poverty, land hunger and threats of disorder by introducing agricultural extension courses, building community clinics and centres and improving infrastructure in villages and small towns. Managed by regional superintendencies in Brazil and national agencies and ministries in the Andean republics, officials responsible for these projects were influenced by the idealism of the agrarian reform movement.[149] This wave of reforms in the countryside was cut short by a shift to the right in Washington and across Latin America, by underfunding and misappropriation of resources, and by a refocusing of attention upon the city. The second generation of measures was authoritarian and conservative. Community action approaches from the top bypassed local elites and targeted the powerless and impoverished, failing to acknowledge initiatives from within the community and from non-governmental sources.[150] Top-down remedial policies of social welfare were criticised by proponents of a 'popular participation' approach, who claimed that action from above was inefficient and wasteful. Optimistic about the capacity of the community for self-action, they called instead for a third wave of policies characterised by 'people's empowerment' and active participation. Communitarians went further. Arguing from the premise that social development was best promoted by people working harmoniously in their communities, 'communitarian populists' urged individuals to foster private

[148]   Landsberger (1969); Stavenhagen (1970).

[149]   Barraclough and Domike (1966).

[150]   Midgley (1995).

interests by working collectively. Communitarian populists differed from collectivists who were encouraging co-operative endeavour and joint-ownership and management. Yet both groups perceived state bureaucracies as inefficient and indifferent, and held community development from above to be insufficiently interactive.[151]

Communities and households have functioned as arenas of mediation, negotiation, production and exchange, with profoundly varied resource endowments. Communities can constitute either instruments of self-defence and self-advancement, which assist national development; or privileged enclave entities that foster sectional goals at the expense of national development. Communities may be understood to be agencies promoting Pareto optimality, or alternatively, as mechanisms boosting the stock of resources available to a specific group at the expense of broader society. Since the mid-nineteenth century indigenous communities have both been defended as the authentic expression of specific cultures and subcultures, and attacked as closed phenomena that impede a buoyant market economy by tying up land and labour and limiting demand for consumer goods.[152] In the late twentieth century, advocates of the benefits of social capital tended to neglect its negative features, for example the particularist preferences and privileged access to resources granted at the expense of universalistic rights of others.[153] Current discussion of communitarian identities carries an element of mythology in urban areas where anonymity prevails over community, and may depend on a stable urban demography that is seldom observed. It also overlooks a wide diversity of 'communities', in particular their capacity for negotiation, absorption, resistance and deflection of reform projects. Migrations further complicate the urban picture. Asymmetrical exchanges of migrants give rise to spatially clustered networks of businesses owned by members of the same community, among them middlemen minorities which occupy economic specialisations abandoned by other businesses. A broader society can benefit from the social capital of immigrants and community-mediated opportunities; but, where access to scarce resources occurs by virtue of membership of migrant networks, new tensions requiring effective social policy can arise.[154]

Deep-rooted patterns of discrimination have militated against the construction of national identity and community. Discriminatory social mores

---

151   *Ibid.*
152   Gros (1991); Portocarrero (1992).
153   Portes and Landolt (2000).
154   Gledhill (1995); Portes (1995).

were embedded in the ideologies and attitudes of external and domestic agents. From the 1890s and 1900s, US firms operating in Latin America preached a 'Social Gospel': sobriety and diligence would be instilled among workers and conformity among the middle class by vocational training, together with the provision of health, education and sports facilities. Although rarely convinced that 'unruly' Latin American populations were 'ready' for the re-ordered social relations that it extolled, a 'coalition of Americanisation' promoted the ideal of a US patriarchal nuclear family as the main building block of a stable environment.[155] These attitudes reinforced the 'scientific racism' then pervasive among positivist policy-makers and intellectuals in Latin America, who viewed the region's racial heritage as an insurmountable obstacle to ambitious projects of social transformation.[156] By the 1910s, immigrant organisations that embodied ideals of 'Europeanisation' and 'social whitening' sharpened pre-existing patterns of class and ethnic discrimination.[157] Racism outlived the abolition of slavery, and black communities, stigmatised as hotbeds of crime, were frequently excluded from the broader nation.[158]

Since the mid-nineteenth century, the state and capitalism have sought to incorporate indigenous communities into wider land and labour markets and to encourage exchange, ambitions that are only incompletely achieved today owing to indigenous resistance, inaccessible upland locations, market weakness and the failures of liberal capitalism. International and national agencies seldom take full cognisance of the diversity of indigenous experience or comprehend that belief systems and cosmologies change more slowly than economic arrangements. Rarely do they connect community discourses about local identity to shifting patterns of power, solidarity and consensus, or grasp the difficulties inherent in binary oppositions between 'western' and indigenous, that simplify and, at times, deny realities of dialogue, mobility and shifting parameters.[159] Agencies often make the glib assumption that the mere opening of a school or health-post confers legitimacy upon the state in the eyes of an indigenous or peasant group. Many national and international agencies overlook histories of ambivalent relationships of peasant communities with the state and the

---

[155] Rosenberg (1982 and 1999); Drake (1991); O'Brien (1996); Miller Klubock (1998).

[156] Halperín Donghi (1999).

[157] Solberg (1970); Reid Andrews (1980 and 1991).

[158] Reid Andrews (1991); Gledhill (1994); Helg (1995); Whitten Jr and Quiroga (1998); Fausto (1999).

[159] Mallon (1992); Harris (2000); van Cott (2000)

market.[160] The consequences of emigration are similarly contradictory, at times weakening, at others strengthening, communal solidarity.[161]

A conscious drive to transform city anonymity into community membership underlay many decisions by governments from the 1960s, embodying a significant change in the premises lying behind urban policy. Before the World Depression of the 1930s, government action had been conditioned by notions of 'respectable' urban society that were founded upon assumptions of stable households. Socially exclusive projects for urban beautification proliferated. There were schemes to build 'garden suburbs' in national and provincial capitals and 'model settlements' in frontier areas.[162] Illusions of a capacity to construct stable urban environments were shattered in the 1930s and 1940s. Export sector crisis triggered sociopolitical upheaval and rural-urban migration that was further aggravated by industrial growth and the concentration of ameliorative state effort in the cities. For insecure regimes of the period, social containment took precedence over the creation of 'recreational public space' in cities. Strikes, riots, hunger marches and popular invasions of city centres began to change elite perceptions of the locus of disorder. The language of the debate shifted from a stress upon the threat posed by dilapidated, insanitary tenements to the dangers associated with sprawling shanty-towns. From mid-century, policy was driven by anxiety about the growth of *favelas*, *barriadas* and *pueblos jóvenes* in and around burgeoning cities and by broader questions of cohesion and order. Decisions taken in the 1960s and 1970s to grant slum dwellers title to property and to provide basic services — roads, water, and electricity — modified the urban landscape.[163] These reforms were legitimised in terms of concepts of modernisation and marginality.[164]

In the late 1970s and 1980s massive mobilisations of community, class and sectional groups underlined the resilience of community, exposed slowness and unevenness in creating channels of community participation and revealed failures of policy-makers to take cognisance of diverse historical, locational and community dynamics.[165] In some countries the origins of 'new social movements' lay in the destruction of representative

---

[160] Baud (1995); Topik (1999).

[161] Portes and Stepnick (1993); Gledhill (1995).

[162] Scobie (1974 and 1988); Joseph and Szuchman (1996).

[163] Hardoy and Satterthwaite (1989); Gilbert (1998).

[164] Perlman (1976).

[165] Eckstein (1990).

institutions, in others in resistance to routine attempts at co-option by the state.[166] The vibrancy and force of grassroots social movements derived to a large degree from the vacuum left by the brutal destruction of top-down vehicles of mobilisation/co-option — political parties, official trade unions and peasant federations — by authoritarian regimes. As political parties recovered during the process of re-democratisation, many new social movements resisted their embrace out of scepticism about the instinctive recourse of machine politicians to clientelistic mechanisms. The momentum of social movements was maintained by the social impact of the debt crises and the NEM. Techniques of containment, co-option and coercion that neutralised opposition and atomised civil society shaped emergent community-based organisations (CBOs) and workplace commit-tees, that spawned a new civic-mindedness. Much optimism about the potential of CBOs to forge social citizenship proved misplaced. The weakness of many CBOs was reflected in the women's movement and teachers' protests. The women's movement seldom developed a single uni-fied organisation to deliver full citizenship for women or to change labour law to take account of women's work.[167] The strategy of unionised teach-ers — to leave discussion of curriculum matters until education funding had improved and teachers were better paid and enjoyed more job securi-ty — can antagonise parents.[168] In spite of recourse to the rhetoric of social empowerment and co-responsibility, governments remained reluctant to accept autonomous representative groups as partners in the policy process. The oppression of military dictatorships reinvigorated traditions of com-munal resistance to the disabling state by demolishing populist agencies of co-option that allowed new movements to flourish. Even Cuba has experi-enced incipient social movements, which according to the regime are spon-sored by European NGOs. These movements have pressed for policies of decentralisation and co-management of autonomous enterprises which are consistent with official revolutionary ideology but are not congruent with top-down structures of a secretive bureaucracy.[169]

Useful at times in extending the access of poor communities to resources and increasing the outreach of government in health and educa-tion, NGOs have well-known limitations: an often lacklustre performance

---

[166]   Castells (1983); Harvey (1993); Piester (1997).

[167]   F. Miller (1991).

[168]   Cook (1996).

[169]   Pérez-Stable (1999); Dilla Alfonso (2000).

and uneven presence; unsustainable interventions and insecure funding; corruption, mismanagement and ineffective systems of planning, monitoring and evaluation. Reluctant to be more than crisis expedients that handled the social costs of the NEM, many NGOs nevertheless felt obliged to undertake wholesale relief and act as permanent alternatives to official social providers. A wide range of scale and purpose can be a source of strength. NGOs may palliate the most serious destitution, promote some bonds of reciprocity and trust and supply financial help and professional advice that are invaluable in confronting the immediate problems of low-income groups. However, diversity of NGO structure and purpose — relief agency, technical innovation organisation, administrator of public service contracts, advocacy network and intermediary institution that supports communities and individuals — can frustrate effectiveness.[170] Rivalries too inhibit co-ordination. And the imposition of alien models can create imbalances and distortions. The overall accomplishment of many NGOs has been meagre, and their role in building a viable democracy has been limited by their own unrepresentative and unaccountable character. Nevertheless, by the 1990s, NGOs were more active in struggles by the poor to obtain both legal rights and access to resources that were not dependent upon patronage-clientelism. This was acknowledged when the World Bank began to use NGOs to channel Social Investment Funds (SIFs) to the poor. However, in the initial stages of SIFs, the Bank was exposed to the criticism that SIFs were misallocated, favouring the 'new poor' like sacked public sector workers and bureaucrats at the expense of the chronic poor. This error has now been rectified.[171] Other criticisms continue. The Bank is widely condemned for reinforcing privatising trends within the social services, depoliticising social policy and promoting an understanding that the role of social policy was confined to poverty alleviation, and was not to involve major redistribution. In addition, the deployment of funds through NGOs engages new social actors in decision-making, with significant positive consequences for active citizen participation, without posing challenges to the authority and legitimacy of the state.[172]

Evidence abounds that potent forces inhibit communal solidarity and stability, a strongly patterned associational life and effective citizenship. Various analysts warn against the deceptive nature of a sharp line between

---

[170] Arrossi (1994).

[171] Graham (1994); Fundación Friedrich Ebert (1998).

[172] Segarra (1997); Hall (1997).

the formal and informal sectors, as well as against over-compartmentalising social and community groups and underestimating the complexity of socioeconomic networks.[173] Linkages and 'social connectedness' can be consolidated in various ways. Voluntarism may sustain civic virtue and social responsibility, if at a heavy cost in wastefulness and duplication of effort.

The harsh realities of the debt crises and adjustment policies of the 1980s and the impact of globalisation in the 1990s and beyond had a variable impact upon poor households. Those with limited material resources have constantly reactivated complex webs of kinship and neighbourhood ties and developed microenterprises in order to survive.[174] Following Gregory, Lustig has argued that, despite a drastic decline in real wages, many Mexican households avoided falls in total income and per capita consumption by working extra hours, by seeking new remunerated activities, by sending more family members into the workforce and by spending remittances from the USA.[175] A view of adaptable households courageously weathering crises does not give enough credence either to diversity among households and inequalities within them, or to associated social and psychological costs.[176] Nor does it sufficiently acknowledge that reduced fertility resulting from urbanisation, international campaigns of family planning and the process of women's emancipation had little positive impact on the health of mothers and children. In addition, optimistic narratives fail to recognise that old solutions no longer apply. Rural-urban migration is not a remedy for rural poverty because cities are losing their capacity for absorption. Furthermore, there was little evidence of sustained development in the 1990s in several countries, and there is less prospect of growth in the near future.[177]

Many poor households fracture in crisis. During short crises ownership of assets like jewellery and livestock reduces household vulnerability; long crises exhaust these 'entitlements'. Other assets, such as a spare room to let, become less negotiable if demand for accommodation for rent falls. A reduction in the hours of available work can reduce access to social goods. Costs of illness or the death of a productive adult can cause profound crisis where access to credit, except from the loan shark, is difficult. Poor

---

[173] MacEwen Scott (1994); González de la Rocha (1994); Clarke and Howard (1999).

[174] Portes and Guernizo (1991); Portes, Dore-Cabral and Landolt (1997).

[175] Gregory (1986); Lustig (1997).

[176] González de la Rocha (1994); Graham (1994).

[177] Chant (1997).

households do not typically remove their children from school; but the costs associated with education — fees, presentable clothing, bus fares, textbooks — can be overwhelming, and the opportunity costs of keeping a child at school during a harvest may be excessive for rural labouring households. One important manifestation of household fracturing is 'denuclearisation': the fragmentation of families into single-person and single parent households further limits the capacity to deal with crises. Moreover, the assumption that the extended family affords support in life-cycle contingencies is tenacious, but probably, in the state of the literature, unverifiable.[178] Different associations exist for different kinds of household: cooperatives for peasants and community associations for indigenous households. For the most part the poorest households are less able to organise for collective action in emergencies like natural disasters and resource degradation than the less poor, and remain over-dependent on casual benevolence and informal philanthropy. In these and other circumstances, social reformers have urged two options on the state. One is to enable households to self-insure and self-protect by extending entitlement to social insurance; the other, to promote household access to finance markets for regulated private insurance made possible by borrowing from government in bad times and repayment in good.[179]

A rare unanimity is observed in the literature that underlines the weakening of social constraints upon women with urbanisation, a rise in female participation in the workforce and an increase in the number of poor, female-headed households. Yet Safa emphasised how paid employment has empowered women only under specific conditions: secure employment and good education. Occupational segregation and wage differentials reinforce workplace gender subordination, which in part occurs as a result of social exclusion and spatial isolation of single mothers.[180] Some empowerment occurs where women negotiate alternative domestic environments and more equitable patterns of sharing of resources and responsibilities within the domestic unit. As poor households that use the earning capacity of adult women prove to be the most resilient in crisis, so the question arises whether older daughters are compelled to neglect education in order to undertake domestic tasks.[181] Recent research stresses the resilience and adaptability of

---

[178]   Chant (1991).

[179]   de Ferranti et al. (2000).

[180]   Safa (1995).

[181]   González de la Rocha (1994); Chant (1997).

patriarchy and the continuing obstacles confronted by women at work, even though they have played an active and often equal role in workplace organisation. It underlines gender-selective patterns of migration and female labour force participation, state policies and family law, and the social norms of gender, marriage, motherhood and female sexuality.[182] Evidence abounds that the ideal of the breadwinning 'good family man' remains powerful, and that residual elements of male dominance are not always upset by new, self-generating money-making activities among women.

Poor households relate to the state often through dysfunctional institutions, with patterns of informal power operating more effectively than patterns of formal, and with men especially being embedded in patron-client relations. Local officialdom often limits access to government and benefits, and local government colludes with elites to prevent benefits reaching their intended destinations.[183] Through the 1990s, Gilbert and Varley reiterated the need for affordable and accessible rental housing, and for more self-help housing with better land security (sites-and-services schemes and squatter upgrading programmes). They stressed, too, the importance of state credit to enable the poor to build, and argued for the creation of more owner-occupier households with space for tenants and sharers.[184] Given the constraints on the housing options of the poor, the prediction of Castells of the early 1980s that mobilisation from below would offset state control has proved over-optimistic.[185] Even when well intentioned, state action can have negative consequences for the poorest households. Legislation to impose an adult minimum wage and abolish child labour may jeopardise household income for the poorest groups. If enforced, minimum wage legislation can price adults out of the labour market while proscriptions of child labour can undermine the capacity of the child to finance his/her own secondary education. Should the priority of law be to abolish child labour or remove its worst excesses? In many instances, rent control has had the unintended effect of reducing the stock of affordable rental housing: should the state instead provide incentives to the 'self-help' landlord?[186]

Poor households view the state at a distance. Poor households and individuals have first-hand experience of the failures of policies that stress a

[182] Craske (1999); Vaughan (2000); Varley (2000).
[183] Tendler (1997).
[184] Gilbert (1991b); Varley (1993); Gilbert (1997).
[185] Castells (1983).
[186] Gilbert and Varley (1989).

pragmatic blend of state provision, self-help solutions, private initiative and NGO assistance. This is especially evident in the administration of policing and justice. Unpredictable policing and 'preventive raids' into crime-ridden neighbourhoods reinforce distrust of the police — identified in opinion polls across the continent as the most unpopular of state institutions. Corruption and violence are associated with 'social cleansing', the dissolution of networks of mutuality and reciprocity and large-scale internal displacements and exile. Violence from outside and within the household provokes a profound disrespect for life, personal freedom and property, and exerts an adverse influence on governability and standards of group behaviour. Increasing inequality and social exclusion are intensifying conflict, which often breaks into new waves of violence in countries that suffered high levels of insurgency in the 1980s. Violence from outside the household has eroded social capital networks between households and within communities, has reduced the human capital endowments of the young, has undermined the internal functioning of households in terms of norms, values and trust and has exacerbated family disintegration and problems of domestic violence. According to the World Bank and the IDB, violence and corruption are among the main constraints on development and efficiency.[187] In the absence of a trustworthy system of judicial protection, households and enterprises are debilitated by corruption and extortion, and develop extra-legal systems of protection and resort to rent-seeking.[188] Attempts to reform creaking judicial systems have been frustrated by political resistance, a defensive professional culture, obstructive and incompetent officials, incoherent legislation, the co-existence of formal rules and informal practices, misallocation of resources and lack of legal aid. These combine to deny access to the courts to low-income groups, women and *los indígenas*. [189]

Towards a Model of Social Liberalism?

To conclude, it can be stated with confidence that, since the end of the Cold War, 'market liberalism' has been in the ascendant in Latin America, having entered a tenuous coalition with ethical socialism and social Catholicism. Conjuring up the bogeys of hyperinflation, class conflict and military coups from the 1970s and 1980s, ideologues of neoliberalism

---

[187]   World Bank (2000); IDB (2000).

[188]   Meertens (1997); Moser and McIlwaine (2000a).

[189]   Fuentes Hernández (1999).

peddle the model of an efficient social policy within the framework of a competitive global economy. The New Social Policy — or rather its outcomes — has become vital to the adaptability and survival of neoliberalism, and has been argued by its advocates to be the key to a more open, just, diverse and mutually enriching society. Indeed, the social component of liberalism is the principal means by which power blocs have temporarily neutralised critics. Standard socialist and reformist Catholic critiques that liberal capitalism possesses momentum but lacks direction and social purpose are temporarily suspended. Until recently, arguments that the values binding society and state are threatened by the pursuit of competitive individualism and the promotion of enlightened self-interest and consumerism were muted and relegated to the periphery of public debate. Yet criticisms that were once blurred have already acquired a new sharpness as the result of economic downturn triggered by currency crises and deepening recession in some countries; and the bland de-ideologised politics of the 'popular-business alliance' in delegative democracies appear to be coming to an end. Although the liberal project has grown in coherence and proved resilient and its critics have often proved inchoate, questions of distribution, stratification and power allocation have exploded in countries as varied as Venezuela, Mexico, Ecuador and Bolivia.

Past models of liberalism have been only unevenly assimilated and incompletely applied in Latin America, and in crises have often given way to alternative forms of political and socioeconomic organisation. Are proponents of market liberalism overconfident in asserting that the current sequence of reforms is firmly embedded, and is more irreversible than its predecessors? Are neoliberals inaccurate in the assumption that their ideas, if near-hegemonic intellectually, have broad public and inclusionary appeal? Earlier versions of liberalism tended to be minimalist in social policy, or, over short periods, treated it as an accessory to stability, only to reject it as a check on macroeconomic efficiency. Habitually, liberals have been bound to 'reform from above and without'. Despite the professed commitment of neoliberals to consultation and accountability, has the formulation and administration of social policy changed radically in reality as well as in rhetoric?

In their drive for 'modernity' are neoliberals — often historically illiterate and present-bound — blind to the failures of their liberal precursors, and insufficiently alert to the improbable viability of many of their schemes? How far has a drive towards professionalisation since the 1960s meant that experts with narrow technically confined areas of competence proliferate, while statesmen and strategists with a view of the long term and an authentic framework of ideas are as rare and undervalued as before? And are experts, who lack a thorough education in modern history and political economy, ill-informed about traditions of defensive and delayed absorption of imported models and narratives of negotiation, accommodation and resistance to them? Indeed, how far have strategists developed endogenous rationalities? Fairly successful efforts were made to construct a 'development strategy from within' during the cepalista years, though outcomes were flawed in terms of equity and stability. Crises in the 1970s and 1980s did much to undermine the self-confidence of Latin American intellectuals and strategists, creating a vacuum that the Washington agencies filled. What policy options will be open to Latin American governments if the agencies suffer a prolonged crisis of confidence, following the failure of policy prescription in various parts of the world and exposures of transparency and accountability deficits in their internal structures and procedures? Market efficiency will be assured — and survive — in Latin America only if it is incorporated in endogenous cultures, through the implementation of successful and sustained social interventions that mobilise constituencies for reform.

With recession, democracy may be threatened by the liberal ethos that is supposedly its ally. Should unfettered market fundamentalism rule, national legislatures be constrained by international agreements and elected politicians be reduced to puppets promoting compliance by gesturing about the domestication of global capitalism, a wave of protest and a lurch to authoritarianism can be predicted, as occurred in the 1930s and 1970s. The constellations of power that render the individual impotent combine to promote mass abstention during elections, apathy between them and a disengagement from politics. Democracy and inclusiveness will be threatened by underestimating the tenacity of authoritarianism. Residual habits of corporatism, the politics of manipulation and conditional access to resources remain, together with the steadfast assumption within the upper class of its right to rule regardless of its past failings. If social liberalism can be generously interpreted as embodying a consensual relationship between government and governed, it can be construed as a durable solution to current problems. If social liberalism is unable to bridge the gaps between government and governed and between rhetoric and delivery, then it is no more than the static, discretionary liberalism of the past and will induce renewed cycles of contradictions and confrontations.

A major test of the social liberal agenda in the early decades of the twenty-first century will be the nature of its interaction with the demands of multiple actors. This presupposes an equitable diffusion of benefits. For almost two centuries, the experience of exposure of many poor communities to the language and practice of liberalism has been a continuum of social and cultural persecution and exclusion, accompanied by a partial integration into the market economy that has involved a loss of resources and autonomy. Absorbing institutionalist thinking from social anthropologists, cultural geographers and political sociologists, policy-makers are beginning to realise that globalisation and 'reform' will have the desired impact only if policy is sensitive to cultural differences, grasping endogenous perceptions of property, exchange and authority. And it will have to take into account the vitality and popular strength of newly empowered actors from the social movements. How well attuned are international and national policy-practitioners to the scepticism of excluded groups who question the benefits of the market and of democracy because they have been exposed to the shadow rather than the substance of liberal capitalism? Or are exclusion, inequality and dispossession intrinsic to the workings of market capitalism? Perhaps this constitutes too negative a vision. A realisation that past models of liberalism were either utopian or chimerical has induced a determination to entrench the rules of the market in politics and economics in order to generalise prosperity.

One of the many challenges confronting advocates of an active social policy is to ensure that the distributional consequences are progressive. Policy-makers also have to confront the dilemmas of reconciling the pursuit of equity with goals of institutional stability and growth, and of formal equality with continuing social divisions. In addition, they need to acknowledge that a progress towards equity can be fast or can be so slow as to be almost imperceptible, and that institutional barriers to equity enhancement are numerous. Whether or not policy will impact positively on distribution depends as much on access and entitlement as on methods of financing. Over a long period, the expansion of social provision was financed in a regressive fashion, often by 'general taxation' — usually inflation. The NEM may have curbed the negative effect of inflation. Whether targeting and the new social policy model will yield more equitable outcomes remains to be seen. A great deal will depend on state capacity and competence.

An active citizenship based on a bundle of political, civil and social rights and obligations is fundamental for the application of an inclusive and social policy framework administered by a capable democratic state. Reducing poverty and delivering equity requires cohesive support from taxpayers, households, communities, enterprises and government at all levels, reinforced by collaborative action by external agencies. The emancipatory potential of social policy will be realised only if negotiations about priorities and allocations engage the entire citizenry, not only policy-making elites and organised lobbies. Simultaneous transitions — from qualified access to primary instruction to universal access to good quality education at all levels, from conditional access to basic social insurance to full participation by individuals and households in viable social security systems, and from modest, spatially haphazard and socially stratified networks of clinics and hospitals to the provision of comprehensive healthcare — will facilitate an ascent to full citizenship that guarantees dynamic institutionality.

CHAPTER 2

Social Policy Delivery:
The New Economic Model and the Reform of the State in Latin America

Pascual Gerstenfeld

Introduction

L ate-twentieth century Latin American societies are mostly characterised by structural transformations in the production system, resulting in important changes in the profile of employment generated, the redefinition of the role of the state and increased processes of economic integration, linked among other things to globalisation, increasing international competitiveness and the pursuit of stability and economic growth.

On the one hand these trends produced a strong expansion of the market as a resource locator and, on the other, a significant increase in the supply of goods and services, with a corresponding increase in people's expectations and propensity to consume.

All of this has been taking place in a climate of consolidation of democracy and greater consensus on the need for 'state' instead of 'governmental' policies, in the sense that economic and social policies require a long-term perspective and stability of rules through different periods of government administrations.

The Economic Context

The 'new economic model', in reality a new context rather than a model, materialised in the middle 1980s, becoming more apparent in the 1990s. Briefly defined as significant and growing commercial liberalisation, accompanied by economic growth; a strong currency valuation and improvements in fiscal stability; an increase – albeit inadequate – in investment levels, with the incorporation of technological advances that produced high levels of manpower substitution, accompanied by relative growth in the service sector, with its concomitant manpower demands. All this, barring rare exceptions, in a context of insufficient levels of internal saving, made up for by foreign debt and a significant increase in direct foreign investment.

The most prominent aspect of the new context, beyond some crises in certain countries, most notably in 1994–95 or 1998–99, turned out to be the recovery of economic growth, with an average increase in gross domestic product (GDP) of 3.3 per cent a year for the period 1991–2000, in contrast to the 1.2 per cent a year of the 1980s. In terms of GDP per capita it meant an increase of 1.5 per cent a year in the 1990s as opposed to -0.9 per cent over the previous decade (Table 2.1).[1] However, this achievement is insufficient to overcome, among others, the serious problem of poverty of the majority of Latin American countries, which would require yearly rates of growth of six per cent to seven per cent, according to the United Nations Economic Commission for Latin America and the Caribbean (ECLAC).[2]

In addition, the commercial liberalisation meant that in the 1990s total exports grew on average at nearly ten per cent per year (three times the rate of GDP), while imports grew at around 13 per cent a year (four times the rate of growth of GDP), also confirming the well-known trade deficit of most Latin American countries (Table 2.1). This deficit incorporates not only investment initiatives, as Latin American countries are mainly 'technology buyers', but also includes a significant increase in household consumption of imported goods.

On the other hand, most states improved their fiscal performance, reducing their annual deficit significantly, while achieving important reductions in their inflation rates. In the 1990s the fiscal deficit stood in general at between one and three per cent of GDP, up to 1997 at generally below two per cent and from 1998 above this value. Also, inflation moved from rates in double or treble figures to single figures in most countries(Table 2.1).

As regards internal investment levels, the gross creation of capital oscillated in this period between 20 and 23 per cent of GDP, with insufficient levels of internal saving, requiring between two and three per cent of GDP of external saving (Table 2.1).

Notable effects on productive transformations in the structure of urban employment included:

i) That the formal sector went from incorporating 58 per cent of urban employment to 53 per cent, particularly due to the decrease of public employment — from 16 per cent to 13 per cent — studied below, to

---

[1] This progress determined that the absolute economic level of most of the countries rose above the level attained before the debt crisis, but one third of them failed to recover their per capita level of production, mainly due to the continuing high rate of population growth.

[2] CEPAL (2000b).

which was added the salary reduction of non professionals, including technicians, whose share diminished from 32 per cent to 30 per cent.

ii)   That the informal sector grew from 42 per cent to 47 per cent, self-employed unqualified workers accounting for three per cent of the five per cent increase, and rose from 22 per cent to 25 per cent of urban employment, a further one per cent increase coming from *microempresas* (very small businesses) and from domestic service employment respectively.[3]

Main Social Trends

The social evolution of Latin America over the last four decades has seen significant advances in key areas, such as increased life expectancy, the reduction of infant mortality, more inclusive basic social services, greater access to basic education and the reduction of illiteracy, with significant differences between countries in terms of individual progress (Table 2.2).

However, it also confirmed the continued existence of profound social inequity, with a great diversity of situations — both in terms of scale and type — but at the same time with certain broadly shared characteristics. Most of the countries share structural poverty, social exclusion, a high and growing informality of employment, a rigid and very unequal distribution of income and very limited social mobility that, along with other factors, is both cause and consequence of the other related phenomena.

In particular, the last decade of the twentieth century was generally positive in terms of the reduction of levels of poverty, but not with regard to inequality of income distribution. For the region as a whole urban poverty decreased from 35 to 30 per cent between 1990 and 1999, and rural poverty fell from 58 to 54 per cent — returning to 1980 levels — unlike urban poverty, for which the 1980 figure was 25 per cent. On the other hand, the crisis of 1998–99 stopped this process of improvement and in some countries levels have deteriorated somewhat. Anyway, the magnitudes of poverty mean immense national challenges, more so when observing the different situations: three-quarters of the countries register levels of urban poverty of 25 per cent or more, some even reaching as high as 66 per cent (Table 2.2).

---

[3]   Table 2 and CEPAL (2000c).

Table 2.1: Latin American Economic Figures in the 1990s

Year	Annual Variation of Gross Domestic Product (GDP)	Annual Variation of GDP per capita	Fiscal Deficit (as % of GDP)	Inflation (annual variation Dec.-Dec.)	Unemployment (as % of Active Economic Population — annual average)	Gross Domestic Investment (as % of GDP)	Gross National Savings (as % of GDP)	External Savings (as % of GDP)	Exports (annual variation rates)	Imports (annual variation rates)	Privatisations (in current million dollars)
1991	3.9	2.0	-0.5	199.0	5.7	19.7	18.1	1.5	0.7	17.7	16.702
1992	3.2	1.3	-1.4	414.4	6.5	21.2	18.7	2.5	8.0	22.8	14.887
1993	4.1	2.3	-1.2	876.6	6.5	20.7	17.4	3.2	9.9	11.7	10.206
1994	5.2	3.4	-2.1	111.1	6.6	21.5	18.3	3.2	16.2	18.8	9.146
1995	1.1	-0.6	-1.6	25.8	7.5	21.0	18.5	2.5	21.2	12.0	3.712
1996	3.7	2.0	-1.1	18.4	7.9	20.6	18.2	2.3	11.6	10.9	12.541
1997	5.3	3.5	-1.3	10.4	7.5	22.3	18.6	3.7	11.3	18.6	24.668
1998	2.3	0.6	-2.5	10.3	8.1	21.4	16.7	4.6	-1.2	6.2	42.291
1999	0.3	-1.3	-3.1	9.5	8.7	20.6	17.2	3.4	5.8	-3.7	12.374
2000	4.0	2.4	-2.3	8.9	8.6	20.7	18.1	2.6	20.1	16.3	18.464

Source: ECLAC, *Estudio Económico de América Latina y el Caribe 2000-2001*, and *Preliminary Overview of the Economy of Latin America and the Caribbean 2000*.

Table 2.2: Some Socioeconomic Indicators of Latin American Countries

Country	Public Social Expenditure per capita 1998-99 (in 1997 dollars)	Public Social Expenditure (annual average of variation) 1990-99	Public Social Expenditure (as % of GDP) 1998-99	Poverty (% of urban household below the poverty line) 1999	Inequality of the Income distribution (urban Gini coefficient) 1999	Informal Sector Employment (urban, as % of total employment) 1999	Public Sector Employment (urban, as % of total employment) 1999
Argentina	1,687	4.2	20.5	13	0.54	47.4	15.6
Uruguay	1,539	7.1	22.8	6	0.44	41.0	16.3
Brazil	1,011	3.2	21.0	26	0.64	46.8	13.3
Chile	827	8.2	16.0	16	0.56	34.4	9.5
Panama	642	3.3	19.4	21	0.56	34.3	23.5
Costa Rica	622	3.4	16.8	16	0.47	39.1	19.7
Mexico	402	5.6	9.1	31	0.54	44.3	14.2
Colombia	381	11.6	15.0	45	0.57	55.9	9.5
Venezuela	313	-1.0	8.6	43	0.50	52.0	15.7
Peru	192	13.6	6.8	—	—	—	10.5
Bolivia	168	—	16.1	42	0.59	65.5	11.9
Dominican Republic	135	9.8	6.6	32	0.52	47.0	10.2
Paraguay	132	11.3	7.4	42	0.57	63.3	...
Guatemala	107	9.4	6.2	39	0.58	...	...
El Salvador	82	—	4.3	34	0.52	50.5	12.1
Honduras	57	-0.6	7.4	66	0.56	53.2	9.5
Nicaragua	57	2.2	12.7	59	0.58	60.1	14.8
Average	491	5.2	12.7	30 *	—	47.3	13.3

Source: ECLAC, *Social Panorama of Latin America, 2000-2001, 1999-2000 and 1998 editions.* Note : * Weighted average

Table 2.2 (continued): Some Socioeconomic Indicators of Latin American Countries

Country	Life Expectancy At Birth (years) 1995–2000	Infant Mortality Rate (death of children aged 0 to 1 years per thousand live births) 1995–2000	Population with Access to Potable Water (% of urban people)	Adult Illiteracy (% of persons 15 years old and above) 1999	Youth Educational Achievement (% of people aged 15–24 with less than 10 years of education) 1999 Urban zones
Argentina	73	22	79	3	43 *
Uruguay	74	18	98	2	51
Brazil	68	42	83	15	70
Chile	75	13	94	4	35
Panama	74	21	87	8	45
Costa Rica	77	12	98	5	59
Mexico	72	31	86	9	61
Colombia	71	30	91	9	47
Venezuela	73	21	84	8	59
Peru	68	45	77	10	—
Bolivia	61	66	79	15	—
Dominican Republic	71	34	79	17	60
Paraguay	70	39	79	7	—
Guatemala	64	46	—	32	69
El Salvador	69	32	74	22	54
Honduras	70	35	—	26	74
Nicaragua	68	43	79	32	72
Average	70	32	84	13	57

Source: ECLAC, *Statistical Yearbook for Latin America and The Caribbean*, 2000 edition; ECLAC, *Social Panorama of Latin America*, 2000–2001 edition; PNUD, *Informe Sobre Desarrollo Humano*, 2001 edition.

As regards income distribution inequality the challenge is even greater, because most of the countries present high or very high levels of inequality, with the exceptions of Uruguay and Costa Rica, which have moderate levels (Table 2.2). Likewise, in the 1990s, the situation has not only failed to improve, but has even deteriorated in several countries.

Both poverty and inequality are the result of multiple factors underpinned, on the economic side, by the scarcity of productive dynamics that produces an incapacity to create adequate quality employment, and therefore a high informal sector accounting for more than 40 per cent of jobs, associated in turn with low levels of productivity and labour income. Since almost 80 per cent of household income comes from labour, it is shown to be the key factor, further skewed by the unequal distribution of assets.

While on the social side, among other factors, the highly hereditary intergenerational transmission not only of economic capital but also of educational capital reduces the socioeconomic opportunities of the majority of Latin Americans for whom it is the only capital available to generate their income. Between half and two-thirds of Latin American urban youth, and even more in the case of their rural counterparts, are already limited by their domestic circumstances in terms of access to opportunities of economic improvement, due to the highly hereditary element in education that emerges as the key factor.[4]

Also, the contrasts in public social expenditure can be observed as a synthetic expression of the different levels of social action in Latin American countries. On the one hand, the great heterogeneity is a consequence of the different product levels (they rank from US$500 to 8,000 per capita a year), in conjunction with the different country efficiency levels that can be measured through the ratio of public social expenditure to product. This latter oscillates from levels of five per cent to 23 per cent. Together with differences in the product, it allows for levels of public social expenditure per capita that range from US$50 a year up to nearly US$1,700 (Table 2.2). This allows the identification of three groups of countries at regional level: a higher group, with a public social expenditure between US$600 and US$1,700 per capita; a middle group with levels at between US$300 and US$400; and a group with low and very low levels, located between US$50 and US$200 per capita.

On the other hand, development in the 1990s was favourable, with significant growth in public social expenditure in most countries, after the

---

4   Gerstenfeld (1998).

strong widespread fall that had characterised the 1980s during the debt crisis. In that decade, this had produced significant fiscal crisis and therefore
strong pressures to diminish public expenditure by reining in the state.

The Reform of the State

Latin American state reforms of the latter twentieth century began in the
1980s with the simple idea of significantly reducing the scope of action,
and therefore the size, of the state. They were guided almost solely by the
objective of reducing the fiscal deficit that was the main government concern at the time of the debt crisis, due to the devastating negative impacts
on growth and welfare of high inflation rates. Also, a second stated objective indicated that this reduction would be allowed to go further, reducing
the cost of the state to society through lower fiscal pressure via tax reduction. This would generate a double stimulus to the commercial private sector: more resources to invest while paying less tax and more areas to invest
in when taking over these same resources from the state.

But in the 1990s, characterised by low fiscal deficits, the idea began to
take root in the region that reform should be orientated to modernising
the state rather than to reducing its size. The main idea behind this new
approach is the premise that without an efficient state it is impossible to
have efficient markets.

This change came fundamentally from the growing importance that
new socioeconomic challenges to the state were acquiring in the context of
the renewed democracies in the region during the second half of the
1980s, with the participation of representative political systems in the discussion and determination of the respective national budgets.

Hence, those challenges emphasised the importance of increasing the
efficiency of the state in those activities where the private sector does not
offer goods and services at a socially acceptable level, does not have an
interest in supplying certain basic social services, lacks the capacity to offer
it, as in the case of justice administration, or would enjoy a natural monopoly. This does not mean that the production of all those goods and services should be completely carried out by the public sector, because many
of these problems can and should be managed with appropriate regulatory systems and appropriate fiscal policies of subsidies and taxes.

Therefore, the idea of strengthening the efficiency and effectiveness of
the state in the implementation of economic and social policies enlarged
the reform agenda, pointing to the necessity for a more modern public sector, incorporating technological advances, the training of civil servants and

the search for greater transparency. The latter aspect has opened a new and very important element in the governmental agenda of several countries, namely the fight against corruption, in the context of the major obstacle that this represents in the move towards an efficient and effective state. Additionally, corruption undermines the state's role as the representative of the collective interest, which is sacrificed in favour of individual self-interest. In 1999 at least six countries of the region carried out some action in this respect, from approving anti-corruption laws to the development of special programmes and the creation of anti-corruption institutions.

The common characteristic of this broad process of state reform is that it tends to be slow, with some countries advancing significantly further than others, though in almost all cases towards the same objective.

This new approach that reevaluates the action of the state in the 'new economic context' is aimed at achieving an efficient public sector of an appropriate size, by virtue of its continued reduction alongside the process of privatisation. As mentioned previously, public sector employment continued to diminish in the 1990s and privatisation continued its vertiginous ascent, reaching a peak in 1998 when it almost doubled the rate of the preceding year, which in turn was more than the sum of privatisations carried out in the first three years of the decade (Table 2.1). The abrupt fall in 1999 is primarily explained by the impact of the economic crisis on the region which saw the postponement or cancellation of a great number of privatisation projects.

In brief, the process of reform, advancing more slowly in some respects than others, points to a state that is:

i)   Less of a supplier, more a regulator that interacts more with multiple profit and non-profit sectors, not only in the economic sphere, but also significantly in the social sphere, as is apparent in the section on paradigms and social policy reform.

ii)   Smaller but with more professional, with an appropriate incorporation to of new technologies, to achieve greater productivity and efficiency.

iii)   More decentralised in certain areas, with increased local government participation in the design and implementation of a range socioeconomic policies.

Social Policies: Paradigms and Reforms

Appropriate economic policies are fundamental for the generation of more and better employment, so that people will be able to satisfy their needs for themselves, but so too is the development of appropriate social policies, since state and society will have more resources for their implementation.

On the other hand, although social policies alone are not enough to achieve equity and to overcome poverty, their role is decisive both directly and indirectly through their influence on economic growth. So, they perform at least three functions:

1.   The incorporation of human capital as a requirement of economic growth, particularly considering the current importance of knowledge as a production factor.

2.   Equity, through seeking more equality of opportunity for those who have different socioeconomic, ethnic, gender or geographical origins.

3.   Emergency or social compensation, defined as satisfaction of basic needs for those affected by crisis, with the aim of maintaining the most human capital possible.

Paradigms

The analysis of Latin American social policy shows that historically it has been characterised by a putative universalism that is rarely achieved, segmented access, a corporatist component that explains the concentration of certain benefits in certain groups and bureaucratic inertia compounded by duplication of functions and the wasting of resources.

Considering this situation, in the first half of the 1980s what could be considered a new paradigm of social policy began to be implemented, known as the 'emergent' paradigm,[5] that aimed to be more compatible with the redefinition of the state, looking for greater efficiency and effectiveness in the achievement of equity and growth.

Those attributes are not always achieved. Even today Latin American countries' social policies are the result of the coexistence of the 'emergent' with those of the traditional paradigm, also denominated 'prevalent' in allusion to its predominance in most policy areas. Also, many social policies contain components that respond to both paradigms. It is interesting to analyse the basic dimensions of social policies according to both paradigms, categorising some of their characteristics to better exemplify the main differences that present their implementation (See Table 2.3).

---

5   Franco (1996).

Table 2.3: Social Policy Paradigms: Comparison of Main Characteristics

	'Prevalent'	'Emergent'
Institutional Form	**State Monopoly** – Finance – Design – Implementation – Control Unified functions Centralisation	Multiple Subsectors – State – Private (commercial) – Philanthropic (NGOs) – Informal (family) Separate functions Decentralisation
Decision-Making Process	**Bureaucratic** – Macro-strategies – 'The state knows what to do' – Users have no say or choice	**By Projects** – Competitive allocation – Tendering – Allocation proposed by users – 'Innovative capacity exists throughout society and every effort should by made to take advantage of it' [Social Investment Funds]
Financing **Source Of Resources**	**The State**	**Co-Financing** – 'No charge=No good' – Recovery of costs: 'who can pay should pay' [Risk: marginalisation of the poor]
Resource Allocation	**Subsidisation Of Supply** – Resources allocated administratively – Absence of competition	**Subsidisation of Demand** – Creation of quasi-markets – Competition – Freedom to choose [Does the consumer have enough information?]
Objective	**Universality Of Supply** – High cost, low impact – Homogeneous available supply favours those who are best-informed and best-organised	**Universality Of Satisfaction** – 'Unequal treatment for those who are socially unequal'
Criterion as Regards Priorities for Expanding the System	**Gradual Expansion from the Top Down** [Segmented access: 'Less social expenditure = less equity']	**The Neediest First** – Instrument: targeting
Beneficiary Population	**The Middle Class Organised Groups**	**The Poor**
Approach	**Centred on the Means** – Social infrastructure – Current expenditure	**Centred on the Ends** – Impact: size of benefits received by the target population, according to ends pursued
Performance Indicator Used	**Public Social Expenditure**	**Cost-Impact Ratio**

Source: Franco (1996), pp. 9–23.

For the *institutional form*, the traditional paradigm assigns all functions to the state (finance, design, implementation, control) with a centralised focus, while the 'emergent' paradigm conceives the participation of multiple sectors in addition to the state, such as the commercial private sector, non-governmental organisations and families and communities, with the decentralisation of activities incorporating the participation of the local governments. As regards decentralisation in education or health, there have been several examples where efficiency and/or equity have not been improved, focusing attention on certain key requirements to obtain better results, such as the initial situation, the form and timing of decentralisation, etc.

Regarding the *decision-making process*, the traditional paradigm starts from the premise that the state best knows society's needs and how to satisfy them. On the other hand, the new paradigm, supported by the experience of the Social Investment Funds, postulates a competitive logic based on projects as the way of taking advantage of the capacity for innovation in society.

In relation to the *financing sources*, traditional social policies are almost exclusively paid for with fiscal resources. While in the emergent vision co-financing is sought, not only to recover costs, but also to stimulate the commitment of the community to the programme. The strong risk in this case resides in the exclusion of the poorest, who are without the ability to pay even subsidised costs.

As for *resource allocation*, the prevalent bureaucratic pattern assigns the flows administratively without further stimuli to efficiency. While the alternative programme outlines what is known as the ' demand subsidy'. This means that the finance provider transfers a purchase power ('voucher') to the beneficiary so that he/she can acquire certain types of goods or services as is most appropriate. This alternative requires the existence of more than one supplier, that is to say the existence of a market or a quasi-market.

Regarding the *objective*, the 'prevalent' paradigm seeks to universalise supply, with homogeneous social goods and services, in the face of a heterogeneous demand — given unequal socioeconomic, geographical and ethnic characteristics — and expanding the system from top to bottom, hence the main beneficiaries are the most organised groups within society, mostly linked to the middle class. The 'emergent' pattern aims to universalise satisfaction, through a heterogeneous supply that is biased in favour of the socioeconomically unequal (positive discrimination), focusing their action peimarily on those in greatest need, namely the poor.

Finally, as regards the *approach and performance indicator* used, the traditional approach focused its attention on the means, such as the construction of schools, health centres, more baskets of food, etc. That is to say that it was more concerned with coverage than with impact, and so the most used indicator is the amount of public social expenditure. On the other hand, the new paradigm focuses on impact, referring to the extent of the benefit received by each beneficiary according to the objectives of the programme. Therefore, the evaluation requires the use of the so-called 'cost-impact' method,[6] that aims to assess the extent of project effectiveness per unit cost.

Reforms

Beyond the coexistence of the social policy paradigms referred to above, further reforms in key social sectors have been spreading in the region in the course of the last decade, so it is useful to have a brief description of these to hand in order to outline the current framework for the evaluation of existing challenges in the context of socioeconomic trends.

In the context of labour reforms the search is for more flexible contracts to reduce labour costs and the costs of dismissal, and to stimulate employment creation. There is consensus that the spread of more flexible labour contracts across most Latin American countries is due more to concrete situations that to any explicit change in regulations. In any case, most countries have a minority group of workers who are broadly protected, while there are broad sectors where labour legislation is not applied in practice, including the informal sector, outsourcing and seasonal workers. The most hotly discussed topics centre on the search for parameters that can provide, on the one hand, flexibility to the companies facing international competition and the integration agreements, and, on the other hand, provide workers with labour stability or mechanisms to protect them from rising unemployment (unemployment insurance, occupational training, etc.).

Education reform is perhaps the most generalised, as it is perceived as positive and necessary, as much by government authorities as by public opinion and international organisations, and so it generally receives substantial funding in terms of international loans and additional public resources.

This has come from the growing consensus regarding the need for more relevant education in terms of productive and social requirements, of appropriate quality and delivered within the required timeframe. This is seen as fundamental to the raising of economic productivity and social efficiency, to increasing opportunities and generating wealth. However, so

---

[6]   Cohen and Franco (1992).

as not to overestimate equity achievements deriving from educational reform, ECLAC's comments should be borne in mind. It claims that more and better education is necessary to promote equity, but this is not enough in itself because other factors, patrimonial, demographic and labour, also interact to a significant extent in the determination of the different equity levels reached by each society.[7] The respective reforms are intended to increase the equity, relevance and quality of the education, as well as efficiency in the use of resources, with changes in: the processes and contents of education; modernisation and decentralisation of administration; the role of the state and the market; professional training; quality evaluation process of supply; and the adjustment of the educational product to the different sociocultural conditions of the beneficiaries and to the new demands of the labour world.

In the health sector two tendencies can be noted in the reform process. First, an increased role of the private sector can be observed in relation to the total supply of health services, and second, there has been an attempt to introduce competition into the operation of public systems. The objective is to promote greater economic efficiency and to encourage the control of costs, through what have been denominated *'cuasi-contratos'* (pseudo-contracts) and 'management commitments'.

The second tendency aims to combine public financing with competition. It aims to abandon the centralised state monopoly of functions related to healthcare, separating and distributing these to different public or private actors, creating certain mechanisms that replicate competition forms among suppliers (pseudo-markets). Additionally, the 'management commitments' imply the definition of health goals, production agreements and performance indicators among the financing public entity and each supplier of services.[8]

Lastly, the pension systems have been another important area of reform. They have been obliged to: operate within overall balanced public finances as well as the pension system itself; to identify risks and to displace them from the public sector to the pension and the administration companies; and to allow freedom of choice to the beneficiary, both in terms of administration of resources and access to service, for both public and private institutions.

---

[7]   CEPAL (1998).

[8]   CEPAL (2000a).

The pension systems reform can be classified as non-structural and structural. In non-structural terms, seeking to perfect the public system with adjustments aimed at contributing to one or more of the following objectives: the extension of cover; standardising conditions for obtaining rights to benefits; the elimination or reduction of financial deficit in the system; improvements in the efficiency of the system's administration; and the offering of more appropriate pensions.

The structural reforms aimed to incorporate, to different degrees, what is known as 'individual full capitalisation', intending to strengthen the relationship between the contribution of each worker and the benefits he or she receives. This component has strong adverse implications for equity, since there is no redistribution between beneficiaries, because the relationship between payment and benefit is at the level of the individual. For redistribution it is necessary to ensure a minimum pension for those lacking the ability to contribute.

The different modalities of structural reform have originated different systems known as 'substitutive', 'mixed' and 'competitive'. The first implies that the new system of individual full capitalisation fully replaces the previous system. In the 'mixed' system the reforms co-exist with the basic and mutual component of the previous system, to which is added the element of individual capitalisation. This sees a basic pension on retirement and a further complementary pension deriving from individual capitalisation. On the other hand, the 'parallel' model breaks the public monopoly of the previous system, which is also modified totally or partially, and a new capitalisation system is created that competes with the public system.[9]

Some Reflections as Conclusions

In conclusion, some challenging or outstanding elements regarding economic and social trends are offered for consideration when evaluating current social policy and reform.

a.   First, social policies have not been able to remove, in most countries, the main factors of socioeconomic inequity. On the one hand, because of the failure to see that economic policies operate in conjunction with social policies and that their interaction should be explicitly considered. Together they have to create more human capital and contribute creatively to the creation of more productive employment,

[9]   CEPAL (2000a).

to effect a change in the very negative growth of the informal sector that includes almost 50 per cent of the active population.

On the other hand, the social policies themselves are not fully integrated, other than in the case of a handful of exceptions. Policy is generally implemented by sector, so that many potential achievements in certain areas are not brought to fruition because they are limited by defects in other areas, as in education, for example, where this has led to results failing to meet expectations.[10]

In some measure the Social Investment Funds have tried to endow their actions with more inter-sector activities, but their scope is very limited due to the relatively limited resources they manage in relation to the total public social expenditure of each country.

b. Considering the very limited socioeconomic mobility in the region, due to the hereditary educational and labour opportunities, policies with components that are premised on a focus on the individual will lead unavoidably to further inequity. This is the case with current pension systems based exclusively on full individual capitalisation, or an extended privatisation of the health sector, among other examples. These cases require the incorporation of at least certain components of basic benefits and instruments of solidarity in the financing scheme, as in the 'mixed' systems described for pension reforms.

c. Although the reforms have brought great advances in the area of social management, accountability and quality control, much remains to be done. There has been progress, for example, in the evaluation of quality in the educational system and the accountability of pension systems, but little or no progress has been made in areas such as health and housing.

d. The reforms implemented in the region in the 1990s were fundamentally stimulated by the renewed relationship between state and society derived from the re-democratisation process of the second half of the 1980s. These reforms have meant raised expectations on the part of policy-makers, although for many these continue to be relatively low. This could be explained, among other things, by the fact that better national performance in fiscal and growth terms was still not able to consolidate clear economic prospects in the long term. This is the reason why the reform agenda is frequently sidetracked by attention

10 Gerstenfeld et al. (1995).

to short-term demands on the part of policy-makers in the economic and social sphere. This situation has become more apparent since 1999, with the new growth crises and their negative fiscal impact that several countries of the region began to experience.

e. As for the finance side of social policy, it is necessary to remember the strong growth in social public expenditure over the last decade, mostly financed by increased fiscal revenues related to growth, in addition to increased levels of public debt. On the other hand, the significance of taxes on consumption in the predominant structure of fiscal revenues in the region makes public expenditure even more sensitive to levels of growth, reinforcing the comments made in the previous paragraph. It is also necessary to point out that both the productive structures and the cultural characteristics of the countries concerned leave little margin in the near future for significant change in the structure of fiscal revenues, particularly as regards taxation policy. Therefore, state action will continue to concentrate on expenditure.

f. The substantial growth in the economic participation of women and the young is transforming the family structure and the roles within it. It is reducing the number of 'bread winner system' households and increasing the number of 'multiple income contribution' households, as well as bringing a substantial increase in the number of single parent homes (*monoparentales*), mainly headed by women. All these changes constitute strong challenges both for labour policy and for the range of social policies (education, health, housing and pensions). They generate new demands that partly require new instruments, or the amplification of existing instruments, often needing to be adapted to new target populations.

g. The social reforms of the last decade have been sustained by the search for more equity, efficiency and effectiveness, but, in many cases, any advances in the last two aspects have been to the detriment of the first, particularly when changes have been inspired more by the need for fiscal balance than by other requirements. ECLAC has highlighted the need for social policy to be guided by certain principles, such as: 'universality' of access, 'solidarity' in terms of financing and 'efficiency' in terms of execution. 'Transparency' of action, with a view to increasing the involvement of different sectors of society and to allow a better evaluation of the results, is also a requirement. [11]

[11]   CEPAL (2000b).

h. Finally, it needs to be pointed out that both the reform of the state and reforms in social policy, with all their successes and failures, or weaknesses, are producing a shift in the Latin American agenda from growth to development. However, with respect to action the transition is slower, even more so in the case of countries with crises of growth, in which short-term priorities have operated to the detriment of longer term development.

CHAPTER 3

Debates on the Effects of Macroeconomic Policies on Poverty

Miguel Urrutia[*]

Introduction

Much criticism of macroeconomic adjustment policies concerns the impact of these on levels of poverty and income distribution. The heterodox theory is that the control of inflation or policies to reduce fiscal deficits or current account deficits decrease the income of the poor. Often a fall in social indicators does occur when an adjustment package is implemented. The question is whether without the adjustment the social indicators would not deteriorate even more. Is a current account deficit sustainable indefinitely? If very rapid growth generates an unsustainable current account deficit, is there any alternative to a monetary policy that moderates growth and produces equilibrium in the current account?

The correct way to address these issues would be to compare the social effects of a set of policies that maintain long-run macroeconomic equilibrium, as against a policy that allows periodic misalignments in macro variables. Either strategy could produce lower unemployment or poverty reduction. The result would depend on many factors.

One possibility is that less variability in the growth of income achieved through permanent macroeconomic equilibrium would reduce uncertainty and therefore generate investment and future economic growth. There is some evidence, however, to support the theory that greater variability in income might generate greater savings in the long run, and therefore greater investment. Most economic historians, however, would conclude that stop-go policies are economically wasteful and generate less income growth and less reduction in poverty in the long run.

In the case of inflation there is a growing literature that shows that low and stable inflation generates higher growth in the long run, and that high variability of inflation rates is particularly harmful to growth. Historical experience also shows that shocks to inflation rates are asymmetrical.

[*] The opinions here expressed are the sole responsibility of the author and do not necessarily represent the views of the Banco de la República or its board of directors.

Prices increase more easily than they stabilise, and the falls in unemployment that accompany expansive policies tend to be less than the corresponding rise when monetary conditions are tightened.

In the following sections the social impact of macroeconomic stabilisation policies will be discussed in greater detail.

Who Are the Poor?

In designing policy it is important to identify the poor and to measure the impact of policies on that group.

In the increasingly urbanised economies of Latin America, the urban poor are made up of the unemployed, households headed by uneducated women and children. In rural areas the poor are agricultural workers and independent farmers with little land.

Rapid economic growth improves the lot of these groups, as does lower inflation. Birth control policies reduce child poverty, which is concentrated in large families of low income, and safety nets help the short-term unemployed, households headed by women with low education and the low-income elderly. Education reduces future poverty and improves future income distribution.

The following sections discuss the impact of macroeconomic policies on these variables.

The Social Impact of Disinflation

There is a very extensive literature on the trade-off between inflation and unemployment and inflation and income distribution. The Phillips curve theory postulates a negative relationship between inflation and unemployment, suggesting that monetary stabilisation policy would have a cost for the less well-off, by raising the unemployment rate.

Although there are serious doubts that a long-run Phillips curve exists, monetary policy-making often assumes that in the short run there is such a relationship. The interesting question, however, relates to the long-term relationship, since if a surge in inflation is not compensated by a hardening of monetary policy inflation may increase permanently. There is strong empirical evidence that permanently high inflation, and certainly hyperinflation, exact a high cost in terms of long-term growth, and therefore have negative welfare effects for the poor.

Cross-section studies across countries show that nations with inflation higher than 15 per cent per annum have significantly lower growth rates than countries with low inflation.[1] Given that a necessary, although not sufficient, condition for poverty reduction is high levels of economic growth, then macroeconomic policy that avoids high inflation is conducive to greater equity.

What are the mechanisms by which inflation reduces economic growth?

i)   Inflation reduces the stimulus for productive work. Inflation reduces the demand for monetary stocks to avoid the costs of inflation, and this leads to a growing proportion of the working population dedicating itself to avoiding the cost of inflation instead of producing goods and services.

ii)   Inflation reduces the information content of the price system, and generates misallocation of resources.

iii) Inflation also increases uncertainty with respect to the profitability of long-term investments, and may increase the long-term real interest rate by incorporating an inflation premium into the cost of capital.

The effect of inflation on investment is particularly relevant, since it has been shown that high inflation produces high levels of volatility, and again cross section studies show that high price volatility has a negative impact on GDP growth rates.[2]

Historical experience shows that once inflation increases above a certain level inertial mechanisms kick-in that tend to increase inflation rates permanently. In Latin America once inflation reached levels of 30 per cent per annum it was highly probable that inflation rates would accelerate and often reach levels of 100 per cent or more. Reversing the process has turned out to be very costly in terms of unemployment and foregone economic growth.

Initiating the disinflation process has a cost. The question is whether the foregone growth in the short run is compensated by the higher growth rates achieved with lower future inflation.

In the case of Colombia, estimates have been made of the long-term relationship between inflation and growth. It has been estimated that reducing inflation by ten percentage points, for example from 25 per cent per year to 15 per cent per year, could increase GDP growth rate by half

---

[1]   See Kormendi and Meguire(1985); Fischer (1991–93); Cozier and Selody (1992); De Gregorio (1993); and Levine and Zervos (1993).

[2]   Barro (1997).

a percentage point per annum.[3] The sacrifice ratio of disinflation has been calculated recently by means of a fairly complete macroeconomic model, indicating that welfare gain from disinflating ten percentage points amounts to an increase in output of 3.9 per cent, in perpetuity.[4]

Another recent study shows a significant negative correlation between inflation and growth in the five Andean Group countries in the period 1970–1999. The correlation between the growth of monetary aggregates and inflation is positive, and that between monetary aggregates and growth of GDP is negative.[5] Although inflation is clearly prejudicial to growth in the long term, Ayala does find a small short-term negative growth effect of disinflation policies in Colombia and Ecuador. No negative effect is found in Venezuela, Bolivia or Peru.

To summarise, decreasing inflation improves growth prospects and, since higher growth tends to facilitate poverty reduction, macroeconomic policies that avoid high inflation improve the welfare of the poor. The example given here was of the effects of price stabilisation policies in Colombia, but the experience of price stabilisation in Brazil[6] and Chile is similar. In both countries lower inflation not only helped to accelerate growth, but also probably improved income distribution.

The clearest effect of low inflation on income distribution is its impact on the assets of different income classes. In general, the poor have little access to the financial system and therefore they are less equipped to defend their liquid assets from the ravages of inflation than are the rich. The better off can also index their incomes more closely to inflation than the poor or the informal sector.

Investment in land is also a means of defence against inflation, and such investments are more available to the well off. Price stabilisation has often reduced the real value of land and real estate, and therefore improved the distribution of wealth as well as improving the economic utilisation of land. Land used as a store of value tends to be inefficiently utilised.

There is a theory that suggests that income concentration leads to greater savings rates and investment rates (Kaldor was an exponent of this idea). Although increasing profit shares could facilitate savings and investment, since the rich and corporations have a greater propensity to invest, the experience of Latin America shows that in these cultures high income

3   Uribe (1994).
4   Gómez and Julio (2001).
5   Ayala (2000).
6   Cardoso et al. (1995).

concentration does not lead to high savings rates, probably because high-income concentrations are consistent with conspicuous consumption. Therefore, income concentration is not a good strategy for growth.

Reduction of Fiscal Deficits

In addition to inflation, the most common macroeconomic imbalances are deficits in the balance of payments current account and fiscal deficits. Often they are related. Fiscal deficits tend to create an excess of expenditure in the economy, and it is this excess of expenditure that tends to generate a current account deficit.

Although current account deficits are often the result of misaligned exchange rates, which overstimulate imports and discourage exports, simply devaluing the exchange rate is often not enough to produce a long-term equilibrium in the external account if the fiscal deficit is not corrected. It is also difficult to envisage a country with low inflation rates if it maintains a high level of fiscal deficit.

Reducing the fiscal deficit, however, has a direct effect on crucial services for the poor. The challenge of stabilisation policies that aim at reducing fiscal deficits is to minimise the impact of such reductions on essential social services.

In countries where government expenditure is still a small proportion of GNP, which is the case in most Latin American countries, probably the best way to achieve fiscal equilibrium is to increase the tax burden. Table 3.1 shows the fiscal burden in a sample of Latin American and OECD countries. As can be observed, the total fiscal burden of Latin American governments is always below 20 per cent, whereas the OECD countries all have fiscal burdens above 25 per cent of GDP. As an example, the total fiscal burden of Colombia is about 18 per cent of GDP, as compared to twice that figure in many European countries.

Tax reforms can be designed to be slightly progressive, although often the best that can be hoped for is that the tax incidence be neutral. Since public expenditure can easily be designed to be progressive, especially if greater emphasis is given to investment on health, education and safety nets, closing the fiscal deficit in Latin America should not negatively affect the poor, if it is done through increased revenues.

Nevertheless, public expenditure can be made more efficient. The gains in efficiency of expenditure in education and health can be substantial, but these gains should be used to increase coverage of these services. The reason why it is difficult in practice to diminish fiscal deficits is that high-income interest groups are capable of resisting increases in the tax burden. Fiscal adjustment in those conditions mean reducing public expenditure, and it is often programmes targeted at the poor that suffer.

In democracies, however, these social programmes, if well established, are defended by large masses of people. For example, governments cannot easily reduce expenditure on health without generating politically effective opposition. Other programmes are more vulnerable, such as programmes of preventive healthcare, where the pressure group is probably limited to health workers and policy-makers who are aware that this is the most efficient health programme available.

The Chilean experience suggests that adjustment programmes can be compatible with growth in social programmes. Eduardo Aninat (1999) has examined the recent experience of Chile and concluded that sound fiscal policy helped reduce poverty. By prepaying its foreign debt and so saving in interest payments, Chile reduced its debt service, which created room in the budget for equity-enhancing spending on basic education and health. Declining inflation raised real incomes and created a 'lower inflation dividend', which directly benefited the poor and those who live on incomes not indexed to inflation. Macroeconomic stability and economic growth helped raise tax revenue. As a result, the amount of resources available for social expenditure increased.

Colombia in the 1990s followed a different strategy: it dramatically increased social expenditure but without fiscal discipline. The result was that when the Asian crisis and the Russian crisis hit in 1997–98, Colombia had the highest fiscal and current account deficits in recent history. Financing these deficits abroad became impossible, and the country entered its first recession in 50 years, unemployment rose to 20 per cent of the labour force and income distribution deteriorated.

The attempt to increase social expenditure without assuring macroeconomic balances determined a reversal of some of the improvements in income distribution and poverty reduction of the previous decades.

The trouble with fiscal deficits is that they must be financed, and therefore are not sustainable. If they persist, the external public debt grows, and international capital markets will stop financing deficits when the debt reaches a certain proportion of GDP. The relationship between debt and GNP will be sustainable at interest rates lower than GDP growth, and in Latin America this has not often been the case. For that reason we cannot afford permanent fiscal deficits.

Macroeconomic Adjustment and Social Indicators

A few years ago I attempted to find the empirical relationship between macroeconomic equilibrium and the social indicator calculated by UNDP.[7] The method used is to find the relationship between the change in the UNDP social indicator (HDI) between 1970 and 1985, and the following variables:

1. Average levels of inflation rates.

2. Fiscal deficits.

3. Government expenditures as a percentage of GDP

4. GDP growth rates.

5. The HDI in 1970 (The assumption being that countries with an initially low HDI would tend to improve it faster.)

The cross-section regressions suggest a significant relationship for the convergence variable, a weak negative relationship between inflation and social progress and a positive relationship between the proportion of government expenditure and GDP and improvements in the index.

This third finding supports the conclusion of the previous section that, up to a point, an increased tax burden that finances government expenditure, often dedicated to social expenditures such as education and health, tends to improve social indicators.

This chapter also tests the hypothesis that countries with greater stability in some crucial macroeconomic variables achieve greater social progress.

The idea is that a country that develops institutional and political arrangements that allow it to avoid large swings in government expenditure or fiscal deficits may be able to achieve greater social progress (regardless of the level of those indicators). For example, the assumption is that large fluctuations in GNP are harmful for social progress.

In relation to this last point, the aim is to to see whether large terms of trade (TT)[8] shocks also hinder social progress, either directly or through the effect on GNP instability. The effect of instability of inflation rates on social progress was also tested.

Interestingly enough, when the measures of instability of some of the macroeconomic variables discussed above are included, it becomes possible to explain a relatively large proportion of the variations in the HDI.

---

[7]   Cárdenas (1995).

[8]   Measured as the ratio of the aggregate price of exports to the aggregate price of imports.

For instance, the following equation produced an R^2 of 0.84 with N= 36 (D.W. = 1.6; F = 13.8***):

(1) $HDI = 74.1 - 0.99HDI70 + 3.15AVGGNP$
         (6.4)*** (-8.59)***   (2.72)***

     $+ 1.74DVGNP - 3.78DVFD + 1.66AVGFD + 1.14AVGG$
              (0.84)   (-1.77)*   (1.79)*   (2.4)**
$0.77DVG - 4.25DVTT + 0.01DVINF$
              (-0.44)   (-1.24)   (0.97)

where the prefixes DV and AVG denote the standard deviation and the average of that variable over the period 1970–85. GNP is the growth rate of output, FD is the fiscal deficit as a percentage of GNP and INF is inflation rates.

The results show, as expected, that high growth of GNP is positively related to improvements in the HDI, as is the level of public expenditure as a proportion of GNP. This latter result suggests that the HDI improves only with the active involvement of the government in social expenditure, a circumstance that is accompanied by high government expenditure as a proportion of GNP.

Instability in the fiscal deficit deteriorates the HDI, as do high average levels of fiscal deficit. The instability in government expenditures and terms of trade variables have the right (negative) signs but are not statistically significant.

In equation (3) coefficients of variation, or the standard deviation divided by the average (CV is the prefix in the case) are used as a measure of instability, instead of deviations. This would be more appropriate in variables such as inflation, which may have very different levels across countries. Equation (3) is an alternative to equation (2) (R^2 = 0.81; N = 36).

                $HDI = 77.0 - 1.0HDI70 + 3.26AVGGNP +$
0.13CVGNP
                (6.78)*** (-8.52)*** (2.82)***   (1.00)
(3) $- 0.3 CVFD +1.99AVGFD + 0.94AVGG - 5.1CVTT$
              (-0.65)   (2.3)**   (2.96)***   (-1.18)
1.31CVINF

              (-0.28)

The results are quite similar. Once again, in addition to average GDP growth, the average relative level of government expenditure is related positively to improvement in the HDI and average fiscal deficits are related negatively with improvements in the HDI. In both equations the initial level of the HDI effects HDI growth negatively and in a significant manner, confirming the tendency for convergence in this social indicator.

Conclusions

There is an abundant literature showing that rapid economic growth diminishes poverty and improves other social indicators such as education and health coverage, reduces unemployment rates and improves housing quality. The impact of growth on income distribution is less clear. On the other hand, there is much evidence to suggest that reasonable macroeconomic stability is probably necessary for sustained growth.[9]

Cross-section studies suggest other factors that are related to growth: market and export orientation, the size and the role of government both in physical and social infrastructure, especially for human capital, and in limiting its role in other areas. Another study described here suggests that macroeconomic stability directly improves social indicators.

In summary, it is possible that macroeconomic adjustment policies may have a negative impact on the poor in the short run, but macroeconomic stability will benefit vulnerable groups in the medium term. The challenge is to minimise the negative social impact of adjustment policies, and it is clearly viable to design adjustment policies with an emphasis on safety nets so as to limit their impact on the poor.

In conclusion, as Stanley Fischer argues,[10] although poverty reduction and equity can be affected by a broad array of macroeconomic policies and structural reforms, fiscal policy is the most direct tool to these ends. The five key ingredients in the IMF's approach to equitable fiscal policy are: fiscal management that supports macroeconomic stability and enhances the prospects for sustained high-quality economic growth — the best way to lower poverty on an enduring basis; implementation of a fair and efficient system of taxation — ideally a system of easily administered taxes with broad bases, moderate tax rates and a minimum number of exemptions; reductions in unproductive expenditure; improvements in the composition of expenditure to promote the reduction of income inequality and increase equality of opportunity; and well-targeted social safety nets.

[9]   Fischer (1991).

[10]   Fischer (1999).

Table 3.1: Fiscal Burden 1990-99. Tax Revenues as a Proportion of GDP

Country		1990	1991	1992	1993	1994	1995	1996	1997	1998p
Colombia	Consolidated	8.8	9.9	10.5	10.8	10.9	10.6	11.0	11.7	11.5
	Central Gov.*1/	1.6	1.6	1.5	1.5	1.4	1.4	1.4	1.3	1.3
	Regional Govs.	1.1	1.2	1.2	1.4	1.6	1.6	1.7	1.7	1.7
	Local Govs	1.9	2.1	2.2	1.9	2.7	3.1	2.8	3.2	3.2
	Contribution to Social Security									
	Total	13.4	14.8	15.4	15.6	16.6	16.7	16.9	17.9	17.7
Venezuela	Consolidated	17.5	17.7	13.2	13.0	13.6	12.5	13.5	17.0	12.0
	Gov.*	0.9	0.8	0.9	0.8	1.0	0.7	0.3	0.4	0.7
	Contributions to Social Security									
	Total	18.4	18.5	14.1	13.8	14.6	13.2	13.8	17.3	12.8
Chile	Consolidated	14.5	16.6	17.3	18.1	17.5	17.0	18.4	17.9	17.9
	Gov.*	n.d	n.d	1.3	1.4	1.3	1.4	1.5	1.5	1.6
	Local Govs.	1.7	1.6	1.6	1.5	1.5	1.3	1.4	1.4	1.5
	Contribution to Social Security									
	Total	16.3	18.2	20.2	21.0	20.2	19.7	21.3	20.8	20.8
Mexico	Consolidated	11.8	11.5	11.6	11.3	10.7	10.7	10.9	11.2	n.d
	Gov.*	2.6	2.6	2.7	2.8	2.7	2.5	2.6	2.8	n.d
	Regional Govs.	0.7	0.7	0.8	0.8	0.8	0.7	0.7	0.7	n.d
	Local Govs.	1.9	2.0	2.1	2.3	2.4	2.1	1.9	1.8	n.d
	Contribution to Social Security									
	Total	16.9	16.8	17.2	17.1	16.6	16.0	16.2	16.5	n.d
Peru	Consolidated	9.2	8.9	10.0	9.8	11.0	11.5	12.0	12.0	12.0
	Gov.*.	0.0	0.0	0.0	0.1	0.1	0.1	0.1	0.1	0.1
	Regional Govs.	0.1	0.3	0.3	0.4	0.2	0.2	0.2	0.2	0.2
	Local Govs.	0.8	1.5	1.6	1.5	1.4	1.4	1.3	1.3	1.3
	Contribution to Social Security									
	Total	10.1	10.8	12.0	11.7	12.7	13.2	13.7	13.7	13.6
Costa Rica	Consolidated	13.1	13.5	15.2	15.3	14.6	15.7	16.0	n.d	n.d
	Gov.*	6.6	6.7	6.5	7.2	7.4	6.8	7.1	n.d	n.d
	Contribution to Social Security									
	Total	19.7	20.3	21.7	22.5	22.0	22.5	23.1	n.d	n.d
Germany	Consolidated	11.6	12.5	12.9	12.5	12.6	12.5	11.5	11.1	n.d
	Gov.*	8.1	7.5	8.1	8.4	8.3	8.4	8.4	8.2	8.1
	Regional Govs.	2.8	2.6	3.0	3.1	3.0	2.9	2.8	2.6	2.9
	Local Govs.	15.4	14.4	15.0	15.1	15.4	15.4	15.5	15.6	n.d
	Contribution to Social Security									
	Total	37.9	37.1	39.0	39.1	39.3	39.2	38.1	37.5	n.d
USA	Consolidated	10.9	10.7	10.4	10.8	11.1	11.5	12.0	12.5	13.1
	Gov.	5.2	5.2	5.3	5.4	5.4	5.4	5.4	5.3	n.d
	Regional Govs.	3.5	3.6	3.7	3.7	3.6	3.6	3.5	3.5	n.d
	Local Govs.	6.7	6.8	6.7	6.6	6.7	6.8	6.7	6.7	6.7
	Contribution to Social Security									
	Total	26.3	26.4	26.1	26.5	26.9	27.3	27.6	28.1	n.d
Sweden	Consolidated	24.6	22.5	19.7	17.7	17.1	19.5	21.2	20.4	22.0
	Gov.*	15.1	16.1	18.7	17.7	16.7	15.8	17.4	16.9	16.7
	Local Govs.	13.8	13.1	15.8	12.9	12.1	14.2	15.6	16.6	13.8
	Contribution to Social Security									
	Total	53.5	51.7	54.2	48.3	45.9	49.5	54.2	53.9	52.5

Table 3.1 (continued)

Country		1990	1991	1992	1993	1994	1995	1996	1997	1998p
Norway	Consolidated Gov.*	22.1	22.3	21.5	21.5	22.5	23.4	23.7	25.2	n.d
		8.5	8.4	8.3	8.3	8.6	8.2	7.9	7.9	n.d
	Local Govs. Contributions to Social Security	10.2	10.1	10.2	9.3	9.2	9.0	8.8	8.9	n.d
	Total	40.8	40.8	40.0	39.2	40.4	40.6	40.5	41.9	n.d
Canada	Consolidated Gov.	15.2	15.2	14.5	13.8	14.0	14.0	n.d	n.d	n.d
		13.4	13.3	12.8	13.2	13.1	13.4	n.d	n.d	n.d
	Regional Govs.	3.5	3.7	3.8	3.8	3.6	3.5	n.d	n.d	n.d
	Local Govs. Contributions to Social Security	4.7	5.1	5.4	5.3	5.4	5.2	n.d	n.d	n.d
	Total	36.8	37.3	36.6	36.1	36.1	36.0	n.d	n.d	n.d
Australia	Consolidated Gov.	23.1	23.2	21.0	20.3	20.1	21.3	22.2	22.7	22.6
		4.8	5.0	5.2	5.3	5.5	5.5	5.6	5.7	5.6
	Regional Govs.	1.0	1.1	1.1	1.1	1.0	1.0	1.0	1.0	1.0
	Local Govs Contributions to Social Security	0.0	0.0	0.0	0.0	0.0	0.0	0.0	0.0	0.0
	Total	28.9	29.3	27.3	26.6	26.7	27.8	28.7	29.4	29.2
UK	Consolidated Gov.	26.8	28.0	27.2	25.8	26.5	27.2	27.6	27.5	29.0
		1.9	1.4	1.5	1.4	1.4	1.5	1.4	1.4	1.5
	Local Govs. Contributions to Social Security	6.2	6.2	6.3	6.0	6.2	6.2	6.2	6.1	6.6
	Total	34.8	35.6	35.1	33.2	34.1	34.9	35.2	35.0	37.0
Switzerland	Consolidated Gov.	9.2	8.8	9.0	8.3	8.9	9.0	9.4	9.4	n.d
		6.7	6.6	6.6	6.9	6.9	6.9	6.9	6.7	n.d
	Regional Govs.	4.7	4.6	4.7	4.9	5.0	5.0	5.0	4.9	n.d
	Local Govs. Contribution to Social Security	10.3	10.6	10.9	12.2	12.2	12.6	12.6	12.5	n.d
	Total	30 9	30.6	31.2	32.2	33.0	33.5	33.9	33.5	n.d
New Zealand	Consolidated Govs.	36.3	33.6	30.9	30.0	31.9	31.5	32.7	31.0	n.d
		n.d	n.d	2.3	2.1	2.1	2.1	2.1	2.1	n.d
	Local Govs. Contributions to Social Security	0.0	0.0	0.0	0.0	0.0	0.0	0.0	0.0	n.d
	Total	n.d	n.d	33.2	32.1	33.9	33.6	34.7	33.1	n.d

n.d: Not available

Source: *Estadísticas Financieras Internacionales del FMI Anuario 1999; Government Finance Statistic Yearbook,* 1999, IMF; Confis and DANE

* Includes Central Government and Decentralised Agencies

1/ Includes earmarked income for SENA, ICBF and ESAP

p: Provisional

CHAPTER 4

Despite the Odds: The Political Economy of Social Sector Reform in Latin America

Merilee S. Grindle

Whether considering health, education or pension systems, and regardless of the extent of change proposed, conventional political economy indicates that reform initiatives are likely to be met with stiff opposition and lukewarm support. This same approach warns that politicians are unlikely to champion change, even though they often recognise that unreformed social welfare policies absorb extensive amounts of state resources and deliver very little for the investment. Standard analyses of political institutions also create expectations that anti-reformists will have important sources of power that are not so readily available to those promoting change. Not surprisingly, given these expectations, political economists generally anticipate that reform initiatives will fail.

How, then, do we account for the introduction of social sector reforms during the 1990s? Despite the political odds against such outcomes, a significant number of countries in Latin America introduced major changes in the way that health and education systems operated and set in motion fundamental changes in the structure of pension systems. In many cases, these policy and institutional changes survived mobilised opposition, acrimonious debates, resistant bureaucracies and changes in political administrations to be implemented with some degree of consistency. Of course, the reforms were not always as thoroughgoing as their proponents hoped nor did they necessarily solve the problems they were expected to address. Nevertheless, the introduction and at least partial implementation of new social sector policies was a notable characteristic of the decade.

This paradox — that the political cards appear to be stacked against change, yet reform has occurred in many countries — needs to be explained. This chapter asks why reforms are adopted more frequently than our political economy models would predict. The social sectors are a classic case in which political calculations based on the identification of winners and losers or on the distribution of power within institutional contexts militate against change. But winners and losers and political institutions are not the only factors at work in efforts to introduce new policies. Indeed, the process of reform offers numerous opportunities to alter the political equations that impede change, although this is generally ignored in current political economy models.

Analysis of the process of reform must be incorporated into political economy approaches if concepts and models are to become more helpful in understanding when and why change occurs. In this process, reformers and their strategic decisions, as well as the organisational characteristics of winners and losers and the constraints introduced by political institutions, become key factors in determining reform destinies. In exploring the process of change, the chapter first discusses conditions in the social sectors at the beginning of the 1990s and the kinds of reforms that were introduced during the decade.[1] The chapter goes on to consider how political economists understand the politics of introducing such reforms. The third part explores the findings of empirical studies of reform initiatives to demonstrate how, in the case of contentious policies, process shapes outcomes. Throughout, 'reform' is used to imply deliberate changes in policies and institutions that supply social sector services; it does not imply a normative judgement about the appropriateness or the goodness of the changes.

Social Sector Reform in the 1990s

Extensive reforms were introduced in the social sectors in Latin America in the 1990s. Table 4.1 lists nine countries that introduced reforms in health services between 1990 and 2000, 14 countries that made significant changes in education policy and 11 countries that reformed their pension systems. Eight countries introduced change in all three social services and three additional countries in two out of three services. These data do not indicate the extent to which reforms were fully implemented, but they do suggest the extent to which reformers were busy promoting policy changes during the decade.

---

[1] The focus throughout this chapter is on health, education and pension reforms. In Latin America, the social sector agenda is broader than this focus implies. Investments in sewers, potable water and nutrition programmes; employment creation; squatter settlement upgrading; land reform; rural roads; environmental protection and conservation; public security; judicial reform and human rights protections; programmes to increase participation of women in the labour force; unemployment insurance; microfinance programmes; and many other policies and programmes also have significant implications for social welfare and poverty reduction. It is likely that exploring a process of reform in these policy areas could also reveal important insights into how change occurs.

Table 4.1: Social Sector Reforms in Latin America

Country	Sector		
	Health	Education	Pension
Argentina	1996	1991	1994
Bolivia	1999	1994	1996
Brazil	1996	1993	1998
Chile	1992	1981	1981
Colombia	1993	1994	1994
Costa Rica	1993	1995/6	1995/6
Dominican Republic			
Ecuador			
El Salvador		1996	1997
Guatemala		1991	
Honduras		1996	
Mexico	1998	1997	1997
Nicaragua	1993	1993	2000
Panama		1997	
Paraguay			
Peru			1993
Uruguay		1995	1996
Venezuela	1994	1989	

Note: Dates for the same reform often vary, depending on the source, and may represent when reforms were legislated or when they were first implemented. In addition, in some countries, reforms were subject to significant re-reforms after they had been in existence for a time. Most dates given above are drawn from World Bank and Inter-American Development Bank sources; see note 18 for additional sources. I am grateful to Geoffrey Davis of the Kennedy School of Government for assistance in compiling this table.

The general content of these reforms was often strikingly similar across countries.[2] In education — particularly at the primary level — decentralisation, the introduction of national standards for students, professional training for teachers, revised curricula and expanded community control

---

2   They differed, of course, in the details of how broad changes were pursued.

were priorities for change.[3] In health, decentralisation, competition among providers, various forms of privatisation, new insurance systems, management autonomy for hospitals and increased community participation figured in many reforms.[4] In pension systems, defined benefit, pay-as-you-go, public systems were usually replaced by multi-pillar systems (mixed public-private systems with both compulsory and voluntary savings components) based on defined individual worker contributory accounts; the size of contributions, the age of eligibility, and the way benefits were calculated were also generally redefined.[5] In all three services, increased efficiency, accountability and quality were enunciated as goals of the reforms; the path toward these objectives meant complex conceptual, organisational and behavioural changes.[6]

Of course, countries differed in terms of how broad and deep the reform designs were. And, in every country, reform was a moving target, often with a history of one or more failed attempts before a successful initiative was launched.[7] Countries also varied in the extent to which they were able to sustain new policies and institutional arrangements. Opposition to reform during its implementation was much in evidence and frequently slowed the impact of new systems and threatened their sustainability. In this regard, pension reforms, while often very contentious as they were being designed and decided upon, were put into effect more easily than reforms in health and education, both of which require longer-term, more extensive, and more complex implementation processes.[8] And, in spite of a region-wide trend toward reform, at the end of the decade, some countries — Ecuador, Honduras, Paraguay and Peru among them — had yet to make

---

[3]   Reimers (2000); Navarro, Carnoy and de Moura Castro (1999); Savedoff (1998).

[4]   González-Rosetti and Bossert (2000); IDB (1996); Savedoff (1998).

[5]   Brooks (2000); Cruz-Saco and Mesa-Lago (1998); Brooks and James(1999).

[6]   Thus, simply providing more resources to provide more services was not viewed as a solution to the problems plaguing the sector.

[7]   Pension reform in Uruguay, for example, failed four times before being adopted in 1996 (Nelson, 1999, pp. 12–13). Colombia's health reform of 1993 got off to a good start, and then progress was paralysed for four years before being given new life with the inauguration of a new administration (González-Rosetti and Bossert, 2000). Bolivia implemented a novel pension reform in 1996, but a new administration rejected much of it after 1997. That country's comprehensive education reform took two administrations to be designed and approved and during a third it was implemented, but only in part (Grindle, 2000c). Ecuador has yet to see a successful education reform, despite a number of initiatives. Argentina's pension reform was put in operation in 1994, but needed to be extensively re-reformed in later years (Nelson, 1999). Similar situations arose in Peru and Colombia. Brazil's pension reform experienced extensive delays before it was finally adopted in diluted form in 1998 (Melo, forthcoming).

[8]   Nelson (1999).

much headway in introducing and implementing important changes in social welfare policies. Despite these caveats, there is no question that social services were high on most government agendas and that significant progress was made in altering their content and administration.

At the outset of this reformist decade there was good empirical evidence that Latin America's social services needed to be improved. While poverty, inequality and inadequate services were endemic in most countries in the region, such conditions became more acute during the 1980s. The decade was characterised by heightened indices of poverty and unemployment, as national policy-makers imposed stabilisation and structural adjustment measures in response to menacingly large debt burdens, spiralling inflation, fiscal crises, stagnating growth and the conditionalities of international financial institutions. At the end of the 1980s 40 million more people in Latin America and the Caribbean lived in poverty than at the beginning of the decade.[9] Moreover, according to the Inter-American Development Bank, the poorest decile of the population lost 15 per cent of its income share during this decade and wealth concentration increased.[10]

Moreover, despite evidence of increased need for social protection, the 'lost decade' witnessed the constriction of social sector budgets as governments sought ways to tame inflation and reduce fiscal deficits.[11] Per capita social spending in the region declined in real terms by ten per cent from 1982 to 1986 and, while spending grew after that period, at the end of the decade it still remained six per cent below what it had been in 1980 on a per capita basis.[12]

On a country-by-country basis, government expenditures in education declined as a portion of GNP between 1980 and 1991 in Costa Rica, the Dominican Republic, Ecuador, El Salvador, Mexico, Paraguay and Uruguay.[13] Teacher pay declined throughout the region and absenteeism increased, as did that of poor children, as teachers and students abandoned

---

[9]　According to a World Bank study, 31 per cent of the population of the region lived below the poverty line in 1989; in 1980, the percentage had been 26.5 per cent (based on a poverty line of US$2 a day) (Psacharopoulos et al., 1997, p. 71).

[10]　IDB (1998), pp. 14–15.

[11]　IDB (1996), p. 47; Cardoso and Helwege (1992), p. 227.

[12]　IDB (1996), p. 47.

[13]　World Bank (1993, pp. 258–9). Comparable data are missing for Argentina, Bolivia, Chile, Colombia, Guatemala, Nicaragua and Venezuela. Spending increased in Panama and Peru. By the mid-1990s, Latin America as a whole was spending more of its GNP on education than East and South Asian countries, but considerably less than was being spent in Europe and Central Asia, the Middle East and North Africa, Sub-Saharan Africa and high income countries (World Bank, 1998, p. 201).

the classroom to find additional means to contribute to fragile household incomes. Textbooks and other educational materials, school breakfasts, teacher training and other critically important inputs suffered significant cutbacks. Educational standards were also low. While some countries — Argentina, Bolivia, Chile, Panama and Uruguay — managed to achieve an average of eight years or more of schooling by the 1990s, this average was five years or less in Brazil, El Salvador and Nicaragua.[14] Secondary school completion rates were below 20 per cent in Honduras and Nicaragua, under 40 per cent in Costa Rica, Paraguay, Brazil, Ecuador, El Salvador, Mexico and Venezuela, and did not reach 60 per cent in Argentina, Chile and Peru.[15] Because education is a critical factor explaining the persistence of inequality and poverty, the failure of the region to provide this service more effectively suggests a more general failure to address divisive social ills.

In health, the lost decade produced declining expenditures as a proportion of total public spending in Brazil, El Salvador, Mexico and Uruguay.[16] For the region as a whole, expenditures on public health amounted to only 1.28 per cent of GDP in 1990, well below the standard in industrial economies, below the percentage expended in much more rapidly growing regions of the world such as East and South Asia, and considerably below percentages in Sub-Saharan Africa, the Middle East and Central Europe and Asia.[17] In the poorest countries, large portions of the population lacked access to medical care; in Haiti, 55 per cent of the population fell into this category, in Guatemala, 40 per cent; in Honduras, 38 per cent; in Ecuador, 20 per cent; and in Panama, 18 per cent.[18] Where health insurance was tied to formal sector employment, economic recession and formal unemployment, coupled with increased participation in the informal sector or in part-time work, left many formerly protected citizens without access to services.

By the early 1990s many ministries of education and health had made no substantial investments in expanded or improved facilities for a decade and were spending almost all of their budgets on salaries for personnel. In practice, this meant schools and health posts fallen into decay, no restocking of textbooks or medicines, no equipment replacement or repairs, and

[14]   IDB (1998), p. 27.
[15]   *Ibid.*
[16]   World Bank (1993), pp. 258–9.
[17]   IDB (1996), p. 336.
[18]   UNDP (2000), pp. 169–71.

demoralised employees working two or even three jobs in order to make ends meet. In addition, a variety of perverse incentives for the performance of social sector professionals continued to undermine the quality and quantity of services available.[19] Access to social services was unequally distributed between urban and rural areas and those who had economic resources continued to flee the public provision of services for private markets for education and health. The 1980s had left behind a striking 'social deficit'.

The condition of pension systems was also bleak. In many countries publicly run systems were the largest fiscal programmes in 1990. These were almost universally pay-as-you-go programmes with defined benefits. By 1990, spending on public pensions averaged 8.5 per cent of GDP in Latin America countries and over 40 per cent of all pension spending was for public employees.[20] During the 1980s and early 1990s, fiscal crises and low growth alerted policy-makers to the costs of these pension systems, which were also under pressure because high rates of unemployment reduced contributions, inflation eroded benefits and an ageing population created fears about future costs.[21] In 1994, the World Bank published an influential treatise, *Averting the Old Age Crisis: Policies to Protect the Old and Promote Growth*, which raised the profile of the problem worldwide and increased the interest of policy-makers in privatising part or all of their pension systems.[22] Additionally, the example set by reform in Chile in the early 1980s encouraged other countries to introduce at least partially privatised systems.[23]

Thus, the need for change in social sector policies was clear by the early 1990s. At the time, large numbers of citizens throughout Latin America were denied access to social protection policies or were doomed to receive only inefficient and ineffective services. The rapid pace of global integration during the decade was a forceful reminder of the role of human capital in advancing productivity, assimilating new technology and attracting foreign investment. Similarly, almost every government in the region was under pressure to demonstrate how new democratic institutions could provide for the economic and social wellbeing of their predominantly poor populations.[24]

---

[19]   Salaries were almost exclusively based on seniority, for example, and appointments and promotions were generally determined by patronage, not merit.

[20]   World Bank (1994a), p. 359.

[21]   Brooks (2000). In Argentina, for example, the value of pensions declined by 64 per cent between 1980 and 1988 (Huber and Stephens, 2000, p. 12).

[22]   World Bank (1994a).

[23]   Nelson (1999), p. 13; Cruz-Saco and Mesa-Lago (1998).

[24]   Grindle (2000b).

But policy reforms do not occur simply because evidence accumulates about the severity of a problem or even about the positive benefits of change for welfare and national development. Indeed, although it was clear in many countries that the provision of health, education and pensions was in dire need of improvement, it was not at all clear how the political basis for such changes could be found. Reform requires concerted action on the part of political decision-makers, action that often engenders opposition more effectively than it does support.

Explaining the Odds: The Political Economy of Reform

Social sector reforms are contentious. That they might ever succeed in being introduced is, according to many analysts, a long shot. Indeed, in comparing the political difficulty of these reforms to earlier macroeconomic policy changes, Joan Nelson has written that, 'Social sector reforms are a different ball game, with far more actors, less leverage, different fields of play, a much longer playing period (with unpredictable time-outs) and uncertain scoring'.[25] In acknowledgement of these difficulties, current political economy concepts and models provide us with excellent reasons to suspect that reform is doomed to failure. Whether approaching the issue of reform from the perspective of rational choice political economy or institutionalist orientations, the case for failure is strong.

Winners and Losers in Conflict Equations

A dominant theme in formal political economy is the way in which proposed changes create material winners and losers.[26] In the generic analytic case of the politics surrounding reform initiatives, losers are clearly aware of their potential losses and quick to oppose change, while winners are much less likely to benefit in the short term or be aware of long-term gains.[27] Losers have incentives to organise to protect the status quo; winners lack clear incentives to organise for change and therefore face difficult problems of

---

[25]   Nelson (1999), p. 36.

[26]   Important theoretical contributions to this perspective are found in Alesina and Drazen (1991); Alesina and Perotti (1994); Fernandez and Rodrik (1991); Geddes (1994); Rodrik (1994); Schamis (1999); Tommasi and Velasco (1996); Weingast, Shepsle and Johnson (1981). For empirical studies adopting this perspective, see individual chapters in Bates and Krueger (1993).

[27]   In the most common cases of reform, there are many winners but they have only a diffuse sense of their common interests in change; there are few losers, but they tend to be concentrated and have a clear sense of what they will lose through change.

collective action. Further, reform is politically difficult because electorally sensitive politicians have incentives to postpone it, given imbalances between the power of winners and losers. In this perspective, whether or not reforms are adopted and implemented is a consequence of the ability of losers to create obstacles to change. In the end, incentives for winners, losers and politicians conspire against most reform initiatives.

In the case of social sector reforms the model has strong empirical referents. Almost all reforms impose at least short-term burdens on politically important groups that readily define themselves as losers. Reforms often seek to redress distributional inequalities by extending services to new groups and imposing limits or fees on long-existing beneficiaries or by reallocating resources among programmes. Health and education reforms, in particular, reallocate power, budgets and jobs and expose public sector workers to new pressures and expectations while altering long-existing rights and career tracts. They usually reassign authority relationships and empower new stakeholders. Pension and health reforms may involve shifting some responsibilities from public to private actors. Pension system changes threaten services that many regard as entitlements and, like education and health, have long been regarded in Latin America as exclusive responsibilities of the state.

These characteristics usually produce strong opposition from important political groups. Most prominent among them are unions, which resist the loss of benefits, jobs and security. It is important that public sector unions are often the largest and most powerful organised groups in a country, a characteristic that is particularly true of teachers' unions. Health providers' unions and associations, although often divided by function or speciality, are composed of particularly important groups. In education and health, providers' unions have often colonised ministries and achieved privileged positions in personnel decisions; in reform, their leaders face loss of power and prestige. Pension reforms are met with hostility by much of organised labour, which fears the loss of security if state-provided pension schemes are privatised and the loss of worker solidarity if individual contributory accounts are established.[28] Pensioners' associations have frequently joined in the protest against reform. As a consequence, nearly everywhere, the announcement of social sector reforms has been met by protests, strikes and vociferous opposition by providers' unions and by organised workers more generally in the case of pension reform.

---

[28]   Nelson (1999), p. 14.

Bureaucrats in social sector ministries also frequently define themselves as losers in proposed reforms, as they may lose their jobs or their responsibilities or be forced to abide by new performance standards. In health and pensions it is not uncommon for government agencies responsible for such services to be collectively opposed to changes that threaten to diminish or restructure their roles. And, where the provision of jobs for supporters is a fundamental characteristic of party systems, as it is throughout much of Latin America, party leaders stand to lose extensive patronage opportunities if new standards and systems are put in place. In addition, opposition political parties have often been outspoken critics of social sector policy changes for both ideological and electoral reasons; the charge that governments are abandoning their responsibilities by privatising social programmes has resonated effectively in political debates in many countries.

Winners — parents with school-age children, those who need more and better healthcare, citizens who benefit from living in a more healthy and well-educated society, new entrants into the labour market, new public or private sector institutions and their employees — are also created by social sector reforms. Characteristically, however, they are not well informed of the benefits that will accrue to them, they are unorganised, they often lack access to policy-making circles and the benefits they will receive are often too distant to be taken seriously. No doubt many winners also distrust government enough to be wary of promises for improvement of services in the future; they have heard many such promises and yet have lived through a decade or more of disappointment with economic conditions and sluggish responses to state policies.

The problem for political economy, of course, is that even in the presence of empirical evidence of strong losers and weak winners, reform initiatives at times become reality. In the face of evidence of substantial reform progress, preserving the integrity of the model has meant appealing to exogenous factors to explain change.[29] In the case of economic policy reforms introduced in many countries, analysts were forced to adduce unusual situations to explain how governments are pushed toward support of new policies — major economic crises, favourable electoral calendars, carrots and sticks brandished by international financial institutions, or risk-inducing party alignments.[30] In other cases, unusual people, whose behaviour cannot be understood by the same rationality that binds other actors, are introduced to explain change — reform 'entrepreneurs,' 'heroes' or 'champions'.[31] Empirically,

---

[29]   Grindle (1991).

[30]   Alesina and Drazen (1991); Geddes (1994); Stallings (1992); Williamson (1994).

[31]   Harberger (1993a); North (1992); Srinivasan (1985).

particular situations and particular people may well be important in explaining reform success; but political economy models have failed to endogenise these factors.

The simple arithmetic of winners and losers also fails to capture the factors that affect the ability of losers to obstruct change. For example, unions vary considerably in their capacity to present a unified front opposing change, in the extent to which they are compromised by their ties to particular political parties and the extent to which they are able to engage in actions that actually obstruct reform. Murillo (1999) has shown how internal conditions in teachers' unions contribute to divergent outcomes in whether unions accept reform or not.[32] Corrales (1998) has found that unions closely identified with governing parties are less able to resist reforms than unions affiliated with opposition parties. González-Rosetti and Bossert (2000) demonstrate that many groups opposing health reform in Chile could not mobilise effectively under the military regime; in Mexico, divisions among unions and health agencies weakened their ability to pension reform. In fact, in many countries decades of bossism, the competing claims of independent unions or the divisive nature of internal reformism, the expansion of the informal sector and a decade or more of recession weakened the power of the union sector generally.[33]

And, although the structure of social sector bureaucracies and the incentive systems that motivate public sector workers usually put them at odds with reform initiatives, not all bureaucrats are rent seekers or passive beneficiaries of patronage jobs. Some may be valuable allies of reform, as Tendler demonstrates in the case of community health in north-east Brazil and Uribe notes among teachers in Colombia.[34] DiUlio (1994) has pointed to the importance of 'principled agents' in public sector organisations, and many others have indicated the importance of managerial and incentive systems that motivate active and engaged public servants in some organisations.[35] Moreover, in many Latin American countries, changes of ministry leadership are accompanied by many changes in middle and upper level ministry staff, giving reform proponents opportunities to salt their organisations with personnel who will support their initiatives.[36]

---

[32] In addition, a network of researchers under the auspices of PREAL is generating extensive new descriptive and analytic work on teachers' unions in Latin America (see, for example, Tiramonte, 2000, and Loyo, Ibarrola and Blanco, 2000).

[33] Arrighi (1996); Lawson (1990); Middlebrook (1995); Murrillo (1996).

[34] Tendler (1997); Uribe (1999).

[35] Evans (1995); Grindle (1997a); Israel (1987).

[36] Unfortunately, the same privilege is available to ministers who wish to halt reform.

The analysis of winners and losers current in rational choice political economy can also misstate the political weakness of winners. One factor that encourages some support for reform is the obvious condition of so many pre-reform social services in Latin America. Widespread public opinion that the current system is broken beyond repair can rob organised resistance of its legitimacy. Empirically, public opinion in many countries has expressed little tolerance for those who oppose health and educational reforms, although it has been more supportive of organised workers opposed to pension reform. Indeed, with the exception of a few countries — Costa Rica principal among them — claims of teachers' unions and healthcare workers have not been widely respected, their images often soiled by their lack of professionalism, the bossism of their unions and widespread public dismay at the dismal state of public services. When teachers went on strike in Argentina in 1997, few citizens did much more than criticise them for the poor performance of local schools; when doctors went on strike in Venezuela in 1997, they were met with public disdain and hostility. In 1999, Bolivian reformers successfully publicised violent union resistance to education reform to call into question the professionalism and legitimacy of the teachers.

Moreover, despite the general passivity of potential winners, in some cases winners are both mobilised and powerful. In some health reforms, for example, private insurers identify their interests with changes that provide more opportunities for the private sector. Similarly in pension reform, is it possible to identify powerful and well-organised interests on the side of reform — insurance providers, domestic and international capital marketeers and foreign investors.[37] In such cases, then, clear and organised winners exist, as well as clear and organised losers. In such cases, the generic analytic case in political economy does not hold.

Rational choice political economy also errs in assuming that reform is a binary choice, either adopted or rejected. In fact, many reform initiatives are negotiated agreements that allow for change to occur in the context of some tolerance by the opposition. This has been clearest in the case of pension reform, in which many governments initially sought to emulate Chile's full privatisation scheme but ended with partially private plans that exempted some of the most powerful opponents of change — public servants, the military, teachers, doctors, bank employees and particularly important unions, such as the oil workers in Mexico.[38] In addition, many

37 Huber and Stephens (2000).
38 *Ibid.*

proposals differentiated between older workers with long term contributions to the pre-reform system, new entrants into the labour market who were usually required to join the new system and other workers who could choose which system they wanted to join.[39] As a result of such changes in Argentina, union opposition declined when they became eligible to manage the new pension funds.

Negotiations were common in education reforms also. In the case of changes involving decentralisation, opposition of teachers' unions was initially very strong. They saw in it poorly disguised efforts to break the unions by forcing them to negotiate separately with numerous regional or local governments or local school boards over salaries and work conditions. But in Mexico, Argentina and a number of other countries decentralisation reforms were negotiated to maintain salary and benefit decisions at central levels. In Chile, after a decade of decentralised union-government negotiation, teachers won back the right to national agreements on salaries and benefits and their unions became more sympathetic to the reforms. Similar situations are apparent in the health sector. In Bolivia, for example, a decentralised health system maintained salary and personnel decisions at the central level. Indeed, most countries that have introduced new health management systems continue to deal centrally with personnel and salary issues. Such compromises may not be optimal in the eyes of reformers, but they do allow other important changes to go forward.

Rational choice political economy provides a powerful and intuitive explanation of the difficulties encountered by reform initiatives. The model is also empirically useful in explaining why opposition to socially beneficial change exists. But the very simplicity of the model may impede its ability to forecast reform outcomes. Effective in identifying winners and losers, it is less able to provide insight into the factors that enhance or weaken the power of these groups, nor does it anticipate the potential for second-best outcomes.

Institutions that Empower Losers

Some political economists have taken the analysis of winners and losers further by exploring the extent to which political institutions explain success and failure in reform initiatives.[40] For example, some have argued that

---

[39]　Nelson (1999), pp. 13–14.

[40]　Institutionalist perspectives generally define institutions as the 'humanly devised constraints that shape human interaction' (North, 1990, p. 3).

differences in power between the executive and legislative branches or differences created by the distribution of power in presidential and parliamentary systems can affect the destiny of reform initiatives.[41] According to other analyses the number of political parties, the degree of party discipline or the extent of centralised control that party leaders have over their memberships can determine reform outcomes.[42] In reforms that must be legislated, the function of legislative committees and rules can create more or fewer barriers to change. These factors, it is claimed, affect the access that winners and losers have to decision-making arenas and determine the value of their political resources.[43]

In the generic case of reform explained by institutionalists, interests defending the status quo tend to be more powerful than those that seek change. This is because anti-reformers are usually winners of prior contests over policy and, as a consequence, they have colonised institutions of power in the society and government. They use these institutions to ensure that policy favours their interests. In cases in which reform is threatened, these same institutions help them defend their interests.[44] In this political economy tradition, institutions are generally treated as rules of the game that constrain the possibility of reform.[45] As in rational choice political economy, then, institutional analyses also provide a model in which the cards are stacked against change.

Empirically, this approach finds ready support. It is common to observe that ministries of education and health are weak compared to public sector unions or that (reformist) ministers come and go while resistant bureaucracies are entrenched. In contrast, pension reforms have been championed by powerful ministries of finance. The weakness of

---

[41]   Lijphart and Waisman (1996); Linz and Valenzuela (1994).

[42]   Brooks (2000); Corrales (1998).

[43]   A large literature considers how institutions affect the fate of policy reforms. See especially Bates and Krueger (1993); Evans (1995); Haggard and Kaufman (1992); Nelson (1990); Steinmo, Thelen and Longstreth (1992).

[44]   In this view, for example, education unions have accumulated sources of power over time that help them maintain their hold over existing arrangements. In contrast, reformers tend to represent interests with less power and little access to institutional sources to influence policy. In most cases, then, reformers must take on the difficult task of building a coalition for change that is equal to or greater than the coalition for the status quo. In the case of education, this is a difficult undertaking because of the problem of mobilising potential supporters, particularly in contexts in which those likely to benefit most tend to be poorly organised or marginalised from political participation – parents, the poor or local communities, for example.

[45]   Grindle (2000a).

Ecuador's executive compared to its legislature has been held to account for numerous failures to approve much needed changes.[46] Colombia's health reform was affected when a new constitution gave the legislature more power than it had traditionally had in its relation to the executive.[47] Policy paralysis in pre-Chávez Venezuela has been accounted for by the extent to which entrenched political parties resisted efforts to redress obvious weaknesses in economic and social policy.[48] Brazil's congress and federal structure have been held to account for the very slow adoption of important policy reforms.[49] Conversely, Chile's early success with major reforms is frequently explained by the lack of institutional constraints under the military authoritarianism of the Pinochet regime.[50]

To their credit, institutional analyses provide for more complex scenarios about change than do rational choice approaches.[51] They acknowledge that institutions have histories that shape values and behaviour and that create ongoing incentives for conflict and cooperation over time. Political institutions at times legitimate formal and informal mechanisms for overcoming resistance to change, such as opportunities for legislative vote-trading and pact-making to provide majority approval for reformist measures. Bolivia, for example, has been able to create effective governing pacts among diverse political parties across different administrations since the mid-1980s.[52] Such a pact was critically important to the ability of a reformist administration in the mid-1990s to carry through a wide range of significant changes, including important education and pension reforms.

Institutional traditions of executive dominance in policy making can also shift power relations among institutions, giving presidents much greater technical capacity than legislatures to design solutions to major national problems. Similarly, presidential decree powers have been an important alternative to legislative approval of many important economic reforms. Informal institutions such as patronage rights and clientelist networks also affect opposition and support for change. In Mexico during the

---

46 Conaghan (1994).

47 González-Rosetti and Bossert (2000), pp. 24–7.

48 Coppedge (1994).

49 Melo (forthcoming).

50 Graham (1998); Huber and Stephens (2000).

51 In rational choice political economy, institutions appear only as contexts in which individuals make constrained strategic decisions.

52 Gamarra (1994).

long dominance of the PRI, for example, ministers were frequently members of political networks (*camarillas*) that allowed them to cooperate in pursuit of policy objectives.[53] Thus, institutional analyses recognise that important variations in institutions can make a difference to the outcome of reforms.

Institutional analyses need to go farther, however, in acknowledging the extent to which timing and strategy can affect the outcome of reform initiatives. In the face of extensive economic crises, for example, reformers have been able to convince reluctant legislatures and political parties to approve changes they would otherwise resist.[54] The strategic linking of unpopular reforms to more widely accepted ones has also been useful in spearheading reform initiatives.[55] As Reimers and McGinn (1997) demonstrate, reformers have sometimes been able to use information as a powerful tool in shaping public, union and bureaucratic tolerance for change. Reformers can also intervene to alter incentives in ways that are more supportive of reform.[56] Similarly, the potential for change can be strengthened through the creation of networks of reformers that actually create the social capital to sustain reform initiatives in environments that are hostile to change. Too often, institutional analyses fail to take into consideration these more dynamic agency possibilities.

More generally, by treating structures and incentives as binding constraints, institutionalists tend to see reformers as narrowly confined. Change often happens, however, when reformers find ways to manoeuvre around such constraints.[57] In fact, institutional analyses underrate the importance of political entrepreneurship and how strategies for coalition building, communication and legislative relations open up or shut off opportunities for introducing politically difficult reforms.[58] In contrast, when reform is viewed as a process, the ways in which winners, losers and reformers interact in complex institutional arenas demonstrates that spaces for strategic action exist and that such actions can alter outcomes.

---

[53] Centeno (1994).

[54] Williamson (1994); Nelson (1990); Haggard and Kaufman (1992).

[55] Graham, Grindle, Lora and Seddon (1999).

[56] Grindle (1997a); Uribe (1999).

[57] Corrales (2000); Graham, Grindle, Lora and Seddon (1999); Grindle and Thomas (1991).

[58] Wallis (1998).

Social Sector Reform as Process

Current political economy models provide insights into the incentives that motivate winners and losers and suggest how institutions shape the political fortunes of reform initiatives. Yet, as the preceding review suggests, they relate to only some of the dynamics that shape outcomes. They fail to provide sufficient insight into the ways in which the characteristics of winners and losers affect the ability to resist or support change or the ways in which institutional constraints can be altered through strategic action on the part of reformers. Considerable empirical evidence suggests that these factors are critical to whether or not reform initiatives are adopted and implemented.

More fundamentally, neither rational choice nor institutionalist perspectives appreciate the importance of reform as a dynamic political process that unfolds over time, a complex chain of decisions subject to the interaction of reform advocates and opponents in particular institutional contexts.[59] In fact, the process through which reforms become part of national agendas, and by which they are designed, adopted, implemented and sustained, has significant implications for reform outcomes. In this process protagonists have different opportunities to influence conflicts and decisions. In many cases, for every action or decision that is taken during a reform process, there is some possibility for altering the conflict equation that surrounds a proposed change.[60]

Approaching policy reform as a process assumes the identification of a specific reform 'episode'. Each episode incorporates several phases across time — agenda setting, design, adoption, implementation and sustaining change. In practice, these phases are interrelated, as when the anticipation of implementation problems affects how policies are designed or when actions taken (or not taken) during implementation alter the meaning and content of policy; in reforms that require ongoing administration, sustaining reforms is merely an extension of implementation.[61] In addition, different actors are important at different phases of the process — teachers' unions may not be important in setting a national agenda for education reform, for example, but they may be critically active participants in the approval, implementation

---

[59] González-Rosetti and Bossert (2000); Graham, Grindle, Lora and Seddon (1999); Reimers and McGinn (1997).

[60] While these decisions have been seen as 'veto points', they can also be understood as strategic moments when reforms can be moved forward (Nelson, 1999, p. 1; González-Rosetti and Bossert, 2000).

[61] Grindle (1980).

and sustainability phases.[62] Moreover, reform episodes are frequently preceded by prior episodes of success or failure that colour the way in which current initiatives are assessed, designed and implemented.

Reform episodes unfold in larger economic, political and social contexts that are characterised by politically relevant individuals, groups and institutions — presidents, ministers, parties, interest groups, legislatures, executive bureaucracies, courts, media and public opinion, other levels of government, etc. Similarly, reform scenarios are influenced by historical legacies of state-society relationships, political cleavages, prior policy initiatives and other social and political conflicts. These factors set the broad rules of the game within which new initiatives will be played out and indicate that a reform episode does not get written on a *tabula rasa*. At each phase in a reform process, institutions shape the incentives faced by actors, including winners and losers, and affect their ability to influence the outcome of conflict.

Nevertheless, while reform scenarios differ according to such factors, case studies of reform have begun to suggest some plausible generalisations about social sector policy changes and how process — as well as winners, losers and institutions — affects the outcome of conflict.[63] Table 4.2, which is explained in the following sections, attempts to summarise the dynamic of these cases. It indicates which actors tend to be most relevant at each phase of the policy process, what institutional arenas are most likely to be the site of conflict and strategic action during each phase, and what critical decisions are likely to be made in those institutional arenas.

---

[62]   Trostle, Somerfeld and Simon (1997).

[63]   The literature on cases of social sector reform is growing. In the following part of the chapter, I rely on a number of sources. For education, see Carnoy and Samoff (1990); Corrales (2000); Gershberg (1998); Graham, Grindle, Lora and Seddon (1999); Murillo (1999); Navarro, Carnoy and de Moura Castro (1999); Navarro, Taylor, Bernasconi and Tyler (2000); Reimers (2000); Reimers and McGinn (1997); Uribe (1999); Winkler (1999); and my own field research in Bolivia, Ecuador, and Nicaragua. For case studies of health reform, see Cruz-Saco and Mesa-Lago (1998); González-Rosetti and Bossert (2000); Jimenez de la Jara and Bossert (1995); Nelson (1999); Tendler (1997). For pensions, see Bertranou (1998); Borzutsky (1998); Brooks (2000); Brooks and James (1999); Graham (1998); Huber and Stephens (2000); Melo (forthcoming); Mesa-Lago and Córdoba MacPas (1998); Nelson (1999); Papadópulos (1998). More generally, see Abel and Lewis (1993); Bulmer-Thomas (1996); and Thorp (1998).

Table 4.2: Participation in Policy Reform Episodes

	Reformers	Losers	Winners	Institutional Arenas	Key Decisions
Agenda Setting	Political Leaders International agencies (pensions)		Ministry of Finance (pensions, health)	Presidency Political parties Ministry Media	Timing Rationale for change Terms of debate Priority
Design	Design team International agencies			Presidency, Ministry, or Interministerial group	Content of change Identification of winners and losers Components to moderate opposition
Approval	Political leaders Minister	Unions Interest groups Opposition parties Political leaders/Legislators	Ministry of finance (pensions, health) Financial interests (pensions)	Legislature Political parties Presidency or ministry Media	Allies Modification of plan Negotiation Approval or rejection
Implementation	Reformist bureaucrats (national & local) Minister International agencies	Bureaucrats Unions Opposition parties Some governors, mayors New ministers?	Beneficiaries Some governors, mayors NGOs Employees of new institutions	Ministry Local/regional governments New institutions	Timing, pace of change Modifications Use of incentives Inclusion/exclusion of participation
Sustaining Reform	Reformist bureaucrats	Bureaucrats Unions Some governors, mayors	Beneficiaries Some governors, mayors Employees of new institutions Vendors, contractors	Ministry Local/regional governments Training institutions New institutions	Incentives Contracts and services Participation of beneficiaries

Agenda Setting

It is certainly possible to point to a series of concerns that brought greater political salience to social sector reforms in the 1990s — increasing awareness among economic technocrats of the rapid pace of globalisation and the importance of human capital development for international competitiveness, the return of all but a couple of Latin American countries to democracy and the increasing presence of civil society in the political arena. Moreover, and as already indicated, conditions in education, health and pension systems were dismal throughout Latin America in the early 1990s. Yet the existence of a problem, or even public awareness of it, does not explain either the introduction of reform initiatives or why some countries introduced reforms sooner than others. Conditions in the social sectors had been deteriorating for some time prior to the 1990s and few countries took action to ameliorate these problems. Why did that situation change?

Case studies of education and health reform suggest that these issues got on public agendas because specific political actors — usually presidents, or ministers with the support of presidents — made specific choices to put them there.[64] There is little evidence that politicians were responding to direct and specific demands or proposals of mobilised groups in the population. Rather, they appeared to have been motivated by convictions about the importance of social sector policies, by concerns about the political legitimacy of the administration, party or regime they headed, or by an interest in reassigning responsibility for difficult problems.[65] In Albert Hirshman's terms, education and health reforms appear to have been 'chosen' rather than 'pressing' reforms in that political leaders decided whether the issue was put on a national policy agenda and given priority or not.[66]

The case for executive initiative in education and health is robust. Protest about the social costs of economic adjustment existed widely in Latin America during the 1980s and 1990s, and does not explain why some leaders chose to take up reform and others did not, nor does it explain the timing of agenda setting in particular countries.[67] Moreover, while many

---

[64]   In attempting to explain economic reforms such as the market-oriented liberalisation policies introduced in many countries after 1980, analysts tested a number of hypotheses about preconditions for reform. For example, they explored whether democratic or authoritarian regimes were more likely to initiate new economic policies, whether change was more likely in institutionalised or new democracies and whether particular kinds of party systems or international conditions were associated with policy changes. They asked if economic reforms were more likely in the context of a deep economic crisis, or at particular moments in an electoral cycle, such as during a political honeymoon in the wake of an election. They hypothesised that high rates of inflation encouraged public tolerance for governments to introduce reforms to 'do something' about the problem. These analyses led to the general conclusion that party systems, electoral calendars and economic crises were often, but not always, important in explaining when reform initiatives emerged in particular countries. In some initial analyses of preconditions for education reform in 16 countries in Latin America, I found little support for claiming that any specific conditions were consistently present at the time of new policy initiatives (Gutierrez, 2000). In fact, conditions in the economy, whether crisis, stagnation, or growth, appeared to differ widely among countries during the four years leading up to the announcement of a reform. Moreover, reform initiatives seem to have been scattered throughout electoral cycles.

[65]   Grindle (2000a). Reassigning responsibility to lower levels of government appears to have been important in a number of decentralisation efforts in education and health and in partial privatisation of pension programmes.

[66]   Hirschman (1981).

[67]   In a study of democratising reforms in three countries in Latin America, I found evidence that political leaders were motivated to support reform because of their concerns about the legitimacy and durability of the governments they led (Grindle, 2000a).

politicians promised improved public services, not all of them took the next step of ensuring that social sector reforms were high on the priority list for public action. International financial institutions encouraged education and health reforms, but in general did not include such issues in their reform conditionalities. The record in many countries indicates that such organisations became important after the issues were on national agendas, not before. And, while politicians may have been influenced by important national and international discussions of the need for change, there is little evidence that they took up reform as a response to direct internal or external pressure. Interest group politics may help explain the destiny of education and health reforms, but it does not indicate how they became priority public issues.

In contrast, the case of pensions conforms more to the profile of a 'pressing' reform. Conditionalities imposed by international agencies were important factors in causing economic ministries to take pension reform more seriously and, at times, economic elites in financial sectors joined the international financial institutions in pressing for privatisation of pension systems.[68] In this case, then, international political economy and interest group politics are better able to explain the emergence of pension system reform on national policy agendas.

With the important exception of pension reforms, then, social sector reforms did not achieve an important place on policy agendas as a result of specific domestic pressures on decision-makers or because of the actions of international financial institutions. Instead, the process was a more exclusive one in which important political actors decided, often for political reasons, that the issues merited more attention.

Designing Reforms

Traditionally, policy design in Latin America has been a closed and executive-centred activity. Current case studies of reform suggest a similar dynamic in education, health and pension reform. Most indicate that proposals for policy change were generated by the executive rather than by legislatures, political parties, interest groups or think tanks. It is not difficult to explain this dynamic. In most Latin American countries alternative sources of policy design are difficult to find. Political parties, legislatures and interest groups lack staff to study and design proposals for change and

---

[68] Huber and Stephens (2000); Nelson (1999), pp. 12–16.

the development of policy think tanks is incipient. Moreover, in many countries, executives dominate legislatures and enjoy long traditions of leadership in policy development.

Although education and health reforms are meant to improve and expand services to citizens, and pension reforms are opened up to greater inclusiveness, participation in their design appears to have been limited. Indeed, most social sector reform proposals were generated by small groups of policy planners that met, debated, designed and introduced new initiatives with relatively little public discussion or involvement. In some cases of education and health, these design teams were located in economic or planning ministries or in the presidential office, but frequently they were adjuncts to education and health ministries, where they worked closely with reformist ministry leadership. Pension reforms tended to emerge from economic ministries, particularly the Ministry of Finance, rather than from the labour or health ministries, or from the specialised agencies that administer social security systems. In some cases, national commissions composed of representatives of important interests met to generate outlines of changes and then turned these plans over to technical teams for further development. While at times unions and others were consulted, in most cases their involvement came after the reform designs had been completed, and sometimes after the policies had been publicly announced.

Conventional political analyses rarely consider the process of policy design to be politically relevant.[69] But social sector reform experiences indicate that design teams are critically important in determining the content of reform initiatives, which in turn defines winners and losers and determines the scope of initial gains and losses. The political leaders who select such teams often give them broad mandates. At the outset of the process, these leaders are sometimes unable to articulate a clear sense of the problem, let alone a solution to it. Designers thus often have considerable latitude to define the problem, generate options and make choices that respond to their own analyses.[70] International agencies, important in purveying ideas about changes to improve the quality and efficiency of social services and in providing funding for new initiatives, generally have their most frequent interactions with these social sector design teams. Thus, many social sector reforms could be considered elite projects, gen-

---

[69]   In contrast, see González-Rosetti and Bossert (2000).

[70]   Increasingly, of course, technical experts are playing important roles inside the 'black box' of policy decision-making in Latin America (Domínguez, 1997; Centeno, 1994; Grindle, 1996; Conaghan and Malloy, 1994; Williamson 1994).

erated by small groups that share concerns about social sector problems in their countries and that are assisted by international officials who claim expertise in the policy area.[71] Who is selected to be part of these teams, the ideas they bring with them and how well they work with one another turn out to be politically important in terms of what kinds of solutions are selected to address social sector problems.

Design teams are also politically relevant because the policy proposals they develop prefigure the conflicts that will emerge when the reform is publicly announced. In the case of education and health reforms, for example, designs that include decentralisation of services usually spark extensive resistance by unions and by elected officials at regional and local levels who may not want to take responsibility for expensive, complex and politically sensitive services. At times, the designers include elements to moderate the potential for such conflicts. For example, they may attempt to decrease opposition and expand the number of winners in a reform initiative by recommending automatic salary adjustments as part of their plan. In pension reforms, design teams have at times recommended the maintenance of special pension programmes for particularly sensitive political interests or by allowing unions to become administrators of the new private pension funds. To the extent that conflict reflects the specific contents of reform proposals, the teams have considerable capacity to create or ameliorate opposition.

The political relevance of a design team, of course, can be a function of how well placed it is in ministerial and bureaucratic hierarchies. For example, social sector reformers make little headway unless they find support from economic ministries, particularly the Finance Ministry. At the same time, if reform teams are located outside ministries of education and health, they may have greater trouble gaining legitimacy from those within them. Studies of economic reforms suggest that the influence of design teams is increased when they share a common view of what needs to be done and diminished when they do not.[72] Their influence is significantly constrained by their dependence on political patrons interested (or not interested) in adopting the specific plans they develop. Nevertheless, these teams participate in a reform process at a critical moment when decisions about content determine initial winners and losers, the scope of change to be attempted and strategies to be considered. That their deliberations are usually closed and only occasionally consultative does not diminish their political importance in a process of reform.

[71]   On this point, see in particular González-Rosetti and Bossert (2000); and Grindle (2000a).
[72]   Nelson (1990); Williamson (1994).

Approving or Rejecting Reforms

Despite the installation of more democratic regimes in Latin America and despite much lip service to more open and participatory policy-making, new initiatives in the social sectors continue to be hatched in relatively closed executive settings. In contrast, when reform initiatives are announced, the dynamic shifts to a much more public arena of conflict and debate. Because they become most engaged at this phase of the policy process, interest groups, including political parties and unions, are almost always forced to be reactive rather than proactive about proposals for change. Nevertheless, the process of approving or rejecting reform initiatives tends to be a relatively inclusive part of the policy process, although usually restricted to already mobilised interests. And, it is here that conventional political economy models can be most helpful in explaining conflict, given their focus on winners, losers and institutions. At the same time, however, the process of approving or rejecting reform offers opportunities to reformers to influence outcomes.

The discourse between reformers and opponents has often been shrill and confrontational. In the case of unions, for example, reformers often claim that the unions are enemies of progress and modernisation and criticise them for their preference for a broken status quo over the promise of change. In response to these charges, the unions have decried hidden agendas about saving money, cutting jobs, breaking the unions and replacing public services with market-driven solutions that will only benefit the better-off. In some cases, contention over reform initiatives forced governments to negotiate adjustments, and in some cases it forced proponents to shelve their proposals, at least for the time being. But often, as suggested already, opponents have been unsuccessful in halting the pursuit of reform because their internal divisions have weakened them or because reformers have been successful in outflanking them.

The legacy of conflict with government and the partisan identity of the unions are important in determining outcomes but so too are the ways in which issue formation, consultation and negotiation strategies affect resistance. Reformers have the advantage of being able to affect the initial terms of debate through decisions about how to introduce new initiatives and what language to use to explain them. To consult with affected interests or not, to negotiate or not, to appeal to broader publics or not, to address economic motivations or social solidarity — these and other strategic choices by reform leaders can have an important impact on the fate of specific initiatives. Negotiation and the modification of reform design are most likely to happen during this contentious part of the policy process.

In contrast to many of the early economic policy reforms, most social sector reforms have been approved or rejected by legislatures.[73] Institutional factors appear to be important in determining the degree of resistance and support these reforms encounter as they are introduced, debated and voted upon in this arena. The strength and discipline of the governing party, the extent to which legislative coalitions exist and traditional institutional relationships between executives and legislatures are factors that have been found to make a difference in a variety of reform initiatives, as suggested earlier. Moreover, the fate of specific reforms may hang on more complex relationships involving broader policy and party agendas. In some cases, executives and reformers have been able to negotiate across policies or to invoke party and coalition support for change even in the face of disagreement with the content of the particular reform. Despite the importance of institutional relationships and legacies, the strategies and choices of reform leaders also influence the outcome of legislative consideration of reform initiatives.

Implementing Reforms

Political economy analysis of the politics of reform focuses almost exclusively on the acceptance or rejection of reform initiatives. Nevertheless, the process of implementation is rife with evidence of political conflict. This is an additional arena in which winners, losers and reformers interact and attempt to influence the destiny of social sector initiatives.

But not all implementation problems are political in origin. The characteristics of social sector policies are important in their viability. New health and education policies are implementation intensive. They are complex in terms of the kinds of services they deliver, the number of goals they seek, the levels of government they incorporate, the number of decisions that must be taken in pursuit of change, the number of actors whose behaviour and attitudes must change if the reform is to go forward and the extent of time required before pay-offs can be anticipated. Pension reforms, in contrast, have been more easily implemented. They are less complex and more easily administered once appropriate new institutions have been created.[74]

---

[73] Many economic policy reforms were put in place by executive decree. While legislation has been the preferred mode of introducing policy change in the social sectors, Gershberg (1999a) presents the case of education reform in Nicaragua, carried out through ministerial action and directives rather than legislation. He compares the costs and benefits of this approach with the legislative strategy followed in Mexico.

[74] On these points, see Nelson (1999).

Problems often emerge because of the way in which social sector policies have been designed. Whether goals are clearly defined and feasible, the extent to which there is broad agreement within government and society about those goals, how complex the policy is and whether required resources and capacity exist — these are all factors relating to design flaws that tend to become evident only during implementation. Governments often have different endowments in terms of managerial and administrative capacity to carry out the reforms. And, of course, problems can emerge around the kinds of incentives that the policy contains for administrators, service delivery personnel such as teachers and nurses, other officials involved in implementing the reforms and beneficiaries. Even popular reforms, if they contain perverse incentives, can easily go awry at this point in the policy process.

But beyond problems related to the characteristics of the reforms and the process of design, political conflict is usually endemic in social sector policy implementation. At the most general level, the implementation phase of policy reform is when bureaucrats have extensive power to reject or sabotage the requirements of new policies — all the more powerful because it frequently occurs silently — when politicians and citizens seek to capture benefits, when stakeholders emerge to demand changes and new directions in policies, when changing ministerial leadership can leave initiatives in the lurch and when politicians can deny resources to policies they do not support. Implementation thus usually involves an extensive array of stakeholders and is often when new social sector policies fall apart or achieve divergent results in distinct localities.

A good example of such complex issues of implementation is the way in which local officials have responded to new responsibilities in education and health reforms. Many of Latin America's governors and mayors, often popularly elected for the first time in history, are now expected to take responsibility for managing complex service delivery programmes and to manage budgets and financing mechanisms. In some cases, regional and local officials have welcomed the new responsibilities as means to improve the delivery of services in their jurisdictions and to enhance their popularity with voters. In other cases, they have turned new responsibilities into political resources, distributing jobs, contracts and resources in ways that recreate old patronage systems at more local levels of government. In still other cases, they have resisted the assignment of new responsibilities because of concerns about conflict with unions, low budget allocations and the high expectations of citizens. But electoral calculations, participation in reform discussions, information and capacity building efforts and finance options can affect the willingness of local and regional officials to implement reform. Again, the strategies and choices of reformers may alter the outcome of new initiatives in this important but difficult and often overlooked political arena.

Sustaining Reforms

The sustainability of new initiatives in the social sectors cannot be taken for granted. To some degree, whether reforms are sustained over time or not is a function of the resources and capacity of responsible government agencies — can they deliver the goods? — and is an issue embedded in design and implementation processes. But sustainability is also affected by the active involvement of new stakeholders — the beneficiaries of social services, politicians who can gain electoral support from the provision of well-functioning services, parties that claim credit for such services, vendors who supply goods and services, new providers and others. Moreover, sustainability can be dependent on the ways in which national and international policy reformers provide support and assistance to agencies implementing reforms and to the local level activists in the cause of reform. In these ways, the process of sustaining reform is an arena that tests the skills and strategies of reformers and winners.

Successful reform initiatives are often characterised by the development of alliances and networks among international, national and local level reformers who strategise about introducing and sustaining change and avoiding or neutralising opposition. In these cases, international and national reformers are able to channel technical assistance and resources to responsive local players and to mediate political conflict at a variety of levels. The support and monitoring activities of local proponents of reform, in turn, are critically important to the international and national level reformers.

Conclusions: Exclusion and Engagement in Policy Reform

Conventional political analysis asks why reform is unlikely to happen. This chapter suggests that a more useful approach is to ask why reform does sometimes occur. In turning the conventional question on its head, researchers are more likely to investigate how winners and losers are posed to support and resist change initiatives, how reform entrepreneurs take actions intended to manoeuvre around institutional and interest group obstacles to change and how the policy process provides opportunities for the interaction of winners, losers and reformers. This perspective helps respond to the puzzle of why reforms sometimes succeed, even when there are powerful interests that oppose them and important institutions that privilege the status quo.

Understanding reform is not a simple arithmetic of weighing winners and losers or assessing the relative power of institutional actors. It is instead a dynamic process in which actors and arenas change with time and the actions of protagonists have the potential to alter equations of power. Winners and losers do exist, institutions do indeed constrain actions, but strategic leadership and action, and perhaps a bit of good luck, can make a difference in reform outcomes.

Assessing what current research indicates about the politics of reform in the social sectors also sheds light on enduring characteristics of policy-making and implementation in Latin America. New social sector policies often promise expanded participation in benefits and improved solutions to historically embedded conditions of poverty, inequality and marginality. Current evidence, however, suggests the continuance of a tradition of an elite-centred process of agenda setting and policy design. Table 4.2 is instructive in this regard. Although policy adoption is a more open part of the process, the most active participants are likely to be well-established interests — political leaders, unions, interest groups and legislators. A wider array of groups and interests may be involved when policies are being implemented, although the process is often dominated by bureaucrats, elected officials and other privileged interests. New stakeholders have a greater opportunity to influence policies once they have been put in place and have begun to demonstrate results. Overall, however, creating and implementing new social sector policies in Latin America has not provided many arenas for the participation of the region's poor and marginalised populations. It can be hoped that they are less excluded from the benefits of new policies.

Chapter 5

Citizenship, Social Policy and Population Change

Bryan R. Roberts[*]

Introduction

This chapter explores the changing conceptualisation of urban poverty in Latin America and the significance of contemporary conditions of poverty for the equality of membership that citizenship implies. I focus on social citizenship and on social rights. In the period of import-substituting industrialisation (ISI) in Latin America, social rights in terms of social security provision, health and education increased and were generally less contested than were either civil or political rights.[1] In the contemporary period in which free trade and free labour and capital markets prevail in Latin America, social rights may now become the most contested part of citizenship. As Marshall (1985) and Esping-Anderson (1990) argue, the development of social rights inevitably conflicts with the competitiveness and income insecurity that fuels the development of the market economy.

The centralised social security, health and educational systems by which social rights were advanced in Latin America during the ISI period are now viewed as needing not just reform but replacement by new ways of securing welfare. Contemporary criticisms of the ISI welfare regimes emphasise their inefficiency and clientelism, arguing that they were overly bureaucratic, too centralised in their administration and did not make enough use of the market, civil society and community self-help.[2] Accompanying these criticisms there is often a bias against basing welfare regimes on universal rights and a preference for targeting welfare to select groups of those in need. A new orthodoxy is now emerging in which social welfare is seen as best provided by reducing the role of government and making welfare conditional on the contributions in time and resources of potential beneficiaries.

Two elements are generally missing from the analyses and recommendations associated with the new orthodoxy. One is a sense of historical

---

[*]   I would like to thank Georgina Rojas for help and advice in constructing the tables and Gonzalo Saravi for his help and advice in the analysis of the Buenos Aires data.

[1]   Roberts (1996).

[2]   CEPAL (1995).

context. As in the CEPAL article cited above, the merits of the new approaches to social policy in comparison to the old are argued in absolute terms and without consideration of the social and economic contexts, which inevitably shape social policy. Indeed, the generalities that justify the new policies of decentralisation and targeting — whether about the capacities of the state versus civil society or about the caring capacity of the community and family — are rarely grounded in careful analyses of actual states, communities or families. The other deficiency is the failure to recognise that citizenship is an evolving process in which the rights recognised by those in power are likely to conflict with those claimed by those without power.[3] In this process, social policy becomes part of the contest over citizenship, in which policy prescriptions from above, including definitions of 'acceptable' citizenship can act to limit and restrict what those below would seek to enlarge. This is not an argument against social policy. Rather it is an argument for placing social policy in its own historical context to appreciate better the possible conflicts of interest between elites, foreign and national, and the people who are the objects of the policies.

The purpose of this chapter is to explore these issues further by first looking at the differences in the conceptualisation of poverty in the 1960s and 1990s. Concepts are essential for making sense of data and deriving policy prescriptions. This is particularly true for the analysis of poverty where measurement alone makes no sense unless it is based on an understanding of what produces poverty and what will best help the poor.[4] But concepts also limit our appreciation of reality by focusing attention on some data at the expense of other data. This happened in the 1960s and is likely to happen in the present period. The accumulation of data on poverty that contradicted some of the assumptions underlying the dominant conceptualisation of poverty in the earlier period led to new concepts that took fuller account of the data. These new concepts also need, however, to be subjected to empirical scrutiny. That will be the purpose of the second part of the chapter, which examines the socioeconomic changes in the cities of Latin America that affect community, family and thus social policy. In the conclusion, I return to the issue of social citizenship and to the relation between social policy and citizenship in the cities of Latin America.

---

3   Jelin (1996a).

4   This is Maria Josefina Huaman's emphasis in her discussion of the need to go beyond poverty measures, *La pobreza: es necesario ir más allá de la medición*.

Changing Perspectives on Poverty

In the 1960s and 1970s the dominant perspective on poverty in Latin America was that of marginality. The term was used extensively in the literature and with different conceptual emphases, as in the differences between Marxist and Modernisation theory perspectives on marginality. There are, however, some common elements to the marginality perspective, notably its concern with macro-structural limitations on development, that provide a contrast with the perspectives that have come to dominate in the 1990s.

In the marginality literature there is an emphasis on three main 'peculiarities' of Latin American development.[5] One is the dependent incorporation/forced modernisation of the Latin American economies. The second peculiarity is the sharp internal inequalities between regions, city and countryside, and between social classes (peasants, indigenous populations, white/European elites). The third concerns the implications of rapid urbanisation, such as low levels of access to formal housing, basic services or jobs, a lack of adjustment to urban life and 'deviant' types of political incorporation, such as populism and clientelism. These peculiarities gave the marginality perspectives of the 1960s and 1970s two characteristic preoccupations: one with the cultural dimensions of marginality and the other with the class dimensions of marginality. Both preoccupations depicted the marginal as incapable of improving their situation through their individual or collective efforts.

To marginality theorists the marginal had a consciousness that put them at odds with the values required for functioning effectively in modern society.[6] The marginal population was also, to use Shanin's (1972) term, an awkward class, difficult to fit conceptually into a stratification typology. Germani viewed the possibilities of progressive change as depending less on the marginal than on cross-class alliances between the other classes, particularly the established middle and working classes.[7] The marginal are unlikely to enter into class alliances for reformist or revolutionary change — they are 'disposable'.[8]

---

5   Germani (1973).

6   On this point, there is relatively little difference between sophisticated modernisation theorists, such as Gino Germani and Marxists, such as Anibal Quijano (1974) or José Nun (1969). The difference between them lay in Germani's greater emphasis on psychological maladjustment or traditionalism in contrast to Quijano's or Nun's emphasis on their lack of class consciousness.

7   Germani (1973), p. 90.

8   *Ibid.*, Cuadro 2, p. 90.

Particularly as used by Gino Germani (1973) marginality was coterminous with lack of citizenship and thus emphasised the responsibility of the
state and of political parties to extend social rights to the marginal population. For Germani, marginality is the condition of not having access to
possibilities to which people are normatively entitled.[9] Referring to T.H.
Marshall, Germani defines marginality in terms of the substantial sections
of the Latin American population who have not benefited from the progressive extension of civil, political and social rights in modern society.
The counterpart of the extension of rights is the multidimensionality of
marginality. The most marginalised are those excluded on all dimensions,
from a decent job, from the protection of the law, from an adequate
income, from education, from political participation and are culturally
marginal to the dominant urban culture.

The solution to marginality other than through revolutionary change
was strengthening the role of the state in ensuring equity. This would be
done progressively, with adequate education, healthcare, jobs and social
security being gradually extended to all sectors of society, beginning with
the urban middle and working classes.[10]

Empirical studies of urban poverty began increasingly to question the
marginality perspective, particularly in its cultural manifestations. In contrast
to Oscar Lewis's (1968) emphasis on the cultural marginality of the very
poor, urban sociologists and anthropologists in the 1960s and 1970s stressed
the capacity of the poor to fend for themselves and to cope with urban life.[11]
These studies showed that migrants along with other poor urban inhabitants
were skilled in organising themselves and in using community organisation
and social relationships to cope with urban life.[12] The poor built the Latin
American city and, to an extent, created their own job opportunities through
the informal sector.[13] Analyses of the urban labour markets in Latin
America in the 1960s and 1970s indicated their capacity to absorb the rapid

---

[9]   *Ibid.*, pp. 34–9.

[10]   Carmelo Mesa-Lago's (1978) analysis of the extension of social security in Latin America shows
       how that extension began with key sectors of the employed population, such as government work-
       ers, transport workers etc. The principle of universal coverage was, however, tacitly accepted and
       had been achieved in the Southern Cone countries by the 1970s. The extension of pension rights
       to all rural workers in Brazil in the 1990s is a recent expression of the universal principle.

[11]   The criticism of Lewis's culture of poverty thesis came also from studies of poor African
       American urban communities, as in Carol Stack's (1974) account of family coping strategies.

[12]   A review of these studies can be found in Roberts (1995), chapter 7.

[13]   Bromley (1979).

growth of the urban labour force that resulted from migration and high birth-rates.[14] Indeed Peter Gregory (1986) was so taken by this capacity that he entitled his analysis of the Mexican case, *The Myth of Market Failure.*

The attention given to the informal sector in Latin America was perhaps the first sign of the changes in perspective that were to come. Beginning with Keith Hart's (1973) article and the ILO mission in Kenya, there was an increasing recognition by researchers and international agencies that self-employment and the micro-enterprise sector was less a problem than a solution for income generation in the cities of developing countries. Hernando de Soto (1989) went even further in the praise of 'informal' enterprises, stressing their merits as innovative and flexible means of delivering services. The attacks on the bureaucratic rigidity of the Latin American state and on the inefficiency of the large enterprises of ISI were fully underway.

The New Paradigms for Viewing Poverty

In contemporary perspectives on poverty, the concept of social exclusion has replaced that of marginality. There is a considerable overlap between the two concepts, but also differences of emphasis. First, social exclusion focuses attention on the processes by which people are excluded from the standards of their society, whereas marginality is more concerned with the situation of exclusion.[15] Marginality explained inequality and poverty as resulting principally from the power of economic and social elites or from the dependency relationship between developing countries and developed countries. Social exclusion, in contrast, pays more attention to the institutional basis of exclusion, such as the way in which educational and health systems are organised or the way in which the labour market is regulated.

In the 1990s public health and educational systems play an inescapable role in the lives of the poor. Education has become the gatekeeper for access to jobs that pay a living wage. Whereas marginality meant lack of contact with welfare systems and government regulation, social exclusion focuses on the ways in which contact with public institutions work to exclude the poor. Remember that part of the intellectual origin of the concept of social exclusion is the attempt to understand the paradox of European welfare systems in which extensive systems of welfare, including unemployment insurance, have not abolished vulnerability and have

[14] Bálan et al. (1973); Muñoz et al. (1983); de Oliveira and Roberts (1994).

[15] See Kaztman et al. (1999).

had negative consequences for community solidarity.[16] The issue has thus become that of the institutional arrangements of the modern state that keep substantial numbers of the population dependent and without adequate access to the opportunities of their society.

Social exclusion is associated with a set of concepts that focus both on the potential for change among the poor and on the limits placed on that potential by the external environment. One of these is the concept of assets.[17] It is closely related to Amartya Sen's (1985) concept of capabilities. Like the 1970s concepts of coping or survival strategies, assets emphasise the potential of the poor in actively shaping their life chances. The concept of assets, however, forces a more precise accounting of resources and strategies than did the earlier concepts. An important dimension of assets is the way in which people handle the resources that they possess. Both capabilities and assets signal the possibility of building upon existing resources, human, social or material, to create the means to exit permanently from poverty.

Vulnerability, in contrast, emphasises the lack of control over the forces that affect one's life that results from assets that are either inadequate or have been made inadequate by changes in the economy or social structure, increasing the vulnerability of the poor. Thus, vulnerability refers to the degree of risk that people have of falling into poverty. Vulnerability, along with the concept of social exclusion, identifies the risks associated with development and modernity. Marginality viewed lack of participation in the institutions of the modern state, such as the formal labour market, health and educational services, as the reason for poverty. In contrast, the exclusion and vulnerability focuses warn that it is the way in which these institutions now operate that poses the real threat to equality. This happens when state deregulation of the labour market generalises insecure job statuses or when state social services or welfare programmes are cut back to make room for market-based ones.

The advantage of the assets/vulnerability approach is that it identifies the range of resources that are needed to overcome poverty.[18] It also draws attention to the economic and social changes that put groups at risk of poverty or downward mobility even when they are currently above the poverty line. The disadvantage of the assets/vulnerability approach is, as

---

[16]   Castel (1997).

[17]   Moser (1997).

[18]   Moser (1998).

Kaztman et al. (1999) point out, that it can focus attention exclusively on the situation of the poor and neglect the responsibilities of other actors, such as state or private agencies. The necessary complements to assets, it can be argued, are rights or entitlements, which the state guarantees irrespective of market pressures or individual interests.

A major difference between the 1960s and the present is the rapid appropriation of policy-relevant concepts by powerful international agencies. Modernisation theories did, of course, influence policy in the 1960s through their emphasis on developing human capital through education and health and through building economic infrastructure. The difference lies in the nature of the concepts that are being appropriated. Modernisation theory and marginality perspectives stressed the need to develop the capabilities of the state to extend education and health or to remedy regional inequalities. The new perspectives are more likely to emphasise working directly with civil society organisations to reduce dependency on the central state.

The new perspectives also encourage the targeting of localities since it is at the community level that social capital is built and assets developed. The new perspectives are consequently highly interventionist in their implications. External agents come to work intensively with communities. It is less a question now of providing schools, for example, than of ensuring that people use them properly. This type of intervention is difficult, complex and labour intensive. It means that there are few urban or rural poor communities that are not subject to external interventions. Furthermore, international or government development agencies need solutions that can be implemented rapidly and in standard ways. This leads to a simplification of concepts through the selective appropriation of some elements to the neglect of others. This has happened with the concept of social capital, which is becoming the panacea for community development.

In its most frequent use by development practitioners, following Putnam's (1993) lead, social capital is viewed as equivalent to civicism. Building social capital is promoting a variety of associational activities and a general climate of trust that reduces transaction costs and facilitates people working together for the common good. As various commentators have pointed out, this view of social capital neglects its downside when solidarity serves purposes such as gang activity or prevents community members taking advantage of external opportunities.[19]

---

[19]   Portes and Landholt (1996); Lechner (2000).

Social capital can be conceptualised as the property of a community, but developing it at the community level depends on a set of factors that give common goals to individuals and households, a cultural and relational basis for trusting each other and low dependence on external patrons.[20] The relevant external environment will usually include the job market and sources of information or aid. When community members are differentiated in these respects, then individual social capital may both be different from community social capital and run counter to it. Earlier uses of the term social capital pointed to its importance for social differentiation. How, for example, the middle classes gained extra advantages by calling on their relationships and information — their social and cultural capital — to gain a comparative advantage over others in their community. Also, close community ties are not always advantageous when they restrict information.

The next section explores the changes in the urban community and family in Latin America that limit the contribution of community and household to the welfare of the poor.

The Changing Conditions of Latin American Cities

In certain respects, the problems that the poor face in the cities of Latin America have not changed dramatically since the 1960s. Levels of poverty are, in general, somewhat lower, but not substantially so. Securing stable formal employment is as difficult in 2000 as it was in the 1960s. Indeed, in the 1990s, the proportions of urban informal employment and unemployment rose in various countries, notably Mexico and Argentina. Urban infrastructure and housing has improved over the period, but the priority for most poor urban inhabitants remains that of upgrading housing or existing infrastructure, as is shown by the participative budgeting priorities of the populations of Brazilian cities, such as Porto Alegre and Belo Horizonte.

In other respects, the changes have been substantial. I shall concentrate on migration, employment structure, household demographics, income inequality and spatial segregation. The analysis focuses on Buenos Aires and Mexico City, examining the contrasts and convergence in their demographic structures.[21]

---

[20]   Durston (1999).

[21]   The analysis is part of a comparative study of Assets and Vulnerability in Buenos Aires, Mexico City, Montevideo and Santiago in co-operation with Carlos Filgueira, Rubén Kaztman and Guillermo Wormald. The research is based on the household surveys of each city for the decade of the 1990s, and on community studies in low-income neighbourhoods in all four cities. I am grateful to Georgina Rojas and Gonzalo Saravi for their help in assembling the data that I present here.

Migration

In the 1960s urbanisation was proceeding rapidly in most Latin American countries, resulting in high rates of urban growth and high rates of rural-urban migration. The urban growth and the rural-urban migration concentrated in the largest cities of each country, often bypassing smaller regional centres. This was the phenomenon of 'peasants in cities' in which in Mexico City, Lima, Buenos Aires or Rio de Janeiro, the city-born viewed their cities as being colonised by rural people, with distinctive cultures and appearances. This was also the period in which these migrants effectively built much of the city to which they came. Through invasion or illegal subdivision migrants settled vast urban areas, building their own homes and, as many studies were to show, installing their own infrastructure. This migration was heavily networked in which relatives and fellow villagers helped each to obtain housing and find work. In Peru, the 'social capital' of interlocking rural-based relationships became the basis of social clubs in Lima, of economic enterprises and of urban community improvement.

The contrast between the 1960s and the 1990s in Mexico City and Buenos Aires illustrates the sea change that has taken place in urban migration. For the sake of comparability, I use the figures for the federal district in each case. In both cities, there are substantial declines in the proportion of their inhabitants born outside the city (Table 5.1). The figures for the outlying parts of the metropolitan areas show a somewhat different rhythm, with in-migration peaking later than in the metropolitan cores. By 1999, however, in both cities, those born outside the metropolitan area are a relatively small minority of the population.

The numbers of those born in the metropolitan areas of both cities in the 1990s conceal a substantial movement within the metropolitan areas. In both cases, this movement is mainly from the central cities to the outlying areas. It is a movement that reflects both the 'flight' of the middle classes from the crowded conditions of the central cities and that of poorer households seeking cheap space in the outer rings of the metropoles. These centrifugal patterns of intra-urban movement differ from the predominantly centripetal rural-urban migrations of the 1960s and 1970s. Whereas the earlier migrations brought people together in the city on the basis of pre-established ties, the new movements are more likely to mean a spatial and often social distancing from family and neighbours. Children move away to establish their own households and relatives seek cheaper or more spacious accommodation on the outskirts of the city. In Mexico City there is also, in the 1990s, a net out-migration of the population of the metropolis to other Mexican cities in the west and the north of the country, and to the United States. These movements can also weaken urban relationships as is reported by Mercedes González de la Rocha (1997) in the case of elderly Guadalajara couples who report 'losing their children to the North.

Table 5.1: Percentage of Urban Population Born in the City Buenos Aires and Mexico City

Approx. Census Year	Buenos Aires Capital	Mexico City DF	Buenos Aires Metropolitan	Mexico City Metropolitan
1950	40.7	52.5	40.0	52.5
1960	50.1	58.1	—	58.5
1970	53.0	66.0	49.1	68.3
1980	61.4	69.8	50.4	*
1990	65.2	74.6	62.1	75.0
1999	70.4	77.0	70.4	79.2

* Comparable information is not available for this Census.
Sources: National Population Censuses for the corresponding years up to 1990; the *Argentine Permanent Household Survey* (EPH), *October Waves of 1999*; and *Conteo de Vivienda*, 1995 for Mexico City

Household Demographics

There are three changes in the structure of households that have particular relevance to social policy. The first is that the average size of household in Latin American cities has decreased sharply since the 1960s. This alleviates the pressure on the household budget, but it also means that there are fewer young household members available to supplement the household budget through paid work. It also means that there are fewer young members to care for the elderly. Since fertility has declined and life expectancy has increased in the period from the 1960s to the end of 1990s, the second change is that the elderly are a higher proportion of the population than in the past.

The third change reflects cultural as well as demographic trends. It is the decrease in the proportion of households composed of a couple and their children and an increase in the proportion of single memberhouseholds, couples alone or single parents.

The extent of these changes can be appreciated by comparing Mexico City and Buenos Aires from the 1980s to the present. Buenos Aires has the higher proportion of its population who are 65 and over. Of its population, 11.1 per cent were 65 and over in 1998 compared with 4.9 per cent of Mexico City's population. In both cities the proportion of the elderly has increased — from 10.8 per cent in 1990 in Buenos Aires and from 3.5 per cent in 1987 in Mexico City. A more marked narrowing of differences between the two cities can be noted in the average household size (Table 5.2). In 1990 41.7 per cent of households in Mexico City had four members or fewer, compared with 64.1 per cent in Buenos Aires. By the late 1990s 58.5 per cent of Mexico City households had four or less members, whereas the proportion in Buenos Aires had only increased to 65.1 per cent. Households in both cities were categorised by a similar measure of occupational class. In Mexico City the higher occupational status households had fewer members both in 1990 and at the end of the 1990s. The trend was less clear in Buenos Aires. The decline in the average size of households was uniform across all occupational classes in Mexico City. In Buenos Aires some occupational classes increased the size of their households during the 1990s — most notably the 'polar' occupational classes of the high and low service classes and the petty bourgeoisie of the self-employed and owners of enterprises of five workers or fewer. It is unlikely that this result can be explained by changes in the fertility of these classes. Rather, it suggests a similar coping behaviour in the face of economic pressures in which children stay longer in the parental household — for educational reasons in the high status households and because of subsistence pressures in the lower status households.

In both cities the proportions of childless and single parent households have increased, whereas extended households have declined. In Mexico City the proportions of single person households, a couple alone and single parent households rose from 8.9 per cent in 1987 to 10.5 per cent in 1990 and to 13.2 per cent by 1999. In Buenos Aires these three types of households accounted for 18.4 per cent of the total in 1990 and 22.6 per cent in 1999. The types of household that have decreased are extended ones in which other relatives or friends live with the nuclear family. Households with two parents and children still remain the majority of households in both Mexico City and Buenos Aires — 54 per cent in Buenos Aires and 58 per cent in Mexico City. However, between 1990 and 1999, the average size of two parent and children households declined from 5.2 members to 4.6 members in Mexico City and from 4.7 to 4.6 in Buenos Aires.

Table 5.2: Size of Nuclear Family* by Occupational Class in Mexico City and Buenos Aires. Changes in the 1990s (%)

Occupational Class of Head of the Household	1990 Family Size				2000 Family Size			
Mexico City	3-4	5-6	7+	Total	3-4	5-6	7+	Total
I. High-Service	51.5	35.4	13.1	100	73.9	24.7	1.4	100
II. Lower-grade Professional	52.1	36.5	11.4	100	69.7	25.5	4.9	100
III. Routine Non-manual	43.4	42.5	14.1	100	59.7	35.3	5.1	100
IV. Petty Bourgeoisie	39.7	45.2	15.1	100	56.3	36.5	7.2	100
V. Skilled Manual	37.6	41.4	21.0	100	53.8	39.5	6.7	100
VI. Semi-skilled Manual	35.4	42.3	22.3	100	54.8	32.9	12.3	100
VII. Low-Service	36.7	44.5	18.8	100	52.3	36.4	11.3	100
Total	**41.7**	**41.6**	**16.7**	**100**	**58.5**	**34.8**	**6.7**	**100**
Buenos Aires								
I. High-Service	74.1	22.4	3.5	100	68.3	27.0	4.7	100
II. Lower-grade Professional	63.3	30.6	6.1	100	65.2	30.1	4.7	100
III. Routine Non-manual	69.4	26.5	4.1	100	79.4	18.1	2.5	100
IV. Petty Bourgeoisie	60.2	33.5	6.3	100	62.3	28.1	9.6	100
V. Skilled Manual	62.7	26.8	10.5	100	64.9	26.4	8.7	100
VI. Semi-skilled Manual	61.8	23.2	15.0	100	61.0	34.9	4.1	100
VII. Low-Service	61.8	26.6	11.6	100	52.9	32.5	14.6	100
Total	**64.1**	**28.9**	**7.3**	**100**	**65.1**	**27.7**	**7.3**	**100**

* Nuclear family = couple + children
Sources: *Mexican National Survey on Urban Employment* (ENEU), Second Quarter of 1990 and 2000; and the *Argentine Current Household Survey* (EPH), October Waves of 1990 and 2000

These changes suggest a decline in the type of large households with enough adults or adolescents to care for very young children or elderly dependents. The pressure on the caring capacity of the household is accentuated by changes in the urban employment structure, particularly the increase in female labour force participation.

Urban Employment

The major changes in employment structures in the cities of Latin America from the 1960s to the end of the 1990s are familiar ones: a decline in manufacturing employment and an increase in service employment. The increase in the latter is both in the high-end services, such as business services, and 'low-end' ones such as personal services. There is also a shift in the nature of employment from manual work occupations to 'white-collar' jobs, mainly in commerce and the services. Accompanying these trends are two sub-trends that are particularly relevant to social policy.

One is the increase in the proportions of women in the labour force who have children at home. Some of these women are single or once married, but the largest proportions are married women with children. In both Mexico City and Buenos Aires, women with children make up the majority of the female labour force (Table 5.3). In Mexico City, there is a clear shift away from young, dependent females as the mainstay of the female labour force and their replacement by women with children. Buenos Aires has the highest rates of female participation, both at the beginning and at the end of the period and the highest contribution to employment by married women without children, reflecting the increase in childless households in that decade.

Table 5.3: Economically Active Female Population by Household Status in Mexico City and Buenos Aires, 1990 and 1999 (%)

	Mexico City		Buenos Aires	
Household Status	1990	2000	1990	2000
Single W/out Children	41.9	35.8	29.0	28.6
Single W/Children	2.3	3.4	3.9	6.2
Married W/out Children	3.8	5.6	10.6	10.3
Married W/Children	34.4	37.8	40.8	36.8
Ex-marr W/out Children*	2.0	1.8	3.3	3.6
Ex-marr W/Children*	12.8	13.3	11.2	12.4
Other Non-single Members**	2.9	2.4	1.2	2.0
Total	100	100	100	100
N (000s)	1,891.8	2,629.7	1,625.6	2,262.9

* Ex-married Women: Those divorced, separated or widowed
** Other Non-single Women: Those non-direct relatives or friends who live in the household
Sources: *Mexican National Survey on Urban Employment* (ENEU), Second Quarter of 1990 and 2000; and the *Argentine Permanent Household Survey* (EPH), October Waves of 1990 and 2000

Part of the explanation of this trend is the diminishing supply of adolescents of both sexes in the labour force as a result of declining fertility and the young staying longer in school. Supplementing household incomes is increasingly done through the employment of the female head, not the children. Cultural changes are also part of the reasons for this shift in the intra-household pattern of employment. Interviews in both Mexico and Buenos Aires suggest that husbands have become less antagonistic to their wives working outside the home. At the same time, the job market for adolescents is bad, particularly in Buenos Aires. Low-income parents recognise both that it is difficult for adolescents to get reasonable jobs and that staying on longer in school is necessary in order to find a good job.

Demography and cultural expectations are creating a situation where women, as the traditional carers, both in the home and in the community, are likely to be less available than in the 1960s. Women are more likely than men to work part-time and intermittently, but the increasing burden of outside employment inevitably cuts down on their time both for the household and children and for community tasks. Remember that many of the programmes that are the mainstay of welfare for low-income families in the cities of Latin America depend on the voluntary work of women. Examples are food distribution programmes such as Plan Vida in Buenos Aires or the Comedores and the Vaso de Leche programme of Lima.

Income Inequality

The second sub-trend is the sharpening of income inequality in the cities of Latin America. The data from Buenos Aires and Mexico City suggest a similar pattern of inequality. When compared with the end of the 1980s the income inequality between the poorest 40 per cent of the population and the richest 20 per cent has increased in both cities.[22] The data indicate that this inequality is closely related to the restructuring of the labour market, which has created a demand for skilled workers in certain sectors of services and manufacturing, but has decreased demand for low-skilled jobs. Cheap imports and the restructuring of distribution with the proliferation of supermarket chains have, for example, reduced the earnings of small-scale businesses in commerce, the services and manufacturing. In the 1980s income inequality in Buenos Aires and Mexico City was lower than in the late 1990s within each of the major employment sectors of the self-employed, workers in micro-enterprises, employees of larger enterprises and owners. Moreover, the self-employed earned comparable incomes to

---

[22]   Bayón and Saravi (2001); Cimillo (2000); Rojas (2001).

those employed in larger enterprises. By the end of the 1990s in both cities income inequality had increased both within sectors and between sectors. Thus, workers in larger enterprises who were in the lowest 20 per cent of income saw their earnings deteriorate with respect the highest 20 per cent of earners in their sector. Furthermore, as a sector of employment, the self-employed saw their earnings worsen over the period with respect to those working in larger enterprises.

The growth in income inequality, particularly between formal (workers and owners in larger enterprises) and informal sectors (the self-employed and micro-enterprise workers), and between the highest and lowest quintiles of earnings, creates the potential for an increasing social segregation in the use of, and access to, services. On the one hand, in those sectors that have benefited from restructuring, there is the capacity to pay for private services in health, education and pensions. In many countries this option is now part of social security systems and is part of the package offered by dynamic private sector firms. On the other hand, a substantial sector of earners and households can only afford publicly provided services. This trend feeds into a broader tend in the spatial organisation of the Latin American cities.

The Spatial Segregation of Cities

There has been some debate about the degree to which Latin American cities are socially and spatially segregated. In the years of rapid urban growth there were opposing tendencies.[23] The middle classes abandoned central cities and located in relatively homogeneous neighbourhoods, but the poor sought space wherever they could find it. Often this was on the outskirts of the cities, but, depending on ecology, it could also be in the middle of cities and in the interstices of middle-class settlement. Thus the favelas of Rio de Janeiro or the squatter settlements of Guatemala or Mexico City were often close to middle class areas.

Good data were not available on recent trends in the spatial segregation of Latin American cities. There are indications, however, that cities are becoming more segregated by socioeconomic status. This can happen without a marked increase in residential differentiation. One tendency is for middle and upper classes to reside in '*barrios cerrados*' (gated communities), where armed guards ensure the security of the inhabitants and filter visits. In Buenos Aires there has been an explosion of such communities

---

[23]   Portes (1989).

in the 1990s, but they are equally evident in Brazil and Mexico. Associated with this form of segregation is that between private and public facilities in health, education, welfare and recreation. Note that the public/private divide is usually a spatial divide also. Deteriorating public facilities concentrate in the poorer areas of cities; whereas private schools and clinics are mainly found in the middle class residential neighbourhoods.

This spatial segregation adds to inequality. As Kaztman has argued, when the poor live in homogeneously poor neighbourhoods, they score lower on a series of health, work and educational indicators than do the poor who live in more heterogeneous neighbourhoods.[24] The suggestion is that in homogeneously poor neighbourhoods, facilities are likely to be worse, are overused and to provide lower levels of health and educational care. Even 'social capital' is likely to be of less utility. Granovetter (1973) showed how even strong ties with friends and neighbours are of little utility if there are no resources to share or no one has access to jobs. The public-private divide also puts the public sector at a competitive disadvantage. Better pay and conditions of work mean that the private sector can recruit the best teachers and medical personnel.

Summary

Each of these changes suggests an important shift in the nature of the problems facing the poor between the 1960s and the 1990s. In the earlier period these problems were severe in terms of inadequate housing, urban infrastructure and jobs. They were problems, however, that could be resolved at least partly by the efforts of households and with the help of friends and neighbours. Urban life might be complex when compared to the countryside, but urban organisation in much of Latin America was relatively informal and little regulated. Electricity, for example, was often obtained for squatter settlements by tapping into the overhead electricity cables.

This informality still continues and in some cases, such as Buenos Aires, it may have become a little more accentuated. In general, however, Latin American cities are more regulated now than they were. They are also larger and more complex. The challenges of finding work and housing or obtaining access to urban services are not so easy to resolve through social networks or through the initiative of self and neighbours. All this is occurring in a situation in which the demographic and labour market changes outlined above are likely to produce more social fragmentation than in the

[24]   Kaztman (1999), pp. 263–6.

past. There were more, but smaller, household units in the 1990s than in the 1960s, whose members, as our own and other's case studies show, do not have the time, the material resources or the numbers to network extensively.

Citizenship in the New Urban Context

In conclusion, I would like to emphasise and develop two further themes that arise from the preceding discussion. The first is the relation between the increasing individualisation that accompanies modernisation and globalisation and the development of a participative citizenship at the local level. This is a theme that Norbert Lechner (2000) takes up in his analysis of the applicability of the notion of social capital to the Latin American and Chilean cases. The second theme is the development of citizenship through external intervention. I shall call this process the rationalisation of citizenship.[25]

The social, demographic and economic trends outlined in the previous section pose considerable obstacles to city inhabitants acting together on a locality basis to improve their conditions of life. The incentives that existed in earlier periods for such locality-based actions, primarily in defence of settlement, are no longer so prevalent. The formalisation/politicisation of locality-based welfare programmes, such as communal kitchens, weakens their contribution to community solidarity. In this context, experiments in participative democracy, such as the setting of budget priorities by meetings of neighbours, have ambiguous implications for the development of vigorous citizen action around themes that are of common interest to low-income people throughout the city.

People may develop a better sense of the responsibilities of citizenship, but action is curtailed to local needs, thus fragmenting political demands. However, there are opposing tendencies that can be built upon to promote citizenship action. In Granovetter's (1973) distinction between the advantages of weak and strong ties for the unemployed, the point is that relationships outside the community — weak ties — can often be more useful as social capital than strong community ties that restrict people to limited information. What the focus on social capital needs, then, is a discovery of the 'weaker' ties that bridge communities and counter the individualising tendencies of urban life.[26] The media, particularly television, may

---

[25] A similar process occurs in relation to social policy, which Judith Tendler (2000) calls the tendency to 'projectise' social policy and thus to avoid the general reforms that are likely to have the largest impact on reducing poverty.

[26] Lechner (2000).

privatise communication, but it can also spread common moralities on such issues as appropriate family size, egalitarian relations between men and women, respect and care for others, as has been shown in studies of Brazilian soap operas. The notion of rights, particularly human and individual rights, is as a result more general than it was in the earlier period.

Such a focus on weaker ties needs to be complemented by recognising the necessary role of the state as the only agent capable of providing the institutional framework that sustains weak relationships in face of the fragmenting impact of market competition. The state has a crucial role in providing the framework to encourage people to act together to advance the equalities of citizenship. Both Lechner (2000) and Tendler (1997) call for more flexible means for providing this framework than was present in the state welfare systems of earlier periods.

Evans (1996) stressed two aspects that need to accompany the new relationship between state and civil society: complementarity between the contributions of each side and the embeddedness of state agencies in local relationships. Evans warns, however, that a successful synergy is less likely when societies are highly differentiated. The threat to this synergy comes from the rationalisation of citizenship, which is an evident part of contemporary community development initiatives.

Rationalisation is a key process accompanying modernisation and the development of the modern state, as described by a long line of analysts from Max Weber to Jurgen Habermas. Essentially, rationalisation is the substitution of instrumental criteria for value-based ones in setting priorities for action. Both bureaucracy and the market are means to an end, but they also become ends in themselves with criteria such as efficiency and clarity of guidelines becoming the justifications for action. This process poses a special threat to citizenship in the modern world. The development of citizenship depends on substantive values, such as those of identity, equality and fellowship, which people redefine and struggle for against the opposing values of entrenched elites.

In the practices of international aid agencies these values can be subordinated to the means needed to pursue them. Detailed manuals provide templates for how to develop a participative citizenship, with precise instructions as to how to involve the citizenry at each step. These agencies are disbursing public funds and they wish to avoid clientelism. Thus, procedures for evaluating and accounting for the delivery of services are put in place. How closely the procedures are followed and how faithfully citizens follow these procedures are used to measure the development of citizenship. The increasing public reflexivity that accompanies modernisation with the rise of experts, along with the proliferation of statistics and surveys, contributes to this rationalisation of citizenship.[27]

Evaluation and accountability mean bureaucracy. Bureaucracy develops internal criteria for success, and these in turn become the bases for careers. The interface between bureaucracies, even development bureaucracies, and their clients is a problematic one because bureaucracies necessarily seek to curtail demand making at the local level in the interests of administering existing resources in standard ways.[28] Community members, their organisations and NGOs have to negotiate this interface, accommodating their own actions to what is made available from above. Jelin (1996) argues that aid agencies' emphasis on the sustainability of NGOs directs NGOs toward projects where the return and efficacy can be more easily measured. Since many of the new development initiatives are targeted, and are not provided as of right, communities and their organisations often compete to devise projects that will bring scarce resources. The writing of projects to guidelines provided by external agencies has become a routine community activity, taking up time and energy that might otherwise be devoted to the door-to-door work of identifying needs and encouraging demands.

The inability of these interventions to develop citizenship is more likely in cities than in the countryside. In poor urban neighbourhoods, there is a considerable gulf between local development programmes and the forces that determine peoples' life chances. Local micro-enterprise programmes are likely, for instance, to be less easy to articulate with the urban economy and market than is the case in a small village. The community impact of programmes and the possibility of them becoming examples for other communities are also likely to be less in cities. In the programmes that I examined in Argentina, not only did projects reach only a small fraction of neighbourhoods that were potential beneficiaries, but also the circle of influence reached only a few blocks beyond the location of the community organisation that administered them. When interviewed, most neighbours living only a quarter of a mile away knew nothing of the programmes.

A considerable part of the problem could be resolved if programmes were rights not competitive resources. Communities would still need to organise to make use of external resources, but once a degree of civic organisation had been reached, then the programmes would come as of

---

27   *Ibid.*.

28   Arce (1993).

right. The criteria would not be set externally, but would be based on the existence of active community organisations. In establishing these, the role of both the state and NGOs is important in making known the possibilities and encouraging community members to make demands. Although communities would run their own programmes, the state needs, as Tendler (1997) argues, to set guidelines and incentives for good implementation.

CHAPTER 6

Some Conceptual and Substantive Limitations of Contemporary Western (Global) Discourses of Rights and Social Justice

John Gledhill

The concept of the individual as a rights-bearing subject of justice clearly has much to recommend it. The defence of the rights of individuals (and a civil society founded on market relations) against the 'Old Corruption' of the Absolutist State that characterised the high-point of bourgeois revolution in Europe might not be dismissed simply as 'progressive' for its epoch. Arguing that globalisation has polarised the gap between rich and the poor to a point that makes a two-class model of the world apposite, Keith Hart has invoked Locke in an argument that distinguishes capitalism from the market economy.[1] Hart looks to the voluntary, horizontal associations of mutual aid and defence of the original industrial working classes in England as a paradigm for a movement that could force the global economy in more humane directions. As a good libertarian he would really like states to disappear, but conceding that to be presently utopian, he pins his hopes on the capacity of the internet to augment our unmediated networking activities as citizens.

What Hart seems to forget about Locke is his ultimate justification for the accumulation of land and capital in the hands of the few. This was the now familiar argument that an increase in social productivity would 'trickle down' to the dispossessed as improved living standards, through distributive mechanisms that today seem more contingent than ever.[2] Locke was also strong on the need for a tutelary state and Church to police the inevitable vices of the dispossessed, whose capacities for social and political citizenship remained distant from bourgeois standards. In the old colonial world that grew up around the expanding mercantile capitalism of Locke's day, the addition of the idea of racial difference neatly reduced an increasing number of human beings to unfitness to enjoy the full panoply of freedoms proclaimed by universalising liberal ideologies. Nineteenth-

---

[1]   Hart (2000).
[2]   Gledhill (1997).

century Latin America repeated the exercise in terms of both race and gender when its newly independent nations adopted liberal constitutions.

Contemporary doctrines of universal human rights and the transcendent value of political democracy are, in principle, blind to differences of gender and culture. They strongly assert the unity of humanity against any racial qualification and reject the idea that rights are consequent on education for the proper discharge of the responsibilities of citizenship. The core idea of seventeenth century liberalism, as defined by Macpherson (1962), was that full freedom could only be enjoyed by those who possessed full 'property of their persons' (were not servants or employees). It has ceased to be meaningful in a world in which few enjoy such social autonomy, and in a sense we seem to have moved on. Yet old battles continue to be fought, in particular those in which the welfare of the many seems to demand circumscription of the freedoms associated with property, economic power and enterprise.

But 'the many' face increasing problems of political representation and action. In contrast to the 'old' working classes, today's 'poor' face a problem of *anonymity* in the sense of a lack of a defined social personality. As Julio Boltvinik puts it:

> While the workers' gains expressed themselves as rights stipulated in legislation — above all, in labour and social security laws — conventional proposals for a fight against poverty take the form of more or less discretionary government policies, not only in Mexico but throughout the world. The poor person appears not as a subject of rights but as a receiver of transfers to which he can only respond with his vote. Where citizenship ends, charity and manipulation for electoral purposes begins.[3]

One effect of this dilemma is to keep the proper role of the national state at the heart of the debate about social justice. I will, however, argue later in this chapter that changes in the nature of 'global governmentality' and transnational class processes greatly complicate the issues of social policy as they have traditionally been discussed — within the framework of nation-states.

Leaving that issue aside for the moment, it is clear that states, located in national societies with different histories, vary in their interpretations of the substance of the 'universal' rights to which they subscribe on behalf of their citizens and may fail to buy into the whole package. The United States, for example, did not buy into the socioeconomic rights embodied

---

[3]   Boltvinik and Hernández (2000), p. 14, my translation.

in the 1948 UN Universal Declaration. The original declaration was anchored in the individualistic premises of the Western liberal tradition.[4] While its ethnocentrism and assumptions about the eventual global diffusion of Western models of 'modernity' have been tempered by subsequent international legislation, the assumption that individuals are the ultimate bearers of rights remains both a strength and a weakness.

As the number of rights it is deemed appropriate to recognise has increased, so has the possibility of extending protection to minorities of various kinds. Women and children have become subjects of rights. This has placed increasing strain on the universalism of legislation. What, cross-culturally, is 'a child'? What effect should we allow the idea that children have a right to a childhood and protection from economic exploitation to have on the immediate welfare of families with working children? Clearly Western social and cultural values have continued to play a prominent role in defining the terrain of 'universal' rights discourse, but this does not, in itself, invalidate the discourse. The issue is, first, whether there is a hegemonic thrust to the way Western rights discourse operates which, when accompanied by other hegemonic impulses in fields such as international commercial law, limits its value for some potential beneficiaries. Secondly, there is the question of whether a partial, Western-orientated field of rights politics actually fails to address the central conditions that perpetuate global social injustice.

Thus, for example, Petras and Morley argue that studies of Latin American dictatorship focused on violations of human rights obscure the way military regimes implemented a form of class domination tied to North Atlantic interests.[5] The political framework of neoliberalism continues to impose a model of capitalist development sponsored by the North through different mechanisms, and even non-governmental organisations (NGOs), at first glance a counter-hegemonic[6] or at least civilising face of capitalist globalisation, may also play a role in this. As professional organisations with their own agendas, both environmentalist and indigenous rights NGOs may subtly disempower those they seek to aid.

---

4   Gledhill (1997).

5   Petras and Morley (1992), p. 160.

6   Analysts from the RAND Corporation have identified the 'swarming' around local social movements of loose networks of acephalous, polycentric and transnational organisations as the major challenge to traditional forms of national and global governance and to US hegemony within the global order (Ronfeldt and Martínez, 1997; Arquilla and Ronfeldt, 2000). It is, however, to highlight that there are significant contradictions even where the support of national and transnational NGOs has been of vital importance to the survival and wider influence of a movement such as the Zapatista Army of National Liberation (EZLN) in Chiapas.

Community leaders become semi-professionalised and detached from their original base as they learn to navigate the new circuits of NGO resourcing. Projects must be adapted to the visions of sponsors, which construct the beneficiaries of funds in ways that reflect social and cultural distance. 'Exotic' Indians preserving a 'traditional culture' may seem more worthy of support than 'acculturated' ones and poor people eager to start individual small businesses may be more attractive than those with a more collectivist ethos.[7] Respect for democratic rights is a necessary condition for open debate about different models of social justice. Yet the value of free and fair elections may seem limited to families facing increasing impoverishment irrespective of their electoral choices. Freedom from arbitrary arrest and inhuman and degrading treatment is a necessary condition for minimum standards of social welfare. But obliging states to respect human rights may not reduce the amount of everyday violence citizens experience if growing impoverishment wears down the fabric of sociality.

The results of some recent Latin American elections do, however, suggest that voting against governments that have reduced living standards, and for parties that promise to create jobs and extend public services, is a meaningful act for significant numbers of citizens from different social classes. There are significant variations in neoliberal models, and some governments claim to be pursuing alternatives to neoliberalism. The experience of Mexico under Carlos Salinas de Gortari (1988–94) demonstrates that bold claims about tackling social inequality by empowering citizens and removing the dead hand of the state from civil society may disguise cynically calculated deployment of 'traditional' practices of clientelism and co-optation — and still darker projects for advancing the concentration of wealth in the hands of a politically connected elite. It is, however, worth considering other ways in which social justice might be founded on broadly liberal conceptions of the rights of individual citizens in society.

Third Way Models: the Problem of 'Society'

To talk about 'social policy' from a conceptual angle invites reflection on the extent to which 'the social' can be considered a transparent category. Mainstream sociology assumes that there is some universal sense in which it is possible to talk about 'individuals', 'groups' and the relations between them that constitute 'the social' or 'society'. The currently fashionable idea

---

[7]   Gill (1997); Ramos (1998); Warren (1998).

of 'social exclusion' rests on the idea that some groups of people are cut off from a flow of *sociality* or interactions with others in a way that prevents 'society' from realising itself in an optimal form. Thus Giddens (1999) has argued that 'social exclusion' should not merely be seen as the physical isolation of certain categories of people, such as low-income families living in run-down public housing. It is also produced by the active self-isolation of more fortunate citizens sequestering themselves in gated communities. Basing a concept of 'social exclusion' on the idea of 'social separation' distinguishes the former from 'poverty' in the sense of relative deprivation and lack of resources. Poor people are not necessarily socially separated. There are a variety of causes and conditions of individual poverty, which may be a transitory state in an individual or family life cycle, removing a simple correlation with social class. For Giddens exclusion is a matter of either social isolation in the physical sense or 'lack of access to normal labour market opportunities'. Even in the absence of physical separation, elites may contribute to its growth by 'withdrawal from their social and economic responsibilities, including fiscal responsibilities'.

As a description of one of the processes that underlay the concentration of poverty in inner-city cores as tax-payers fled to the suburbs in the United States, this way of looking at the relationships between poverty and social exclusion/separation has virtues. But Giddens's arguments seem less convincing transferred to a Latin American context in which levels of mass poverty are very high, while concentration of wealth is commensurately narrow, but gives the wealthy a healthy ranking on international scales. Although there are virtues in decomposing the category 'poor people' analytically, doing so in a way that shifts the question of income inequality from the centre of analysis is questionable. These are countries in which households (and often, in particular, their female members) are obliged to bear the weight of economic adjustments in the absence of comprehensive public welfare systems. Equally disturbing is the moralising and 'normalising' thrust of Giddens's concept of social citizenship and proposed 'Third Way' remedies for 'social exclusion'.

If elites cannot be coerced into accepting their fiscal responsibilities, 'the rest of us' (the 'merely affluent') must be urged to adopt more philanthropic attitudes, while those suffering deprivation must accept those 'normal labour market opportunities' that global capitalism is willing to provide. 'Society' must be made to 'function' in terms of a minimal normative consensus on individual rights and social responsibilities. Defrauding the welfare system or participating in the black economy clearly do not fit into the kind of normative consensus Giddens has in mind and he does not shrink from employing 'underclass' rhetoric in discussing such behaviours. Yet they may provide individuals with a superior subjective sense of personal worth as socially situated actors and improved material opportunities to participate in the culture of consumerism. Giddens's sociology seems to have little interest in what it might *mean* to be a former worker in a downsized traditional industry living in a post-industrial economy, a *puertorriqueño* in New York, a provincial *cholo* in Lima or a Cambodian surrounded by Mexicans and Central Americans in Stockton, California. Yet struggles to infuse personal and collective lives with meaning seem central to urbanised mass societies in the twenty-first century.

The Third Way critique of neoliberalism thus ultimately shares its concern to efface the distinct social personalities and projects of the poor and excluded and make them individual manageable subjects of bourgeois governmentality as worker-consumer-citizens. As a more 'liberal' doctrine than that of the conservative right, 'Third Wayism' does not advocate the combination of extreme deregulation of the market economy with a state that is coercive in a totalising way in the moral sphere. Rights to diversity can be recognised in areas such as sexual preference and 'life-styles' consistent with the continuing commodification of social life and personhood. But the rights of corporate capital to restructure the world (and its boundaries) are considered only marginally negotiable.[8]

Latin America evolved its own 'Third Way' model as a response to the social and political polarisation threatened by Washington consensus neoliberalism, exemplified by the discussions of the Grupo Mangabeira think-tank.[9] Whether the emphasis is on micro-credit schemes, targeted anti-poverty programmes or restoring and extending access to public services, the distinctive feature of *alternativa latinomericana* is that it envisages a fiscal equilibrium with public spending at a level of 30 per cent of GDP.

---

[8]   As far as North-South relations are concerned, Giddens follows the lead of analysts who argue that that even a major cut in Northern per capita incomes could not increase average incomes in developing countries significantly. He reinforces this contention with a 'blame the victim approach', arguing that: 'Most of the problems that inhibit the economic development of the impoverished countries don't come from the global economy itself, or from self-seeking behaviour on the part of the richer nations. They lie mainly in the societies themselves – in authoritarian government, corruption, conflict, over-regulation and the low level of emancipation of women (Giddens, 2000, p. 129).

[9]   The initiative of Brazilian political scientist, Roberto Mangabeira, the group included Vicente Fox, now president of Mexico, and his foreign minister, Jorge Castañeda, then aligned with the centre-left Party of the Democratic Revolution. Other members of the group included Rodolfo Terragno, subsequently prime minister of Argentina, and the Chilean Ricardo Lagos, subsequently president. As governor of Guanajuato state, Fox had introduced a 'bank of the poor' and promoted literacy schemes financed by business taxation, the kinds of schemes advocated by Third Wayers.

This would represent a substantial increase for countries such as Mexico. Leaving the impact of recession aside, fulfilment of Vicente Fox's electoral promises to the three in every five Mexicans living below the poverty line and 25 million in extreme poverty, depends on fiscal reform. The proposals sent to Congress and still stalled at the time of writing were disappointingly regressive given that non-oil taxation stands at only 11 per cent of GDP, less than half its US level and only just over a third of the average in the EU. Congress was also asked to approve the costs of servicing the US$44 billion of private debt to be transferred to the public purse under the bank rescue scheme. At present the rich are not taxed on their capital gains, but receive compensation for their losses.

The ultimate goal of a market society of possessive individuals for whom assistance from the state is a means towards achievement of self-realising autonomy can be presented in ways that resonate with Latin American political cultures and experience. Yet it still sits uncomfortably with many of the historically evolved characteristics of specific Latin American 'societies' and the relations that articulate and construct 'groups' and social identities within them in the context of capitalist globalisation. The most obvious issue is that of 'ethnic' distinctions.

Indigenous Peoples and the Rights of the Colonised

Clearly not merely the absolute size of both aboriginal and black populations, but also the way ethnicity is constructed politically and influences social interactions varies between countries.[10] The social meanings of eth-

---

10   Mexico contains the largest absolute number of people professing an 'indigenous' identity of any Latin American country. But they are constructed not merely as a minority but as a minority that is spatially, socially and historically 'peripheral' to the mestizo core of 'the nation', while 'blackness' is a largely suppressed category in the construction of 'Mexicanness'. There is no Mexican equivalent of the contrast between the 'coldness' of the Bogota elites and the 'hotness' of a Caribbean-orientated coastal region suffused with blackness and dangerous forms of miscegenation in the case of Colombia (Wade, 2000). Although blackness could theoretically have been used to construct the Pacific coast and hot country zones of western Mexico as a significant 'other' to the interior highland zones, the colonisation of parts of the western highlands by black insurgents has faded entirely from historical memory. Twentieth century nationalist constructions focused on a particular, *ranchero*, image of *mestizaje* as an icon for 'difference' relative to the most significant Mexican 'other', the USA, while official 'indigenismo' celebrated the subsumption of an indigenous civilised past by the mestizo future in the demographic centre of the country. The latter tactic turned the suffering peasant into a revolutionary hero, heir to a 'great tradition', while simultaneously reasserting the nineteenth century liberal model of 'whitening as progress'. The peasant Indian and the once civilised Indian can also be distinguished from the 'wild' or truly 'primitive' Indian (Ramos, 1998). Thus even the category 'indigenous' can itself become the basis for a variety of images of 'alterity', which, in countries such as Brazil, become means by which the colonisers themselves mythologise their own identities.

nic categories such as 'ladino' or 'mestizo' vary in time as well as space, and the ethnic identities that people adopt also shift historically. The most striking change is the replacement of local (community) identities and the categories of the colonial ethno-racial hierarchy with more inclusive ethnic labels that enable citizens who retain 'indigenous' identities to reconceive themselves as 'nations' or 'peoples'. This is not a simple linear development. Not all indigenous groups embrace these more inclusive categories with enthusiasm, and less inclusive forms of ethnic identity can be or become of more strategic value in the shifting politics of resource appropriation and official recognition.[11] Ethnic factionalism remains common in contemporary indigenous rights politics. Nevertheless, a new generation of leaders has articulated itself to global movements for special rights for indigenous people.

Indigenous movements complicate the issue of inclusion and exclusion in Latin America in various respects. Firstly, indigenous demands for recognition in a pluri-cultural nation are based on the premise that having been colonised gives certain citizens special status and rights. There is a significant problem in defining which citizens qualify to be the bearers of such rights in the first place.[12] This is magnified (and subject to political manipulation) where mestizo citizens feel themselves to be disadvantaged by any special status that might be accorded their neighbours.[13] Secondly, the rights demanded are themselves problematic for both the neoliberal and 'Third Way' state. In the case of Mexico it has not proved too difficult in practice to allow indigenous communities to elect political representatives by means other than the ballot box (although the virtues of these arrangements from the democratic standpoint are contested). But it is a different matter to define territorial units in which different legal procedures might apply, especially if they are ethnically mixed, and to define the point at which the jurisdiction of such processes should give way to those of the national legal apparatus. Islands of even limited indigenous sovereignty become even more problematic when they are associated with collective rather than individual rights to manage or control access to

---

11   Collier (1997).

12   Gledhill (1997).

13   In the case of Chiapas an increasing assertiveness on the part of indigenous people towards mestizos within their communities that predates the Zapatista uprising has left a bitter legacy as the latter felt themselves increasing marginalised socially and as having lost economic advantages. Where these families did not simply leave for the towns, local relations have become extremely antagonistic, and the wider implications for patterns of violence and the continuing strength of some of the paramilitary movements within the state are far from negligible (Moguel and Parra, 1998).

resources, especially resources previously claimed as 'national patrimony' or which are becoming increasingly valuable to outside interests. This is another point at which the postcolonial definition of the rights of the descendants of aboriginal people becomes highly politicised and subject to contention between different indigenous groups.

The case of the Lacandón Indians of Chiapas and their conflictive relations with their Chol and Tzeltal-speaking neighbours provides a good illustration of these problems.[14] The Lacandones have been constructed as living representatives of a 'primitive' Maya pagan forest culture. This not only made them a privileged object of protection and cultural conservation, but enabled the Mexican government to use this tiny group as the putative 'owners' of a biosphere reserve initially intended to give the state control over the extraction of timber resources. The ancestors of today's Lacandones appear to have migrated into the region from Yucatán in the eighteenth century.[15] Yet they have also appropriated their image as descendants of the ancient Maya (as crafted by romanticising archaeologists and ethnologists) to claim a privileged relationship with the region's archaeological sites. Like other 'postcolonial tribes' that have acquired the status of 'living social fossils' — notably the Yanomami of Venezuela and Brazil —[16] the Lacandones and their 'culture' have joined the flora and fauna as objects of conservation.

The way that the Lacandones have responded to the employment opportunities made available by the forest conservation department and state agencies administering the archaeological sites has, in practice, produced a considerable change of life-style. So has the intervention of the Summer Institute of Linguistics and their conversion to Seventh Day Adventism. But they can still capitalise on their 'exotic' image in the world of commodities by marketing themselves. The special rights accorded to them as 'custodians' made them proxies for control by state agencies over the biodiversity and 'national patrimony' of the region. The struggle for a share in the benefits of these resources on the part of other, more numerous, indigenous groups, has increasingly taken the form of striving to wrest control from the bureaucrats and invest it in local organisations. The politics such situations unleash may, however, become increasingly tangled and divisive.

---

[14] My understanding of this evolving situation is based on the research of Tim Trench, a post-graduate student.

[15] de Vos (1995), p. 338.

[16] Whitehead (2000).

A large proportion of the worlds' indigenous peoples inhabit regions of high tropical biodiversity, which may also, as in the case of the Selva Lacandona, be areas with significant oil and mineral resources, and at the same time be attractive to cattle ranchers and landless peasant colonists. The conservation strategies recommended by environmentalists may be threatened by small farmers as well as by those extracting timber or pasturing cattle commercially on thin tropical soils. The 'conservation' of small populations of indigenous 'exotics' along with the existing ecosystem is, on the other hand, desirable from the point of view of promoters of ecotourism, although they are again opposed to 'destructive' peasant farming. Pharmaceutical companies may also have an interest in 'conservation', but the interests of bio-prospectors is of shorter duration, since the objective is the extraction of genetic material. Oil and mineral extractive industries have become more sensitive to environmental damage in recent decades. But Mexico has a dismal record of attempting to combine natural resource conservation with extractive activities, as illustrated by the history of PEMEX operations across the state border in Tabasco under the political *cacicazgo* of governor Roberto Madrazo.[17] Where, as in Amazonia, extractive industries such as gold mining develop on the basis of attracting prospectors and workers from the disadvantaged sectors of national society — and indigenous people present obstacles rather than assets for 'development' — the results may be genocidal rather than ethnocidal.

Nevertheless, the interest of transnational companies in forms of resource extraction that bring previously marginalised groups into the front line of the global economy has stimulated a growth of movements that tie specific historical identities to territory. Any population that can claim or construct its cultural distinctiveness and distinctive practices of resource use is likely to gain NGO allies and can articulate itself to the global environmentalist movement. This is one of several respects in which rural people have been able to regain space for negotiating the terms of their incorporation into the global economy at an historical moment in which the peasant farmer or small-scale fisherman appeared on the verge of economic extinction.[18]

Such struggles are, however, often uphill at best where the economic stakes are high and outcomes reflect the complicity of national political actors. Even where they do have an impact, the outcomes do not necessarily involve any managerial control. Where arrangements are agreed to

[17]　Weinberg (2000), pp. 218–20.

[18]　Kearney (1996).

pay royalties or provide compensation, these may simply accelerate social change and empower particular factions at the expense of others. Where states privatise management of 'cultural patrimony' and 'natural resources', this may increase levels of conflict between competing organisations representing indigenous groups. Even relatively corrupt state agencies are in principle subject to wider public accountability and their policies and practices can more readily be challenged through formal channels of political representation. Private companies that cut deals with particular groups at the expense of others may provoke protests from the excluded, but the state can treat this more as a public order issue than a question of its own social responsibilities. Indeed, it may be increasingly obliged to do that by international law as the penalties for allowing local protest movements to damage the interests of transnational companies mount.

The Transnational Dimension

This last observation underscores the extent to which globalisation is reducing the sovereign power of states in certain areas (although it does not demonstrate the increasing irrelevance of national states in global governmentality but a change in the way hegemonic centres exercise hegemony). The other side of the coin is the way struggles for recognition of the rights of colonised peoples and environmentalist causes can be facilitated by transnational organisations, some of which are forged by indigenous people themselves, as in the case of Oaxaca.[19] Transnational coalitions which link concerned Northern citizens to citizens of Latin American countries can influence issues ranging from the position of migrants and refugees, to environmental rehabilitation and local battles against transnational corporations. Such concerned citizens may become increasingly 'disloyal' to their own national state and increasingly 'global' in their outlook on social justice, but tensions over control and leadership, along with cross-cultural miscommunication, are likely to emerge in such alliances.[20] The emergence of a 'global public sphere' has transformed debates about rights and social justice at one level. The languages of 'human rights', 'women's rights', 'environmentalism' and even 'globalisation' itself have diffused widely, but this does not guarantee that all the actors ascribe the same meanings to the vocabulary that they now share.

[19] Kearney (2000).

[20] Cunningham (1995).

If we take an historical perspective, it seems obvious that Latin American societies have been internalising 'global' discourses for a long period of time, and not simply at the elite level. The rising up of 'El Pueblo' in the 'backward' Peruvian province of Chachapoyas offers a striking example.[21] Here 'modernity' was a project of the periphery in a society with a weak national state in which arbitrary rule based on ethno-racial hierarchy could be challenged locally by selective local appropriation of the ideals of liberalism. The *chachapoyano* ideal of individual freedom was social autonomy, expressed in terms of masculine virtues and an implicit anti-capitalism, the idea that all should retain full property of their persons and 'be beholden to no one'. Although the *chachapoyanos* rapidly became disillusioned with the national state, the fact that they demanded that the state make law and government real illustrates a more widespread tendency.

In considering the apparent paradox that some Guatemalan indigenous people have positive recollections of the rule of Jorge Ubico, Rachel Sieder (2000) shows how both male workers and women in Alta Verapaz sought to make the new legal apparatus installed by the dictatorship work for them, against local plantation owners. The fact that the new legislation was intensely patriarchal in tone and intent did not prevent subalterns seeking to use it to claim rights not to be abused in certain ways. The law was not an abstraction, but a set of concrete possibilities that could be realised by appealing to agents whose interests were distinct from those of the *finqueros*, and with whom some kind of communication could be established. No doubt the fact that the supplicant was an Indian influenced the form and substance of this communication in important ways, so that the application of the law remained tied to particular political and social conditions which were reproduced through the administration of justice. Yet the fact that elites are not homogeneous, and subalterns are active agents exploring the possibility of changing their situations, made an 'articulation of discourses' possible.

This does not, however, entail any complete fusion of meanings or a move towards a shared notion of the rights-bearing citizen as possessive individual. As Neil Harvey has argued: 'although the struggle for rights appears to distinguish recent popular movements from their predecessors, we cannot assume any universal meaning of rights to which these movements appeal'.[22] The 'rights' enshrined in liberal democracy are rights assigned to, and constitutive of, individuals. An indigenous rights politics ori-

---

[21]   Nugent (1997).

[22]   Harvey (1998), p. 24.

entated around mutual respect for 'difference' within the pluri-cultural nation and defence of the cultural and material resources of indigenous communities, in contrast, threatens to reassert the collective rights and legal personalities expunged by liberal constitutions in the nineteenth century.[23]

It might appear that while indigenous rights politics complicate the visions of 'progress and modernisation' that once underpinned the confident assimilationism of Latin American social reformers and nation-builders, this remains a sideshow. Most Latin American countries are now overwhelmingly urbanised (Guatemala being a conspicuous exception, as well as in having an indigenous majority).[24] As I will argue later, however, the assumption that urban and rural 'society' are separate domains whose contours should be taken as given may not be a desirable one for either national or more global perspectives on social justice. The environmentalists have also offered us good grounds for thinking that urban people (globally) should be preoccupied about the ecological impacts of rural transformation. Nevertheless, even where indigenous movements are strong, demands may be subverted by suborning leaderships and/or offering jobs and social development funding to supporters of indigenous movements as individuals. Subcomandante Marcos mocked Vicente Fox for imagining that indigenous people in Chiapas would be content to be converted into 'mini-micro-empresarios': 'Here, and under many other Mexican skies, being indigenous is not only about blood and origin, but also about a vision of life, death, culture, the land, history, tomorrow.'[25] Yet the problem facing Fox seems to be less an unshakeable commitment to defence of an alternative form of life on the part of indigenous people than the sheer cost of securing a pragmatic solution to the problems of material livelihood faced by Mexico's 10.5 million indigenous citizens.

Many of them are not, in fact, residents of rural places. Leaving aside transmigrants in the United States, Mexico City has continued to attract an increasing number of indigenous migrants as conditions of personal security as well as economic possibilities have diminished in rural areas. Boltvinik and Hernández (2000) have highlighted the dismal record of Mexican neoliberalism in terms of the growth of poverty even in the most

---

[23]   Gledhill (1997), p. 90; Escobar (1999).

[24]   The absolute numbers of rural people in countries such as Mexico and Brazil are not, of course, by any means inconsequential, even with urban-rural ratios of 74:26 and 81:19, respectively.

[25]   Letter from Subcomandate Marcos to President Vicente Fox Quesada, *La Jornada*, 3 Dec. 2000.

'dynamic' centres of the export economy. It seems unlikely that citizens who can gain leverage in seeking entitlements by virtue of their identities will cease to do so, even if their identities and interests are also shaped by the economic niches that they occupy in the city.

This does, however, leave a majority of citizens in Mexico with the problem of finding alternative ways of seeking leverage. To return to the point made by Julio Boltvinik, the mass of socially anonymous 'poor' face extreme difficulties in converting themselves into subjects of 'rights' rather than receivers of discretionary transfers. This is why the politics of identity has become so central to the contemporary politics of rights, while self-help solutions remain the principle means by which most people seek to alleviate their poverty. Cross-border migration has been a classic individual solution to the problems of household reproduction, and broadened its social and geographical composition significantly from the 1980s onwards. The flow northwards has continued to increase, despite the militarisation of the border. During the 1990s the spatial distribution of Mexicans within the United States diversified rapidly, with new movements to the midwest and a greater range of cities in the north-east. Even traditional destinations such as Chicago now have an increasingly visible Mexican presence in ethnically mixed districts previously associated with other groups. It is dangerous to exaggerate the extent to which 'mobility' is a defining feature of the contemporary world, but NAFTA itself illustrates why 'mobility' should be seen as an important issue in the discussion of 'rights'.

Mobility and the Limits of the Nation as an Arena for Defining Social Justice

Capital has enhanced its 'rights' relative to labour by securing the compliance of the international nation-states system hegemonised by the USA in reducing the barriers to the flow of capital to cheap labour zones. States police their borders against the free movement of labour, but do not do so in a completely resolute way. As Heyman (1998) has pointed out, there is a marked difference in the intensity of border surveillance and Immigration and Naturalisation Service activity in the interior of the USA. Border regulation principally serves to determine the conditions under which undocumented migrant workers work and, through immigration laws that are increasingly discriminatory, to increase their exploitability. Enforcement practices ensure that the undocumented find work only as a result of 'relatively successful conspiracies to avoid the law'. Immigration policy is driven less by political economy than by the way class is entangled with 'race' and 'long waves of anxiety' about threats to national 'integrity'. Seen from south of the border, however, migration is not merely a way of solving an immediate problem of household survival, but sometimes integral to strategies for improving social position and reconstructing local economies and forms of social life.

The forms such reconstruction takes are regionally and culturally variable. The mestizo members of the Zacatecas Federation of Migrants in Mexico have an outlook that makes them natural subscribers to a small-business driven development model.[26] Oaxacan migrant organisations, in contrast, have pursued projects orientated to rebuilding an ethnic community that keeps the Mexican state and nation at arm's length.[27] Nevertheless, as people with an indigenous identity particularly well equipped to present themselves as a 'community of suffering', they have an exceptional capacity to mobilise public sympathy in the United States and thereby gain concessions from the Mexican government by a different route. Transmigrant networks may bolster rather than undermine national political regimes in the 'home country', especially where the migrants are subject to social exclusion in the 'host country', but their implications do vary substantially in different contexts. In the case of Mexico and Central America, migration to the United States (or from Central America to Mexico) is an important factor in national economies, not only from the viewpoint of the households involved in it, but also from the point of view of national government policy. Governments can make (implicit) assumptions about the extent to which negative impacts of domestic policies may be offset by migrant remissions. Yet this is not simply an economic question, let alone one that can be reduced to whether domestic earnings plus migrant earnings or remissions equal 'household survival'.

The qualitative social, cultural and political impacts of migration, particularly of a sustained 'living lives across borders' kind, change many of the parameters under which social policy operates. Migration has complex differentiating effects on local communities, affecting the fabric of everyday sociality. Migration changes evaluations of different styles of life and promotes different kinds of divisions and solidarities among people, within communities and across the former boundaries of communities and nationalities. It produces new experiences of exclusion, but also new kinds

[26] Smith (1998).

[27] Besserer (1999).

of engagements, such as those that some migrants have experienced with trades unions in the United States, as a result of the efforts of organisations such as 'Justice for Janitors'.

Structurally, we might think of labour moving across borders as part of a transnational class process (governed by the 'non-economic' conditions mentioned above) which also articulates with the new class processes associated with the movement of capital south. The latter include the 'maquiladora-isation' of the productive economies of countries such as Mexico, Guatemala and Colombia, the impacts of new extractive enterprises, and the tourism-casino-real estate developments that turn some regions of Latin America into playgrounds for more affluent consumers in this global network of flows. But they also include the financial sectors (which have their own direct and indirect effects on class structures) and the international legal frameworks which regulate (or systematically fail to regulate) the conditions under which people, commodities, capital, information and symbols move through the circuits. It is important that not all these flows belong to the 'legal' economy and that the structure itself maintains the distinctions between 'legal' and 'illegal' flows that influence their economic values.[28]

Transnational relations of different kinds are therefore both the conduits through which ideas about social justice flow and processes that circumscribe the rights and opportunities that individuals enjoy. Some transmigrants live their lives under conditions in which the rights accorded to citizens under the sovereignty of national states now seem inadequate guarantors of welfare. Some mobile people are mobile precisely because their civil or human rights are violated. But a good deal of the discussion of mobile people must focus on the way global economic conditions both limit their opportunities 'at home' and shape their lives, qualitatively as well as in terms of income, in ways that constitute denial of social justice as seen from a global perspective.

Such a perspective also needs to emphasise, however, that an *inability* to move is a common and disadvantaging condition for labour, and for the social solidarity of poor people, under current conditions. Individualised and immobilised victims of corporate downsizing and international relocation of production and services may be drawn into a politics of resentment against new immigrants in their own struggle to defend their entitlements as citizens of national states. This is another respect in which the nation-state remains central to the structuring of our social and political

[28]   Gledhill (1999).

worlds. Yet it might be argued that states now play their direct and indirect regulatory roles within a new form of globalised sovereignty of the kind postulated by Hardt and Negri (2000). In this view, rights doctrines would be part of the new global hegemonic process in just the same way as more obvious expressions of 'Northern' hegemony such as international trade and arbitration law and (selective) military 'police actions'. This is again not an argument against the value of Western concepts of human rights. It is an argument for understanding the limitations of rights politics within the structure of global power relations that shape the responses of 'the citizen' within the national state.

What the anger of the immobilised citizen locked within the national framework of rights and entitlements starkly reveals is the problem faced by 'multi-cultural societies' which have porous boundaries but constitute themselves in fractured ways. 'Majorities' (vocal or 'silent') confront coalitions of minorities in what, nationally and perhaps internationally, tends to become a zero sum game in terms of the distribution of benefits.

Concluding Remarks

Many of the migratory movements discussed in the later stages of this chapter erode clear distinctions between urban and rural people at the same time as they erode the meaningfulness of confining 'social policy' to national frames of reference. As I remarked earlier, the taken-for-grantedness of evolving patterns of spatial distribution of population for social welfare in the qualitative sense also needs to be questioned. A variety of social movements in both the North and the South are currently demanding a re-evaluation of the relationships between the urban and rural components of contemporary societies. Some, such as the Sem Terra movement in Brazil, offer visions of 'alternative rural modernities' that reflect the unwillingness of substantial numbers of 'socially excluded' people to rest content with the imperatives of global capitalism. It is easy to dismiss such projects as utopian, and to note that the socially excluded frequently improvise their own strategies for becoming 'mini-micro-empresarios' without any support from the state (or advice from Anthony Giddens). But the lesson we might draw from that is that socially excluded people tend to be more imaginative about alternative models of livelihood than today's liberal or social democratic academic analysts, because most of them have to work, and being poor is very hard work indeed. The only complacency here is on the part of those who take structures for granted, and leave individuals to take what they can get.

PART B:
HEALTH AND SOCIAL SECURITY

CHAPTER 7

Globalisation, Equity and Health in Latin America

Antonio Ugalde, Nuria Homedes and Anthony Zwi

Introduction

The twentieth century witnessed an impressive reduction of infant mortality and increased life expectancy across nations,[1] and within nations across social classes and ethnic groups. Almost everywhere public health interventions have been responsible for lowering rates of communicable diseases. In Latin America, with few exceptions, immunisation coverage against polio, measles, pertusis, tetanus and diphtheria is above 80 per cent. New technologies, some of them extremely simple and inexpensive, such as rehydration salts, have contributed to reductions in infant and child mortality. Health expenditures that were severely cut during the crisis of the 1980s steadily increased in the following decade in most countries.

In spite of these positive developments and many other advances there are signs that all is not well in the Latin American health field. Compared to other countries of similar level of development, Latin America lags behind in life expectancy (four per cent), infant mortality (17 per cent) and healthy years of life lost (14 per cent).[2] Access to healthcare continues to be a problem for many. In several countries of the region access to prenatal care and the percentage of institutional deliveries is low, and a large proportion of deaths are not medically certified, indicating relatively poor access to health services (see Table 7.1). Expensive technologies, some of which are life saving, are not available to many, and relatively large proportions of the population do not have access to tertiary care.

In Latin America infant mortality has decreased, but continues to be unacceptably high for many populations, and around 150,000 children under the age of five die every year due to acute respiratory infections, diarrhoea diseases, nutritional deficiencies, dengue, malaria and tuberculosis. New communicable diseases have appeared, and the old ones — thought to have been eradicated or to be under control — have returned. Sixteen to 18 million are infected with Chagas'; haemorrhagic dengue is now endemic in 15 countries when in 1970 it was endemic in only seven;

---

[1] Ahmad et al. (2000).

[2] Medici (2000).

there are one million cases of malaria per year; 1,100 people are infected daily with tuberculosis (TB) and 200 die daily as a consequence of TB; between 1991 and 1999 there were 1.2 million cases of cholera; and polio, thought to be eradicated in the Americas, has recently resurfaced in Haiti and the Dominican Republic.[3] Many of these diseases could be prevented and cured for as little as a dollar a day.[4] 15 per cent of the cancers could be avoided if the infection associated with them was prevented (helicobacter pylori, papilloma virus and hepatitis B and C). In addition, only six Latin American countries report screening all donated units for HIV and hepatitis B and C, this means that annually, around 50,000 units are transfused that have not been screened for HIV or hepatitis B, and around 1,500,000 that have not been screened for hepatitis C.[5]

Table 7.1: Health Expenditures, Access to Prenatal and Delivery Care, and Mortality Under Registration in Latin America

	Per capita health expenditures[1] (US$)	Total health expenditures as % of GDP[1]	Access to services[2]		Mortality under registration[3]
			Prenatal	Institutional deliveries	
Argentina	880 (1999)	11.4 (1999)	96	95	4.4
Bolivia	51 (1997)	5.0 (1997)	53	28	—
Brazil	417 (1998)	8.7 (1998)	86	92	19.0
Chile	297 (1997)	6.0 (1997)	100	100	0.0
Colombia	180 (1996)	8.2 (1996)	83	96	16.4
Costa Rica	239 (1996)	8.9 (1996)	92	97	0.0
Cuba	60 (1991)	6.2 (1992)	100	100	0.0
Dominican Rep.	133 (1996)	8.0 (1997)	98	95	48.0
Ecuador	71 (1995)	4.6 (1995)	—	59	24.3
El Salvador	146 (1998)	7.4 (1998)	59	67	22.9
Guatemala	92 (1997)	5.3 (1998)	54	35	5.8
Haiti	24 (1996)	5.6 (1996)	68	46	—
Honduras	49 (1995)	7.3 (1995)	84	54	51.9
Mexico	141 (1996)	4.1 (1995)	—	84	7.2
Nicaragua	58 (1996)	13.3 (1996)	87	87	49.0
Panama	236 (1996)	7.7 (1996)	94	89	20.0
Paraguay	143 (1996)	7.5 (1996)	69	36	43.6
Peru	100 (1995)	4.9 (1996)	67	56	47.0
Uruguay	603 (1997)	9.9 (1997)	98	99	2.1
Venezuela	345 (1995)	9.9 (1995)	74	95	2.1

Sources: Columns 1 and 2, PAHO, Public Health Policy Programme, Division of Health and Human Development www.paho.org. Columns 3, 4 and 5 PAHO, Health Situation in the Americas. Basic Indicators 1998. 2. 1995 data; 3. 1990-5 data.

[3]   *Morbidity and Mortality Weekly Report* (2000); PAHO (1999a).
[4]   PAHO (1999b).
[5]   PAHO (1999a).

Table 7.2: Fertility Rates, Physical Infrastructure, Selected Mortality Data and Incidence of Selected Infectious Diseases in Latin America

	Total Fertility Rate[4]	Access to potable water[1] (%)		Adequate sewerage treatment[1] (%)		MM[5]	IM[3]	Mortality <5 years due to (%)		Total adjusted mortality[6]	Adjusted mortality due to transmissible diseases[6]	TB Incidence[2]	Cholera cases[3]	Dengue cases[3]
		Urb.	Rur.	Urb.	Rur.			EDA	IRA					
Argentina	2.6	71	24	80	42	44	21	2.1	5.8	706	48	38	637	—
Bolivia	4.3	84	24	64	19	390	69	17.6	14.8	1,230	—	134	1,632	539
Brasil	2.2	80	28	74	43	114	40	6.9	8.0	866	93	55	2,884	254,109
Chile	2.4	97	25	98	94	25	13	1.2	12.6	628	75	28	4	—
Colombia	2.7	95	41	81	27	87	24	9.3	11.2	765	61	27	1,508	24,290
Costa Rica	2.9	100	100	100	100	29	12	4.3	—	535	36	18	2	14,279
Cuba	1.6	98	75	95	79	33	8	1.3	7.3	629	51	14	—	3,012
Dominican Rep.	2.8	80	46	—	—	110	45	—	—	756	—	75	—	608
Ecuador	3.1	82	51	71	37	159	39	11.5	14.0	725	121	—	65	3,871
El Salvador	3.1	78	26		59	60	40	11.3	5.8	745	95	29	—	423
Guatemala	4.9	97	48	94	50	190	38	21.0	19.5	1,072	—	—	1,263	5,385
Haití	4.6	47	41	47	16	457	74	—	—	1,431	—	91	—	—
Honduras	4.2	91	66	95	71	148	42	—	—	809	—	72	90	11,873
Mexico	2.7	93	61	88	30	48	23	7.6	14.5	703	84	—	2,356	53,541
Nicaragua	3.8	52	12	36	54	124	47	19.6	11.3	817	141	71	1,283	3,126
Panamá	2.6	99	73	99	81	84	16	6.7	6.7	649	—	—	—	2,628
Paraguay	4.1	70	6	20	44	123	36	11.2	13.9	853	—	43	—	—
Perú	3.0	84	33	89	37	265	43	9.1	20.1	868	—	174	3,483	1,397
Uruguay	2.2	89		56	—	19	18	2.6	8.5	732	—	22	—	—
Venezuela	3.0	79	79	74	60	56	22	18.1	8.6	698	80	25	2,551	33,654

Source: PAHO, *Health Situation in the Americas. Basic Indicators 1998.* 1. 1995 data; 2. 1996 data; 3. 1997 data; 4. 1998 data; 5. 1992–97 data; 6.1990–95 data; 7. 1993–96 data.

MM= maternal mortality; IM= infant mortality

The deficit in sanitation in the Americas is acute, particularly in rural areas, only 69 per cent of the region's population has appropriate sewage disposal and only ten per cent of the wastewater collected receives any type of treatment prior to its final disposal (Table 7.2). Other important environmental problems include food contamination, inadequate disposal of solid wastes, precarious housing and exposure to accidents and occupational diseases. Around 300 workers die daily due to accidents and occupational hazards, and less than five per cent of the occupational diseases are reported. The mental component of health has not improved. On the contrary, mental and behavioural problems are on the rise.[6]

Many of the above-mentioned conditions disproportionately affect the poor and many could be effectively treated at reasonable cost. The health gap between the poor and the wealthy continues to grow.

Responding to the Crisis of the 1980s: the Reforms

Traditionally most governments in Latin America provided medical care — including tertiary care — free or at a very low cost to the poor and the indigent. It was recognised that the public services were deficient, inefficient and of variable quality, but the services were available to those in need, who represent half of the Latin American population. The economic crisis of the 1980s brought to light, perhaps more clearly than ever before, that the health conditions of the region did not correspond to the level of socioeconomic development or to the magnitude of health-related expenditure. The inefficiency of the public sector was highlighted as the principal cause of the problem, while the structural aspects were disregarded. Loans to bail out the economies of Latin America were tied to the acceptance of the structural adjustments that included a reduction in social spending and the transformation of, and decrease in, the role of the state. The decline in health expenditures contributed to a deterioration of health services, and hospital equipment and sanitation services declined alongside worsening administrative systems and personnel training.

The Economic Commission for Latin America and the Caribbean (ECLAC/CEPAL) attributed the overall decline of public healthcare services to the events described above.[7] According to CEPAL, the worsening health situation can also be related, in large part, to the new neoliberal policies and budget cuts. CEPAL also concluded that, given the collapse of the

---

6   PAHO (1999c).
7   CEPAL/ECLAC (1994).

public health sector induced by neoliberal policies, citizens had no other choice but to go to the private sector to seek quality services,[8] reinforcing the view of public sector failure. The impact of the structural adjustments was particularly harsh on the poor. The World Bank (WB) recognised this but refused to accept responsibility, blaming governments for faulty policies and failure to increase unemployment.[9] In order to cushion the negative impact of structural adjustments the WB introduced adjustment mitigation loans which, according to some observers, caused additional suffering to the poor.[10] The WB asked rhetorically: 'Do the poor suffer as a consequence of such adjustment policies as cuts in public spending ... How is health affected? The answers to these questions are complicated ....'[11] Social scientists in the field did not find it 'complicated' to document the devastating impact of the WB structural reforms on the poor.[12]

In the same period the WB in Latin America became — as in other regions of the world — the most influential policy-maker and the leading contributor or lender to the health sector.[13] The International Monetary Fund (IMF) and the World Bank capitalised on the unquestionable failures of the public sector to forcefully promote their own solutions based on neoliberal ideology. WB loans were offered to assist countries in carrying out health reforms. The Inter-American Development Bank (IDB) subsequently joined ranks with the WB in funding and setting policies for the health sector in much of Latin America.

In order to find solutions to the health problems of the region, most governments of the region, under pressure from and funded by the multilateral banks, USAID and other international agencies, launched health reforms that were strikingly similar and grounded in neoliberal principles.[14] Generous research contracts from the above institutions drew in prestigious academic centres to provide assistance and 'technical expertise'. The countries of the region have much in common, but also many cultural, political, historical, social and economic differences. That the reform blueprints were much the same for all countries illustrates the centralisation of global policy-making.

8   *Ibid.*, p. 40.
9   World Bank (1993), p. 45.
10   Rich (1994).
11   *Ibid.*
12   Danaher (1994); Lezama (1991); Reyna (1990); Zamora (1990).
13   Buse (1993); Rao (1999); Ugalde and Jackson (1995).
14   Homedes et al. (2000).

The declared goals of the reforms were the improvement of quality, equity, efficiency and user satisfaction; all within conditions of financial sustainability. The proposed strategies included a change in the role of the public sector from direct provider to regulator, promotion of the private provision of services, decentralisation, changes in health financing and subsidised universal coverage of selected medical interventions. This chapter only examines the impact of reform initiatives on health equity.

Earlier comprehensive health sector assessments and research had identified other key interventions to achieve the same goals, but for reasons that will be explained later, they were not supported or excluded. Among them were innovations in human resource deployment and policies (such as de-emphasising the need for specialisation and moving professionals to rural areas), extension of preventive and promotional programmes, shifts in expenditure from hospital to ambulatory care, expansion of services and coverage in rural areas, control over the use of expensive technologies and use of generic medicines and essential drugs lists. Most of these policies were aimed at benefiting the poor. For example, the Mexican Social Security Institute (IMSS) organised an ambitious family physician programme to reduce emphasis on medical specialisations and to enhance comprehensive primary care; the Mexican Ministry of Health extended social security to the peasantry under the name IMSS-Coplamar;[15] Ecuador designed an innovative social security programme for rural communities known as the Seguro Social Campesino;[16] and the Dominican Republic began a generic drugs programme and public pharmacies (*boticas populares*) that lower considerably the costs of essential drugs for the poor.[17]

Before examining the reasons why some interventions were included and others excluded from the neoliberal reforms, it is useful to examine briefly the relationship between globalisation and health.

Globalisation and Health

As in other areas, it is not possible in the health sector to have a full understanding of the positive and negative changes that are taking place in Latin America without examining the dynamics of global change. The transformation of international governing structures, communication innovations,

[15]   Lozoya Legorreta et al. (1988).

[16]   Córdova Jiménez (1980).

[17]   Ugalde and Homedes (1988).

the broadening of international commerce and the new mobility of capital across international borders are part of the concept of globalisation. An increasing number of scholars are exploring the impact that these processes have on world health.[18]

Frequently, globalisation is defined as an economic process of interdependence of countries worldwide caused by the increasing cross-border transactions of goods and services and of international capital flows. Other authors consider that economic interdependence is only one dimension of globalisation. For them, globalisation implies a weakening of the nation-state, along with the breaking down of the cultural and political barriers that separate nations. It is not clear what type of global political structure is likely to follow the economic and trading blocs currently in the process of configuration.

Neoliberal globalisation is best explained as a logical step in the history of human domination, that is a new process of colonisation through which transnational dominant classes control labourers cross-nationally. It is not possible to understand the current modality of globalisation without understanding the role of the transnational dominant classes. The economic elites of developing nations have the same interest in promoting neoliberal globalisation as those of the industrial nations, and both benefit from it. It is understandable that they speak the same language and promote similar policies, a fact that is increasingly being recognised by scholars such as Wade (2001) and explains the behaviour of Third World governments. Their instruments of domination are the multinational corporations and the international organisations, in particular, the multilateral banks and more recently the World Trade Organisation. The main beneficiaries of the economic policies and activities of these institutions are the transnational elites.[19]

Many analysts have linked the worsening of wealth distribution to globalisation.[20] Table 7.3 presents CEPAL's estimates of the Gini index of wealth distribution that tend to be lower — i.e. less wealth concentration — than the WB's estimates.[21] As can be seen, during the last two decades the concentration of wealth in the region showed a tendency to increase. For the countries for which information is presented only a handful experi-

---

[18] Yong Kim et al. (2000), Bezruchka (2000), Labonte (1999), Yach and Bettcher (1998), see also *The Lancet* vol. 351, 7 February 1998 with a collection of articles on the topic, and Lee (1998) for a comprehensive bibliography on the subject.

[19] Oxfam (2001); Dollar and Kraay (2001); Kliksberg (2000).

[20] Wade (2001).

[21] Korzeniewicz and Smith (2000).

enced decreases, while increases in some countries such as Argentina, Mexico, Panama and Venezuela are pronounced. It is recognised that income distribution in Latin America is worse than in other regions, and that Brazil has the worst in the world. Some WB economists argue that there is no reason to be concerned about wealth disparities within countries because the lower income deciles do not have less income than in the past.[22] Most social scientists disagree with this view. On the one hand, in a number of Latin American countries the situation has worsened for the indigent, and secondly history shows that social problems, including political violence, result from unacceptable wealth disparities.

Poor wealth distribution is of concern for several reasons. Some authors suggest that countries with poor income distribution are less healthy than those with a more equitable distribution, or to express it in positive terms, other things being equal, egalitarian societies enjoy better health status than those that are not.[23] Data on mortality, homicides and some specific diseases and mental health conditions seem to support this hypothesis in 'advanced' societies. But there are doubts regarding the validity of this proposition for Latin America. It is known that violence has increased dramatically in the region: male homicides specific mortality rates per 100,000 increased between 1984 and 1994 from 32 to 38 in Central America and the Latin Caribbean, from 47 to 97 in the Andean region and from 42 to 55 in Brazil.[24] If the proposition is applicable to Latin America, it would appear that the transnational elites and the institutions that serve them are creating health problems by widening wealth disparities. This contradiction is important to understanding the characteristics of the neoliberal reforms.

Many policy-makers consider economic growth to be a prerequisite for the solution of social problems. However, economic growth does not guarantee in itself the expansion of productive opportunities for the poor and the raising of their income.[25] In the health sector it has been confirmed that policies that improve the average health of a population may not reduce health inequalities; indeed, they may increase them because those who are better off seem to profit more from the available services.[26]

---

[22] Dollar and Kraay (2001).

[23] Wilkinson (1996).

[24] PAHO (1998).

[25] Sen (1998).

[26] Acheson (2000).

Table 7.3: Evolution of the Gini Coefficient and Health Expenditures as Percentage of GDP

Country	Year	Gini Coefficient		Households with income below average (%)	
		Urban	Rural	Urban	Rural
Argentina*	1980	0.365	—	66	—
	1997	0.439	—	73	—
Bolivia**	1989	0.484	—	71	—
	1997	0.455	0.531	73	—
Brazil	1979	0.493	0.407	74	72
	1996	0.538	0.460	77	73
Chile	1987	0.485	0.387	74	74
	1996	0.473	0.402	74	75
Colombia***	1980	0.518	—	75	—
	1997	0.477	0.401	74	71
Costa Rica	1981	0.328	0.355	65	66
	1997	0.357	0.357	66	67
Ecuador	1990	0.381	—	70	—
	1997	0.388	—	70	—
El Salvador	1995	0.382	0.355	70	65
	1997	0.384	0.317	70	67
Guatemala	1986	0.464	0.472	72	76
	1989	0.479	0.432	73	73
Honduras	1990	0.487	0.465	73	75
	1997	0.448	0.427	73	72
Mexico	1984	0.321	0.323	70	71
	1996	0.392	0.334	73	69
Nicaragua	1997	0.443	—	74	—
Panama	1979	0.399	0.347	67	67
	1997	0.462	0.440	73	74
Paraguay****	1986	0.404	—	71	—
	1996	0.389	—	70	—
Dominican Republic	1997	0.432	0.392	74	69
Uruguay	1981	0.379	—	69	—
	1997	0.300	—	68	—
Venezuela	1981	0.306	0.288	66	67
	1997	0.425	0.349 (1994)	72	69 (1994)

Source: CEPAL, *Indicadores Económicos* (Santiago de Chile: CEPAL, 1999).
* Gran Buenos Aires; ** 1989 17 Urban centers in Bolivia and 1997 all urban centres;
1980 eight most important cities; * Asunción.

Globalisation and Health Reforms

While many observers claim that neoliberal health reforms have been largely successful in Latin America, the opposite can be argued. Objectives have not been fully realised nor policy effectively applied. For example, in Mexico health inequities continue to be pronounced several years after the introduction of reform-related changes.[27] In Argentina social security reforms have produced fragmentation in the system and increased inequities.[28] Indeed, the WB found in 1996 that the Redistribution Fund created in Argentina in 1970 to increase solidarity among the social funds was producing the opposite effect.[29] Colombia has allocated more energy and resources than other countries in the region to implement a health reform, but several years after initiating the reform there are doubts whether the government has the political will to correct inequities in the geographical distribution of health resources.[30]

Neoliberal reform strategies include three key interventions — privatisation, decentralisation and basic packages of services — and exclude one other: pharmaceutical policies.

Privatisation

The delegation of responsibilities to the private sector is rationalised as a means of increasing efficiency and reducing corruption. In fact, it increases the share of health costs borne by users through co-payments, deductibles and regressive municipal taxes that have a very negative impact on the poor by raising further barriers to access to services. Transnational elites are the primary beneficiaries of the privatisation of healthcare delivery. Foreign insurance and health corporations are entering the Latin American market with expectations of large profits. There are well-documented accounts of the links between privatisation, World Bank policies and the profits of transnational corporations to support this analysis of globalisation and health. In Brazil, Aetna owns a large number of managed care groups through Sul America Seguros — the largest insurance company in the country with 1.6 million managed-care enrolees and US$1.2 billion in revenues in 1996. In Argentina, Galeno Life TIM, a managed-care firm controlled by the Exxel Group, had revenues of US$ 181 million; in Chile, Cigna had over 100,000 enrolees, and in Guatemala, 40,000.31 US firms are rapidly positioning themselves for the day the Mexican Institute of Social Security decides to privatise the delivery of care in that country.

It has been recognised that a large percentage of Latin Americans, perhaps as much as 50 per cent, lives in poverty. This population cannot

27   Frenk (1998).
28   Giordano and Colina (2000).
29   World Bank (1997).
30   Yepes (2000)

afford emergency or hospital care, or care for chronic diseases. Even WB economists have acknowledged that there is a need to subsidise care for rural populations and an undefined number of the urban poor. Programmes of privatisation have introduced and expanded the use of user fees and co-payments for many services that previously were provided free — or nearly free — of charge. Field studies from many countries indicate that user and recovery fees and co-payments are barriers to the utilisation of health services among the poor. Newbrander asks: 'Do user fees have an inequitable effect on the poor? Do user fees reduce the access of the poor to health services? The studies show that the answer to both questions is yes, even when protection mechanisms are in place.'[32] The poor who decide to pay user fees have to sacrifice other necessary goods such as food. By forcing the poor to reduce food intake and other essential goods, privatisation generates additional illness.

As indicated above, Colombia has allocated more energy and resources than other countries in the region to implementing a health reform. Between 1993 and 1997 there were large increases in hospital use, while social security coverage increased substantially, most impressively among the lowest decile — from three to 44 per cent.[33] For Céspedes-Londoño et al. this data shows that the reform is succeeding in correcting health inequities in access to services. This statement is questionable. The same study also demonstrates that utilisation rates correlate positively with income decile — the lower the income, the lower the utilisation — and suggests that co-payments constitute a barrier to utilisation for the insured poor. This case tends to add validity to the thesis that policies to improve the healthcare of a nation may not reduce health inequities. Moreover, Céspedes-Londoño et al. fail to indicate that between 1990 and 1996 total per capita health spending increased from US$ (current) 86 to 180, and that private health expenditure as a percentage of GDP fell from 3.86 to 3.67 while total spending rose from 6.86 to 8.17 per cent. Whether the utilisation increases were due to the reforms or to expenditure growth remains a moot question. Private health expenditure by income decile is unavailable, but it is plausible to argue that the reforms enabled the better off to reduce expenditure on healthcare. On the other hand, the poor who had spent very little on health before the 1993 reform because they received free care from the Ministry of Health were now compelled to pay. When

31   Iriart et al. (2001), Stocker et al. (1999).

32   Newbrander, Collins and Wilson (2000), p. 166.

33   Céspedes-Londoño, Almeida, Travassos et al. (c. 2000).

social insurance regimes are based on co-payments, the terms coverage and utilisation cannot be used inter-changeably. Reform in Colombia may have accentuated inequities. Furthermore, for the 47 per cent of Colombians who do not have health insurance, access to care may today be more difficult than before the reform when, in theory at least, the Ministry made provision for them. To sustain the argument that equity has improved, data on access to services before and after the reform are required.

Chile is perhaps the country where privatisation was most eagerly promoted. That the private sector does not improve equity is confirmed by the Chilean reform. Chileans may opt to joint private insurance companies (ISAPRES), some of them subsidiaries of transnational corporations; otherwise they are covered by the National Health Service. ISAPRES function like any private insurance company: services depend on the premium paid and participants have to pay co-payments and deductibles. Most people who join a private scheme belong to the middle and upper classes. About a quarter of Chileans have chosen private insurance, but they account for approximately one half of total health expenditure. This inequality illustrates the highly criticised imbalance of spending on health. In addition, cross-subsidies from the state to the ISAPRES further intensify inequality. For example, a large proportion of ISAPRES affiliates use the public sector — particularly accident and emergency facilities and maternity services — because they give more consumer satisfaction because they are of higher quality, cheaper or more widely available than private provision.[34] A further example of cross-subsidisation is 'cream-skimming': ISAPRES exclude expensive patients (the elderly and those with chronic and terminal conditions) who are forced to rely on the public sector. Although the government is trying to resolve these problems — and has declared cream-skimming to be illegal — cross-subsidies benefit the multinational corporations, represent a burden for the public sector and generate health inequities.

In Brazil privatisation of healthcare delivery began in the early 1980s and now more is spent per capita on healthcare than in many countries in the region. Yet a very large percentage of the population does not have access to services: about 22 per cent of the urban population and those located in the poorer parts of the countryside have no access to physicians. To redress these inequalities, the Ministry of Health is considering establishing a year of compulsory service, known as *pasantía*, for newly qualified doctors.[35]

---

[34]   Barrientos (2000).

[35]   Csillag (2001).

The recent literature on developed and developing countries suggests that public funding is more equitable than private, and that co-payments and user fees create inequities. The role of the private sector in the delivery of services, especially ancillary services such as catering, laundry, security and accounting, is less controversial so long as there is capacity to enforce contracts.

Decentralisation and Equity

Decentralisation is promoted within the rationale of democratisation and citizen participation, and rests upon the hypothesis that decisions made on the ground better satisfy users by avoiding the expensive mistakes of distant bureaucrats ignorant of local needs. The result is a more efficient use of resources and a higher quality of services. Studies of decentralisation demonstrate that predicted improvements seldom occur.[36]

Bossert suggests that in Chile the transfer of municipal common funds from wealthy to poor municipalities increased equity.[37] Before making such an affirmation it is necessary to know who pays the taxes in the wealthy municipalities and who benefits in the poorer ones. First, if property taxes are paid by poor residents, the poor of wealthy municipalities are subsidising poor municipalities. Secondly, it is important to know who benefits from these transfers. If poor municipalities use these resources to fund services that disproportionately favour the wealthy, it cannot be asserted that the transfers increase equity. If municipal and provincial authorities spend these resources on high salaries for health professionals, on the purchase of expensive technologies for urban hospitals that are inaccessible to the rural poor, or on the payment of higher prices for medicine, equipment and other inputs that were previously purchased at lower prices by central authorities (see below), the outcome will also be inequitable.

The misallocation of funds at local levels in ways that do not improve equity has been documented in Bolivia,[38] Colombia[39] and Peru.[40] It is also possible that decentralisation has fostered bossism and corruption. It is not surprising that highly aggregated data allow for different interpretations, or that several studies argue for Chile that decentralisation has not

36   Ugalde and Homedes (2001).
37   Bossert (2000).
38   Ruiz Mier and Giussani (1996).
39   LaForgia and Homedes (1992).
40   Altobelli (2000).

had an impact on inequity.[41] Decentralisation has derailed some already successful programmes for the poor. Gershberg reported that decentralisation in Mexico severely damaged IMSS-COPLAMAR, a successful centralised programme for the rural poor.[42] In Mexico and Bolivia decentralisation has increased inequities by concentrating services in urban areas, providing services for the better off and tending to respond to powerful pressure groups rather than the poor.[43] Frequently, hospitals have been favoured at the expense of primary care, and townships have received more per capita resources than their rural hinterlands.

It has been suggested that decentralisation is a means of privatising health services. In countries like Mexico,[44] Costa Rica,[45] El Salvador[46] and Guatemala programmes of decentralisation include, or are scheduled to include, privatisation through the contracting out of healthcare delivery. From the above discussion it is clear that decentralisation is an undeniable need in some circumstances. But before launching a programme of decentralisation, policy-makers need both to recognise its complexity and to be certain that the political and economic enabling factors are in place that will assure a positive equity impact.

Basic Packages of Services

Recent health reforms have limited the range of publicly funded services. The *canastas básicas* (a basic package of health services) in most countries are restricted to prenatal care and delivery, family planning, acute respiratory infections, rehydration salts and immunisations. The *canasta* does not satisfy many other health needs like access to essential drugs, timely response to acute episodes,and care of chronic diseases. Mexico is unusual in having one of the most comprehensive packages. Other countries have decided to finance an enlarged *canasta* through health insurance but coverage is rarely complete. For example, in Colombia coverage does not extend to 36 per cent of the population.

In contrast to the *canasta básica* concept, it can be contended that all the Latin American economies, with the exception of Haiti, have sufficient

---

[41]   Lenz and Sánchez (c. 1998); Duarte Quapper and Zuleta Reyes (1999); Larrañaga (1999); Duarte (1995).

[42]   Gershberg (1998a).

[43]   Holley (1995); González-Block et al. (1989).

[44]   Gómez-Dantés (2000).

[45]   Castro Valverde and Sáenz (1998).

[46]   Zamora (2001).

resources to provide universal primary care and relatively sophisticated tertiary care to the vast majority of their citizens if their resources are efficiently used. The argument has been made that until very recently the majority of governments allocated limited resources to health, preferring to spend unreasonably large proportions of their revenues on unproductive activities such as the armed forces. Additionally, globalisation policies favour the exodus of capital to industrial nations, impoverishing the Latin American economies. With appropriate economic policies Latin American countries could have sufficient resources to fund an adequate, universal healthcare system. It follows that it is difficult to justify the inequitable concept of the *canasta básica*.

Since the 1960s, with remarkable consistency, numerous assessments of healthcare sectors across the region identified common problems that reduce efficiency and generate waste. More equity would have been achieved if healthcare reformers had searched for solutions to these problems, instead of ignoring them and implanting neoliberal models that within a few years began to show similar shortcomings to their predecessors.[47]

Pharmaceuticals, Globalisation, Reform and Equity

The study of the pharmaceutical industry illustrates how multinational corporations benefit at the expense of the Third World poor, incrementing health inequities. There are two basic reasons that make the study of pharmaceuticals particularly important from an equity point of view. The first one is the relatively large amounts of money that patients spend on medicines. In 1995 the Latin American pharmaceutical market amounted to US$18,058 million, representing about seven per cent of the world market, and 78 per cent of the pharmaceutical market was private;[48] proportionately the poor spend a higher percentage of health expenditures on drugs than the more affluent. Secondly, due to multiple factors a large percentage of drugs are not used adequately. Among these factors one can mention excessive self-medication especially among the poor who use pharmacies as the first source of healthcare;[49] inadequate patients' compliance with physician's advice that tends to be higher among the poor due to low educational levels and poorer communication with providers;[50] and

[47]   Atkinson (2000); Gómez-Dantés (2000); Lloyd-Sherlock (2000).

[48]   PAHO (1998).

[49]   Lalama (1999).

[50]   Homedes and Ugalde (1993).

the purchase of incomplete treatment regimes, a very frequent occurrence among the poor.[51] At the same time, the pharmaceutical industry also contributes to unnecessary expenditures and inadequate use of pharmaceuticals through aggressive marketing strategies, oligopolistic behaviours, pressures to register products that do not add therapeutic value, sales of irrational combinations of active ingredients, restrictions to local production of generics through excessive patent protection rights, opposition to compulsory licensing and parallel importing. These practices create access barriers to needed medications and preclude the adequate use of drugs.

Contrary to what affects other activities in the health sector (for example, financing and delivery systems), there are very clear guidelines on how to efficiently run the pharmaceutical system of any given country. However, countries that have tried to rationalise the use of pharmaceuticals have faced tremendous opposition from physicians, the pharmaceutical industry, and misinformed communities. It is very clear that improvements in equity, efficiency and quality of care require improvements in drug policies.

The promoters of health reforms have not explained the reasons why interventions in the pharmaceutical sector have not been included as a basic component of the reforms. Their exclusion is most unfortunate because recent global changes are threatening the access to needed drugs and the appropriate use of available drugs, especially among the poor in developing countries. The changes that we have identified include: (1) a decrease of public expenditures on medicines, while total pharmaceutical expenditure has increased significantly; (2) the regionalisation of markets and its impact in the registration of new products; (3) the increasing pressures of the industry to avoid regulations and preclude access to generics; and (4) the decentralisation of the health sector.

Private Expenditures on the Increase

The pharmaceutical market has expanded very rapidly. In developed countries a large proportion of the drug market is publicly funded. In the past, in Latin America, medicines could be obtained through social security or were subsidised by the public sector or institutions serving the poor. However, as a result of health reform, government is imposing higher user fees and co-payments for services and medications. Currently, only selected drugs are publicly financed, such as drugs to treat priority programmes (malaria and

---

[51]   Ugalde and Homedes (1988).

tuberculosis) and medications that are used for maternal and child services; and, even in these instances, resources are not always sufficient.

Self-medication is likely to continue to increase as countries privatise the provision of services and charge deductibles and co-payments to health service users. The results are the increase in sales of expensive medicines when cheaper drugs are available and sales of medication with limited therapeutic value; a higher percentage of families' income spent on pharmaceuticals; and, very probably, increases in the detrimental effects associated with poor use of pharmaceuticals such as iatrogenia and increased antibiotic resistance.[52]

Regionalisation of the Markets and Regulation

Deciding which medicines should be in the market is a complex process and WHO recommended the use of essential drug lists. According to WHO developing countries need only about 270 products to deal with prevailing health problems. There have been some criticisms regarding this number, some authors suggest that the number should be higher. Although the majority of countries have developed essential drug lists, only a few have used them to guide registration and purchasing practices, and their utilisation has been limited to the public sector.

Current world economic policies limit the ability of countries to resist the entry into their markets of the increasing number of products that are released each year. In the past, approval of new products took an unreasonable amount of time. Pressures to expedite the process led to the adoption of streamlined procedures that permit the registration of unnecessary drugs. For example, Colombia established a Provisional Medicinal Drug System that led to an overload of approval requests and the appearance on the market of products of questionable utility and quality. Peru streamlined the registration process in 1992 and allowed products of little therapeutic value to enter the national market.[53]

At the same time, under international pressures the Latin American countries are using regional trade agreements (the Central American Common Market, the Andean Group and MERCOSUR) to significantly alter drug registration requirements and procedures. All three regional co-operation forums are advancing with plans to harmonise regulatory statutes in order gradually to allow for the free circulation of pharmaceutical products among

---

[52]   Heinick et al. (1998); Lexchin (1995); López-Linares and Phang Romero (1992).

[53]   PAHO (1998).

the countries.[54] This could have been a perfect opportunity to determine what drugs satisfy the needs of Latin American consumers, establish streamline procedures for their registration and exclude the rest. Latin American health reformers could have utilised this opportunity to strengthen pharmaceutical policies, including the use of essential drugs lists and generic drugs. Unfortunately, under pressures from pharmaceutical firms, the countries with softer drug regulation procedures tend to impose their criteria within their own regional markets, thus subverting the process.

The International Conference on Harmonisation of Technical Requirements for Registration of Pharmaceuticals for Human Use (ICH) was established during the 1990s to harmonise technical requirements for registration of new products.[55] The composition and the operations of ICH have raised concerns. ICH has been criticised for being more concerned about getting medication onto the market as quickly as possible, while paying insufficient attention to drug safety, drug information and to monitoring drug use. In addition, ICH has been accused of favouring the large industry, unnecessarily increasing the requirements for generics, and for its lack of accountability and openness.[56]

Industries' Opposition to Regulation and Generics

The financial success of the pharmaceutical industry depends on its ability to innovate and sell its products. The innovation capacity is limited, only a handful of new active ingredients are commercialised each year, and their numbers have been declining.[57] Consequently, the pharmaceutical industry needs to increase sales and engages in aggressive marketing strategies.[58] The percentage of sales that pharmaceutical companies invest in marketing has been increasing (from 17 per cent in 1973 to 24 per cent in 1989).[59] In the USA, according to recent estimates, pharmaceutical companies invest between US$8,000 and US$13,000 a year per physician in marketing their products.[60] The industry is now the main source of drug information available to pre-

---

54   *Ibid.*, pp. 299–300.

55   Stolley and Laporte (2000).

56   *Ibid.*

57   Casadio Tarabusi and Vickery (1998).

58   Stolley and Laporte (2000).

59   Ballance (1992).

60   Stolberg and Gerth (2000).

scribers and through direct to consumers advertising (DTCA) is becoming an important source of information for consumers. DTCA aims to increase self-medication with brand name medicines and to encourage clients to request the prescription of brand name medicines from their providers.

WHO has advocated the use of generics and many countries have managed to control costs by substituting the prescription of brand names for their generic formulation. Argentina, Brazil, Colombia, Ecuador and Venezuela have made great strides in that regard, but opposition from physicians and the industry has presented formidable obstacles. The problems are fostered by the public's view — often induced by prescribers and the industry — that generic products are of lower quality. In addition, many countries allowed local manufacturers to produce generics. This strategy fostered the development of local industry and facilitated access to affordable pharmaceuticals.

The industry has used all possible legal loopholes to safeguard brand names and maximise profits.[61] One of the most recent and far-reaching tools has been the Trade-Related Aspects of Intellectual Property Rights (TRIPs) Agreement imposed by the World Trade Organisation (WTO). Under the TRIPs Agreement all member states have to make patent protection available for at least 20 years. Many WHO member states have expressed concerns about the effect that the TRIPs or its interpretation will have on drug prices.[62] South Africa,[63] Central America[64] and Brazil[65] are already experiencing the impact of TRIPs on access to HIV/AIDs medicines. The impact of TRIPs in access to pharmaceuticals raises significant human rights issues and constitutes the basis for a worldwide campaign spearheaded by Oxfam, Health Action International (HAI) and Medicines sans Frontieres (MSF) to allow parallel importing and the local production of generics.[66] According to Oxfam (2001) the main beneficiaries of TRIPs are the transnational pharmaceutical corporations.

The passing of TRIPs and the recent mergers of major pharmaceutical manufacturers strengthen the oligopolistic nature of the sector which, in addition to raising the global costs of medicines, will have the upper hand in their negotiation with governments and regulatory agencies.

[61] Gottlieb (2000).

[62] Supakankunti et al. (1999); Dumoulin (1999).

[63] Bond (1999).

[64] Stern (2001).

[65] Aith (2000).

[66] Pécoul et al. (1999).

Decentralisation of the Health Sector

The decentralisation of drug procurement as occurred in India, or the deregulation as happened in Peru and Bolivia, increased the presence of useless combination drugs or even dangerous drugs that had been withdrawn from markets in other countries.[67] On the other hand, countries that have maintained the centralisation of procurement have reduced costs. For example, Costa Rica was able to save between 40 and 60 per cent of pharmaceutical expenditures by improving drug selection and procurement. Similarly, the Caribbean islands joined together to carry out international tenders through the Caribbean Development Bank. In the first year they saved 44 per cent over previous prices.[68] Significant savings can be observed when purchasers use international bidding procedures, except in the case of patented drugs that are protected by monopoly power.

The decentralisation of the health sector has forced countries to devise new drug procurement systems, but it is too early to evaluate the results. One can anticipate that if the purchase of drugs is decentralised, purchasers will not benefit from economies of scale.

Health reforms have missed an opportunity to improve health equity by excluding drug policies that when implemented in developed and developing countries have had a positive impact on health, and particularly on the health of the poor. Recent global economic policies further jeopardise the prospects of access to affordable medications in developing nations. Behind those economic policies are the interests of powerful multinational manufacturers and international agencies. The problems affecting the pharmaceutical policies today are beyond the control of individual countries, only a well-orchestrated international effort can assist countries in reverting or balancing current trends. The global reform effort could have provided the structure for this type of development. The failure to include pharmaceutical policies highlights the real interests of the World Bank, USAID and the other agencies that are promoting neoliberal reforms. Their stated objective is to help world poverty eradication, but their actions indicate that they are more interested in the welfare of the transnational elites and their corporations than in the welfare of the poor.

---

[67]   Laing (1999).

[68]   World Bank (1993), p. 146.

Conclusions

This chapter has analysed some aspects of the health reforms that were promoted by institutions that serve the transnational elites and found that health reforms are not succeeding in reducing health inequities. Gómez-Dantés (2000) indicates that financial reforms in Mexico raise concerns about the possibility that they will be met at the expense of the poor and public health activities. This appreciation concurs with our research in other countries of the region.

By its very own ideological principles, as a new step in the history of world exploitation, the neoliberal globalisation creates inequities. Most countries have increased the percentage of their GDP allocated to health, but access to care has not increased correspondingly. With the exception of Chile and Costa Rica — two countries that had almost full coverage before the neoliberal reforms — most other countries in the region continue to have large percentages of the population without health coverage.

Under the excuse of public sector inefficiencies, those who benefit from a laissez-faire state have promoted health reforms that, according to many studies, appear to be generating health inequity, while providing transnational corporations the opportunity of collecting hefty profits.

Because globalisation in its present form is based on neoliberal principles, it is understandable that policies that affect negatively the interests of transnational corporations were quietly left out of the reform packages. We have used the case of the essential drugs lists and generic drugs to illustrate this point. There are other examples of policies that were left out because they would have reduced corporate profits. Examples include policies to prevent occupational accidents and hazards, the provision of adequate sewage systems, control of food contamination and the rationalisation of high-tech medical equipment purchases. On the other hand, other types of intervention that did not have the potential to benefit the transnational corporations have also been left out; examples of these policies are human resources interventions and health education programmes. The exclusion of policies such as these demonstrates the limited interest of the transnational elites in the promotion of the health of the masses.

Globalisation is the result of technological advances and is consequently irreversible, but the neoliberal economic principles under which it was born are reversible.

CHAPTER 8

Health, Equity and Social Exclusion in Argentina and Mexico

Peter Lloyd-Sherlock

As a region Latin America has performed relatively well in terms of basic health indicators, even during the crisis years of the 1980s. However, this apparent success belies profound and complex problems of inequity and solidarity, which are rooted in wider processes of political and social exclusion. This chapter provides a short regional overview of some of these issues. Given the complexity of the topic, generalisations are elaborated from the experience of two countries, Argentina and Mexico. Though different, both countries are broadly representative of the key issues and problems faced by Latin America as a whole. The chapter begins by referring to the difficulty of conceptualising health, particularly with reference to exclusion and equity. It then examines equity and health from a number of different angles, including progress towards universal provision of formal services, geographical variations for different health indicators, the segmentation of healthcare systems and the historical and political context within which these problems of equity occur. The concluding section looks at recent reform experiences and finds little evidence that these issues are being effectively addressed.

Health, Equity and Universality

Health is a complex and problematic concept in any part of the world, not just Latin America. This becomes particularly challenging when we attempt to relate health to ideas about equity and social exclusion. The most widely accepted definition of health comes from the World Health Organisation (WHO), which sees it as: 'a state of complete physical, mental and social wellbeing, and not merely the absence of disease or infirmity'.[1] This constitutes an embracing and ambitious approach to understanding health, and serves to rebut the narrower, more negative conceptions sometimes found among health professionals. The WHO approach stresses that population

[1]   WHO (1948).

health is influenced by much more than formal health service provision, and must be understood with reference to general economic, social, environmental and cultural conditions. This is of particular significance in Latin America, whose wider context of development has rarely been propitious to good health for poorer and more vulnerable groups.[2]

However, the WHO approach to health is not easily translated into obvious policies or clear strategies, and quantitative indicators are unable to capture the complexity of such a concept. Consequently, a more limited approach to measuring and understanding health is usually taken. In regions of extreme resource scarcity, particular attention is given to developing basic packages of services, essential drugs and selective primary healthcare. In Latin America the focus is rather different, and the traditional conservative, curative/negative approach to health still tends to predominate.

Table 8.1: Basic Health and Demographic Indicators, Latin America and the Caribbean, 1960–95

	1960–65	1970–75	1980–85	1990–95
Infant mortality, per 1,000 births	101	81	57	40
Life expectancy at birth (years)	56.8	60.9	64.9	68.1

Source: United Nations (1999)

Taking this narrower definition Latin America appears to have performed reasonably well as a region over recent decades.[3] Of particular significance has been a large fall in infant mortality (Table 8.1). The region's performance fits within a wider picture of epidemiological transition. This involves a shift in the main causes of sickness and death from infectious diseases, under-nutrition and inadequate hygiene to a post-transition phase, where diseases of 'wealth and modernity' (including chronic disease, road accidents and stress) are more prominent.[4] Key motors of this change have included socioeconomic change, wider access to sanitation and clean water and the extension of some basic health services, such as immunisation programmes. The timing of this epidemiological transition has varied

2   Morley (2001); Gwynne and Kay (1999).

3   PAHO (1998).

4   Phillips (1990).

across the region. Southern Cone countries are now at a much more advanced stage of transition than poorer Andean and Central American ones. This is seen in Table 8.2, which shows changes in the prominence of two causes of diseases associated with different phases of the transition.

Table 8.2: Percentage of Healthy Life Years Lost, by Selected Causes, 1980 and 1994

	Central America and the Latin Caribbean		Mexico		Southern Cone	
	1980	1994	1980	1994	1980	1994
Intestinal and infectious diseases	18	11	17	5	less than 2	less than 2
Cancers	2	4	3	7	11	15

Source: PAHO (1998).

While the region's general health performance may have been good, a recent report by the Pan American Health Organization (PAHO) observed that: 'The characteristics and speed of this improvement have not been the same in all countries or in all population groups in any one country'.[5] Consequently, organisations such as PAHO have attached a high priority to improving equity in the region.

But what does equity mean when applied to health? Perhaps ideally, this should consider the degree to which economic and social policies reduce health differences within a population (once one has standardised for things like age and sex). However, in current Latin American health policy discourse equity is usually understood in a much narrower sense, to be the guarantee of minimum levels of health and access to services for poorer and more vulnerable groups. To some extent, this approach resonates with universalist agendas. These were given impetus by the 'Health for All by the Year 2000' pledge made at the landmark 1978 Alma Ata conference. Every country in Latin America signed up to this commitment, and it is echoed by constitutional guarantees across the region. During the 1980s and 1990s policy rhetoric made much of this 'mission' for the region.[6] The challenge of universal healthcare was considerable: the Pan American Health

---

5   PAHO (1998), p. 1.
6   IADB (1996); PAHO (1998).

Organization estimated that by the early 1990s 130 million people in Latin America and the Caribbean still had no access to any form of modern healthcare services.[7] However, references to 'Health for All' became fewer as the deadline approached, and there were no public attempts to take stock or evaluate progress towards universal access during 2000. In this light, it is difficult to know how seriously we should take similar pledges made by international agencies such as UNFPA's goal of reproductive healthcare for all women by 2015 or the UK government's aim to halve world poverty by 2020. Do such 'mission statements' provide an effective policy focus, or do they give a misleading impression about the solvability of what are often deeply-rooted social problems? Possibly the answer is both.

So how has the region fared in terms of universalising access to healthcare? Clearly, the starting point for different countries has been very variable. In the case of Argentina, it is often stated that access to basic services is all but universal. However, some studies report increasing exclusion of more vulnerable groups.[8] By contrast, in some of the poorest countries it is thought that the majority of the rural population remains unserved.[9] The case of Mexico falls somewhere between these two extremes, but its efforts to extend access do not give cause for optimism.

Estimates for 1978 show that around 45 per cent of Mexicans lacked access to formal healthcare services from any source.[10] Efforts to extend coverage to the rural population during the 1980s were led by a scheme known as IMSS-Solidarity. This was managed by Mexico's main social insurance fund (the Instituto Mexicano del Seguro Social or IMSS), but was fully financed by the federal government. Claims about the success of this initiative vary. Some studies suggest that 89 per cent of the population could access services by 1990. However, data on actual levels of utilisation suggest coverage was only 56 per cent. There were also doubts about the quality of care provided by IMSS-Solidarity. Its services were never legally defined, and the scheme was not subject to external supervision. The scheme was politically important to IMSS, as it strengthened its redistributive and universalist credentials, and provided an important source of employment.

---

7   Mesa-Lago (1992).

8   Stillwaggon (1998).

9   Data on access are very poor for much of Latin America. While some information is available about the supply of services (numbers of doctors, beds, etc), much less is known about actual levels of utilisation by different population groups.

10   Tamez and Molina (2000).

Consequently, IMSS resisted efforts to integrate the programme with Ministry of Health initiatives for unprotected urban groups.[11]

During the 1990s the Mexican Ministry of Health implemented two further extension programmes. The first of these, el Programa de Apoyo a los Servicios de Salud para la Población no Asegurada (PASSPA), ran from 1991 to 1995 and aimed to improve primary healthcare infrastructure in the country's four poorest states.[12] Official sources claim that PASSPA extended potential regular access to healthcare to around two million people. However, the Ministry of Health's own programme evaluation was never made publicly available. A second initiative, el Programa de Extensión de Cobertura (PEC), ran from 1996 to 2000 and aimed to offer a package of 12 basic health services to the entire population which remained unserved. PEC had a broader geographical base, extending to 18 states, and was claimed to have reached around six million people during its first two years. Again, no evaluations have been made publicly available to support this claim, and the credibility of the six million figure remains highly questionable. Gómez-Dantés (2000) argues that even if official data is to be believed, key features of PASSPA and PEC raise concerns about equity. These include issues about the narrowness of the basic health package being offered the poor, and the fact that both programmes were largely financed by the World Bank rather than the Mexican government. This raises questions about the commitment of the Mexican state to provide a good standard of care to all its citizens. It also suggests that the Alma Ata ideal of universal healthcare may have been replaced by a narrower neoliberal safety net approach of poor services for the poor.

Geographical Indicators of Health and Equity

A second way to examine equity is through geographical variations in health at the sub-national level. As most Latin American countries are characterised by sharp regional disparities in wealth and human development, it is to be expected that health conditions will also vary. Tables 8.3 and 8.4 give sub-national data for infant mortality and life expectancy at birth for Argentina and Mexico in the mid-1990s. In the case of Argentina, the probability of a child dying in the first year of life in the poor province of Chaco was more than double that in Buenos Aires city. Variations in life expectancy across Mexico are less acute, although they still account for over six years between

---

[11]   González Block and Ruiz (1998).

[12]   Gómez-Dantés (2000).

the richest and poorest states. In the relatively prosperous Nuevo León, life expectancy is almost on a par with developed countries (74.3 years in 1990). In Chiapas it is slightly below that of Western Asia (68.3 years)[13]

Table 8.3: Infant Mortality per 1,000 Live Births by Province, Argentina, 1996

	Infant mortality per 1000
National average	20.9
Buenos Aires City	14.7
Chaco	34.4

Source: INDEC (1998)

Table 8.4: Life Expectancy at Birth by State, Mexico, 1994

	Life expectancy (years)
National average	71.6
Chiapas	67.5
Nuevo León	73.7

Source: Frenk (ed.) (1997), Appendix A.

These general demographic figures give a crude indication about health patterns, particularly with regard to mortality. However, they give no information about variations in the overall health status of the surviving populations. One way this information can be captured is with reference to the epidemiological profiles of different groups or geographical areas in a country. Ideally, epidemiological data should include the overall extent of ill-health and premature mortality, as well as the types of factors which cause these problems. Good epidemiological information is not available at the sub-national level for many Latin American countries (this itself should be a matter of concern). One exception is Mexico, and data for regional health variations are presented in Table 8.5. The health indicator used, the Disability Adjusted Life Year (or DALY) is a composite measurement of premature mortality and general population health.[14] This epi-

---

13   UN (1994).

14   For further information about DALYs see World Bank (1993). Paalman et al. (1998) identify a number of weaknesses and potential biases with this indicator.

demiological information points to a higher level of regional inequity than suggested by demographic statistics. For example, the overall burden of disease in the rich state of Nuevo León compares favourably to that of developed market economies (estimated at 117 per 1000 in 1990), while the poor state of Chiapas is closer to India (344 per 1000).[15] These differences have led some commentators to refer to the 'epidemiological polarisation' of Mexico and other Latin American countries.[16] The extent of this polarisation might be revealed by data which are more geographically desegregated or which compare the situation of different socioeconomic groups. Unfortunately, such data are not available for Mexico or Argentina.

Table 8.5: DALYs Lost per 1,000 Inhabitants by Cause and by Region, Mexico, 1994

	Communicable diseases, nutrition and reproductive	Non-communicable diseases	Accidental and non-accidental injuries	Total
National average	44.4	68.6	30.7	143.7
Chiapas	90.9	83.5	31.8	206.2
Nuevo León	23.8	60.9	23.4	108.1

Source: R. Lozano (1997)

Geographical inequities in health can also be examined with reference to the distribution of infrastructure and personnel. Care should be taken when interpreting such data for several reasons. First, as mentioned above, formal healthcare service delivery is only one of many things which may influence health outcomes in a population, and should not be taken as a proxy for health status. Second, crude measurements of things such as the supply of hospital beds ignore important variations in what a bed may actually consist of, which might range from an intensive therapy unit to a trolley in a corridor. Third, such data tell us little about the overall resource mix in service provision. Most of Latin America suffers from an extreme bias towards curative hospital-based care, and towards specialist physicians rather than generalists and nurses.[17] Using data on beds and doctors may

---

[15]   World Bank (1993).

[16]   Frenk (2000).

[17]   Abel and Lloyd-Sherlock (2000).

serve to promote the misconception that this is what good health is all about. Finally, regional variations may be a misleading reflection of inequity, as hospitals in large cities may function as national referral and teaching centres, serving populations from less well-endowed regions.

Table 8.6 gives some data for the regional distribution of healthcare infrastructure for Argentina. Data are given for the province of Buenos Aires instead of Buenos Aires City, to avoid the national referral effect mentioned above.[18] While this province is less prosperous than the capital and contains significant pockets of poverty, it is still relatively affluent compared to northern provinces such as Chaco. According to Table 8.6, Chaco province is well-served in terms of hospital beds and out-patient clinics. Whether the quality of these facilities is on a par with standards elsewhere in the country is another matter. Stillwaggon (1998) found very wide variations in the facilities and quality of care provided by Argentine clinics, some of which even lacked running water. The high level of infant mortality in Chaco reported in Table 8.3, is suggestive of both the low quality of services there, and their failure to compensate for the wide range of socioeconomic and environmental risks faced by the local population.

Table 8.6: Regional Distribution of Hospital Beds and Out-Patient Establishments in Argentina, mid-1990s

	Hospital and clinic beds 1000 population* (1995)	Out-patient establishments per 1000 population* (1997)
National average	4.8	0.18
Buenos Aires province	4.0	0.12
Chaco	5.0	0.38

*includes public and private sectors.
Source: calculated from INDEC (1998).

In most Latin American countries the geographical distribution of trained medics is strongly biased towards richer regions and urban centres. Efforts to reduce this imbalance through, for example, obliging newly-qualified physicians to take a 'rural year' have had little effect.[19] Data from Mexico reveal the

[18] The province of Buenos Aires surrounds, but does not include, the city of Buenos Aires.
[19] Abel and Lloyd-Sherlock (2000); Nigenda (1997).

extent of this problem. In 1996 there was one physician for every 1,108 inhabitants in Chiapas, compared to a ratio of one to 625 in Nuevo León. Moreover, within Chiapas there were large geographical disparities, and in municipalities where indigenous groups accounted for over 70 per cent of the population the ratio was one physician to 3,246 inhabitants. While trained physicians should not be seen as the be all and end all of healthcare provision (although both they and their patients often think so), such an imbalance is suggestive of a major 'quality gap' between privileged and excluded areas.

A Systemic View of Inequity and Health

The formal healthcare delivery system is only one of many things that may influence population health. However, it is clear that the structure of healthcare systems across the region has significantly contributed to problems of inequity. Traditionally, most Latin American healthcare systems have been highly segmented, and it is usually possible to identify at least three separate sectors. This structure conforms to the wider conservative/corporatist orientation of the region's welfare regimes.[20] Public provision is theoretically financed by general revenue, and aims to provide universal, basic coverage. A range of occupation-specific health insurance programmes provide additional protection to the formal urban labour force and their dependants. These may be administered by the public sector (usually by a separate agency from the Ministry of Health) or, as is the case in Argentina, by organisations such as trade unions. Finally, private health insurance has become increasingly significant in the region, although its coverage remains largely confined to relatively wealthy groups.[21]

Typically, Latin American social and private insurance programmes account for almost as much health expenditure as the public sector, but only provide for a relatively privileged minority of the population.[22] Tables 8.7 and 8.8 provide data on social and private insurance coverage for Argentina and Mexico, and show that the people living in poorer areas are much less likely to be protected. The situation is particularly acute in the Mexican state of Chiapas, where health insurance still remains an option for only a small elite.

[20] Esping-Andersen (1996); Barrientos (2001).

[21] Most studies overlook other potentially important health sectors, such as traditional medicine, homeopathic medicine and informal caring. Given the brevity of this chapter and the scope of its topic, these sectors are not included.

[22] Lloyd-Sherlock (2000a).

Table 8.7: Population Lacking Health Insurance by Province, Argentina, 1991

	% population lacking cover
National average	36.9
Federal Capital	19.7
Chaco	52.2

Source: INDEC (1995).

Table 8.8: Population Lacking Health Insurance by State, Mexico, 1995

	% population lacking cover
National average	62.1
Nuevo León	37.7
Chiapas	84.7

Source: Frenk (ed.) (1997).

It is a widely held view in Latin America that groups lacking social insurance programmes cover make no financial contribution to it, and so these schemes have neither a positive or negative impact on equity or distribution. Indeed, it is sometimes argued that the existence of the social insurance sector frees up public resources which can be directed towards unprotected groups. Both of these assumptions are flawed. First, there are many ways in which the non-insured subsidise the social insurance schemes. Where states make a matching insurance contribution to that levied on the payroll, this must be financed through some form of general taxation. Also, employers may recover payroll contributions by raising the prices of their merchandise to the cost of the entire population. Large proportions of occupation groups included in social insurance succeed in evading their contributions but are still able to obtain benefits, either as a result of frequent contribution amnesties or due to administrators' failure to identify evaders.[23] Furthermore, Latin American governments have frequently resorted to baling out social insurance funds which have run into financial problems. In the case of Mexico, the 1995 Social Security Law raised direct government funding of the main social insurance fund from

---

23   Mesa-Lago (1991a).

four to 33 per cent of its total income.[24] In Argentina, the government has over recent years provided substantial support to the ailing health insurance scheme for older people.[25] Finally, social insurance programmes usually capture a number of substantial indirect subsidies from the public health sector, such as the training of doctors and the dumping of chronic or expensive conditions on public hospitals.

The segmented structure of healthcare delivery systems has led to very large disparities in per capita financing. For example, in 1994 Mexico's social insurance fund for oil workers spent more than 20 times the per capita rate of the Ministry of Health.[26] In many cases, significant variation can also be found across the social insurance sector. Until recently Argentina contained several hundred separate funds, each with monopolistic ties to occupation groups. In 1994 average revenue per beneficiary in these funds ranged from US$5 to US$80. In recognition of this, a mechanism had been set up to redistribute resources between the funds, but this was found to actually worsen the disparities.[27]

These financing inequities translate into marked variations in the range and quality of services provided by different parts of the healthcare system. In many countries it is possible to observe a polarisation within the public sector, with a small number of world-class 'flagship' facilities (usually located in major cities), and a rump of poor quality, under-resourced services. Relatively privileged groups are often able to make selective use of the high quality parts of the public sector, and in some cases are able to crowd out poorer groups (especially when hospitals are granted financial autonomy to recover costs from patients).

Problems of equity have been exacerbated by the rapid growth of private insurance plans in the region.[28] The uncritical acceptance of such schemes, both on the part of policy-makers and the population at large, is a matter of concern. Often these funds are directly imported from the USA and Chile, both of whose health systems are notoriously inequitable. The capacity of Latin American states to regulate this burgeoning, complex and highly profitable industry is highly questionable. In Argentina, there is no official entity responsible for regulating or even over-seeing the private

---

24   Gómez-Dantés (2000).

25   Lloyd-Sherlock (1997a).

26   Gómez-Dantés (2000).

27   Barrientos and Lloyd-Sherlock (2000).

28   Stocker et al. (1999); EIU (1999).

health insurance sector.[29] No reliable data exist for affiliation, types of health plan or the quality of care, and there is considerable anecdotal evidence of widespread abuses by some insurers. The cheapest health plans, at around US$60 a month, are beyond the means of most Argentines, while premia for groups such as elderly people start at around US$150.

The sectoral fragmentation of healthcare in most countries is also associated with a marked bias towards expensive curative provision rather than more cost-effective areas, such as prevention, promotion and basic services. Neither the social nor private insurance sectors are inclined to emphasise the latter. Even in the public sector, there is little evidence of any reorientation towards primary healthcare. A study of Mexico's public sector estimated that 68 per cent of its resources were devoted to curative services between 1992 and 1994, and only seven per cent went to prevention.[30] Argentina has the highest ratio of doctors to per capita GDP in the world, yet easily preventable diseases such as Chagas' are still endemic in poor rural districts, and immunisation against conditions such as measles is well below that of neighbouring countries.[31] Such an approach to healthcare is both inefficient and concentrates resources on more privileged groups, rather than distribute them equitably.

Historical and Political Perspectives

The preceding sections have examined health inequities from a range of different perspectives, as far as the data allow. To understand some of the deeper causes of inequity, it is necessary to look at much wider historical and political processes of exclusion. Writing about social policy in the West, Lavalette and Pratt (1996) observe that 'social policies are intimately bound to the societies in which they develop and reflect the priorities of those systems'. The same can be said for healthcare in Latin America, a region which has historically been characterised much more by elitist political traditions than by pluralism and inclusion.[32] In this context, it may be more enlightening to examine cases where health policies have taken on a more equitable and universal hue, rather than focus on the wider backdrop of exclusion. In this way, it may be possible to identify a number of cir-

[29] Ahuad et al. (1999).
[30] Hernández et al. (1997).
[31] World Bank (1997).
[32] Wynia (1990); O'Donnell et al. (1986).

cumstances in which profoundly inegalitarian social and political systems take an interest in the health of poorer and less powerful groups.

One such spur to solidarity may arise when a health problem is perceived as a public risk against which privileged groups are unable to insulate themselves. Fears of epidemics of infectious diseases, such as cholera and yellow fever, were a driving force behind many of the early public health measures in the region. Often, these responses had a strongly authoritarian and repressive tinge, which viewed the poor as vectors of both moral and epidemiological infection.[33] The global HIV/AIDs pandemic could represent a contemporary health risk of a similar nature.[34] However, rates of seroprevalence remain relatively low in Latin America (0.5 per cent compared to over five per cent in Sub-Saharan Africa in mid 1996), and as yet HIV/AIDS has not come to be seen as a major health threat to privileged groups, saving some parts of Brazil. The region's most significant contemporary infectious diseases, such as Chagas', TB and dengue, are inherently unlikely to affect groups other than the poor. The low priority given these contrasts with the massive response to what were relatively small cholera outbreaks in the early 1990s (fresh fruit and ceviche are not only eaten by the poor). Rather than infectious disease, the main public health risk to richer groups is that of crime and violence. Along with road accidents, injury and death through crime and violence accounted for 40 per cent of Colombia's total burden of disease in 1994.[35] Even so, most studies of violence in the region show that poorer people are more likely to be affected.[36]

During the second third of the twentieth century the development of health services in Latin America was driven by a rapid growth of social insurance. This was associated with the 'selective populism' pursued by what were still essentially elitist systems, as part of a limited exercise of political legitimation and alliance building. A key element of this strategy was the extension of social protection to parts of the formal sector workforce. This occurred in a highly selective and stratified fashion, reflecting the complexity of power structures and alliance building.[37] The creation of national insurance funds dove-tailed with the human capital concerns of large employers who were keen that the burden of provision should not

33   Prieto (1996).

34   Izazola Licea (1997).

35   Yepes (2000).

36   Golbert and Kessler (2000).

37   Mesa-Lago (1978).

fall directly on themselves.[38] They were also supported by local and international pharmaceutical and medical equipment industries, which predicted the process would create the basis for a burgeoning and highly lucrative market. Moreover, in most countries the extension of health insurance was relatively costless for the state, since services were mainly funded by pension fund surpluses. This was a major contributory factor in the pension fund crises of the 1980s and 1990s.

Studies of social insurance in some developing countries outside the region claim that its gradual extension can be understood as a prelude to the creation of a more universal system.[39] There are few signs that this was the case in Latin America. Even in populist regimes where elite interests appeared, albeit temporarily, to be in abeyance, few efforts were made to include rural labour in the spoils being offered to other groups. For example, in Peronist Argentina strikes by sugar workers demanding greater social protection were violently put down. More was done for the rural sectors in Mexico under Cárdenas, but this proved to be short-lived, and provision lagged well behind provision for more powerful urban constituencies. In more recent years, few would dare to hope that these countries are still on the road to universal health insurance.

The use of health services as a tool of political legitimation had much to do with the segmentation of the region's healthcare systems, the pre-eminence of social insurance and the urban bias of provision. It also led to widespread problems of clientelism, political patronage and sometimes extreme corruption within individual parts of the health system. This has been particularly evident in the better-resourced social insurance sectors, parts of which are still struggling to overcome this unfortunate legacy. Argentina's health fund for pensioners, which manages an annual budget of over US$2 billion, has become notorious as a vehicle for political patronage and financial abuses on a grand scale. At the same time, its capacity to service affiliates has been steadily eroded.[40]

The above casts some light on the relationships between the development of health provision and wider political processes in Latin America. From this, it is clear that the commitment of states to extending effective healthcare has been highly conditional on a range of other factors, and should not simply be taken for granted. Current reformers should ask

[38]   Lewis (1993).
[39]   Mills (1998).
[40]   Bonvecchi et al. (1998); Lloyd-Sherlock (1997a).

themselves whether these relationships have changed significantly in recent years, and whether regardless of the rhetoric, states are any more committed to goals of equitable health than in the past.

Recent Reforms

Many Latin American countries have recently embarked on what are claimed to be sweeping reforms of the health sector. In some respects, this current wave of reforms should not be seen as a radical departure from the past. Most countries have a long history of (usually failed) attempts at fundamental healthcare reform. However, there are some important differences with previous experiences. First, there has been a shift away from primary healthcare and universalism towards policies that are more consonant with neoliberal agendas. This has involved radical changes in the role and responsibilities of the state. Second, multilateral lending agencies and finance ministries now play a much larger role in designing health reforms. As a result, the old reform language has been replaced by a three-way policy mantra of efficiency, equity and quality. All of these currents have contributed to the emergence of a recognisable health sector reform package, which includes redefining public and private spheres of action, as well as promoting new management strategies and decentralisation.[41] This package has been put forward as a coherent set of evidence-based, technical and politically neutral solutions to the region's many healthcare problems. However, the actual experiences of different countries in implementing the reforms and their impacts suggest that the reality is rather different.

Attempts to decentralise health services in Latin America illustrate the potential dangers of poorly conceived reforms. In theory, decentralisation should promote accountability, participation and responsiveness to local needs, and thus reduce exclusion.[42] However, the few published empirical appraisals show that it more often serves to foster inequality. Gonzalez-Block et al (1989) found that decentralising healthcare administration had significantly reduced service provision and utilisation for the poor in Mexico's two poorest states and increased it for the wealthy (who dominated local decision-making). Reducing central government financial responsibility for health services in Argentina has led to large disparities in per capita spend between different provinces.[43] Conversely, the author was

---

[41]   Homedes et al. (2000).

[42]   Mills et al. (1987).

[43]   Lloyd-Sherlock (2000b).

unable to find any case where decentralisation was proved to have promoted equity (however equity might be understood and measured).

Cost recovery schemes are another key weapon in the arsenal of health sector reform. These usually take the form of requiring patients to pay an out-of-pocket fee at the point of service. Theoretically, cost recovery may increase overall funding, and exemptions for poor and vulnerable groups reduce the risk of exclusion.[44] A study of user fees in public hospitals in Buenos Aires found that these operated through essentially informal arrangements, and that state regulation was almost entirely absent. Hospitals were given complete freedom to interpret the policy, and no systems were in place to protect the rights of vulnerable social groups.[45] As with decentralisation, this points to the dangers of implementing complex reforms in a context of weak state institutions and flawed governance.

In some countries reforms have sought to radically restructure the entire healthcare system, replacing its traditional segmentation with a new configuration. This includes reducing the divisions between social insurance and private insurance, while reasserting the role of public provision as a safety net of last resort. In Argentina the virtual merger between social insurance and private funds has meant that the previous stratification based on occupation group has been replaced by one based purely on income. Mexico's reforms have permitted private health funds to operate within a pluralistic social insurance sector, leading to a large-scale influx of US-based organisations targeting 'niche' population groups.[46] Across the region, the proliferation and high-profile marketing of personal health plans is changing the popular perception of healthcare from a public good to an item of private consumption.

Rather than upgrade the role of the publicly financed health sector, reforms have sought to reduce it to a decentralised, residual safety net. As such, it is likely that the gap between healthcare for groups with insurance and the rest of the population will widen. Moreover, in many countries rising poverty, unemployment and informal working will increase the size of the population lacking social insurance. There is an urgent necessity to invest substantial amounts in public health facilities which have been eroded over the past two decades. At the same time, reforms should seek to counter the strong bias towards curative services, strengthening areas such

[44]   World Bank (1993).

[45]   Lloyd-Sherlock and Novick (2001).

[46]   Laurell (2001).

as primary healthcare, prevention and health education. The role of the state as regulator of the health system as a whole remains highly questionable in most countries. As well as the new challenges created by the growth of private financing and provision, this includes issues such as environmental health and monitoring the responsibilities of employers in increasingly deregulated economies. Whilst advocates of reform pay much lip-service to state regulation, decentralisation and privatisation have tended to undermine what was already a weak capacity.

As with all aspects of social policy, the current wave of health reforms should be understood as part of much wider processes of social and economic transformation in Latin America. Deepening inequality and social exclusion do not give grounds for optimism that significant progress can be made towards equitable and socially inclusive health. There are inevitably lags between the shift towards neoliberal development models and their health impacts. However, it is likely that the effects of recent economic and social policy will become increasingly evident in the health status of poor and excluded groups. The prognosis for Latin America in the early twenty-first century is not good.

CHAPTER 9

Intergenerational Transfers in Income, Health and Social Security: The Experiences of Brazil, Mexico and Colombia

Maria Cristina Gomes da Conceição

Introduction

This chapter compares household income structure and intergenerational support in three countries — Brazil, Colombia and Mexico. It also analyses the institutional settings. Differences in institutional support, especially social, economic and institutional resources, define opportunities and limits to family support. In order to understand this interplay between macroeconomic and institutional settings and household patterns, these societies are compared through aggregated social indicators, household indicators and individual indicators. Brazilian society has a stronger social security system and formal labour market than Mexican and Colombian societies. Mexico compensates for the lack of institutional support and formal labour market with the North American Free Trade Agreement (NAFTA), emigration and remittances from the United States; Colombia's economy is influenced by informal and illegal activities, subsidies for adult generations and monetary donations among individuals.

Each institutional-household pattern offers different opportunities to each individual, according to their role in the household and according to their stage of life. Heads of household in the three countries mainly work in adulthood (in the formal or informal labour market).

Later on, most heads of household in Brazil retire, while the majority do not retire in Mexico and Colombia. Instead of receiving a pension, Mexican male heads of household keep on working until an advanced age, while their female counterparts receive financial support from relatives living in Mexico or abroad. Colombian male heads of household generally carry on working until the age of 65 after which retirement is progressively more frequent. Female heads of household do not retire, but generally receive donations.

In Brazil the universal coverage of the pension system guarantees homogeneity in the domestic income structure, while in Mexico and Colombia a very diversified income structure emerges among heads and other household members, showing important differences according to gender and the role assumed by individuals in the household.

Income and Social Benefits in each Society

Similarities in Socioeconomic and Political Contexts

There are a number of similarities among the three countries. Brazil, Mexico and Colombia are classified as medium income countries. Brazil and Mexico are in the upper-medium group and Colombia is a lower-medium income country.[1] In 1999 Brazil, Mexico and Colombia were in eighth, twelfth and thirty-seventh position in the world respectively as regards Gross National Product (see Table 9.1). The Colombian GNP is ten times lower than that of Brazil and seven times lower than that of Mexico. Historically, the annual rate of exports (in terms of volume and value) has grown at different rates, but it grew fastest in Mexico between 1929 and 1981. In the following period, from 1981 to 1995, this growth was higher in Colombia, compared to the other two countries.[2] The three countries have substantial external debt, but Colombia's is five and seven times higher than that of Mexico and Brazil, respectively . On the other hand, Brazil has the biggest population and GNP (Table 9.1).

The proportion of urban population is bigger in Brazil than in Mexico or Colombia. In 1990 the capital of Colombia, Bogotá, had a population of 5.7 million,[3] while Brazil and Mexico have had cities (Rio de Janeiro, São Paulo and Mexico City) of more than 10 million inhabitants since 1980, and these comprise some of the most important industrial and service centres in Latin America.[4]

a) In the three countries the formal labour market has never covered the Economically Active Population. In recent decades the formal labour market has decreased sharply, although labour laws are oriented exclusively to formal labour and labour policy is based on minimum wages.[5] Therefore, as citizenship is 'conditioned' to having a formal employment, social benefits are restricted to small and specific groups of the population.

b) Inequality in income distribution persists and poverty is still increasing even after significant falls in birth-rates (approximately from 6 to 2.5 children per woman in the last two decades in the three countries).[6]

---

1   World Bank (1997).

2   Thorp (1998a).

3   DANE (2000).

4   Miró (1984).

5   *Ibid.*; Maddison (1993).

6   For further information about fertility trends in Brazil, Mexico and Colombia, see Martine (1996), Zavala (1992) and Rodríguez and Hobcraft (1990), respectively. Relationships between declines in fertility and poverty in Latin America are studied by Carvalho and Wood (1988), Stern and Tuirán (1993); United Nations (1991).

c) Housing is financed and built mainly by the private sector and is most-
    ly inadequate.[7] The proportion of owners is slightly higher in Mexico
    (68 per cent) than in Brazil (62 per cent).[8]

d) Population in the three countries shows low levels of education and
    an unequal distribution of education by sex and social groups.[9]

Table 9.1: Macroeconomic and Demographic Indicators

	Brazil	Mexico	Colombia
Population 1991 (millions)	151	83	33
Population 1999 (millions) [1]	168	97	42
Urban Population (%)	81	74	73
GNP Increase (% 1970–80)	8.1	6.3	5.4
GNP Increase (% 1980–91)	2.5	1.2	3.7
GNP 1970 (millions of dollars)	35.5	38.3	7.2
GNP 1991 (millions of dollars)	414.1	282.5	41.7
GNP 1999 (millions of dollars) [1]	742.8	428.8	93.6
GNP Rank in 1999[1]	8th	12th	37th
GNP per capita 1991	2,940	3,030	1,260
GNP per capita 1999[1]	4,420	4,040	2,250
External Debt 1990 (millions)	120	104	17
External Debt 1998 (millions) [1]	232	160	33
External Debt as % of GNP 1999[1]	29	39	32

Public Expenditures (% GDP)	1980 1991	1980 1991	1980 1991
Total	20.9 35.1	17.4 18.1	13.5 15.1
Defence	4.0 3.5	2.3 2.4	6.7 —
Education	— 3.1	18.0 13.9	19.1 —
Health	8.0 6.7	2.4 1.9	3.9 —
Housing, Leisure and Welfare	32.0 25.0	18.5 13.0	21.2 —
Economic Services	24.0 3.2	31.2 13.4	27.1 —
Other	32.0 57.9	27.6 55.5	22.0 —

Source: World Bank (1993d)

1 World Bank (2000a)

---

7   For further information about the quality of housing in Mexico see Martha Schteingart and
    Camas (1998), and for Colombia see interview with Puyana (2001).
8   Maddison (1993).
9   World Bank (2000).

Differences in Inequalities among Countries

In spite of these similarities, there are important differences in levels of inequality between the countries. Distribution of income and resources has been dramatically unequal between areas, households and individuals in the three countries. However, Brazil has one of the most acute levels of income inequality in the world. In 1998 the Gini Index of inequity was higher in Brazil (60) and Colombia (57) than in Mexico (54) (see Table 9.2). Different sources of information reveal a range of indicators of inequity, which confirm the worse social situation in Brazil,[10] compared to Mexico and Colombia.[11]

Land distribution is more equitable in Mexico.[12] Taxes and transfers are more progressive in Mexico, with several benefits and subsidies; even though their distribution is selective. Brazil shows the most regressive economy compared to the other two countries.[13]

The level of education has increased to a greater degree in Mexico[14] over the last five decades, compared to Brazil.[15] In 1998 the adult illiteracy rate for both sexes was 16 per cent in Brazil as against nine per cent in Colombia. In Mexico only seven per cent of men and 11 per cent of women were illiterate in that year (Table 9.2).

Although the Economically Active Population represents a similar proportion of population in the three countries, the proportion of the labour force comprising the Economically Active Population is higher in Brazil and Colombia, and female participation in the labour force is higher in these two countries, compared to Mexico.

In 1995 formal work was much more frequent in Brazil than in Mexico or Colombia, for both sexes (Table 9.2). In spite of women working substantially

---

[10] See World Bank (1996, 1997a, 2000a) and United Nations bulletins from 1993 to 1999.

[11] Some authors argue that Mexicans compensate for poverty with the option to emigrate temporarily to the USA in search of work and higher salaries (Maddison, 1993; Wong, Soldo and Capoferro, 2000).

[12] Land distribution has been an important element deriving from the revolution, and it legitimated the Mexican political system for decades. This has been a 'weak point' for various Brazilian and Colombian governments up to the present day (Maddison, 1993; Gutelman, 1978; and Camacho, 1980).

[13] Subsidies as income distribution mechanisms represented 6.1 per cent of the GDP in Brazil, more than two times than Mexico (14.1 per cent of the GDP) (Maddison, 1993).

[14] Improvements in levels of literacy in Mexico began some years after the Revolution and reached a maximum between 1930 and 1980. In Colombia the maximum was reached between 1950 and 1974 (Cataño, 1989), but in Brazil only between 1950 and 1990. Historically the Mexican educational system has persisted and extended its coverage, promoting a better distribution of education among areas and citizens, compared to other Latin American countries such as Brazil (Thorp, 1998a).

[15] Maddison (1993).

less than men in the three countries, the percentage of women in the labour force differs according to their role in the household. Higher proportions of female household heads were working in Colombia and Mexico[16] than in Brazil. However, there are greater proportions of spouses working in Brazil than in Mexico or Colombia. [17]

Table 9.2: Socioeconomic and Demographic Indicators

Populational Data	Brazil	Mexico	Colombia
Gini Index 1996	60	54*	57
EAP – Age 15–64 as per cent of total population 1999	65	62	63
Labour Force as per cent of EAP 1999	72	67	69
Females as per cent of labour force 1999	35	33	38
Total Fertility Rate 1998	2.3	2.8	2.7
Contraceptive prevalence rate 1998	77	65	72
Life expectancy at birth (years) 1998			
Males	63	69	67
Females	71	75	73
Infant mortality rate (per 1,000 live births)			
1980	70	51	41
1998	33	30	23
Adult illiteracy rate (per cent) 1998			
Males	16	7	9
Females	16	11	9

Source: World Bank (2000a)
* 1995 data
Formal Labour as per cent of labour force are own calculations from PNAD/1995 (IBGE); ENIGH/1994 (INEGI); ENIG/1994/1995 (DANE).

History and Rules: Unequal Distribution of Institutional Benefits in Social Security

In all three countries the social security system has been created from the corporative insurance system and savings cooperatives, which have been

---

[16]   In Brazil proportions of female heads of household are 54 per cent, 34 per cent and three per cent, at between 20–39, 40–59 or over 60 years old respectively. For the same age groups, Mexican female heads are present in greater proportions: 56 per cent, 46 per cent and 19 per cent, respectively (Gomes, 2000). And 51 per cent of all Colombian female heads of household work.

[17]   Gomes (2000).

centralised by governments at different times. In Mexico a significant process of incorporation of corporative systems began in 1941 with Lazaro Cárdenas' government, in Colombia centralisation occurred in 1946 through a National Congress decision, and in Brazil they were finally centralised by the military dictatorship in 1967.[18]

Centralised systems developed standard norms, according to the specific economic and political context in each country. Taxes are paid in different proportions, by employers (80 per cent in Brazil, 70 per cent in Mexico and 74 per cent in Colombia), workers (20 per cent in Brazil, 25 per cent in Mexico and 26 per cent in Colombia), and government (ten per cent in Brazil, five per cent in Mexico).[19]

These resources have been invested and directed by subsequent nationalist governments that centralised health and pensions resources in corporative institutes and used these resources to promote industrialisation and welfare.[20] The main social security benefits are pensions (in cash) and health resources and services.

Between the 1950s and 1970s decreases in mortality[21] and fertility led to increases in the economically active population, and the political economy of import substitution industrialisation increased rates of formal employment in the three countries. These two associated trends promoted increases in the number of taxpayers and in tax values, with the doubling of the taxes collected through the social security system. In the next period, in the 1980s and 1990s, tax collection fell due to falls in formal employ-

---

[18]   For the history of the Brazilian social security system see Oliveira and Fleury (1989) and Lewis (2000); for Mexico see García Cruz (1962); for Colombia see H. Jaramillo (1994).

[19]   For further information on Brazil see Beltrão et al. (1996), for Mexico see Gomes (1997). In Colombia the level of participation of the government in taxation depended on the type of system – solidarity or individual saving system (Law no.100).

[20]   'Military administrations favoured institutional consolidation and a massive expansion of the social insurance regime in order to expand mechanisms of forced savings'. And 'social insurance was subsumed within a larger social policy framework of state provision of social goods and social services – education, healthcare, social assistance, social security and housing' (Lewis, 2000). Regarding the health system, most of the services and hospitals in the three countries were built with resources derived from social security, corporative insurance and savings cooperatives in Latin America, with the aim of developing human capital among associates (see Oliveira and Fleury, 1989).

[21]   Increased life expectancy in Latin America is the result of improvements in health resources and services. Between the 1940s and 1970s life expectancy increased by more than 15 years in the three countries, due mainly to improvements in healthcare (antibiotics and immunisation). Between 1969 and 1979 life expectancy in these populations increased by a further five years, because of health improvements on the one hand, but also because better income, education and nutrition contributed to a decrease in mortality (Over, 1992).

ment, in the number of taxpayers and reduction in wages and tax values. On the other hand, expenses tripled due to the Latin American economic crisis, reinforced by inflation and increases in the number of beneficiaries (related to increased life expectancy). Currently, most of these taxpayers have survived beyond 60 years of age and have retired.[22] These results were not as envisaged in the 1940s, when average life expectancy stood at about 40 in all three countries.[23] Co-habitation among couples and the accumulation of several generations simultaneously force institutions to recalculate intergenerational transfers.

Pension criteria are different in Brazil, where retirement is based on the period of time worked (30 years for women and 35 for men). On the other hand, in Mexico and Colombia retirement is based on age: 55 for women and 60 for men in Colombia, 65 for both sexes in Mexico. Pension values are mainly at around the minimum wage: 70 per cent of retired people in Brazil, 90 per cent in Mexico and 40 per cent in Colombia receive one minimum wage or less.[24] This trend towards homogeneity hides a paradox: although small and powerful groups account for most social security resources receiving high pensions,[25] the majority who receive one minimum wage gain great advantages from this small income. Beltrão at al. (2000a) observe the social impact of low pensions in Brazilian rural areas, where this income has empowered elderly individuals in economic and domestic relationships.

Over the last ten years each country has experienced different reforms in its social security system. In Brazil the current government could not eliminate the principle of retirement based on years worked because of corporative and politic pressures and in the end reforms merely offered the option to retire after 30 years of working, with proportional benefits at different ages.[26] In Mexico the reform transferred the public and solidarity funds to individual accounts in private banks.[27] In Colombia the reform of the pensions system created two non-exclusive solidarity funds,

---

[22]   Gomes (1997); H. Jaramillo (1994); Ruezga Barba (1994); Beltrão at al. (1996); F. Oliveira (1994).

[23]   For further information about mortality in these countries see Livi-Bacci (1990 and 1992); Camposortega (1993); and Antunes (1993).

[24]   For further information about Brazil see Beltrão et al. (1996, 2000); on Mexico see Gomes (1997); for Colombia data is calculated from INEGI (1994/1995).

[25]   For example, Beltrão et al. (1994, 1996) show that in Brazil a small group of retired workers from the legislative and judicial system receive more than 30 times the minimum wage as a pension, and account for a high percentage of the total expenditure on pensions in the social security system.

[26]   See Beltrão et al. (2000).

[27]   See Laurell (1996, 1997).

both managed by government: one being a 'defined benefits regime' and the other an 'individual saving regime'. Clients (beneficiaries) can switch between systems (Law no. 100).

Limited results of reforms to solve shortages in social security systems led to alternative solutions, created especially by the socially excluded. Mexico compensates for informal labour, low wages and deficiencies in the social security system with the North American Free Trade Agreement (NAFTA) and emigration to the United States. Colombia compensates for the shortfall with illegal commerce. In Brazil there is a trend for individuals to keep on working after retirement. Although Mexico and Colombia could not universalise pensions and health benefits, they do have a significantly better performance in education and per capita income distribution compared to Brazil. Moreover, Mexico has much better health results in terms of life expectancy and infant mortality, as well as better land distribution and broad subsidies. Brazil is ahead only in the universal coverage of pensions and healthcare. As a result, there are different political and institutional contexts in which Brazilians have disadvantages in income distribution, education and health results, compared to Colombians, and more still compared to Mexicans. In other words, Brazilian families have fewer monetary and social resources in their daily life, except in terms of getting pensions.

In terms of combined results, Mexico shows a lower total and female participation in the labour force, lower contraceptive use and higher fertility. However, some social indicators such as the Gini Index, life expectancy and infant mortality indicate better results in health and equity in Mexico, compared to Colombia and Brazil. The same social indicators in Brazil confirm that it lags behind most Latin American countries.

The Appropiation of Institutional and Labour Resources and Benefits by Social Actors

In this section the concept of social reproduction is applied to analyse the unequal distribution of resources and benefits, and the ways that social actors use these resources in the domestic sphere. The social structure is conceptualised as a mix of roles[28] and resources,[29] implicit in the social process of social reproduction. The conditions described previously shape contexts that have specific socioeconomic, institutional and labour characteristics in every

---

[28]　Rules are 'generalisable procedures' known and used by actors in several circumstances, as a formula that orients their actions and social relationships.

[29]　In this article we analyse only monetary resources.

unequal society. The unequal distribution of economic and institutional resources in each society close and open different opportunities for social actors in their daily life, in several ways. At the same time, as social actors are able to change their circumstances, they use, appropriate, reproduce and transform the rules and resources available in the social structure.

The domestic positions and resources of each individual in the household are articulated to examine the patterns of this process of resource appropriation. Typical and atypical shapes of distribution of rules and resources emerge in domestic relationships, with different combinations of normative and non-normative patterns, specific to each member of the household: heads, spouses, children and other relatives.

Patterns of Distribution of Rules and Resources in Domestic Relationships

The distribution of monetary resources in domestic relationships is taken from National Surveys of Income and Expenditures that provide information about domestic economy.[30]

The norm among adult men is to be the household head and to receive a wage (formal or informal) in much higher proportions than women in the three countries do. Adult women are mainly spouses and the majority do not work.[31]

However, in Brazil this pattern changes progressively with age. Most householdheads of both sexes over 60 years old are retired. The proportion of Brazilian heads who receive other types of income is very low: some women heads receive donations, mainly at the beginning of the life course, while some men receive investments during their active life (see Figure 9.1).

[30]   Sources of information are: PNAD/1995 (IBGE); ENIGH/1994 (INEGI); ENIG/1994/1995 (DANE). These surveys offer information about types and level of income. In this section the income structure is studied by types, for different members of the household and according to their domestic role. The type of income (presence or absence) is taken into account to construct income structures for heads, spouses, children and other relatives of the head. In each country there are different questions and different available data about types of income. In all countries people were asked about income from formal and informal work, pensions, investments and donations. However, there is only information about international remittances for Mexico, and only information about alimony and subsidies for Colombia. The level of income for each type of income is also different. However, it is not the main focus of analysis in this section. The level of income will be considered in the next section.

[31]   Gomes (2000).

Figure 9.1: Heads of Households' Income Structure by Sex and Age

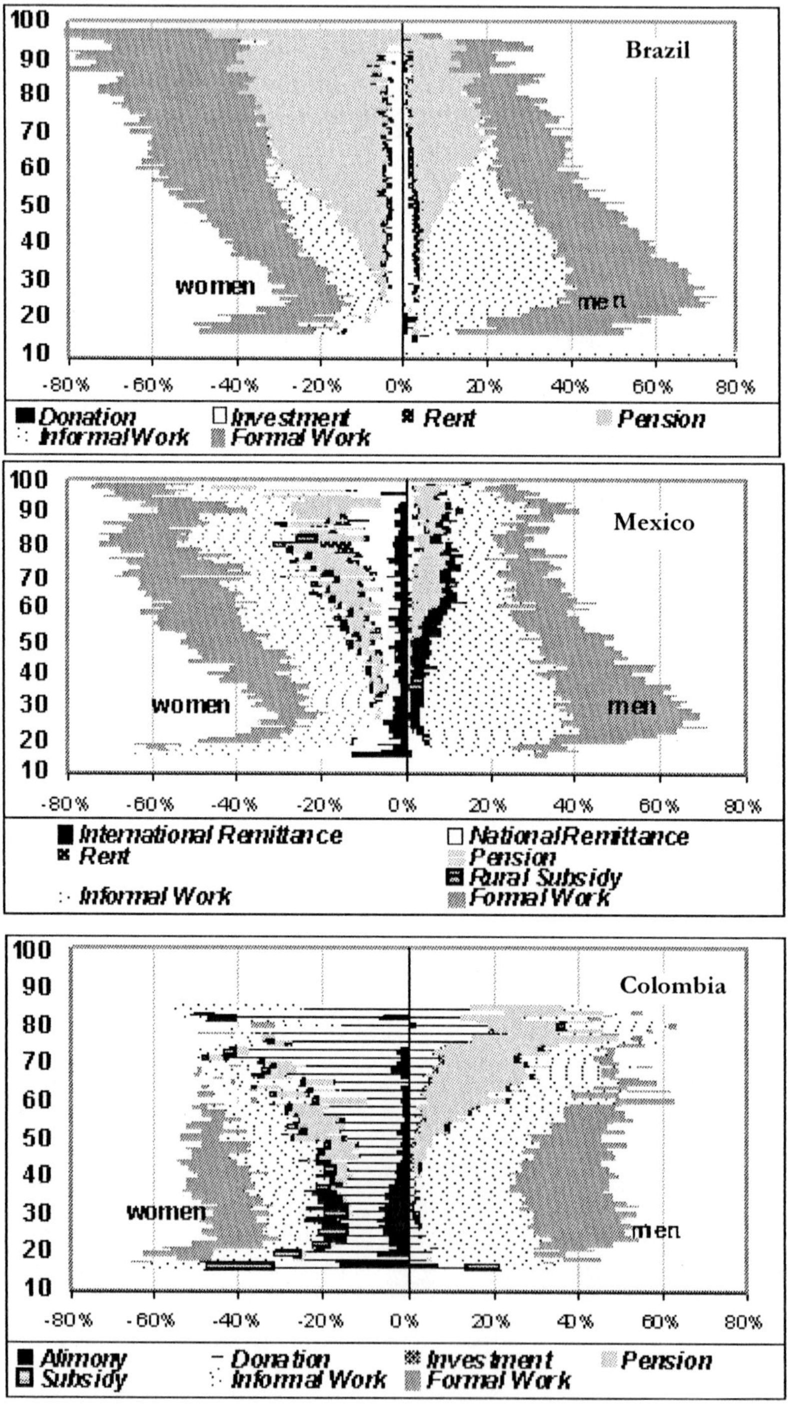

Brazil

women   men

| -80% | -60% | -40% | -20% | 0% | 20% | 40% | 60% | 80% |

■ Donation   □ Investment   ▩ Rent   ▨ Pension
∴ Informal Work   ▨ Formal Work

Mexico

women   men

| -80% | -60% | -40% | -20% | 0% | 20% | 40% | 60% | 80% |

■ International Remittance   □ National Remittance
▩ Rent
            ▨ Pension
            ▩ Rural Subsidy
∴ Informal Work
            ▨ Formal Work

Colombia

women   men

| -80% | -60% | -40% | -20% | 0% | 20% | 40% | 60% | 80% |

■ Alimony   – Donation   ▩ Investment   ▨ Pension
▨ Subsidy   ∴ Informal Work   ▨ Formal Work

In Mexico the normative pattern for male household heads is to work in all phases of the life course, to an advanced age. Heads of both sexes work and get wages in all the age groups. In adulthood, substantial proportions of male heads receive support from Procampo.[32] However, even at advanced ages the majority of male and female heads keep on working and do not retire. Therefore, a higher diversification of income structure appears from a young age, persisting and increasing until the end of the life course. At advanced ages diversification of sources of income is the most important trend: retirement, national and foreign remittances are common among male and female heads .

Differences between countries are mainly due to the level of cover of formal employment and pension system. In Brazil the formal labour market and the pensions system cover the majority of workers and those who are retired. Therefore, this institutionalised context homogenises the domestic income pattern, according to the phase of the life course — formal work at the beginning and retirement at the end of the life course shape a homogeneous pattern for male and female heads of household. In Mexico and Colombia the higher levels of informal employment do not permit the majority to retire. Therefore, actors have to look for other types of income at advanced ages. In Mexico common alternatives are agricultural support (Procampo) in adult life, and national and international remittances at the end of the life course. In Colombia male and female heads mainly work in the informal labour market during adult life, but only men retire at an advanced age. Women receive donations, alimony and subsidies throughout adulthood, and at an advanced age the main pattern is to receive mainly monetary donations from other individuals.

As non-head of household spouses are mainly women,[33] only wives are analysed. In Brazil many wives have formal employment, and after the age of 60 a substantial proportion retire. On the contrary, in Mexico wives work more in informal employment, and they keep on working to an advanced age, while a substantial proportion receive national remittances. In Mexico they work or receive subsidies in adult life and receive mainly donations towards the end of the life course(see Figure 9.2).

---

[32] Procampo is a government subsidy programme,to improve land productivity in agriculture.

[33] Non-head of household spouses are mainly women. However, there is a small proportion of men who assume the role of partner in the household in all three countries (less than 10 per cent of the total of spouses). Their income structure is shown but this result is not analysed.

Figure 9.2: Spouses' Income Structure by Sex and Age

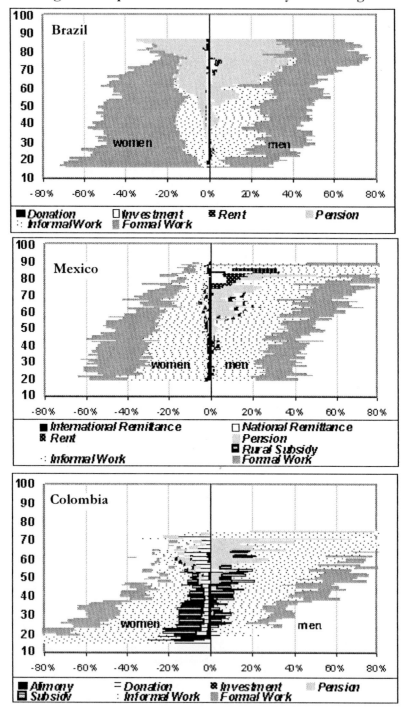

Figure 9.3: Children's Income Structure by Sex and Age

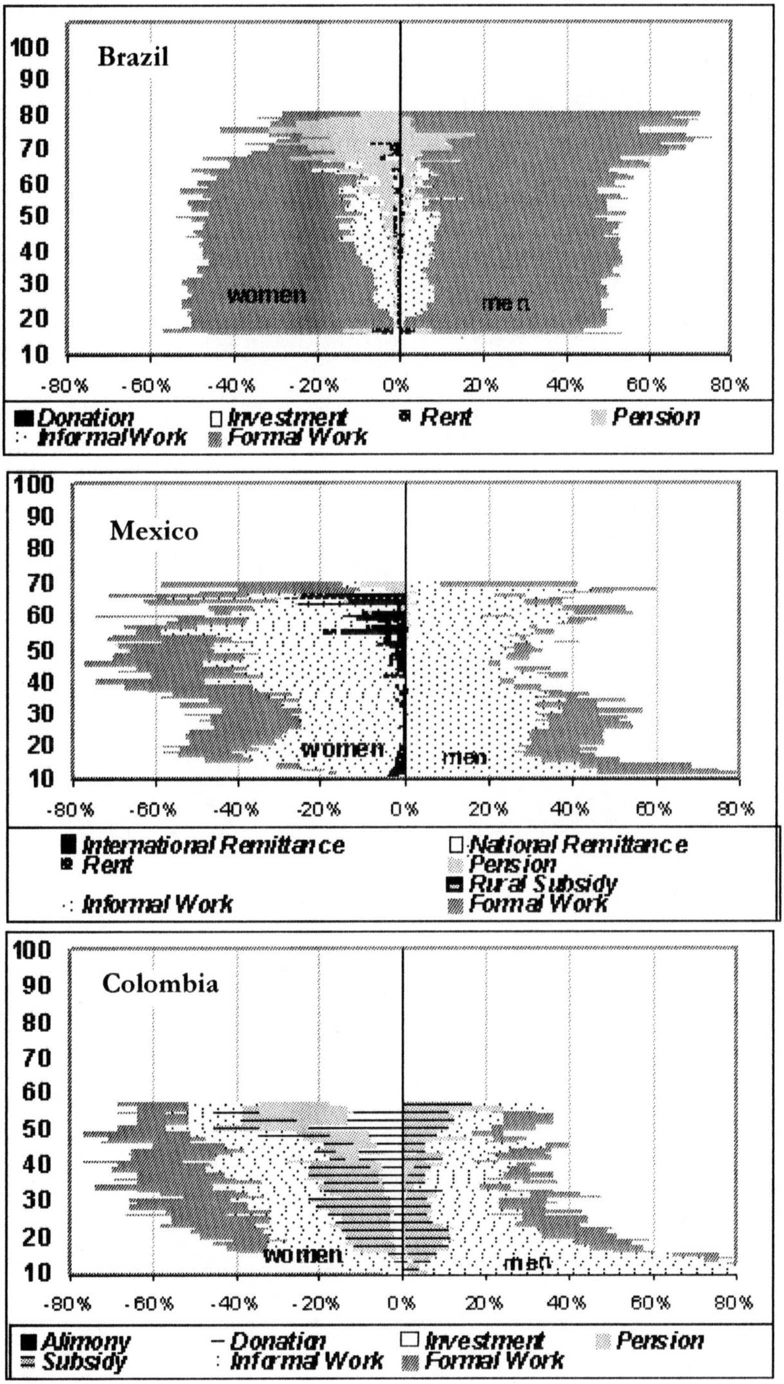

Figure 9. 4: Other Relatives' Income Structure by Sex and Age

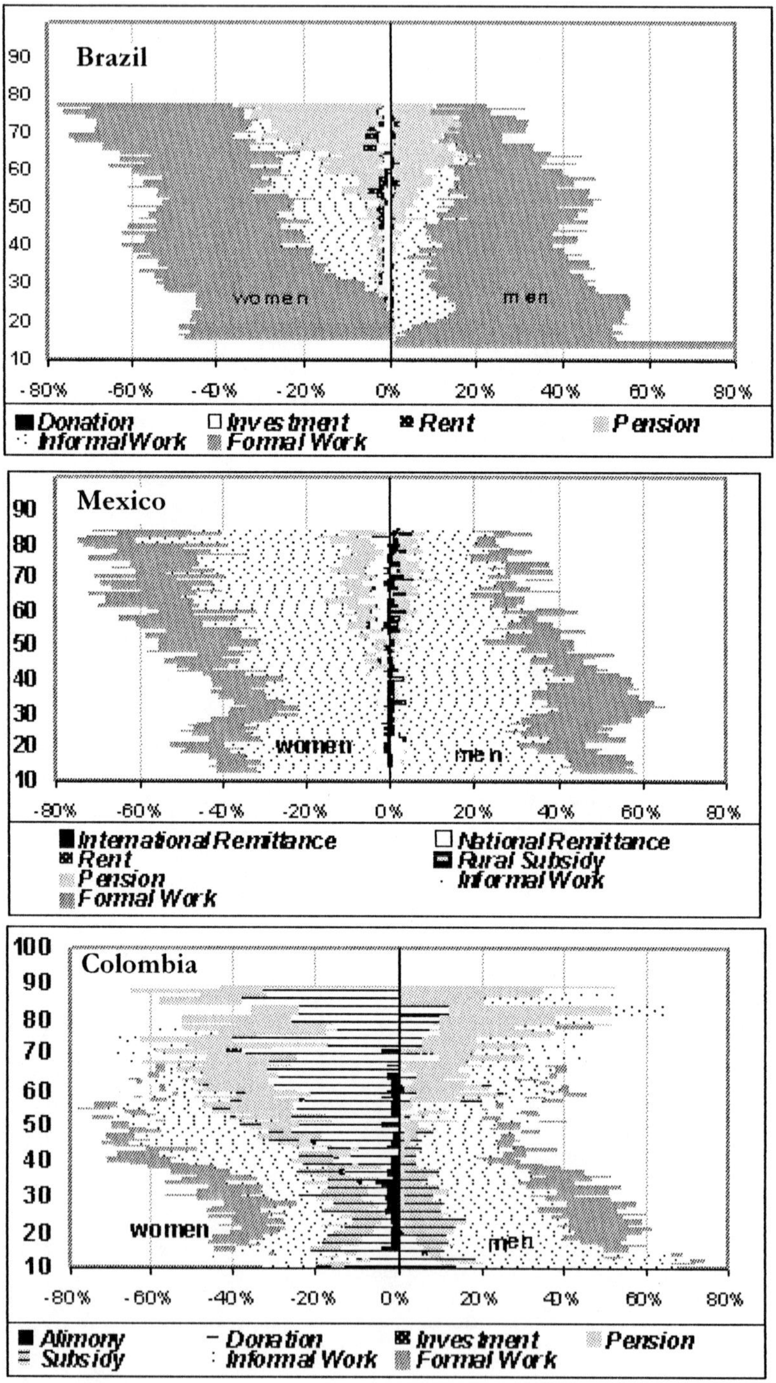

Adults who live with parents work, and trends reproduce the formal pattern and institutional retirement, especially for women in Brazil. The informal labour market and other sources of income are very frequent in Mexico, especially Procampo for men and international remittances for adult women and older children in the household. In Colombia informal work and subsidies hardly affect the typical pattern of income among children from adulthood to old age (see Figure 9.3).

Other relatives reveal a similar formal and institutional income pattern in Brazil, an informal and non-institutional pattern in Mexico, and an informal and subsidised income pattern in Colombia, where donations act as alternatives to interchange among individuals(see Figure 9.4).

Co-residence and Intergenerational Transfers

The next section analyses one type of intergenerational support — co-residence of individuals between the ages of 30 and 59 and individuals of over 60,[34] that is generations of adults and elderly individuals who live in the same domestic space. At present Brazil, Mexico and Colombia are in the third phase of the demographic transition, life expectancy has increased progressively, intergenerational crossover is more likely,[35] and co-residence is a type of intergenerational support. Multivariate models are used in order to uncover the different weights of demographic and socioeconomic elements in the development of intergenerational co-residence. Variables in the model are individual characteristics of the elderly individual of the household[36] and characteristics of the domestic group, indicating the conditions under which each generation gives or receives transferences.

The socioeconomic inequality in developing countries is taken into account, in conjunction with the probability of co-residence and its breakdown. In this way a main question is: how and under what conditions

[34]   Intergenerational transfers encompass interchanges among individuals, households, generations and institutions. Types of intergenerational support include financial transfer, health and physical care, interchanges of domestic and public services, co-residence, etc. (Tuiran and Wong, 1994; Soldo and Hill, 1995).

[35]   At present several Latin American countries are in the third phase of demographic transition, where there is a large proportion of adults as compared to infants, the young and the elderly. In the next two decades the current large adult generation will age, and the median age of the population will increase progressively (Livi-Bacci, 1990, 1992).

[36]   In these developing countries there are no specific surveys to study co-residence, and a proxy method was developed to use real, but limited, data. All households that have at least one elderly individual were selected (therefore, it is possible to use these individuals' characteristics for all cases in the sample). However, only some households have an adult individual (the co-residence cases), other household do not (the no co-residence cases), and it is not possible to use adult characteristics in this model.

dogenerations of adults and elderly individuals divide the household space in developing countries? There are three important domains to be taken into account in this discussion:

1. The sociological hypothesis about the evolution of types of family assumes that the increase in individualism and drop in the value of the family in modern societies promote falling levels of marriage and rising divorce rates. Therefore, extended or co-resident households would be less likely today than in the past. They are considered to be indicators of modernisation. Indicators linked to this hypothesis are having a partner (married or otherwise) and levels of education. [37]

2. Demographic factors affect the explanation of intergenerational co-residence. Increases in life expectancy allow the intersection of parents, adult children and grandchildren, because co-habitation could increase the availability of relatives to co-reside. This intersection promotes changes in intergenerational, institutional and domestic commitments and expectations. The demographic indicators are age and sex.[38]

3. Moreover, economic factors are also part of this explanation. Even though individuals prefer to live in their own household, away from their parents, the capacity to fulfil this preference is restricted by economic opportunities and limits. Therefore, the decision to live in a separate household depends on the ability to pay for and to maintain an independent household. Type of individual income, level of household income and area of residence are some socioeconomic indicators.[39]

Socioeconomic and demographic indicators are independent variables in the model, whereas the dependent variable (to be explained) is the co-residence between two generations: adult individuals between the ages of 30 and 59, and elderly individuals over 60 who live in the same household.

Co-residence among Generations — Related to Some Types and Levels of Income

Among atypical households,[40] intergenerational co-residence represents a type of interchange among generations. In Brazil co-residence occurs mainly among

---

[37]   Goody (1969 and 1972)

[38]   Goldani (1989); Tuiran and Wong (1994); Soldo and Hill (1995); Grundy (1999).

[39]   *Ibid.*

[40]   In all three countries most households are nuclear and biparental (parents with children), the typical domestic arrangement. But there are also atypical arrangements: nuclear and mono-parental, co-resident, unipersonal and empty-nest households (Gomes, 2000).

those individuals over 60 who are getting on in age, those with a low level of education and those who work or receive donations and investment income, and in households with a higher adult-equivalent income (see Table 9.3).

Table 9.3: Odds Ratio for Co-Residence between Individuals over 60 and Individuals 30–59 Years Old (Not the Partner of the Head)

		EXP. B	
	Brazil	Mexico	Colombia
1. Age and Sex			
Men 60–69	Reference		
Men 70–79	1.56***	1.75***	0.72
Men 80+	1.76***	0.42***	1.13
Women 60–69	0.92	2.00***	1.12
Women 70–79	1.65***	2.33***	1.94***
Women 80+	1.23*	1.16	1.02
2. Marital Status			
Divorced	Reference		
Widow	1.33***	—	—
Married	0.31***	—	—
3. Level of Education			
Illiterate	Reference		—
Uncompleted Basic School	2.75***	1.39**	—
Completed Basic School	2.48***	1.23	Reference
High School or more	1.80***	1.20	1.71***
4. Kind of Income			
Work	0.63***	0.49***	0.88
Pension	0.91	0.80	0.94
Investment	0.33*	0.80	0.94
Rent	2.45	0.59*	—
Donation (included National Remittance)	0.46***	0.40***	1.46***
International Remittance	—	0.31***	—
Alimony	—	—	0.56
Subsidy	—	—	0.43**
5. Level of Income			
No Income	Reference		
1/3 Minimum Wage	0.12***	2.00***	Reference
3/5 M. Wage	1.09***	1.80***	0.19***
5/8 M. Wage	2.95***	3.60**	0.49***
9+ M. Wage	9.96***	7.01***	1.13
6. Rent of Residence			
Rent			
7. Area of Residence			
Rural	Reference		
Urban		0.81	
-2Log Likelihood initial=23682.54	18402.04	2700.04	22549.72
Fitness	18156.43	2557.67	18907.13
–2LL	5265.87***	360.32***	1132.82***
% no co-residence	90.15	94.63	96.80
% co-residence	46.52	36.18	8.28
% Total	76.08	74.63	68.26

* p< 0.05, ** p< 0.01, *** p< 0.001

In Mexico co-residence is not always higher at more advanced ages. It is less likely among men over 80 than among men of 60 to 69 (the reference group). Co-residence is more likely among women than among men, among elderly individuals who work or receive donations than among those who do not and it is more likely in households with a higher adult-equivalent income. Elderly individuals who receive rents and remittances show a lower probability of co-residence than elderly individuals who do not receive theses types of income (Table 9.3).

Colombia shows a very different pattern of intergenerational co-residence compared to the two other countries: the age and sex of elderly individuals are not related to co-residence, but the higher the level of education and donations of the elderly increase the probability of co-residence. On the other hand, a higher level of adult-equivalent income in the household decreases the probability of intergenerational co-residence (Table 9.3).

In Brazil and Mexico intergenerational co-residence is related to ageing, female relativesand the higher availability of resources. As a special case, in Mexico, co-residence is related to the ageing process, but only up to the age of 80. After this age co-residence is not a likely type of interchange among generations. Therefore, the relationship between the higher level of income and co-residence is not clear. Do the benefits of intergenerational co-residence end when people reach the age of 80 in Mexico? Or are elderly individuals abandoned by adult generations at advanced ages?[41] On the other hand, in Colombia co-residence is not as related to a more advanced age or the higher availability of resources, but it is more likely among elderly individuals who receive donations from other.

In other words, ageing in contemporaneous developing societies leads to an intergenerational crossroads, but it does not necessary imply intergenerational co-residence in extended households. In Brazil and Mexico co-residence emerges among elderly individuals with better positions in the income and social structure, but it is not frequent among individuals who need to receive monetary donations. This set of results indicates that in Brazil and Mexico there is the same trend observed in developed countries: co-residence occurs in households in which individuals of over 60 have a higher level of resources and can meet the needs of adult co-residents.

---

[41]   In spite of rates of institutionalisation in *asilos* (old peoples homes) being very low in Mexico (see, for example, Gomes, 1998), some authors show that in Mexico there are strong problems in commitments across generations. Reyes (1999) and Blasco and Varley (2001) analyse small Mexican communities and observe specific cases of intergenerational competition due to restricted land, resulting in domestic expulsion, abandonment and abuse towards the elderly from their adult relatives.

Some 'modernisation characteristics' indicate the opposite of this hypothesis: divorced (a data available in Brazil only) and better-educated individuals over 60 (in Brazil and Colombia) have higher probabilities of co-residence with adult generations in extend households. On the other hand, these results indicate that socioeconomic and demographic factors affect the explanation of this phenomenon.

CHAPTER 10

Ideology and the New Social Security in Argentina

Rubén M. Lo Vuolo

Introduction

The notion of ideology refers to a set of beliefs at once both justificatory and explanatorythat helps to make assessments and make sense of situations arising in the environment in which people lead their lives. According to the 'weakest' of its meanings, such a concept is neutral, as opposed to what is 'pragmatic', where doctrinairism and dogma prevail. In its 'strongest' version, the ideas around ideology have been blended with notions of falseness, alluding to images of the world as determined mainly by domination relations in a society.[1]

Ideology has always been a driving force for social research and regulatory prescriptions in terms of public policy. Nevertheless, this is often hidden while it claims a sort of indisputable truth and proven technical consistency in certain generally accepted formulations, in particular when such formulations are communicated by 'experts' sitting in institutions and holding posts that give them acknowledged political power. Moreover, the 'the end of ideologies' belief has been popularised by making reference to a seemingly universal agreement on the interpretations and procedures required for the organisation of modern societies.

Such beliefs, being fundamentally ideological, are nothing new. Back in the 1950s and 1960s they already provided a rich source of debate.[2] However, at the time the 'end of ideologies' tended to refer to a synthesis based on welfare state institutions, as an essential part of a mixed economy and political pluralism. Nowadays, in contrast, a similar prophecy is used to give support to policies advocating the retrenchment of the welfare state.[3]

This has to do with a paradigm shift from the organisation principles that have provided an identity and outlined the development processes for modern societies.[4] This new paradigm comes across as 'conventional' ideology,

---

1   See Stoppino (1998), pp. 755–70.
2   Remember, for instance, the popular work by Bell (1964).
3   See Pierson (1994). For the Argentine case, see Lo Vuolo (1998).
4   My idea of paradigm here is similar to the one set out by Kuhn (1962) to analyse the history and the role of scientific 'communities' in the development of science. This deals with interpretation models that provide convenient solutions to certain problems for a period of time. The notion of

designating a set of opinions and procedures that see themselves as true postulates out of convenience or the defence of certain groups' interests.

Conventional ideology is more in tune with the strongest view of the concept and, in my opinion, it is the most consistent when it comes to explaining the paradigm shift in social security that has been taking place in Latin America in the last couple of decades. I have named this new conventional ideology in the field of pensions as 'New Pension Orthodoxy' (NPO).[5]

The NPO is an essential feature of the multiple and conservative criticism of welfare state social protection models. Even though such criticism comes mostly from industrialised countries, it is in Latin America and Eastern Europe where all of its practical varieties have been experienced. Thus, in terms of pensions, the reference that is inevitably invoked is the Chilean experience of 1981 under the dictatorship of Augusto Pinochet, along with the successive reforms throughout Latin America inspired by the Chilean model. These reforms have coincided in doing away with the exclusivity of 'Pay-As-You-Go' (PAYG) public systems. They have differed from one another, though, in that they have been totally or partially substituted or supplemented by a private scheme of individual fully-funded pension funds (IFF).[6]

The Chilean model would be at the extreme of total substitution and should be the ultimate goal for the NPO. The privately managed pension funds companies (AFPs for the Chilean case and AFJPs for the Argentine case) collect mandatory contributions plus a commission and a premium for disability and survivors insurance. The accumulated funds are invested in the financial markets. They comply with specific regulations under the control of a state supervisory agency. Given the fact that they manage a 'defined contribution' plan, the value of the future pensions is uncertain and it will depend on the rate of return of the pension assets, on the contributions made by the workers throughout their whole working life and on the actuarial methods used to estimate the regular benefits (which are associated with the life expectancy of the insured and their dependants). The government adds on 'recognition bonds' on account of the contributions made to the old

---

'principles of organisation' is taken from Habermas (1973, p. 7). It refers to very abstract regulations and properties characterising a particular degree of social development; coming about in non-evolutionary leaps. These principles limit a society's capacity to learn and change without losing its identity.

5   Lo Vuolo (1996) The idea of orthodoxy implies a general conformity to the current doctrine in terms of pensions and it refers to Latin America. Orthodoxy may be different in other cases.

6   The Chilean model would be 'substitutive', together with Bolivia (1997), Mexico (1997) and El Salvador (1997). Peru (1993) and Colombia (1994) would be 'parallel' models and both the Argentine (1994) and the Uruguayan (1996) reforms would be 'mixed' models. See works included in Cruz-Saco and Mesa-Lago (1998) and Mesa-Lago (1998a).

system, which also accumulate in the individual accounts. In parallel, there is a welfare policy funded by general taxes for those who fail to reach the number of years of compulsory contribution required by the regular system, as long as they can prove their need. This programme grants neither definite nor acquired rights; yet, it makes a selection of potential beneficiaries and allows for a very low benefit to a limited number of people.[7]

The NPO advocates the substitution of systems based on the Chilean model for all of the existing pension systems. Since the Chilean reform is linked to a bloody dictatorship, the Argentine reform is very important for the NPO, in as much as it is the first country in Latin America to promote this kind of model under a democracy. In addition, the 'mixed' design of the Argentine reform triggered off a debate that still persists: is it an alternative to the NPO model or a strategy geared to ultimately setting it up?

This chapter is going to argue that the second of the above definitions is the most convincing. The reform process undergone by social security in Argentina should not be seen as an ideological alternative to the NPO but as one that is consistent with the relevant postulates of NPOs. Another argument is that the subject goes beyond the specific field of social security and is connected to the expectation of imposing a sort of 'asset-based citizenship' replacing the political and social (even labour) citizenship that is typical of welfare state fundamentals. Instead of an organic solidarity of interdependence among all citizens, implemented by means of shared public rights, an asset-based citizenship feeds from an individual economic conception of rights enforced by holding bonds representing ownership rights. In the case of pension funds, both solidarity and interdependence occur in the financial market by common interest at a value established by the market for the workers' savings.[8]

This change of paradigm has serious operational difficulties. The Argentine experience demonstrates that the NPO models reduce coverage, are expensive, do not fight evasion, are legally uncertain, depend strongly on government action and do not guarantee sound capital markets that can protect financial funds. To a great extent these problems stem from the fact that the models' objectives relate less to social security than to the intent to set up an accumulation model driven by finance, which — being fed by workers' savings — transfers much of the risk of the economic activity to the workers.

The analysis of the pension system reform in Argentina is particularly important, not only for Latin America but also for other less developed

---

7   The welfare benefit in Chile has amounted to 10.5% of the average wage.
8   See Orléan (1999), pp. 235–57.

countries. Indeed, the Latin American experience has been replicated in many other countries.[9] However, it should also be studied by the industrialised countries, in as much as the NPO advocates an ideology with universal ambitions and is premised on objective problems common to traditional models of social protection.[10]

Ideology and the New Social Security Orthodoxy

The widely circulated World Bank report, 'Ageing Without Crisis',[11] serves to summarise the NPO ideology in its compilation of the main arguments and proposals.[12] At the same time, it works as a 'users' manual' for all to follow in order to set up the paradigm shift successfully.

The main criticisms of PAYG systems in the report are that they are not equitable because they would see a drop in the value of benefits, they would provide generous cover for the modern sector of employment but would not reach the poor, who, nonetheless, would be financing the system because the payroll taxes on salaries would be transferred to the consumer through prices. Concern about the elderly poor is only relative because: a) poverty would not affect the elderly as much as working people and children; and b) pensions would cut resources to assist the two latter. As a result, income should not be redistributed among the elderly poor using pension system resources.

The report further argues that PAYG systems would also lack 'generational equity' because they would be unable to process the demographic transition. Thus, they would provide the first generation of contributors with generous benefits on account of the high sustaining ratio between working contributors and retired beneficiaries at the beginning of the system. However, it postulates that subsequent generations would invariably have to endure lower benefits due to the decline of such rate (caused by the ageing population and the weaker incentive to employment demand that is attributed to the growth of payroll taxes over wages).

Similarly, according to the report, these systems would show high administrative costs and a notoriously inefficient fund allocation (as a result of the restrictions on portfolio management and the lack of trained

9   Pension fund reforms in Central-Eastern Europe have been inspired by both the Argentine and Chilean cases (Müller, 1999).

10   The importance of the Latin American experience in the international comparison of social policy reforms has been pointed out by Esping-Andersen (1996) and Huber (1996).

11   Banco Mundial (1994).

12   Beattie and McGillivray (1995) make a critical outline of this document.

staff). In addition, they would foster political clientelism and they would entail the 'political risk' of having their revenues used for other purposes. 'Legal insecurity' would be a congenital characteristic of systems under public administration. The above, along with the lack of a tight link between contributions and personal benefits would generate 'moral-hazard' situations that would not provide incentives to contribute to the system.

All of these shortcomings would have repercussions resulting in major economic distortions. Savings would be discouraged, curtailing economic growth and the development of capital markets. Financial deficits would increase, forcing a transfer of resources from other taxes and public debt and generating 'crowding out' effects. At the same time, Aaron's rule would be reversed upon the ageing process of the population, helping IFF schemes to get higher rates of return than the implicit rate in PAYG systems.[13]

Given the above diagnosis, the report further proposes that other systems in line with those of IFFs be substituted for all public pension systems. These compulsory savings plans would collect defined contributions although they would not guarantee the value of benefits. Those without access to such plans would have the option of paying a minimum social assistance pension depending on a 'means test' (Chile) or a uniform and universal basic pension (Argentina). The latter is not recommended because it is more costly (it pays benefits to more people and detracts from resources to accumulate funds in the private administrating agencies.)

According to the NOP set out in the report, these systems: i) would be able to endure the demographic transition because it would end transfers from generation to generation; ii) would not be exposed to political manipulation because the funds would be owned by the affiliates and managed by private companies; iii) would benefit contributions, which would encourage affiliation and payment, thus increasing coverage and collection; iv) would pay higher benefits owing to the high yield of the funds; v) would be cheaper and more efficient thanks to the competition among the privately managed pension funds; vii) would take care of the elderly poor without using the contribution system's funds; and viii) would promote savings, capital markets and economic growth.

This way the goal of social security is changed: it is no longer aimed at guaranteeing a certain income level during retirement, but a greater accumulation of savings and financial yield throughout the workers' active life.

---

13   Aaron (1966) states that the implicit rate of return in PAYG systems consists in adding the population growth rate and the average wage growth rate. Such an addition would result in higher values than the market rate of return and show a certain 'advantage' of the yields of PAYG systems.

The new paradigm proclaims that the accumulation of the workers' savings in private institutions would help to finance productive investment, unleashing a virtuous circle of economic growth, higher employment rates and wages, a larger savings capacity and better pensions in the future.

Even the subtitle of the apologetic report of the World Bank anticipates this change of paradigm as follows: 'Policies to Protect the Old *and* Promote Growth'. This is not limited to pensions. For the World Bank policies to fight poverty also depend on the enforcement of their 'healthy' policies to promote economic growth.[14] Even when its macroeconomic adjustment policies might have negative social impacts — an effect clearly evident in Latin America — these would only be short-term. In the long run everyone will benefit from the enforcement of these policies.[15]

Both the economic and the social security paradigm proclaim their universal benefits.[16] They both need and are conditional on each other. Their common instrument is individual savings institutionalised into 'investment funds'.

The Argentine Reform: a Different Strategy for the Same Ideology

All of the above statements have been made public so as to justify the Argentine reform implemented by Carlos Menem's Peronist Administration (1989–99).[17] The environment was particularly appropriate, for a situation of social anomie derived from the 1989–90 hyperinflation added to the typical 'systemic crisis' of the oldest systems in Latin America.[18] This atmosphere notably broadened the boundaries of tolerance that the government used to have to implement dramatic institutional changes.

For example, the Argentine reform took place under a democratic regime which, owing to exceptional circumstances, was concentrating political power as follows: 'administrative emergency' extraordinary legislation; an absolute majority in the legislative authority; a majority in provincial governments; and practical control of the supreme court, all of which endowed former president Carlos Menem with a political power with very few checks and balances.[19] Even though the political coalition that set up

---

14 World Bank (1993a) XII.

15 World Bank (1993b), p. 122.

16 The claim of universality of a certain economic paradigm ignores the existence of opposing paradigms that acknowledge different epistemologies (Katouzian, 1980).

17 In Schulthess and Demarco (1993) – two officials who are highly responsible for the Argentine reform – the official justification of the project is available for consultation.

18 Mesa-Lago (1989).

19 Menem issued more 'necessity and urgency' decrees than any other elected president in Argentine history, and he also managed to impose a constitutional reform that enabled his later re-election.

the reforms drew on the economic and financial world as well as on the domestic and foreign technocracy, the key elements that contributed with electoral endorsement included the historic pillars of Peronism, such as the unions and most of its 'base' structure. The most powerful union organisations became 'business units' linked to privatisations (including the social security reform).[20]

Such a political atmosphere was combined with an economic context just as peculiar. Hyperinflation was followed by the so-called Plan de Convertibilidad, which pegged the local currency to the US dollar, forcing the Central Bank to back up 100 per cent of the monetary base with reserves in foreign currency and validating contracts in foreign currency.[21] Ever since 1991 both business and capital flows have been completely liberalised.[22] Similarly, by the end of 1994 most of the state-owned generalised input-producing companies and utilities had been either privatised or handed over 'under concession'.

The macroeconomic dynamics of the Plan de Convertibilidad can be explained by means of a simple model observing the balance of payments, the international interest rate and the so-called 'country risk'.[23] The result of the balance of payments depends on the net capital income and most of its variance (variation rate of the Central Bank reserves) can be explained by the variance of the capital account and particularly by the private capital account. The international financial variance explains most of the real product variance.

According to such dynamics, during the first phase of the Plan de Convertibilidad (1991–94) the net capital income flowing into the country generated a consumption and growth boom fuelled by the 'income' effect of the currency stabilisation and the 'wealth' effect as a consequence of real and financial asset revalorisation in dollars. The international liquidity at much lower rates compared to the rates in the 1980s was multiplied by the good business resulting from the privatisations, the public debt restructuring and the support offered by multilateral agencies to the structural reforms dramatically implemented by the government.

20   This resulted in the break-up of the union movement into other union groups opposing the official politics.

21   In September 1992 the new articles of agreement of the Central Bank were issued, so establishing its autonomy, eliminating official guarantees on deposits and setting very tight limits to the purchase of public bonds.

22   Quantitative restrictions to imports were eliminated and tariffs were lowered, on average, from 26.5% in October 1989 to 9.7% in April 1991.

23   A model of this kind can be consulted in Frenkel and González Rosada (1999). The 'country risk' premium is herein defined as the difference between the yields of Argentine sovereign bonds and the 10-year US Treasury bond.

It is within this exceptional context that the social security reform process in Argentina should be considered. In June 1992 the executive authority sent a bill to the legislative authority proposing a reform very similar to the Chilean model. The prevailing environment at that point was one of strong political power concentration, social anomie, extraordinary fiscal revenues, public asset privatisations, sudden business and financial openness, massive capital income and economic boom financed by external savings. The interactive game among the various political players holding veto power modified the original content of the bill until Congress passed the National Integrated Pension System Act (Ley Nacional del Sistema Integrado de Jubilaciones y Pensiones – SIJP) in October 1993 as a 'mixed' system, the main characteristics of which are the following:[24]

1. Workers may choose between a new PAYG Public Pension Regime (RPP) and the new mixed Capitalisation Regime (RC). Those who do not expressly make a choice get registered under the RC automatically and are assigned to one of the so-called Administradoras de Fondos de Jubilaciones y Pensiones (AFJPs).

2. Originally, all members were entitled to two benefits: a) a Uniform Basic Pension (PBU), which would pay the same amount to every beneficiary; and b) a Compensating Benefit (PC), which would recognise the years of contribution to the 'old system'. Additionally, the Capitalisation Benefit (HC) in individual accounts is paid out to the members registered under the RC system and, in order to acknowledge the years of contribution to the new system, the Additional Benefit on account of Permanence (PAP) would be paid out to people choosing RPP.

3. The government is in charge of funding PBU, PC and PAP. AFJPs or the retirement insurance companies pay HC, according to the beneficiary's choice of either a retirement plan scheduled in fractions or a life pension.

4. Minimum ages for retirement go up to 65 for men and 60 for women, provided they can prove at least 30 years of service and duly paid contributions, accordingly.

---

24 To analyse the relevant political actors during the drafting process and debate of the Argentine Pension Reform, see Alonso (2000).

5.   The Aporte Medio Previsional Obligatorio (AMPO), calculated as the quotient between the total amount of collected contributions and the total number of contributors was created. The AMPO would establish an automatic adjustment mechanism for the system's variables, including RPP benefits, minimum and maximum contributions, and contributions by the self-employed.

6.   One AFJP is created within the National Bank of Argentina (Banco de la Nación Argentina) offering a guarantee of minimum yields.

7.   The government is responsible for the collection of contributions.

The 'mixed' model act was the beginning of a new story. Measures were systematically applied in order to undermine the public component of the system and to bring it closer to the pure NPO's private model: i) RPP takes over the loss-making systems for provincial employees and special regimes (such as the armed forces); ii) a reduction of employers' contributions financing RPP;[25] iii) an increase in the contribution amount of the lowest category for the self-employed, which drove out the most difficult workers to oversee and control; iv) no transfer of committed resources coming from other taxes.[26]

In 1995 the so-called 'Pension Solidarity' Act was passed, establishing that only the payment of pensions up to the amount authorised in the budget would be guaranteed and that, under no circumstances, would it be linked to salaries. That was the end of AMPO's automatic adjustment and the historical connection between retirement payment and salaries. The peculiar solidarity promoted by this act can be taken to refer to the sympathy that the retired citizens must feel for the budget. The stance of the Supreme Court — as controlled by the executive branch — is that no one can claim 'acquired rights' from the federal government.

All of these measures led to multiple lawsuits that have accumulated uncertain debts, which are being settled with by the equally questionable means of issuing government bonds.[27] Together with all those measures

25   From 16 per cent down to five to ten per cent depending on the area and activity. The annual fiscal cost of this measure has been estimated at over one per cent of GDP (between 1995 and 1999, due to these reductions, the public regime lost more revenues than the total fiscal deficit for 2000).

26   The formal commitment was to transfer ten per cent of value added tax, 90 per cent of personal property tax, 20 per cent of income tax, part of co-sharing taxes and 30 per cent of the income resulting from the privatisations of state-owned companies to the public system. The funds that were effectively transferred were significantly lower.

27   At the beginning of 2000, there were an estimated 100,000 pending lawsuits and claims by the retired citizens who chose not to be paid with bonds, which accounted for 0.7 per cent of GDP (Clarín, 20 January 2000).

that went on to degrade the state component of the mixed system, the Peronist administration would constantly advertise the need for a deeper reform eliminating the public system option, 'fencing in' PBU and replacing it with a social assistance benefit.[28] However, consensus to turn the proposals into new legislation was never achieved.

It was the new administration — the Alianza —that implemented this project on taking office in December 1999. In November 2000 a bill was sent to Congress under the framework of the previous Peronist administration.[29] Disregarding due consideration by the legislature, on the last working day of 2000 President Fernando de la Rúa signed a new 'necessity and emergency' decree moving towards the elimination of the public component of the hitherto mixed Argentine pension model.[30]

The following were the main provisions: i) PBU was abolished for future pensions; ii) a supplementary pension was created that could only be collected by those meeting the requirements for admission to retirement, although benefits were somewhere between the minimum and the maximum therein established; iii) a minimum universal means tested benefit was created for people not receiving any pension benefits and — gradually — shown to be over 70 years old, 'poor' and 'needy'; iv) those contributing to the system for fewer years than required are allowed to receive a proportional benefit. At the same time: i) the market share for every AFJP is limited to 27.5 per cent, without specifying whether this refers to the number of members or accumulated amount; ii) the 'fixed' component of the commission is eliminated and the new criterion for allocation of the undecided to AFJPs gets established; iii) AFJPs are authorised to invest in public debt securities 50–60 per cent of the total investments.

The approval of this new reform has been introduced to the country as a 'condition' imposed by the IMF prior to approval of a financial operation to 'bail out' the Plan de Convertibilidad, within a long economic recession context, a higher country risk, a growing fiscal deficit, difficulties in servicing the public debt and an imminent financial crisis. This financial operation envisaged a 'commitment' by the AFJPs to 'lend' more money to the Treasury, which justified the increase of the legal authorisation to do it.

28 These proposals have been communicated in international and local fora. See, for example, the interview with the then secretary of fiscal equity, Ms. Carola Pessino (*Clarín*, 17 April 1999).

29 In the election campaign the Alianza had criticised the initiatives of the previous Peronist administration. However, shortly after taking office, it had already adopted its guidelines. See, for example, the interview with the secretary of the Treasury, Mr Mario Vicens (*Clarín*, 20 February 2000).

30 The main difference between the bill and the decree is that the former encouraged the total elimination of the public system and PBU.

In addition to improving the financial situation among other emergencies, the government argued that the fiscal situation would be improved, but the estimates indicate that such an improvement is not very relevant in the face of the budget troubles.[31] The true outcome is that the mixed model in Argentina is almost over and all of the benefits expected by future retired citizens have been reduced, opening a new door for another wave of lawsuits that would result in a greater debt and future fiscal burden.

The decree is making progress towards consolidating the AFJPs' power which, with the money transferred from taxes, consolidate their position as lenders to the government and umpires of the country's fate. The problems of social security, worsened by the changes that have been implemented, are left behind in second place. The connection between the new paradigm in social security and the ideology that fuels the economic policy is once again visible.

The Argentine Reform: a Universal Ideological Paradigm

After successive administrations, the reform-oriented process in Argentina is not an alternative to NPO, but a continuing process. This process is in line with World Bank advice that wherever radical reforms cannot be implemented once and for all, 'gradual strategies' and 'politically feasible tactics' should be pursued by means of a sequence that allows for a partial privatisation of the pension system and a legitimate phasing-out of the public regime.[32]

Eroding the financial capacities of the public component of the Argentine mixed model was a key policy in such a gradual strategy. In 1994 70 per cent of pension expenditure was covered by contributions coming from employees and employers, whereas in 1999–2000 only 35 per cent was being met in this way. However, during that time AFJPs collected revenues equal to 6.8 per cent of GDP; pensions remaining frozen at 1992 rates. The 'fiscal crisis' discourse of the pension system shows two contradictory sides: it is used to reduce benefits but not to draw resources from the public system.

The decline in both quantity and value of the benefits was reflected in the increasing number of elderly people returning to the employment market and those joining the poverty ranks.[33] This makes sense because

31   The latest estimates available point out that the present value of all the expected savings from the new decree, in the next five years, would be tantamount to one third of the interest of the public debt as estimated only for 2001.

32   World Bank (1997b), pp. 145–53. These tactics match the ones that relate to the Politics of Welfare State's Retrenchment (Pierson, 1994) and emphasise the actions by the strategic players of the reforms (Müller, 1999).

33   The Secretariat for the Elderly of the Argentine government estimates that 85 per cent of retired people can not afford the cost of a basic basket.

retired people fall in the lower deciles of income distribution and are more sensitive to marginal modifications to their income.[34] Contrary to the assumptions of NPO, the elderly are very vulnerable to poverty situations, at least in countries like Argentina.

Rather than providing solutions to problems, the reforms in line with NPO ideology not only transfer them to other social arenas but also push them into the future, as demonstrated by the relentless issuing of public debt securities to pay for lawsuits resulting from illegal measures. While retired people compulsively collect public bonds instead of benefits, those bonds can be used to pay fiscal debts, including debts incurred on account of defaulting contributions to the social security system.

The rate of evasion by contributors rose: leaving aside the unemployed, only one in three individuals subject to do so makes contributions to the SIJP. Besides, 93 per cent of RC affiliates (77 per cent in the public regime) are wage earners, who have been compulsively included and forced to pay because their contribution gets discounted from their salary slip. Independent workers — who account for the largest evading group and are where the presumed 'incentives' attributed to individual capitalisation of contributions should most be reflected — are not motivated to join RC.[35] Given that the contribution rates for this group were raised disproportionate to their incomes and the benefits as promised to them, it can be stated that the self-employed who earn the lowest income have been thrown out of the system altogether.

Cutting down on employers' contributions did not lead to improvements in the labour market, but to eroded resources in the public regime. Throughout the 1990s unemployment, underemployment and all casual forms of employment rose remarkably: 60 per cent of EAP are not contributing to social security in Argentina.

Neither the stimuli nor the competition among AFJPs worked as prophesied in the NPO ideology: more than 70 per cent of the new entries to RC are 'undecided' who fail to choose either one of the two regimes and/or an AFJP in particular.[36] Savings did not rise either. The savings rate of the 1990s is lower than that of the so-called 'lost decade' of the 1980s.

---

34 The difference in the average income of retired people between the first (the lowest) and the third deciles is 35 per cent, while it is 97 per cent for wage earners and 120 per cent for the self-employed.

35 Given the design of the new pension system, this situation was foreseen in Barbeito and Lo Vuolo (1993)

36 SAFJP (2000). The criteria for allocation was based on each AFJP's market share, and when the new decree was signed it would be the one charging the lowest commission according to the member's income level.

What did go up was the external savings (which went from negative figures in the 1980s to record-breaking positive values) and public debt (growth of which is fast increasing). The capital markets did not show a positive response either, in spite of the now privatised state-owned companies listed in the stock exchange that slowly migrated to more important markets.[37] After the booming first stage of the Plan de Convertibilidad, both volume and profitability at the Buenos Aires Stock Exchange fell, in particular in the wake of the so-called 'Tequila' effect.

Only a small proportion of pension funds is invested in stocks, a growing percentage of which are from foreign companies. Most of the portfolio consists of Federal Government Bonds and term deposits. Public debt securities make up the most substantial part of the AFJPs' portfolio. In addition to covering its deficit, the government went on issuing debt to settle debts with providers, retired people and many social programmes funded by borrowing from banks and other international agencies.

However, the profitability of the funds has grown, though not without the wild swings typical of spasmodic movements caused by the financial market. Nevertheless, mainly due to commissions, the actual value of individual accounts is below the money that was originally paid as contributions.

The administrative cost of the new system is very high and around 50 per cent is spent on marketing.[38] The difference among AFJPs in terms of the lowest and the highest commissions would amount to 98 per cent for low income workers; in some cases, the commission paid was estimated as being over 50 per cent of the contribution.[39] Likewise, since the AFJPs' commissions include not only a fixed component but also a variable one, they have a greater impact on low income workers for the most part.

The degree of market concentration rose systematically. Out of the original 26 AFJPs only 13 were left by June and four of these would keep 66 per cent of the affiliates. On top of that, almost all of the disability and death insurance policies are contracted out to companies linked to the AFJPs themselves.[40] Although the cost of these premiums dropped steadily, the commissions to affiliates were not adjusted proportionately and it is very uncommon for affiliates not to take out life insurance with the insurance companies that oversee their AFJPs.

The results of the Argentine reform are far from what the NPO had

37   Since 1990 over 100 companies have left the Buenos Aires Stock Exchange.
38   The average commissions are 3.37 per cent of salaries (over 30 per cent of total contributions).
39   Report by the Secretariat of Industry, Commerce and Mining (Clarín, 8 August 1998).
40   Rofman (1999).

predicted and most of the current problems derive from the 'change' and not from the legacy of the previous system. However, the measures taken since the new system was launched have served to 'deepen' such change. This path is politically permeable and strongly dependent on the continuous actions taken by the government to change the rules.

Ideology and the New Social Security: Asset-Based Citizenship and Financial Solidarity

The new social security paradigm gives priority to high financial profitability over socioeconomic security, the capitalisation of savings for those with an income over broadening coverage, a fixed 'minimum profitability' for the financial capital — typical of benchmarking practices — over guaranteeing basic, universal and sufficient benefits for every citizen.

Clearly, the main goal of pension reforms such as Argentina's is to create pension funds at any expense and to encourage changes in the social organisation principles from a 'citizenship of rights' to an 'asset-based citizenship'. The aim is then to consolidate the power of finances in the economic and social dynamics regulation. The main player in this project, the direction of which is geared to strengthening the market's role in political and social organisation, is the government, through transferring resources, creating profitability and continually changing the rules of the game.

This asset-based citizenship seeks to substitute each individual's claims in terms of securities for their social rights. The necessary solidarity to keep social cohesion would not come from the participants of the same labour division process or the same political rights' system. The identification would be with the financial markets where prices are fixed for the claims representing the citizens' individual assets. The government hands the 'arbitrator' role over to the financial market to take care of the social values that organise the hierarchies and the 'functionings' of people in a particular society.[41]

The organisational solidarity and social co-operation imposed *ex ante* by institutions is expected to be replaced by the employees' sympathy for the enterprise they get their regular paycheque from, and for the financial system where their savings are capitalised (including pension funds in the first place). This model is built on a strictly 'contract-oriented' ideology that presumes that the contractor (the AFJPs) is going to act always as driven by the ruling interests and that society comprises a set of intertwined con-

---

41 'Functioning' means the variety of things handled (controlled) by people in their being or doing in life (Sen, 1993).

tracts where everyone is seeking personal benefit. This sort of contractual solidarity is by no means as 'natural' as some may think; and that is why in practice the parties end up being forced to enter contracts. It is the state, in the use of its political clout, that ends up deciding on the contract and modifying its provisions; there is no 'freedom to choose' here.

The creation of an autonomous power for finance is the core of this project in pursuit of the transformation of liquid capital possession into capacity for social control. The physical capital becomes liquid as long as the bonds representing such capital are diversified and traded in the financial markets on a daily basis. The claims (debt) define the direction of production, investment and work; in other words, most of the fundamental economic and social relations.[42] This new paradigm requires that all the financial markets join the international strategies of institutional fund diversification and reduce the leeway for monetary and fiscal policies as much as possible — as is the case of the Plan de Convertibilidad and the projects for dollarisation in Latin America.

The NPO ideology is consistent with the multiple ways of transferring the economic activity risk onto the workers, for instance, through labour precariousness (insecurity of labour income) and pension funds (insecurity of retirement income). The value of pensions is uncertain and depends on the asset value of pension funds upon retirement. However, at the same time that the risk is transferred to the workers, the financial system is fed by the workers' compulsory savings in pension funds.

The contradictions of this paradigm are many. While it announces long term profitability as its driving force, it surrenders to the financial markets, which are driven to a great extent by short-term profitability and speculation against pensions. This is more serious in the so-called 'emerging' markets, which are heavily indebted and depend on the external flow of funds. The continuous interventions by government authorities to sustain a volatile and insecure system have shown how vulnerable the project is. This is even more worrying when proven that, as in the Argentine case, neither savings nor capital markets react as forecast.

---

42   A supplement to this project is subordinating the banking power to the financial power, and removing the former from the production system. This is particularly clear in Anglo-Saxon countries rather than in countries endorsing the 'German' model (Orléans, 1999, pp. 194–235). See also Lordon (2000).

While Argentina is still lacking domestic savings and depending on external savings, it is most likely that Argentine workers' savings are increasingly destined to end up in foreign capital markets; and from that point to financing production systems overseas. Social security helps to feed so-called 'financial globalisation', which means a movement that tends to add liquidity to a global market accessible to every economic agent that is sufficiently solvent to capture funds from it.

The risks for countries such as Argentina are very significant. While it excludes people from its coverage, it constantly requires income transfers and shrinking rights to solve its increasing problems. The consolidation of the new pension system in Argentina is done at the expense of transferring the problems to other sectors and into the future. This is a very risky way to build an 'asset-based citizenship', and it challenges the very political organisation as a system that defines the core values through which citizenship can be accessed.

CHAPTER 11

Gender Relations and Social Security in Southern Brazil

Anita Brumer

Introduction

The alterations in the Brazilian social security system in the last few decades occurred in a context of rapid and significant change, which took place both in the country itself and throughout the world, in economics, politics and the demographics of social relations. As shown by Oliveira et al.,[1] among the aspects that have a direct bearing on social security in Brazil are the decline in fertility[2] and increasing life expectancy at birth (which led to a rapid ageing of the population structure),[3] affecting the period of enjoyment (and receipt of benefits) of retirement. At the same time, the changes that occurred in the economy modified the forms of professional insertion (creating new categories and increasing the number of self-employed, 'informal' workers and the unemployed) and altered the values of wages and services, with an effect on the volume of social security revenues and expenditures.

Both political and financial factors can explain variations in social security systems in different countries. This is why the Brazilian social security system, which underwent a parametric reform of the state-run, pay-as-

---

[1] de Oliveira et al. (1997), p. 1.

[2] According to the census performed by the Brazilian Institute of Geography and Statistics (IBGE), fertility rates dropped from six children per woman in the 1950s to 4.7 in the 1970–75 period, and to 2.7 in the period 1990/95. In rural areas, where fecundity rates are usually higher than in urban areas, during 1980–85 the highest rate was in the north, 6.8, and the lowest was in the south, 3.6; between 1985 and 1990, the rates in these regions were respectively 6.0 and 3.1 (Teixeira et al, 1994). In Rio Grande do Sul, the southernmost state of Brazil, in 1970, the average number of children per woman between the ages 15 and 44 in this rural area was 5.62; it was 3.78 in 1980, 2.78 in 1990 and 2.62 in 1995, according to calculations performed by experts from the Economy and Statistics Foundation (FEE), a state government agency, based on various IBGE censuses.

[3] Deere and León (2000, p. 20) indicate that in Latin America 'in 1950, average life expectancy for women was 53.5 years, increasing to 71.4 in 1990. The rise in life expectancy for men was less impressive, increasing from 50.2 in 1950 to 66.2 in 1990, so that the gender gap in favour of women increased'. These rates varied by country and, in Brazil, by region and state – for example in the south and the south-east (life expectancy of 72.5 years for women and 65.0 for men, in 1990) compared to the north-east and the north (life expectancy of 67.7 years for women and 60.8 for men, in 1990) (IBGE, 2000).

you-go system, aiming to improve its efficiency and equity, differed from others in the continent. According to Kay (2001), the Brazilian reform differed from those initiated in Chile, in 1981, and in Colombia, Peru, Argentina, Uruguay, Mexico, Bolivia and El Salvador, in the 1990s. These countries have been depicted as occupying 'the vanguard of global social security reform', introducing 'private individual investment accounts to complement or replace state-run pay-as-you-go systems'.[4]

The focus of this chapter on rural social security may be set out as follows: 1) rural workers were one of the last occupational groups to be included; 2) the inclusion of this group occurred, in different periods, as a result either of state 'concession' or of a 'conquest' by mobilised workers; and 3) rural social security involves income distribution, transferring resources from the urban to the rural sector.

The social security model adopted in urban areas, where workers typically have formal wage-earning jobs and regular incomes, cannot be applied to the countryside, where workers do not have regular incomes, and many are subsistence farmers, with the result that they are not generally classified as wage-earners. Furthermore, according to the dynamics of economic development in Brazil, in the last few decades, the rural sector has been subordinated to the urban, and has the task of 'financing investments, by transferring resources from the agrarian to the industrial sector', which leads to the 'exclusion of a vast number of family farmers'.[5] Hence, the capacity of the rural sector to provide contributions to social security is very low, rendering it practically impossible to balance contributions and benefits. According to Schwarzer,[6] as indicated by international experience, universal coverage can only be achieved if alternative structures are created to provide financing, that are alternative to, or complement, deductions from income.[7]

---

4   Kay (2001) explains the differences in the reforms introduced in Brazil and elsewhere in political terms. In Brazil, private accounts were broadly opposed by both supporters and opponents of President Cardoso when he first discussed the topic in 1994: in neighbouring countries, privatisation found political support (Kay, 2001, p. 3).

5   Schwarzer (2000), p. 74.

6   *Ibid.*

7   Schwarzer (2000) presents a typology of rural social security schemes prevailing in the world: 1) the 'Beveridgian Model', in which the rural population is included in old-age security by means of a claim on a universal pension, based upon an encompassing citizenship/residence criterion (basic universal model), exemplified by Finland and Canada; 2) the model based on Bismarckian contributive principles that differentiate between urban and rural occupations when designing contribution or eligibility principle – in this case, either the urban sector subsidises the rural one or the National Treasury covers the difference (contributive differentiated model), exemplified by Germany; 3) the 'Bismarckian Undifferentiated Model', in which the access and benefit legal designs are exactly the same for rural and urban occupational groups (contributive model), exem

Despite these difficulties, over the last 30 years a number of laws were approved to extend social coverage to rural workers, both wage earners and self-employed, giving them the same social rights as urban workers. These advances were so substantial that Schwarzer claims that the rural subsystem[8] of Brazilian Social Security is an exception among developing countries. It alone has a significant degree of coverage, with precision targeting. As a result, it is exceptionally effective in combating rural poverty in Brazil.[9]

The inclusion of rural workers was later than that of urban groups, and the inclusion of women rural workers was later than that of men. This occurred mainly because women had to be 'recognised' as rural workers to be included as beneficiaries of social insurance. This recognition was hindered by the lack of corroboration of their working status: most of their work was not visible, considered either as 'help' to men or confined to the domestic sphere. Initially considered 'dependent', either on their parents or on their husbands, women are gradually being seen as 'autonomous', with rights of their own. With this change of perspective, they are included as social security beneficiaries.

The central purpose of this chapter is to show the evolution of the rural social security system in Brazil, stressing advances achieved by rural working women. In doing so, it becomes important to examine the background of these advances, emphasising their character as a 'donation' (by the state), or 'conquest' (by the workers). The study also analyses the social effects of rural social security on its beneficiaries, focusing on the south, and speculates about future outcomes.

Evolution of Rural Social Security in Brazil

Social security includes social insurance, 'constituted by a schedule of payments, in money and/or services provided/rendered to an individual or his dependants, as a partial/total compensation for the loss of working capac-

---

plified by the United States; 4) the model in which some form of coverage is given to the rural sector through assistance pensions, based on 'focalisation' criteria (means test) rather than on universal or contributory rights (assistance model), exemplified by Chile and Costa Rica. The Brazilian case does not fit any of these models exactly, given that its urban security system is contributory and its rural security system is similar to the first model presented above: the benefit is a flat rate of one minimum wage and has no correlation with the individual's earnings in his/her working life or with effective contributions.

8   The rural subsystem of social security includes three different groups: farmers who are also employers, self -employed family farm workers and wage earners. Schwarzer refers here mainly to the second group.

9   Schwarzer (2000), p. 72.

ity, generally due to a contributive connection'.[10] Together with the policies and actions which aim to provide healthcare to the population and social care to the needy, social insurance is part of the ensemble of policies and actions that form the social security of a given country. The way this is done depends, in each case, on the institutional history of the country and on the circumstances and the play of forces among the power groups that make up society.

The first law referring to social security insurance established old age retirement pensions and other benefits for railway workers in 1923 (the Eloy Chaves Law). The connection to the system was institutional, but each railway company operated its own system. During the 1930s the connection to the social security system came to be made by occupational category and benefits extended to include widow's pensions. The system came to involve almost all urban wage-workers and a majority of the self-employed.[11] The administration of retirement and pensions institutes since the 1930s has been managed by the state, which appoints senior administrative personnel, defines the organisational format of the whole social security system, fixes contribution levels and determines fund investment strategy.[12]

According to Santos, when introducing the first social insurance legislation, the main concern of the government was the drive to accumulate savings, seeking, on the one hand, 'to conciliate politics of accumulation that would not exacerbate social inequalities to threatening heights', and, on the other hand, 'to establish a policy focusing on equality that would not endanger, and if possible, stimulate the effort of accumulation'.[13] As a result of this, coverage was extended to almost all urban workers and to the majority of the self employed, but some occupational categories were excluded, among them rural workers, domestic workers and autonomous professionals. The exclusion of rural workers was due to the lack of organised social movements until the late 1950s: and the exclusion of other occupational categories was explained by the difficulties caused by fragmentation and dispersion.

During the 1960s the first initiatives to extend social security coverage to rural workers were taken. In 1963 the Fundo de Assistência ao Trabalhador Rural (Fund for Assistance to Rural Workers) was established and, in 1969, the Basic Plan to help workers in sugar cane agribusiness was implemented

---

10   de Oliveira et al. (1997), p. 4.
11   *Ibid.*, p. 7.
12   *Ibid.*, pp. 1–12.
13   dos Santos (1979) p. 33.

— it was later extended to other rural activities. In practice, social security coverage for rural workers did not take effect because the necessary resources (financial and administrative) were not addressed by the legislation.

Measures regarding the organisation of rural workers were adopted in several laws in the 1960s, which permitted the unionisation of rural workers and enabled them to press for rural social security. These measures included the Administrative Ruling 395 of 17 July 1965, which established procedures for the foundation, organisation and recognition of the unions and outlined their purposes; the Decree-Law 276 of 1967, which established a sales tax on rural products at the rate of one per cent to be used to finance medical and hospital care for rural workers; and the Decree-Law 789, of 27 August 1969 which redefined Administrative Ruling 395, which introduced single, county-wide unions for each category of workers and farmers. These laws facilitated the regulation of rural unions and gave an impulse to the organisation of rural workers and rural producers/employers. In 1966, the National Institute of Social Security (INPS) was created, absorbing the separate institutes that operated the social security system, apart from the Instituto de Previdência e Aposentadoria dos Servidores do Estado (IPASE) which was responsible for federal civil servants. Workers' representatives were excluded from the administration of the INPS, which was managed by state civil servants.

In 1971, the Rural Assistance Programme (PRORURAL) was launched, absorbing the responsibilities of Fundação Rural (FUNRURAL), which had administered social insurance and health services for rural workers. Among other measures, PRORURAL provided retirement and disability pensions for rural workers over the age of 70, worth half the regional minimum wage; a pension for dependants that was equal to 70 per cent of that for direct beneficiaries, together with assistance for funerals; healthcare services, including medical-surgical and hospital care and dental treatment; and social services in general. Women would only benefit directly if they were heads of family (something very rare in southern Brazil) or rural wage-earners. The inauguration of this programme clearly showed that 'land distribution would be a second step, a later stage after all assistance to workers had been regulated'.[14] According to dos Santos PRORURAL was different from the urban social security system in at least three aspects: 1) it was financed only by a tax on rural merchandise supplemented by

---

[14]   Part of the speech given by President Médici on the occasion of the launch of PRORURAL, in National Conference of Brazilian Bishops – Episcopal Committee (CNBB-CEP) (1976), p. 102.

other levies on urban companies; 2) rural workers did not contribute in a direct way to the fund; 3) benefits were standard for all rural workers.[15]

During the 1970s, as indicated by Oliveira et al.,[16] social security coverage was extended to occupational categories left out of previous plans. Among measures taken were: the inclusion of domestic workers (1972); the compulsory registration of self-employed workers (1973); the provision of support for people over 70 and for uninsured disabled persons (1974); and the extension of social security and social care benefits to rural employers and their dependants (1976). Summing up, 'at this point social security began to cover all people with paid activities in the country',[17] although workers in the informal sector and the unemployed remained excluded from the system.

Dos Santos uses the expression 'regulated citizenship' to characterise the politics of social and economic policy in Brazil between the 1930s and 1980s. With this expression, he means 'the concept of citizenship, whose roots are, not in a code of political values, but in a system of occupational stratification. Moreover, such a system of occupational stratification is defined by legal norm. In other words, citizens are all those members of the community who are localised in any of the occupations *recognised and defined in law*'.[18] As indicated by Coradini, the main characteristic of institutional changes during this period was the unification or administrative centralisation of public and para-official bodies acting in the sphere of 'social welfare'.[19] Among new measures were the creation of the Ministry of Social Security and Social Welfare (MPAS – Ministério de Previdência e Assistência Social) in 1974, which set out to centralise social security policies; the establishment of the National Social Security System (SINPAS) and the National Institute of Social Security (INPS) in 1977, which superseded FUNRURAL and IPASE. The INPS was redefined as the monopoly provider of benefits.[20]

The 1988 Constitution, complemented by Laws 8,212 (Plan of Costs) and 8,213 (Plan of Benefits) of 1991, provided universal access to old age and invalidity pensions for both genders in the rural sector. Yet claimants still had to prove their status as 'producer, partner, share-cropper and ten-

---

[15]   dos Santos (1979), p. 115.

[16]   de Oliveira et al (1997), p. 8.

[17]   *Ibid.*

[18]   dos Santos (1979) p. 75.

[19]   Coradini (1989), p. 62–3.

[20]   *Ibid.*, p. 63.

ant farmer, prospector and artisanal fisherman, as well as their respective spouses who carry out activities in a familial economy situation, without permanent employees'.[21] In this sense, 'the risks covered by social security, as well as the minimum and maximum values of the benefits provided, become the same for all contributors to the system, and thus the inequalities resulting from the previous plan that distinguished between the urban and rural population disappeared'.[22] Female rural workers now had the right to a retirement pension at 55, regardless of whether or not their spouses were already beneficiaries. Men also had their benefits extended, the retirement age being lowered from 65 to 60, and they acquired the right to a pension in the case of the death of their wife if she had social security. Also important for the rural population was the provision of social assistance in 1996: people aged 67 and more, as well as those with a physical disability received the equivalent of a minimum wage even if they had not previously contributed to the social security system.[23] The legislation of 1988 continued the process of broadening the notion of citizenship that had been initiated with the creation of PRORURAL in 1971, so that all citizens have social rights, independent of contributions. In short, a full transition from social insurance to social security was in prospect.

In 1990 the MPAS was dismantled and its functions divided between the Ministry of Social Assistance and Health and the Ministry of Work and Social Insurance (MTPS). The MTPS included agencies like the National Institute of Social Security (INSS) that had previously absorbed the functions of the INPS and the IAPAS. In 1992, a new social administrative reform was carried out, dividing the MTPS in two new ministries, the Ministry of Work and the Ministry of Social Insurance, the latter incorporating the INSS.

Among other features, the legislation of 1988 conceded maternity pay to female rural workers: however, this was vetoed by the president when the social security law was put into effect in 1990. Owing to pressure by female rural workers' movements on congressmen, their right to pay during maternity leave became law in 1993, and was put into effect in 1994. According to this legislation, female rural workers should receive a benefit equivalent to one minimum wage a month for four months on the birth of a child.

The rural social security system differs from the urban in several specific respects. First, the rural system is non-contributory, financed by sales taxes. Secondly, the retirement age for rural male workers is now 60, and

---

[21]   Federal Constitution (1988), art. 195, par. 8.

[22]   de Oliveira et al. (1997), p. 10.

[23]   Delgado and Schwarzer (2000), pp. 197–8.

for females 55, while for urban workers it is set at 65 and 60 respectively. Thirdly, unlike their urban counterparts, rural workers are not required to complete a basic minimum period of work in order to gain entitlement, but have to prove that they have worked for a period similar to that of urban workers, by presenting documents proving the use of land (property title or partnership or leasing contract), sales invoices, or a statement of employment issued the rural union and confirmed by the INSS. As a result, rural workers now enjoy benefits approaching those of urban workers.[24]

Table 11.1 shows the impact of rural social security reform in the 1990s. First, between 1991 and 1998 the number of benefits of all kinds practically doubled. Growth was particularly rapid between 1991 and 1993, years before the impact of ageing became particularly pronounced.[25] Secondly, the unit value of benefit increased considerably, from US$44.1 in 1991 to US$ 108.5 in 1998; but today it stands at around US$80.00, owing to the devaluation of the Brazilian currency. Finally, as regards overall expenditure on rural social security benefits, there was a significant rise — from US$180 million a month in 1991 to US$750 million a month in 1998 — that is almost US$10 billion a year in 1998.

Table 11.1: Distribution of Rural Social Security Benefits in Brazil from 1991 to 1998

Years	Amount of Monthly Benefits Paid (in US$ millions)	Total Number of Benefits Mantained (in thousands)	Number of Age Benefits (in thousands)	Monthly Value of the Rural Benefits (in US$)
1991	180.0	4,080.4	2,240.5	44.1
1992	234.4	4,976.9	2,912.8	47.1
1993	403.8	6,001.0	3,855.9	67.3
1994	526.8	6,359.2	4,176.2	82.8
1995	637.8	6,332.2	4,126.8	100.7
1996	705.2	6,474.4	4,102.2	108.9
1997	725.3	6,672.3	4,140.2	108.7
1998	749.8	6,913.1	4,305.3	108.5

Source: *Anuário Estatístico da Previdência Social* (AEPS) - 1991 a 1998 (apud Delgado and Cardoso Jr., 2000, p. 3; 2001, p. 228).

---

[24] Schwarzer (2000) p. 77.

[25] Delgado (1997); Delgado and Cardoso Jr. (2000), p. 21.

In spite of the advances achieved by rural workers, the distribution of benefits, compared with other groups, remains inequitable. In 2001, the average monthly benefit received by urban workers was US$148, that paid to rural workers was US$73. In the same year, the average monthly benefit received by pensioned state civil servants was US$768; the average for the military was US$1,158; for personnel in the judiciary, the average was US$2,547.[26] In addition, as Oliveira et al. have underlined, the inequality of the social security benefits system in Brazil is compounded by the fact that the poor subsidise the better off: the poor usually start working younger and die younger — thus receiving fewer years of pension entitlement.[27] Benefit criteria also discriminate against the poor as a pension is usually based on an average of the best earning years. For the poor, wages hardly rise during their working life, whereas other income groups usually enjoy salary increments and have their pensions calculated on the basis of their years of highest earnings. When income distribution is considered the situation is no better. Hoffmann (2001) indicates that, according to the 1998 National Research by Household Sampling (Pesquisa Nacional por Amostra de Domicílios, PNAD), in rural areas, the richest decile enjoys 47.2 per cent of total rural income. The fact that there are 'a few with very much and many with very little' may help to explain the paradox that the increase in the number of beneficiaries of social security has reduced rural poverty, while having very little impact on equity.[28]

The Role of the State and Civil Society in the Evolution of Rural Social Security

In Brazil the social security system has undergone considerable changes, 'at times as the result of political achievements in the democratic context, at others as the result of the paternalistic and authoritarian action of the State'.[29] Some analysts have sought to explain why social security benefits were extended so late to rural workers compared with urban, and why this process occurred mainly during the military regime which was authoritarian and conservative.[30] In his synthesis, Schwarzer indicates that this delay

---

26 Matijascic (2001).

27 Oliviera et al. (1997), p. 34.

28 Hoffmann (2001).

29 de Oliveira et al. (1997), p. 6.

30 Malloy (1976); Malloy and Parodi (1993); Schwarzer (2000).

may be explained by the lack of organisation and political leverage of the rural population, which constituted the majority of Brazilians until at least the 1970s.[31] On the other hand, earlier studies give five reasons for the action of the military regime: 1) the social security technocracy absorbed the ILO principle of universalisation of coverage; 2) the regime sought to avoid the social tensions caused by modernisation policies of the 1950s and 1960s that resulted in high levels of social exclusion; 3) sections of the military aimed to co-opt rural workers unions; 4) development strategists were determined to prevent an intensification of the rural-urban migration; 5) consistent with the national security doctrine, there was an intention of integrating the rural sector into the national development project, maintaining 'social peace' by creating 'social justice'.[32]

These interpretations are convincing but incomplete. First, the process of extending benefits to rural workers began before the military regime, with the Fund for Assistance and Social Security for Rural Workers (1963) founded during the populist government of João Goulart, and continued after the end of the military regime. Hence, the process was not exclusive to the military dictatorship. Throughout, social legislation remained an instrument by which the state tried to eliminate direct confrontations between capital and labour: technocratic centralisation ensured the dominance of capital in all productive sectors.[33] Secondly, from the mid-1950s to the 1964 military coup, social upheaval in rural Brazil was intense, centred mainly on the struggle for land. As a result, there appears to be a certain relationship between 'social struggles' and the 'concession of benefits'. Though, extending the analysis of the influence of the union movement on labour legislation by Rodrigues, the consequences of organised social struggles for the evolution of legal entitlements 'were not immediate', nor did actors remain 'exempt from the extra-legal influences resulting from political and social events'.[34] Consequently, according to Houtzager, the issue facing governing elites was how to modernise an archaic sector that was widely perceived as posing a major bottleneck for development and a breeding ground for agrarian radicalism.[35] During the military regime, union action and the struggle for land were severely

---

31   *Ibid.*, pp. 74–5.
32   Malloy and Parodi (1993).
33   Brumer (1985), p. 216.
34   Rodrigues (1968), pp. 4–5.
35   Houtzager (1998).

repressed, which may suggest that the formation of PRORURAL in 1971 was a co-optive concession by the state rather than the result of worker struggle, as Malloy, Parodi and Schwarzer have argued.[36] The contention of these scholars is that social security was a secondary issue in the rural milieu during the military period. It should be remembered that before the 1960s, little rural unionisation occurred.

Although not illegal, and encouraged by leaders of social movements like Francisco Julião, rural unions hardly existed due to an indeterminate juridical status that precluded effective organisation.[37] Furthermore, subsequent legislation, for example, the Rural Workers' Statute and Land Statute, which 'regulated' the formation of rural unions, originated largely in demands of the previous populist period.[38] As an advisor of the National Confederation of Agricultural Workers (CONTAG) observed, 'these conquests were not the result of gifts from the Government of the period, but the result of struggles and the frequent mobilisation of workers in several states of the Country'.[39]

Advances in social security in the state of Rio Grande do Sul, namely, pressure for the extension of the benefits of social security to rural wage-workers and self-employed workers, originate in the First Congress of Rural Workers held by the old Rio Grande do Sul Agrarian Front (FAG) in 1962.[40] These demands, with small differences in emphasis and specific issues, were present at all rural worker meetings and congresses that followed. During the 1960s, and early 1970s, claims of rural workers sounded like a 'demand' in the sense of 'asking the government' (and not in the sense of 'rights'). 'In most of the documentation [the issue of social security] appears as an "administrative" problem in the sense of information and management of the appropriation of the "benefits" by the "insured" through their unions, as well as demands by the unions regarding the conditions under which their members could enjoy them.'[41] Perhaps this was

---

36 In some aspects the laws enacted during the military regime were a step backward from previous concessions already given to rural workers, such as the provision of 3% of the national tax revenues to be allocated to land reform, according to article 28 of the Land Statute of 30 November 1964 (prepared before the military coup d'état but discussed and approved by the Congress during the first phase of the military regime, that was more favourable to workers than the following one) that was eliminated from the February 1968 Law.

37 Julião (1962), pp. 50–8, 69–80.

38 Coradini and Belato (1981), p. 162.

39 Gorenstein (1981), p. 237.

40 Coradini (1989), pp. 329–30.

41 *Ibid.*, pp. 331–2.

due to the general political situation, which limited both union action and discourse, and to the influence of the conservative wing of the Catholic Church regarding rural unionism.[42] After 1976, in Rio Grande do Sul, the issue of rural heath and social security benefits was subsumed in broader struggles and public manifestations that became particularly intense from 1979–80.[43]

The interest of the state in co-opting the rural worker unions was manifest in agreements to supply medical care, that were designed to legitimise a given stratified and contradictory social structure became clear with the implementation of PRORURAL.[44] Thus unions became 'service agencies' rather than bodies representing class interests[45] and were dependent on government agencies.[46] At the same time, the interest of unions regarding assistance to rural workers was having trouble in justifying its legitimacy in the union discourse which considered itself more 'representative of a class'.[47] Unsurprisingly, divisions within the union movement occurred. 'Service provider' unions were opposed by independent organisation such as the Movement of Landless Peasants (MST — Movimento dos Trabalhadores Rurais Sem Terra), with a Leninist orientation, that entered the political void created by the lack of emphasis given by the CUT to organising landless farmers.[48]

From the late 1970s, when the 'political opening' of the military began, there was an intense mobilisation of rural workers seeking the provision of healthcare and broader access to social security benefits. Initially, unions focused on the implementation of the law concerning free medical and hospital services. This reflected the absence of public health centres in most municipalities of the interior and the unwillingness of doctors to provide free care except to the very poor.[49] Unions similarly were preoccupied with the low value of rural retirement pensions (considered humiliating by rural workers), and campaigned under the slogan 'we are not half a man to receive half a minimum wage'.[50] By the early 1980s union

---

42 *Ibid.*, p. 331.
43 *Ibid.*, p. 334.
44 Coradini (1996), p. 185.
45 Delgado and Schwarzer (2000), p. 190; Schmitt (1996).
46 Coradini (1989), p. 59.
47 Coradini (1996), p. 184.
48 Fox (1996), p. 21; Schmitt (1996).
49 Coradini (1996), p. 180.
50 Coradini (1989), p. 280.

demands expanded to include the extension of retirement pay to female rural workers. Indeed, the mobilisation of women became part of a broader political strategy.[51] Intense mobilisation ensued. Thousands of protestors converged on Brasilia to lobby congressmen. This action was a major factor in determining the social content of the 1988 Constitution.[52]

The beginning of the mobilisation of female rural workers hails back to the women's movement that began in the late 1970s as part of the national struggle to restore democracy and evolved into a movement for women's rights and the elimination of sexual discrimination. Their achievements included the creation of the National Council of Women's Rights (CNDM) in 1985, during the Sarney administration. The CNDM was active in the debates preceding the constitutional reform of 1988, which embodied a progressive approach to gender issues.[53] The mobilisation of female rural workers, particularly in the south, was also important at the beginning of the 1980s. Its main purpose was to obtain rights to social security, such as retirement pensions and maternity pay. As the movement gained momentum, pressure for these rights was subordinated to demands for full recognition of the status of women as rural workers in their own right. The classification of women as rural social security beneficiaries was rendered more difficult owing to the incompatibility of the 'organisation of family work' and the regulatory framework for health and pensions. The rationale presented by union leaders and rural workers, both 'male' and 'female', was based on the familial and interdependent character of agricultural work. Legislation, however, was based on assumptions of distinction between the individual 'worker' or 'the head of the family', and his/her 'dependants'.[54]

With the Collor administration (1990), the state adopted a neoliberal approach to social security. Social rights were increasingly seen as a 'problem' and less as an 'obligation'. It was argued that 'social rights' presented a 'threat to democracy' both because the rising cost of social benefits posed an obstacle to budgetary stability and because they reflected a discredited corporatist tradition. Information about the social security deficit was frequently published in the press. The social achievements of the 1988 law were depicted as being responsible for 'excesses' that weakened the effectiveness of the state by perpetuating 'injustices'.[55]

---

[51]   Brumer (1990, 1993).

[52]   Brumer (1993); Teixeira et al. (1994); Stephen (1996, 1997).

[53]   Barsted (1994), p. 40.

[54]   Coradini (1989), p. 280.

[55]   Nogueira (2000).

In 1995–96 rural social security 'benefits were contained'. Changes in INSS procedures were designed to control fraud — particularly in the award of benefits. Examples of fraud include: falsification of documents;failure to declare non-agricultural income; and making claims on behalf of family members who were ineligible to receive rural health and social security benefits. As a result, there was a significant increase in the rate of benefit requests rejected. Before the mid-1990s procedures were simple. The main document necessary for rural workers to claim retirement benefits was a statement of entitlement, issued by the union and endorsed by the Municipal District Attorney.[56] The new arrangements involved more complex documentation. Claimants had to produce evidence of rural employment and/or land ownership or tenancy.[57] Rarely did these documents carry the name of women. Silva reports that in mid-1996, after repeated pressures from unions and protracted negotiations with INSS/MPAS, female workers were once again able to claim benefits by presenting documents that named their partner. They could also establish entitlement (if they were unmarried) by showing similar documents that named their father. However, the rural social security reform of 1998 established that a woman claimant had to prove independent affiliation to a union for at least nine years — a period which has subsequently been increased at intervals. The new law also did away with the possibility of including non-rural work in the minimum period of entitlement. Through these measures the government aimed to control the increase of spending on rural social insurance. It should be stressed that since the mid-1980s rural worker unions in the state of Rio Grande do Sul — which took up the advocacy of social security rights as one of their main aims — have advised their members to record systematically their sales in the names of both husband and wife, plus their children.[58]

Some Results of the Implementation of Rural Social Security in Southern Brazil

Agriculture in southern Brazil is characterised by small family farms, producing for the market and independent of adjacent large agricultural and livestock operations. These productive units are inserted in the international market as well as in the national market. Based on family labour, small farms respond to economic crises in different ways from large companies.

---

[56]   Silva (2000), p. 110.

[57]   *Ibid.*, p. 111.

[58]   Brumer (2000).

In the last two decades Brazilian agriculture has faced many challenges. During the early 1980s agriculture policy was marked by a lack of credit and the removal of subsidies, with significant adverse effects for medium and big producers, and for export crops. Producers less affected were those producing for the internal market, thanks to the existence of minimum prices. In the second half of the decade, new policies of deregulation and trade liberalisation, favoured subsidised agricultural imports. Although the application of the Plan Real in July 1994 curbed inflation and stimulated consumption, with positive results for the production of crops for the internal market, the main beneficiaries were importers. The overall result of these policy changes and the concurrent economic crisis was a substantial contraction in the area under cultivation and the incomes of small farmers — which fell by almost 40 per cent.[59] Given deteriorating conditions, access to social insurance became crucial. Social insurance benefits came to represent practically one half of income in 90 per cent of the households surveyed in the south.[60]

Several researchers analysed the results of a household survey undertaken by the Institute of Applied Research (IPEA) during the second semester of 1998, in partnership with the Paraná Institute of Economic and Social Development (IPARDES) and the Department of Rural Socioeconomic Studies (DESER). The survey involved a sample of 3000 households containing members in receipt of social security benefits in the three southern states — Paraná, Santa Catarina and Rio Grande do Sul. The aim of the survey was to assess the 'living and economic reproduction conditions of families that benefit from rural social security in the south of Brazil'.[61] Analysis of the survey data confirmed that 85 per cent of southern families above the poverty line were recipients of at least one rural social security benefit.[62] Meanwhile, among families below the poverty line, only 60 per cent of households were in receipt of a benefit.[63] This demonstrates the importance of social security benefits in lifting rural households above the poverty line. This is because: a) households in receipt of benefits tended to receive more than one, that is an average of

---

[59] Graziano da Silva, Balsadi and Del Grossi (1997), p. 50.

[60] Delgado and Cardoso Jr. (2000), p. 12.

[61] http://www.ipea.gov.br.

[62] The poverty line was defined as half a monthly minimum wage per capital (equivalent to approximately US$60 in 1998).

[63] Delgado and Cardoso Jr. (2000), p. 33.

1.78 benefits per household; b) households in which there were beneficiaries of rural social security were associated with productive establishments, usually in agriculture; and c) households receiving at least one benefit contained members in remunerative employment.[64] This last point deserves special comment. Unlike other countries, in Brazil individuals who receive a pension rarely stop working, mainly because the value of the benefit is insufficient to cover all basic needs. However, working after retirement occurs more among men than among women. In southern Brazil, while 48.1 per cent of male beneficiaries declared 'no occupation', the figure for female beneficiaries was 74.5 per cent.[65] The explanation for this difference probably lies in the invisibility of female domestic work.

The lower the level of household income, the greater the importance of social security benefits.[66] Furthermore, Sugamosto and Doustdar stress that 'one of the main functions performed by social insurance concerns its contribution to the economic and social reproduction of family units, since 63.5 per cent of the beneficiaries are heads of households, and that income from the social security benefits in the southern region represent 41.6 per cent of the average family income'.[67]

One of the characteristics of rural social security in southern Brazil is that 63.2 per cent of the recipients are female and 36.8 per cent are male.[68] The main explanations for the predominance of women as beneficiaries of rural social security are: 1) the minimum age to enter the system is five years lower for women than for men (respectively 55 and 60 years); 2) as they generally live longer, 'besides being beneficiaries by right of retirement, women still tend to inherit pension rights on the occasion of the death of their spouse more often than men'.[69] Among the female beneficiaries of rural social security in the south, 66 per cent receive the benefit of 'retirement due to age',[70] and are mostly 55 or over (only 8.4 per cent of the female beneficiaries are younger than 55).[71] As regards marital status, 52.8 per cent of the female beneficiaries of rural social security are

---

64   *Ibid.*, p. 34.

65   Silva (2000), p. 126.

66   Delgado and Cardoso Jr. (2000), p. 25.

67   Sugamosto and Doustdar (2000), p. 149.

68   Delgado and Cardoso Jr. (2000), p. 18.

69   *Ibid.*, p. 19.

70   Sugamosto and Doustdar (2000), p. 142.

71   Delgado and Cardoso Jr. (2000), p. 20.

widows (there are more widows than widowers), 39.8 per cent are married, 4.2 per cent are unmarried and 3.1 per cent are separated.[72]

Another characteristic of rural social security beneficiaries is that 51.0 per cent have an urban domicile (usually in the county town), while 49.0 per cent reside in the rural area.[73] It should be emphasised that approximately one quarter of the interviewees in the study declared that they had moved their domicile at least once since they had first received benefits, generally from the rural area to the urban.[74] Analysing the reasons for migration, Delgado and Cardoso Jr. indicate that 'generally, migration from the rural to the urban area is related to the need of the beneficiaries or members of their families to live close to places that provide free health-care services (70.8 per cent of the cases) and education (15.2 per cent). On the other hand, in a lesser degree, migration from one municipality to another appears to be related also to a search for urban jobs (7.3 per cent of the cases) and to the proximity to relatives' homes (3.3 per cent).'[75]

Furthermore, almost all family farmers benefiting from rural social security applied part of benefit-income to activities related to farming, 'showing the important role of farming insurance in financing family farms, thus establishing itself as an agricultural insurance'.[76] In addition, as bearers of pension rights, older people became valued members of the household.[77] Pensioners were no longer dependants, but were able to help family members and neighbours with loans and gifts. In the interior of Rio Grande do Sul maternity pay, received by women for four months after childbirth, was also used in family reproduction. This was different from the practice among female urban wage-workers, who stopped working at this time and dedicated themselves exclusively to domestic tasks and taking care of their babies. Rural workers continued to carry out their usual activities

Receiving retirement pay, pensions and maternity benefit in their own right has enabled rural women to decide for themselves how they are going to spend it, thus increasing their personal power. The elderly were no longer dependants of their companions, children and other relatives who were still actively employed, becoming suppliers and managers of one of the few

---

[72] Sugamosto and Doustdar (2000), p. 142.

[73] Delgado and Cardoso Jr (2000), pp. 18–19.

[74] *Ibid.*, pp. 39–40.

[75] *Ibid.*, p. 42.

[76] Sugamosto and Doustdar (2000).

[77] Delgado and Cardoso Jr (1999).

resources that existed in the family production unit. They were now one of the few members of the household with a regular monthly income.

However, some surveys undertaken in the interior of Rio Grande do Sul have indicated that men and women use their benefit money differently.[78] This is why there is an additional effect of the access of rural women to social security. Whereas men use the money they receive for personal expenses, women first try to ensure the support and improve the quality of life of their families. In this sense, the benefit of rural retirement to women provides a guarantee for their own reproduction and that of their families, while only part — although probably the major part — of the benefits received by the men does the same. Another symbolic value of women's access to rural social security as direct beneficiaries is the perception that they participated in these conquests, thus increasing their awareness of their rights. However, it should be said that neither the mobilisations in which they have participated nor the conquest of social rights, nor even the increased perception of 'rights' in general, make these women question gender relations in their day-to-day personal relationships.

Issues for Reflection

'The role of social and union movements that lead to achieving a minimum of rights in the sphere of social and agrarian policy and, mainly, their maintenance in the different struggle of the current situation, is the most significant novelty of the 1990s in the country, whose first fruits have become known and been harvested.'[79] This raises concerns about what happens to social security in the current Brazilian situation. Attempts by the government to reduce the social security deficit, and other measures that included the removal of agricultural subsidies, have impoverished the rural population, transforming access to social security benefits into agricultural insurance and reproduction insurance. Social benefits have become essential to the maintenance of rural activities and probably helped curb rural-urban migration. Since these benefits are perceived as 'conquests' and not as 'donations', workers fight to maintain them, and to voice their opposition to attempts to change the rules or remove 'rights' already acquired. Thus, it can be foreseen that, on the part of the government, attempts will continue to control the access of potential beneficiaries through new demands as to proof of time

[78]   Brumer (2000).
[79]   Delgado and Cardoso Jr. (2000), p. 16.

worked and increase in the time needed to be able to retire, to avoid fraud and increase the amount of contributions; on the part of the rural workers, the main emphasis will be on healthcare, although the latter has improved since the services were decentralised by means of the Sistema Único de Saúde (SUS), it is still very precarious in the rural areas.

Another issue involves the participation of rural unions in the management of rural social security, on which they base their main claim to work with the farmers and their legitimacy. It is unlikely that they will give up their institutional connection and patronage to take action and make claims that may be considered illegal. Thus, it is improbable that they will become more combative than they are now. However, as mechanisms for the 'management' of rural social security, they will certainly take a vanguard role in the struggle to maintain established rights and to broaden and achieve new social security rights for self-employed rural workers.

Finally, it is important to stress that for those groups excluded from social security, like female agricultural wage earners and informal farm workers without a work permit, there is no solution in the short term. For these groups, the only possible legal ways forward are the professional register and access to social assistance programmes (programmes of minimum rent or distribution of basic food packages). At the same time, as stressed by Matijascic (2001), even though women are allowed to retire five years younger than men and have a higher life expectancy, the government is unlikely to try to change their relatively favourable circumstances owing to the greater difficulties they face in gaining access to the labour market.

PART C:
EDUCATION

CHAPTER 12

Ideology and Education:
Equity and Efficiency

Marcial Bóo

Introduction

The expansion of education provision in Latin America from 1950 to 2000 was political, and part of the wider incorporation of the population into society. As early as the late nineteenth century it was recognised that the extension of the vote to all citizens entailed, as an inevitable consequence, the diffusion of education to all.[1] It is no coincidence that, at the beginning of the twentieth century, the slowest improvements in literacy rates occurred in countries such as Peru, Chile and Bolivia, where illiterates were disenfranchised. From 1950, the increasing integration of the population into literate Latin American society through urbanisation, changing occupational profiles and the breakdown of traditional communities, ensured that formal education, and literacy in particular, was seen as a means of sharing economic benefits. The positive correlation between earnings and education became increasingly apparent, symptomatised socially by the use of epithets such as '*doctor*' and '*licenciado*' which reaffirmed the importance of education as a marker of social class. Indigenous, rural populations, as well as those in marginal urban areas, concluded that the hegemonic groups had attained their position of privilege partly due to extensive formal education. The increase in demand for education was cumulative. Once it was believed that social mobility came through education (rather than through marriage, occupation or residence), the demand for formal, state-sponsored education could not decrease. A return to a pre-literate society would be inconceivable.

Given these dramatic societal changes and the change in the perception of education engendered by them, formal enrolment ratios and literacy rates were bound to increase.

This analysis of education provision in Latin America in the second half of the twentieth century demonstrates the impact of these societal pressures towards expansion and how they have been influenced by eco-

---

[1]   Rama (1983), p. 18.

nomic and political priorities. By examining the statistical evidence of education enrolments and expenditure, I argue that each Latin American country is passing through one of five phases of educational development, from a period prior even to an expansion of primary education provision when literacy rates are below 50 per cent and fewer than one in 20 adults have any university-level study, through to a period when primary education is universal with literacy rates approaching 100 per cent and between a third and half of young people going on to post-secondary education. This empirically-based classification forms a descriptive and explanatory model of the nature of education expansion, capable of incorporating external economic and political influences on education provision as well as the internal development of formal education within each country.

In terms of the causes of this pattern of expansion, I argue that macroeconomic and political factors promote or inhibit the expansion of education, yet are insufficient as explanations of the nature of the expansion. Instead, the considerable inertia within the educational system ensures that education provision rarely responds to short-term political initiatives nor immediately to economic growth. It is this educational inertia, a sociological phenomenon, which has a determining influence on the expansion of education in the longer term.

In terms of the consequences of this pattern of education expansion, I argue that an understanding of the five phases of education development can ensure that education policy-makers take into account not only economic exigencies and ascendant political ideologies, but also the historical nature of education expansion within their countries. Different policies are required for different educational phases. This has not always been demonstrated. Tertiary education, for example, has been given priority in many countries out of step with their educational phase. This has had the effect of inhibiting the successful expansion of mass education provision, particularly at secondary level, and reducing allocative efficiency and social equity. I show how expansion has taken place more efficiently and equitably through a balanced use of resources appropriate to the particular phase of educational development, funding educational levels in line with changing underlying demand.

The analysis below relies on education statistics published by governmental and international sources (and sourced in the bibliography), including literacy and enrolment rates, and education expenditure as a proportion of Gross National Product. There are difficulties in the use of these indicators. Gross enrolment rates can exceed 100 per cent, for example, when more pupils are studying than there are in the relevant age cohorts (due to some older pupils still being in learning). More significantly, enrolment rates say nothing of the quality of the education experience. Literacy rates are a poor proxy for this[2] with a definition that has changed markedly over time[3] and a weak correlation with educational attainment.[4] Education expenditure statistics share many of the methodological and comparative differences of all public accounts, covering far less than the World Bank's laudably inclusive definition,[5] and usually omitting the at-times substantial expenditure within the private education sector.

Nevertheless, despite the substantial difficulties involved in a statistical analysis of education for a region comprising 20 countries over 50 years, the study of education indicators reveals a number of trends which, at this necessarily broad level of analysis, can only be measured using these less-than-adequate statistical tools. Indeed, the fact that these trends reveal a pattern which is mirrored to a greater or lesser extent in each of the countries under consideration lends credence to their value.

Trends in the Expansion of Education in Latin America

There have been substantial increases in enrolment ratios and literacy rates in Latin America in the twentieth century. Average enrolment in basic education in Latin America averaged 30 per cent in 1900 and rose to 50 per cent by 1950. By 2000 average primary enrolment was well over 90 per cent. Expansion was particularly fast in the period 1950–65. Secondary and tertiary education also expanded rapidly during this period, such that by 1980 average tertiary enrolments stood at over three times their 1950 level (from five per cent to 16 per cent), with average secondary enrolments increasing from 15 per cent to 25 per cent. Some examples illustrate the speed of the expansion. In Chile, gross enrolment rates for the three education levels increased from 66 per cent, 18 per cent and 1.5 per cent in 1949–50 to 99 per cent, 69 per cent and 19 per cent in 1992. In Honduras, the corresponding figures for 1950 were 22 per cent, three per cent and 0.5 per cent, increasing to 112 per cent, 33 per cent and nine per cent in 1992. In turn, more widespread school attendance facilitated an increase in literacy rates across the region. In Chile, for example, literacy rates climbed

2   OECD (2001), p. 20.
3   Barton (1994), p.78; Street (1995), p. 23.
4   Archer and Costello (1990), p. 201.
5   World Bank (1995a), p. 235.

from 70 per cent in 1950 to 95 per cent in 1995. The corresponding figures for Honduras are 29 per cent and 66 per cent.

Although there are still considerable numbers of children who are not in school, and although literacy rates exceed 90 per cent in only half the countries of the region, these are significant changes in the availability and the role of formal education in the region. Yet even a cursory examination of the statistics reveals that the expansion of formal education provision and its success, as measured by literacy rates, have not taken place uniformly across the region. If these data are disaggregated however and temporal changes are analysed for each country, a number of patterns emerge. These patterns show: a) that a period can be discerned when primary enrolments begin to expand more rapidly than previously; b) that after the period of rapid primary expansion, secondary enrolments begin to expand more rapidly; c) that tertiary enrolments begin to expand after the period of secondary enrolment expansion; d) that prior to the period of primary enrolment expansion, a greater proportion of the population is deemed literate than is enrolled in primary education; and e) that increases in adult literacy occur at a slower rate than increases in primary enrolments and there is no clear correlation between the two. This information, standardised across the region, is represented graphically in Figure 12.1, where point 2 marks the beginning of rapid primary expansion, point 3 the beginning of rapid secondary expansion, and point 4 the beginning of rapid tertiary expansion.

Figure 12.1: Gross Enrolment Ratios and Adult Literacy Rates in Latin America Standardised Over Time.

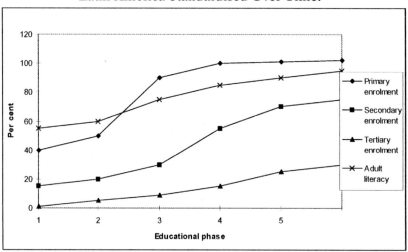

Figures 12.2–12.4 provide examples from Peru, Mexico and Argentina. Each diverges from the standardised model. Peru moved quickly from primary to secondary expansion, but proceeded more slowly to tertiary expansion. Mexico experienced declining enrolments in education levels sequentially starting with a decline in primary enrolments in the late 1970s. Argentina, with historically high literacy rates, passed through its educational phases earlier than the other countries. The standards pattern is nonetheless clear in all three examples.

Figure 12.2: Gross Enrolment Ratios and Adult Literacy Rates in Peru, 1950–95

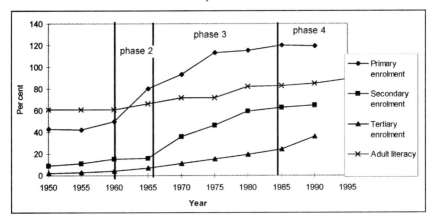

Figure 12.3: Gross Enrolment Ratios and Adult Literacy Rates in Mexico, 1950–95

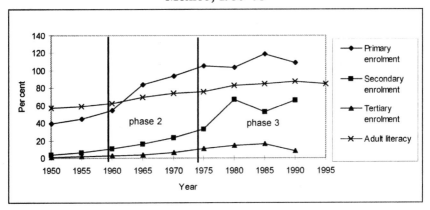

Figure 12.4: Gross Enrolment Ratios and Adult Literacy Rates in Argentina, 1950–95

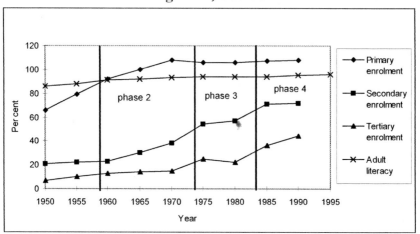

Since 1950 there have also been substantial, yet regular, changes in the pattern of funding for education in Latin America. Per capita spending on education depends on two factors: the amount spent on education as a percentage of GNP, and the level of national income itself. The former has tended to increase during periods when economic and political theory stressed the value of human capital, particularly during the 1960s and in the early 1990s. The latter is contingent on macroeconomic growth and in Latin America coincides with the period up to the early-1970s. Nevertheless, around 1950, average education expenditure as a proportion of GNP stood at only 1.4 per cent. In almost all the countries of the region, primary education was allocated over half of the government's total education budget. During the 1960s and early 1970s, overall education expenditure increased in a number of countries of the region to between two per cent and four per cent of GNP, and by 1976, the average for the region, but with wide variation, stood at 3.4 per cent. By 1992, the average had declined slightly to just over three per cent of GNP. By this time, many countries' education budgets had been reallocated to secondary and tertiary education with a corresponding decline in the allocation to primary education.

As with enrolment data, patterns in governments' education expenditure are visible, linked with the five phases of education development. These patterns show: a) that in initial stages of educational development (phase 1), government spending is focused on the primary sector which receives approximately half of the total government education budget; b) that high spending on primary education precedes the expansion of primary enrolment ratios; c) that as primary enrolment expands (phase 2), the government education budget is increasingly reallocated to secondary and tertiary education; d) that this shift in expenditure towards secondary and tertiary education continues until the period in which secondary and tertiary enrolments have both begun their period of expansion (phases 3 and 4), and e) that for those countries which have experienced all three periods of enrolment expansion (phase 5), the education budget has tended to move once more towards the primary sector. These patterns are represented graphically in figure 12.5.

Figure 12.5: Education Expenditure Standardised by Educational Phase

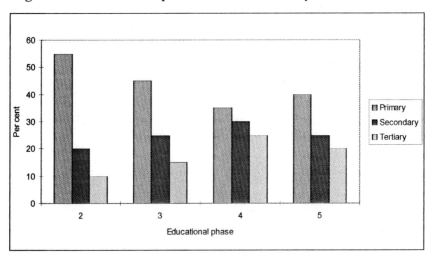

Figures 12.6–12.8 provide examples from Chile, Columbia and Paraguay. None exactly follows the standardised model in Figure 12.5. In Chile particularly, a disproportionate amount of overall expenditure is allocated to tertiary education, but the movement in the budgets largely follows the standard pattern. In both Colombia and Paraguay it is possible to see a relative decline in primary compared to secondary education expenditure as secondary enrolments increase in educational phase 3 which took place in the 1980s in both countries.

Figure 12.6: Education Expenditure by Level, Chile, 1950–90

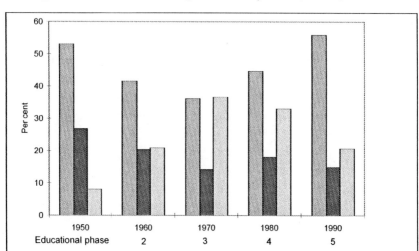

Figure 12.7: Education Expenditure by Level, Colombia, 1950–90

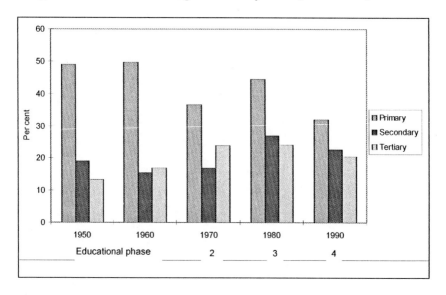

Figure 12.8: Education Expenditure by Level, Paraguay, 1950–90

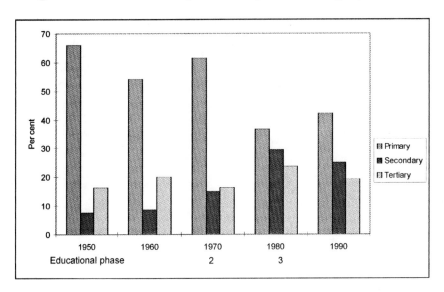

These trends in enrolment ratios, literacy rates and education expenditure define the series of educational stages or phases through which Latin American countries have passed since 1950. The characteristics of these phases are described in Table 12.1.

Phase 1 is characterised by little state involvement in education. Education expenditure is low overall and caters principally for the children of the dominant classes, particularly in the case of the scant secondary and tertiary education provision. When funding for education begins to increase, primary education is the main recipient, tending to receive approximately half of the national education budget. Nevertheless, in most instances, funding per pupil remains poor due to limited national resources and competing development priorities. This, coupled with inadequate teacher education and limited capital stock, often implies poor quality provision.

Phase 2 is characterised by the rapid expansion of primary education provision and a corresponding increase in adult literacy to above 50 per cent. This phase has, historically, marked the beginning of state involvement in educational provision, and in early instances the beginning of significant state involvement in the economy generally. Education expenditure slowly increases as a share of government expenditure with funds gradually moving into secondary and, in some cases, tertiary education, particularly following the improvement of primary enrolment ratios.

Table 12.1: Phases of Educational Provision in Latin America

Phase	Dominant Characteristic	Enrolment ratios (%)			Adult Literacy (%)	State Priorities
		Level 1	Level 2	Level 3		
1	Limited state involvement in education	< 50	< 15	< 5	< 50	Initially little state education, with secondary and tertiary education catering only for dominant groups; later, mainly primary level education expenditure
2	Expansion of primary provision	50–80	15–25	5–10	50–70	Primary education expenditure declines; funding moves to secondary level; some additional tertiary funds.
3	Expansion of secondary provision	80–90	25–55	10–15	70–85	Funds move to tertiary level, often from the primary budget.
4	Expansion of tertiary provision	90–100	55–70	15–25	85–90	Overall education budget declines due to alternative development demands.
5	Consolidation of education provision	100	> 70	> 25	> 90	Consolidation of state education provision; concerns about quality of education; concerns about cost of universal provision leading to attempts to limit state expenditure

Phase 3 signals the consolidation of primary enrolment ratios and a continued increase in adult literacy. Substantial secondary expansion enables up to half of the population to receive some post-primary education. In many countries, overall education expenditure rises, and the increase in funds for tertiary education tends to be drawn from the primary education budget. Primary (gross) enrolment rates are at or over 100 per cent. In Phase 4, the tertiary sector becomes increasingly important with enrolments rising to 25 per cent of the population, and the sector tending to receive a disproportionately high proportion of overall funds.

Phase 5 is one of consolidation, such that primary provision becomes universal, secondary provision comprehensive and tertiary education provision satisfies most economic development needs. Education expenditure remains static or begins to decline. Educational success can no longer be measured in terms of enrolment ratios and rates of literacy as these targets have largely been met. Questions of the quality of education provision thus become the dominant themes of state education policy discourse, together with issues of cost-effectiveness and rates of return to investment. In these cases the state has often begun to initiate a process of withdrawal from education provision, through, for example, the reduction of state financing, the increase in teacher-student ratios, cost-recovery and the selective privatisation of (initially) tertiary education provision.

Table 12.2: Latin American Enrolment Ratios, Literacy Rates and UNDP Ranking, 1995

Educational phase	Country	Primary enrolment (%)	Secondary Enrolment (%)	Tertiary Enrolment (%)	Adult Literacy (%)	UNDP Education Index
5	Uruguay	108	83	50	97.3	0.90
5	Argentina	108	72	44	96.2	0.90
4–5	Chile	99	69	19	95.2	0.87
4–5	Cuba	102	82	21	95.7	0.85
4	Panama	106	63	22	91.8	0.83
4	Costa Rica	103	43	26	94.8	0.85
4	Peru	119	65	36	88.7	0.84
4	Colombia	117	61	14	91.3	0.83
4	Ecuador	123	55	20	90.1	0.83
3–4	Mexico	109	66	8	85.0	0.81
3	Venezuela	96	35	29	91.1	0.84
3	Paraguay	109	34	8	92.1	0.80
3	Bolivia	108	37	23	83.1	0.76
3	Brazil	111	43	12	83.3	0.78
3	Dominican Rep.	97	37	19	82.1	0.78
2–3	Nicaragua	103	41	9	65.7	0.63
2–3	El Salvador	78	26	17	71.5	0.64
2–3	Honduras	112	33	9	72.7	0.67
2	Guatemala	84	24	8	55.6	0.50
1–2	Haiti	56	22	1	45.0	0.38

Sources: columns 1–4 UNESCO, (1995); column 5, UNDP (1995).

This model of educational phases, a descriptive 'ideal type', facilitates a detailed understanding of educational change over time, not only by allowing a more thorough analysis of snapshot education statistics, such as those for

1995 in Table 12.2, than is possible using indicators such as the UNDP's, included in Table 12.2 for comparative purposes, but also by enabling comparisons to be made between countries over time, as in Figure 12.9.

Figure 12.9 Educational Phases in Latin America, 1950–95

Group	Country	Phases (1950 ⟶ 1990)
A	Uruguay	2 · 3 · 4 · 5
	Argentina	2 · 3 · 4 · 5
	Chile	2 · 3 · 4 · 5
	Cuba	2 · 3 · 4 · 5
B	Panama	2 · 3 · 4
	Costa Rica	2 · 3 · 4
	Peru	2 · 3 · 4
	Colombia	2 · 3 · 4
	Ecuador	2 · 3 · 4
C	Mexico	2 · 3
	Venezuela	2 · 3
	Paraguay	2 · 3
	Bolivia	2 · 3
	Brazil	2 · 3
	Dominican Rep.	2 · 3
D	Nicaragua	2 · 3
	Honduras	2 · 3
	El Salvador	2 · 3
	Guatemala	2
	Haiti	

The groupings of countries in figure 12.9, nominally A–D, share certain characteristics. Group A Southern Cone countries (Uruguay, Argentina and Chile) had the historical advantage of high literacy rates and substantial primary provision, in part a product of the widespread understanding of the importance of education and literacy which was brought with the immigrants at the beginning of the twentieth century. They now demonstrate high standards of overall education and are facing many of the educational dilemmas currently being faced in the developed world, including the need to improve the quality of the provision. Cuba is included in this group, although it has attained the corresponding high level of educational achievement through a wholly different path and is facing correspondingly different problems.

The second grouping of countries (Group B: Panama, Costa Rica, Peru, Colombia and Ecuador) has demonstrated substantial educational progress over the last 50 years from low enrolment ratios in all three sectors and low levels of adult literacy to standards of educational provision which come close to those of the more advanced educational members of the region. For a third group of countries (Group C: Mexico, Venezuela,

Paraguay, Bolivia, Brazil and the Dominican Republic) success has been hard to achieve for a number of reasons. The 'lost decade' of the 1980s hit the countries of this group particularly hard – educational levels stagnated and slipped in Mexico and Venezuela particularly, due to difficulties in the macroeconomic environment, while Brazil has unsuccessfully contended with its enormous population and widespread corruption. This has had most impact on the difficulty these countries have had in consolidating the expansion of secondary education (phase 3). Finally, a fourth group of countries (Group D: Nicaragua, Honduras, El Salvador, Guatemala and Haiti) is still struggling to increase the provision of education to primary-age children and, at the same time, to increase adult literacy. These countries only began their educational effort in earnest in the 1970s – hampered by meagre national income, war, debt and the existence of a strong non-literate culture.

Factors Affecting the Expansion of Education Provision

Despite the difficulties of classifying countries by educational phase of development, taxonomies of this kind have a substantial theoretical pedigree. Rostow's (1960) model of developmental stages is well known and Mesa-Lago (1986) produced a similar taxonomy of countries in Latin America with respect to the historical development of social security provision. Within education, Anderson and Bowman (1966, 1973) posited a 40 per cent threshold for literacy rates, beyond which economic take-off and industrial expansion become possible. Blat Gimeno (1983) has also classified education in Latin America according to the proportion of qualified teachers in the primary sector, and Borsotti (1983) according to countries' educational profiles in rural areas. The expansion of state involvement in welfare provision in Latin America has also been well documented, with, for example, Bresser Pereira (1993) positing a cyclical model of state intervention. Ultimately, however, the recognition that 'in Latin America there are several time-scales in the same place'[6] necessitates an analysis capable of coping with latitudinal differences within a longitudinally coherent framework.

Traditionally, longitudinal explanations of the rapid increase in educational provision, particularly in the 1960s, have focused on economic and political factors. The strong positive correlation between economic growth

---

6   Blat Gimeno (1983), p.18, quoting Peruvian President Haya de la Torre.

and the expansion of educational provision has been documented by many. Growth in GNP per capita obviously facilitated greater welfare expenditure in the late 1950s and 1960s and helped to pay for the expansion of education provision. This goes part of the way to explain the growth-enrolment correlation. Causation between education and economic growth has nonetheless proved difficult to establish.[7] Nor is there a clear correlation between increased government funding for education and educational results. Both Colombia and the Dominican Republic, for example, experienced rapid economic growth of around five per cent per annum in the 1960s, with education expenditure increasing from around ten per cent of government expenditure at the beginning of the decade to around 15 per cent at the end. Yet literacy rates in the same period increased from around 64 per cent in both countries by over fifteen percentage points in Colombia and by less than five points in the Dominican Republic. Favourable economic circumstances do not therefore constitute a sufficient condition for improvements in national education provision.

Politically, the growth in education provision has been linked to the waxing and waning of interest in education as a developmental priority. In the 1950s, economic planners began to see in education a means of creating wealth.[8] The belief that education automatically led to increased prosperity, welfare, security and economic development was taken up by economists and fostered by the United Nations and by international and multilateral lenders who were willing to invest in projects to develop human resources.[9] It was recognised by politicians and economists alike that modern industry required a mobile, literate, technologically-equipped workforce and that the modern state was the only agency capable of providing this through its support for a mass, public, compulsory and standardised education system.

The debate on education and development reached its peak in the 1970s following the spectacular increases in enrolment in the region. Yet expansion created the new phenomenon of 'educated unemployment' and the 'educated poor' leading many to question the automatic correlation between education and development. It came to be recognised that planners had been over-optimistic of the ability of education to neutralise social inequalities and foster economic development. With hindsight, the relationship between education and economic development was deemed

7   Psacharopoulos and Woodhall (1985).

8   Blat Gimeno (1983).

9   Hall (1986).

to be 'based on a false analogy with European experience where it was assumed that educational expansion had preceded the industrial revolution rather than vice versa'[10] and Solari was able to assert towards the end of the decade that 'most writers are prepared to agree that new investment in education ... exerts little or no influence on the output of the school system'.[11]

The breakdown of the political welfare consensus in the 1970s was exacerbated by the economic crisis of the early 1980s. Governments cut expenditure on non-interest items, particularly health and education, creating a sustained attack on welfare provision through the increased use of cost-recovery mechanisms, a policy much in keeping with the ascendant neoliberal orthodoxy. The 1970s belief that literacy was a sound economic investment, which would lead to increased productivity received scant attention in the recessionary 1980s. Expenditure on education, even in those countries where it maintained its share of the overall government budget, declined in absolute terms. In some countries its share was also reduced. Primary and secondary enrolment ratios in the region during the 1980s stagnated or declined in over half the countries of the region with minimal improvements, or even slight declines, in literacy rates in a few. Overall, levels of educational attainment at the end of the decade were similar to those of the mid-1970s.

Economic and political factors have therefore acted on education by encouraging or impeding the expansion of provision. Yet explanations of the increase in education provision in Latin America that focus on economic and political factors alone fail to take into account the structural nature of education systems nor how they have developed over time, and do not explain either the increased demand for education or the highly divergent way in which education expanded in the different countries of the region.

Education is a long-term enterprise and, as a complex organisation with hundreds of thousands of personnel and millions of customers, is unlikely to respond immediately to short-term political or economic cycles. Indeed, considerable inertia must be overcome among the teaching profession itself on whose motivation, enthusiasm and commitment the successful operation of the education system largely depends. Particularly in situations where teachers suffer from low prestige, poor training and unfavourable relative incomes, political initiatives and increased expenditure are unlikely to produce rapid results unless solutions are offered to

---

[10]   *Ibid.*, 71.

[11]   Solari (1977), p. 75.

existing teaching and learning problems that match aspirations and are considered feasible and desirable to existing practitioners. In education, as elsewhere, vested interests are strong and institutions often oversized and therefore slow to change even when policy objectives are strong and clear. Moreover, as the completion of the educational process by any one educand can take around six years for each level, there is an inevitable lack of phasing between political and educational time cycles. Thus even in the 1980s, improvement in certain education indicators in Latin America is visible, with literacy rates continuing to increase in most countries of the region. These increases reflect increased investment in, and prioritisation of, education dating back as far as the early 1970s.

This positive inertia in education with regard to adult literacy rates is also a consequence of wider sociological changes, such as the changes in perception of education among the population at large. Massive urbanisation during the post-war period greatly increased both the expectations and the availability of education provision. The greater population concentration, first, reduced individuals' opportunity costs of attending school through the reduction in travelling time for example, and second, facilitated governments' provision of education through economies of scale and the reduced logistical and financial complexities of ensuring full primary enrolment for a highly-dispersed rural population. The concentration of the urban poor, together with the growing political power of the urban middle classes, put pressure on urban authorities to provide primary schooling. The increased educational provision in urban areas promoted, in turn, even greater migration to the cities where economic opportunities were perceived to be greater and welfare amenities more widespread.

High literacy rates, therefore, have not 'caused' economic take-off, as suggested by Anderson and Bowman (1966, 1973), nor necessarily led to educational expansion, but are instead indicators of societal change alongside other social indicators such as degree of urbanisation with which adult literacy rates correlate. It is worth noting that in both ancient Greece and medieval England literacy has been an important indicator of social homogeneity in the transition between one form of social organisation and another.[12]

As such, improvement in literacy rates do not respond directly to government education initiatives nor to increases in expenditure on education. Figure 12.1 (above) reveals that in the early stages of educational expansion, more of the population is literate than is enrolled in primary education, suggesting that the acquisition of literacy practices is partially, if not

[12]   Street (1995), p. 15.

wholly, extra-scholastic. The rapid increase in primary enrolments in phase 2, that of primary enrolment expansion, has only a limited effect on levels of literacy. A consequence of this lack of correlation between literacy rates and other education variables is that it is unlikely that literacy rates *per se* can function as a measure of the success of a country's education policies, as posited by the UNDP amongst many others.

Seen in this perspective, a model which groups Latin American countries by educational phase acquires greater explanatory power. The observation that differences in enrolment ratios and adult literacy rates have remained reasonably consistent over time between countries suggests that historical factors act as more important determiners of the present educational situation than the particular political or economic cycle which the region is currently experiencing. In other words, as with the hypothesis of inertial inflation,[13] the current education situation can be described as a function of: a) the immediately-previous education situation, as well as of the factors discussed above, namely: b) political initiatives; c) the economic situation; and d) societal changes which affect demand for education. This is where an historical model of Latin American education can allow a detailed analysis of long-term education trends, taking account of latitudinal differences between countries and locating them within a structurally-coherent longitudinal framework.

The model of Latin American education presented here thus shows that the favourable political and economic conjuncture of the 1950s and 1960s encouraged the expansion of education provision. Similarly, expansion was impeded by the debt crisis and the cuts in welfare expenditure of the 1980s. These large-scale, external influences had a clear impact on each country's education system, but the nature of this impact was determined by the phase of educational development through which the country was passing. Thus, the 1960s for example marked the beginnings of secondary enrolment expansion in Group A countries, where primary enrolment expansion had already taken place. In Group B and C countries, on the other hand, it was primary education expansion which characterised this decade. Similarly, the 1980s saw little improvement in education provision in many countries, yet while the countries of Group C experienced difficulties with the consolidation of secondary education expansion, it was primary expansion that was impeded in the countries of Group D.

When education first became the subject of developmental debate in the late 1950s, little account was made of how educational systems had devel-

---

13   Williamson (1985).

oped over time and it was regarded as inevitable that the expansion of primary education would in time put pressure on secondary education, stimu-
lating expanded secondary provision and thence tertiary education.[14]
Instead, discussion focused on the discrepancies within all levels of education in comparison with those of the developed world, and on the question
of where investment in education would have the highest social rate of
return. For some, and especially for the middle classes for whom secondary
education led inevitably to university, the funding of secondary and vocational education represented the key to development. Others, encouraged by
loans from international organisations, perceived the developmental gap at
the level of the technocratic and business elites, and therefore supported the
increased funding of national universities. Hence, although in principle it
was accepted that the expansion of primary education and the spread of literacy were fundamental, if not moral, governmental responsibilities, in practice, stronger vested interests led to alternative funding priorities.

Yet by working against the historical pattern of education expansion,
Latin American governments' preferential expenditure on tertiary over secondary education reduced the efficiency of their education programmes
with inequitable consequences. The result has been that secondary schools
function in many countries largely as a conduit to universities, with curricula based on western models of certification inappropriate for and contributing little towards indigenous national development needs. The preferential
funding of tertiary education is regressive and therefore inequitable for a
number of reasons. First, given that historically the expansion of secondary
education has involved the incorporation of students representing the first
generation of their family to attain that level of education, the expansion of
tertiary enrolments before secondary, or even primary, enrolments have been
consolidated serves to widen education, and hence income, distribution.
This trend is exacerbated by the fact that secondary schools in middle-class
urban areas are in general less underfunded than most and enrolment ratios
in those schools are invariably higher.[15]

Second, given that typical unit costs at primary level are between two
and ten per cent of those at tertiary level, and that expenditure on primary
education has a higher rate of return, spending on lower levels of education is
potentially more wide-reaching and allocatively efficient.[16] Third, since private
rates of return in education are higher than social returns, the facts that pub-

---

[14]   Solari (1977).

[15]   Hardiman and Midgely (1982), p. 190.

lic subsidies increase with the level of education and that university educands in particular have increased their share of public funds, suggest that those who can afford the opportunity cost and who have benefited from high-quality (often private) secondary education, reap excessive benefits. Even today in Brazil, for example, university tuition is free to the learner despite the fact that each university student costs 18 times more than government expenditure per student at the primary and secondary level combined.[17]

Fourth, it may be inappropriate to development needs for a country to produce excessive university graduates when demand for their expertise is low. And fifth, the data above which indicate that the underfunding of secondary education is linked to poor secondary enrolment increases, also suggest that in the medium term further success at tertiary level could be hampered by the lack of enough suitably-educated secondary graduates. Collectively, these factors imply that educational phase 3 — that of secondary enrolment expansion — cannot be bypassed in the attempt to foster development through education. Venezuela, for example, has still not managed to increase gross secondary enrolments above 40 per cent, largely due to its prioritising tertiary over secondary education (see Figure 12.9).

The belief that primary education expansion should be consolidated before secondary expansion begins has been voiced since Sarmiento speaking of Argentina one hundred years ago. It is not the case that full enrolment is necessary at one level before expansion begins at the next. But in education unlike, say, in industry, it is impossible to omit either basic or intermediate systemic development and still ensure comprehensive and effective third-level attainment. An efficient national university system requires large numbers of well-educated candidates from which to select its intake. Adequate primary and secondary provision therefore underpins success at tertiary level. Yet to argue in favour of a series of developmental stages within education does not necessarily deny countries currently experiencing secondary expansion the benefit of other countries' experience, nor condemn them to permanent comparative educational underdevelopment. Debates about the quality of provision, for example, are taking place across the continent. It does, however, mean that there are necessarily different policy implications for the different countries at different periods of educational development.

Argentina and Chile, for example, having largely consolidated enrolment expansion have shifted much of their focus to improving the quali-

16   UNESCO (1991a), p. 69.
17   Cardoso and Helwege (1992), p. 29.

ty of provision, which was at the heart of Argentina's 1993 Federal Law of Education, and on cost-recovery, particularly at university level, which both Argentina and Chile, as well as others, are working towards. On the other hand, the countries of Group B, including Peru, Colombia and Panama, and those of Group C, including Mexico, Paraguay and Brazil, while clearly able to benefit from the experience of other countries' measures to increase quality and reduce cost, nonetheless have a more immediate and important focus — reaching and bringing in to learning all its primary and secondary-age children. Countries such as Brazil cannot hope to maximise its graduate achievement if the stock of students is drawn from a massively underfunded secondary sector accounting for less than ten per cent of total education expenditure since the late 1970s and in which only half of all secondary-age pupils are enrolled.

The good news, of course, is that almost regardless of governments' education policies, long-term adult literacy rates as well as enrolment ratios tend to increase in Latin America as a result of societal change and the positive effects of educational inertia. Macroeconomic and political stability are necessary but not sufficient conditions for this educational success. But there are clear lessons for governments from this process of educational change. First, the high political prioritisation of education and the targeting of poorly-educated population subgroups both tend to boost enrolment increases, particularly at primary and secondary level. Second, due to the inertia within educational systems, national education policies should remain reasonably consistent over time and formulated for the longer term, rather than as a consequence of short-term political and economic exigencies. And third, to ensure an efficient and equitable allocation of resources, attempts must be made to make education spending less regressive. Data on the historical expansion of education in Latin America demonstrate how this can be done. The countries of the region have passed through clearly discernible educational phases over the last 50 years, and funds more accurately targeted at the level of education appropriate to the country's particular educational phase are more likely to satisfy societal demand, and hence lead to the more rapid expansion of education provision.

The expansion of education provision in Latin America from 1950 to 2000 has therefore been the result of a number of interacting factors. The economic and political environment has certainly had a significant impact on the rate of expansion. But it is the wider societal environment, including increasing urbanisation and national homogeneity, which have had a more significant influence, creating strong long-term pressure towards increasing literacy and enrolment rates. This inertia is demonstrated in a series of five educational phases, such that the expansion of primary provision precedes that of secondary provision, which in turn precedes tertiary expansion. Analysis of expenditure priorities in the region reveals that when funding has not matched educational phase, the success of expanded provision has been compromised. As a consequence, further expansion of Latin American education in the twenty-first century, particularly in primary and secondary education, depends not just on favourable politics and economics, but on an understanding by policy-makers both of their countries' current educational profile and of its historical development.

CHAPTER 13

Education Reform in Latin America: Decentralisation or Restructuring?

Andrew Nickson

Introduction

Popular dissatisfaction with public education in Latin America has been growing for several decades and there is general agreement among policy-makers at the highest level that the basic (primary and secondary) educational system of the region is in need of serious reform. Despite the fact that enrolment rates and the share of education in total public expenditure are both high in most countries, several major problems have been identified. First, low allocative efficiency, as measured by the extremely high per capita expenditure on university education. Secondly, low productive efficiency, as measured by high repetition and drop-out rates, and low number of classroom hours per year. Thirdly, low effectiveness of a 'poor quality' education, as measured by a theoretically based curriculum de-linked from the world of work, and imparted by poorly-qualified teachers who receive minimal in-service training. Fourthly, high 'vertical' or social inequity, as evidenced by a two-tier system whereby students from the top three deciles of the population, who have been privately financed through primary and secondary school, dominate the publicly-funded university system. Finally, high 'horizontal' or territorial inequity, as measured by striking disparities in coverage (i.e. average years of schooling and adult illiteracy rates) between urban and rural areas.

Decentralisation as a Panacea

During the 1970s and 1980s educational specialists began to place the blame for many of these problems on the highly centralised organisation of the educational system. This thinking reflected the new fashion for decentralisation and for strengthening local government in the region, itself the result of a fortuitous coalition of the following pressure groups: fiscal federalists bent on reducing the fiscal imbalance at the macro level by transferring greater fiscal responsibility to lower tiers of government; technocrats bent on improving service delivery by overcoming the gross inefficiencies in the form of high transaction costs resulting from the need to seek approval from the ministerial headquarters before even minor decisions could be taken at the local level; and political radicals keen to bridge the gulf between the state and civil society through participatory forms of democracy.[1]

A broad consensus emerged that was based on a shared belief that educational decentralisation would lead to improved productive and allocative efficiency, as well as greater effectiveness and equity. However, decentralisation, which was now seen as a key strategy in order to alleviate the problems within the education sector, can be defined in four very different ways:[2] policies that deconcentrate decision-making to sub-national directorates of the central government; policies that delegate decision-making to autonomous public entities; policies that devolve decision-making to local government; and policies that privatise decision-making to the business sector or the not-for-profit sector.

Although the reform rhetoric at the time emphasised devolution of service responsibility to local government, in practice most decentralisation during this period took the form of limited de-concentration of decision-making powers within ministries of education, from central headquarters to regional field offices. With the notable exception of Chile, policies that devolved decision-making to autonomous public entities, to local government or to the private sector were noticeable by their absence.

The New Public Management

At around the same time a quite separate panacea — known as the New Public Management (NPM) — was emerging in New Zealand and the United Kingdom for solving the problems of the public sector. The NPM paradigm provided the foundation for the major educational reform in both countries — the 1988 Education Reform Act in the UK and the 1988 Picot Report in New Zealand.[3] Through the leverage of IMF structural adjustment programmes and the powerful intermediaries of the World Bank and Inter-American Development Bank, the ideas associated with the NPM began to be forcefully impressed on Latin American governments. After decades of inertia, this policy transfer process kicked off a major process of state reform in the region during the 1990s.

---

[1] Nickson (1995).

[2] Rondinelli et al. (1984).

[3] Bullock and Thomas (1997).

NPM has become a collective term used to describe a bundle of management techniques introduced to the public sector, many of which are borrowed from the private sector.[4] The essence of the state reform process in Latin America is encapsulated by three main tenets that have been shaped by the NPM paradigm. This states, first, that in order to overcome chronic macro-economic imbalance, the overall role of the state in the economy should be reduced. Second, within the framework of this reduced role, the state should retreat from involvement in productive sectors of the economy but strengthen its involvement in social sectors. Third, in those sectors where the state retains a strong involvement, the state should switch from a direct provider role to that of strategic 'conductor', at one and the same time regulating and enabling the delivery of services by other providers.

Under the NPM, the reassignment of roles to the actors in the process of service delivery (different levels of government and field administration, the private sector and the not-for-profit sector) is based on principal-agent theory. This involves a split between the purchaser (the central ministry) and the providers (the rest), which is driven primarily by the effort to capture gains in economic efficiency, equity and effectiveness. In the case of the education sector, the central ministry switches from its former direct provider role into a new role as strategic director of the educational system as a whole through its ability to 'purchase' service from other providers.[5] Two new functions are paramount. First, there is the concern for effectiveness through the introduction of national standards (for example, a national curriculum and national standards of teacher training) and measurement of outcomes (for example, national testing). Second, there is the concern for equity through the introduction of a system of compensatory financial transfers designed to counter vertical and horizontal inequities. In addition, special investment grants are targeted on children in greatest need. Meanwhile, the providers, including sub-national levels of government, deconcentrated units of the central ministry, public schools, the private sector and not-for-profit bodies, assume a new role in administrating various aspects of the delivery of educational programmes on behalf of central government, to which they are held accountable.

---

[4]   Ferlie et al. (1996); Hood (1990); Walsh (1995).

[5]   This is often referred to as 'ministry without schools' – *ministerio sin escuela.*

Recent Educational Reform in Latin America

In the 1990s educational reform was once again on the political agenda in Latin America.[6] Sweeping new educational laws were passed in several countries: Argentina (Ley Federal de Educación, 1993), Bolivia (Ley de Reforma Educativa, 1994), Colombia (Ley General de Educación, 1994) and Mexico (Ley General de Educación, 1993). The contemporary educational reform process in Latin America, as reflected in the above laws, incorporates major features of the NPM. These include compensatory financing schemes to improve equity, strengthening of the national curriculum, shifting the emphasis from coverage to the quality of education, evaluating educational outcomes through national testing, focusing on the school at the centre of reform, increasing the number of years of compulsory education, shifting the focus of concern of educational information systems from collection of data on inputs to data collection on outcomes and restructuring central ministries of education, via the removal of operational functions and the incorporation of a new strategic role.

But the 'take-up' of the NPM paradigm by educational policy-makers in Latin America has not been simply the product of external pressure. It has been assisted by the recognition that greater regional competitiveness in the 'knowledge-based' global economy requires a more skilled labour force and a growing consensus that basic education is a 'missing ingredient' that is holding back the overall development of Latin America. Recent studies suggest that more education would not only substantially raise economic growth rates, but also reduce the extremely high level of income inequality found in the region.[7] There is also growing agreement that closing the 'education gap' in Latin America is not simply a question of increasing public spending but allocating those resources in a more efficient and equitable manner. The bloated bureaucracies of central ministries of education and the centralised decision-making powers that they contain are now seen as major obstacles to educational reform.

The following review briefly examines the roles of decentralisation and NPM in six Latin American countries (Argentina, Bolivia, Chile, Mexico, Nicaragua and Venezuela) that have witnessed the most far-reaching educational reforms in the region in recent years.

---

6   Peru was the only major exception.

7   Inter-American Development Bank (1998).

Argentina

From 1978 onwards responsibility for the financing and administration of federal primary schools in Argentina was gradually transferred to provincial governments. This was carried out in an authoritarian manner by military rulers who dictated the terms and conditions of the transfer. By contrast, the transfer of responsibility for secondary schools from 1992 was carried out in a democratic context through negotiation between federal and provincial authorities. The pressing need to reduce the overall fiscal deficit was the motive force in both cases.[8]

Nevertheless, the transfer of responsibility provided the basis for a redefinition of roles between tiers of government along the lines of the NPM. This was spelled out in the 1993 Federal Education Law, the first national education law in the history of the country. Major features of the law included: the introduction of ten years of compulsory education between the ages of five and fourteen; a basic national curriculum; the introduction of quality control through a new system of national testing, Sistema Nacional de Evaluación de la Calidad (SINEC); a Social Education Plan to provide compensatory finance to schools identified as in need; and a national plan for teacher training. The Federal Education Pact signed on 11 September 1994 between the federal and provincial governments provided the political support for implementation of the new law. With the noticeable exception of the province of Córdoba, the role of local government in the educational reform process has been extremely limited.

The recent experience of educational reform in the province of Buenos Aires, the third largest educational authority in Latin America, highlights the limitations of transferability of the NPM in the context of an administrative culture dominated by patronage and the 'spoils system'. The province was the last of the 23 provinces to receive the transfer of federal schools, and this was only completed in 1994. In 1998 it administered 15,500 schools with four million pupils. There is a longstanding tradition of devolved School Management in the province that operates through school boards (*consejos escolares*) in each of the 134 municipalities.[9] Members of these boards are elected for a six-year term coterminous with

---

8   Filmus (1998).

9   The School Boards were first established in 1875 by Sarmiento. As director of education of the Provincial Government of Buenos Aires (1856–61), he had been strongly influenced by the education model pioneered by Horace and Mary Peabody Mann in Massachusetts, which combined funding from the centre with a high level of local autonomy.

municipal authorities. Until 1994 they had powers to appoint and dismiss teachers, and to create new schools in their jurisdiction.

The 1994 Provincial Education Reform considerably reduced the powers of School Boards and tightened the control over them by the provincial education authorities. First, the previous six-person membership of each board was altered to a range between four and ten, depending on the number of schools in each municipality. Second, their power to appoint and remove teachers was removed. Third, the previous ban on teachers standing for election to School Boards was removed. The provincial government justified the reforms on the grounds that the School Boards had appointed teachers on political criteria rather than merit. However, the transfer of responsibility for appointments to district inspectors of the provincial education service is unlikely to solve this problem, since these posts are occupied principally by leading members of the teachers' union.

The transfer of responsibility from the federal government did little to improve either productive efficiency or equity. The sole criteria used to distribute financial resources within the province is the size of the school (i.e. enrolment and number of grades) while the socioeconomic conditions of the children are not considered. As a result, there is widespread adulteration of statistics (for example, by raising enrolment figures) in order to justify extra teachers and higher grades. Similarly, the geographical distribution of educational personnel (teachers and administrators) still bears little relationship to relative need because current labour laws disallow transfers of personnel, except at the instigation of the staff member. As a result, schools in the poorest municipalities continue to have the lowest qualified teachers.[10]

Since 1994 the provincial authorities have identified 'vulnerable' schools by applying five indicators of socioeconomic need, based primarily on where children live. This is used as a basis for distributing 'extra' resources, but not for the basic distribution of grant aid, nor for teacher training. On the contrary, financial resources continue to be distributed primarily on the basis of clientelist relations between provincial authorities and local leaders.[11] As a result, there is no linkage between plan objectives and actual expenditure, and no evaluation of the implementation and impact of expenditure. Consequently, the distribution of educational resources by the Provincial Department of Education is still not based on criteria of efficiency, equity and effectiveness.

---

10 Arango (1998).
11 Tiramonti (1996).

Bolivia

Decentralisation to the local level is commonly undertaken as a means of democratisation and of increasing citizen participation, especially of ethnic or disadvantaged minorities.[12] This was certainly the case in Bolivia, which underwent a radical state reform process during the 1990s, the cornerstone of which was the 1994 Popular Participation Law (Ley de Participación Popular — LPP). The reform process was designed to end the system of 'informal apartheid' under which 80 per cent of the population living in rural areas were bereft of any political representation at the municipal level. This political discrimination was mirrored by the extremely low coverage and poor quality of educational services in rural areas in comparison to urban areas.

The state reform process gave community organisations considerable influence over local schools. For the first time in the history of the country, the LPP formally recognised the network of deep-rooted community organisations in rural areas, which were henceforth given the generic title of Organizaciones Territoriales de Base (OTBs). The law also granted a novel supervisory role to new directly-elected municipal surveillance committees, Comités de Vigilancia (CVs). The law also granted them sweeping powers to review current and capital expenditure on education at the local level. In practice this has meant ensuring that contracts for new school buildings are awarded and implemented in a transparent fashion, as well as monitoring the chronic absenteeism of rural school teachers. In the event of alleged irregularities, the CVs may request that central government transfers to municipalities be suspended pending an investigation. The LPP also encouraged the involvement of parents and community organisations in school management through the creation of School Boards (Juntas Escolares — JEs). The law granted a high degree of flexibility over the membership and organisational structure of the JEs in order to reflect the heterogeneity of cultural traditions, especially in rural areas. By 1997 School Boards, comprising a total of 50,000 members, were operating in 11,081 state schools, equivalent to 80 per cent of the total.[13]

The LPP also gave limited powers over education to municipalities. Ownership of all school buildings was transferred from central to local government, which henceforth became responsible for teaching materials,

[12]   Winkler (1989).
[13]   Molina (1997).

the maintenance of school buildings and equipment and the construction of new schools. An Education Reform Law passed at the same time strengthened relations between schools and local government. The boundaries of the district offices of the Ministry of Education were redrawn to correspond with municipal boundaries. Local Educational Boards (Directorios Locales de Educación — DILEs) were created in all municipalities, comprising the mayor, a representative of the departmental office of the Ministry of Education and a representative of the vigilance committee.

The Bolivian case presents an example of educational decentralisation motivated primarily by the desire to strengthen local democracy rather than as part of any long-term strategy of educational reform along the lines of the NPM paradigm. In part due to the absence of any such strategic vision from the centre, by 2000 this experiment was beginning to run out of steam. The DILE had been abolished and replaced by a municipal-wide educational board, Junta Distrital (JD), the members of which were drawn exclusively from civil society. The respective roles and responsibilities of the OTBs, the CVs and the new JD remained unclear, leading to widespread confusion. The municipal education departments remained starved of human and financial resources and were coming under the increasing control of the education office of the departmental government. And in both administrative tiers staffing was subject to rampant political clientelism.

Chile

Educational reform in Chile has been one of the most far-reaching in Latin America to date and is clearly based on the NPM paradigm. For this reason, it merits special discussion. The basic principles were laid down during the military dictatorship of General Pinochet and have been followed by the successive civilian governments since the return to democracy in 1990. In 1980 a presidential decree authorised the transfer of responsibility for administering basic education to municipalities, including personnel, school buildings and finance. According to this decree, teachers were henceforth contracted by municipalities as employees covered by the general labour law.[14]

The 1980 reform also authorised private sector participation in the delivery of basic education, through the novel arrangement of privately-

---

[14] With the return to democracy, a 1991 Statute for Educational Professionals (*Estatuto de los Profesionales de la Educación*) gave back to teachers in municipal schools the special labour rights and career prospects as public employees. Teachers employed in private schools receiving municipal subsidy remained under the general labour law.

owned but publicly-subsidised schools, known as Centros Educativos Particulares Subvencionados. These were henceforth allowed to compete for enrolment with municipal schools. Under this new arrangement, the role of the central ministry is to inspect and supervise the operation of the educational system. Inspection refers to matters such as compliance with basic requirements for all educational establishments as well as compliance with specific requirements imposed on municipal and private subsidised schools in order to be eligible for the state subsidy. Supervision refers to compliance with national educational objectives and curriculum norms, as well as support to schools and teachers with the aim of raising the quality of education. The inspection and supervisory functions are carried out by de-concentrated units of the central ministry — in the form of 13 regional secretariats and 40 provincial departments.

The state subsidy to municipal and to private, subsidised schools is calculated by multiplying a capitation per student by the average effective attendance during the previous three months of the school year. The capitation is based on a centrally determined unit of account known as the Unidad de Subvención Escolar (USE). The subsidy expressed in USEs is determined for each type or level of education, but is weighted according to the type of school (one or two shift), geographical region and if the school is rural. Municipalities may top up this central subsidy to schools under their direct control with grants from their own resources on a voluntary basis, although few do so.[15]

This arrangement delegates to parents or guardians the right to choose which school their child attends. At the same time, this parental decision defines the destination of the state subsidy. This has given rise to competition between municipal and private, subsidised schools as they compete for enrolment up to a maximum of 45 children per class, the maximum level permitted by the state subsidy.[16] As a result of this competition, enrolment in municipal schools has gradually fallen as parents have opted to enrol their children in private, subsidised schools. By 1998, 55 per cent of enrolment in basic education was in municipal schools, 34 per cent in private, subsidised schools and nine per cent in private non-subsidised schools.

A comprehensive national testing system, Sistema de Medición de Calidad de la Educación (SIMCE), one of the first in the world, was introduced in 1992. The results for each school are published in the press. A national sys-

[15]   Parry (1997).

[16]   Although not in rural areas, where there is no competition.

tem for school performance evaluation, Sistema Nacional de Evaluación del Desempeño de los Establecimientos Educacionales Subvencionados (SNED), was introduced in 1996. This measures school performance according to factors such as effectiveness, improvement as measured by SIMCE scores, initiative, improvement in working conditions, equal opportunities and the involvement of parents and guardians. Schools that perform well on the SNED inspection receive a special monthly bonus, which must be spent entirely on the teachers who work there. Such schools are selected every two years, and now cover about 25 per cent of the total enrolment.

The Chilean reforms, which had been initially aimed at privatising the whole system of basic education have now settled down to a co-existence between the public and the private, subsidised schools, characterised by three main features. First, there has been a far-reaching administrative decentralisation of primary and secondary education, under which responsibility has been passed to local government, but which is also aimed at encouraging school autonomy. Second, a strong central ministry now carries out a regulatory and enabling role, enforcing rules and regulations, supervision, technical support and providing extra resources for redistributive purposes, while avoiding direct administration of schools. Third, the private sector has an active presence in the delivery of basic education. This takes the form of a non-subsidised sector, in which the Catholic Church has traditionally predominated, and a more recent sector, motivated by profit, which receives a state subsidy.

Mexico

Until 1992 the federal government in Mexico financed and directly administered the lion's share of primary and secondary education throughout the country. There were only six states where the federal government financed less than half of the combined (federal and state) expenditure on education. But after two decades of gradual administrative de-concentration by the Ministry of Education (Secretaría de Educación Pública — SEP), responsibility for all primary and secondary schools that were previously federally-funded was suddenly transferred to all 31 states. The political agreement, Acuerdo Nacional para la Modernización de la Educación Básica (ANMEB), was rushed through in just two days — 18 and 19 May 1992.[17] The massive transfer covered 630,000 employees (514,000 teachers

---

[17]   Merino (1998).

and 116,000 administrators), who had responsibility for 13.4 million students and 100,000 schools. The 1993 National Education Law that accompanied this transfer re-enforced the role of the centre in the educational reform process, through the imposition of national standards in teacher training, prescribed textbook, and a national curriculum. A compensatory programme, Programa para Abatir el Rezago Educativo (PARE), was set up to channel extra funds to the four poorest states.

In order to promote parental and community participation in education, the ANMEB called for the establishment of local councils at the level of the individual school (Comité de Participación Social) and for each municipality (Comité de Educación Municipal). Despite the national directive, hardly any of these councils ever came into operation. The proposed school-level committees overlapped with the well-established parent associations (Asociaciones de Padres), while the proposed municipal-level committees failed to gain the confidence of the necessary diverse range of stakeholders because of the exclusive political practice of the ruling party, the PRI. As a result, the reforms have not yet led to school autonomy, and nor has local government become actively involved. Their impact on overall efficiency and equity within the educational system has been minimal to date.[18]

The transfer of responsibility for basic education to state level has not even improved allocative efficiency, even though basic pay and conditions of teachers under the formerly federal system and under the new state system have been equalised. During the transition period, semi-autonomous agencies were created at the state level to assume responsibility for the payroll of the former federally-funded teachers, while the payroll of state-level teachers continued to be administered by the state education secretariats. Over time, a number of states succeeded in unifying these two bodies, but even where this has happened, the two payrolls themselves have not been integrated. In practice, this means that personnel administration of teachers under the former federal programmes continues to be treated separately from that of state-level teachers. This has led to gross misallocation of teachers between schools. The main explanation for this situation is the factional power struggles within the powerful Mexican teachers union. [19]

One striking exception to this negative panorama is the state of Aguascalientes, where substantial improvements have been achieved in educational performance since 1992. With the active support of the state

[18]   Pardo (1998).
[19]   Santizo (1997).

governor, a dynamic reform team succeeded in carrying out a raft of major reforms along the lines of the NPM. A new educational secretariat (Instituto de Educación) was granted substantial autonomy. The secretariat's capacity to design and monitor the reform programme was based on a detailed data base, *clave única*, for every child in school and the results of an annual testing programme for all children in primary six and secondary three that was introduced in 1996, the first of its kind in Mexico. Its power was strengthened by the de-concentration of educational administration within the state to a network of regional co-ordinators. Each of these was given overall responsibility in their area of jurisdiction for nursery, primary and secondary education as well as for the inspection service. Its capacity to implement reform relied heavily on greater control over the educational inspectorate, whose role was gradually converted from a purely disciplinary one into a supportive role. A 'co-option' strategy of actively selecting influential union activists to occupy positions as co-ordinators and supervisors was successful in avoiding opposition from the powerful teachers' union.[20]

Nicaragua

The most radical educational reform in Latin America began in Nicaragua in 1993. It combines the basic premise of the NPM, through the devolution of responsibility to school councils, with a strong neoliberal slant, through the introduction of fees charged to parents. The reform programme initially involved merely the transfer of responsibility for administering the payroll for state schools to municipalities. This transfer was carried out in only ten out of the 143 municipalities before it was quickly abandoned in favour of granting a high degree of autonomy in management and financial decision-making directly to schools.[21] The directors of the new 'autonomous schools' (Centros Autónomos) receive capitation grants directly from the central ministry to cover teacher salaries and non-salary costs. By 1997 50 per cent of secondary schools and 13 per cent of primary schools were classified as 'autonomous'.[22] Parents have a voting majority on school councils and the school director is always a member. Schools with less than 500 students have five-member councils, including three parents and one teacher. Schools with more than 500 students have seven-member councils, including four parents and two teachers.

---

[20]   Alvarez (2000).

[21]   King and Ozler (1998).

[22]   Castillo (1998). Secondary schools only became eligible for autonomous status from 1995.

Democratic practice varies, with parents' representatives directly elected in some cases, while in others they are appointed by the director or ministry officials.[23] In theory, the school councils can recruit and dismiss the director, although in practice most directors remain centrally appointed. Community participation in school management is strong.[24] School councils have powers over budget, personnel and planning functions. They also determine the level of fees charged to parents for attendance and/or examinations, the proceeds of which are used to raise teacher salaries or to cover other costs. Fees are mandatory in secondary schools but voluntary in primary schools, although in practice there is wide variation in their application.

The 'strategic' role of central government in the new institutional arrangement, as envisaged by the NPM paradigm, is still underdeveloped. A crucial role is played by the local-level ministry of education officials appointed to each municipality in promoting and monitoring the implementation of the reform process. Equity considerations are still haphazard, although there is a systematic financial preference in favour of poor autonomous schools through capitation grants and the disbursement of additional funds for school infrastructure repairs.[25] Although the ministry can now count on a detailed performance audit of all autonomous schools, there has not yet been any reform of the national curriculum, and no national system of testing has been introduced. Nor is there any national programme for pedagogical improvement, although teachers would welcome this. [26]

Venezuela

In 1989 a decentralisation law was passed that envisaged the gradual transfer of responsibility for social services, including education, from the federal to state governments. In the case of education, a key aim was to cut back the bloated administrative payroll of the central ministry, thereby releasing funds for urgently needed investment. At that time, 50 per cent of primary and secondary enrolment was accounted for by federal schools, 20 per cent by state schools, 28 per cent by private and religious schools and only 2.5 per cent by municipal schools.[27] Municipalities were given little consideration in the transfer process — in fact the limited educational

23   Gershberg (1999).
24   Arcia and Belli (1998).
25   Gershberg (1999).
26   Fuller and Rivarola (1998).
27   Gamus (1998).

powers of local government were removed by a municipal reform law passed in the same year. The transfer of educational responsibilities has been extremely slow since 1989. This was primarily because the absence of any unified system of pay and conditions for federal, state and municipal teachers galvanised trade union opposition to the transfer. By 2001 responsibility for basic education had been transferred to only three out of 22 states: Aragua, Lara and Nueva Esparta.

But some improvement in educational administration could take place even in those states where responsibility for basic education was not transferred. In 1989 the first directly elected governor in the state of Mérida began a pilot project for strengthening basic education among those schools — half of the total number and one-third of total enrolment — that were directly controlled by the state government. By 1994 it had provided extra resources for 22 targeted schools in poor areas. Features of the programme included the introduction of a double shift system (most school children in Venezuela only attend for a half day); two school meals per day; improvement to school buildings; and introduction of computers. The project was able to overcome opposition from the powerful national teachers union by appealing directly to its members. [28]

Decentralisation, Local Government and the NPM

Any discussion of decentralisation cannot be divorced from the particular historical context in which that discussion takes place. In the 1980s the pressure for decentralisation in Latin America was driven primarily by 'political factors', namely the benefits that the devolution of service provision, by strengthening local government, could contribute to the democratisation process.[29] This discussion, which influenced policy towards the education sector as well as towards other social sectors, was particularly pertinent in countries emerging from authoritarian rule, where there was a strong recognition among policy-makers of the scale of the 'democratic deficit' that had to be met. Under this approach, the particular needs of the sector — whether education or health — were subsumed within this wider concern for strengthening local democracy.

However, in the 1990s the parameters of this debate were overtaken by events. The issue of decentralisation itself has ceased to be self-standing

---

[28]   Knavery (1995).

[29]   Rojas (2000).

and has become a factor within a far more fundamental debate on 'state reform'. As shown above, the state reform process itself has been strongly influenced by the ideas of the New Public Management (NPM). The pressure for decentralisation has now become primarily driven by economic rather than political factors, and is much more focused on the needs of individual sectors, in pursuit of increased welfare benefits from public expenditure, as measured by indicators of efficiency, equity and effectiveness. The particular impact that these new organisational arrangements will have on municipalities in particular, and local democracy in general, has now been relegated to secondary consideration.

As in other sectors, the driving force for educational reform has come from above. Social movements have been notably absent in shaping the reform agenda and in the process of its implementation. The pursuit of these new NPM objectives has led to changes in the organisational arrangement for carrying out both existing and new functions. Under the complex 'reshuffling' of responsibilities that has taken place, some functions have become more centralised while others have become more decentralised. The above review of the recent experience of six countries suggests that staff appointments, payroll management and financing have tended to become more decentralised. On the other hand, the introduction of a stronger national curriculum, linked to national testing and achievement standards, suggests a move towards greater centralisation. The traditional approach to this question sought to determine whether the movement over a range of different functions amounted 'on balance' towards greater centralisation or towards greater decentralisation.[30] This uni-linear perspective of the territorial dimension of decentralisation is now too simplistic and is redundant as a methodology for policy analysis. It needs to be replaced by a far more complex multidimensional mosaic that is inherent in the new functional perspective on decentralisation that has been introduced by NPM reforms.

Two recent comprehensive surveys of education decentralisation in Latin America in the 1990s confirm this new perspective. The first of these, covering seven countries, started from the premise that 'Decentralization of educational services ... is undoubtedly a megatrend in the region'[31] yet concluded that '... there is no simple dichotomy between centralized and decentralized systems but rather a variety of

---

[30]   McGinn and Street (1986); Tedesco (1988); Prawda (1993); Espínola (1994).

[31]   Di Gropelli (1999), p. 160.

options. Indeed the only common trend seen in all the systems for the provisions of services is the strengthening of the regulatory role of the state ... and the transfer of the direct management of the services to subnational levels'.[32] The second survey, covering six countries, acknowledged that 'some educational functions are decentralized even within centralized systems, and others are centralized even within decentralized systems'.[33] The study concluded that:

> In sum, there is growing evidence that at least some of the characteristics of education decentralization reforms that focus on school autonomy, as opposed to municipal or regional autonomy, contribute to high-performing schools. Decentralization to subregional governments may also yield some educational benefits by allowing greater innovation and greater flexibility to adapt resource allocation to local prices, but they have not yet been proved. [34]

These regional trends mirror a similar process already evident from a study of 14 OECD countries where the NPM paradigm is more pronounced:

> The distinction between centralization/decentralization is too crude to be useful in capturing current international developments in educational administration. What we see happening in many systems, e.g. the U.K., Australia, Canada, is a restructuring of the educational systems in the sense that in some domains authority is given to the school (e.g., in the area of teaching methods), whereas in other domains centralized measures are taken (e.g. a national curriculum or a national assessment programme).[35]

It is clear from the above that under the current educational reform process in Latin America the transfer of functional responsibilities to local government, hitherto the litmus test of decentralisation when viewed from the 'territorial' perspective, is becoming of relatively minor importance. Instead, a new actor — the school itself — is emerging as a major player. This is most pronounced in Nicaragua and in some Brazilian states, especially Minas Gerais, where control over some resource categories have also been transferred directly to schools since the mid-1980s.[36] More recently, community-based school councils actively participate in the routine man-

---

[32] *Ibid.*, p. 164.

[33] Winkler and Gershberg (2000), p. 206.

[34] *Ibid.*, p. 218.

[35] Meuret and Scheerens (1995), p. 2.

[36] Paes de Barros and Mendoça (1997).

agement of schools, including the appointment of school directors.[37] As a result, there is growing evidence in Latin America that local government is being bypassed in the educational reform process.[38] If devolution to local government in the 1970s and 1980s was a rhetorical device that masked mere de-concentration to regional offices of the Ministry of Education, devolution to schools in the first decade of the twenty-first century may actually weaken the limited educational functions of local government.

Conclusion

The criticism that under the guise of decentralist discourse, governments in Latin America today are re-centralising educational powers (i.e. through the imposition of national curriculum, national testing and school inspections) is ill-conceived. This unilinear perspective, locked in the mindset of the 1970s and 1980s, is no longer adequate to address the complex organisational consequences of the education reform process now under way in the region. A far more pertinent question is whether the state in Latin America has the institutional capacity to perform the new regulatory and enabling roles that it is now obliged to assume under the NPM reforms.[39]

Three examples illustrate this challenge in the case of education. First is the question of financial management. Given the enormous disparities in access to resources, even within the public educational system, the granting of greater autonomy for schools as part of the new decentralisation process will necessarily lead to greater diversity of outcomes unless the central funding agency is able to recognise such differences between schools and adjust grants accordingly to provide more resources to poorer schools in order to compensate for these disadvantages. Paradoxically, this can only be achieved by strengthening administrative capacity at the centre (i.e. the Ministry of Education). If this does not happen, there is a risk that greater school autonomy will worsen rather than improve the prevailing horizontal inequities. Second is the question of pedagogic management. The ability of the central funding agency to translate the results of national examinations into the policy-making process is crucial in order to improve the overall effectiveness of the educational system.[40] Third is the question of human resource management. The underlying philosophy of

---

[37]   Guedes, Lobo and Walker (1997).

[38]   Di Gropelli (1999); Winkler and Gershberg (2000).

[39]   Batley (1999).

[40]   For example, in Argentina the results of the national testing programme, SINEC, are not incorporated in educational policy-making.

granting greater school autonomy presupposes an 'enabling' capacity by the centre to shift the organisational culture at the school towards 'team management' and 'management by objectives'.

In the various OECD countries where the NPM originated and has spread rapidly, the implementation of these sophisticated 'strategic' roles by central ministries of education is carried out by professional career civil servants. Yet in Latin America NPM-type reforms in the education sector, as in other sectors, have not been accompanied by the introduction of a career civil service, comprising merit-based recruitment and with promotion linked to individual performance and in-service training. Despite repeated attempts in this direction, civil service reform remains '... the area (of public sector reform) where success has been hardest to achieve'.[41] In this respect, the observations concerning the system of educational administration in Latin America made by a researcher over 25 years ago are still relevant today: '... the minister of education is careful to appoint to sensitive offices only educators with the right political persuasions and whose party loyalty can be counted upon ... The unfortunate consequence of this situation is that the educational institution is an extension of the political institution and, therefore, educational decisions are often made for good political rather than good educational reasons.'[42]

The persistence of clientelist-based practices of recruitment and promotion within the public administration system throughout much of the region has led observers to question the transferability of the NPM paradigm to Latin America. There is a real danger that NPM discourse may simply be used as a 'discourse tool' within a personalistic game played by politicians adept at using reform as a convenient 'socially constructed narrative' to meet their own ends.[43] As one writer put it, Latin America is caught up in a paradigm shift from 'old' public management to NPM, but without ever having itself experienced the classic features of Weberian bureaucracy associated with the former.[44] It is therefore not surprising that a recent review attributed the contrast between the significant educational reforms carried out in Latin America since the mid-1980s and lack of positive results to date to problems associated with policy implementation.[45]

[41] Rowat (1996), p. 9.
[42] Hanson (1974), p. 209.
[43] Spink (1999).
[44] Méndez (1997).
[45] Gajardo (1999).

Successful professionalisation of educational management remains limited with the exception of Chile, where a cadre of educational administrators now exists at the central and regional level. Indeed, civil service reform remains the crucial missing piece in the jigsaw of state reform in the region. Until it is seriously addressed, the impact of NPM in the education sector, as in other sectors, will remain limited.

CHAPTER 14

Paradoxes of Chilean Education Reform, 1989–2000[*]

Ernesto Schiefelbein and Paulina Schiefelbein

The Chilean voucher system developed in the 1980s was modified in the last decade by three reform waves that eventually improved key inputs of the educational process, but international reports published in 2000 showed that educational achievement has not got better. The voucher system created incentives for parents to choose the best school for their children among the local supply of schools (as part of the free-market economic model implemented by the military regime), but teaching methods have not changed. In theory, bad schools would improve in quality or go out of business, but the process may be too slow. Therefore, paltry quality improvements and the return to democracy triggered three distinct reform processes in the last decade.

The 1990 reform was embedded in the transition from autocratic to democratic government. Sociologists were the intellectual authors of this initiative, which focused on improving the working conditions of teachers and supporting their creativity. The 1994 reform focused attention on the classroom effectiveness and the need for better instructional materials, more learning time and improvements in the teaching/learning process. In this case, education research was the driving force. The third reform was the unlikely result of discussing and approving several laws and ordinances in the second half of the decade. In 1996 Congress approved funds for extending the daily schedule and a new curriculum was decreed for grades 1–8 (basic education). In 1998 a new curriculum was also decreed for grades 9–12 (secondary education).

The decade began optimistically, but ended gloomily. In the late 1990s the government even announced that primary education problems were solved, but three comparative reports published in 2000 by reliable international institutions revealed few improvements in achievement in basic education and low functional literacy levels of the adult population. Local authorities (and many international observers) had assumed that the quality of Chilean primary education had improved to expected standards and

[*] The authors have benefited from conversation with Larry Wolff, Noel McGinn, Himelda Martínez, Mark Hanson and Robert McMeekin.

moved forward to finalise the development of the education sector in the second half of the decade. The World Bank also funded a secondary education project and a reform of higher education. Thus, the three gloomy reports on comparative international testing published in 2000 shocked many observers and the reports have not been widely commented, nor has the lending institution disclosed its failure. In fact, policies similar to those that proved inefficient in the case of Chile are still being used in other Latin American countries.

Therefore, it is time to review the lessons of the 1990s and to go back to the drawing board. The continued study of educational reforms in Chile is important because it operates a nationwide voucher system and the government has 'correctly' applied all the conventional (national and international) wisdom. So, this chapter starts with a brief glimpse at the aims and interests behind each reform effort and closes reviewing possible causes of the poor outcome in Chile and reliable strategies for effective improvement.

Motives Shaping each Reform Process and the Sobering Reality of Testing

The 1990 reform was part of the political platform of the democratic government that replaced the autocratic government of Pinochet. The intellectual authors of this initiative were sociologists, who focused on teacher motivation and creativity, curriculum design and remedial programmes. Quality improvements in 1981–90 had been poor; there was an unequal distribution of learning; little social mobility for the poor or reduction of poverty was in evidence; and the private sector was demanding a better-trained labour force.[1] But the main element of the platform was the improvement of benefits for teachers.[2] Even though a careful decision to support the 'decentralisation process carried out in the 1980s' was included in the campaign platform, the new government 'reversed the deregulation of the teaching labour market'.[3] The so-called Teachers Law (Estatuto Docente), enacted in 1991, established centralised bargaining, a common structure of wages throughout the school system and made it practically impossible to lay off ineffective teachers. At the same time the World Bank lent money for 'positive discrimination' to the most inefficient 900 primary

---

[1]   Schiefelbein (1991).

[2]   Schiefelbein and Schiefelbein (2000a), p. 413.

[3]   Cox (1999), p. 35.

schools for allocating grants to school designed projects (Proyectos de Mejoramiento Educativo — PME) assuming that teachers alone were able to shape interesting learning experiences; and for developing a national computer network.

The second democratic government that took office in 1994 maintained the whole team implementing the World Bank project, but made public that 40 per cent of Grade 4 students could not understand simple sentences. The press used this figure to make public opinion aware of the magnitude of the educational problem. The time was ripe because the UNESCO Regional Office for Education had carried out a comprehensive research programme in the early 1990s after Latin American ministers acknowledged low achievements in most countries and requested advise.[4] Chilean managers were aware that functionally illiterate workers constrained their possibility to compete in a global market.[5] They knew that most Chilean workers below the median salary were unable to communicate in writing or learn from their job manuals.[6] On the other hand UNESCO had evaluated a successful project implemented in Colombia and replicated it in Chile and other countries.[7] The data and reports gathered by UNESCO were analysed in a national committee with a fair representation of education stakeholders.[8] A national consensus on a reform strategy (that complemented all inputs provided in the World Bank project) was reached in September 1994. This consensus focused on the classroom level (including teaching methods and processes, well-tested materials, additional learning time and use of computers to share best teaching practices) and an efficient allocation of teachers.

The 1995–98 period was supposed to be the implementation of the consensus reached in 1994, but eventually new elements were introduced shaping up to a third reform wave. A long bargaining process between the government and the teachers' union concluded in 1995 with increased teachers' wages linked to the amount of time worked and the flexibility to adjust the teaching staff to enrolments. In 1996 the students' daily schedules increased from five to seven chronological hours when parliament unanimously approved a law. However, the time extension recommended

---

4   UNESCO (1992, 1996).
5   ECLAC–UNESCO (1992); Apec (1999).
6   OECD (2000).
7   UNESCO (1996); Schiefelbein (1992).
8   Brunner et al. (1994).

in the 1994 consensus was used for 'more of the same' rather than for processes that would change the role of the teacher (for example to use the additional time in project preparation and implementation). In the same year an updated curriculum was enacted for grades 1–8, but no learning guides for implementing relevant classes was designed and tested. A large school building programme to provide class space for the expanded daily schedule started in 1997 and was at the half way stage in 2000. A new curriculum for grades 9–12 was also approved in June 1998.

In spite of great optimism about the impact of the reforms fuelled by positive World Bank mission reports on the excellent implementation of every component of the projects and apparent impacts, Chilean educators reported that the teaching processes had not changed.[9] These misgivings were confirmed when the Grade 4 national testing showed in 2000 that increments were rather small.[10] Such findings were later on confirmed by the TIMSS international report[11] and two international reports on adult functional literacy levels.[12] From being the example to be followed the Chilean experience became a hot potato. It was the time to review the causes of the stagnation and to find effective strategies. An analysis of each of the three reform waves is presented below.

The 1990 Reform

The 1990 strategy was embedded in the transition from an authoritarian to a democratic government and the demands made by political parties and unions (Social Debt). The first democratic government elected in 1990 designed its strategy after a long internal debate. The educators wanted to keep the decision-making process closer to the community. Those more politically oriented and supporters of the Estado Docente (Teaching State) defended a centralisation process. Eventually, the platform of the democratic candidate upheld the decentralisation route, but promised participatory opportunities for teachers and parents as well as a national salary agreement for teachers. The strategy was also influenced by world events such as the fall of the Berlin Wall, the UNESCO-led Major Project on Education for the region and the World Conference on Education for All held in Jomtien.[13] A project was prepared and negotiated with the World

---

9   Schiefelbein and Schiefelbein (2000d).
10   SIMCE (2000).
11   IEA (2000).
12   OECD (2000); UNESCO (2000).

Bank to develop primary education, as soon as the new democratic government took power.

Participation was introduced through elected mayors (*alcaldes*) and grants to locally developed 'improving school projects (ISP)'. The decentralisation policies of the military government had relocated power in the hands of *alcaldes* (appointed by the central government) rather than promoting community participation and accountability. Therefore the election of mayors returned power to the community. The ISPs were eagerly supported by the World Bank missions (which objected to the successful Colombian model based on well-tested textbooks with detailed instructions for students to carry out attractive learning processes). The World Bank staff assumed that projects prepared at the school level would raise the performance, even though 'we know very little about the effects of choice on learning'.[14] Leading scholars like Basil Bernstein and Martin Carnoy visited the country and validated the government decision. Eventually, regional staff appointed by the Ministry of Education made the selection of projects and, therefore, once again centralisation broadened its role.

The new government had also promised to raise teachers' salaries. The military government's reduction of the power of the teachers' union had resulted in declining salaries, a pattern seen in other countries.[15] Nearly ten per cent of the teaching staff had been dismissed in 1974–80 accused of militant leftist tendencies, and the training of new teachers was transferred to universities. However, the military regime overlooked the fact that low salaries attract people from the lower half of the socioeconomic distribution, which is usually closer to leftist political positions. So teachers backed the election of the democratic government and the new government 'reversed the deregulation of the teaching labour market'.[16] The so-called Teachers Law (Estatuto Docente) established centralised bargaining, a common structure of wages, and made it practically impossible to lay off ineffective teachers.

In sum, by the end of 1993 the government had improved the conditions of education because it had: (i) raised teachers' salaries; (ii) started an educational computer network (ENLACES) that reached some 300 schools in 1993; (iii) provided books, classroom libraries and materials; (iv) granted some US$10,000 to each of approximately 2,000 education

---

13   Cox (1999), p. 30.
14   Patrinos and Ariasingam (1997), p. 4.
15   Cox (1999), p. 25; Hanson (1997), p. 9.
16   Cox (1999), p. 35.

improvement projects (PME) designed at the school level and selected at the provincial level; (v) provided positive discrimination to 900 low-achieving schools; and (vi) extended pre-school through centralised public agencies.

The 1990 reform strategy assumed (as it was also assumed in the military regime) that each teacher alone (using only all his/her knowledge and experience)would be able to design highly rewarding experiences in each class so that students' learning would be maximised. Unfortunately, no attempt was ever made to help teachers gain access to well described and detailed lesson plans, written by other teachers, that could be adapted to classrooms around the country.[17] In the Chilean educational culture each teacher was expected to start preparing lesson plans from scratch. This work culture widely differs from other professional fields, such as music (where masterpiece scores are readily available); medicine (where surgery manuals describe in detail all the steps of each operation); or drama and ballet (where the scripts of each play are readily available to recreate the production). The assumption that each school works in isolation is reflected even in the lack of mechanisms for principals and teachers to visit the best or worst schools in the municipality, or for establishing mutual visits and discussions. In fact, schools had no practical advice whatsoever to improve their teaching methods, except for very general conferences.

No changes were proposed in the early 1990s for textbooks, even though they did not conform to the main characteristics of a good learning process. For example, textbooks distributed to schools: (i) did not suggest activities that students should carry out to grasp the main concepts; (ii) did not use prior knowledge; (iii) did not contain instructions for effective group work; (iv) presented no options for the student to make decisions about how to engage in the learning experience; (v) there were no demands (or few instructions given) for writing conclusions or reporting the work carried out; (vi) they did not include activities to be carried out with the family; and (vii) provided limited opportunities for students to self-evaluate their work. Acceptance of traditional books constrained the teachers' ability to change the predominant frontal teaching method used throughout their whole education, including the pre-service teacher training institution.

Adding to the poor quality problem, there was a gap in the late 1980s between the *total number of school hours per year* available in Chile for teaching and learning compared to the total in developed countries. In Chile, the school year included some 160 effective school days and a daily schedule

---

[17]   Page et al. (2000).

of five chronological hours. In developed countries, the school year included 180 to 200 school days and six to seven hours per day. Therefore, the learning time for Chilean students was one-third shorter than the time available for students in most developed countries. The new government in 1994 raised these issues.

The 1994 National Consensus

The 1994 strategy focused on the learning process aiming to complement the on-going World Bank primary education project. It was based on the analysis of data showing the poor performance of the educational system; specific guidelines presented by UNESCO to the ministers of education in 1993; and the evaluation of the strategy by a High Level Interagency Mission that visited Chile in April 1994.[18] The mission included ten internationally well known educational reform practitioners.[19] Their endorsement was instrumental in the construction of the national consensus on proposed reforms agreed later on in a Presidential Commission appointed in mid 1994[20] and in the unanimous support in Congress for approving funds in 1996 for an extended daily school schedule.

The minister made the country aware of the education problems and the feasible solutions. At the outset, the issues were widely discussed in the mass media. Newspapers and TV stations reported the inability of 40 per cent of Grade 4 students to understand simple written messages and highlighted that most of them were children from families below the average socioeconomic level. Municipalities operating the decentralised system were not able (alone) to cope with that problem. Fortunately, UNESCO had successfully tested in marginal schools some interactive materials that helped students to be actively involved in sound learning experiences. Newspapers and TV stations reported those experiences showing that learning problems could be solved. Public opinion eventually accepted that teacher centred whole-class instruction (frontal teaching) should be blended with active learning.[21] In addition, bidding on textbook procurement eventually included half a dozen required criteria linked with active learning; the World Bank project was revised to make sure that all schools would have computers to access the Internet (in fact the whole project

[18]   Tedesco et al. (1994).
[19]   Schiefelbein (1997, 1996).
[20]   Brunner et al. (1994).
[21]   Schiefelbein (1992).

should have been deleted but such an action could have been used as an excuse for future failures and a similar project would be eventually designed), and a small set of *descriptions of the best learning experiences* was developed by the best teachers of the country. Also, the 'available time for learning' gap (with developed countries) was included as a key element in the National consensus.[22]

The 1994 strategy focused on the solution of daily problems of teachers compelled to generate each week some 20 to 30 successful learning experiences; one in each new class session. This approach was based on massive research carried out over the past decade by the UNESCO Regional Office for Education.[23] Such research identified a massive failure in reading as well as proven successful classroom strategies that could cope with such an enormous problem of low student achievement. The UNESCO findings were transformed into a checklist to identify the necessary changes in classroom activities and linked cultural variables. For example, the 'Teachers Law' (enacted in the early 1990s) was identified as an obstacle and a bargaining process was started to allow municipalities to re-allocate teachers according to changes in school enrolments

In Chile, teachers' salaries had been relatively low (in the 1980s and early 1990s) with respect to other jobs requiring four years of university training. Therefore, teacher-training institutions had to prepare students selecting the teaching career because there were no other alternatives open to them. Subsequently, principals (or municipalities) have to screen applicants that mainly graduated in the lower quartile from their secondary education. The pool of talent was severely limited. Thus, there was a vicious circle that would keep average salaries low and consequently prevent the educational system from hiring the best-qualified high school graduates of each generation. Thus, salaries were gradually raised (doubled in the decade) so that better candidates might be attracted to the teaching profession.

Other cultural variables (or myths) restricting improvement in education were also socialised. Several misleading 'expectations' were identified and criticised, including:

(i)   Why should each teacher generate interesting learning experiences from scratch and why was access to the best lesson plans on specific subjects not organised in order to make them available to teachers throughout Chile?

22   Brunner et al. (1994).

23   UNESCO (1992, 1996).

(ii) Why were textbooks designed to provide 'bits of knowledge that teachers could use in certain moments of the learning experience they design' rather than being directly addressed to the student that should carry out a personal learning experience?

(iii) Was the traditional amount of 'school time available for learning' enough for the expected level of learning, bearing in mind the amount of time allocated in developed countries?

(iv) Was it realistic to expect that each school could act alone to design its own curricula, as well as implementing the best teaching strategies available or should several curricula be available for certain schools (not willing or able to design their own curricula) to select from among them?

(v) Should students be competing with their classmates in order to advance towards their personal development or it is feasible to use group-work to sharpen thinking processes, improve writing, discuss options and reach consensus?

(vi) Should students learn because there is a teacher transmitting their wisdom (i.e. the locus of control of the learning process is external to the students) or because the students are immersed in a challenging experience?

(vii) Are the parents marginal to the main activities of the school or are they sharing their culture and characteristics for students to enrich their class discussions?

(viii) Was it fair to assume that teachers working extra hours tests and homework (when frontal teaching was delivered) provide formative evaluation or should it be an activity carried out as part of the class-work mainly during group-work?

Some 'vicious circles' were made evident. Because many teachers were accustomed to evaluating students' work in their homes, they tried to minimise the amount of extra work devoted to evaluation. Therefore, language tests emphasised spelling and grammar isolated from the use of language for communication, because it took less time to grade those tests. A survey showed that the average Chilean primary student write about six pages of compositions (freestyle writing) in the whole school year. In any case, there was little formative evaluation to help students to improve their future performance. Most of the time, evaluation was limited to a grade to be reported in a card.

The 1994 strategy supported the sharing of teachers' best experiences. It was requested that the 'ENLACES' computer network include a mechanism for teachers to share their best lesson plans and for easy retrieval of past experiences (unfortunately the designers of the network eventually omitted this mechanism in their design). A national contest for the 'best lesson plans' was carried out in 1994 and 1995 with support from UNICEF and UNESCO, along with a system of national awards (prizes) for the best teachers. Those prizes were effective to counterbalance the ethic of competition among teachers that inhibits sharing of 'best practice'. With all these materials and case studies available, schools were expected to be able to prepare their own curriculum. However, the lack of a website in ENLACES to accumulate and share lesson plans reduced the effort to a journal of limited diffusion.[24] However, textbook design started to change through a new bidding process that included specifications for support of relevant learning process, but only in 2001 were editors asked to include data on the evaluation of their use as part of the bidding process.

In summary, the 1994 strategy questioned the main characteristics of the traditional organisational culture and proposed systematic changes. They were highlighted and supported by the Interagency Mission in early 1994[25] and later on by the National Presidential Commission for Education.[26] The tasks of the following ministers of education were to implement these agreements in the ensuing years, including legislation on extension of the daily schedule and salaries.

The 1995–2000 Agreements on Legislation and Management

In the 1995–2000 period efforts were mainly focused on extending the daily schedule, improving management and implementing new curricula. All in all it was a huge task that turned attention away from classroom processes. Two weeks were added to the length of the school year and the daily schedule increased 40 per cent (from five to seven hours per day). The latter involved building more space, because schools were used in two shifts. These activities depleted the energy of authorities and eventually the time extension (recommended in the 1994 consensus) was used for 'more of the same' rather than for processes that required a different role from the teacher (for example to use the additional time in preparing and implementing education projects).

---

[24] Noguera (2000).

[25] Tedesco et al. (1994).

[26] Brunner et al. (1994).

Poor management of public schools also proved to be too difficult to handle. For example, even though a dozen world experts recommend that the best teacher should be teaching the first grade,[27] new (inexperienced) teachers were (and are) assigned to the first grade. Thus, children did not achieve a good command of reading and writing skills. Also the amount of time teachers spent in the classroom was (and is) less than the official time they should work, particularly in the case of marginal rural or urban teachers. It is not easy to supervise if teachers really teach the required amount of time in schools operating in areas that are isolated or without telephones. Finally, the local use of huge amounts of resources has likewise proved to be difficult to supervise. Municipalities were financing ten per cent of their school budgets with their own resources,[28] but the figure varied according to the wealth of each one. On the other hand, the large size of this financial activity has attracted vested interests of political bosses and kinship groups (*padrinos*). Some teachers are hired according to their political partisanship or family ties. In any case, there are no objective indicators of teachers' performance; therefore, evaluation of teachers at the municipal level is not based on objective information.

Curricula were updated and further decentralised in 1996–98. The new curricula included a core of topics covering some 60 per cent of the learning time. Though most local schools used the curricula suggested by the Ministry, each school principal was able to determine the curricula to be used in the remaining 40 per cent of the available learning time. Changes in curricula imposed additional pressures on teachers. If the learning processes were poorly implemented with a simple curricula, a more complex curricula (implemented by the same group of teachers) could only create havoc in most cases. By the same token, if many students could not master basic skills it would be even more difficult to develop critical skills amongst primary or secondary school pupils,

Frontal teaching and lack of learning materials had constrained student's achievement, mainly in schools operating in population areas below the average socioeconomic level. These constraints were probably linked to the 40 per cent of Grade 4 students that were unable to understand the main message of a short article on the first page of a national newspaper. This poor performance was far below the expected increments in quality generated through competition with private educational initiatives. But several other

27   Schiefelbein, Wolff and Schiefelbein (1998).
28   Winkler and Rounds (1996), p. 366.

comparative education achievement reports have been published at the turn of the century. They can be used to assess the effects of all these reforms.

Main Outcomes after the Last Decade of Reforms

The reform process has generated both positive and negative outcomes, but the expected improvement in the quality and functioning of the educational system derived from market choice, public choice, local bargaining and a national testing system did not materialise. The positive side includes management aspects, enrolments, time to learn, testing and more resources and inputs. The support of the decentralisation process continued, there had been an impressive expansion of private education (45 per cent of total enrolments) and total enrolments (98 per cent net enrolment for the 6–13 years age group), and the World Bank projects have been fully and opportunely implemented. There are more school days attended by students (180 days) and teacher's salaries are now close to the international average (over twice the per-capita income). There is also an efficient payback of vouchers; a well administered testing system; more public resources (4.8 per cent of GDP); a larger share of public resources allocated to primary education (near 40 per cent); and central bureaucracy has been reduced.

The negative side includes seven key issues:

(i)   40 per cent of additional time has been used (or wasted) to teach 'more of the same'.

(ii)   Textbooks are still traditional and their use should be organised by the teacher.

(iii)   There is no accumulation of 'good teaching representations', nor incentives to add new ones.

(iv)   There is no increase in community and parent participation, this remains as little as before, and there is no role for parents in education decision-making.

(v)   There are isolated areas in which no public choice is available, and the dumping of poor students into the public schools adds to class heterogeneity.

(vi)   There are few advances in the quality or level of achievement and many students are not going to reach the minimum levels of training required for working

(vii) Pre-service teacher training is delivering new teachers ready to continue with the traditional 'frontal' teaching prevailing at all education levels.

Technical secondary education managed by private industry is graduating students that are in demand by the labour market. Available fragmentary evidence suggests that results are good, even though the unit cost is sometimes twice as much as the cost of municipal technical secondary schools.[29]

Several institutional advantages were used in implementing the reforms. Management capacity is adequate for operating resources and the level of public corruption is low. As a result, an efficient pay back of vouchers has operated, including effectively penalising schools for inaccurate reporting of student attendance.[30] The use of standardised government accounting has helped the monitoring of expenses and budgeting. Past experience and management ability were also the basis for the design and operation of a well administered testing system.[31] Since 1995, testing information has been widely published in newspapers.

> Intermunicipal variations in fiscal capacity generated inequities in per pupil school expenditures' because municipalities provided a small supplement to the school attendance grants they received.[32] However, 'the relatively large size of the central government school attendance grant (almost 90 per cent of total financing) ensures all pupils receive a relatively high minimum level of school services'.[33]

Not all students can choose the school they attend. In one-third of the total of 327 municipalities there are no subsidised private schools and only one-fifth have paid private schools. Furthermore, private schools are concentrated in urban areas. In 91 predominantly rural municipalities, students have no choice but to attend public schools.[34]

Subsidised private schools used to charge illegal fees in various forms.[35] A law was enacted in the early 1990s to allow all schools to charge fees not exceeding 50 per cent of the voucher value. This law may compound problems mentioned in the following paragraph. It may be necessary to find ways to assure equality of access to opportunities for good education.

---

[29] Cox (1999), p. 25.

[30] Winkler and Rounds (1996), p. 373.

[31] Cox (1999), p. 26; Winkler and Rounds (1996), p. 373.

[32] Carnoy (1998), p. 318.

[33] Winkler and Rounds (1996), p. 373.

[34] Carnoy (1998), p. 317.

[35] *Ibid*, p. 327.

Despite the legal prohibition of student selection in any voucher school, private subsidised and more recently municipal schools tend to select the better pupils. Most of the low achieving pupils have to be taken by the public system, but recently students with lower than average grades have been required to enrol in private subsidised schools. The advantage of more homogeneous groups was estimated to be six percentage points, after controlling for average socioeconomic background of students.[36]

There are negligible improvements in pupil performance measured by achievement tests.[37] Measured in terms of scores of the private students from high socioeconomic levels, there has been a slight reduction in the gap with respect to students in public schools.[38]

On the other hand, there was an increase in total real spending on education during the 1990s from 5.4 per cent in 1990 to 7.4 per cent in 2000.[39] Resources per students doubled for a (practically) constant achievement level. Therefore, the cost-effectiveness was rather low.

Furthermore, there are no differences in the value added by private and public schools,[40] that was assumed to be the main source of improvements in quality. While 'subsidised private schools appear to be more cost-effective than municipal schools' given their lower unit costs, the differences disappear when profits 'captured by the owner/director of the school' are included.[41]

Lessons Learned and Final Comments

It is no longer appropriate to see reforms in Chile as a 'model' for education policy across Latin America, but as an excellent case to learn about 'what works' and which are the problems of a mechanical implementation of the 'conventional wisdom'. For example, we have learned about active reactions of an educational system to incentives (in terms of expansion of private schools) and lack of reactions in terms of quality or closing learning gaps. The introduction of the voucher programme led to a large number of schools changing status from paid-private to subsidised-private.

---

[36]   *Ibid.*, p. 320.

[37]   OECD (2000); UNESCO (2000); SIMCE (2000).

[38]   Schiefelbein and Schiefelbein (2000).

[39]   Cox (2001), p. 8.

[40]   Mizala and Romaguera (1998); Carnoy (1998).

[41]   Winkler and Rounds (1996), pp. 368, 373.

Later on, reductions in the real value of the voucher led to paid-private schools regaining their earlier market share. [42]

Sharing of the successful learning experiences designed by individual (or groups of) teachers may be an effective way to accumulate educational knowledge but mechanisms for such processes should be provided on the internet or in data banks.

The approval of special curricula (presented by leading schools) could feed a 'data bank of programmes of study' that other schools could use to select the learning activities that best fit their specific needs. Therefore 'several curricula' could be equally acceptable for a subsidised school to fulfil the corresponding requirement to get subsidies.

We are now aware that achievement scores of students in public schools should not be compared with those in subsidised-private schools, because 'private schools have a continuing advantage in terms of student background characteristics.[43] However, better-designed teaching strategies may eventually bridge those gaps.

There is a need to check with stakeholders of public education the 'commitment' of privately educated officials to 'delivering' reform in the public sector. Those officials have delayed ten years the access of deprived children to computers similar to those used by their children in their homes and it may have been a contestable decision. The same has happened with the use of learning guides (as in the Colombian *Escuela Nueva*) that have proved to be highly cost-effective for students from deprived families. It is always dangerous to make decisions that do not affect the decision-makers or their siblings.

We have also learned about preconditions to take into account for implementing a voucher system. Management capacity and sound financial accounting in the original public system have also been important in implementing the decentralisation reform. The reach and reliability of the banking system should also be considered.

International lending banks should revise their policies and strategies for improving education. Those institutions should spend more time and resources to evaluating the cost-effectiveness of the projects approved and implemented. Each country cannot pay for carefully designed research evaluations that should be used by all countries of each region.

---

[42] *Ibid.*, p. 373.
[43] *Ibid.*

The evidence from these reform processes in the last decade can help educators and economists to design realistic proposals for improving the quality of education outcomes; training better teachers; regulating competition among public and private education, making explicit who should pay for schooling (in which cases part of the cost should be borne by taxpayers rather than by direct beneficiaries), and which could be the type of vouchers used to transfer subsidies. The educational experiments in Chile are extremely interesting and worthy of study to improve effectiveness in educational change.

PART D:
HOUSEHOLD AND COMMUNITY

CHAPTER 15

Housing Policy and Legal Entitlements:
Survival Strategies of the Urban Poor[*]

Alan Gilbert

Introduction

Millions of Latin American families face a severe shelter problem. They live in homes without adequate sanitation, with an irregular electricity supply, built of flimsy materials and without adequate security. Millions more live in solid and serviced accommodation but in overcrowded conditions. Housing problems affect both large and small cities and are perhaps most serious in the countryside. Apart from the households living in shacks, overcrowded tenements and accommodation without adequate services, millions more would claim to have a housing problem. They live in houses that do not match their hopes and needs: they have difficulty paying their rent or mortgage, they have a long journey to work, their home is too small, they wish to own a house rather than to rent.

Defining the precise extent of the problem is difficult and is perhaps a less than useful task. Nevertheless, efforts to do this underline just how serious the housing situation is. According to the United Nations' Commission for Latin America and the Caribbean (UNECLAC, 1996) there were 100 million independent homes in Latin America and the Caribbean in 1995, of which one-quarter were deficient in terms of their construction or servicing. In addition, there were 28 million families that were forced to live with another family. Adding the qualitative and the quantitative deficits together reveals a housing shortage in Latin America equivalent to 54 per cent of the existing housing stock.

This chapter is concerned with how governments and ordinary households have attempted to face up to this appalling housing shortage. The chapter has three sections. The first provides a brief history of housing intervention in Latin America and how shifts in policy bear a passing resemblance to changes in economic and social policy in general. The sec-

*   I should like to acknowledge the help received from the Inter-American Development Bank, the Economic and Social Research Council and the Department for International Development for providing the resources that I used to collect and prepare much of the material included in this chapter.

ond section considers some of the weaknesses of current thinking about housing. The final section considers how low-income families have attempted to resolve their housing problem through their own efforts. Data from Bogotá are used to demonstrate how they have not only provided their own shelter but have also developed their own social safety net. In the absence of adequate forms of state assistance, they use the house as a source of supplementary income, to guard against the problems of old age and as a refuge for themselves and their adult children at times of economic stress.

A Housing Policy Void in Latin America?

The rhetoric that has peppered most politicians' statements about the shelter situation suggests that governments must have given high priority to housing in their budget allocations. In practice, most have spent very little, at least, in the period since 1980. Indeed, Table 15.1 shows that some countries have dedicated virtually nothing to housing.

Table 15.1: Public Spending on Housing by Country, 1980–95

Percentage of GDP	Country (period)
Above 2%	Costa Rica (1986–94: 3.2% in 1989), Mexico (1992–94) Dominican Republic (1987–92), Venezuela (1980–2)
1–2%	Argentina, Brazil (1980–92), Chile (twice went lower), Ecuador, Mexico (1984–91), Nicaragua (1981–85), Panama (1980–84), Venezuela (1983–90)
0.5–1%	Colombia only twice went over 1%, Costa Rica (1980–85), Guatemala (1993–95), Honduras (1983–89), Mexico (1980–83), Nicaragua (1986–7), Panama (1985–94)
0.2–0.5%	El Salvador (1980–84), Honduras (1981–2, 1990–95), Paraguay, Dominican Republic (1980–86), Uruguay
Less than 0.2%	Bolivia, El Salvador (1985–94), Guatemala (1980–92), Nicaragua (1990–95), Peru (1981–90)

Source: Cominetti and Ruiz (1997: Tables 3 and 7)

With few exceptions, housing has seldom been a priority for most Latin American governments. Indeed, housing has always occupied an uneasy position in policy-makers' minds. Whereas education, healthcare and pensions are clearly regarded as social issues, housing occupies an awkward position somewhere between the economic realm and the social. The consequence of its intermediate position is that housing is neglected both by economic and by social planners. Economists do not consider investment in housing to be as important as the generation of exports or the encouragement of employment. Social planners do not consider housing within their remit. It is true that most politicians include housing in their electoral promises, yet they are less ready to increase the government budget when it comes to paying for the promised housing investment.

Why does housing occupy this intermediate position? Housing is difficult for some economists to accept as an integral element of macroeconomic policy because they regard it primarily as a private rather than a public good, and as a consumption item rather than an item of investment. Compared with issues critical to increasing national production such as generating exports, increasing savings or developing power or transport networks, housing investment seems to rank low on most economists' list of priorities. Good housing for all certainly does not make the economy more competitive. It is only at times of recession that some economists are occasionally attracted to the sector as a potential source of jobs.

But why do social planners not embrace housing more enthusiastically? Part of the answer lies in the way that social policy developed. In most of the world, it developed as a means of dealing with exceptional groups of people. Poverty programmes dealt with the very poor. Education dealt with the young and not even all of the young (pre-school children were omitted). Health dealt with the sick or the pregnant. Pensions dealt with the old. The problem with housing is that it was comprehensive; everyone needed a house. There might occasionally be a special housing programme to remove slums but it was exceptional. More typically public housing programmes evolved merely as part of special interest pleading. Housing for the military, housing for government workers. Public housing programmes were motivated more by political demands than by social philosophy.

However, the critical problem facing those who would embrace housing as social policy has always been cost. Housing is exceptionally expensive because everyone requires a home and because housing is an expensive item to produce. The per capita cost of housing compared to the per capita cost of providing primary education or even hospital care is high. Since few governments beyond Northern and Western Europe have ever been prepared to spend a great deal on social programmes, it was usually ruled out as a serious contender for social policy. While many Latin

American constitutions talk of decent housing as a human right, social practice has rarely matched those lofty words.

Despite the peculiarities of the housing sector, it is difficult to understand how housing cannot be regarded as a social issue. To state the obvious: the quality of housing is a critical factor in determining the state of health; a home is a critical element in maintaining a feeling of personal and family esteem; housing takes up a substantial component of the family budget; for the fortunate home-ownership is the principal source of capital accumulation; the location of housing helps determine access to good schools, jobs and social facilities; housing is a key indicator of social class — to an extent where one lives is what one is; maintaining family solidarity is more difficult in poor housing conditions; housing is an important element in how the poor protect themselves from economic hardship; and urban protest is often based on issues related to the house and its environment.

In sum, an effective social policy cannot be developed without considering the roles that housing and the home play in people's lives.

A Brief History of Housing Intervention in Latin America

Even if few governments have spent much on housing, most have adopted a similar strategy towards the housing sector. In general terms this has been one of benign neglect. Most governments have left responsibility for building housing to the private sector and to civil society. Governments have built some housing but most of their effort has gone into regulating private sector construction or into making good the problems that urban sprawl and self-help settlement have created.

Rent control

Until the 1940s, and in places even later than that, most urban Latin Americans lived in rental housing. As such, the first kind of housing policy to develop was concerned with the problems of regulating tenements. Governments were drawn into struggles between landlords and tenants over perennial sources of dispute such as eviction, maintenance and the level of the rent. Rent controls were introduced quite early in some countries, and became ubiquitous during the 1940s as part of the effort to combat war-induced price rises.

Most economists regard rent controls with genuine hostility.[1] Summarising the findings of a major economic investigation into the

---

[1]   Aaron (1966); Grimes (1976); UN (1979).

effects of rent control, Malpezzi and Ball state that 'rent control fails to meet the goals sought by its advocates', particularly because 'it restricts the supply of housing.'[2] All too often it also fails to redistribute income, partly because landlords are not much better off than tenants and partly because the tenants who benefit are more affluent than the tenants who lose out because of the consequent supply constraints. Building regulations have had a similar effect.[3] In practice, rent control has been only one of a number of factors discouraging investment in rental housing and in any case has rarely been applied effectively in most Latin American cities.[4] Indeed, the vast growth of rental housing in self-help settlements testifies to the fact that in those areas the legislation is never applied.[5] Even in the 'notorious' case of Mexico City, the rent controls only apply to a tiny proportion of the housing in the city.

Even though rent controls are largely ineffective, few Latin American governments have ever been prepared to abolish them. And, even where substantial changes have been made, it is debatable how much difference the reform has made. In Santiago, Pinochet's removal of rent control in 1975 never unleashed a flood of investment into the housing sector.[6]

Encouraging Owner-Occupation

The post-war period has seen a huge expansion in the number of home-owners in Latin American cities. Gradually, government after government established institutions to finance the construction of housing by the private sector. Many of these institutions were modelled on the US Savings and Loans Institutions, an approach that was pushed very hard by USAID under the Alliance for Progress. Later more sophisticated institutions were set up in Brazil and Colombia, which, by guaranteeing savers a positive return on their money, attracted huge sums into housing construction.[7] With the numbers of middle-class families growing rapidly, home ownership became the norm in the more affluent sectors of Latin American cities.

Official encouragement of a shift from renting to ownership was justified on the grounds that most Latin Americans express a strong preference for

2 Malpezzi and Ball (1991), p. xiii.
3 Gilbert and Varley (1991).
4 Coulomb (1985).
5 Gilbert (1983).
6 Paquette-Vassalli (1998).
7 Jaramillo (1992); Sandilands (1990); Shidlo (1990); Valenca (1992).

home ownership.[8] Table 15.2 suggests that the aim of converting Latin American countries into 'nations of homeowners' has been extremely successful. Even in the larger cities, where housing tends to be more expensive, rates of home ownership have increased dramatically during the last half-century.

Table 15.2: The Development of Owner Occupation in Selected Cities since c. 1950 (percentage of households owning their home)

City	1947–52	1970–73	1990–93
Mexico City	25	43	70
Guadalajara	29	43	68
Bogotá	43	42	54
Medellín	51	57	65
Santiago	26	57	71
Rio de Janeiro	33	54	63
Buenos Aires	27	61	72

Source: Gilbert (1998a, p. 92) based on census data.

Building Social Housing

During the inter-war years, many Latin American governments established public agencies to build social housing. Ostensibly social housing was intended for the poor but, in practice, most went to unionised groups like the army, the police, dockers and government workers. Colombia established ICT in 1939, Venezuela set up the Banco Obrero in 1928 and the Dirección de Pensiones Civiles began building homes for its Mexican affiliates from 1926. By the 1950s, few Latin American countries lacked at least one public housing agency. Such agencies achieved their apogee when US monies flooded into the region under the Alliance for Progress.

Initially, Latin American governments built social housing for rent but it soon became obvious that they were rather poor landlords. Rents were set too low and seldom rose in line with prices. Maintenance of the hous-

[8]   Gilbert (1983); Beijaard (1995); van Lindert (1991); Gilbert and Varley (1991); Gilbert et al. (1993).

ing estates was deficient and many rapidly turned into new kinds of slum. In Mexico and Venezuela, the tenants did not even pay their rent. And, since governments were reluctant or unable to evict non-paying tenants, public housing agencies ran up very large debts. The history of governments acting as social landlords in Latin America is not a happy one.[9]

Most Latin American governments decided to sell the rental units to the tenants and resolved that in future they would build only for sale. This improved their performance although not by much and few commentators have many kind words for public housing agencies at any time in their history. Mayo, for example, criticises public housing projects in the 1960s because they 'were small in scale, largely unaffordable by the poor, poorly targeted, and largely inefficient. Moreover they followed the typical paradigm of government housing programmes at the time — relying on government to design, produce and allocate the housing "solutions" which contributed little to addressing the needs either of the poor or of the broader economy.'[10] By the 1980s, paralleling broader economic thinking about government failure, the whole concept of public housing agencies in Latin America had fallen into disrepute. In the early 1990s, the World Bank was explicitly recommending that: 'privatisation of housing production should go hand in hand with the overall privatisation of public sector enterprises'.[11] USAID was denouncing the activities of 'centralised bureaucracies' and praising the virtues of the market.[12]

Turning a Blind Eye

Helping the middle class to become homeowners and providing social housing for more powerful working class groups may have helped political stability and encouraged economic growth. However, such a policy did little to solve the housing problems of the poor. When the poor remained in the countryside, their housing problems could be ignored. But with migration bringing millions to the cities, the housing problem began to get serious. Without the resources or the ability to build houses for all the newcomers, the governmental response was simple: leave it to the poor to find their own solution. The newcomers responded by moving into rental tenements and later by building self-help housing alternatives.

9   UNCHS (1989); Gilbert and Varley (1991).
10   Mayo (1999), p. 41.
11   World Bank (1993c), p. 62.
12   Kimm (1993), p. 49.

Self-help solutions provided shelter but generated problems for the authorities insofar as they led to the proliferation of un-serviced settlements founded upon a wide variety of informal, and sometimes downright illegal, forms of land tenure. The answer to that was generally to ignore the mounting illegality and to gradually find some way of servicing the settlements. Unless the poor protested or some kind of physical or health problem was created for the rest of the city, the new settlers could be largely left to their own devices.[13]

Although much has been made of the way poor people invade land in Latin American cities, land invasions rarely threatened the dominant social order. The reason why was that invasion settlements normally occupied public land of low value. Indeed, most of the cities where land has been invaded, lowland Peru, the Caribbean coastal areas of Colombia and Venezuela, the hillsides of Rio de Janeiro, have been cities where public land was either plentiful or had no alternative use. Under such circumstances, politicians were not only prepared to turn a blind eye to the process but were active in encouraging it. In Lima, large-scale land occupations were first stimulated by the Odría administration in the 1940s.[14] Similarly, in Venezuelan cities, the main political parties have directly encouraged the invasion of public land over many years.[15] Even when urban land was relatively scarce, the run-up to a close election could see every political party encouraging their supporters to occupy land — the 1970 election in Chile being a major case in point.[16]

However, in many cities invasions were not the normal way in which poor people obtained land. In most of Colombia and Ecuador, in the south of Brazil and in Mexico, most families bought plots on which to build their homes.[17] These self-help settlements were illegal only in the sense that they offended the planning regulations. The illegality consists of a lack of services, something that could be easily resolved by the authorities providing infrastructure. Elsewhere, perfectly decent and well-serviced homes simply lacked properly registered title deeds; they were illegal only in a technical sense.[18]

---

[13]   Gilbert and Gugler (1982).

[14]   Collier (1976).

[15]   Ray (1969); Gilbert and Healey (1985).

[16]   Kusnetzoff (1987, 1990).

[17]   Doebele (1975); Gilbert (1981); Gilbert and Ward (1985); Beijaard (1995).

[18]   Azuela (1989); Jones and Ward (1998); Fernandes and Varley (1998).

With the growth of bus transportation, with servicing capacity increasing in the 1970s and with sustained economic growth, it could be argued that self-help housing was a form of 'architecture that worked'.[19] And since few self-help settlements seemed to contain nests of revolutionaries,[20] most resource-starved governments were more than happy to accept such a judgement.

From Demolition to Upgrading (plus improved servicing)

Every so often, turning a blind eye to the proliferation of self-help settlement was inconvenient. It was unacceptable when a new government was committed to maintaining 'order and progress', particularly when self-help settlements occupied land next to high-income neighbourhoods as in Caracas or Rio de Janeiro.[21] It was unwelcome when the self-help settlements were populated by members of the political opposition, as in the campamentos of Santiago, or when they occupied land that was destined for some other purpose, road building, a hospital or even a private housing development.

Under such circumstances, governments would demolish slum settlements. They would rehouse most of the people but in settlements far from the city centre where the population would have difficulty maintaining their existing social and economic networks.[22] The opposition of alternative planners and architects was ignored at such moments, particularly by military governments untrammelled by the need for popular support. It was only the gradual return of democracy in the 1980s that reduced the incidence of slum removal programmes; generally democratic governments have been more reluctant to send in the troops.

There is now broad agreement that in situ upgrading schemes are far superior to slum removal projects.[23] First, upgrading maintains existing social and economic networks. When families are removed from their existing neighbourhoods, essential community support mechanisms or 'social capital' are likely to be destroyed. Move businesses and they are liable to fold. Second, upgrading is relatively cheap, government spending undoubtedly reaches the

---

[19]   Turner (1967, 1968a, 1968b).

[20]   Portes (1972); Cornelius (1975); Ray (1969).

[21]   Coulomb and Sánchez (1991); Dwyer (1975); Hardoy and Satterthwaite (1981); Myers (1978); Perlman (1976); Valladares (1978).

[22]   Valladares (1978); Rodríguez and Icaza (1993); Scarpaci et al. (1988).

[23]   Abrams (1964); Skinner et al. (1987); World Bank (1993c); Van der Linden (1986).

poor and it is increasingly clear that the poor can be persuaded to pay for the costs of servicing.[24] As such, upgrading programmes now form part of the conventional wisdom of urban planning and both the Inter-American Development Bank and the World Bank are very active in this area.[25]

From Illegality to Legality

If the authorities have sometimes been prominent among the actors helping to promote land invasion and other forms of informality, many have subsequently been eager to remove that illegality. Indeed, few governments, whether authoritarian or democratic, have been reluctant to woo popular support by 'generously' distributing property titles to illegal settlers. The military government in Chile gave out more than 500,000 land titles between 1979 and 1989 and the two democratic governments that succeeded it had distributed a further 150,000 titles by 1998.[26] In Peru, the new Commission to Formalise Informal Property (COFOPRI) managed to register some 1,134,000 urban land titles from 1996 to 2000.[27]

Two motives are associated with the delivery of title deeds. The first is to accelerate the speed of housing improvement by guaranteeing people tenure of their land. The second is to increase poor people's access to formal sector credit, which will also increase their capacity for undertaking improvements on their homes. As de Soto (2000) argues the poor have accumulated considerable amounts of savings, most of which are concentrated in real estate. What they lack is legal title to this property: 'The poor inhabitants of these nations — five-sixths of humanity — do have things, but they lack the process to represent their property and create capital. They have houses but not titles; crops but not deeds; businesses but not statutes of incorporation.'[28]

He is not wholly wrong. People do have a problem when they lack title deeds. 'The registration of property rights in squatter settlements is …important in making land and house transactions possible and giving occupants legal protection. It encourages the buying and selling of housing and makes it possible for households to move to a dwelling that suits their needs and their budgets. It also increases the choice of tenure available to

24   Lee (1994).

25   Rojas (1995); see World Bank's upgrading web pages.

26   Rugiero (1998), pp. 31 and 51.

27   Calderón (2001).

28   de Soto (2000), pp. 6–7.

households, allowing them to own or rent as they see fit.'[29] How much difference such programmes make in practice is much less obvious (see below).

Enabling Markets to Work

Integrating self-help housing into the formal economy through the offer of title deeds is one part of a wider effort to transform housing from a state-led sector into one that follows the rules of the market. Latin American cities need well-functioning markets that will remove the inefficiency, dishonesty and distortions brought about by excessive government interference. Effective markets will also allow good housing projects to work by improving the environment into which they are introduced. In the past, far too many projects failed because of the poor economic and financial environment. For example, good social housing were liable to downward raiding because the middle class could not find affordable private housing or could not find the finance to buy the housing that they could afford.

The parallel with structural adjustment policies is clear. Just as poverty alleviation was impossible in an environment of rapid inflation, so housing policies would fail unless an appropriate economic and housing environment could be established. During the 1990s, Washington's advice on housing and infrastructure policy recommended an 'enabling approach to housing, in which the primary policy goal is to create a "well-functioning housing sector" that serves the needs of all key stakeholder groups'.[30]

The World Bank's (1993) Housing Sector Paper continues to be the base document around which most thinking about housing revolves.[31] The key sentiment is 'to redirect developing-country governments from engaging in building, marketing, financing and maintenance of housing units toward facilitating expansion of the private sector's role in such activities'.[32] In order to facilitate private sector engagement, governments need to work on 'property rights development, mortgage finance, targeted subsidies, infrastructure for urban land development, regulatory reform, organization of the building industry, and institutional development'.

Around the globe few governments argue against this approach for three principal reasons. First, most accept that past attempts at public housing provision were highly flawed. Second, most economists in govern-

---

29 World Bank (1993), p. 117.
30 Mayo (1999), p. 39.
31 Inter-American Development Bank (1993, 1999b).
32 World Bank (1993c), p. 62.

ment recommend that greater reliance be placed on market forces, that there is a need to raise productivity and that, in a globalising world, the key to success is greater competitiveness. If greater market-led efficiency is the principal goal, it is clearly nonsensical to fund inefficient public housing agencies or even to permit specialised forms of housing finance. Third, under the new rules of global competition most governments believe that they should keep taxes low and limit government expenditure. Under such a strategy, there is little or no room for public construction or housing finance.

Capital Subsidies to Increase the Demand for Formal Housing

In the new context, few governments in Latin America now wish to build social housing. But many wish to improve the local housing situation and to discourage the continued growth of self-help housing. Insofar as there is an answer it consists of providing poor families with up-front subsidies with which to buy homes or serviced plots. Such an approach is wholly compatible with the enabling approach and requires little of government beyond the offer of subsidies and the maintenance of economic and financial stability. The forerunner of a capital subsidy policy for housing was developed in Chile during the 1970s; a direct outcome of the introduction of Chicago School economics into public administration in that country.[33] Despite its neoliberal economic agenda, the Pinochet government was prepared to continue the long tradition in Chile of subsidising housing. However, in future housing provision had to be market led and more firmly embedded in more competitive economic and financial systems.[34]

On the supply side, public housing would no longer be contracted by the state but would be built by the private sector responding to market signals. Instead of builders producing what the public sector asked for, they would have to compete to produce what consumers wanted. Private enterprise would produce cheaper units than under the public contracting system and provide a choice of housing for the poor.

On the demand side, subsidies would be given to poor families who would use the subsidy to buy housing on the market. The system devised to allocate the subsidies was intended to guarantee that the recipients were poor and that they were prepared to help themselves. The test of the latter was their readiness to accumulate savings; the longer their savings record and the higher

[33]   Almarza (1997); Haramoto (1983); Valdés (1995).

[34]   Arellano (1982).

their savings the more likely they were to get a subsidy. The public housing ministry would issue guidelines and applications forms that would explain how people would become eligible for a subsidy. Because the rules for allocating subsidies were to be manifestly open and transparent, any form of political favouritism or corruption would be impossible.

From 1977 on, the new demand-side subsidy mechanism was consolidated into Chilean practice. It was not an immediate success and took some years, and many modifications, before its best results were achieved under the democratic governments of the 1990s. The Concertación governments have boasted that Chile is the only Latin American country that is managing to cut its housing deficit.

Gradually, the influence of the Chilean housing subsidy model spread to other Latin American countries. Costa Rica, Colombia, Ecuador and Panama all adopted subsidy models strongly influenced by Chilean practice,[35] and there was considerable interest elsewhere, in Guatemala, Paraguay, Uruguay and Venezuela. Institutions like the World Bank, the Inter-American Development Bank and particularly USAID were influential in different ways in diffusing the Chilean 'housing model'. By 1993, a Chile-type model had become acknowledged 'best practice'. In principle, the model embraced three elements that were highly approved in the new development environment: explicit targeting at the poor, transparency and private market provision.[36]

Some Problems with Post-1990 Thinking

It is difficult to praise Latin America's past housing policy very highly. Demolition programmes were often brutally implemented, informal housing solutions occupied land that was expensive to service and electoral rationality was more important than people's needs in determining most forms of governmental action. In addition, few of the public housing agencies that were established in the region were effective. Many had their good moments but over time became over-politicised and inefficient. As such, the current approach to housing in the region has to be an improvement. Nevertheless, a whole series of questions must be posed about its likely effectiveness.

---

[35] Held (2000); Pérez-Iñigo González (1999).

[36] World Bank (1993c), p. 126.

Upgrading: an Excellent Policy but is it Replicable?

Most slum upgrading programmes aim to keep families in their existing homes and to improve the quality of their neighbourhoods. A number of writers have questioned whether these two goals are compatible and have suggested that the market mechanisms unleashed by such programmes will drive poor people out of their newly improved homes.[37] Middle-class households will buy the newly distributed title deeds, transforming the settlement and destroying the community. In practice, this seems to have happened very rarely and most owners have remained in the improved settlement.[38] More likely is that improvements in the quality of settlements and the subsequent charges levied on owners, have led to rents being raised and the departure of poor tenant families, although there is little information available on this phenomenon. However, even tenants may benefit from upgrading in the sense that owners tend to increase the amount of rental accommodation available in improved settlements.[39]

Few now question the utility and necessity for slum upgrading programmes and the Inter-American Development Bank and the World Bank have been actively financing upgrading programmes for a number of years. Insofar as they have reservations about the approach it has nothing to do with its potential to improve people's lives. The problem lies in the difficulties of replicating these projects on a city-wide or on a national basis. Because slum upgrading is a relatively complex operation too many governments have proved themselves to be less than adequate to the task.[40] In addition, there is the problem of how to guarantee cost recovery. Most upgrading projects benefit from large subsidies 'making large-scale implementation unimaginable for most governments' and few have managed to attract private investment on a large scale.[41]

Does Legalisation Make Much Difference?

Some writers on the political left have argued that issuing title deeds can harm the poor because it leads to down-raiding by higher income families, the displacement of tenants because of rising rents and the introduction of service charges and property taxes.[42] But there is not much evidence to

---

[37] Harms (1982); Durand-Lasserve (1997); Payne (1989).

[38] Baken et al. (1991), p. 21.

[39] Skinner et al. (1987).

[40] Werlin (1999).

[41] Mayo (1999), p. 41.

support these arguments and the real point about title deeds is whether issuing them really makes much difference. In general, I would argue that the poor gain rather little from their precious pieces of paper. First, there are major doubts about whether possession of a legal title accelerates the process of housing improvement. There is plenty of evidence to show that most settlers improve their homes without possessing anything resembling a title deed.[43] In Bogotá, settlers build homes when all they have is a receipt for their payments for the plot of land. These people have been prepared to build because they had confidence that their tenure was secure. Although there is no doubt that the granting of legal title sometimes gives previously insecure settlers reassurance and thereby unleashes investment, it is sometimes spontaneous investment that brings about title deeds.[44]

Second, does the issue of a legal title open the doors of banks and lenders to the informal settlements? In practice, formal financial systems face various barriers in reaching the poor, most notably the non-profitability of lending small sums of money. In addition, 'mortgage lenders have difficulty verifying self-employed income and developing an accurate estimate of self-employed income from analysis of tax returns',[45] and many lenders do not believe that poor people will repay their loans.[46] Even micro-lending does not often reach self-help settlements and certainly not to finance the sale of used housing.[47]

Third, it may not even be true that the poor are desperate for loans. Repaying a loan is a burden that may endanger the household's whole financial viability.[48] As such, many poor families are less than enthusiastic about borrowing from formal lending agencies or indeed from anyone else. Admittedly, recent experience in Lima suggests that titling can lead to an increase in formal sector loans. Of the approximately 200,000 families awarded legal titles in 1998 and 1999, some 23.8 per cent had taken out loans to expand or renovate their homes.[49] This impressively high figure makes Lima appear very different from Bogotá, where many fewer families seem prepared to borrow against the title of their house and where

---

[42] Burgess (1982).

[43] Gilbert and Ward (1985); Payne (1989); Razzaz (1993); Varley (1987).

[44] Hirschman (1984).

[45] Ferguson (1999), p. 187.

[46] UNCHS (1996), p. 370.

[47] Almeyda (1996), p. 128.

[48] Rogaly and Johnson (1997).

[49] Calderón (2001); Conger (1999); Panaritis (2001).

lending agencies seem to be less convinced of the virtues of land titles.[50] However, Calderón points out that the vast bulk of the lending came from state institutions and that 'there is no connection between the official registration of property and access to loans from private banks'.

The self-help settlements of Latin America will hardly disappear if title deeds cease to be allocated or if housing credit fails to reach them. But the quality of the housing may improve if more credit is available. More lending is necessary if the process of self-help construction is to be encouraged and if more rental accommodation is to be generated. More credit is also essential if the poor are to make real money from their homes for, without credit, successful self-help consolidators will be unable to sell their homes and therefore to make capital gains. Would it not be ironic if, having struggled for years to build self-help homes, these self-help consolidators are robbed of the opportunity to cash in their principal capital asset and even to move house?

Fourth, the fact that so many Latin American governments have begun to distribute title deeds on a large scale raised the suspicion that this approach has not been adopted primarily to help the poor. Arguably, the real motive behind titling programmes has been to expand the property tax base and to start charging for services.[51] Others have pointed out that because land titling is cheap, especially when the beneficiaries are charged for the service, it always represents a housing strategy that is far more economical than providing either proper homes or, even, infrastructure and services.[52]

Where are the Sites and Services Programmes?

In most Latin American cities there is no realistic alternative to self-help or progressive housing because most poor people cannot afford the price of a finished house.[53] In Colombia, even with the aid of a housing subsidy, most families can only buy the cheapest social-interest house if they are prepared to devote an excessively high proportion of their income to the mortgage repayment.[54] If they cannot afford a formal house, the only formal alternative is to offer them the opportunity to buy a serviced plot, with or without a 'core' house that they can improve over time.

---

[50]   Gilbert (2000).

[51]   Ward (1989).

[52]   Fernandes and Varley (1998).

[53]   Van der Linden (1986).

[54]   Gilbert (1997).

'Sites and services' is an approach that has been financed by the development banks for several decades.[55] It is the natural corollary to slum upgrading. Governments should anticipate and prevent the formation of slums by providing the poor with a way to develop their housing incrementally in an ordered way. Such an approach saves on servicing costs because some services are installed before settlement. It is even acceptable to provide plots without services providing the layout of the settlements permits services to be installed cheaply after the population has begun construction.[56] Anticipating urban development by providing organised areas for settlement should also help prevent the occupation of hillsides or of low-lying land liable to flood, both of which are dangerous for the settlers and expensive to service. Building advice can be given to the settlers through technical assistance and some economies of scale can be obtained through wholesale provision of building materials. In an imperfect world, the logic underlying a 'sites and services' approach is impeccable.

Unfortunately, relatively few such schemes have been developed in Latin America, particularly in the largest cities, and few governments have backed such an approach in a big way.[57] Ironically, given the logic of the argument, the essential problem has been that the cost of such schemes has been too high.[58] Costs have been high because few governments or funding agencies have been prepared to reduce minimum standards sufficiently to keep costs low; most Inter-American Development Bank projects, for example, have insisted that all beneficiaries have full legal title to their property and that a full range of infrastructure and services is provided before occupancy. Such schemes have offered 'too much security' at a price the poor could not afford.[59] By contrast, illegal developers have offered the poor a much inferior product but one that is popular insofar as it fits their budget.

The second major problem is that there has been insufficient land available on which to establish progressive housing developments in suitable locations.[60] The Bank itself accepted this explanation at a time when it had already begun to phase out this approach.[61]

---

55   Rojas (1995).

56   Jacobs and Savedoff (1999), p. 32.

57   Van der Linden (1986).

58   Danière (1992), p. 178.

59   Johnson (1987).

60   Werlin (1999).

61   World Bank (1992).

The great challenge for governments in Latin America, therefore, is to make serviced, or at least serviceable, land available at prices the poor can afford.

Strengths and Weaknesses in the Chilean Model

The Chilean programme has been producing more than 100,000 houses per annum and has worked very well in a number of ways.[62] Nevertheless, even though the programme has improved greatly over the years,[63] it is not without substantial blemishes even today.[64]

The introduction of a savings requirement in Chile made a great deal of sense. It increased the sense of responsibility among Chilean families, it increased the savings rate and it controlled, arguably in a legitimate way, people's expectations of when they would obtain government help. But if the savings requirement worked well in Chile as a criterion of eligibility for the subsidy, it did not help the majority of poor families obtain credit because the banks were reluctant to lend to them.[65] Given the reluctance of private banks to lend to the poor, the government was forced to offer complementary loans to beneficiaries of the Basic Housing Programme at a preferential rate.

Despite the generosity of the subsidy — at first it was 75 per cent for basic housing units — few Chileans paid back all that they owed on their mortgages. Indeed, the Chilean government suffered extensive defaults and, in October 1992, three-quarters of all beneficiaries were more than 90 days behind with their payments to the Ministry of Housing and Urbanism.[66] Between 1979 and 1997 the government renegotiated loans seven times and yet around 60 per cent of borrowers are still three months behind in their payments.[67]

In Chile, private investors were extremely reluctant to invest in low-income housing because of the low profit margins. Indeed, the amount of disinterest in the Basic Housing and Progressive Housing Programmes, together with the reluctance of banks to lend to the poor, forced the government to develop land and directly hire private contractors to built the

62   Ducci (2000); Rojas (1999).
63   Haramoto (1983); Rugiero (1998).
64   Crespo et al. (2000); Ducci (1997); Rojas (1999).
65   Rojas and Greene (1995).
66   Almarza (1997), p. 23.
67   Rojas (1999), p. 7; Persaud (1991), p. 5.
68   Rojas and Greene (1995), p. 40.

houses before assigning them to low-income households.[68]

In Chile, because the cost of each housing solution was so cheap, the quality and location of the dwellings was often extremely poor. Most of the flats that constituted the bulk of the basic housing programme were both small (averaging 40 square metres in size) and poorly constructed.[69] The walls were extremely thin, bathrooms were located by the front door to save on plumbing costs and, in the worst cases, builders did not use enough cement.[70]

The subsidy system and the owner-occupation programme accentuated the already acute level of residential segregation in Chilean cities.[71] In Santiago, because most of the subsidised schemes were developed on cheaper land at the fringe of the city, opportunities for owner-occupation were being created far from the major areas of employment. Distant location increased travel times for most of the beneficiary families and became a major source of complaint.[72] A further problem was that the subsidy system aggravated already low rates of residential mobility. [73]

In Santiago, the housing subsidy programme also aggravated the problem of low-density urban sprawl. The removal of strict land-use controls on the urban periphery of Santiago in 1979, in order to reduce land prices by creating a free market in land, emphasised that tendency without reducing prices.[74] The limited provision of rental housing in the low-income suburbs further encourages the desire for home ownership on the periphery.[75] Such low-density development tends to increase the length of the journey to work and to raise the cost of infrastructure provision.

Over the years, Washington institutions have generally applauded the Chilean subsidy programme. The World Bank was heavily involved in financing and modifying the Chilean housing programme and it was sympathetic to many of the ideas underlying the policy. The capital subsidies approach promised to encourage the private sector to provide housing for low-income groups, reduce inefficiency, ensure that subsidies reached the poor, match housing supply to housing needs and to encourage poor people to help themselves by saving for their home. By the late 1980s, the

[69] Richards (1995).

[70] Ducci (1997), p. 108.

[71] Richards (1995).

[72] Rodríguez and Icaza (1993).

[73] Richards (1994).

[74] AUCA (1979); Trivelli (1987); Smolka and Sabatini (2000).

[75] Paquette-Vassili (1998).

Bank had become disenchanted with the Chilean experience on the grounds that the Chileans were not actually doing what they promised to do.[76] However, other Washington agencies rallied to the cause, particularly USAID, which always seemed to be much happier about the Chilean model.[77] The Inter-American Development Bank has subsequently encouraged a Chile-like model in several countries, including Colombia, Costa Rica, Paraguay, Uruguay and Venezuela.[78]

The problem with attempting to diffuse the Chilean model to other parts of Latin America is that the latter often lack many of the fundamentals that have permitted the Chilean model to be as successful as it has been in Chile. Few Latin American countries are as prosperous as Chile, most have weaker and more corrupt bureaucracies, they are less committed to transparent subsidy mechanisms and their servicing capacity is much inferior. Many Chileans who have acted as advisers to other Latin American governments have returned home in despair.

Increasing Access to Serviced Land

Land prices seem to be rising very quickly in Latin America and in cities like Bogotá, Rio and Santiago there are frequent complaints that it is impossible to find land on which to build low-cost formal housing.[79] Of course, there are times when land prices fall, but over the past 50 years such moments have been comparatively rare.[80] The reason for land price inflation is that 'under conditions of sustained high urban growth, urban land has enjoyed a level of demand well in excess of formally sanctioned supply, guaranteeing a good rate of return on investment. The relative weakness of urban administrative structures in preparing and maintaining land ownership records, regulating land title transfers or implementing land taxation procedures, enables land investors to operate with relative impunity, thereby further increasing profit margins without a consequent increase in risk.'[81] In addition, most Latin American cities suffer from the hoarding of urban land. Perhaps one-third of the land in Buenos Aires, nearly one-quarter in Quito and a staggering 44 per

---

[76]   Persaud (1991); Renaud (1988); Gilbert (2001).

[77]   Kimm (1993).

[78]   Ferguson et al. (1996).

[79]   Allen (1989); Fedelonjas (1988); Trivelli (1987); Smolka and Sabatini (2000).

[80]   Gilbert (1996), pp. 88–9.

[81]   Payne (1989), p. 45.

[82]   Clichevsky (1999), p. 2.

cent in Rio de Janeiro remains vacant.[82]

Despite the fact that so much vacant land is being held for speculative purposes few Latin America cities have instituted policies to deal with the problem. Even where the authorities do manage to distinguish between vacant and developed land in their tax systems, as in Buenos Aires and Quito, owners of vacant land are protected from higher taxes 'through a series of loopholes and "exceptions"'.[83]

> Washington's answer to these problems seems to be to simplify plan-
> ning regulations in an effort to make the land market work more effec-
> tively.[84] Both development banks are arguing along similar lines to de
> Soto (1989) that most Latin Americans would benefit from removal of
> the excessive numbers of rules and regulations. No doubt, Turner
> would rally to the cause because he long ago argued the case for more
> 'prescriptive' as opposed to 'proscriptive' regulations; policies that tell
> people what they ought to do rather than what they should not do.
> However, Chilean experience with simplifying regulations in Santiago
> suggests by itself, this policy will do little to improve the quality of the
> housing stock. Unless there is an adequate expansion of services and
> infrastructure, the efficient market will merely produce higher prices
> for serviced land. In addition, some kind of planning control is vital.

It seems to me that Washington is over-reacting to the era of 'government failure' and is making too much of the virtues of the market. If no market works perfectly, land and housing markets often work much less well than most. Governments should not eschew intervention when it is nec-essary and the current conventional wisdom has probably also gone too far in damning government incompetence. Not all government agencies per-form badly. And, now that the state has been 'rolled back' and many of the more inefficient state operations closed down, there is an urgent need to establish some efficient state agencies.

But where Washington is most in error is in failing to recognise that establishing an efficient land and housing market can cause problems if done in the wrong places. No doubt in a totally equal society, market mech-anisms would work very well, even in the area of land and housing. Unfortunately, Latin American societies are far from equal and the ten-dency is that they, like most societies in the world, appear to be getting

[83]   *Ibid.*
[84]   World Bank (1993).
[85]   Inter American Development Bank (1999b); Londoño and Székely (1997).

even more unequal.[85] In such a context, the danger is that the creation of efficient land and housing markets will lead to even greater inequality than before. Improving the quality of housing, therefore, does demand the removal of inefficiency from the land market, but it also requires a great deal else if that policy is to be effective.

The Lack of a Rental Housing Policy

Millions of families in Latin American cities live in rental housing most of which has been created in the older self-help housing areas. Most self-help developers eventually let out rooms to supplement the family income and as many as half of all households rent accommodation in cities like Bogotá and Quito. Despite this fact, few Latin American governments have considered how they might stimulate production and improve the quality of rental housing.[86] Since the incomes of most landlords and landladies differ little from those of their tenants, equity is not a significant issue. Since rental housing tends to offer tenants better location, services and infrastructure than does self-help housing,[87] support for rental housing promises to improve the quality of shelter in most cities. Finally, direct investment in rental housing will help to increase housing densities, thereby reducing suburban sprawl and illegal forms of land occupation.

Encouraging rental housing is part of the wider need to use shelter as a means of increasing family incomes.[88] Very little has been done to assist the small-scale retailer, producer and landlord. Helping small builders, landlords and shopkeepers clearly fits most governments' development priorities and would provide direct help to a particularly deprived group, female-headed households. Since 'home-bound women' are prominent among the small-scale business people in many Latin American self-help settlements and often make up a majority of the landlords, helping home-based enterprises is critical.[89]

The Role of the Home in Bogotá

In a context of extensive poverty, without an adequate social security system and where there is a severe shortage of well paid or sometimes any form of

---

[86] UNCHS (1989; 1993).

[87] Lemer (1987).

[88] McCallum and Benjamin (1985); Gilbert (1988); Strassman (1987).

[89] Moser (1996), p. 47; Gilbert and Varley (1991).

work at all, Latin American families favour home ownership because it provides a kind of safety net. Despite the difficulties, expense and hard work involved in building a home, a consolidated self-help house serves as an effective hedge against personal disasters, security against old age and as a supplementary source of income. Evidence from two surveys in Bogotá demonstrates how well home-ownership serves these functions.[90]

Not surprisingly, most *bogotano* families are happy to own their home and most tenants aspire to owner-occupation.[91] Notwithstanding the fact that many tenants who could afford to be owners often eschew that option for many years, there can be little doubt that the aspiration to be a home-owner is very strong. Self-help settlers in the south of Bogotá speak of the 'glory of the house', claim that 'he who has a house is a king', and testify that 'anything purchased is worth it'.

What is so special about home ownership? When presented with a list of specific reasons why they bought their home, two answers tended to dominate. Three-fifths of interviewees mentioned that ownership gave them something to leave to the children or referred to the security that ownership offered for one's old age. Leaving property to the children was clearly something that most household heads felt was part of their duty as parents. Although few had made wills or were very clear about the possible complications involved in inheriting property, there was little doubt about the sincerity of their feelings. Similarly, the role of ownership in guarding against the risks of old age was vitally important. As one owner put it: 'for those with nothing, to have a secure roof for oneself and the children is a good investment'.

One-fifth of interviewees mentioned a third motive: the advantage of not having to pay rent. As one grandmother put it: 'by getting a plot of land, one is no longer humiliated by having to pay rent. They can't throw you out, insult you or humiliate you.' Home ownership is also useful in times of financial hardship insofar as it allows an extended family to absorb kin who find themselves in difficulty. If a son loses his job he and his family can sometimes move back into the parents' house. If the daughter's husband leaves home, she can move back to the parents' home with the children.

Home ownership is popular, therefore, because it allows low-income families to overcome or to survive penury. Buying a house means that you avoid paying rent. Although it can be argued that rents are not especially high, they constitute a regular commitment that have to be paid every

[90]   Gilbert (1999).

[91]   Gilbert and Varley (1991); Gilbert et al. (1993).

month whatever the household's economic situation. If the main earner loses his or her job, then sooner or later, the family will be asked to move out of their room. Although building a home brings considerable hardship, the costs involved can often be deferred. While it is not possible to postpone paying the monthly service charges or the monthly instalment to the illegal subdivider, (subdividers normally offer 90 per cent credit on the illegal plot to be paid off over four years), it is possible to slow the pace of house construction and to buy bricks and glass when economic circumstances improve. When funds are scarce the family makes do with deficient accommodation, when times improve they add on a room or fix the roof.

Ownership offers a way to increase economic security for all poor families but only some take up the option of building a self-help home. Some prefer to buy a small formal sector house while others live with kin or rent accommodation. What determines the timing and the route into ownership? Part of the answer lies with personal and family characteristics. Some female-headed households may feel that they lack the ability or know-how to build or organise the construction of a self-help home. Some downwardly mobile middle-class people may feel that living in an illegal subdivision is not a feasible option for them. Some families do not want to inflict months or even years of living without services on their young children. There are lots of other reasons why people might eschew the self-help housing option.[92]

But, to judge from the evidence in Bogotá, there is an additional factor that is really very important: the kind of work undertaken by the major income earners in the family. Most owners of formal sector housing are workers who are affiliated to a formal enterprise and have regular incomes. Such workers can obtain a mortgage and sometimes benefit from inclusion in a social housing project. By contrast, there are relatively few formal sector workers in the self-help settlements, where the majority are employed in some kind of informal employment. There are very few government workers and the predominant kind of formal work is factory employment.

A further advantage of ownership, particularly in the self-help areas, is that the home can be used to generate income. Many owners operate businesses from the premises: shops, workshops and cafes. In addition, a few rent out space to other people to run a business. In some of the self-help settlements as many as one home in five was operating some kind of money earning activity in the house. Although home businesses were more common in the self-help settlements, plenty of shops and commercial

---

[92] Gilbert and Varley (1991).

activities had also been opened in the formal housing estates as well.

By far the most common source of income in the self-help areas, however, is rent from lodgers. According to Table 15.3 more than half of the houses have tenants and on average those houses have two tenants each. There is a major difference, however, between the formal and the self-help settlements in terms of the incidence of renting. Whereas a mere 11 per cent of the formal houses contain tenants, two-thirds of the self-help houses have them. In the latter, there are more tenant families than owners. Clearly, letting rooms is a substantial source of income for many and a dominant source for a few.

Table 15.3: Proportion of Tenants in Each Settlement

Barrio	Houses visited	% with tenants	Average number of tenants in houses containing tenants	Total tenants
Atenas	93	62.4	2.2	125
Britalia	103	68.9	2.3	162
Casablanca	38	68.4	1.4	36
Olarte	101	64.4	1.6	101
Sub-total	335	65.7	1.9	424
Villa Andrea	19	10.5	1.0	2
La Coruña	80	11.3	1.0	9
Sub-total	99	11.1	1.0	11
Total	434	53.2	1.9	435

Source: Gilbert (1999)

The Problems with Self-Help Ownership

Apart from the well-documented problems with self-help ownership — the time it takes, the high cost of acquiring building materials and services and the dangers posed by building in certain locations — there is another. In Bogotá, and I suspect everywhere else, self-help settlers lose out on one of the fundamental advantages of home-ownership — the ability to accumulate capital.[93]

---

[93] Gilbert (1999).

Most families in developed countries purchase accommodation at least in part because it is regarded as a good investment.[94] In the higher income areas of most Third World cities anecdotal evidence suggests that such a motive is equally important. Although self-help owners say that their homes are increasing in value, few are very clear about what their house is worth. They do not know what their homes are worth because there are so few sales in the neighbourhood. As such, self-help ownership is of limited help in increasing the tradable assets of poor families.

Sales are very uncommon in the consolidated settlements of Bogotá. Owners advertise very infrequently in the property pages of the main newspapers but there are also few signs of real estate activity in the neighbourhood. While signs appear in the windows of homes all over the north of Bogotá welcoming offers, very few notices can be seen in the low-income self-help suburbs. The infrequency of sales is reflected in the very low rates of residential mobility. Most families move in and stay forever. Their poor colleagues living in formal sector homes move more frequently.

I have argued elsewhere that the difference in the marketability of houses in formal and informal settlements can be explained in terms of the housing finance.[95] It is extremely difficult to sell a consolidated self-help home because there is little credit available and the limited credit that is available is very expensive. Finance is available for many things in Bogotá, including the purchase of consumer durables and undeveloped land. But the amount of credit required to buy a house is of a different dimension compared to that needed to buy a television or to pay a medical bill. Without credit, very few families can contemplate finding a sum of between US$20,000 and US$50,000, the amount required to buy the two or three storey houses that were available in the four self-help settlements where I was working.

If the lack of credit is the constraint on buying and selling, why is credit not readily available for this kind of housing? The essential reason is that the major lending agencies will lend only a limited amount of money for self-help housing in Bogotá. Banks are reluctant to lend because the properties do not have title deeds, many lack planning permission and the owners do not have regular incomes or not incomes that can be easily verified. Even the self-help homes that have all of the necessary legal documents receive little or no funding. The result is that the poor of Bogotá are

---

[94]   Saunders (1990); Rohe and Stewart (1996); McLaverty and Yip (1993).

[95]   Gilbert (2000).

unable to dispose of their consolidated homes. They can generate an income from their home but not the capital gains that might provide them with a much more effective safety net.

Conclusion

Looking for a housing 'solution' in Latin America is much like searching for the Holy Grail, a challenging but ultimately futile pursuit. Inadequate housing will always exist in poor countries, as it does in most parts of the developed world. What makes the housing problem even more intractable in Latin America is that the principal causes lie outside the sector itself; for example, the poverty of so many Latin Americans is the main cause of most of the really bad housing. In the past, we might have assumed that poverty would not always remain with us. Unfortunately, poverty and particularly inequality are no longer temporary phenomena waiting to be washed away by the trickle-down benefits of economic growth. Unlike the mixed economy model of yesteryear, the New Economic Model appears to have institutionalised inequality; it is a stain that will never be removed. Such inequality is not only undesirable in itself but in Latin America appears to generate increasing poverty.[96]

If it is not possible to solve the housing problem or, given the persistence of poverty, even to reduce it substantially, governments might still do a great deal more to make things better. To do so, however, requires that they think a little more clearly than now, be prepared to eschew populist solutions and be willing to adopt some policies that will upset influential groups in society. Washington thinking is often helpful in that respect. Unfortunately, many potential routes to improvement are closed off by current Washington practice: small public land banks and higher taxes on undeveloped land are not currently popular.

Both Washington and most Latin American governments should think more creatively about both the economic and social benefits of housing investment. At present few seem prepared to spend much on housing or to think beyond the idea of using housing to generate jobs in the formal sector or to provide subsidies for the very poor. Certainly, few have serious policies with respect to self-help housing even though the building of informal homes creates a lot of labour-intensive work. Nor are governments used to thinking about how ordinary people use their homes: how homes are

---

[96] IADB (1999b); Londoño and Székely (1997).

used as substitutes for non-existent pensions and insurance policies and how large numbers of Latin Americans earn part or all of their living from their home. Most governments need to rethink their assumption that homes are merely residences and incorporate incentives for new forms of home-based work into their employment and development programmes.

CHAPTER 16

Cuba: the Retreat from Entitlement?

Claes Brundenius

Introduction

The collapse of the Soviet Union and the dissolution of the 'socialist bloc' at the beginning of the 1990s, and the subsequent downsizing of economic ties with Cuba, made the island extremely vulnerable and the result was a deep depression (GDP dropped by more than 30 per cent between 1990 and 1993).[1] In contrast to the rest of Latin America the Cuban economy had been growing during the first half of the 1980s, so while Latin America was talking of a lost decade (with negative per capita growth as a result of the debt crisis and declining terms of trade), the economic outlook for Cuba was cautiously optimistic by the end of the 1980s. By 2001 there was talk of a lost decade for Cuba (the 1990s), although the economy started to recover in 1994; and GDP has during the last two years shown a rather vigorous growth of 5–6 per cent per annum. However, the economy still needs to catch up another 15 per cent to reach the 1989 levels of output.

But it is not only the collapse of the 'socialist camp' in Eastern Europe that has made economic recovery so difficult and cumbersome. The continuation of the US embargo (having now lasted for more than 40 years) has made Cuban integration with the international economy increasingly more difficult, and its negative effects on the social situation in the island have been considerable.[2]

Although the Cuban economy is steadily recovering, to a large degree thanks to economic reforms introduced, many necessary reforms have also taken their toll in terms of social consequences. The reforms have, however, not had the same effect on all Cubans, some social groups have been harder hit than others, and there are even new social groups that have benefited from the new situation. 'The Special Period in Time of Peace', as the recovery period is officially called in Cuba, has led to increasing inequalities that are of great concern to the government. Are these inequalities just temporary? Can they be reversed, or are they likely to stay for a longer time? These are some of the issues discussed in this chapter.

---

1   The term GDP has been used in Cuban official data since the early 1990s. Previously, the Cuban practice was to use the concept of Gross Social Product (GSP).

2   See, for example, Olof Palme Center (1998).

The Cuban Social Welfare System before 1994

Cuba had a cradle-to-grave welfare system until the beginning of the 1990s that was not only functioning reasonably well, but it also covered practically the whole Cuban population. In this sense the Cuban welfare system was unique in Latin America. Major benefits consisted of free education and health services, low rents (a maximum of ten per cent of household income), free or cheap community services (like day-care centres) and practically free access to culture, sports and arts events.

Social policies were among the major concerns of the revolutionary government that overthrew the corrupt Batista dictatorship in 1959. Thus a Law of Social Security was passed already in 1963, whereby all citizens would receive social benefits, in stark contrast to the situation in pre-revolutionary Cuba. The law was designed to give 'adequate protection in cases of maternity, illness, accidents at work and at home, disablement, old-age and death'.[3] Men and women who had been working for at least one year had the right to a pension, on reaching the age of 65 and 60, respectively (the retirement age was changed in the 1970s, to 60 and 55, to conform with the practice in other socialist countries). The retirement age is, however, voluntary in Cuba, and anyone can, if she or he so prefers, continue working.

The government also made an early commitment to increase health services (free of charge to all citizens) and education of medical personnel accelerated. Another important area was housing policy. Already in March 1959 average housing rents were rolled back by up to 50 per cent and an Urban Reform followed in 1960 whereby over half of urban tenants became owners of their homes.[4]

It should also be mentioned that all Cubans have had a rationing card since 1962, through which they, in principle, acquire many essential food items (and at times also other items like detergents, clothes, etc.) at highly subsidised prices. The only problem with this system was that in bad times the supply of goods was far from enough to cover the monthly needs of the population. The situation was especially bad at the beginning of the 1970s, and then again after 1990, when the so-called 'Special Period in Time of Peace' started. However, at the end of the 1970s, and practically until the end of the 1980s, the system functioned reasonably well, and most families even had enough money left over from the monthly pay check to supplement their food basket in the 'parallel market', or in the

3   Minrex (1966), p. 286.
4   Hamberg (1990), p. 235.

short lived peasants' market (1980–84), and they often also had money left to spend on leisure and vacation, or to save (either by hoarding or in savings accounts with low interests). It should also be mentioned that practically all workers and employees in the state sector have subsidised canteen meals at and children have free meals in the many boarding schools.

But there is 'no such thing as a free lunch', even in socialist Cuba.[5] All the social reforms had to be financed somehow. With the nationalisation of practically all remaining private businesses in 1968 (with the exception of small agricultural holdings), it was thought that the nation would function as one big enterprise, with just one account belonging to an all embracing and benevolent state. Taxes had been abolished so government expenditure was to be financed from surpluses produced by the state enterprises. This system remained intact more or less until the crisis in the 1990s. Since a substantial number of state enterprises were running with chronic deficits, one might wonder how this welfare system could be sustained.

A partial explanation could be found in the very generous preferential trade agreements with the Soviet Union (sugar for oil). It has even been claimed that Cuba's commitment to social goals (such as full employment, social equity and universal provision of social services) were achieved 'at significant economic cost, and it was largely feasible with enormous Soviet aid'.[6] Although this might be somewhat exaggerated, it is still no doubt true that when the Soviet subsidy vanished practically overnight in 1991, the Cuban welfare system became very vulnerable.

Retreat from Entitlement? Reforms after 1993 and their Impact on Social Welfare

The reform process started only in 1993–94 when it became clear to the Cuban leadership that the transition process in the former Soviet Union was irreversible, but above all because the economic situation in the island had become untenable, and both the economic and political systems were at the risk of collapsing. A 'structural adjustment' of public finances took place that brought down the budget deficit from minus 30.4 per cent of GDP in 1993 to minus 6.9 per cent within a year, and has since then stabilised around minus 2–3 per cent per year. The reduction of the deficit was primarily the result of a gradual downsizing of public sector employment and phasing out subsidies to loss–making State Owned Enterprises

---

5   Benjamin et al. (1984).

6   Mesa-Lago (2000), p. 557.

(SOEs). The latter alone amounted to 32.7 per cent of GDP in 1993. Between 1993 and 1994 alone, state employment declined by 500,000 (out of 3.5 million), and subsidies to loss-making SOEs were cut by 2,000 million pesos (from 5,400 million).

Changes have also occurred on the income side. Thus, the government has introduced new indirect taxes and also some targeted personal income taxes (see further below). As a result of these reforms, there are undoubtedly many people who are enjoying fewer benefits now than say ten years ago. But this is not really as a result of a 'retreat from entitlement', but rather *it is the result of entitlements being worth less than before.* There are a number of reasons for this. Let us start with a look at the social security system and how it functions in Cuba today.

Social Security in Cuba Today

The social security system has not changed very much although pensioners no longer receive the full amount (100 per cent of the last pay cheque). A retired person today receives 80 per cent of that amount and there is also a deduction made depending on number of years worked. That is, one receives the full 80 per cent only if one has worked for 15 years or more. The number of people depending on pensions in Cuba had increased from 1.1 million in 1990 to 1.4 million by the end of last decade. At the same time the average pension has increased in nominal value from about 84 pesos per month to 95 pesos.[7]

However, this change is not the most important change for most pensioners. Whether it is 100 per cent or 80 per cent of the old salary is not decisive, nor is the increase per se. It is the erosion of the worth of the peso that has made pensions worth so much less. While it was possible to live on the pension (although not especially well perhaps) in the 1980s, this is just impossible today. Had it not been for the rationing card, subsidised meals at special canteens and help from relatives and friends, the situation of most pensioners would be just unbearable.

Other Reforms Affecting Family Budgets

Although most social services are still free in Cuba (such as education and health services), the government has introduced fees for some communal services that were free before. One such case is day-care services that were earlier free of charge. Families now have to spend a certain percentage of

---

[7]   Togores (1999).

the wage income for such services. Although this in money terms might seem little (perhaps 10 pesos per month), it is still an additional burden on many already tight budgets. The government has not excluded plans to introduce fees for other communal services in the near future, too.

A new tax system is also being introduced gradually with the enactment of the Tax System Law (Law 73) in August 1994. This new system modified both direct and indirect taxation. The aims were to protect the lowest income groups, to promote productivity and help to diminish excess liquidity.[8] The direct taxes apply both to business and private persons. Companies (also SOEs) now have to pay a 35 per cent profit tax, although with a more simplified, but also more controversial, system for small business (so-called *cuentapropistas*, or self-employed).

A personal income tax was also introduced, for the first time since it was abolished after the Revolution, with a progressive scale, from five per cent for incomes below 3,000 pesos a year (the value of the peso will be discussed below), with a marginal rate of 50 per cent on annual incomes over 60,000 pesos per year (equivalent to about 25 times the annual average wage). The tax is in principle applicable to *all* incomes, although it has been decided to exempt wages and pensions paid in national currency for the time being.[9]

The most controversial tax is the tax on self-employed activities. These pay a flat rate whatever the size of profits. Typical rates are 100 pesos a month for a taxi driver and 500 pesos for private restaurant owner, with an additional 20 per cent for each family helper. However, the rate can be extended to up to 1,000 dollars per month for private restaurants (*paladares*) that cater to tourists. Such restaurants can make more than 5,000 dollars per month according to unofficial estimates.[10] The same type of flat rate is applied to renting of rooms (real-estate rental was legalised in 1997), where those with a license to rent rooms pay a fixed tax per month (some in dollars).

Law 73 also modified several indirect taxes. Thus, a special surcharge on certain 'unnecessary' consumer items such as tobacco and alcoholic beverages was introduced already in 1994. Likewise, a special surcharge has been applied in relation to electricity consumption (50 per cent of the population did not pay at all for various reasons). Now there is a progressive rate mounting with level of electricity consumption per household.

---

8   CEPAL (2000).

9   There was even a referendum taken prior to the Party Congress in 1997 to determine whether the Cubans were in favour or not of paying reintroducing taxes on their (state) wages and salaries. Not surprisingly an overwhelming majority voted against.

10   CEPAL (1997).

Transportation prices have also increased (intercity-bus prices as much as 116 per cent) and so have gasoline prices, postal rates and water supply rates.[11] The state also adds a tax of 140 per cent on all items sold in the 'dollar shops' (Tiendas de Recaudación de Divisas — TDR).

The Government Social Budget

In spite of this shock treatment with price increases and new tariffs and taxes, the government has continued its strong commitment to welfare policies, and there has been an honest attempt to maintain the social safety net for the most needy, even in times of crisis during the Special Period. This commitment is illustrated by the social spending of the government in the 1990s (Tables 16.1 and 16.2).

Table 16.1: Cuba: Government Social Budget in Current Prices, 1989, 1993–2000 (m. pesos)

	1989	1993	1994	1995	1996	1997	1998	1999	2000
Total Government Current Income	12,188	8,196	10,873	10,720	11,564	11,574	12,014	12,891	13,934
Indirect taxes	5,547	3,611	5,595	6,165	5,513	5,330	5,543	6,336	n.a.
Direct taxes	0	414	572	910	1,497	2,173	2,684	3,084	n.a.
SS Contributions	676	925	881	898	959	1,071	1,025	1,115	1,170
Other income*	5,964	3,246	3,825	2,746	3,595	3,000	2,762	2,356	n.a.
Total Government Current Exp.	10,844	12,529	11,495	12,064	10,770	10,824	11,481	12,331	13,396
Education	1651	1,385	1,335	1,359	1,421	1,454	1,510	1,830	2,125
Health	905	1,077	1,061	1,108	1,190	1,265	1,345	1,553	1,726
Social Security	1,094	1,452	1,532	1,594	1,630	1,636	1,705	1,786	1,786
Social Assist.	101	94	94	119	128	135	145	158	165
Total Social Exp.	3,751	4,008	4,022	4,180	4,369	4,490	4,705	5,327	5,802
Social as % of Total	34.6	32.0	35.0	34.6	40.6	41.5	41.0	43.2	43.3

* Primarily 'contributions by state enterprises'
Source: CEPAL (2000: Table A.13); *Anuario Estadístico de Cuba 1999*, Table IV.4; and ONE (2001)

[11]   *Ibid.*

The social budget (as defined by education, health, social security and social assistance) has increased every year in current prices during the Special Period. It has also increased its share of total current expenditure, from 35 per cent in 1989 to 43 per cent today. Education increased its share of current expenditure from 15.2 per cent in 1989 to 15.9 per cent in 2000; health has increased from 8.3 per cent to 12.9 per cent, social security from 10.1 per cent to 13.3 per cent in the same period. Expenditure under the item 'social assistance' are quite low but it is not unlikely that this budgeted item will increase considerably in the future.

Table 16.2: Cuba: Government Social Expenditure in Constant Prices, 1989, 1993–2000 (m. pesos)

	1989	1993	1994	1995	1996	1997	1998	1999	2000
Total Gov. Current Exp.	10,930	10,806	8,136	7,746	6,998	7,152	7,334	8,478	9,156
Education	1,664	1,194	945	872	924	961	964	1,258	1,452
Health	912	929	751	712	773	836	859	1,068	1,180
Social Security	1,103	1,253	1,085	1,023	1,059	1,081	1,089	1,228	1,221
Social Assistance	102	81	66	76	83	89	93	109	113
Total Social Exp.	3,781	3,457	2,847	2,683	2,839	2,967	3,005	3,663	3,966
Social Exp. Per Capita	357	316	260	244	257	269	270	328	354

Source: Same as Table 16.1 (constant prices calculated by the author using the implicit GDP deflator)

The situation looks a bit different if social expenditure is considered in constant prices.[12] Social expenditure has been rising as a percentage of total expenditure, of course, but it dropped in real terms from 3.8 billion pesos in 1989 to a bottom low of 2.7 billion pesos in 1995 (a drop of almost 30 per cent). Since then, however, social expenditure has recovered slowly but steadily, and by 2000 amounted to four billion pesos, or five per cent above the 1989 level. Social expenditure per capita declined between 1989 and 1995 from 357 to 244 pesos (a drop of 32 per cent) but had by 2000 increased again to 354 pesos (or just about the same as in 1989).

---

[12]　Current prices deflated by the implicit GDP deflator.

The commitment to social transfers is clear if compared with other budget items. Thus, defence spending as a share of total government expenditure fell from 11.6 per cent in 1989 to 5.1 per cent in 1995, although this have again risen slightly in the last three years (7.0 per cent in 2000).

Many Social Indicators Continue to Improve

One can not doubt that the Cuban government has striven to maintain a social safety net to protect the most vulnerable sectors of the population. However, when the crisis was at its most serious in the mid-90s, a large majority of the population was having difficulties in getting the necessary intake of calories, proteins and vitamins, and many people were, if not starving, seriously under-nourished. In 1993, the average Cuban got only 1,940 calories per day, and only 48 grams of proteins (well below the levels recommended by the World Health Organization — WHO). By 2000, however, the levels were almost restored to normal, or 2,585 calories and 68 grams of protein.[13]

Table 16.3: Cuba: Social Indicators, 1989–99

	Life Expectancy	Infant Mortality	Inhabitants per Physician
1989	74.6	11.1	303
1990	74.6	10.7	275
1991	74.7	10.7	252
1992	74.7	10.2	231
1993	74.7	9.4	214
1994	74.7	9.9	202
1995	74.8	9.4	193
1996	74.8	7.9	183
1997	74.8	7.2	176
1998	74.8	7.1	175
1999	74.8	6.4	172

Sources: *Anuario Estadístico de Cuba*, 1996, 1997, 1998 and 1999;
Anuario Demográfico de Cuba, 1998

[13] J-L. Rodríguez (2000).

Another indication that Cuba has managed to provide its citizens with a minimum of social protection, even in times of serious economic crisis, is that many social indicators have continued progressing during the whole 'Special Period' (see Table 16.3), in stark contrast for instance to the development of most republics of the former Soviet Union after the collapse. Thus, life expectancy has increased and stabilised at a level of 75 years (only paralleled by Costa Rica and Chile in Latin America). Infant mortality has steadily gone down and is now the lowest in the developing world (6.4 per thousand live births in 1999), and also lower than in many developed countries. The density of physicians has also continued to progress, and Cuba is now almost unique in the world with only 172 inhabitants per doctor. It is noteworthy that the 'family doctor' system especially has been extended all through the 'Special Period'.

A Bifurcated Economy and a Heterogeneous Labour Market

The Cuban economy is steadily recovering from its deep depression between 1990 and 1993 and the reform process has no doubt played an important role in this recovery. However, this reform process has also forced the government to sacrifice, at least temporarily, important 'sacred pillars' on which the former socialist economy was based. In this respect there are two new main features in the new, more market-oriented, economy that distinguish it from the old centrally planned economy. First of all, the legalisation of holding and trading in foreign exchange in 1993, that led to the bifurcation, or partial 'dollarisation', of the economy. A growing share of merchandise is now sold for dollars (or convertible pesos) in special shops, or TRDs, which is a mechanism used to collect dollars in circulation (by putting a 140 per cent tax on top of the price of the goods sold in the shop, whether national or imported).

Secondly, a more diversified, mixed labour market has emerged, partly as result of the gradual dollarisation of the economy, but was also as a consequence of the opening up of the economy to international tourism, to foreign direct investment, to the cooperativisation of large parts of agriculture and the opening up of private employment opportunities, although until now on a rather limited scale.

While 94 per cent of the civilian labour force was occupied in the state sector in 1989, the share had declined to 78 per cent in 1999 (see Table 16.4). The biggest increase has taken place in the cooperative sector (up from 1.7 per cent in 1989 to 8.5 per cent ten years later), and private sector employment has increased its share from 4.2 per cent in 1989 to 13.0 per cent in 1999. The private sector consists primarily of private farmers (for example, all tobacco farms are private, and have always been) and a slowly growing self-employment sector. It is mainly those employed in the new emerging sectors of the economy that have money to spend in the dollar sector of the economy (that is, the TRDs and the tourism sector).

Table 16.4. Occupied Civilian Labour Force by Type of Ownership, 1989, 1995 and 1999 (thousand)

	1989		1995		1999	
	thousand	%	thousand	%	thousand	%
State	3,641.1	94.1	2,902.8	80.8	2,985.2	78.0
Of which 'mercantile corporations'*	—	—	71.6	2.0	140.2	3.7
Joint Ventures	—	—	13.8	0.4	19.8	0.5
Cooperatives	64.5	1.7	348.8	9.7	324.9	8.5
Private	164.6	4.3	325.8	9.1	496.4	13.0
Of which self-employed (licensed)	25.2	0.7	138.1	3.8	156.6	4.1
Total Occupied Civilian Labour Force	3,870.2	100.0	3,591.0	100.0	3,826.3	100.0

* a new type of, more independent, SOE

Source: *Anuario Estadístico de Cuba, 1989* (CEE, 1990: Table IV.1); *Anuario Estadístico de Cuba ,1999* (ONE, 2001: Table V.1)

A More Unequal Society in the 1990s

However, a growing number of Cubans do get access to dollars, or other foreign currency. Thus, while only 33.5 per cent of the Cubans had dollars to spend in 1996, the percentage gradually increased to 49.5 per cent in 1997, to 56.3 per cent in 1998 and to 62.0 per cent in 1999.[14] On the other hand, the great majority of these have only small amounts of dollars, in most cases (72.4 per cent) less than two dollars per month. Although most Cubans with access to dollars still get them either through family remittances, or as a result of working in, or being close to the tourism sector or

[14] Añé (2000).

other 'emerging sectors', a growing number of workers also receive incentives in the form of convertible pesos (equivalent to dollars) on top of their monthly peso pay-cheque. In 1999, no less than 1,079,000 state employed took part in such schemes, with an average hard currency addition of US$19 per employee and month. It should be noted that although the peso is officially at parity with the dollar, it is exchanged at a parallel (officially administered) market at 20 pesos (January 2001), so the US$19 addition in practice means a doubling of the monthly salary.

Family remittances from abroad are an important source of income for many Cubans. However, it is not known with exactitude how many receive remittances and what is the average size of transfers. The statistical office (ONE) has carried out a household survey annually since 1996, and the survey asks questions about foreign exchange holdings, and origin. The data are, however, classified, but even if they were made public, they would probably not tell the whole story. It is likely that many people avoid answering truthfully to such pertinent questions, even if they are guaranteed full confidentiality by law. But the government has made estimates of the total flows of family remittances. Thus, official data claim that remittances have increased from practically zero ten years ago to about US$725 million in 1999, equivalent to about 16 per cent of total exports of goods and services.

The new economic situation in Cuba, the 'Special Period', has no doubt led to drastic income gaps and inequalities. It is, however, extremely difficult to measure with exactness the increase in inequality. There are many reasons for this. First of all, it is tricky to compare income inequalities today with the income distribution before 1989 (when data were primarily based on wage data). Another reason is that estimates in the 1990s have so many unknown variables, such as amount of income in dollars other than wages, for instance, through family remittances, or income earned either *legally*, as tips and through self-employment, or *illegally*, for example, through prostitution or sales of stolen goods.

The government increasingly includes state-employed workers and employees in an incentive scheme that a comprises a convertible peso component (equivalent to dollars) in the salary. In 1994 there were about 115,000 workers who benefited from such incentive schemes, valued at US$3.1 million (US$27 per worker). By 1999 this number had increased to 1.1 million workers, representing about 32 per cent of the labour force employed by the state, with a total amount of US$52.3 million (or US$48 per worker). This might still be considered to be a modest supplement to the wage or salary, but on the average it means (with an exchange rate of

20 pesos per dollar) an addition to the average monthly pay of about 40 per cent. Many workers and employees also receive incentives in the form of non-monetary supplements, such as toiletry and clothes.[15]

Income Inequalities before and after the Crisis

Income inequalities narrowed considerably in Cuba after the Revolution.[16] Thus, while the share of the poorest 40 per cent only amounted to 6.5 per cent in 1953 (or very reminiscent of the shares in Latin America at that time, and also in most cases still today), this share increased to 17.2 per cent in 1962, to 24.8 per cent in 1978 and to 26.0 per cent in 1986.[17]

Table 16.5: Income Distribution in Cuba by Quintile Groups: 1986, 1989, 1996 and 1999

Quintiles	1986	1989	1996	1999
Lower (0–20)	11.3%	8.8%	4.8%	4.3%
Second (21–40)	14.7%	14.5%	9.1%	8.2%
Third (41–60)	17.0%	18.7%	13.2%	12.2%
Fourth (61–80)	23.2%	24.1%	18.5%	17.1%
Upper (81–100)	33.8%	33.9%	54.4%	58.1%
Upper/Lower	3.3	3.8	11.3	13.5
Gini	0.22	n.a.	0.399	0.407

Source: All data (except 1986) from Añé (2000); 1986 data from Brundenius (1990)

Income inequalities have, however, again started to increase (Table 16.5 above). Thus, according to official estimates (based on the household surveys mentioned above), the income share of the poorest 40 per cent dropped from 23.3 per cent in 1989, to 13.9 per cent in 1996 and to 12.5 per cent in 1999.

A look at the top of the scale reveals that the upper quintile not surprisingly increased its shares of total incomes in the same period, or from

---

[15] *Ibid.*, p. 13–14; and J-L. Rodriguez (2000).

[16] Brundenius (1984 and 1990).

[17] Brundenius (1990), Table 10.4.

33.9 per cent in 1989 to 54.4 per cent in 1996, and to 58.1 per cent in 1999. It should be stressed that the 1996 and 1999 data are based on the sum of income earnings in pesos + income in dollars + 42 pesos (the latter a proxy equivalent to free education and health services and subsidy of food and housing). This of course makes the data more meaningful per se, considering the new context, but on the other hand they make them more difficult to compare with the pre-1990 data.

Income inequalities are also often expressed in a concentration coefficient, the Gini coefficient. Here also we see a clear trend. Between 1953 and 1962 the Gini declines from 0.55 to 0.35, continues to decline to 0.25 in 1978, and then further to 0.22 in 1986. There are no available data until 1996 but these data (based on the same source as mentioned in Table 16.5) show a drastic increase of the Gini coefficient after 1990. In 1996 the Gini was, according to these estimates, 0.399, then declined slightly to 0.394 in 1997 and to 0.385 in 1998, but then again increased slightly to 0.407 in 1999.[18] Although these data should be interpreted with caution, it clear that income inequalities dramatically increased in Cuba in the 1990s, and especially after 1994 when most of the reforms were introduced.

Growing inequalities are also reflected in the savings accounts. Thus many Cubans save money in the Cuban Savings Bank, Banco Popular de Ahorro. Until 1993 it was only possible to save money in peso accounts, but after 1993 it has also become possible to open accounts in foreign exchange. It goes without saying that Cubans with access to dollars, or working in the new emerging sectors of the economy, are the ones who account for the lion's share of the money deposited in the savings bank. According to the bank's own annual reports, there was an increasing concentration of money deposited, that is, a small number of deposits accounted for increasing shares of all the money deposited.

Slightly more than 60 per cent of the deposit holders had less than 200 pesos (or dollar equivalent) in their accounts in 1994 and their holdings amounted to only 4.4 per cent of total holdings in that same year. By 1997, this group with small savings accounted for 66.5 per cent of all deposit holders, while their share of holdings declined even further to 2.4 per cent. On the other side of the extreme, those deposit holders with more than 10 000 pesos in their accounts increased their share of total holdings from 36.0 to 46.4 per cent in the same period (Table 16.6).

---

[18] Añé (2000).

Table 16.6: Deposits in the Cuban Savings Bank by Size of Holdings, 1994 and 1997

	Share of deposits (%)		Share of holdings (%)	
Size of holdings	1994	1997	1994	1997
Less than 200 pesos	61.7	66.5	4.4	2.4
201– 2,000	24.2	20.9	17.8	12.6
2 001–10,000	11.9	10.2	41.8	38.6
10 001– 20,000	1.7	2.0	20.0	23.3
More than 20,000	0.5	0.9	16.0	23.1

Source: Bank data quoted in Togares (2000)

Who are the Winners and Losers and Can the Losers also become Winners?

The winners so far are: people receiving family remittances, peoples working in the tourism sector (especially taxi drivers), in private agriculture, in some self-employment sectors, in the new emerging sectors (especially joint ventures and prioritised sectors such as energy, telecommunications and biotechnology).

The losers so far are: people living on pensions alone, the unemployed, those on sick leave, those working in 'traditional sectors' (with income only in pesos), that comprise most state sectors, and also most medical personnel and teachers. The latter group is rather surprising in this context, considering the important role they are playing in the Cuban society. One reason is no doubt that being a doctor, a nurse or a teacher is considered (especially by Fidel Castro himself) to be a self-sacrificing vocation. However, there are signs that this policy is about to change.

Human Capital: a Precious but Dwindling Asset

One of the Cuban Revolution's main achievements is the investment it has made in human capital. Cuba has today the most educated work force in Latin America. However, there are worrying signs: it tends to be poorly utilised and there are also signs that the human capital is dwindling.

Thus, a recent phenomenon has become the preoccupation of the Cuban government. Since the beginning of the 1990s an increasing number of young people neither go to work nor continue education after compulsory school.[19] A glance at official statistics sheds some light on this phenomenon. By contrasting demographic data with employment and educational statistics it is possible to get an idea of the problem with the young people. If we look at some of the characteristics of young people in their twenties (age cohort 20–29), several trends are clear (Table 16.7).[20]

a.   The total numbers in the cohort are declining (contributing to the ageing of the population problem discussed above).

b.   But surprisingly, the number of inactive young people is increasing in both absolute numbers and in relative terms (until 1998).

c.   The young people are inactive not only because they do not attend university (or other higher learning institutions), but also because they apparently do not work.

d.   Apparent inactivity rates are (not surprisingly) higher for women than for men, but the number of inactive men increased more rapidly between 1988 and 1998 than in the case of women (with 35 per cent compared to 23 per cent).

e.   There may have been a reversal of the trends at the end of the 1990s. Student enrolments again started increasing in 1999, and so did labour force participation rates for both men and women.

Although the trend now may be reversing, the problem with many inactive young people remains. The reasons for this apparent inactivity (one third of all 20–29 year olds in 1999, 23 per cent of the men and 46 per cent of the women) are not self-evident. One reason could be that there are fewer university places available in disciplines that are in demand (like social sciences), coupled with the fact that the downsized state sector offers few tempting job opportunities. It thus could be that many of those listed as 'inactive' are actually doing unregistered work of both the legal and illegal kind. In addition, many young people, who have finished their basic higher education, may be doing jobs that have nothing, or very little, to do with their educational background (some kind of 'internal brain drain'). Finally, it should also be stressed that the data in Table 16.7 only refer to full time enrolments (that is the rule in Cuba). However, the government is increasingly now also introducing university courses 'at distance', often complemented with lectures broadcast over TV.

---

[19]   Also analysed in Brundenius (2000).

[20]   The data in Table 16.7 refer to annual averages (or to situation at 30 June each year). Seasonal variations are not known.

Table 16.7: Characteristics of the 20–29 Age Cohort, 1988, 1996, 1998 and 1999 (thousand)

	1988	1996	1998	1999
Total Age Cohort	2,203.4	2, 122.2	1,971.4	1,873.9
In Labour Force*	1,351.9	1,264.5	1,103.7	1,125.1
Students	250.6	111.6	102.6	106.8
Inactive	600.9	746.1	764.7	642.0
Inactive/Total	27.3%	35.2%	38.8%	34.3%
Males	1,112.2	1,071.7	995.0	945.5
In Labour Force*	797.6	776.6	676.5	688.0
Students	107.6	44.5	38.8	40.0
Inactive	207.0	250.6	279.7	217.5
Inactive/Total	18.6%	23.4%	28.1%	23.0%
Females	1,091.2	1,050.5	976.4	928.4
In Labour Force*	554.3	487.9	427.6	437.1
Students	143.0	67.1	63.8	66.8
Inactive	393.9	495.5	485.0	424.5
Inactive/Total	36.1%	47.2%	49.7%	45.7%

* Economically active population (includes unemployed and non-civilian labour force)
Source: Brundenius (2000: Table 7) plus updates based on Anuario Estadístico de Cuba 1999 (ONE, 2001), Tables II.3, V.2, V.11, XV.8, XV.9

There is no doubt that Cuba will have to make much better use of its highly qualified labour force in the future. However, there is additional problem that is perhaps even more serious. One of Cuba's main future problems might be to have to cope with dwindling human capital formation and there might not be enough highly qualified manpower in a few years when the economy has fully recovered! This is so for a number of reasons. One is that the growth of the population in Cuba is very low (0.4 per cent per year at present). Secondly, the population is ageing, a problem shared with many developed countries in Europe. In a way one could say the Cuban Revolution has been 'victim of its own success'. Efficient family planning coupled with expansion of health services to cover the whole population have led to low fertility rates and low mortality rates (although low infant mortality rates have helped to keep nativity rates up). The result is that the working age population is now stagnating, or even declining, and in the not so distant future Cuba will have difficulties finding enough people for the jobs created. Fortunately Cuba still has a large stock of human capital but with the slowing down of higher education enrolments there is a risk that this source of economic growth might erode rapidly.

This means that a large number of highly educated Cubans will leave the labour force in the coming ten years, and this will exert pressure for a far more efficient utilisation of the labour force than in the past. The only short-term solution to increase the working age population in the coming years would be to increase the retirement age to 65 for both men and women (from today's 55 for women and 60 for men). To retire at the age of 65 is quite common in many countries (for instance in most OECD countries), a drastic change with many financial implications in Cuba, and it might not be so popular either among Cubans about to retire.

Future Prospects: Challenges of a New Kind

Even if the Cuban economy continues to recover and achieves a high and sustained rate of growth, Cuba's welfare system will still be confronted with a series of challenges in the coming years. It is bound to change in many respects. The 'cradle to grave' provisions will have to adapt to a new economic reality. Cuba's strength lies in the solid base it has in its educational and health systems with an important reserve (so far) of highly educated people. With the ageing of the population, however, a larger burden will be laid on the shoulders of a stagnating (and for a while even declining) working age population to support a growing population of retired people. This will require a new type of pension system where perhaps a growing share of the funds will be financed through individual contributions.[21] In addition, the retirement age will no doubt have to be extended to make the system work.

In order to maintain a social welfare system that covers the whole population, Cuba will have to introduce a modern tax system, including the introduction of direct income taxes, a shocking novelty for most Cubans. The direct taxes will have to be progressive in order to cope with the growing income differentials described earlier. Another problem is that there is so far no unemployment insurance scheme in Cuba, since full employment has been not only a goal but a sacred principle in the government's social-

---

21   There is already a debate in Cuba about imposing contributions on workers (in addition to enterprise contributions). According to an article in *Time*, 20 February 1995 (quoted in Mesa-Lago 2000, p. 323), such contributions are envisaged in the new Tax Law, but have not been implemented so far. 'Castro has explained the delay based on the crisis and the need to change the workers' mentality, but he said the contribution would range from 5% to 7%.'

ist strategy (supported by the trade unions).[22] Nevertheless, with the gradual introduction of mixed forms of property (joint ventures, and perhaps in the near future purely private companies), there might be a need for market type unemployment schemes as well.

Finally, there are still many other problems related to social policies that have to be dealt with. One such problem is for instance housing policies. The housing situation, especially in Havana, is chaotic with unclear rules of ownership and tenants' rights. So far it is illegal to sell properties but this is also about to change. In sum, Cuba is confronted with a series of new challenges in its attempt to maintain and develop its universally admired social welfare system of the past. One outcome could be that the future social welfare system in Cuba will more and more resemble the welfare systems of most parts of the European Union. There could be worse outcomes than that.

---

[22] In the past laid off workers, however, have been paid 100% of their salary the first month after being 'rationalised' and 60% thereafter until a job is found (with a three year limit). Workers who refuse reassignment are dismissed with one month's wages, and 'young unemployed graduates have the option of retraining, continuing their studies, or waiting for job [a monthly subsidy is paid to them]' (Mesa-Lago 2000, p. 323).

CHAPTER 17

Whose Crisis? Public and Popular Reactions to Family Change in Costa Rica[*]

Sylvia Chant

Introduction

The concerns of this chapter are inspired by a report on family change commissioned by the United Nations Research Institute for Social Development (UNRISD) in the run-up to the 1995 World Summit on Social Development. The task of writing the review devolved to feminist anthropologist, Henrietta Moore, whose optic on the issue is encapsulated succinctly in its opening paragraph.

> Is the family in crisis? There is a widespread perception at the present time that something has gone wrong with the family. High rates of divorce, increased marital conflict and the escalating costs of welfare programmes, coupled with rising crime, drug-taking and anti-social behaviour among the young, are all taken as evidence that the family and the social values on which it is based are in decline. How accurate is this picture? Does it reflect a form of 'moral panic' rather than a description of an empirical situation?[1]

In the analysis which follows, Moore raises numerous issues which caution against the uncritical acceptance of 'crisis' and 'panic' as concepts which might depict reactions to family change at a world scale. One important proviso is that crisis discourses tend to be 'public and often produced by the state and/or elite groups'.[2] How well these might converge with local understandings and experiences of family life is questionable. A second major qualification relates to the fact that the general perception of 'family crisis' is one which has very specific Euro-American origins.[3] While Moore stresses that this does not preclude the fact that families in other

[*]   I am grateful to Monica Budowski, Nikki Craske, John Gledhill, Matthew Gutmann, Gareth Jones, Cathy McIlwaine, Diane Perrons and Eugenia Rodríguez for their comments.

[1]   Moore (1994), p. 1.

[2]   *Ibid.*, p. 6.

[3]   *Ibid.*, p. 25.

regions might be undergoing change and/or difficulty, she also maintains that there are many countries in which 'there is no public discourse of family decline'.[4] How long this might last, however, is uncertain, given that the notion of family crisis has already come onto some national and internation-al agendas, harbouring direct consequences for policy initiatives in its wake.[5] In the USA, for example, recent responses have included renewed assertion of the superiority of heterosexual marriage as the most desirable arrange-ment for child-rearing, cuts in welfare to lone mothers and proposals to restrict access to divorce.[6] The current emphasis in international agencies such as the World Bank on combating poverty through building 'social capi-tal' might also be regarded as a means of arresting 'family decline', given the central focus on strengthening kin and community relationships.[7]

With this in mind, the aim of the present chapter is to interrogate the relevance of what appears to be a rapidly-spreading 'global stereotype' in the context of Costa Rica. Having experienced shifts in family and house-hold organisation consonant with those occurring in many other parts of the world, have these changes also been interpreted in Costa Rica as signs of 'family crisis'? To what extent do they constitute a source of anxiety in popular, as well as policy-making, circles? Have recent social policies attempted to adapt to contemporary transitions, and if so, how? In order to explore these questions I draw on interview surveys with low- and mid-dle-income families, and on discussions with government officials and rep-resentatives of civil society organisations.[8]

The discussion is divided into four parts. The first considers the main sources and concerns of 'crisis discourses' which have developed around

---

4   *Ibid.*, p. 26.

5   *Ibid.*

6   See Stacey (1997).

7   See World Bank, (2000), chapter 7; also Gledhill (2000), p. 22; Molyneux (2002).

8   The interviews in question were carried out under the auspices of two projects conducted in Costa Rica during 1999: 'Institutional Perspectives on Family Change in Costa Rica', funded by the Central Research Fund and London School of Economics, and 'Youth, Gender and Family Crisis in Costa Rica', funded by the Nuffield Foundation (Award no. SGS/LB/0223). Aside from my thanks to these organisations for supporting the projects, I am indebted to Wagner Moreno, Faculty of Social Psychology, University of Costa Rica in Guanacaste for his valuable collaboration in interviewing and analysis on the latter project, and to the members of our field team – Sonia Alvarado, Emma Hernández, Juan José Morales and Lisette Ondoy – for their painstaking work on transcription. The chapter also utilises some survey work conducted for a field-based pilot project on 'Men, Households and Poverty in Costa Rica' carried out in the sum-mer of 1997, co-funded by the Nuffield Foundation (Award no: SOC/100 [1554]), and ESRC (Award no. R000222205).

recent trends in household and family organisation at an international scale. The second explores popular responses to family change in Costa Rica with reference to interviews conducted with 176 men and women from low- and middle-income groups in Guanacaste province. The third section examines attitudes towards, and responses to, family change on the part of public institutions such as government agencies, NGOs and the Catholic Church. The final section re-visits the utility of 'crisis' as an organising concept for current household transitions in Costa Rica itself, and at a wider, global level.

Although there is an extensive literature on the importance of disaggregating concepts of 'household' and 'family', the former generally being used to describe a residential unit, and the latter 'a set of normative relationships',[9] the main reason why I use the terms interchangeably in the bulk of the chapter is because 'family crisis' discourses tend to refer, if not explicitly, to changes in residentially-based forms of family life.

'Layering the Crisis': from the Global to the National

Despite the generalised projection of 'crisis' in some quarters, it is clear, as Moore suggests, that this is not a view that is necessarily widely shared, even if there is reasonably widespread consensus that a number of contemporary processes are undermining 'traditional' forms of family organisation in many parts of the world. These processes include globalisation, neoliberal economic restructuring, the changing nature of work, rising female labour force participation, increased access to population control and post-1960s feminist movements.[10]

A Crisis for Whom, about What and Why?

Yet although there is evidence of immense diversity in the functions and forms of families in different places and historical periods and accordingly no *single* type of family which can be held up as 'traditional',[11] this is not the case as far as family crisis discourses are concerned. Instead, crisis discourses are specifically, if not always explicitly, tied to crisis in a particular

---

9   Roberts (1994), p. 10.

10   See Beck and Beck-Gernsheim (1995); Castells (1997); Gledhill (2000); Moore (1994).

11   See Chant (2002); Cicerchia (1997); Dore (1997); Gudmundson (1986); Kuznetsoff (1980); E. Rodríguez (2000) on Latin America; Collier et al. (1997); Harris (1981); Roberts (1991) more generally.

Eurocentric ideal of household arrangement, notably the patriarchal family unit comprising a married couple and their children.[12] Concerns mainly, although not exclusively, on the part of conservative and right-wing sectors in Europe and the USA to uphold this normative model mean that other family forms, such as lone mother households, have fallen subject to considerable criticism and stigmatisation.

While feminists have pressed the point that 'the social pathology of the lone mother is just as imaginary as the social desirability of the nuclear family',[13] and that lone mother households are extremely diverse,[14] dominant projections are both monolithic and negative.[15] Coupled with rising levels of divorce and increased conjugal conflict, lone motherhood is routinely linked with a breakdown in social and family values, rising crime, violence and drug-use (particularly on the part of men), and, in places where there has been concern to cut social expenditure, such as the UK and USA, increased poverty, with the corollary of growing dependency of mothers and children on the state.[16] While the wellbeing of children is seen to be threatened in 'fatherless families', there is also the concern for the effects on society of 'familyless fathers' sprung from the 'civilising' and 'stabilising' effects of marriage and responsibility for offspring.[17] It is evident, accordingly, that it is not only concerns to cut welfare bills which have driven 'family crisis' discourses, but moral, political and ideological agendas. Stacey's (1997) hard-hitting analysis of the evolution of the 'family values' campaign in the USA during the 1990s, for example, indicates that attempts to (re-) assert the supremacy of a white, middle class, heterosexual, model of nuclear family life are sometimes only thinly underlain by anti-racial, homophobic and anti-feminist motives.[18]

Patterns of social and household change which have given rise to concern and anxiety in parts of Europe and North America are also found in Latin America. In many countries in the region, a growing incidence of lone motherhood and female household headship has been accompanied

---

[12]   See Castells (1997), p. 222; Moore (1994); Stacey (1997), p. 466. A major irony here is that the male-headed nuclear family unit is often held up as a product rather than precursor of economic development and modernity (see Baylies, 1996, p. 77).

[13]   McIntosh (1996), p. 150.

[14]   Chant (1997); Feijoó (1999); Phoenix (1996).

[15]   See Baylies (1996); Chant (1999a).

[16]   See Duncan and Edwards (1994); Phoenix (1996); Roseneil and Mann (1996); Smart (1996).

[17]   See Laws (1996), p. 64; also Morgan (1995); Stacey (1997); Westwood (1996).

[18]   See also Duncan and Edwards (1994); Phoenix (1996) on the UK.

by, and embedded in, falling levels of legal marriage, rising numbers of out-of-wedlock births, greater rates of divorce and separation and mounting involvement of women in the historically male preserve of family 'breadwinning'.[19] In some cases, such as Guatemala, there is also evidence from grassroots surveys that high levels of crime and violence, and the 'perverse socialisation' of children, are thought to derive from women heading households, or working outside the home.[20]

Trends in Family Patterns in Costa Rica: Ingredients for a Discourse of 'Family Crisis'?

As far as Costa Rica is concerned, the 'traditional nuclear family' comprising male breadwinner, female housewife and an average of three children is described as having been the dominant family unit until as recently the 1970s,[21] even if only 50 per cent of households actually conformed to this model at the time.[22] Subsequent decline, to around one-third of households today, has been driven by a combination of increases in people living alone, a rise in complex or extended households and mounting numbers of one-parent units, nearly all of which are headed by women.[23] Although lone mother households and female-headed households are not synonymous,[24] the proportion of households headed by women climbed from 16 per cent of the total in 1973, to 22 per cent in 1997.[25]

Contributing to the decrease in patriarchal family units, marriage rates dropped from 30.8 to 23.5 per 100 between 1980 and 1994,[26] and divorce rates rose from 9.9 to 21.2 per 100 between 1980 and 1996.[27] Official figures also indicate that the proportion of births outside marriage in Costa

---

19   For examples see Arriagada (1998); Benería (1991); Cerrutti and Zenteno (1999); Folbre (1991); Geldstein (1997); González de la Rocha (1995); Jelin (1991a); Kaztman (1992); Safa (1995).

20   Datta and McIlwaine (2000), p. 43.

21   CMF (1996), p. 20.

22   The 'norm' of the nuclear household is historically quite recent in Costa Rica. According to the historian Eugenia Rodríguez (1999), the monogamous nuclear family only became a powerful concept with the national liberal project of Costa Rica in the late 19th and 20th centuries, although Catholic marriage was first introduced in the mid-18th and early 19th centuries in the Valle Central (see also Budowski, 2000a, p. 61; Rodríguez, 2000).

23   Fauné (1997), p. 92; Pereira García (1998), p. 187.

24   Chant (1997).

25   Budowski and Guzmán (1998).

26   MIDEPLAN (1995), pp. 5–6.

27   PEN (1998), p. 210.

Rica increased from 23 per cent in 1960 to 38 per cent in 1985, and to 49 per cent in 1998.[28] Moreover, nearly one in three children now have a *padre desconocido* (unknown father).[29] This is mainly due to the rise in births among unmarried mothers, and is significant insofar as traditionally, only formally acknowledged children received their father's family name and entitlement to paternal support.[30] Aside from an upward trend in children with unregistered paternity (from 21 per cent to 30 per cent between 1990 and 1999),[31] teenage motherhood is on the rise, with 60 per cent of single parents in the country being under 25 years of age, and 16 per cent under 18 (see also note 28). In addition to these transitions, there have been major changes going on inside the family, particularly with respect to gender divisions of labour. In 1980, for example, there was only one female worker for every three men in the 20–39 year age cohort, but the gap had narrowed to one in two by 1990.[32] Between 1980 and 1995, the share of the labour force made up by women in Costa Rica rose from 24.3 to 30.5 per cent,[33] and in the non-agricultural sector, where women are most likely to be employed, the increase was from 30 to 36 per cent between 1980 and 1994.[34] Despite the fact that women's average wages are lower than men's, that women are more likely to be unemployed and that the rate of male labour force participation has remained relatively stable for many years (at around 80 per cent of men of working age), unemployment has risen among men since the late 1980s (from 4.5 per cent to 5.8 per cent between 1989 and 1995). The most notable increases in male unemployment are in the 15–25 year and 45–70 year age groups, with periods of unemployment also becoming longer.[35]

What Evidence of a Discourse of 'Family Crisis' in Costa Rica? Initial Impressions

Given current trends in Costa Rican family patterns, it is possibly surprising that, on the surface at least, there has been significantly less public discussion on the subject than in other contexts. For the most part, this also

28 Budowski and Rosero Bixby (forthcoming). Out-of-wedlock births are mainly concentrated among younger age groups, with 74.8 per cent of the total in 1996 occurring to women who were 29 years or younger (DGEC, 1997, p. 25). This, coupled with other evidence discussed in the text, points to a progressive weakening of marriage-based parenting over time.

29 INAMU (2001), p. 9.

30 Budowski and Rosero Bixby (forthcoming); also below.

31 INAMU (2001), p. 9.

32 Dierckxsens (1992), p. 22.

33 Fauné (1997), p. 58.

34 Standing (1999), p. 159.

35 Arias (2000), p. 26, Table 1.

been relatively free of the cataclysmic terms common to conservative discourses in the North.[36] By the same token, although there may be little talk of 'family crisis' *per se*, the phrase *desintegración familiar* (family breakdown) is found quite frequently. This is usually linked with the absence or irresponsibility of one or both parents, normally fathers, as encapsulated in the term *paternidad irresponsable* (irresponsible fatherhood). Beyond this, the language used in press, policy and academic documents suggests that 'proper' families should comprise two parents and their children, with *familia completa* (complete family) describing these units and *familia incompleta* denoting their one-parent counterparts.[37]

Notwithstanding the assumptions and biases encompassed in these terms, if signs of 'family crisis' are measured by their coverage in the public domain, then in Costa Rica these do not devolve so much on family form, as on *intra-family* relationships, particularly those between parents and children. For example, a number of press and academic articles in recent years have revealed concern about declining parental involvement in the daily care and socialisation of children. One reason given relates to rising economic pressures and growing work burdens on parents. This, coupled with the spread of new technology and media access is deemed to have created a potent cocktail for the socialisation and wellbeing of Costa Rica's youth. For example, a study conducted on adolescent depression in 1999 by a consortium of national and international agencies concluded that one of the main reasons for rising rates of depression among the young was that 'parents have abandoned their role through overwork; the television and computer have taken the place of parents' (my translation).[38] This is endorsed by other recent research which has asserted that the hierarchy and hegemony of the family is being displaced by communication media, especially television, and is, in turn, leading to a weakening of traditional support systems for children and adolescents.[39] Indeed, Costa Rica has one of the highest rates of access to television and personal computers in Latin America, at 387 television sets per 1,000 people in 1998 and 39.1 personal computers (the regional averages for Latin America and the Caribbean in the same year were 225 and 33.9 respectively).[40]

[36] See Chant (1999a)

[37] See Sagot (1999), p. 101 for examples.

[38] This study, '*Depresión en Jóvenes*', was conducted by the University of Costa Rica, the Pan American Health Organisation, the Ministry of Health and the Costa Rican Social Security Institute, and was reviewed on publication in *La Nación*, 22 September 1999, p. 8a.

[39] See Tiffer (1998), p. 116; also Moreno (1997).

[40] World Bank (2000), pp. 310–11, Table 19.

While it is recognised that parents are often powerless to maintain influence over children in the face of increased economic pressure and/or the rapid spread of technology, the fact that women work (and may do so out of choice) has sometimes been singled out for attention, especially by men. A more extreme example of this is a man's response to an article on feminism and politics (by Iris Zamora Zumbado) published in one of Costa Rica's national newspapers, *Al Día*, on 9 August 1999:

> To be 'equal' with men, women abandon their homes and neglect their children, leaving them in the hands of strangers who don't care how they grow up. Doña Iris, have you realised that there are alarming levels of violence and drug addiction among the young, because their mothers aren't there to guide them, and while the latter destroy themselves with excessive consumption of drugs and alcohol, the women are engaging in political debate alongside men? Is this the way to improve the country? How ironic!

Although outbursts such as this are relatively rare, some academic sources have also attributed a range of social problems to family change. For example, a recent social psychology article on access to further education in Guanacaste province levels that: 'Disorganisation and disintegration of the family are the cause of declining moral values, economic pressures and social problems such as prostitution, alcoholism, drug addiction and violence'.[41] These latter issues, in turn, are of major consequence to Costa Rican society more generally, with nearly one-quarter of the population ranking delinquency (including violence) and/or drugs as Costa Rica's biggest contemporary problem.[42] Certainly, violence of various types seems to have increased in recent years. On the one hand, there are more denouncements of intrafamily violence (although this is partly due to increased consciousness of, and support for, the rights of women and children — see below), and on the other, there is evidence of a rise of violent muggings and murders, possibly as a result of increased ownership of arms in the country.[43]

[41]   Loaíciga Guillén (1994), p. 10, my translation.

[42]   The figures derive from an opinion poll conducted by Borge y Asociados in 1999 to ascertain levels of satisfaction with the present government and prospective voting preferences for the next election in 2002. The results were published in the newspaper *Al Día*, 2 Sept. 1999, and showed the following rankings for Costa Rica's principal contemporary problems: cost of living (25 per cent), economic situation (19 per cent), delinquency (16.4 per cent), corruption (10.2 per cent), unemployment (7.2 per cent), drugs (6.8 per cent), poverty (6.6 per cent) and government (2.4 per cent).

[43]   See PEN (1998), p. 44.

Charges of the interrelationship between declining family values and anti-social behaviour have perhaps reached their most extreme expression among sectors of the Catholic community, whose 'Movimiento Familiar Cristiano' (Christian Family Movement)[44] holds that increased sexual freedom is responsible for the decline in social values in the country.[45] Falling rates of marriage, increased illegitimacy, prostitution, and the rising visibility of homosexuality are related concerns among the Catholic establishment, with the recently retired archbishop of San José, Monseñor Roman Arrieta, making frequent appeals to the public to set good examples to their young by eschewing the evils of libertinism and modern consumerism, and respecting family traditions.[46] The Church is not alone in these exhortations. In the wake of an outbreak of concern over domestic violence during August 1999, for example, President Miguel Angel Rodríguez (1998–2002) made several announcements on radio and in public rallies of the need to defend the family as a cornerstone of Costa Rican society, and to safeguard its principal mission of protecting children (see also later).

In order to establish better the extent to which there is a sense of 'family crisis' in Costa Rica, the opinions of people garnered in the surveys are arguably more revealing, especially those at the grassroots whose voices often fail to reach conventional media channels.

---

[44] The Latin American *Movimiento Familiar Cristiano* (MFC) originated in Argentina in 1948, started in Costa Rica with a small group in 1958, and became a full-blown regional movement in the 1960s (Rodríguez Cháves, 1999). The objectives of the movement are to promote 'human and Christian values in the family and in the community', and to provide assistance to families (MFC, 1997). These services include a range of programmes designed to strengthen marriage and to help people lead 'Christian family lives', such as pre-nuptial courses, support groups, matrimonial retreats, 'family integration' weeks, and a marriage advisory service (see also Napolitano, 1998 for a discussion of the MFC in Mexico).

[45] Schifter and Madrigal (1996), p. 62. In the context of research on lone motherhood in Costa Rica and the rise in births unacknowledged by fathers, Budowski (2000b) observes that the Catholic Church has been much more outspoken about these trends than any other single group in the country, viewing them as the outcome of 'sinful' behaviour, and as highly threatening to the moral and social order. This contrasts with what Budowksi classifies as the 'liberal' discourse, which regards women as effectively powerless victims of male irresponsibility, and two much more widespread discourses, which she terms 'anti-poverty/welfare' and 'feminist'. The 'anti-poverty/welfare' discourse is primarily concerned about children growing up in poverty, while the 'feminist' discourse sees continued emphasis on the two-parent family as antithetical to women's interests given its common association with financial insecurity for women and children and domestic violence.

[46] The Church has also withdrawn its support from a government programme called 'Young Love', aimed at preventing adolescent pregnancy and discussed later in the text. This is mainly because the teaching and training materials are alleged to go against what was earlier approved by the Church (*La Nación*, 24 December 2000, p. 5A).

Popular Reactions to Family Change in Guanacaste

In examining popular reactions to family change, this section draws from a 1999 survey of 176 low- and middle-income men and women from three broad age bands (see Table 17.1; also footnote 8).

Table 17.1: Interview Sample by Age, Gender and Socioeconomic Status

	Parents/adults		Adolescents/young adults		Children/young adolescents	
	(>25 years)		(14–24 years)		(10–13 years)	
	Male	Female	Male	Female	Male	Female
Middle-income	8	20	8	38	4	7
Low-income	14	21	20	15	6	15
TOTAL	**22**	**41**	**28**	**53**	**10**	**22**

The setting of the survey was the province of Guanacaste in the north-west of the country, where poverty and un- and under-employment have routinely been higher than in most other parts of Costa Rica.[47] This is mainly due to the fact that until the 1990s, when international tourism began to take off along the Pacific coast, the province was reliant on a small number of agricultural activities (cattle-ranching, rice and sugar production), with limited or only seasonal demand for labour. This has historically forced a large percentage of low-income men into periodic out-migration, resulting in instability in household composition and livelihoods.[48] Phenomena such as men's summary termination of remittances, their desertion of spouses and children, heavy drinking and multiple sexual partnerships, are widely attributed to the economic and physical hardships of migration combined with the psychological and emotional stresses on couples engendered by frequent and/or prolonged periods of separation. Formal marriage has traditionally been less common in Guanacaste than in other parts of Costa Rica, with only 30.9 per cent of women in unions with male partners formally married in low-income settlements in Guanacaste in the 1980s, compared with 73.3 per cent at a national level.[49]

---

[47]   See Aguilar et al. (1988); MEIC (1998).

[48]   See Chant (1992, 2000); Moreno (1997), p. 9.

[49]   Chant (1997), p. 170.

Similarly, whereas in Costa Rica as a whole in 1996, 52.8 per cent of births occurred to married women, in Guanacaste this was only 34.7 per cent.[50] Accordingly Guanacaste is possibly less representative of Costa Rica than other parts of the country.

As far as the survey itself is concerned, this consisted mainly of focus group discussions, organised as *'talleres'* or 'workshops', in which participants were invited to reflect on gender and the family in Guanacaste at the end of the twentieth century, and how things had changed (or not) in their own lifetimes.[51] The workshops seemed to create an important space for people to explore and debate matters important in their lives but which were normally confined to close friends and relatives and/or not discussed in depth or in any systematic way at all. Parents in particular found reassurance in the fact that the problems they were facing with their own families were also experienced by others.

Concerns about 'the Family' in Guanacaste

The two themes which surfaced most frequently in the sessions, and over which there was most consensus were: first, the decline of 'family values' such as 'respect', 'morality', 'honesty' and 'loyalty', and second, the mounting difficulties of inter-generational communication and parental control over children. While people often found it hard to pinpoint precise reasons for these patterns, four main sets of processes emerged as significant.

Technology and Mass Media as Influences on Family Life

Mirroring discussions in the national press (see earlier), the decline in inter-generational communication and family values was seen to reside in the increased influence of television and other forms of mass media such as the internet over children and youth. These had exposed them to 'undesirable influences' such as violence, individualism, materialism, consumerism, sexual licentiousness and 'global culture'.[52] *Telenovelas* (TV soap operas), for example, were held responsible for setting bad examples of 'libertine behaviour' and 'offensive language'. Growing access to technology and mass media also meant that children had much more in the way

---

50 DGEC (1997), p. 25.

51 See Chant (1999b) for fuller details.

52 Klak (1999, p. 111) notes for Middle America in general that media flows from the North have increased since the onset of neoliberal economic restructuring.

of stimuli than they had done in the past, which detracted from a formerly narrow range of activities and fixed reference points.[53] As noted by
Andrey, a 16 year-old schoolboy interviewed in a mixed group of low-
income adolescents in the village of Bernabela:

> Well, I think that families have been breaking down, that they have dis-
> integrated. People in the past were more cultured. But with changes in
> technology, television, prostitution, pornography ... all this has made a
> lot of men and women ... want to experiment in other areas. And fam-
> ilies are getting lost in the process ... There are many people who say
> why am I going to stay home if I can be ... I don't know ... watching a
> film or something? In other words, young people have other options
> which don't have anything to do with the family, because they see the
> family as boring ...

Similar sentiments were expressed by young middle-class adults taking university degrees in psychology in Liberia, with Fiorella (aged 21) observing
that she had hardly sat down to a family meal in ten years. In her household everybody had either a television or computer in their own room, and
usually retired there to eat alone. Another student, Angie (aged 23)
described technology as a 'double-edged sword', alienating people and
impeding the need for human contact.

The wedge driven between adults and children by new technology
seems to be greatest among low-income groups in which many parents
have not had more than primary schooling. These parents feel threatened
by their children's greater education and technological abilities. They not
only feel ill-equipped to teach their children in the way their own parents
did, but unable to exert authority. Tentatively, it might be suggested that
whereas in the past, children feared their parents, nowadays, parents are
tending to fear their children.[54]

Lack of Time and New Work Patterns

Leading on from this, a second major factor held responsible for problems
of communication between parents and children was lack of time. This
was not only a result of orientation to an increasing range of extra-domes-
tic activities, but also due to economic pressures and the need for both parents to generate income. The increased rarity of families eating together,

---

[53] See also Pereira García (1998), p. 45.

[54] See also Moser and McIlwaine (2000a & b) on Colombia and Guatemala.

for example, was often attributed by older people to the fact that mothers were no longer a 'constant presence' in the house. As stated by Sonia, a 46 year-old chemistry lecturer:

> ... Of course it [family life] has changed! In the sense that it now takes a little more effort to maintain family unity. It takes a little more effort to sit down and eat together, because of differences in hours, because the woman works the same as the man ... Normally, in my era, my mother was always in the house. She was a housewife. There was a fixed person who took on this role in the home, almost always.

Interestingly, women tended to emphasise that even if they did make an effort to organise family meals, it was harder to get children to eat at home given their growing tastes for foreign and/or fast food such as chips and hamburgers. By the same token, many women felt guilty at the thought they might be neglecting children, and low-income mothers in particular consoled themselves with the fact that at least they only worked part-time or from home, or left their children with relatives. The poor's perception of the middle classes, alternatively, was that children spent most of their time with domestic servants. Notwithstanding that better-off people have always employed domestic servants and nannies this was deemed to be a source of guilt for parents, and in the modern age, translated into their buying their children everything they asked for as a means of compensating. This, in turn, was seen as exacerbating the evils of modern consumerism, as well as contributing to a new generation of undisciplined youth. As observed by Don Carlos Luis, a 62 year old farmer from the village of 27 de Abril:

> There are many cases where the sons and daughters of teachers or professional couples are the most unruly. Why? Because the parents are never in the family home to see what they are doing. They can give them financial support and everything, but this isn't enough.

Something of a vicious circle seemed to be in operation here, with parents working harder and making bigger sacrifices than in the past to oblige their children's demands for cash or consumer goods, but at the same time, so doing partly to assuage guilt for the reduced amount of time spent at home.

The Role of the State in Parent-Child Relationships

Another very important factor identified as having diminished parental control over children was the increased influence of the state in child protection, such as the abolition of corporal punishment and the extension of children's rights. The role played by organisations such as the National Child Protection Agency (Patronato Nacional de la Infancia — PANI) in enforcing bans on the use of physical discipline at home and at school received particular attention. For many parents, especially fathers, lack of ability to use physical force was perceived as having greatly diluted their power to exert authority, which, in turn, had led to a loss of values, and the increase of 'deviant' social behaviour among the young such as prostitution

Similar sentiments were found in a national study on lifestyles and public opinion of nearly 1,300 urban households carried out in 1996 by a team of Costa Rican psychologists and the Centre for Women and the Family. A total of 46 per cent of the sample declared that the state ought not to intervene in family problems, and another 42.6 per cent stressed that it was men's role to exert authority within the family.[55]

Development and International Tourism in Guanacaste

A fourth set of factors highlighted as leading to a decline in family values related to the conversion of Guanacaste from a subsistence-oriented agricultural economy, to a 'modern' economy increasingly reliant on 'science', external capital and international tourism. Consumerism, and the influx of foreign visitors, residents and business owners, often observed to have 'loose morals' and 'anti-social' habits, such as recreational drug use, were also deemed to have played an important part in undermining 'traditional' patterns of behaviour This arose not only from the pernicious effects of 'demonstration', with Doña Imelda, a 52 year old retired primary school teacher from the village of 27 de Abril declaring 'we Costa Ricans like to copy', but also from social interaction, especially among the young.

Adult Men's Concerns about Changes in Family Relationships in Guanacaste

If the above represent concerns shared across the class and age spectrum of respondents, another issue raised predominantly by adult men was mounting rates of conflict between husbands and wives (whether legal or common-law). One of the main reasons given by male respondents for this state of affairs was that new legislation and social programmes had increased women's rights in their homes and in wider society. Many felt

---

[55]   Dobles Oropeza (1998), p. 36.

that these interventions had gone 'too far' and that women were 'abusing' their new privileges.[56] As expressed by one male participant in 27 de Abril:

> Equality in the law, equality between men and women, has brought with it a whole host of problems for the family. Why? Because where you have couples in conflict, the woman can even kill her husband. Whoever saw a woman hitting her husband in the past? Whoever heard of a husband killing his wife? This didn't happen before ... Husbands beat their wives. Sure, they beat them, but not ... shall we say..to the point of such aggression ... God forbid! If a man [now] so much as touches his wife he can go to prison for it!

The other major factor held responsible by men for women's declining submission was their growing participation in the labour force. While women's opportunities for employment have increased as services have become a more important part of the regional economy, in relative terms, and particularly due to the decrease in agriculture, men's have declined.[57] For many men this has made them feel that their wives are less likely to stay with them, especially if they themselves cannot find work, which has eroded their sense of self-worth and seriously disrupted the order of family life.[58]

Men's increasing difficulties of securing employment, coupled with women's rising labour force participation, was regarded as extremely threatening by adult male respondents and bears out the findings from a more dedicated study of men and masculinity I had carried out in 1997 (see footnote 8). Many men in this survey had talked about feeling less needed and appreciated by their wives and children, and having less say and authority in the home. Martín, a 30 year old bricklayer, for example, had declared that: 'A woman who has her own money loses affection for her husband. Many marriages have been ruined because of this'. In turn, Luis, a 33 year old waiter, stressed that when a man cannot provide for his wife and children, his self-image and his image in the eyes of others 'isn't worth anything'.[59] While *machismo* is often heralded as a stabilising influence on

---

56   In the nationwide study carried out by the Psychology Institute of the University of Costa Rica cited in the penultimate section, 54.1 per cent of the sample felt there was equality of opportunity between men and women in Costa Rica, with this view being held much more strongly by men than women (Dobles Oropeza, 1998, p. 36).

57   The average wages of male workers in Guanacaste are 13 per cent lower than in San José (Arias, 2000, p. 21). Moreover, as of 1998, unemployment in Guanacaste was 7.2 per cent, and underemployment, 19.8 per cent, compared with national levels of 5.6 per cent and 13.1 per cent, respectively (MEIC, 1998).

58   See also Salas (1998), p. 66.

59   See Chant (2000).

the family, however, it is important to point out that present day discourses of family crisis tend to leave unpacked the social conditions of the past, and particularly, to gloss over the vulnerabilities women faced when patriarchal relations were stronger. Indeed, as might be expected, many women were in favour of changes that had taken place in the sphere of their civil and economic rights, and did not view these as playing a significant role in contemporary family problems.

Summary Comments on Popular Reactions to Family Change

In summing up the findings from this section of the research, many people in Guanacaste are confused and concerned about the changes taking place in family life. Such reactions may clearly have been obtained in earlier historical periods, not only because family patterns have arguably never been stable, but because a tendency to romanticise the past may well repeat itself across generations. Yet this does not diminish the fact that there is still a marked sense of concern about current trajectories, particularly the loss of control over children and youth, the lack of time for parent–child communication and declining family values. People also feel unable to deal with these matters, mainly because the processes responsible are regarded as so big and intractable. Although people view changes going on in families as having an important part to play in negative social tendencies, however, much more emphasis was placed on the way in which wider societal phenomena were impacting *upon* families and stripping them of the power to determine their own lives. Echoing a point made earlier, therefore, it is not so much a crisis *in* the family that is at stake at the present time, but a crisis *for* the family induced by 'external' and/or structural factors such as globalisation and development.

This is not to say that a sense of crisis *about* the family *per se* is entirely absent, however, especially for men, who claim to be worried about rising levels of conjugal conflict. As I have argued elsewhere, however, family break-up itself is not the primary concern for men — especially given the historical instability of family life in Guanacaste — but the fact that decisions within and over family life are perceived to be increasingly out of their own hands as a result of increases in women's employment, rights and legal protection.[60]

---

[60]   *Ibid.*; Dobles Oropeza (1998); also McCallum (1999) on Brazil; Safa (1999) on the Dominican Republic. In relation to research on Salvador da Bahia, Brazil, McCallum (1999, p. 275) notes that: 'In local talk, about sexual mores and parenting, the dominant theme is the 'liberal' and 'decadent' character of the modern age. Modernity is equated with a loss of control over female sexuality and reproduction'. McCallum further argues that discussion about 'women's loss of restraint and respectability functions as a brake upon pressure for change' (*ibid.*).

The historical legacy of family patterns in Guanacaste could, in turn, be one of the most important reasons why many issues central to 'mainstream'/Euro-American discourses of 'family crisis' — declining levels of marriage, rises in out-of-wedlock birth, increased numbers of households headed by lone mothers and so on — did not emerge as problematic in the course of our discussions, or at least in any direct and/or significant way. Adolescents and young adults from low-income groups in our survey, for example, tend to see *uniones libres* (consensual unions) as preferable to marriage given the instability of conjugal relationships and the expense attached to divorce. Although middle class people marry more frequently, youth from this sector overwhelmingly profess that there is little difference between formal and informal partnerships, and are open in principle to the notion of diverse forms of family organisation.

Other conceivable reasons for scant concern about household form in the survey include the fact that even if households are not especially stable in Guanacaste, families tend to be large and to retain strong extended family networks, especially with consanguineal kin. This provides large stocks of 'bonding social capital' on which households can draw, thereby rendering their actual composition less significant than it might otherwise be.

Another potentially important reason why people are not overly concerned about departures from an 'ideal' family form is because they have been less penalised by the state for belonging to 'alternative' household units as time as gone on (see below).

In respect of the areas in which the majority of respondents felt they could benefit from more assistance from the government, one pertained to achieving a better balance between work and family life, the other in facilitating better communication between parents and children. Although amenities for child and after-school care are increasingly available, and there are various sources of family guidance such as state-run Escuelas de Padres (Parents' Schools) and the Catholic Church's Movimiento Familiar Cristiano, many participants expressed a desire to receive more publicly-provided help in these domains, even if they could not necessarily identify what this might entail.

Public Reactions and Responses to Family Change[61]

Although public interventions can only go so far in addressing people's needs, and some have clearly been more neglected than others, consider-

---

[61] The primary fieldwork for the Central Research Fund project (see footnote 8) consisted of consultations with 14 representatives from different state and non-governmental agencies and organisations in Costa Rica during March and April 1999.

able progress seems to have been made in some dimensions of social policy in Costa Rica in respect of working with, rather than against, the direction of family change at the grass roots. My interviews with government officials and representatives of NGOs indicated not only a general tolerance of shifts towards greater diversity in family form and internal relations, but a willingness to strengthen arrangements that furthered the interests of women and children. The moralising sentiment so often attached to nuclear family protagonism in the North was also conspicuous by its absence. Collectively these attitudes are perhaps best exemplified by various statements in the section on social relations and values in Costa Rica's 1998 *State of the Nation* report. One is that while there may be a majority of married nuclear households in the country (which in fact there is not), this does not mean that families are fulfilling their functions adequately. Another is that the rise in lone parent households does not necessarily imply disadvantage for children. Another is that since 'traditional families' are often based on inegalitarian relations, dissolution can mean escape from the hazards of domestic violence.[62]

Over and above considerable reference to women's and children's rights and how families are evolving in such a way as to guarantee these better, many respondents stressed that there was no more a 'crisis in the family' in Costa Rica now than at any moment in the past. Families in Costa Rica have always been dynamic and plural, as well as subject to debate.[63] If anything, as stated by Jorge Sanabria of PANI, there was simply more visibility of intra-household problems at present as the 'private' domain had come under greater scrutiny. Moreover, rather than holding 'the family' to account for current social problems, there seemed to be widespread recognition of the way in which structural and global factors such as increased consumerism, media and communications technology had played a major role in undermining people's orientation to their families, and in turn, 'family values' and cohesiveness. For example, Ludwig Güendel of the United Nations Childrens Fund (UNICEF) pointed out that 20 years ago the state was the biggest employer of middle class people in Costa Rica. However, the influx of multinational firms accompanying neoliberal economic restructuring had brought in its wake an aggressive enterprise culture which has increased competition, driven people to work long hours at the expense of family life, and made them more materialistic. Patricia Arce of

62   PEN (1998), p. 210.
63   See E. Rodríguez (2000).

the National Institute for Women (Instituto Nacional de las Mujeres — INAMU), felt that the increase of poverty and insecurity of work had also undermined family solidarity. These interpretations echo those of the grassroots in their emphasis on the factors giving rise to problems *for* families, rather than the problems which arguably arise from family change *per se*.

While addressing the structural problems facing Costa Rican society was felt to be beyond the remit of organisations in the survey, quite a lot has been done to at least improve the immediate material and social difficulties facing poorer families in the form of legislation and social policies and programmes.

Family Legislation and Social Programmes

Costa Rica's reputation as a state which has been particularly sympathetic to women's issues and a leading promoter of women's rights is commonly held to derive from the convergence of a number of complementary developments since the second half of the twentieth century. These include the abolition of the army with the country's new Constitution of 1948, which as Budowski (2000b) argues, dismantled one of the most powerful masculinist symbols. Other important factors include the buoyancy of the country's women's movement, the United Nations Decade for Women 1975–85, and long-standing respect for civil opinion.[64] The inauguration of the Centre for Women and the Family in 1986 helped to galvanise the groundswell of feminist momentum in the country, playing an important part in the passing of the Law for Social Equality in 1990, a landmark piece of legislation which aimed not only to promote, but to guarantee, women's equality with men.[65] Within the next few years several new laws and amendments to existing ones entered the statute books with direct consequences for women's and children's rights within the family. These included the Law Against Domestic Violence (Law no. 7586), the Law for the Protection of Adolescent Mothers (Law no. 7739), the Law for Women in Conditions of Poverty (Law no. 7769), reforms to articles 84, 85 and 89 of the Family Code, recognising children born outside marriage (Law no. 7538), the addition of articles 242–46 to the Family Code acknowledging the legal validity of consensual unions and the reform of Article 5 of the Family Code eliminating the equivalence of women and minors.[66] Many of the new laws were established and/or

---

[64] *Ibid.*

[65] See Chant (1997), pp. 136–7.

[66] See CMF (1996), p. 22; Colaboración Área Legal (1997).

were buttressed by plans and programmes such as the National Equal Opportunities Plan (Plan Nacional para la Igualdad de Oportunidades entre Mujeres y Hombres —PIOMH), and the National Plan for the Attention and Prevention of Intrafamily Violence (Plan Nacional para la Atención y Prevención de la Violencia Intrafamiliar — PLANOVI). Many also came into being in 1996 mid-way through the administration of President José María Figueres (1994–98). Aside from the maintenance of feminist pressure within and outside government agencies, the breakthroughs for women during Figueres' regime are widely attributed to the fact that the first lady, Josette Altman de Figueres, and second vice president, Rebecca Grynspan, were both dedicated advocates of women's issues.[67]

The Figueres administration also saw the beginning of explicit government assistance to female-headed households, with the launch of the Programa de Formación Integral para Mujeres Jefas de Hogar en Condiciones de Pobreza (Comprehensive Training Programme for Female Household Heads in Conditions of Poverty) in 1997 as part of the Plan Nacional de Combate a la Pobreza (National Plan to Combat Poverty). This initiative was undoubtedly spurred in part by an increase in poverty among women-headed households from the mid-1980s,[68] and the fact that the Costa Rican state takes very seriously its obligations to children. The programme had high profile promotion and support, being inaugurated with the first public festival for female household heads on International Women's Day on 8 March 1997.[69] The programme's implementation involved not only various government organisations, principally the Social Welfare Institute (Instituto Mixto de Ayuda Social — IMAS) and INAMU, but NGOs and the Catholic Church. Budowksi notes that incorporating 'the important players in civil society ... was part of the new public management strategy to draw upon different resources available in current society and appeal to social responsibility'.[70]

The programme offered a temporary stipend for women to enable them to take training courses in self-esteem and assertiveness, and employment and income-generating skills. While arguably limited in its coverage and impacts,[71] Juan Diego Trejos, of the Instituto de

---

[67]   Budowski (2000a), p. 69.

[68]   While female-headed households were only 20.1 per cent of poor families in 1986, they were 27 per cent by 1995 (Trejos and Montiel, 1999, p. 10).

[69]   Palacinóo (1997).

[70]   Budowksi (2000a), p. 70.

[71]   See Budowksi and Guzmán (1998).

Investigaciones Económicas of the University of Costa Rica, who had been involved in drawing up the Poverty Plan, declared that the programme had given greater legitimacy to 'non-standard' households. Moreover, in encompassing notions of 'empowerment' and embracing moves towards strategic gender interests, it also demonstrated an unusually strong commitment to women's rights.[72] Even if the evaluation of the programme (in which Trejos also participated) concluded that it was difficult for an isolated intervention to battle against structural conditions of gender inequality,[73] a new version 'Creciendo Juntas', which has been extended to cover women 'in conditions of poverty' more generally, was launched in 1999. This has been accompanied by two ancillary programmes aimed at the young, both promoted by the current first lady, Lorena Clare de Rodríguez. The first of these, Amor Jóven (Young Love), is concerned with preventing adolescent pregnancy; the second, Construyendo Oportunidades (Building Opportunities), seeks to (re)integrate teenage mothers into education and to provide special programmes of state support for their children.[74] Aside from these initiatives, two other of the six main strategic areas of the Solidarity Plan are oriented to family assistance: one geared to strengthening family cohesion (Programa de Fortalecimiento Familiar), which assigns basic income supplements to families in extreme poverty, the other (Programa Infancia y Juventud) which provides assistance for children and youth from low-income families, principally in the form of day care, 'after-school' clubs and youth development centres.

Accompanying efforts to alleviate household poverty and childcare problems, domestic violence has also received an unprecedented level of attention in Costa Rica during the last two administrations. PLANOVI (see earlier), which was launched in 1996, marked a major victory for feminists who had been campaigning to get the problem of intra-family violence recognised seriously for years, and whom had hitherto had to draw on the resources of externally-funded NGOs such as the Centro Feminista de Información y Acción (CEFEMINA) for shelter and telephone help-lines. Commitment to following through the goals of the plan is also evident in the present regime. In August 1999, for example, when news broke that on top of 3,321 denunciations of domestic violence to the Women's

---

[72]   Budowski (2000b).

[73]   Marenco et al. (1998), p. 153.

[74]   see Chant (1999a, 2000); also IMAS (1998, 2001).

Delegation within the first seven months of the year, there had been 18 murders of women by spouses or boyfriends (predominantly motivated by sexual jealousy or by women having left their partners), President Rodríguez, in an address to INAMU, declared that violence against women, boys and girls constituted one of the most serious and destructive manifestations of gender discrimination, as well as constituting a grave threat to 'the basic structure of Costa Rican society: "the family"'.[75] More recently, in April 2001, the Law for Responsible Fatherhood (Law no. 8101) was passed, whereby men who do not voluntarily register themselves as fathers now have to undergo a compulsory DNA test at the Social Security Institute. If the result is positive they not only have to pay alimony and child support, but are liable to contribute to the costs of the pregnancy and birth, and to pay their children's food bills for the first twelve months of life.[76]

Factors Accounting for State Responses to Family Transitions in Costa Rica

As far as the factors responsible for recent responses to family patterns and problems are concerned, it has been argued that the magnitude of changes in household form and internal organisation in Costa Rica has obliged the public sector to broaden and diversify its actions for the development and wellbeing of families.[77] Additional influences have been the increase of poverty among some segments of the population, such as women-headed households (footnote 68), and concerns about the vulnerability of children unacknowledged by their fathers.[78] At one level, therefore, motivations can be argued to be pragmatic, with strategies to strengthen families of all types an instrumental means of helping people weather an increasingly competitive economic environment. Yet these reasons are insufficient in themselves to account for the fact that Costa Rica stands out as having policies that are notably more friendly to 'alternative families' than many of its Latin American neighbours, and which have often served as a platform for promoting the rights of women and children.

Factors identified by respondents as having made Costa Rica distinctive in this regard revolved around what they perceived as the progressive and

---

[75]   *Diario de Extra*, 8 September 1999, p. 2.

[76]   See INAMU (2001).

[77]   CMF (1996), p. 20.

[78]   Budowski (2000b).

consensus-driven nature of Costa Rican political culture, including respect for democracy and human rights, the attempt to contain social unrest and extremes through social inclusiveness and redistribution, the presence of a healthy civil society, including feminist groups, and the absence of military violence. Along with the fact that relative to other Central American countries, changes in family form have been more gradual,[79] these features have accorded government agencies in Costa Rica the will, time, space and resources to adapt more sensitively and effectively to transitions. Added to this, the creation of the Centre for Development of Women and the Family (Centro de Desarrollo de la Mujer y la Familia — CMF), and particularly its conversion into an autonomous state institution as INAMU in 1998, has provided an important space for feminists within government decision-making.[80]

Partly because of the existence of CMF/INAMU, the state seems to have been highly receptive to voices from the feminist lobby in civil society, including their repeated demands for 'strengthening the family as a means of generating equality of opportunity between men and women' and encouraging acceptance of family diversity.[81] As noted earlier, the inauguration of PLANOVI was in large part the result of campaigns by feminist organisations such as CEFEMINA. Zeneida Ballesteros, the CEFEMINA representative I interviewed, also informed me that while the Catholic Church maintains that there is a need to *'velar por la familia tradicional'* ('look out for the traditional family'), where there is violence, incest and/or abuse, this is not deemed to be a Christian arrangement. Indeed, one of CEFEMINA's support groups (in Cartago) actually held their first meetings on Church premises. Moreover, the Catholic Church has been very outspoken about domestic violence. In his pre-retirement final homily to the Virgen de los Angeles in August 1999, for example, the archbishop of San José, Monseñor Roman Arrieta, called for an end to domestic violence, alongside a rallying call to save contemporary

79   See PEN (1998), p. 43.

80   See Budowksi (2000a), p. 71.

81   CMF (1996), p. 20. In a recent manifesto drawn up by a coalition of Costa Rican feminists, for example, there were renewed calls for the state to recognise a wider vision of the family, to acknowledge that members of the same household do not necessarily share the same interests and to appreciate that adherence to the figure of *'hombre jefe de familia'* (male family head) reproduces inequality and perpetuates violation of the rights of women and children (Grupo Agenda Política de Mujeres Costarricenses, 1997, p. 42).

youth from drugs and *'degeneración moral'* ('moral degeneracy'). Protestant churches in Costa Rica have also aligned themselves with the cause of preserving 'family integrity'.[82]

Last, but not least, aside from being one of the earliest signatories of Global Convention of the Rights of the Child in 1989,[83] the fact that Costa Rica is home to the regional headquarters of UNICEF is also significant, with one of the organisation's main missions at present being to promote the family as a 'space for recognising, reproducing and reinforcing rights'. Similarly the regional headquarters of another international agency with a potentially strong input to family interventions, the United Nations Institute for the Prevention of Crime and the Treatment of Delinquency, is also located in San José, from which it has mounted various programmes geared to eliminating domestic violence in the Central American region.[84] The proximity of sources of international funding for progressive gender and family initiatives could also help to explain the presence of so many forward-looking social programmes in the country.

Summary Comments on Public Reactions to Family Change

In general terms, social policy in Costa Rica has tended to work with, rather than against, the tide of grassroots change, and has also attempted to create a fairer deal for women and children within families. In this way, public agencies have not only been adaptive, but proactive on behalf of conventionally 'minority' groups. In turn, their performance makes Costa Rica stand out as a salutary example, not only to many of its Latin American neighbours, but to countries elsewhere in the world. This is not to suggest, of course, that there is nothing left to be done.

Among the most pressing issues arising out of the grass-roots research in Guanacaste, for example, is the better integration of men into new patterns of family life. Although the National Institute for Women (then the

---

[82]   See also Chant with Craske (2002), chapter 6. Protestant churches have been increasing in numbers and followers in Costa Rica in recent years, with about nine alone in Guanacaste, including the Emmanuel Bible Church, Assembly of God, Church of God and the World Missionary Movement. Attempts to safeguard family cohesion and welfare have included income-generating activities and efforts to reduce alcoholism, which is often linked with violence and family conflict (interview with José Blas Díáz Castillo, Emmanuel Bible Church, Liberia, 14 September 1999).

[83]   Güendel (1999), p. 5.

[84]   See ILANUD (1999).

CMF) promoted a nationwide survey on masculinity and 'responsible fatherhood' in 1996,[85] and there has been discussion of a 'gender re-socialisation' component in both the programmes for female household heads/women in poverty thus far, the latter did not get off the ground. With the dropping of 're-socialisation', the programme assumed the status of a women's, rather than a gender programme.[86] While the Law for Responsible Paternity may well make men more conscious of the fact that fatherhood carries financial obligations (which is already inscribed in the Family Code), it might also be helpful to expanding definitions of men's roles within a re-negotiated family. As noted by Salas in the context of a research project on masculinity and domestic violence with 200 men, the fact that so many men have been ousted from their position as breadwinners by 'criminal programmes of economic and structural adjustment', is a major factor in perpetuating male displacement and the consequences that this entails, such as domestic violence (my translation).[87] Strategies might draw from those proposed by UNICEF to encourage men's greater involvement in parenting, which include: 'Identification of culturally acceptable and positive images of men and women that can potentially demonstrate a balance of roles and responsibilities between men and women'.[88] Aside from benefiting men, there are potentially important outcomes for women, who stand to gain some alleviation from their increasing load of financial, domestic and childcare responsibilities within families.[89] As for children, more participation from both parents in their everyday lives is likely to bring about less gender-typed socialisation.[90]

Greater assistance to parents in managing the work/life balance and bridging the technology gap that currently exists between many of them and their children are also important priorities. Much could be done, for example, by extending current initiatives such as increasing the provision of day care. If a rhetoric of more flexible family life is to be translated more effectively into practice, then encouraging the sharing of childcare across a broader cross-section of people, including kin, friends, neighbours and professional carers, could be of major practical and ideological

---

85   See CMF (1996); Gomáriz (1997).

86   Budowski and Rosero Bixby (forthcoming).

87   Salas (1998), p. 66.

88   *Ibid.*, p. 33.

89   *Ibid.*, p. 26.

90   *Ibid.* p. 27.

benefit. Since it is not just the *quantity* of time parents, or other carers, spend with children, but *quality* of time, more attention also might be given to parents' needs, which have arguably been rather neglected in comparison with those of children in Costa Rica. It is hardly surprising that computers are regarded as taking over the educational and socialisation roles of parents, if parents have little knowledge of the tools their children are using. Here initiatives for life-long learning and education in new technology in accordance with the demands of a rapidly globalising society could not only help facilitate parent-child communication, but also extend parents' employment opportunities. In turn, labour laws could be made more supportive by allowing for paternity as well as maternity leave, permitting time off to care for sick children, and so on.[91]

Last but not least, existing legislation oriented to strengthening the position of women and children should undoubtedly be subject to greater monitoring and enforcement, and might also be accompanied by ancillary programmes to ensure their effectiveness. As noted by Budowski in relation to her assessment of the first programme for female household heads, attempts to raise this group's self-esteem are unlikely to be fulfilled by concentrating on the target population alone, and need to be accompanied by initiatives to break down discrimination in wider society.[92] Related to this, the question of 'family values' requires further attention. As Vega has argued,[93] although there is lip-service in Costa Rica to family diversity, the daily-used term 'family' conjures up an impression of a uniform institution comprising of a married, monogamous couple with distinctive gendered duties.[94] Indeed, fairly common reference in public and policy circles to 'family disintegration' suggests that there remains, covertly if not overtly, an idealisation of the 'traditional' two-parent patriarchal unit. The normative persistence of these values in wider society is, in turn, borne out by various surveys and opinion polls throughout the 1990s,[95] and can conceivably act to depress the legitimacy of other types of household arrangement.

---

[91]   See UNICEF (1997), p. 26.

[92]   Budowski (2000a), p. 259.

[93]   Vega (1987, cited in Moreno, 1994, p. 4).

[94]   See also Güendel and González (1998), pp. 19–20.

[95]   A survey carried out by the CMF in 1997 revealed that 73 per cent of men, and 75 per cent of women felt that men should provide for the households, and 75.4 per cent and 78.2 per cent of men and women respectively stressed that women's main responsibilities should be home and family (PEN, 1998, p. 44). This echoes a poll conducted earlier in the 1990s which indicated that the marriage-based nuclear family, comprising male breadwinner and female homemaker was favoured by three out of four people in the country as the most desirable arrangement for raising children (Fernández, 1992; see also Budowski, 2000a; F. Muñoz, 1997).

Concluding Comments: Reflections on 'Crisis' as an Organising Concept for Family Transitions

As noted earlier, discourses of 'family crisis' have been less pronounced in countries outside Europe and North America, possibly because one of the main sources of anxiety — how to cut the welfare bill in the wake of the increased marketisation of economies and the rolling back of the state — is less imperative, particularly in countries of the South, where substantial programmes of social assistance have been few and far between. Costa Rica presents something of an anomaly in this regard insofar as it is one of the few developing societies where basic welfare coverage has been pretty much in place since the mid twentieth century. Yet despite pressure on public finances, and ongoing decline of the patriarchal household, there is little evidence of a 'family crisis' discourse, either at the grassroots or at the level of public institutions, at least of the type which has prevailed in the North. Moreover, the Costa Rican state has actually managed to increase resources to 'non-standard' low-income households at a time when many countries in the North are cutting back.[96] Even if the Figueres and Rodríguez administrations have both expressly identified that they have no wish to provide 'perverse incentives' for the formation of female-headed households, the move to extend the reach of social interventions to 'non-standard' families reveals, in my view, some significant underlying breakthroughs.[97] These include, first, acceptance of the notion that the traditional functions of the family do not need to be wedded to a particular household form. This, in turn, has arguably arisen from: a) the recognition (undoubtedly fomented by feminist pressure groups) that patriarchal household arrangements can increase rather than diminish the vulnerability of women and children; and b) acknowledgement of the fact that families are not synonymous with households, and that where family ties remain strong, these can bolster individual household units. In short, an appreciation of, and concern for, the quality of family relationships seems to have taken precedence over any atavistic attachment to a normative

---

[96]   Budowski (2000b).

[97]   Although it seems that government assistance for female-headed households in Costa Rica has been strongly motivated by concerns to better the position of women and children, it is also important to bear in mind that, as in other countries in Latin America where there have been similar initiatives for lone mothers, such as Chile, Honduras and Puerto Rico, another important influence has been the way in which neoliberal restructuring has promoted the reduction of public expenditure on universal social programmes in favour of targeted schemes for poverty alleviation (see Budowski and Guzmán, 1998; Chant, 2002).

family form. A second factor relevant to support for 'non-standard house-holds' in a time of change, is that the rights and welfare of children occupy such a prominent place in Costa Rican social policy that if the state upholds its commitments to children, the actual constitution of households is arguably less significant. Third, by assisting families in need in the short-term, this can enhance security and stability, thereby helping to preclude the break-out of problems of 'crisis' proportions in the longer term.

Leading on from this, resisting the use of 'family crisis' as a general description of popular and public reactions to current transitions in Costa Rica resides in the observation that different groups have different responses to family change. Echoing Moore's argument that '... if there is a crisis in the family, it can only be a multiple set of crises in many different families',[98] it is clear that an operational concept of 'crisis' needs to be differentiated and tied much more specifically to who is concerned about family transitions, which particular aspects of them, and why. Arguably, change only constitutes crisis when the interests of a given set of stakeholders are threatened, or where people find it difficult to adhere to idealised norms and experience a profound sense of failure at being unable to do so. In this light it is no surprise that men in Guanacaste have a much greater sense of 'family crisis' than women, or indeed that the Catholic Church stands out on something of a limb compared to other civil society organisations. While 'crisis' might be extremely pertinent to particular groups of men and some segments of the religious establishment, however, this does not merit a generalised projection.

Another finding of the research carrying important warnings about the indiscriminate use of crisis, is that in public arenas and at the grass roots alike, it seems that there is more concern about the influences *on* the family (exerted by 'development', globalisation and so on), than the social problems emanating *from* family transitions. This presents a challenge to the conservative/Euro-American way of deflecting the attention from structural social and economic problems from society to individual families.[99] In turn, it suggests that for countries such as Costa Rica which are often unable to resist the penetration of global economic and technological forces, a 'crisis *for* families' rather than a 'crisis *in* the family' might be a more appropriate terminology. Indeed, allowing a small but powerful set

[98]   Moore (1994), p. 25.

[99]   *Ibid.*, p. 27; also Roseneil and Mann (1996).

of interest groups in the North to persist in spreading panic about the family may take energy away from the arguably more relevant task of addressing some of the global processes giving rise to 'family problems' in the first place. Further comparative work in Latin America and in other regions of the South could make a valuable contribution in this regard.

While not denying that people in Costa Rica are experiencing difficulties in dealing with issues like the work-life balance, and the technology-driven inter-generational rift between parents and children, and that the public sector might take further measures to respond to people's needs at the grassroots, I would argue that 'family crisis' is not a particularly relevant concept in the country and should accordingly be resisted. The fact is that steps have already been taken in Costa Rica to circumvent the escalation of problems in families to crisis proportions. While the problems of designing social policy for a complex household universe are significant, especially at a time when families themselves are under greater pressure to fall back on their own resources, there are lessons from Costa Rica that might usefully be taken up by other countries in Latin America, not to mention elsewhere in the world.

CHAPTER 18

Rural Poverty and Policy:
Mexico and Colombia Compared [*]

Alicia Puyana

Introduction

Until December 1994 it seemed that the liberal economic model established in Latin America had produced expected results in terms of lower
inflation, GDP growth, fiscal discipline and a more fluid functioning of
the market. A closer examination of these economies revealed results that
are not altogether positive. As in 1982, in December 1994 Mexico sounded the alarm by sinking again into severe crisis. That Argentina, another
radical 'reformer', Paraguay, Venezuela and Colombia should also suffer
disarray in their economies, is reason to call for thoughtful consideration
of how to orient economic policies if recessions, persistent levels of
unemployment and poverty are to be overcome.[1]

This chapter explores 'Dutch Disease Effects',[1] attributable to changes
in oil and coffee windfalls and the impacts derived from the macroeconomic reforms, on tradable sectors, poverty and employment of rural population. Adjustment policies and structural reforms have sought to eradicate the causes of macroeconomic imbalances and establish the bases for
sustained growth necessary to alleviate mass poverty

The two nations comprise nearly 30 per cent of the region's population
and gross domestic product. Both are examples of relatively high political
stability, though their systems differ. Mexico established a one party system
and developed its own brand of economic 'populism.' Colombia's liberal-
conservative two-party system has been labelled *exclusionist* and is prized by
conservative, orthodox macroeconomic management. Up to 1998
Colombia attained a consistent, although mediocre, rate of growth and rel-

---

[*]   Jorge Horbath provided assistance with econometric work.

[1]   'Dutch Disease' is a conceptual model based on the experience of countries that have experi-
      enced negative consequences to their economies because of 'bonanza' effects of raw material
      exports, such as those experienced by the Netherlands as a result of the discovery of gas
      deposits. Tradable sectors, mainly industry and agriculture, contract due to the impact of the
      revaluation of the real exchange rate induced by the inflow of foreign resources and the expan-
      sion of public expenditure.

atively low inflation rates. Mexico adjusted the economy radically, but only in 2000 managed to avoid the 'sexsenal' crisis. Colombia took a moderate route and freed its domestic market at the beginning of the 1990s, when Mexico was well into negotiating the North American Free Trade Agreement. Up to 1996 Colombia's GNP per capita increased, while Mexico experienced an alarming drop. Mexico and Colombia suffer similar degrees of poverty and extreme levels of inequity and today's tendencies suggest that in both countries the situation is getting worse.

That in both countries rural poverty is so similar is worth analysing due to the contrasting historical and institutional experiences which marked the development path of the rural sector. Mexico implemented a radical agrarian reform in 1933, while Colombian land reform cannot be considered a success. The Colombian agrarian sector is one of the main sources of foreign currency (despite the oil boom) and the powerful Colombian Coffee Federation managed to defend coffee producers and the entire sector from the most extreme discriminatory elements of the import substitution industrialisation (ISI) but has proved powerless to solve the actual crisis induced by the fall of international coffee prices. In Mexico, such a private institution never existed, but the peasant's organisation, the Confederación Nacional de Campesinos was one of the pillars of the political system. Mexican northern landowners always managed to extract substantial rents.

Both countries export oil and coffee and have suffered from the instability of international prices. Both saw bonanzas and oil richness as the key element to overcoming underdevelopment and backwardness by providing the resources to finance modernisation, industrialisation and urbanisation. Both overestimated the magnitude of the bonanzas and promoted a too large absorption of oil revenues overstretching public expenditure.

This chapter is organised as follows: the next section reviews some of the topics in the debate on poverty and growth, pointing at different approaches for the assessment of poverty and inequality. The third section presents a review of the experiences of adjustment and macroeconomic reform most relevant for the rural sector and examines the effects of such policies in terms of overall and sectoral economic growth. It further analyses the effects of investments, technology, credit, exchange rate and expenditure in the preservation of the bimodal mode of production. It is assumed that land concentration aggravates poverty and induces productive inefficiencies. The final section offers some conclusions.

The Debate on Poverty

From the initial policies towards poverty in developing countries,[2] there has been considerable progress in the political debate on poverty, the understanding of the linkages between poverty, income concentration and growth and in the methods for measuring poverty.

The 'right to development'[3] establishes that 'certain welfare conditions must be met in order to achieve the ... worth of liberty ... Unless certain basic welfare conditions are met and resources and opportunities provided, we cannot seriously claim that society is preserving and protecting everyone's freedom'.[4] The reasons are mainly two: 'the first is the impaired capacity for formulating and pursuing a conception of the good, and the second is that a person that lacks these basic goods is subject to intimidation's by the rich and powerful, especially if others depend on her'.[5] By now it is established that the basic objective of economic growth is the reduction of poverty and the satisfaction of basic needs.[6] These objectives become legitimate political objectives and, as such, the state and the international community have the obligation to guarantee their fulfilment.

Although there is agreement that the reduction of poverty is essential to the development of human resources, there is not a clear consensus about the role the state, or the market, should play in the achievement of human development. It is important that arguments about the nature of the state and its role are put forward now, when market mechanisms are assumed to perfectly allocate resources and to guarantee growth and redistribution. Many economists contest this.[7] What is lacking is an open and frank discussion about the linkages between structural reforms and poverty, which is different to the argument that without reforms the situation could have further deteriorated or to insisting on the creation of 'safety

---

2   Galbraith (1979).

3   Nussbaum and Sen (1993).

4   Kasgaaard (1993).

5   *Ibid.*.

6   IDB/UNDP (1993).

7   Stiglitz, (1991) hints that the 'pathologies of capitalism': the conditions of life in the less developed economies, where more than three quarters of humanity live and the periodical episodes of unemployment in developed countries, should suggest to us that the market is always slightly inefficient and that only extreme cases of inefficiencies are detected. He adds that 'issues of efficiency and equity cannot be neatly separated, these issues of political economy can not be ignored. These, and not the issue of whether the market economy attains the ideal of Pareto Efficiency ought to be the focus of debate in democratic societies.'

nets' to support the poor. An important contribution to this debate is ECLAC's project on the impact of economic reforms, which concludes that taking all reforms together a slightly negative effect was detected. The most important factors contributing to the expansion of poverty and inequality are recessions — which thus far reforms have not helped prevent — and inflation.[8]

When it was obvious that poverty was growing, it was accepted that adjustment programmes ought to be complemented with actions to alleviate the impact on the 'new poor', to knit 'safety nets' and to better target social expenditure. Taking effects as causes, the emphasis was put on education, nutrition, health and housing as the sources of poverty. But the causality relationship is the reverse. Until recently, no mention was made to alter the character of the adjustment programmes by reducing the scope of the pro-cyclical measures to overcome the crisis. As new studies show, policies to reduce poverty, in addition to improving education, health and housing, supporting the creation of employment and productivity growth, must address other elements that reproduce poverty, making the process of economic growth systematically unequal. These are factors that influence the pattern of primary distribution of income and reduce the impact of actions in education and health, such as the concentration of assets ownership and the economic structure, i.e. the labour intensity of production or the rural/urban terms of trade.[9] One can add international specialisation in commodities and manufactures with low technology,[10] resulting in worsening terms of trade and shocks. A new stream of analysis concentrates on the negative effects of assets concentration on growth, income distribution and investments on human and physical capital.[11]

There is a renewed interest in the validity of the Kuznets argument about the increasing poverty and income inequality during the early phases of development. Recent studies show no conclusive results. Anand and Kanbur (1986) found that cross-sectional data were best fit by a U-shaped curve, not an inverted U as suggested by Kuznets (1955). Studies analysing changes over time for several developing countries, grouped by levels of income, concluded that inequality increases in the low-income countries as

---

[8]   Morley (2000).

[9]   Lipton (1991 and 1993) '… poverty in the rural sector tends to be explained more by low access to physical assets (particularly land), farm technology, non-farm employment opportunities, healthcare and schooling, rather than by labour-market failures (Lipton and Ravallion, 1993)'.

[10]   Sheahan (1990).

[11]   Deininger and Olinto (2000).

in the high-income countries. No clear tendency was observed for inequality to increase more in the early stages of economic development than in later stages.[12] Linked to the theory that savings were the catalyst of growth, for decades the prevalent view was that income inequality promoted savings and, therefore, induced growth. That assertion was challenged by the experiences of the Asian countries, which combined fast growth with no worsening of income distribution. When studying the opposite causality: from inequality and poverty to growth, there is the suggestion that income and assets (land) inequality are negatively associated with per capita income growth.[13] The post-war expansion of the Taiwanese economy is explained by redistribution of income by the way of land reform. The World Bank has stressed the need to redistribute land as a condition for growth in developing transition economies. Redistribution of human capital is another way to reduce income concentration and reinforce growth. ECLAC suggests that in the 1990s the reduction of poverty turned out to be less sensitive to economic growth, and redistributive actions became of paramount importance.

Progress has been achieved in defining how to measure poverty and what to measure. If the question is how poor are the poor, it is not sufficient to use a *head count*, or to calculate the *incidence of poverty*, the proportion of the total population that is poor. The *intensity of poverty* or the *poverty gap* shows how much more income poor people need to pass the poverty line; the *distribution of poverty* shows the income concentration among the poor. These measures show where the problem is greater and growing and allows policymakers to take the appropriate steps and to focus actions. The *poverty line*, indicates when the income received by individuals or households is lower than that needed to satisfy basic needs, and *extreme poverty* is when income is insufficient to meet food needs. The *satisfaction of basic needs*, as an indicator of the social gap (UBN — *unsatisfied basic needs*), measures poverty in terms of the characteristics of goods and services, and is heavily biased towards housing and less appropriate for rural areas. The construction of poverty maps is adequate when there is no need to establish differences among poor people. Finally, the *Integrated Poverty Measure* (IPM) combines the *poverty line* and the UBN, since they complement one another.

---

[12]   Fields (1991).

[13]   Alesina and Rodrik (1994).

Only One 'Década Perdida'

Due to extreme income concentration in Latin America, growth would have to reach unprecedented sustained highs to make any real impact on poverty levels. However, such extreme inequality is shown to be of a destructive 'character ... associated with low aggregate growth and worsening poverty', as the experiences of the region (and those of Mexico and Colombia) indicate. Since the late 1990s, growth rates in Latin America have been higher than in the early 1980s, but growth has been insufficient to abate poverty and inequality levels.

Table 18.1: Incidence of Poverty in Latin America

year	Households in poverty %			Households in indigency %			Gini coefficient
	total	urban	rural	total	urban	rural	
1970	40	26	62	19		34	0.58
1980	35	25	54	15	9	28	0.55
1986	37	30	56	17	17	30	
1990	41	36	56	18	13	33	0.58
1994	39	34	55	17	12	33	0.58
1997	36	30	54	15	10	31	

Source: CEPAL, *Panorama Social de América Latina.* 1994, 1996 and 1999

There is abundant evidence that in Latin America poverty increased during the 1980s and no signals of clear recovery were evident up to 1994. The effects of the 1995 Mexican crisis reduced or even reversed the improvement registered during 1992–94. By the end of the 1990s income concentration, measured by the Gini coefficient, is practically the same as in 1970 (Table 18.1). In 1997, the incidence of poverty and extreme poverty was similar to that of 1980, with a clear upward trend registered in urban areas coinciding with important reductions in rural areas. Despite this divergence, both indexes remain on the whole considerably larger for rural areas. By 1997 out of a total of 204 million poor, 78 million lived in the countryside. In the case of extreme poverty, the situation is reversed. In 1997, out of 90 million extreme poor, 47 million lived in rural areas.

Measured by incidence there is no doubt that poverty is a more rural-con-
centrated phenomenon, but decreasing. Policies to alleviate poverty, if
focused on trends, might be urban oriented, if on incidence, the emphasis
should be rural. Given the critical situation in both areas, no one should be
excluded. Two factors explain the poor results in poverty reduction: insufficient growth and 'persistent inequalities that have inhibited the poor
from participating in the growth that did occur'.[14]

Poverty in Mexico and Colombia. Conflicting Criteria[15]

In Mexico, three criteria are used to set poverty lines, (Table 18.2, column 1).
The results are contrasting: 1) failure to satisy basic needs as reflected in the
poverty lines of Hernández Laos-Boltvinik (per capita monthly income of
US$79.00) and of Levi-Alarcón (with a per capita income of US$70.00); 2)
ECLA and ECLA-INEGI's relative nutritional poverty (US$53.00); 3) the
World Bank's (WB) absolute nutritional poverty (US$20 per capita per
month for urban population). The WB level is considered mere subsistence,
not covering all the poor or those in extreme poverty. Table 18.3 shows how
the incidence and the population to be included is reduced (from Levy's 79.3
per cent in 1989 to 26 per cent according to World Bank) and so too are the
resources needed to overcome poverty. Considering extreme poor, in 1984,
the differences will be between 23.6 per cent of the population (Levy-
Alarcón) and 7.3 per cent (the World Bank — if Lustig-Mitchell or
Boltvinik are considered the gap is even larger).

Poverty in Mexico is considered a predominantly rural or urban phenomenon as a function of: a) the criteria for the urban-rural cut-off.
Population density leads to a distribution of 60 per cent urban to 40 per
cent rural (high-low), while by adopting the urban-rural limit of 15,000
inhabitants per locality, the structure will be 70:30 per cent; b) different
poverty lines; poverty lines for rural environment diminish the poverty
level in comparison to what the result would be if equal lines were applied.
The World Bank rural poverty line is almost 50 per cent lower than the
urban one; c) The absolute level of poverty lines: the lower the line, the
more predominant isrural poverty (Table 18.4).

14   Chen and Ravallion (2000).

15   This section develops the work by Puyana and Boltvinik (1995). Data are presented in tables
      18.2–18.4.

Table 18.2: Mexico: Poverty Lines According to Several Studies (constant 1984 prices)

Study	PL	EPL	EPL/PL	% of level 5	
			%	PL	EPL
CEPAL 77-84 (urban)	36	18	50	45.5	38.4
CEPAL 77-84 (rural)	26	15	57.2	33.2	32
INEGI-CEPAL (1984) urban	53	26			
INEGI-CEPAL (1984) rural	40	23			
Hernández Laos-Boltvinik	79	47	59.3	100	100
Levy-Alarcón	70	17	23.9	88.7	35.7
World Bank-urban	20	10	50	28.7	24.2
World Bank-rural	15	7			

PL: Poverty line (us month)   EPL: Extreme poverty line (us month)
Source: Puyana and Boltvinik, 1995.

Hernández Laos and ECLA studies conclude that during the period 1968–81 the incidence of poverty was reduced by a third (Table 18.3) Economic growth during 1970–81 was accompanied by decreases in income concentration and poverty, and improvements in the UBN. From 1981 to 1994, economic stagnation erupted together with increases in income concentration, poverty and deceleration in UBN. During 1968–81, the three variables determining the income of poor population (rate of employment, average wage per worker and participation of wages in GDP) raised per capita income. The basic mechanism for the reduction in poverty was the creation of more productive jobs. In 1981–91, and after the 1995 crisis, the rate of employment and the returns to labour as a percentage of GDP moved unfavourably; the deterioration of workers' living standards is explained by the drop of 31.2 per cent in the share of wages in GDP, aggravated by increases in the rate of dependency. Income concentration, measured by the GINI coefficient deteriorated and in 1999 was higher than in 1978.

Table 18.3: Mexico: Trends in the Incidence of Poverty in Percentage of Total Population

STUDIES	1963		1968		1977		1984		1989		1992		1996		1998	
	P	EP	P	EP	P	EP	P	EP	P	EP	P	EP	P	EP	P	EP
CEPAL (persons) 1/			N.D.	N.D.	39.5	13.6	37.4	13.4							47.0	19.0
CEPAL (household)			34.0	12.0	31.6	10.4	29.9	10.2							38.0	13.0
INEGI-CEPAL							42.5	15.4	47.8	18.8	44.1	16.1	43.0	16.0		
Hernández Laos-Boltvinik	77.5	69.5	72.6	56.7	58.0	34.0	58.5	29.9	64.0	N.D.	66.0	N.D.	66.0	N.D.		
Levy-Alarcón							81.2	19.5	79.3	23.6						
World Bank							16.6	2.5	22.6	7.3						
Lustig-Mitchell I 2/							2.3	0.4	6.7	1.1						
Lustig-Mitchell II 3/							38.1	15.7	50.6	27.1						
Boltvinik (MMIP)							69.8	40.3	73.8	47.3	75.1	50.7				

1/ 1968 by CEPAL 70 and Oscar Altimir 1979. Data for 1977-84 CEPAL-PNUD (1990).

2/ According to poverty lines by the World Bank. 3/ Based on COPLAMAR poverty line, as in Hernandez Laos.

Table 18.4: Mexico: Rural and Urban Poverty Incidence According to Different Criteria

STUDIES	Poverty incidence % of total population		Extreme poverty incidence % of total population		% of total national poor population		% of total national extreme poor	
	High Density	Low Density	High Density	Low Density	High Density	Low Density	High Density	Low Density
CEPAL (1984)	30.2	50.5	7.5	24.1	52.1	47.9	36.3	63.7
INEGI-CEPAL (1992) 1/	36.7	54.9	9.6	25.6	53.3	46.7	39.1	60.9
Hernández Laos (1984)	49.6	76.1	20	52.9	59.4	40.6	47	53
Alarcón (1989)	70.7	92.8	11.8	42.1	54.4	45.6	31.2	68.8
World Bank (1989)	14.1	27.9	N.D.	N.D.	56.5	43.5	N.D.	N.D.
Boltvinik (MMIP:1989)	66	88.1	38.6	68	51.8	48.2	44.9	55.1

1/ High density=Localities larger than 15,000 inhabitants. Low density=Smaller than 15,000 inhabitants.
High density=Localities larger than 100,000 inhabitants. Low density= Smaller than 100,000 inhabitants.

Source: Puyana and Boltvinik 1995.

Trends in UBN also reveal the contrast between the two periods. If considering current household incomes, the decade of the 1980s was one of worsening worker's welfare. There were improvements in education, housing, health and social security, although at a lower rate than in the 1970s. A non-mercantile access predominates in BN, either by means of public transfers (education, healthcare, water and drainage), or because of self-production (housing). During the crisis, BN satisfied by public transfers behaved differently from private wages. Adjustment in education, health and sanitation did not imply the reduction in the volume of employment and services. The contraction of real expenditure was implemented at the expense of real wages, a deceleration in the growth of services and a decrease in quality.

In Colombia income concentration has not improved. From 1978–99, the urban and total Gini coefficients deteriorated, from 0.49 to 0.57. While urban poverty lines calculated by the National Administrative Department of Statistics (DANE) and CEPAL are near US$38 and US$39, respectively; the World Bank uses a US$21 urban line, resulting in lower incidence: 14 per cent urban and 7 per cent rural (See Table 18.5).[16] In terms of UBN, all studies show lower urban poverty and a better situation both in level and dynamics. The UBN have fallen quite intensively, from 72 per cent in 1970 to 24 per cent in 1995. Urban UBN fall faster than rural ones despite urbanisation. The World Bank attributes all the reduction in rural poverty to redistribution, while the growth component tends to increase poverty. In the urban sector, growth is more relevant, contributing some 60 per cent of the total decline in poverty (Table 18.6).[17] Increases in poverty and inequality during the 1990s are related to the deceleration of GDP growth, instability of coffee and oil prices, the crisis in the agricultural sector, caused by reductions in international prices of tradable, and the inflow of imports. The oil boom and the revaluation of the peso to control inflation contracted the production of labour intensive tradables. From 1990–97 the real exchange rate for imports was revalued, in Colombia by 47 per cent. In Mexico revaluation reached 27 per cent in 1994 and was reversed in 1995 by 52 per cent. In both countries terms of trade declined.

---

[16]   With a 50% increase in the poverty line of the WB, national incidence index will grow from 18% to 48% while that of rural poverty from 31.2% to 64.6% and in the cities the change would be from 9.9% to 36%.

[17]   World Bank (1994a).

Table 18. 5: Colombia: Urban And Rural Poverty Incidence

Studies	Total National			Urban			Rural	
	PL: US$ per head monthly	Millions persons	% total	PL: US$ per head monthly	Millions persons	% total	PL: US$ per head monthly	Millions persons	% total
CEPAL- persons (86)	35.0	12.2	37.1	38.9	8.0	65.8	27.6	4.2	34.2
DANE- persons (90)	33.6	16.1	45.4	37.0	10.0	62.3	28.0	6.1	37.7
Fresneda-PL (92)	33.4	17.9	48.7	37.0	10.7	60.0	28.0	7.2	40.0
BIRF-PL1 (92)	16.1	6.2	16.9	21.0	1.9	30.6	14.0	4.3	69.4
BIRF-PL3 (92)	25.8	15.8	43.0	32.0	6.9	43.7	21.0	8.9	56.3
DNP-PL (95)	54.4	21.3	54.9	69.0	12.4	45.9	34.0	8.9	76.0
CNP-PL (97)		22.9	56.9		13.7	48.0		9.3	78.7

Source: Puyana and Boltvinik (1995) and DNP (2000).

Table 18. 6: Colombia: Incidence of Poverty According to Several Studies in Percentage of Total Population

STUDIES	1970 P	1970 EP	1972 P	1972 EP	1978 P	1978 EP	1980 P	1980 EP	1986 P	1986 EP	1988 P	1988 EP	1990-91 P	1990-91 EP	1992 P	1992 EP	1994 P	1994 EP	1995* P	1995* EP	1997 P	1997 EP	1999 P	1999 EP
NATIONAL LEVEL																								
Cepal-Households	45.0	18.0					38.6	16.1	37.9	17.3											45.0	20.0		
Cepal-Pers.	N.D.	N.D.					42.3	17.4	41.9	18.8											51.0	24.0		
DANE PL-Pers. 2/			60.0								50.9		48.9		52.8	20.5	51.8				51.5	18.3	53.8	18.7
DANE-UBN-Pers.2/			72.5				55.4		42.9		39.4		36.3		35.5		31.0	8.2	24.2	7.5				
DANE-MMIP											62.0													
Fresneda-LP-Pers.					56.3	23.3									53.6	20.5								
BIRF-LP-Pers.1/					52.5	23.6					46.9	18.7	44.6	16.9	45.7	17.7								
Sarmiento-LP-Pers. 3/	60.0						59.0		55.0		59.0		57.0		56.0		54.0		55.0				57.0	
URBAN MEAN																								
Cepal-Households	38.0	14.0					35.5	13.3	35.9	15.2			35.0	12.0	38.0	15.0					40.0	15.0		
Cepal-Pers.	N.D.	N.D.					39.7	14.5	40.2	16.6											45.0	17.0		
DANE PL-Pers. 2/			42.4								44.0		42.0		46.0		45.0				39.1	8.3	45.2	11.0
DANE-UBN-Pers.2/			61.1				43.3		30.8		27.7		25.0		24.4		19.0	2.9	14.3	2.7				
DANE-MMIP-7 Cities.											43.7		40.0											
Fresneda-LP-Pers.					48.6	14.5									46.4	13.0								
BIRF-LP-Pers.1/					38.9	12.1					32.4	8.0	31.1	7.8	32.1	8.0								
Sarmiento-LP-Pers. 3/	51.0						49.0		45.0		51.0		48.0		47.0		45.0		46.0				48.0	
RURAL MEAN																								
Cepal-Households	54.0	23.0					45.4	22.4	42.4	22.3											54.0	29.0		
Cepal-Pers.	N.D.	N.D.					47.7	23.5	44.5	23.4											60.0	33.0		
DANE PL-Pers. 2/			86.0								68.2		67.0		69.5		71.8				78.9	42.9	79.7	45.9
DANE-UBN-Pers.2/			89.2				79.0		71.3		68.7		66.0				15.7		38.3	14.3				
DANE-MMIP											77.9													
Fresneda-LP-Pers.					70.0	39.0									69.5	37.0								
BIRF-LP-Pers.1/					69.9	38.4					66.3	33.1	62.6	29.0	64.6	31.2								
Sarmiento-LP-Pers. 3/	72.0						76.0		74.0		75.0		76.0		74.0		75.0		76.0				78.7	

* DNP, Aug 1997.

1/ The study uses three poverty lines equal to 1, 1.5 y 2.0 times the basic food basket by DANE.

2/ Libardo Sarmiento (1995) *Pobreza rural y reformas económicas y sociales.*

3/ Libardo Sarmiento, *Concentración de la Pobreza. Tres años del salto social,* Consejo Nacional de Planeación,. Nov. 1997.

Rural Development and Poverty

Colombia and Mexico present similar and high levels of rural poverty, as illustrated above. From 1980–99 the situation worsened both in terms of poverty and extreme poverty. This chapter aims to explore some of the reasons for such an outcome.

Here it is proposed that three elements collided to repress the growth of agriculture and to discriminate against small and peasant producers: *Dutch Disease* induced by oil (and, in Colombia, coffee too) *bonanzas*; *the urban bias* of import substitution industrialisation and the export oriented model; and the concentration of land property.

Figure 18.1: International Oil and Coffee Prices

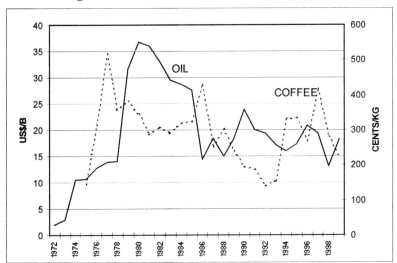

Source: New York Board Of Trade, Agricultural Options Report and Word Bank. (Oil: 1976-84 Forties, 1985-98 Brent).

Dutch Disease and Agricultural Growth

Radical changes in the international coffee and oil markets made prices highly *unstable* (Figure 18.1). In oil, due to the expansion of supply, the reduction of exploration and development costs and the fall in the oil intensity of the global economy and the erosion of the power of OPEC to support prices for longer periods. In coffee, the liberalisation of the market, the entry of new low cost producers and a stagnating world demand are responsible for the collapse of prices. From Figure 18.1 it appears that the different paths of coffee and oil prices would counterbalance each other. This may not be the case because of the different systems of production. While coffee is intensive in domestic productive factors, especially in labour and land, and is produced in small peasant units, oil is intensive in capital, external technology and highly qualified manpower.

The effects of price changes on economic growth are highly asymmetric. Positive shocks stimulate growth in the short term, and do not induce sustainable expansion of incomes. Negative shocks have significant negative effects on growth (Figure 18.2) through investments, capacity utilisation, uncertainty and the rate of absorption of new technology.[18] The reduction of oil rent depresses public expenditure, as in 1986 and in 1997. The poor are not able to protect themselves from negative shocks, since they do not have insurance or savings.

Figure 18.2: Growth Rates of Total and Agricultural Value Added

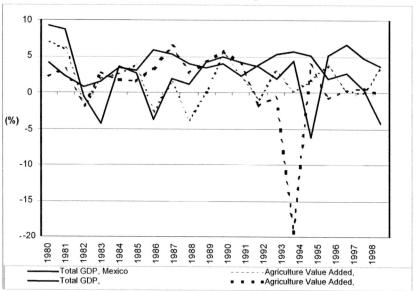

Source: World Development Indicators. World Bank (2000) *Indicadores Básicos De Banco Interamericano de Desarrollo* (2000).

Dramatic increases in foreign earnings and wage increases in the booming sector may cause real exchange rate revaluation, wage increases and other

[18]   Dehn (2000).

distortions in the economy which may decrease the competitiveness of the non booming sectors, and induce policy responses that are difficult to reverse once the boom has subsided.[19] Real revaluation in Colombia and in Mexico did occur and was induced by the expansion of public expenditure, which was intensive in non-tradables, public services and construction. '... the exchange related appreciation that accompanied the commodity boom and government spending hurt agricultural producers, increasing polarisation rather than reducing it' (Figure 18.3).[20]

Figure 18.3: Real Exchange Rate Index

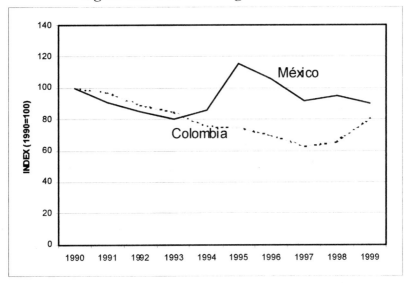

Source: Cuentas Nacionales De Colombia (DANE), México (INEGI), Estadísticas Básicas Del BID (2000).

The impact of revaluation on agriculture stems from the high tradability of the sector. In effect, almost 75 per cent of the Mexican and Colombian agricultural production is made up of tradable goods. Therefore, the revaluation of the real exchange rate, induced by external shocks, favours mechanisation and the extensive use of industrial inputs by lowering their cost relative to labour and land. It reduces labour absorption, helping again better-situated landowners and activities that are less labour intensive, arti-

[19]   Schiff and Valdés (1998).

[20]   Bisinwanger and Deininger (1997).

ficially increasing the rentability of larger farms. The result is an increase in the land to labour ratio and in the capital to labour ratio. In this environment, the benefits from the increments in export volume (and in prices when they occur), tend to be concentrated, and do not favour the poor.

In many case, Colombia and Mexico are no exceptions, imports of food were subsidised and the equilibrium between demand and supply re-established but with lower internal production and reduced employment of domestic factors. After the 'bonanzas', the contraction of agriculture resulted from agriculture's sensitivity to labour market pulls and from its character as a tradable sector. Therefore, food tended to become more costly during and after the boom despite rising imports.[21] When real revaluation takes place in parallel with the reductions of import tariffs and transferences, and drastic falls in international prices, as was the case during the late 1980s and 1990s, the impact on tradables is magnified. Mexico and Colombia did devaluate their currency (in 1994 and 1997 respectively) and signs of agriculture recovery are detected. These symptoms are not strong enough to reverse the contraction of the sector.

The ISI and the Urban Bias.

By establishing the well known policy instruments to favour the growth of industry as the leading sector and key element to modernising the economy, a discrimination against agriculture was set in motion through direct or indirect taxation, control of food prices and agricultural inputs for industry, subsidised credit and numerous tax incentives, all of which led to real exchange rate revaluation and worsening relative prices for agriculture. Public investment in agriculture did not reverse the impact of the ISI policies. During this period agriculture's contribution to GDP and employment fell (Figure 18.4). Oil riches, and oil and coffee bonanzas, provided the resources needed to keep the industrialisation ideal alive, to pay for subsidies and costly tax incentives, to invest in expensive industrial capital intensive projects, such as refineries, aluminium plants, plastics, and metal mechanics, as the way to *sow the bonanzas*. This was especially true for the bonanzas of the 1970s and 1980s experienced by both countries when it was evident that the ISI needed to be substantially modified. Small-scale, poor peasants, dispersed and disconnected, did not have the strength to oppose such policies, and to confront the alliances between rich landowners, industrialist and urban workers.[22]

---

[21]   Gelb (1988).

[22]   Bisinwanger and Deininger (1997).

Figure 18.4: Agricultural Value Added and Employment as Share of Total GDP and Employment

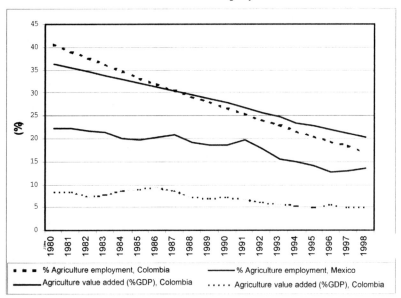

Source: Cuentas Nacionales de Colombia (DANE) 1987-1995 y México (INEGI) 1988-1996. Indicadores Del Desarrollo Mundial. Banco Mundial (1997).

Macroeconomic reforms aimed at dismantling the ISI were expected to eliminate discrimination against agriculture and to stimulate sectoral productivity growth, but adjustment programmes were too severe, induced recessive growth, affecting internal demand for agricultural produce, and did not eliminate the urban bias of the ISI. Some agricultural producers benefited from protection and subsidies during the ISI, in much the same way as the industrial sector did. Agricultural inputs for industry or large-scale modern production for exports were granted all types of subsides, inducing higher real rates of protection. Producers of such goods were able to orchestrate opposition to preserve some of these support policies.[23] As a result, the effects of adjustment reforms upon agriculture were ambiguous.[24]

During 1981–86 sectoral growth was higher than during import substitution, but insufficient to reduce rural poverty and migration or to reverse the contraction of the sectoral contribution to GDP. In Colombia and Mexico, the participation of the agricultural sector in GDP continued to fall, as did agricultural income and employment (Figure 18.4). In Mexico

[23]   Jaramillo (1998).
[24]   Schiff and Valdés (1998).

agriculture represented only four per cent of total GDP. In Colombia, the retreat of agriculture accelerated during the 1990s, falling to 12 per cent of GDP in 2000. In both countries this share is considerably lower than that expected from the Chenery Norm.[25] Agricultural employment in Colombia represents 17 per cent, which is ten per cent lower than expected.[26] In Mexico rural employment concentrates 20 per cent of the total labour force. In both countries, but especially in Mexico, agricultural productivity is lower than industrial productivity (Figure 18.5). As a result of slow sectoral growth and lagging productivity and despite migration, rural income remains only a fraction of the median wages in industry. In Mexico in 1999 rural income was only 30 per cent the urban income. In both countries returns to labour are declining as a percentage of GDP.[27] This is related to lower labour productivity and slower productivity growth in agriculture. Growth in agriculture has resulted more through the incorporation of capital and land, and not by incorporating employment (Figure 18.6).

Figure 18.5: Agricultural and Industrial Labour Productivity in Mexico

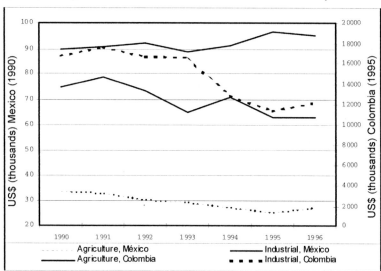

Source: Cuentas Nacionales de Colombia (DANE) y México (INEGI) y Estadísticas Básicas Del BID, 2000.

---

25 Syrquin and Chenery (1989). In Colombia the share of agriculture in GDP could be 17% and in Mexico 14% (Puyana and Thorp, 2000).

26 Puyana and Thorp (2000).

27 In Mexico, payments to labour in agriculture represent 0.3 per cent of GDP an in Colombia six per cent, while agricultural employment accounts for 20 and 17 per cent respectively.

Figure 18.6: Mexico and Colombia: Value Added in Agriculture Index and per capita

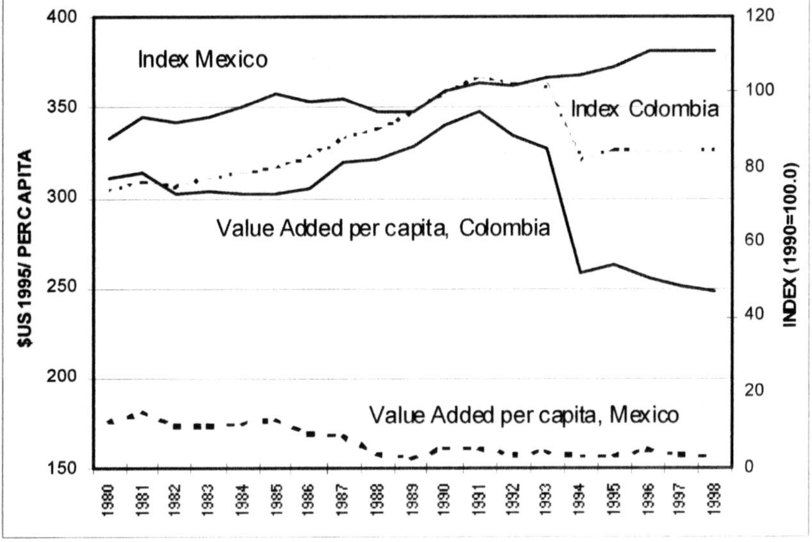

Source: World Development Indicators, Word Bank (2000).

Adjustment programmes were aimed at improving the terms of trade for agricultural production, which could increase rural incomes. By eliminating overvaluation, and the implicit taxes on agriculture stemming from protection to industry, it was expected that labour intensive tradables productionwould be stimulated. In this sense, these policies could reduce poverty. This was offset by a worsening of international prices of both importables and exportables, the reduction in subsidies and in investments and by recurrent episodes of revaluation, related to the trajectory of oil prices and the inflow of *capitales golondrina*. Thus, the positive effects of 'putting the prices right' were less than expected or never manifested. The explanation of the lack of response of agricultural sector to the reforms is that they 'were not structural enough'. Reforms aimed at changing relative prices — market relaxation — by the reduction of state interventions — state compression — leaving the elements that constitute the most important sources of market imperfection untouched: i.e., market suppression. In general, market suppression results more from private actions which structural adjustment did not affect: '… ranging from locally monopsonic trading or credit to quasi-feudal extraction'.[28] In these cir-

---

28   Lipton (1991 and 1993).

cumstances, market interventions are needed to reduce private and overall market suppression. As it happened, due to power structure, and in conditions of budgetary constraints, market relaxation was accepted if the costs of the reduction of the state, in the form of the reduction of public expenditure, was borne mainly by 'rural people'. The instability of coffee and oil prices and foreign investment flows exacerbated the impact of structural adjustment, negatively affecting growth, employment and the participation of wages in total income. The evolution of the border and domestic terms of trade between agriculture and industry systematically turned negative to agriculture (Figure 18.7).

Figure 18.7: Mexico and Colombia: Relative Agriculture Domestic and Border Prices

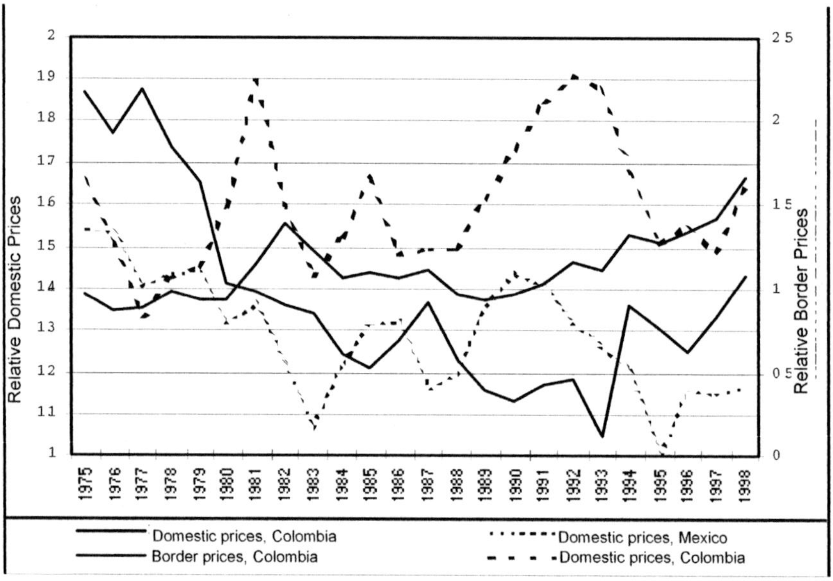

Domestic prices, Colombia   • • • • • • Domestic prices, Mexico
Border prices, Colombia   – – – • Domestic prices, Colombia

Source: *World Development Indicators*, Word Bank (2000).

Land Ownership

Despite historical and institutional characteristics, both countries show a high concentrationof land property, which marks the development options for the agricultural sector and the distribution of the benefits of growth.[29]

[29]   Recent figures show a Gini coefficient of land tenure of 84% for Colombia and 61% for Mexico, which is nevertheless quite high (Deininger and Olinto, 2000, Table 2).

New analysis of rural development and rural organisations suggest that allocation efficiency itself depends on the distribution of wealth since... 'the inseparability of efficiency and distribution considerations is a general result for economies with imperfect information and missing markets'.[30] There is large and significant negative correlation between land concentration and growth, and a positive and significant correlation with income concentration, suggesting that concentration of wealth has growth limiting effects and tends to reconcentrate incomes. Furthermore, high land (and other assets) concentration reduces the effects of policies to stimulate aggregate growth such as investments in human capital. Concentration of assets has a negative impact on growth by reducing efficiency of allocation of factors of production. It is the concentration of assets, more than the concentration of income, that creates the effect of inequality of growth, by making it impossible to access credit markets to finance productive indivisible investments.[31]

In Colombia after 40 years of land reform, the concentration of property remains extremely high in international terms.[32] One million peasants (or 62.4 per cent of the total) own 1.15 million hectares (or 5.16 per cent of total), the average size of this holding being 3.2 hectares, while 1.6 per cent of farmers concentrate 23.3 per cent of land, with an average size of around 1,000 hectares. This pattern of property induced a bimodal mode of production, in which most of the land is operated by a few large farms and makes the tendency towards disparities in income in rural households and farm holdings more severe. Big landowners have easier access to credit, subsidies, technological development and extension programmes, which discriminates against small and poor peasants.

The prevalence of bimodal land structure in Colombia, despite the established superiority in efficiency and productivity of family farms,[33] results from policies designed to support the growth of large, modern capitalistic farming of the ISI, the restrictions on leasing, the eviction of tenants and the incentives to keep land as anti-inflationary insurance. Due to the failure to impose taxes on land in the presence of generous incentives, the market price of large farms exceeds the capitalised value of farm profits. As a result, a poor smallholder or landless worker would not be able to

---

30   Hoff et al. (1993).

31   Deininger and Olinto (2000).

32   *Ibid.*

33   Berry and Cline (1979), Deininger (2000).

finance the purchase of land out of farm profits, even in the event of credit being available from the owner or the bank. Redistribution of land with compensation to the owners was made impossible by the existence of subsidies and benefits, the delivery of public goods and services (irrigation programmes, technical assistance for the appropriation and adaptation of the 'green revolution innovation', credit and purchase programmes) channelled disproportionately to large farms. In Colombia the 'expropriation with compensation was impossible thanks to the distorted institutional framework that allowed large farms to externalise part of the costs of modernisation. During the first 30 years of implementation of the Law 135 approved in 1961, the Instituto Colombiano de la Reforma Agraria (INCORA) distributed one million hectares which benefited 63,000 families, the largest share of which corresponded to legalisation of property rights in new colonisation areas in the Caquetá, Putumayo, Urabá and Amazonian regions. Colonisation was intense during the second half of the twentieth century: more than 300,000 square kilometres of land, almost a quarter of the Colombian territory, were opened by new settlers. Expulsion of peasants by guerrilla warfare and paramilitary activities and the accumulation of land by drug-dealers may have aggravated land concentration.

The Integrated Rural Development Programme favoured mainly a small number of family farms, with enough land and proximity to markets to take advantage of the programme. It did not affect the structure of property or the poverty of the majority of small landowners. When the policy biases that favour large farms are removed, the artificially elevated productivity will disappear and the possibility for a more dynamic land market emerges, making possible a market-oriented land reform.[34]

The bimodal pattern of land structure resulted in a substantial misallocation of resources. During 1950–87, the growth pattern was capital and land intensive; with half of the rate of growth in labour productivity explained by increases in yields per hectare and a sharp contraction in the ratio of land to labour. Compared to other countries at the same level of development, Colombia has lower employment in agriculture and rural-urban migration has been among the most intense in developing countries. Nevertheless, migration has reduced neither rural poverty nor unemploy-

---

[34] In South Africa, agricultural development under apartheid was bimodal, capital intensive and with very slow productivity growth. When subsidies were reduced, due to fiscal constraints, the majority of large-scale farms proved to be inefficient, and that inefficiency was a result of its scale. Those results are considered in the process of redistribution of land. (Christiansen and Cooper, 1995).

ment. This factor is considered by some authors as one of the sources of violence in Colombia.[35] As a result some remarkable effects have appeared: Colombian agriculture is more efficient than that of the USA sector.[36] Land concentration and the political power of big landowners inhibited the effects of structural reforms and resorted to lobbying for protection and preferential credit, to overcome the inability to adapt to the new conditions.[37]

According to the 1991 census 52 per cent of Mexican territory belonged to *ejidos* or was communal land. There were 1.3 million private productive units and three million classified as social and *ejido* property. Thirty four per cent of landowners, with plots smaller than two hectares, in 1994 concentrated 3.8 per cent of land, and 40.06 per cent land owners with plots above five hectares owned 85 per cent of land. Concentration is even more pronounced in the central and northern regions. Concentration of land property has one major effect: three million landless peasants, who are marginalised from all agricultural development programmes and will not benefit directly from the Salinas reforms. As in Colombia, *minifundios* do not have access to credit and the investments in irrigation systems did not favour them. In general, *ejido* and *minifundios* are located in low quality or dry areas, producing only for subsistence. Despite the land reform, the bimodal model of agricultural development was applied, favouring larger units, with capital-intensive methods of production.[38] Technology was developed with the aim of increasing yields without considering costs or total factor productivity. These results respond to the character of the Mexican land reform which resulted from social pressures, became a tool of political control and was not complemented by policies to foster rural development. In such an environment, the rural poor always suffered from unequal access to land, irrigation, technology and education. Migration, especially international migration, softens but does not eliminate discrimination. Even after including remittances and non-agricultural income, it is land, and the size of the plots, that is the the factor that explains why 47.3 per cent of rural house-

---

[35] Deininger (2000).

[36] Taking productivity as the relationship of the ratio of the agricultural GDP to total GDP/agricultural employment to total employment, in the USA it is 0.68; in Colombia, 0.84; in Chile, 0.78; and in Mexico, 0.33. The same productivity as in US agriculture could be reached in, Colombia with 280,000 more employees, but Mexico would have to reduce it by 19.4 million. The same productivity could be reached by expanding Mexican agricultural GDP above 30%, and contracting Colombian GDP to 15% or by a combination of the two options (Puyana and Thorp 2000, p. 125).

[37] Deininger (2000).

[38] Tomich et al. (1995).

holds live in poverty and 26 per cent of them in extreme poverty.

The Salinas administration implemented radical measures with respect to agricultural land tenure, considered one of the most important steps toward modernisation of the Mexican economy. The initiative aimed to normalise communal and *ejido* land property to allow its sale or renting. This was a large-scale agrarian reform entailing major political, social and economic effects. A probable result is that there will be a tendency to sell plots, reconstituting larger properties within the *ejidos*. A greater sectoral differentiation is already evident since small-scale and poor peasants do not respond in the same measure to market signals, because they protect themselves from price changes by diversifying production and maintaining a margin of subsistence agriculture.[39] Procampo was established in 1994 to replace, within a 15-year period, the price support system on grains by direct payments to all producers, with a limit of one hundred hectares. It is a concentrating mechanism since larger producers will receive the largest share of the support.[40]

In the last ten years the Mexican agricultural sector has experienced major reforms: the reduction of subsidies, the liberalisation of the national market, entry to the General Agreement on Tariffs and Trade (GATT), the signing of the North American Free Trade Agreement (NAFTA), and the rationalisation or privatisation of institutions dedicated to trade or processing of agricultural products. The internationalisation of the Mexican agriculture imposed a heavy burden upon peasants: Mexican transferences per hectare and per capita to agricultural producers represent only 25 per cent of the total transferences in the Organisation for Economic Co-operation and Development (OECD) countries.[41] The direct subsidies given by Procampo, might be transferred to landowners in the form of rents. Rural workers and small peasants will lose income.[42] As a consequence of international competition, the demand for labour will fall and *ejidatarios* and landless workers will migrate.[43] To alleviate this impact, an intensive plan for public rural investments will be required to create jobs, such as the construction of small irrigation systems for poor peasants, conservation of roads and social infrastructure.

[39]   López (1995).

[40]   OCDE (1997).

[41]   *Ibid.*.

[42]   Romero (1995).

[43]   OCDE (1995 and 1997).

One effect of land concentration is the misallocation of land and labour. Agricultural land is being transferred to livestock. Sixteen per cent of Colombian area is suitable for crops but only four per cent is cultivated. On the other hand, livestock is occupying 35 per cent of the land, when only 13 per cent is appropriate.[44] A similar, but less intensive, process is observed in Mexico.[45] The rapid expansion of livestock has been stimulated by a generous support policy. During 1980–92 beef and milk absorbed 82 per cent of the total support given by the Colombian government to nine farm commodities, and in 1994 US$700 million were transferred from the government, or the consumers, to livestock farmers. In Mexico, equivalent subsidies to livestock given in 1995 represented 66 per cent of total subsidies to agriculture; support through subsidies to consumers of beef, pork and poultry represented 73 per cent of the total.[46] By subsidising capital inputs and livestock the government has stimulated large farming and the reduction of labour absorption. In subsidising tractors and public irrigation schemes, by credit, tax incentives and a revaluated peso, an over-mechanisation of agriculture took place. In Colombia, small-scale, poor farmers are being displaced from arable land and forced to open new frontiers, deforesting marginal land and the cordillera skirts and seeking refuge in illegal crops.

One way of discriminating in favour of large farms against small landowners is subsidised credit. Credit to agriculture was sharply reduced during adjustment programmes, and in 1992 represented only 0.02 per cent of the sectoral GDP. Credit is concentrated in three activities: two exportables: coffee and meat, and one importable: milk, the three together accounting for 93 per cent of the credit provided between 1980and 1992.[47] In Colombia, only eight per cent of total credit was directed to small peasants, a figure similar to that of Mexico. In Colombia, only 5.6 per cent of small farmers received some type of technical assistance.[48]

There exists a deficit in public investment in the rural sector, aggravated by the budgetary constraints thatboth countries are experiencing. In Colombia, investment in agriculture is only a fraction of total public

---

[44] World Bank (1996).

[45] OCDE (1997).

[46] In 1995 the Mexican government allocated 28.5 billion pesos to support agriculture and livestock producers. The main beneficiaries were modern large-scale farmers (OCDE, 1997, p. 20–2).

[47] Puyana and Thorp (2000).

[48] Valdez and Wiens (1996).

[49] Ishan et al. (1994).

investment (five per cent in 1996). Compared with the participation of agriculture in total GDP (18 per cent), a deficit in investments equal to 80 per cent results.[49] In Mexico the situation is better, with total investment in agriculture representing five per cent of the total, slightly above the ratio of agriculture to total GDP. If some preference to agricultural development is to be implemented, as new approaches to growth and development advise, sectoral investments in Colombia must grow considerably in order to overcome the imbalance. In Mexico, some increment would be advisable with an emphasis on financing small farmers

Social Public Expenditure and Rural Poverty

In most Latin American countries social expenditure shrank during the adjustment programmes, and only in 1991 recovered the levels registered at the beginning of the 1980s. The drop in GDP and the adjustment processes during the 1980s led to a decline in public expenditure dedicated to the social sectors, both per capita and as a proportion of total expenditure.[50] To evaluate the social impact of adjustment I shall estimate the *allocation ratio* (the ratio of social expenditure actually reaching the poor to total social expenditure), and the *social focalisation ratio* (the ratio of social expenditure actually reaching the poor, divided by the share of population living under the poverty lines, both from Stewart, 1992); the equity index is calculated as the *allocation ratio* to GDP divided by the share of population living under the poverty line.[51] Values equal to one represent neutrality and higher than one, some redistribute effects of expenditure (Table 18.7).[52] The *allocation ratio* has increased in both countries since 1980, although with some instability. The *social focalisation ratio*, when calculated in reference to population under the poverty line, suggests a considerable deficit, lower in the case of Colombia, but growing. If considering the population under the extreme poverty line, which would mean that social expenditure would be directed only to that population, the situation is the opposite. On applying the *equity index* substantial gaps are registered, suggesting that in both countries social expenditure is not even neutral, since in order to reach neutral levels social investments going to the poor would need to be doubled.

[50]   Grosh (1990).

[51]   Birgegaard (1998).

[52]   Birgegaard (1998, p 84), suggests that a 'project would be designed as poor oriented only when the benefits that reach the poor are not less than the proportion of the poor population in the total population'.

Table 18.7: Colombia and Mexico: Focalisation of Public Social Expenditure

Concept	1980	1988	1990	1994	1996	1999
C O L O M B I A						
Population in poverty %	59.10	59.10	58.20	54.40	55.00	55.00
Population in extreme poverty %	25.50	27.20	24.70	20.70	20.30	20.90
Social Allocation ratio*	19.80	17.80	32.10	27.20	38.40	31.30
Social expenditure as % of GDP	4.75	5.14	5.55	6.83	9.02	9.50
Social focalisation ratio**						
Population in poverty	0.34	0.35	0.60	0.50	0.70	0.57
Extreme poor	0.84	0.65	1.50	1.20	1.89	1.50
Equity index***						
Population in poverty	0.08	0.09	0.10	0.13	0.16	0.17
Extreme poor	0.18	0.19	0.22	0.33	0.44	0.45
M E X I C O						
Population in poverty %	38.71	46.56	46.42	45.11	50.11	50.00
Population in extreme poverty %	13.09	18.01	17.83	14.48	13.02	13.00
Social Allocation ratio*	35.11	17.77	18.87	40.71	21.73	31.82
Social expenditure as % of GDP	7.15	6.27	6.86	8.99	5.05	7.00
Focalisation coefficient**						
Population in poverty	0.91	0.38	0.41	0.90	0.43	0.64
Extreme poor	2.68	0.99	1.06	2.81	1.67	2.45
Equity index***						
Population in poverty	0.18	0.13	0.15	0.20	0.10	0.14
Extreme poor	0.55	0.35	0.38	0.62	0.39	0.54

Source: own calculations based on Departamento Nacional de Planeación (Colombia) and INEGI (Mexico).

* Public social expenditure = % of total public expenditure without social security.
** Social expenditure as % of total expenditure reaching the poor divided by the share of the poor in total population.

*** Social expenditure reaching the poor to GDP in % PIB, divided by the share of the poor in total population

I ran multiple correlation models to establish if rurality, a higher proportion of rural population, was correlated to per capita GDP, and to indicators such as the index of quality of life (Índices de Calidad de Vida — ICV, calculated by Misión Social del Gobierno Colombiano) and the marginalisation index (Índice de Marginalidad, used by the Mexican government in programmes to combat poverty). These indicators were correlated with social public expenditure at municipal level.[53] High and negative correlation between rurality and income and between social investments and rurality or per capita incomewas found, showing that expenditure is not related to poverty levels.[54] In Mexico during 2000, per capita total social public expenditure in backward regions reached 5,000 pesos, while the expenditure in the most developed regions amounted to 12,000 pesos. A similar situation was registered for Colombia. In general, it seems that criteria used to allocate social expenditure maintain the urban bias and are utilitarian, aiming at the most effective use of resources and faster results. Preference would be given, therefore, to less marginalised groups or to regions where the social indicators are relatively better and which have a better infrastructure. Comparatively small investments will push their levels higher, but a larger number of people will not necessarily be above a certain level of welfare.[55]

Actions to solve the interrelated problems of land concentration and rural poverty are not considered by government officials, who believe that the strategy should be concentrated in promoting faster productivity growth by intensifying mechanisation and the use of chemical inputs. For them and for a number of outspoken personalities[56] land reform is an outdated, populist policy unsupported by any economic rationality. Instead of redistributing land, both governments are implementing subsistence cash transference schemes. The main voices promoting a market oriented land redistribution and an end to macroeconomic policies that discriminate against peasant producers, come from the World Bank. In Colombia, the Fuerzas Armadas Revolucionarias de Colombia (FARC) are asking for the redistribution of 'unproductive latifundia', a luke-warm proposal compared with the World Bank recommendation.

---

[53]   The number of observations is over 1,000 for Colombia and 2,000 for Mexico.

[54]   Stadistics and results are available on request.

[55]   Roemer (1993). The principle of utilitarianism is applied by several non-governmental organisations, which look for instance at countries (or regions within countries) in which social, public infrastructure, communications and community participation are more developed to establish social programmes. They consider those externalities basic for success. That leaves backward regions out of reach (Puyana, 1996).

[56]   In Colombia, former president Alfonso López M and the representatives of the Sociedad Colombiana de Agricultores and the Fedración de Ganaderos, and in Mexico many members of the Salinas and Zedillo governments, represent such opinions.

Conclusions

Poverty in Mexico and Colombia is associated with growth dynamics, and with the drop in the participation of wages in income. The difficulties in achieving higher and sustained rates of growth have made it very hard to reduce poverty. The concentration of property, the Dutch Disease effects of oil bonanzas and the ISI incentives to industry explain to a large extent the development path followed by agriculture and the incidence of poverty and inequality in rural population.

Social expenditure, although more focused than before, has not solved the general social deficit nor the social debt towards the rural sector. Expenditure is implemented with efficiency criteria that benefit the less poor and the regions with better infrastructure. As a result of concentration of land, agricultural development in both countries has established a bimodal structure, which is not the most inefficient in terms of allocation of productive factors. It displaces labour and tends to be extremely intensive in scarce resources, capital and technology, while depressing investments, and excluding small-scale and poor peasants from growth.

Agricultural growth has been unstable, falling quite fast against total GDP. Terms of trade in Colombia and in some periods in Mexico have been declining. Exchange overvaluation has prevented the manifestation of the benefits of liberalisation. Frequent external shocks, *bonanzas* and distortions, accompanied by revaluation, burst of imports of food and all the discriminatory elements of the ISI explain the fall of agriculture in GDP and in employment, low productivity and low incomes. The export-oriented model did not eliminate the urban bias, the preferences for large overcapitalised farms or the discrimination against poor peasants. Concentration of assets may put up insurmountable barriers to sustainable growth and to the reduction of poverty. The elimination of the policy instruments that discriminate in favour of large-scale farming and the implementation of a land reform with efficiency criteria are needed as the way to stimulate agricultural growth and reduce rural poverty.

Bibliography

Aaron, H. (1966) 'Rent Controls and Urban Development: a Case Study of Mexico City', *Social and Economic Studies*, vol. 15, pp. 314–28.

Abel, C. and Lewis, C. (1993) *Welfare, Poverty and Development in Latin America* (Basingstoke: Macmillan).

Abel, C. and Lewis, C.M. (eds.) (1991) *Latin America, Economic Imperialism and the State: the Political Economy of the External Connection from Independence to the Present* (London: Institute of Latin American Studies).

Abel, C. (1996) *Health, Hygiene and Sanitation in Latin America, c.1870-c.1950* (London: Institute of Latin American Studies).

Abel, C. and Lloyd-Sherlock, P. (2000) 'Health Policy in Latin America: Themes, Trends and Challenges', in P. Lloyd-Sherlock (ed.), *Healthcare Reform and Poverty in Latin America* (London: Institute of Latin American Studies), pp. 1-21.

Abrams, C. (1964) *Man's Struggle for Shelter in an Urbanizing World* (Boston, MIT Press).

Acheson, D. (2000) 'Health Inequalities Impact Assessment', *Bulletin of the World Health Organization*, vol. 78, pp. 75–6.

Adelman, J. (ed.) (1999) *Colonial Legacies: the Problem of Persistence in Latin American History* (New York, London: Routledge).

Aguilar, G., Arias, D., Burgos, J.C., Cervantes, S. and Echeverría, J. (1998) *Diagnóstico funcional: plan de acción para la Cuenca del Río Tempisque, vol IV: Socioecónomica* (Liberia/San Jose: Asociación para el Manejo de la Cuenca del Río Tempisque/Ministerio de Ambiente y Energía).

Ahlawalia, L. et al. (1979) 'Economic Development and Income Distribution', *Journal of Development Economics*.

Ahmad, O.B., Lopez, A.D., and Inoue, M. (2000) 'The Decline in Child Mortality: a Reappraisal', *Bulletin of the World Health Organization*, vol. 78, pp. 1175–90.

Ahuad, A., Paganelli, A. and Palmeyro, A. (1999) *Medicina prepagada. Historia y futuro* (Buenos Aires: Ediciones ISALUD).

Aith, M. (2000) 'La ley de patentes puede crear conflicto entre Brasil y EE.UU', *Folha de Sao Paulo*, 12 Feb.

Albala-Bertrand, J.M. (1993) 'Evolution of Aggregate Welfare and Development Indicators in Latin America and the OECD, 1950–85', in

C. Abel and C.M. Lewis (eds.) *Welfare, Poverty and Development in Latin America* (Basingstoke: Macmillan), pp. 33–47

Albert, B. (1988) *South America and the First World War: the Impact of the War on Brazil, Argentina, Peru and Chile* (Cambridge: Cambridge University Press).

Alesina, A. and Drazen, A. (1991) 'Why Are Stabilizations Delayed?' *American Economic Review*, vol. 81 .

Alesina, A. and Perotti, R. (1994) 'The Political Economy of Budget Deficits', *NBER Working Paper*, no. 4637.

Alesina, A. and Rodrik, D. (1994) 'Distributive Politics and Economic Growth', *Quarterly Journal of Economics*, vol. 109.

Alesina, A., Ozler, S., Roubini, N. and Swagel, P. (1996) 'Political Instability and Economic Growth', *Journal of Economic Growth*.

Allen, E. (1989) 'The Flood which became a Disaster: Housing and the Poor in Rio de Janeiro', *Centre for Housing Research Discussion Paper no. 25*, University of Glasgow.

Almarza, S. (1997) *Financiamiento de la vivienda de estratos de ingresos medios y bajos: la experiencia chilena*, CEPAL Serie Financiamento del Desarrollo 46 (Santiago).

Almeyda, G. (1996) *Money Matters: Reaching Women Microentrepreneurs with Financial Services* (New York: UN Development Fund for Women and Washington, DC: IDB).

Alonso, G. (2000) *Política y seguridad social en la Argentina de los '90* (Buenos Aires: Miño y Dávila Editores /FLACSO)

Altimir, O. (1982) *The Extent of Poverty in Latin America* (Washington, DC: World Bank).

Altimir, O. (1997) *Poverty in Latin America: Long-Term Trends* (New York Human Development Report Office, United Nations Development Programme).

Altimir, O. (1997) 'Desigualdad, empleo y pobreza en América Latina: efectos del ajuste y del cambio en el estilo de desarrollo', *Desarrollo Económico*, vol. XXXVII, no. 145, pp. 3–30.

Altimir, O. (1998) 'Inequality and Poverty in Latin America; an Overview' in V. Tokman and G. O'Donnell (eds), *Povery and Inequality in Latin America: Issues and New Challenges* (Notre Dame, Ind.: University of Notre Dame Press), pp. 3–20.

Altimir, O. and Piñera, S. (1982) 'Análisis de descomposición de las desigualdades de ingreso en América Latina', *El Trimestre Económico*, vol. XLIX, no. 4, pp. 813–60.

Altobelli, L. (2000) 'Community Management of Health Facilities', paper presented at the workshop organised by the World Bank, *The Challenge of Health Reform: Reaching the Poor*, San Jose, Costa Rica, 24–26 May.

Alvarez, L.M. (2000) 'La implementación de una reforma educativa en el estado de Aguascalientes', *Gestión y Política Pública* (México), vol. 9, no. 2, pp. 257–301.

Anand, S. and Kanbur, R. (1986) 'Inequality and Development: a Critique' (Yale University Economic Growth Center).

Anderson, B. (1991) *Imagined Communities: Reflections on the Origin and Spread of Nationalism* (London: Verso)

Anderson, C.A. and Bowman, M.J. (eds.) (1966) *Education and Economic Development* (London: Frank Cass).

Anderson, C.A. and Bowman, M.J. (eds.) (1973) 'Human Capital and Economic Modernisation in Historical Perspective', in *Proceedings of the Fourth Conference of Economic History, 1968* (Paris: Mouton).

Andreu, F. (1994) 'The International Community in Haiti: Evidence of the New World Order', in R. Sieder (ed.), *Impunity in Latin America* (London: Institute of Latin American Studies), pp. 33-43.

Añé, L. (2000) 'Cuba: reformas, recuperación y equidad', paper presented to Second Symposium on *Reforma Económico y Cambio Social en América Latina y el Caribe*, Cali, Colombia, 23–24 Nov.

Angell, A. and Graham, C. (1995) 'Can Social Sector Reform Make Adjustment Sustainable and Equitable? Lessons from Chile and Venezuela', *Journal of Latin American Studies*, vol. XXVII, no. 1, pp. 189–219.

Angell, A., Lowden, P. and Thorp, R. (2001) *Decentralising Development: the Political Economy of Institutional Change in Colombia and Chile* (Oxford: Oxford University Press).

Aninat, E, Bauer, A. and Cowan, K. (1999) 'Addressing Equity Issues in Policymaking: Lessons from the Chilean Experience', in V. Tanzi, K. Chu and S. Gupta (eds.), *Economic Policy and Equity* (Washington, DC: IMF).

Annino, A. (ed.) (1995) *Historia de las elecciones en Iberoamérica, siglo XIX* (Buenos Aires: Fondo de Cultura Económica).

Antunes, N. (1993) 'Model Life Table Representation for Brazilian Mortality', PhD Thesis, Faculty of Medicine, London School of Hygiene and Tropical Medicine, University of London.

Apec Education Forum (1999) 'The Relationship between Education Reform and a Changing Economy', International Seminar on Education Reform, Bureau of International Cultural and Educational Relations, Ministry of Education, Taipei.

Arango, A. (1998) 'La Provincia de Buenos Aires en Argentina. Descentralización y autonomía escolar: la ilusión después de la ilusión?', paper presented at the 3rd International Congress of the Centro Latinoamericano de Administración para el Desarrollo (CLAD), Madrid, 14–17 Oct.

Arce, A. (1993) *Negotiating Agricultural Development* (Wageningen, Holland: Agricultural University).

Archer, D. (2000) 'Discovering new Definitions of Reflect: the First Central American meeting', *Education Action,* issue 12, pp. 9–11 (London: Action Aid).

Archer, D. and Costello, P. (1990) *Literacy and Power: The Latin American Battleground* (London: Earthscan).

Arcia, G. and Belli, H. (1998) *Rebuilding the Social Contract: School Autonomy in Nicaragua* (Washington: World Bank), LCHSD paper series, no. 40.

Arditto Barletta, N., Bléjer, M.I. and Landau, L. (1984) *Economic Liberalization and Stabilization Policies in Argentina, Chile and Uruguay* (Washington, DC: World Bank).

Arellano, J.P. (1982) 'Políticas de vivienda popular: lecciones de la experiencia chilena', *Colección Estudios CIEPLAN* 9, pp. 41–73.

Arias, O. (2000) *Are All Men Benefiting from the New Economy? Male Economic Marginalisation in Argentina, Brazil and Costa Rica* (Washington, DC: World Bank, LCSPR).

Arnaut, A. (1994) 'La federalización de la educación básica y normal (1978–1994)', *Política y Gobierno* (México), vol. 1, no. 2 .

Arquilla, J. and Ronfeldt, D. (2000) *Swarming and the Future of Conflict* (Santa Monica: The RAND Corporation and National Defense Institute), text available on-line at http://www.rand.org/publications/DB/DB311/DB311.pdf.

Arriagada, I. (1998) 'Latin American Families: Convergences and Divergences in Models and Policies', *CEPAL Review,* no.65, pp. 85–102.

Arrighi, G. (1996) 'Workers of the World at Century's End', *Fernand Braudel Center Review*, vol. 19, no. 3 .

Arrossi, S. (ed.) (1994) *Funding Community Initiatives* (London: Earthscan).

Atkinson, A. (1996) *Incomes and the Welfare State: Essays on Britain and Europe* (Cambridge: Cambridge University Press).

Atkinson, S. (2000) 'Decentralization in Practice: Tales from the North-East of Brazil', in P. Lloyd-Sherlock (ed.), *Healthcare Reform and Poverty in Latin America* (London: Institute of Latin American Studies, University of London), pp. 78–93.

AUCA (1979) '*Política(s) de desarrollo urbano*', *Arquitectura, Urbanismo, Construcción, Arte* 37, Special edition.

Auty, R. (1993) *Sustaining Development in Mineral Economies. The Resource Curse Thesis* (Routledge, London).

Ayala, R. (2000) 'Análisis de los efectos de las políticas monetarias adoptadas por los países andinos entre 1970 y 1999', *Boletín del Fondo Latinoamericano de Reservas*, no. 34, pp. 133–47.

Azuela, A. (1989) *La ciudad, la propiedad privada y el derecho* (Mexico City: El Colegio de México).

Bacha, E.L. and Klein, H.S. (eds.) (1986) *A transição incompleta: Brasil desde 1945*, 2 vols. (Rio de Janeiro: Paz e Terra).

Baken, R-J., Nientied, P., Peltenburg, M. and Zaaijer, M. (1991) 'Neighbourhood Consolidation and Economic Development of Informal Settlements', *IHS Working Paper*, no. 3.

Balán, J., Browning, H. and Jelin, E. (1973) *Men in a Developing Society* (Austin: University of Texas Press).

Balance, R, Pogany, J. and Forstner, H. (1992) *The World's Pharmaceutical Industries* (Aldershot: UNIDO, Edward Elgar).

Baldwin, P. (1990) *The Politics of Social Solidarity: Class Bases of the European Welfare State* (Cambridge: Cambridge University Press).

Banco Mundial (1994) *Envejecimiento sin crisis. Políticas para la protección de los ancianos y la promoción del crecimiento* (Washington, DC: Banco Mundial).

Barahona de Brito, A. (1997) *Human Rights and Democratisation in Latin America: Uruguay and Chile* (Oxford: Oxford University Press).

Barbeito, A. and Lo Vuolo, R. (1993) 'La reforma del sistema previsional argentino, el mercado de trabajo y la distribución del ingreso', *Estudios del Trabajo*, no. 6, second semester.

Barman, R. (1999) *Citizen Emperor: Pedro II and the Making of Brazil, 1825-91* (Stanford: Stanford University Press).

Barraclough, S. and Domike, A. (1966) 'Agrarian Structure in the Latin American Countries', *Land Economics*, vol. LXII, no. 4, pp. 391–424

Barrera, M. (1999) 'Political Participation and Social Exclusion of the Popular Sectors', in P. Oxhorn and P.K. Starr (eds.), *Markets and Democracy in Latin America: Conflict or Convergence?* (Boulder: Lynne Rienner Publishers), pp. 81–102.

Barrientos, A. (1996) 'Ageing and Personal Pensions in Chile', in P. Lloyd-Sherlock and P. Johnson (eds.), *Ageing and Social Policy: Global Comparisons* (London: Suntory and Toyota International Centres for Economics and Related Disciplines), pp. 44–60.

Barrientos, A. (1998) *Pension Reform in Latin America* (Aldershot: Ashgate).

Barrientos A. (2000) 'Getting Better after Neoliberalism: Shifts and Challenges of Health Policy In Chile', in P. Lloyd-Sherlock (ed.), *Healthcare Reform and Poverty in Latin America* (London: Institute of Latin American Studies), pp. 94–111.

Barrientos, A. (2001) 'Welfare Regimes in Latin America', paper presented at Social Policy in Development Contexts Workshop, University of Bath, March.

Barrientos, A. and Lloyd-Sherlock, P. (2000) 'Reforming Health Insurance in Argentina and Chile', *Health Policy and Planning*, vol. 15, no. 4.

Barro, R. (1997) 'Determinants of Economic Growth. A Cross-Country Empirical Study' (London: MIT Press).

Barros Nock, M. (2000) 'The Mexican Peasantry and the Ejido in the Neo-Liberal Period', in D. Bryceson, C. Kay and J. Mooij (eds.), *Disappearing Peasantries? Rural Labour in Africa, Asia and Latin America* (London: Intermediate Technology), pp. 159-75.

Barsted, L.A.L. (1994) 'Em busca do tempo perdido: mulher e políticas públicas no Brasil, 1983–1993', *Revista Estudos Feministas*, Special Issue (October), pp. 38–53.

Barton, D. (1994) *Literacy: an Introduction to the Ecology of Language* (Oxford: Blackwell).

Bates, R. and A. Krueger (eds.) (1993) *Political and Economic Interactions in Economic Policy Reform* (Cambridge, Mass.: Blackwell Publishers).

Batley, R.A. (1999) 'The New Public Management in Developing

Countries: Introduction and Implications for Policy and Organizational Reform', *Journal of International Development*, vol. 11, pp. 755–65.

Baud, M. (1995) *Peasants and Tobacco in the Dominican Republic 1870-1930* (Knoxville: University of Tennessee Press).

Baylies, C. (1996) 'Diversity in Patterns of Parenting and Household Formation', in E. Bortolaia Silva (ed.), *Good Enough Mothering? Feminist Perspectives on Lone Motherhood* (London: Routledge), pp. 76–96.

Bayón, C. and Saravi, G. (2001) 'Cambios en la estructura de oportunidades, modelo económico, reformas sociales y mercado de trabajo en Argentina', paper for conference on *Activos disponibles, estructura de oportunidades y vulnerabilidad social en América Latina*, Montevideo, Uruguay, 14-15 Aug.

BCC (1999) *Informe Económico 1998* (Havana: Banco Central de Cuba).

BCC (2000) *Informe Económico 1999* (Havana: Banco Central de Cuba).

Beattie, R. and McGillivray, W. (1995) 'Una estrategia riesgosa: reflexiones acerca del informe del Banco Mundial titulado *Envejecimiento sin crisis*', *Revista Internacional de la Seguridad Social*, nos. 3 and 4, pp. 7–28.

Beccaria, L. and Galín, P. (1998) 'Competitiveness and Labour Regulation', *CEPAL Review*, vol. LXV, pp. 71–84.

Beck, U. and Beck-Gernsheim, E. (1995) *The Normal Chaos of Love* (Cambridge: Polity).

Becker, G.S. (1964) *Human Capital: a Theoretical and Empirical Analysis* (Princeton: Princeton University Press).

Beijaard, F. (1995) 'Rental and Rent-Free Housing as Coping Mechanisms in La Paz, Bolivia', *Environment and Urbanization*, vol. 7, pp. 167–82.

Bell, D. (1964) *El fin de las ideologías* (Madrid: Tecnos).

Bellamy, R. (1993) 'Citizenship and Rights', in R. Bellamy (ed.), *Theories and Concepts of Politics* (Manchester: Manchester University Press), pp. 43–96.

Beltrão, K.I. and Oliveira, F.E.B. (2000) *Factor previdenciario ¿Problema o solución para el Sistema de Seguridad Social de Brasil?*, in Encuentro de la Sociedad Mexicana de Demografía (SOMEDE), Mexico.

Beltrão, K.I., Barreto, F.E.B. and Médici, A.C. (1994) 'El sistema de seguridad social brasileño: problemas y soluciones alternativas', in F.E.B. de Oliveira (ed.), *Sistemas de seguridad social en la región: problemas y alternativas de solución* (Rio de Janeiro: BID and Instituto Brasileiro de Pesquisas Economicas Aplicadas), pp. 59–104.

Beltrão, K.I., Passinato, M., Tereza, M. and Oliveira, F.E.B. (1996) *Projeções da situação econômico-financeira da previdência social 1995–2030 e impactos de políticas institucionais alternativas* (Rio de Janeiro: Instituto de Pesquisas Economicas Aplicadas).

Beltrão, K., Sonoê, P. and Oliveira, F.E.B. (2001) 'La familia rural y la seguridad social en Brasil: un análisis con énfasis en los cambios constitucionales', in C. Gomes (ed.), *Procesos sociales, población y familia* (Mexico City: FLACSO and Porrua), pp. 324–44.

Benería, L. (1991) 'Structural Adjustment, the Labour Market and the Household: the Case of Mexico', in G. Standing and V. Tokman (eds), *Towards Social Adjustment: Labour Market Issues in Structural Adjustment* (Geneva: International Labour Organisation), pp. 161–83.

Benjamin, M., Collins, J. and Scott, M. (1984) *No Free Lunch. Food and Revolution in Cuba Today* (San Francisco: Institute for Food and Development Policy).

Bergquist, C. (1986) *Labor in Latin America: Comparative Essays on Chile, Argentina, Venezuela and Colombia* (Stanford.: Stanford University Press).

Bernasconi, A. (1999) 'Second-Generation Reforms in Chile', *International Higher Education*, no. 15 (The Boston College Center for International Higher Education), pp. 13–15.

Berry, A. and Cline, W. (1979) *Agrarian Structure and Productivity in Developing Countries* (Baltimore: Johns Hopkins University Press).

Berry, R.A. (ed.) (1998) *Confronting the Income Distribution Threat in Latin America: Poverty, Economic Reforms and Income Distribution in Latin America* (Boulder.: Lynne Rienner Publishers).

Bertranou, J. (1998) 'Mexico: the Politics of the System for Retirement Pensions', in M.A. Cruz-Saco and C. Mesa-Lago (eds.), *Do Options Exist? The Reform of Pension and Health Care Systems in Latin America* (Pittsburgh: University of Pittsburgh Press).

Besserer, F. (1999) 'Estudios transnacionales y cuidadanía transnacional', in G. Mummert (ed.), *Fronteras fragmentadas* (Zamora: Colegio de Michoacán), pp. 225–38.

Bethell, L. (ed.) (1991)*The Cambridge History of Latin America. Vol. VIII: 1930 to the Present* (Cambridge: Cambridge University Press).

Bethell, L. (ed.) (1994) *The Cambridge History of Latin America. Vol. VI, Pt. 1: 1930 to the Present* (Cambridge: Cambridge University Press).

Bezruchka, S. (2000), 'Is Globalization Dangerous to our Health?' *Western Journal of Medicine*, vol. 172, pp. 332–4.

Bielschowsky, R. (1988) *Pensamento econômico brasileiro: o ciclo ideológico do desenvolvimentismo* (Rio de Janeiro: IPEA/INPES).

Bin Wong, R. (1997) *China Transformed: Historical Change and the Limits of European Experience* (Ithaca, NY: Cornell University Press).

Birsdall, N. (1999) 'Comments', in V. Tanzi et al., *Economic Policy and Equity* (Washington, DC: International Monetary Fund), pp. 85–92.

Birdsall, N. and Graham, C. (eds.) (2000) *New Markets? New Opportunities?: Economic and Social Mobility in a Changing World* (Washington, DC: Brookings Institution Press, Carnegie Endowment for International Peace).

Birdsall, N. and Jaspersen, F. (eds.) (1997) *Pathways to Growth: Comparing East Asia and Latin America* (Baltimore: Inter-American Development Bank).

Birdsall, N. and Sabot, R.H. (comps.) (1996) *Opportunity Foregone: Education in Brazil* (Baltimore: Inter-American Development Bank).

Birdsall, N. et al. (eds.) (1998) *Beyond Trade-Offs — Market Reform and Equitable Growth in Latin America* (Washington, DC: Inter-American Development Bank : Brookings Institution Press).

Birgegaard, L.E (1998) *The Impact of Development Projects on Poverty* (Paris: OCDE).

Bisinwanger, H.P. and Deininger, K. (1997) 'Explaining Agricultural and Agrarian Policies in Developing Countries', *WORLD BANK*, w.p. no. 1765.

Blasco, M. and Varley, A. (2001) '"¿Cosechan lo que siembran ?" Mujeres ancianas, vivienda y relaciones familiares en el México urbano', in C. Gomes (ed.), *Procesos sociales, población y vida doméstica* (Mexico City: FLACSO and Porrua), pp. 301–22.

Blat Gimeno, J. (1983) *Education in Latin America and the Caribbean: Trends and Prospects, 1970–2000* (Paris: UNESCO).

Boltvinik, J. (1995) *Reformas macroeconómicas en América Latina y sus efectos sobre los niveles de pobreza* (OIT).

Boltvinik, J. (1994) 'Poverty Measurement and Indicators of Development', in R. Van der Hoeven et al. (ed.), *Poverty Monitoring an International Concern* (St. Martin's Press, UNICEF).

Boltvinik, J. and Hernández Laos, E. (2000) *Pobreza y distribución del ingreso en México* (Mexico City: Siglo XXI Editores).

Bonato, A. (1996) *Previdência social: inclusões e exclusões* (Curitiba, Pr: DESER).

Bond, P. (1999) 'Globalization, Pharmaceutical Pricing and South African Health Policy: Managing Confrontation with US Firms and Politicians', *International Journal of Health Services*, vol. 29, no. 4.

Bonvecchi, A., Charosky, H., Garay, C. and Urribari, D. (1998) 'Instituto Nacional de Servicios Sociales para Jubilados y Pensionados. Un análisis de sus condiciones de viabilidad organizacional, institucional y política' (Buenos Aires: Fundacíon Argentina para el Desarrollo con Equidad).

Bóo, M. (1996) 'The Expansion of Education Provision in Latin America, 1950–1995' (unpublished University of London, Institute of Latin American Studies, MA dissertation).

Borsotti, C.A. (1983) 'Development and Education in Rural Areas' *CEPAL Review*, vol. 21, pp. 113–32

Borzutsky, S. (1998) 'Chile: The Politics of Privatization', in M.A. Cruz-Saco and C. Mesa-Lago, *Do Options Exist? The Reform of Pension and Health Care Systems in Latin America* (Pittsburgh: University of Pittsburgh Press).

Bossert, T. (2000) *Decentralization of Health Systems in Latin America: A Comparative Study of Chile, Colombia, and Bolivia* (Cambridge, Mass.: International Health Systems Group, Harvard School of Public Health), available at http://www.hsph.harvard.edu/ihsg/region.html#5

Brading, D. (ed.) (1980) *Caudillos and Peasants in the Mexican Revolution* (Cambridge: Cambridge University Press).

Bresser Pereira, L.C. (1993) 'Economic Reforms and Cycles of State Intervention' *World Development*, vol. 21, no. 8, pp. 1337–53.

Brock, C. and Lawler, H. (eds.) (1985) *Education in Latin America* (London: Croom Helm).

Bromley, R. (ed.) (1979) *The Urban Informal Sector: Critical Perspectives on Employment and Housing Policies* (Oxford: Pergamon Press).

Brooks, S. (2000) 'Social Protection and the Market: a Political Economy of Pension Reform in Latin America and the World', paper prepared for the 2000 meeting of the Latin American Studies Association, Miami, March 16–18.

Brooks, S. and James, E. (1999) 'The Political Economy of Pension Reform', paper prepared for a World Bank Research Conference, September 14–15.

Brumer, A. (1971) *Sindicalismo rural e participação dos agricultores em sindicato, em Candelária, Rio Grande do Sul, Brasil* (Porto Alegre: Centro de Estudos e Pesquisas Econômicas/IEPE/UFRGS) (MA dissertation).

Brumer, A. (1985) 'As lutas no campo, no Rio Grande do Sul (1964–1883)', *Revista do Instituto de Filosofia e Ciências Humanas da UFRGS*, vol. 13, pp. 198–218.

Brumer, A. (1990) 'Considerações sobre uma década de lutas sociais no campo no extremo sul do Brasil (1978–88)', *Ensaios FEE*, year 11, no. 1, pp. 124–42.

Brumer, A. (1993) 'Mobilisation and the Quest for Recognition: the Struggle of Rural Women in Southern Brazil for Access to Welfare Benefits', in C. Abel and C.M. Lewis (eds), *Welfare, Poverty and Development in Latin America* (Basingstoke: Macmillan), pp. 405–20.

Brumer, A. (2000) *Gênero e agricultura: a situação da mulher na agricultura do Rio Grande do Sul*, paper presented at the XXII International Congress of the Latin American Studies Association (LASA), Miami, FL, March 16–18.

Brundenius, C. (1984) *Revolutionary Cuba: the Challenge of Economic Growth with Equity* (Boulder and London: Westview Press).

Brundenius, C. (1990) 'Some Reflections on the Cuban Economic Model', in S. Halebsky and J.M. Kirk, *Transformation and Struggle. Cuba Faces the 1990s* (New York: Praeger).

Brundenius, C. (2000) *The Role of Human Capital in Cuban Economic Development, 1959–1999* (Copenhagen: Centre for Development Research), CDR Working Paper Series no. 00.8.

Brundenius, C. and Monreal, P. (2001) 'The Future of the Cuban Model: a Longer View', in C. Brundenius and J. Weeks, *Globalization and Third World Socialism: Cuba and Vietnam* (London: Palgrave/Macmillan).

Brunner, J. et al. (1994) 'Informe para su excelencia el Presidente de la República Don Eduardo Frei Ruiz-Tagle' (Comisión Nacional para la Modernización de la Educación, Ministerio de Educación, Santiago, Chile).

Budowksi, M. (2000a) '"Yo Valgo": the Significance of Daily Practice: the Case of Lone Mothers in Costa Rica' (Berne: Swiss National Science Foundation), End of Award Report, Grant no. 82–04–27891.

Budowski, M. (2000b) 'Lone Motherhood in Costa Rica: a Threat for Society or a Chance for Change?', revised draft of paper delivered for publication of the proceedings of the Symposium 'Order, Risk and Catastrophe', Berne, 11–13 Oct. 1999.

Budowski, M. and Guzmán, L. (1998) 'Strategic Gender Interests in Social Policy: Empowerment Training for Female Heads of Household in Costa Rica', paper prepared for the International Sociological Association, XIV World Congress of Sociology, Montreal, 26 July–1 Aug.

Budowski, M. and Rosero Bixby, L. (forthcoming) 'Fatherless Costa Rica? Child Acknowledgement and Support Among Lone Mothers', *Journal of Comparative Family Studies*.

Bullock, A. and Thomas, H. (1997) *Schools at the Centre? A Study of Decentralisation* (London: Routledge).

Bulmer-Thomas, V. (1994) *The Economic History of Latin America since Independence* (Cambridge: Cambridge University Press).

Bulmer-Thomas, V. (1996) *The New Economic Model and Its Impact on Income Distribution and Poverty* (Basingstoke: Macmillan/Institute of Latin American Studies).

Bulmer-Thomas, V., Craske, N. and Serrano, M. (1994) 'Who will Benefit?' in V. Bulmer-Thomas et al. (eds.) *Mexico and the North American Free Trade Agreement Who Will Benefit?* (London: Macmillan/Institute of Latin American Studies), pp. 203–32.

Burgess, R. (1982) 'Self-Help Housing Advocacy: a Curious Form of Radicalism. A Critique of the Work of John F.C. Turner', in P.M. Ward (ed.), *Self Help Housing : a Critique* (London : Mansell), pp. 56–98.

Buse, D.K. (1993) 'The World Bank and International Health Policy: Genesis, Evolution and Implications', Masters thesis, London School of Economics and London School of Hygiene and Tropical Health.

Buxton, J. and Phillips, N. (eds.) (1999a) *Case Studies in Latin American Political Economy* (Manchester: Manchester University Press).

Buxton, J. and Phillips, N. (eds.) (1999b) *Development in Latin American Political Economy: State, Markets and Actors* (Manchester: Manchester University Press).

Cahnman, W.J. and Heberle, R. (eds.) (1971) *Ferdinand Toennies on Sociology: Pure, Applied, and Empirical: Selected Writing* (Chicago: University of Chicago Press).

Caldeira, T.P.R. (2001) *City of Walls: Crime, Segregation and Citizenship in São Paulo* (Berkele: University of California Press).

Calderón, J. (2001) 'Official Registration (Formalization) of Property in Peru (1996–2000), Issue 1, Coping with Informality and Illegality in Human Settlements in Developing Cities', ESF/N-AERUS International Workshop, Leuven/Brussels, 23–26 May..

Camacho, G.B. (1980) *La cuestión agraria en Colombia*, Masters thesis in Sociology, FLACSO, Mexico.

Camposortega, S. (1993) *Análisis demográfico de la mortalidad en México 1940–1980* (México City: El Colegio de México).

Cárdenas, E. (1996) *La política económica en México, 1950-1994* (Mexico City: Fondo de Cultura Económica).

Cárdenas, E., Ocampo, J.A. and Thorp, R. (eds.) (2000a) *An Economic History of Twentieth Century Latin America, Vol. 1: The Export Age: the Latin American Economies in the Late Nineteenth and Early Twentieth Centuries* (Basingstoke: Palgrave).

Cárdenas, E., Ocampo, J.A. and Thorp, R. (eds.) (2000b) *An Economic History of Twentieth Century Latin America, Vol. 3: Industrialization and the State in the Post-War Years* (Basingstoke: Palgrave).

Cardenas, M. and Urrutia, M. (1995) 'Macroeconomic Instability and Social Progress', R. Dornbusch and S. Edwards (eds.), *Reform, Recovery, and Growth* (Chicago: University of Chicago Press, NBER), pp. 79–114.

Cardoso, E. and Helwege, A. (1991) 'Populism, Profligacy and Redistribution', in R. Dornbusch and S. Edwards (eds.) *The Macroeconomics of Populism in Latin America* (Chicago: University of Chicago Press), pp. 45–70.

Cardoso, E. and Helwege, A. (1992) 'Below the Line: Poverty in Latin America', *World Development*, vol. 20, no. 1, pp. 19–37

Cardoso, E., Barros, R. and Urani A. (1995) 'Inflation and Unemployment as Determinants of Inequality in Brazil: the 1980s', in R. Dornbusch and S. Edwards (eds.), *Reform, Recovery, and Growth* (Chicago: University of Chicago Press, National Bureau of Economic Research), pp. 151–74.

Cardoso, F.H. and Faletto, E. (1979) *Dependency and Development in Latin America* (Berkeley: University of California Press).

Carnoy, M. (1998) 'National Voucher Plans in Chile and Sweden: Did Privatization Reforms Make for Better Education?', *Comparative Education Review*, vol. 42, no. 3.

Carnoy, M. and Samoff, J. (1990) *Education and Social Transition in the Third World* (Princeton, NJ: Princeton University Press).

Carpio, J. and Novacovsky, I. (eds.) (1999) *De igual a igual: el desafío del estado ante los nuevos problemas sociales* (Buenos Aires: SIEMPRO, FLACSO, Fondo de Cultura Económica de Argentina).

Carpio, J., Klein, E. and Novacovsky, I. (1999) *Informalidad y exclusión social* (Buenos Aires).

Carranza Valdés, J., Gutiérrez Urdaneta, L. and Monreal, P. (1996) *Cuba: Restructuring the Economy – A Contribution to the Debate* (London: Institute of Latin American Studies).

Carvalho, J.A.M. and Wood, C.H. (1988) *The Demography of Inequality in Brazil* (Cambridge: Cambridge University Press).

Casadio Tarabusi, C. and Vickery, G. (1998) 'Globalization and the Pharmaceutical Industry', *International Journal of Health Services*, vol. 28, pp. 67–105.

Castaneda, T. (1990) *Innovative Social Policies for Reducing Poverty: Chile in the 1980s* (Washington, DC: The World Bank).

Castel, R. (1997) *Les metámorphoses de la questione sociale* (Paris: Fayard).

Castells, M. (1983) *The City and the Grassroots* (Berkeley: University of California Press).

Castells, M. (1997) *The Power of Identity* (Oxford: Blackwell).

Castillo, M. (1998) *La descentralización de los servicios de educación en Nicaragua* (Santiago: ECLAC).

Castro Martins, T. and Juárez, F (1995) 'The Impact of Women's Education on Fertility in Latin America: Searching for Explanations', *International Family Planning Perspectives*, vol. XXI, pp. 52–57.

Castro Valverde, C. and Sáenz, L.B. (1998) *La reforma del sistema nacional de salud. Estrategias, alternativas, perspectivas* (San José: Ministerio de Planificación y Política Nacional).

Cataño, Gonzalo (1989) *Educación y estructura social: ensayos de sociología de la educación* (Bogotá: Plaza y Janés and Asociación Colegio de Sociología).

CEE (1990) *Anuario estadístico de Cuba 1989* (Havana: Comité Estatal de Estadísticas).

Centeno, M.A. (1994) *Democracy within Reason: Technocratic Revolution in Mexico* (University Park, PA: The Pennsylvania State University Press).

CEPAL (Comision Economica para America Latina y el Caribe) (1994) *Salud, equidad y transformación productiva en América Latina y el Caribe*, Serie Documentos Reproducidos no. 41 (Washington, DC: Organización Panamericana de la Salud).

CEPAL (Comision Economica para America Latina y el Caribe) (1995) *Modelos de desarrollo, papel del estado y políticas sociales: nuevas tendencias en América Latina.* (Santiago: Cepal Document LC/R.1575).

CEPAL (Comision Economica para America Latina y el Caribe) (1995) *Panorama social de América Latina 1994* (Santiago, Chile).

CEPAL (Comisión Económica para América Latina) (1997) *La Brecha de la equidad – América Latina , El Caribe y la Cumbre Social* (Santiago).

CEPAL (Comision Economica para America Latina y el Caribe) (1998) *Panorama social de América Latina – 1997* (Santiago de Chile: Publicación de las Naciones Unidas LC/G.1982-P, Feb.).

CEPAL(Comision Economica para America Latina y el Caribe) (1999) *Panorama social de América Latina – 1998* (Santiago de Chile: Publicación de las Naciones Unidas LC/G.2050-P, May).

CEPAL (Comision Economica para America Latina y el Caribe) (2000) *Equidad, desarrollo y ciudadanía* (Santiago).

CEPAL (Comision Economica para America Latina y el Caribe) (2000) *La economía cubana. Reformas estructurales y desempeño en los noventa* (second and expanded edition) (México: Fondo de Cultura Económica).

CEPAL (Comision Economica para America Latina y el Caribe)(2000a) *La brecha de la equidad: una segunda evaluación* (Santiago de Chile: Publicación de las Naciones Unidas LC/G.2096, May).

CEPAL (Comision Economica para America Latina y el Caribe) (2000b) *Equidad, desarrollo y ciudadanía* (Santiago de Chile: Publicación de las Naciones Unidas LC/G.2071/Rev.1-P, Aug.).

CEPAL (Comision Economica para America Latina y el Caribe) (2000c) *Panorama social de América Latina – 1999–2000* (Santiago de Chile: Publicación de las Naciones Unidas LC/G.2068-P, Aug.).

CEPAL (Comision Economica para America Latina y el Caribe) (2000d) *Estudio económico de América Latina y el Caribe* (Santiago de Chile: Publicación de las Naciones Unidas LC/G.2102-P, Aug.).

CEPAL (Comision Economica para America Latina y el Caribe) (2000e) *Preliminary Overview of the Economies of Latin America and the Caribbean* (Santiago de Chile: United Nations Publications LC/G.2123-P, Dec.).

CEPAL (Comision Economica para America Latina y el Caribe) (2001a) *Panorama social de América Latina – 2000–2001* (Santiago de Chile: Publicación de las Naciones Unidas LC/G.2138-P, Sept.).

CEPAL (Comision Economica para America Latina y el Caribe) (2001b) *Estudio económico de América Latina y el Caribe* (Santiago de Chile Publicación de las Naciones Unidas LC/G.2139-P/E, Sept.).

CEPAL (see also UN Economic Commission for Latin America [and the Caribbean])

Cerrutti, M. and Zenteno, R. (1999) 'Cambios en el papel económico de las mujeres entre las parejas mexicanas', *Estudios Demográficos y Urbanos*, vol. 15, no.1, pp. 65–95.

Céspedes-Londoño, J.E., Almeida, C., Travassos, C. et al. (c. 2000) 'Efectos de la reforma de la seguridad social en salud en Colombia sobre la equidad en el acceso y la utilización de servicios de salud', unpublished paper.

Chalmers, D.A. et al. (eds.) (1997) *The New Politics of Inequality in Latin America: Rethinking Participation and Representation* (Oxford: Oxford University Press).

Chalmers, D.A., Martin, S.B. and Piester, K. (1997) 'New Structures of Representation for the Popular Sectors?' in D.A. Chalmers et al. (eds.), *The New Politics of Inequality in Latin America: Rethinking Participation and Representation* (Oxford: Oxford University Press), pp. 543–82.

Chant, S. (1991) *Women and Survival in Mexican Cities: Perspectives on Gender, Labour Markets and Low-Income Households* (Manchester: Manchester University Press).

Chant, S. (1992) 'Migration at the Margins: Gender, Poverty and Population Movement on the Costa Rican Periphery', in S. Chant (ed.), *Gender and Migration in Developing Countries* (London: Belhaven), pp. 49–72.

Chant, S. (1997) *Women-Headed Households: Diversity and Dynamics in the Developing World* (Basingtoke: Macmillan).

Chant, S. (1999) 'Population, Migration, Employment and Gender', in R.N. Gwynne and C. Kay (eds.), *Latin America Transformed: Globalization and Modernity* (London: Arnold), pp. 226–69.

Chant, S. (1999a) 'Women-Headed Households: Global Orthodoxies and Grassroots Realities', in H. Afshar and S. Barrientos (eds), *Women, Globalisation and Fragmentation in the Developing World* (Basingstoke: Macmillan), pp. 91–130.

Chant, S. (1999b) 'Youth, Gender and "Family Crisis" in Costa Rica', report to the Nuffield Foundation, London (Oct.).

Chant, S. (2000) 'Men in Crisis? Reflections on Masculinities, Work and Family in Northwest Costa Rica', *European Journal of Development Research*, vol. 12, no. 2, pp. 199–218.

Chant, S. (2002) 'Women, Men and Household Diversity', in C. McIlwaine and K. Willis (eds), *Challenges and Change in Middle America: Perspectives on*

Development in Mexico, Central America and the Caribbean (Harlow: Pearson Education), pp. 26–60.

Chant, S. and McIlwaine, C. (1995) *Women of a Lesser Cost: Female Labour, Foreign Exchange and Philippine Development* (London: Pluto Press).

Chant, S. and McIlwaine, C. (eds.) (1998) *Three Generations, Two Genders, One World: Women and Men in a Changing Century* (London: Zed Books).

Chant, S. with Craske, N. (2002) *Gender in Latin America* (London: Latin America Bureau).

Chen, S. and Ravallion, M. (2000) 'How did the World's Poorest Fare in the 1990s?', *World Bank*, w.p. no. 2409.

Christiansen, R.E. and Cooper, D. (1995) 'Land Reform in South Africa: Process and Product', in D. Umali and C. Maguire (ed.), *Agriculture in Liberalizing Economies: Changing Roles for Governments* (World Bank).

Cicerchia, R. (1997) 'The Charm of Family Patterns: Historical and Contemporary Patterns in Latin America', in E. Dore (ed.), *Gender Politics in Latin America: Debates in Theory and Practice* (New York: Monthly Review Press), pp. 118–33.

Cimillo, E. (2000) 'Empleo e ingresos en el sector informal en una economía abierta: el caso argentino', in J. Carpio, E. Klein and I. Novacovsky (comp.), *Informalidad y exclusión social* (Buenos Aires: F.C.E./O.I.T./ Siempro).

Claramunt, M.C. (1997) *Casitas quebradas: el problema de la violencia doméstica en Costa Rica* (San José: Editorial Universidad a Distancia).

Clarke, C. (2000) *Class, Ethnicity and Community in Southern Mexico: Oaxaca's Peasantries* (Oxford: Oxford University Press).

Clarke, C. (ed.) (1991) *Society and Politics in the Caribbean* (Basingstoke: Macmillan/St Antony's College Oxford).

Clarke, C. and Howard, D. (1999) 'Cities, Capitalism and Neoliberal Regimes', in R.N. Gwynne and C. Kay (eds.), *Latin America Transformed: Globalization and Modernity* (London: Arnold), pp. 305–24.

Clarke, C. et al (eds.) (1990) *South Asians Overseas. Migrations and Ethnicity* (Cambridge: Cambridge University Press).

Clichevsky, N. (1999) 'Vacant Land in Latin American Cities', *Landlines*, vol. 11, Jan.

CMF (Centro Nacional para el Desarrollo de la Mujer y la Familia CMF) (1996) *Plan para la igualdad de oportunidades entre mujeres y hombres (PIOMH) 1996–1998* (San José: CMF).

CMF (Centro Nacional para el Desarrollo de la Mujer y la Familia) (1997) *Mujeres, pobreza y política públicas* (San José: CMF).

CNBB-CEP (Conferência Nacional dos Bispos do Brasil – Comissão Episcopal da Pastoral) (1976) *Pastoral da terra; posse e conflitos* (São Paulo: Paulinas).

Cohen, D. (1998) *Radical Heroes: Gramsci, Freire and the Politics of Adult Education* (New York and London: Garland Publishing, Inc. Taylor and Francis)

Cohen, E. and Franco, R. (1992) *Evaluación de proyectos sociales* (Mexico City: Siglo XXI Editores).

Cohn, A. (1995) 'NGO*s, Social Movements and the Privatisation of Health Care in São Paulo*', in C.E. Reilly (ed.) *New Paths to Democratic Development in Latin America. The Rise of NGO-Municipal Collaboration* (Boulder: Lynne Rienner), pp. 85–98.

Colaboración Area Legal (1997) 'Pulso legislativo: nuevos proyectos de ley', *Otra Mirada* (Centro Nacional para el Desarrollo de la Mujer y la Familia, San José), vol.1, no. 2, p. 51.

Colclough, C. and Manor, J. (1991) (eds.) *States or Markets? Neo-Liberalism and the Development Policy Debate* (Oxford: Oxford University Press LDS –DSS).

Collier, D. (1976) *Squatters and Oligarchs: Authoritarian Rule and Policy Change in Peru* (Baltimore: Johns Hopkins University Press).

Collier, D. (ed.) (1979) *The New Authoritarianism in Latin America* (Princeton: Princeton University Press).

Collier, G.A. (1997) 'Reaction and Retrenchment in the Highlands of Chiapas in the Wake of the Zapatista Rebellion', *Journal of Latin American Anthropology*, vol. 3, no. 1, pp. 14–31.

Collier, J., Rosaldo, M. and Yanagisako, S. (1997) 'Is There a Family? New Anthropological Views', in R. Lancaster and M. di Leonardo (eds), *The Gender/Sexuality Reader* (New York: Routledge), pp. 71–81.

Collier, R.B. and Collier, D. (1991) *Shaping the Political Arena: Critical Junctures, the Labor Movement and Regime Dynamics in Latin America* (Princeton: Princeton University Press).

Cominetti, R. and Ruiz, G. (1998) 'Evolución del gasto público social en América Latina: 1980–1995', *Cuadernos de la Cepal*, no. 80.

Conaghan, C. (1994) 'Loose Parties, "Floating" Politicians, and Institutional Stress: Presidentialism in Ecuador, 1979–1988,' in J. Linz and A. Valenzuela (eds.), *The Failure of Presidential Democracy* (Baltimore: Johns Hopkins University Press).

Conaghan, C. and Malloy, J. (1994) *Unsettling Statecraft: Democracy and Neoliberalism in the Central Andes* (Pittsburgh: Pittsburgh University Press).

Conger, L. (1999) 'Entitled to Prosperity', *Urban Age* (Fall), pp. 7–10.

Consejo Nacional de Planeación (1997) *El salto social: la sociedad pide cuentas* (Bogotá, Colombia).

Cook, M.L. (1996) *Organising Dissent: Unions, The State and the Democratic Teachers' Movement in Mexico* (University Park: Pennsylvania State University Press).

Cooper, F., Holt, T.C. and Scott, R.J. (2000) *Beyond Slavery: Explorations of Race, Labor, and Citizenship in Post-Emancipation Societies* (Chapel Hill: University of North Carolina Press).

Coppedge, M. (1994) *Strong Parties and Lame Ducks: Presidential Partyarchy and Factionalism in Venezuela* (Stanford: Stanford University Press).

Coradini, O.L. (1989) *Representações sociais e conflitos nas políticas de saúde e previdência social rural* (Rio de Janeiro: Museu Nacional/UFRJ), PhD thesis.

Coradini, O.L. (1996) 'Ambivalências na representação de classe e a noção de *trabalhador rural*', in Z. Navarro (org.), *Política, protesto e cidadania no campo; as lutas sociais dos colonos e trabalhadores rurais no Rio Grande do Sul* (Porto Alegre: Editora da Universidade/UFRGS), pp. 171–88.

Coradini, O.L. and Belato, D. (1981) 'Observações sobre os movimentos sociais no campo, hoje', in Assembléia Legislativa do Estado do Rio Grande do Sul, *Seminário Nacional 'A questão da terra'* (Porto Alegre: Comissão de Agricultura e Pecuária, Assembléia Legislativa do Estado do Rio Grande do Sul), pp. 161–6.

Córdova Jiménez, C. (1980) *El seguro social campesino en el Ecuador*, paper presented at the I Jornada Internacional del Intercambio en Seguridad Social, Quito, 21–24 May.

Cornelius, W. (1975) *Politics and the Migrant Poor in Mexico* (Stanford: University of Stanford Press).

Cornelius, W.A. (1996) *Mexican Politics in Transition: the Breakdown of a One-Party Dominant Regime* (San Diego: Center for U.S.-Mexican Studies, University of California).

Corrales, J. (1998) *Party-Accommodating Transitions to the Market: Executive-Ruling Party Relations and Economic Reforms in Latin America* (unpublished paper, Amherst College, Amherst, MA).

Corrales, J. (2000) 'The Politics of Education Reform Implementation: Bolstering the Supply and Demand; Overcoming Institutional Blocks' (Washington, DC: World Bank).

Côrrea, S. with Reichmann, R. (1994) *Population and Reproductive Rights: Feminist Perspectives from the South* (London: Zed).

Cortés, F. (2000) *Procesos sociales y desigualdad económica en Mexico* (Mexico City: Siglo Veintiuno Editores).

Coulomb, R. (1985) 'La vivienda de alquiler en las áreas de reciente urbanización', *Revista de Ciencias Sociales y Humanidades*, vol. 6, pp. 43–70.

Coulomb, R. and Sánchez, C. (1991) *¿Todos proprietarios? Vivienda de alquiler y sectores populares en la Ciudad de México* (Mexico City: CENVI).

Coutinho, L. and Ferraz, J.C. (1994) *Estudo da competitividade da indústria brasileira* (Campinas).

Cox, C. (1999) 'Market and State Principles of Reform in Chilean Education: Policies and Results', in Apec Education Forum, *The Relationship Between Education Reform and a Changing Economy*; International Seminar on Education Reform; Bureau of International Cultural and Educational Relations, Ministry of Education, Taipei.

Cox, C. (2001) 'Educación y Ministerio II: la respuesta a Gonzalo Vial', *Diario La Segunda*, 8 Jan., p. 9.

Cozier, B. and Selody, J. (1992) 'Inflation and Macroeconomic Performance: Some Cross-Country Evidence', mimeo (Bank of Canada).

Craske, N. (1999) *Women and Politics in Latin America* (Oxford : Polity).

Cravey, A. (1998) *Women and Work in Mexico's Maquiladoras* (Lanham: Rowman & Littlefield.)

Crespo, G., Gross, P., Hernández, M., Trucco, C. and Sugranyes, A. (2000) *Consulta sobre la política habitacional en Chile: informe final, Oficina de desarrollo urbano para Sur América, Rudo* (Santiago: USAID).

Cruz-Saco, M.A. (1998) 'Introduction: Context and Typology of Reform Models', in M.A. Cruz-Saco and C. Mesa-Lago, *Do Options Exist? The Reform of Pension and Health Care Systems in Latin America* (Pittsburgh: University of Pittsburgh Press).

Cruz-Saco, M.A. and Mesa-Lago, C. (1998) *Do Options Exist. The Reform of Pension and Health Care Systems in Latin America* (Pittsburgh: University of Pittsburgh Press).

Csillag, C. (2001) 'Brazil's Government to Redress Health-Care Inequalities', *Lancet*, vol. 357 (9253), p. 370.

Cueto, M (ed.) (1996) *Salud, cultura y sociedad en América Latina* (Washington, DC: Organización Panamericana de la Salud).

Cueto, M. (ed.) (1994) *Missionaries of Science: the Rockefeller Foundation and Latin America* (Bloomington: Indiana University Press).

Cunningham, H. (1995) *God and Caesar at the Rio Grande: Sanctuary and the Politics of Religion* (Minneapolis and London: University of Minnesota Press).

Danaher, K. (ed) (1994) *50 Years is Enough: the Case Against the World Bank and the International Monetary Fund* (Boston: South End Press).

DANE (1995) *Encuesta nacional de ingresos y gastos* (Bogotá: DANE).

DANE (2000) Home page: www.dane.gov.co.

Daniere, A. (1992) 'Determinants of Tenure Choice in the Third World: an Empirical study of Cairo and Manila', *Journal of Housing Economics*, vol. 2, pp. 159–84.

Datta, K. and McIlwaine, C. (2000) '"Empowered Leaders"? Perspectives on Women Heading Households in Latin America and Southern Africa', *Gender and Development*, vol. 8 no. 3, pp. 40–9.

de Ferranti, D. et al. (2000) *Securing Our Future in a Global Economy* (Washington, DC: World Bank).

De Gregorio, J. (1993) 'Inflation, Taxation, and Long Run Growth', *Journal of Monetary Economics*, vol. 31, pp. 271–98

de Haan, A. (1998) 'Social Exclusion: an Alternative Concept for the Study of Deprivation', *IDS Bulletin*, vol. XXIX, pp. 10–19.

de Janvry, A. and Sadoulte, E. (1993) 'Path Dependent Policy Reforms: from Land Reform to Rural Development in Colombia', in K. Off et al. (eds.), *The Economies of Rural Organisation* (Oxford: Oxford University Press, for the World Bank).

de Janvry, A. and Sadoulet, E. (1999) *Poverty and Inequality in Latin America: a Causal Analysis, 1970-1994* (University of California, Berkeley: IADB).

de Janvry, A. et al. (1994) *The Political Feasibility of Adjustment in Ecuador and Venezuela* (Paris: Development Centre of the Organisation for Economic Co-operation and Development).

de la Fuente, A. (1999) 'Myths of Racial Democracy: Cuba, 1900-1912', *Latin American Research Review*, vol. XXXIV, no. 3, pp. 39–74.

de la Fuente, A. (2001) *A Nation for All: Race, Inequality and Politics in Twentieth-Century Cuba* (Chapel Hill: University of North Carolina Press).

de la Peña, G. (1994) 'Rural Mobilisations in Latin America since c.1920', in L. Bethell (ed.), *The Cambridge History of Latin America*, vol. VI, part 2 (Cambridge: Cambridge University Press), pp. 379–482.

de Oliveira, F.E.B., Beltrão, Kaizô I. and Ferreira, Mônica G. (1997) *Reforma da Previdência* (Rio de Janeiro: IPEA) (Texto para discussão, 508).

de Oliveira, O. and Roberts, B. (1994) 'Urban Growth and Urban Social Structure in Latin America, 1930–1990', in L. Bethell (ed.), *The Cambridge History of Latin America*, vol. VI (Cambridge: Cambridge University Press), pp. 253–324.

De Soto, H. (1989) *The Other Path: The Invisible Revolution in the Third World* (New York: Harper Row, London: IB Tauris).

De Soto, H. (2000) *The Mystery of Capital* (New York: Basic Books).

de Souza Martins, J. (1990) 'The Political Impasse of Rural Social Movements in Amazonia', in D. Goodman and A. Hall (eds.), *The Future of Amazonia: Destruction or Sustainable Development?* (Basingstoke: Macmillan), pp. 245–63.

de Vos, J. (1995) 'El Lacandón: una introducción histórica', in J.P. Viqueira and M. Umberto Ruz (eds.), *Chiapas: los rumbos de otra historia* (Mexico City: Universidad Nacional Autónoma de México), pp. 331–61.

Deere, C.D. (1997) 'Reforming Cuban Agriculture', *Development and Change*, vol. 28 .

Deere, C.D. and León, M. (2000) *Gênero, propriedad y empoderamiento: tierra, Estado y mercado en América Latina* (Bogotá: Tercer Mundo).

Deere, C.D. and Meurs, M. (1992) 'Markets, Markets Everywhere? Understanding the Cuban Anomaly', *World Development*, vol. 20, no. 6.

Dehn, J. (2000) 'The Effects on Growth of Commodity Price Uncertainty and Shocks', *World Bank*, w.p. no. 1967.

Deininger, K. (2000) 'Making Negotiated Land Reform Work: Initial Experience from Colombia, Brazil and South Africa', *World Bank* (w.p. no. 2040).

Deininger, K. and Olinto, P. (2000) 'Asset Distribution, Inequality and Growth', World Bank (w.p. no. 2375).

Delgado, G. (1994) *Agricultura e comércio exterior: rumo da regulação estatal e suas implicações para a regulação alimentar* (Rio de Janeiro: Rede Interamericana Agricultura e Democracia) (Cadernos temáticos do Fórum Alternativo para a Agricultura Brasileira)

Delgado, G. (1997) *Previdência rural: relatório de avaliação socioeconômica* (Brasília: IPEA) (Texto para discussão, 477).

Delgado, G. and Cardoso, J.C. Jr (1999) *O idoso e a previdência rural no Brasil: a experiência recente de universalização* (Brasília: IPEA) (Texto para discussão 688).

Delgado, G. and Cardoso, J.C. Jr (2000) *Principais resultados da pesquisa domiciliar sobre a previdência rural na região sul do Brasil* (Rio de Janeiro: IPEA) (Texto para discussão, 734).

Delgado, G. and Cardoso, J.C. Jr (2001) 'Universalização de direitos sociais no Brasil: a previdência rural nos anos 90', in S. Leite (org) *Políticas públicas e agricultura no Brasil* (Porto Alegre: Editora da Universidade/UFRGS).

Delgado, G. and Schwarzer, H. (2000) 'Evolução histórico-legal e formas de financiamento da previdência rural no Brasil', in G. Delgado and J.C. Cardoso Jr. (orgs.), *A universalização de direitos sociais no Brasil: a previdência rural nos anos 90* (Brasília: IPEA), pp. 187–210.

Departamento Nacional de Planeación (DNP) (1997) *Evolución de la pobreza en Colombia* (Bogotá, Colombia).

DGEC (Dirección General de Estadísticas y Censos) (1996) *Encuesta de hogares* (San José: DGEC).

DGEC (Dirección General de Estadísticas y Censos) (1997) *Estadística vital 1996* (San José: DGEC).

Di Gropello, E. (1999) 'Educational Decentralization Models in Latin America', *CEPAL Review*, no. 68 (Aug.), pp. 155–73.

Di Tella, G. and Dornbusch, R. (eds.) (1989) *The Political Economy of Argentina, 1946-1983* (Basingstoke: Macmillan in association with St Antony's College, Oxford).

Dierckxsens, W. (1992) 'Impacto del ajuste estructural sobre la mujer trabajadora en Costa Rica', in M. Acuña-Ortega (ed.), *Cuadernos de política económica* (Heredia: Universidad Nacional de Costa Rica), pp. 2–59.

Dilla Alfonso, H. (2000) 'The Cuban Experiment: Economic Reform, Social Re-Structuring and Politics', *Latin American Perspectives*, vol. XXVII, no. 1, pp. 33–44.

DiUlio, J. Jr (1994) 'Principled Agents: the Cultural Bases of Behavior in a Federal Government Bureaucracy', *Journal of Public Administration Research and Theory*, vol. 4, no. 3 .

Dobles Oropeza, I. (1998) 'Algunos elementos sobre la violencia en la familia en Costa Rica: un estudio nacional en sectores urbanos', in E.

Rodríguez (ed.), *Violencia Doméstica en Costa Rica: Mas Allá de los Mitos* (San José: FLACSO Sede Costa Rica, Cuaderno de Ciencias Sociales no. 105), pp. 31–52.

Doebele, W. (1975) 'The Private Market and Low-Income Urbanization in Developing Countries: the "Pirate" Subdivision of Bogotá', *Harvard University, Department of City and Regional Planning Discussion Paper* D75–11.

Dollar, D and Kraay, A. (2001) 'Trade, Growth, and Poverty', Development Research Group, The World Bank, unpublished report, March.

Domínguez, J. (ed.) (1997) *Technopols: Freeing Politics and Markets in the 1980s* (University Park, PA: Pennsylvania State University Press).

Domínguez, J.I. and Lowenthal, A.F. (eds.) (1996) *Constructing Democratic Governance: Latin America and the Caribbean in the 1990s* (Baltimore: Johns Hopkins University Press).

Dore, E. (1997) 'The Holy Family: Imagined Households in Latin American History', in E. Dore (ed.), *Gender Politics in Latin America: Debates in Theory and Practice* (New York: Monthly Review Press), pp. 101–17.

Dornbusch, R. (1993) 'Introduction', in R. Dornbusch (ed.), *Policymaking in the Open Economy: Concepts and Case Studies in Economic Performance* (Oxford: World Bank/Oxford University Press), pp. 1–16.

Dornbusch, R. (ed.) (1993a) *Policymaking in the Open Economy: Concepts and Case Studies in Economic Performance* (Oxford: World Bank/Oxford University Press).

Dornbusch, R. and Edwards, S. (1991) 'The Macroeconomics of Populism', in R. Dornbusch and S. Edwards (eds.), *The Macroeconomics of Populism in Latin America* (Chicago: University of Chicago Press), pp. 7–14.

dos Santos, W.G. (1979) *Cidadania e Justiça; a política social na ordem brasileira* (Rio de Janeiro: Campus).

Draibe, S. (1985) *Rumos e metamorfoses: estado e industrialização no Brasil, 1930-1960* (Rio de Janeiro: Paz e Terra).

Drake, P.W. (1991) 'From Good Men to Good Neighbors: 1912-1932', in A.F. Lowenthal (ed.), *Exporting Democracy: the United States and Latin America* (Baltimore: Johns Hopkins University Press), pp. 3–40.

Drake, P.W. (ed.) (1994) *Money Doctors, Foreign Debts and Economic Reforms in Latin America from the 1890s to the Present* (Wilmington, Del.: SR Books).

Duarte, D. (1995) 'Asignación de recursos per cápita en la atención primaria', *Cuadernos de Economía* , vol. 95, pp. 117–24.

Duarte Quapper, D. and Zuleta Reyes, M.S. (1999) 'La Situación de Salud Primaria en Chile', unpublished manuscript.

Ducci, M.E. (1997) 'Chile: el lado obscuro de una politica de vivienda exitosa', *Revista Latinoamericana de Estudios Urbanos-Regionales (EURE)*, vol. 23, pp. 99–115.

Ducci, M.E. (2000) 'Chile: The Dark Side of a Successful Housing Policy', in J. Tulchin and A.M Garland (eds.), *Social Development in Latin America: The Politics of Reform* (Boulder: Lynne Reinner), pp. 149–73.

Dumoulin, J. (1999) 'Les brevets et les prix des medicaments. Revie de la literature', Colloque de L'Association Internationale de Droit Economique (AIDE), Brevets Pharmaceutiques, Innovation et Sante Publique, Toulouse, France, 28–30 Jan.

Duncan, K. and Rutledge, I. (1977) 'Introduction: Patterns of Agrarian Capitalism in Latin America', in K. Duncan and I. Rutledge (with C. Harding) (eds.), *Land and Labour in Latin America: Essays on the Development of Agrarian Capitalism in the Nineteenth and Twentieth Centuries* (Cambridge: Cambridge University Press).

Duncan, S. and Edwards, R. (1994) 'Lone Mothers and Paid Work: State Policies, Social Discourses and Neighbourhood Processes' (Gender Institute, London School of Economics), mimeo.

Durand-Lasserve, A. (1997) 'Regularizing Land Markets', *Habitat Debate*, vol. 3, no. 2, pp. 11–12.

Durston, J. (1999) 'Building Community Social Capital', *CEPAL Review*, vol. 69, pp. 103–118.

Dwyer, D.J. (1975) *People and Housing in Third World Cities* (Harlow: Longman).

Eaton, K. (2001) 'Decentralisation, Democratisation and Liberalisation: the History of Revenue Sharing in Argentina, 1934-1999', *Journal of Latin American Studies*, vol. XXXIII, no. 1 (2001), pp. 1–28.

Eckstein, S. (ed.) (1989) *Power and Popular Protest: Latin American Social Movements* (Berkeley: University of California Press).

Eckstein, S. (1990) 'Urbanisation Revisited: Inner-City Slums of Hope and Squatter Settlements of Despair', *World Development*, vol. XVIII, no. 2, pp. 165–81.

Eckstein, S. (1994) *Back from the Future: Cuba under Castro* (Princeton: Princeton University Press).

Eckstein, S. (1998) 'Communist States as Ideocracies? Lessons from Cuba', in S. Mainwaring and A. Valenzuela (eds.), *Politics, Society and Democracy in Latin America* (Boulder: Westview Press), pp. 49–70.

ECLAC (Economic Commission for Latin America and the Caribbean) and UNESCO (United Nations Educational, Scientific, and Cultural Organization) (1992) *Education and Knowledge: Basic Pillars of Changing Production Patterns with Social Equity* (Chile).

ECLAC (Economic Commission for Latin America and the Caribbean), see also CEPAL and UN Economic Commission for Latin America and the Caribbean.

Edwards, S. (1995) *Crisis and Reform in Latin America: from Despair to Hope* (Oxford: Published for the World Bank [by] Oxford University Press).

Edwards, S. and Lustig, N. (eds.) (1997) *Labor Markets in Latin America: Combining Social Protection with Market Flexibility* (Washington, DC: Brookings Institution Press).

EIU (Economist Intelligence Unit) (1999) *Healthcare Latin America* (London: The Economic Intelligence Unit).

EIU (Economist Intelligence Unit) (2000) *Cuba. Country Report*, Nov. 2000 (London: The Economic Intelligence Unit).

EIU (Economist Intelligence Unit) (2001) *Cuba. Country Report*, Feb. 2001 (London: The Economist Intelligence Unit).

Emmerij L. (ed.) (1997) *Economic and Social Development into the XXI Century* (Washington, DC: Inter-American Development Bank).

Escobar, A. and Álvarez S.E. (eds.) (1992) *The Making of Social Movements in Latin America: Identity, Strategy and Democracy* (Boulder: Westview Press).

Escobar, A. (1999) 'An Ecology of Difference: Equality and Conflict in a Globalized World', in L. Arizpe (ed.) *World Culture Report* 2 (Paris: UNESCO)

Esping-Andersen, G. (1990) *The Three Worlds of Welfare Capitalism* (Cambridge: Polity Press).

Esping Andersen, G. (1996) 'After the Golden Age? Welfare State Dilemmas in a Global Economy', in G. Esping-Andersen (ed.), *Welfare States in Transition. National Adaptations in Global Economies* (London: Sage/UNRISD).

Esping-Andersen G. (ed.) (1996) *Welfare States in Transition: National*

Adaptations in Global Economies (London: Sage).

Espínola, V. (ed.) (1994) *La construcción de lo local en los sistemas educativos descentralizados* (Santiago: CIDE).

Estudio Binacional México-Estados Unidos sobre Migración (1997) Several authors, governments of Mexico and USA.

Evans, P. (1979) *Dependent Development: the Alliance of Multinationals, the State and Local Capital in Brazil* (Princeton: Princeton University Press)

Evans, P. (1995) *Embedded Autonomy: States and Industrial Transformation* (Princeton: Princeton University Press).

Evans, P. (1996) 'Government Action, Social Capital and Development', *World Development*, vol. 24, no. 6, pp. 1119–32.

Fabienke, R. (2000) 'Labor Markets and Income Distribution during Crisis and Reform', in C. Brundenius and J. Weeks, *Globalization and Third World Socialism: Cuba and Vietnam* (Basingstoke: Macmillan).

Fajnzylber, F. (1983) *La industrialización trunca* (Mexico City: Centro de Economía Transnacional/Editorial Nueva Imagen).

Fajnzylber, F. (1990) *Unavoidable Industrial Restructuring in Latin America* (Durham, NC: Duke University Press).

Falkingham, J. and Hills, J. (eds.) (1995) *The Dynamic of Welfare: the Welfare State and the Life Cycle* (New York, London: Prentice Hall/Harvester Wheatsheaf).

Fauné, M.A. (1997) 'Costa Rica: las inequidades de género en el marco de la apertura comercial y la reestructuración productiva. Análisis a nivel macro, mesio, micro', in D. Elson, M.A. Fauné, J. Gideon, M. Gutiérrez, A. López de Mazier and E. Sacayon, *Crecer con la mujer: oportunidades para el desarrollo económico centroamericano* (San José: Embajada Real de los Países Bajos), pp. 51–126.

Fausto, A (1999) *A Concise History of Brazil* (Cambridge: Cambridge University Press).

Fedelonjas (1988) *El valor del suelo urbano en Bogotá, 1959–1988* (Bogotá: Federación Colombiana de Lonjas de Propiedad Raíz).

Feijóo, M.C. (1999) 'De pobres mujeres a mujeres pobres', in M. González de la Rocha (ed.), *Divergencias del modelo tradicional: hogares de jefatura femenina en América Latina* (Mexico City: Centro de Investigaciones y Estudios Superiores en Antropología Social), pp. 155–62.

Ferguson, B. (1999) 'Micro-Finance of Housing: a Key to Housing the

Low or Moderate-Income Majority?', *Environment and Urbanization*, vol. 11, pp. 185–99.

Ferguson, B., Rubinstein, J. and Dominguez-Vial, V. (1996) 'The Design of Direct Demand Subsidy Programs for Housing in Latin America', *Review of Urban and Regional Development Studies*, vol. 8, pp. 202–19.

Ferlie, E. et al. (1996) *The New Public Management in Action* (Oxford: Oxford University Press).

Fernandes, E. and Varley, A. (eds.) (1998) *Illegal Cities: Law and Urban Change in Developing Countries* (London: Zed Books).

Fernández Kelly, M.P. and Portes, A. (1992) 'Continent on the Move: Immigrants and Refugees in the Americas', in A. Stepan (ed.), *Americas: New Interpretive Essays* (Oxford: Oxford University Press), pp. 248–74.

Fernández, O. (1992) 'Qué valores valen hoy en Costa Rica?', in J.M. Villasuso (ed.), *El nuevo rostro de Costa Rica* (Heredia: Centro de Estudios Democráticos de América Latina).

Fernández, R. and Rodrik, D. (1991) 'Resistance to Reform: Status Quo Bias in the Presence of Individual-Specific Uncertainty', *American Economic Review*, vol. 81 .

Ferriol Muruaga, A. (1997) 'Política social cubana: situación y transformaciones', *Temas*, no.11 (Havana).

Ferriol Muruaga, A. et al. (1998) 'Efectos de políticas macroeconómicas y sociales sobre los niveles de pobreza: el caso de Cuba en los años noventa', in E. Ganuza, L. Taylor and S. Morley (eds.), *Política macroeconómica y pobreza en América latina y el Caribe* (Madrid: Mundi Prensa Libros).

Ferriol Muruaga, A. et al. (1998a) *Cuba: crisis, ajuste y situación social, 1990–96* (Havana: Editorial de Ciencias Sociales).

Ffrench-Davis, R. (1973) *Políticas económicas en Chile, 1952-1970* (Santiago: Ediciones Nueva Universidad).

Ffrench-Davis, R. (1988) 'An Outline of a Neostructuralist Approach', *CEPAL Review*, vol. XXXIV, pp. 37–44.

Ffrench-Davis, R., Muñoz G, O. and Palma J.G. (1994) 'The Latin American Economies, 1950-1990', in L. Bethell (ed.), *The Cambridge History of Latin America*, vol. VI, part 1 (Cambridge: Cambridge University Press), pp. 159–252.

Fields, S. (1991) 'Growth and Income Distribution', in G. Psacharopoulos (ed.), *Essays on Poverty, Equity and Growth* (Oxford: Pergamon Press).

Figueras, M. (2000) *Colaboración internacional: doctrina y política cubanas*, paper presented to Latin American Studies Association XXII International Congress, Miami, 16–18 March.

Figueredo, J. and de Haan, A. (eds.) (1998) *Social Exclusion: the Way Forward in Policy and Research* (Geneva).

Filmus, D. (1998) 'La descentralizión educativa en Argentina: elementos para el análisis de un proceso abierto', *Reforma y Democracia* (Caracas), no. 10 (Feb.), pp. 149–172.

Fischer, S. (1991) 'Growth, Macroeconomics, and Development', *NBER Macroeconomics Annual*, vol. 6, pp. 329–64

Fischer, S. (1993) 'The Role of Macroeconomic Factors in Growth', *Journal of Monetary Economics*, vol. 32, pp. 485–512.

Fischer, S. (1999) 'A View from the IMF', in V. Tanzi, K. Chu and S. Gapta (eds.), *Economic Policy and Equity* (Washington, DC: IMF), pp. 13–18.

FitzGerald, E.V.K. (1994) 'ECLA and the Formation of Latin American Economic Doctrine', in D. Rock (ed.), *Latin America in the 1940s: War and Postwar Transitions* (Berkeley: University of California Press), pp. 89–108.

Folbre, N. (1991) 'Women on their Own: Global Patterns of Female Headship', in R.S. Gallin and A. Ferguson (eds), *The Women and International Development Annual*, vol. 2 (Boulder: Westview), pp. 69–126.

Foster, G.M. (1965) 'The Peasants and the Image of Limited Good', *American Anthropologist*, vol. LXII, no. 2, pp. 121–46.

Foweraker, J. (1981) *The Struggle for Land: a Political Economy of the Pioneer Frontier in Brazil from 1930 to the Present Day* (Cambridge: Cambridge University Press).

Foweraker, J. (1993) *Popular Mobilisation in Mexico: the Teachers' Movement, 1977-87* (Cambridge: Cambridge University Press).

Foweraker, J. (1994) 'Measuring Citizenship in Mexico', in M Serrano and V. Bulmer-Thomas (eds.), *Rebuilding the State: Mexico after Salinas* (London: Institute of Latin American Studies), pp. 79–98.

Foweraker, J. and Craig, A. (eds.) (1990) *Popular Movements and Political Change in Latin America* (Boulder: Lynne Rienner).

Foweraker, J. and Landman, T. (1997) *Citizenship Rights and Social Movements: a Comparative and Statistical Analysis* (Oxford: Oxford University Press).

Fox J. (1994) 'The Difficult Transition from Clientilism to Citizenship', *World Politics*, vol. XLVI, no. 2, pp. 151–84.

Fox, J. (1996) 'A política e as novas formas de organização camponesa na América Latina', in Z. Navarro (org.), *Política, protesto e cidadania no campo; as lutas sociais dos colonos e trabalhadores rurais no Rio Grande do Sul* (Porto Alegre: Editora da Universidade/UFRGS), pp. 15–28.

Foxley, A., Aninat, E. and Arellano, J.P. (1980) *Las desigualdades económicas y la acción del estado* (Mexico City: Fondo de Cultura Económica).

Franco, R. (1996) 'Social Policy Paradigms in Latin America', *CEPAL Review*, no. 58 (April), pp. 9–23.

Fraser, N. and Gordon, L. (1994) 'Civil Citizenship against Social Citizenship', in B. van Steenbergen (ed.), *The Condition of Citizenship* (London: Sage), pp. 90–107.

Frenk, J. (ed.) (1997) *Observatorio de la salud. Necesidades, servicios, políticas* (Mexico City: Fundación para la Salud).

Frenk, J. (1998) '20 años de salud en México', *Nexus* (Mexico) Jan., pp. 85–91.

Frenk, J. (2000) 'Structured Pluralism: Towards an Innovative Model for Health System Reform in Latin America', in P. Lloyd-Sherlock (ed.) *Healthcare Reform and Poverty in Latin America* (London: Institute of Latin American Studies).

Frenkel, R. and O'Donnell, G. (1994) 'The "Stabilization Programs" of the International Monetary Fund and Their Internal Impacts', in P.W. Drake (ed.), *Money Doctors, Foreign Debts and Economic Reforms in Latin America from the 1890s to the Present* (Wilmington: SR Books), pp. 159–74.

Frenkel, R. and González Rosada, M. (1999) 'Liberalización del balance de pagos. Efectos sobre el crecimiento del empleo y los ingresos en la Argentina', *Serie de Documentos de Economía*, no. 11, Centro de Investigaciones en Economía, Universidad de Palermo-CEDES.

Fuentes Hernández, A. (1999) *Reforma judicial en América Latina: una tarea inconclusa* (Bogotá: Corporación Excelencia en la justicia).

Fuller, B. and Rivarola, M. (1998) *Nicaragua's Experiment to Decentralize Schools: Views of Parents, Teachers and Directors* (Washington: World Bank, working paper series on impact evaluation of education reforms, no. 5).

Fundación Friedrich Ebert (1998) *Economía social de mercado: su dimensión social* (Caracas: Editorial Nueva Sociedad).

Gajardo, M. (1999) *Reformas educativas en América Latina: balance de una década* (Santiago: PREAL).

Galbraith, J.K. (1979) *The Nature of Mass Poverty* (New York: Oxford University Press).

Gamus, E. (1998) 'La trayectoria de la descentralización educativa en Venezuela: nuevos desafíos', paper presented at the 3rd International Congress of the Centro Latinoamericano de Administración para el Desarrollo (CLAD), Madrid, 14–17 Oct.

García Cruz, M. (1962) *Evolución mexicana del ideario de la seguridad social* (Mexico City: Instituto de Investigaciones Sociales, UNAM).

García Méndez, E. and Salazar, M.C. (comps.) (1999) *Nuevas perspectivas para erradicar el trabajo infantil en América Latina: seminario regional post-Oslo* (Bogotá).

Garfield, R. and Holtz, T. (2000) 'Health System Reforms in Cuba in the 1990s', in P. Lloyd-Sherlock (ed.), *Healthcare Reform and Poverty in Latin America* (London: Institute of Latin American Studies).

Geddes, B. (1994) *Politicians' Dilemma: Reforming the State in Latin America* (Berkeley: University of California Press).

Gelb, A. et al. (1989) *Oil Windfalls. Blessing or Curse?* (New York: Oxford University Press for the World Bank)

Geldstein, R. (1997) *Mujeres jefas de hogar: familia, pobreza y género* (Buenos Aires: UNICEF–Argentina).

Gereffi, G. (1990) 'Paths of Industrialization: an Overview', in G. Gereffi and D.L. Wyman (eds.), *Manufacturing Miracles: Paths of Industrialization in Latin America and East Asia* (Princeton: Princeton University Press), pp. 3–31.

Germani, G. (1968) *Política y sociedad en una época de transición* (Buenos Aires: Editorial Paidós).

Germani, G. (1973) *El concepto de marginalidad* (Buenos Aires: Ediciones Nueva Visión).

Gershberg, A.I. (1998) 'Fostering Effective Parental Participation in Education: Lessons from a Comparison of Reform Processes in Nicaragua and Mexico,' *World Development*, vol. 27, no. 4.

Gershberg, A.I. (1998a) *Decentralization and Recentralization: Lessons from the Social Sectors in Mexico and Nicaragua. Final Report*, submitted to the Inter-American Development Bank, RE2/S02, 15 Jan.

Gershberg, A.I. (1999) 'Decentralization, Citizen Participation, and the Role of the State: The Autonomous Schools Program in Nicaragua', *Latin American Perspectives*, vol. 26, no. 4 (July), pp. 8–38.

Gershberg, A.I. (1999a) 'Education "Decentralization" Processes in Mexico and Nicaragua: Legislative versus Ministry-Led Reform Strategies,' *Comparative Education*, vol. 35, no. 1.

Gerstenfeld, P. (1998) 'Oportunidades de bienestar y movilidad social en América Latina: percepciones y realidades', in R. Franco and D. Rivarola (eds.), *Inequidad y política social* (Asunción, Paraguay)

Gerstenfeld, P. et al. (1995) *Comparación regional del impacto de las características del hogar en el logro escolar*, CEPAL, Serie Políticas Sociales, no. 9 (Santiago de Chile: CEPAL, LC/L.924, Dec.).

Giddens, A. (1999) 'Social Change in Britain: Inequality and Social Democracy', Tenth ESRC Annual Lecture, available on-line at http://www.esrc.ac.uk/esrclecture10/socialchange.html.

Giddens, A. (2000) *The Third Way and Its Critics* (Cambridge: Polity Press).

Gilbert, A.G. (1981) 'Pirates and Invaders: Land Acquisition in Urban Colombia and Venezuela', *World Development*, vol. 9, pp. 657–78.

Gilbert, A.G. (1983) 'The Tenants of Self-Help Housing: Choice and Constraint in the Housing Markets of Less Developed Countries', *Development and Change*, vol. 14, pp. 449–77.

Gilbert, A.G. (1988) 'Home Enterprises in Poor Urban Settlements: Constraints, Potentials, and Policy Options', *Regional Development Dialogue*, vol. 9, pp. 21–37.

Gilbert, A. (1991a) *Landlord and Tenant: Housing the Poor in Urban Mexico* (London: Routledge).

Gilbert, A. (1991b) 'Renting and the Transition to Owner Occupation in Latin American Cities', *Habitat International*, vol. XV, no. 1, pp. 87–99

Gilbert, A. (1992) *Cities, Poverty and Development: Urbanization in the Third World* (Oxford: Oxford University Press).

Gilbert, A. (1994) 'Third World Cities: Poverty, Employment, Gender Roles and the Environment during a Time of Restructuring', *Urban Studies*, vol. XXXI, pp. 605-33.

Gilbert, A.G. (1996) 'Land, Housing and Infrastructure in Latin America's Major Cities', in A.G. Gilbert (ed.) *The Mega-city in Latin America* (Tokyo: United Nations University Press), pp. 73–109.

Gilbert, A. (1997) 'Employment and Poverty during Economic Restructuring: the Case of Bogotá, Colombia', *Urban Studies*, vol. XXXIV, pp. 1047–70.

Gilbert, A. (1998) 'Colombian Housing Policy during the 1990s', in E. Posada-Carbó (ed.), *Colombia: The Politics of Reforming the State* (London: Macmillan/Institute of Latin American Studies), pp. 155–82.

Gilbert, A.G. (1998a) *The Latin American City* (London: Latin America Bureau and New York: Monthly Review Press), revised and expanded edition.

Gilbert, A.G. (1999) 'A Home is for Ever? Residential Mobility and Home Ownership in Self-Help Settlements', *Environment and Planning A*, vol. 31, pp. 1073–91.

Gilbert, A.G. (2000) 'Financing Self-Help Housing: Evidence from Bogotá, Colombia', *International Planning Studies*, vol. 5, pp. 165–90.

Gilbert, A. (2001) 'The Origins and Evolution of Housing Subsidies in Chile', forthcoming.

Gilbert, A. and Varley, A. (1989) *The Mexican Landlord: Rental Housing in Guadalajara and Puebla* (London: Institute of Latin American Studies).

Gilbert, A.G. and Varley, A. (1991) *Landlord and Tenant: Housing the Poor in Urban Mexico* (London: Routledge).

Gilbert, A.G. and Gugler, J. (1992) *Cities, Poverty and Development: Urbanization in the Third World* (Oxford: Oxford University Press), second edition.

Gilbert, A.G. and Healey, P. (1985) *The Political Economy of Land: Urban Development in an Oil Economy* (Aldershot: Gower Press).

Gilbert, A.G. and Ward, P.M. (1985) *Housing, the State and the Poor: Policy and Practice in Three Latin American Cities* (Cambridge: Cambridge University Press).

Gilbert, A.G., Camacho, O.O., Coulomb, R. and Necochea, A. (1993) *In Search of a Home: Rental and Shared Housing in Latin America* (London: UCL Press and Albuquerque: The University of Arizona Press).

Gill, L. (1997) 'Relocating Class: Ex-Miners and Neoliberalism in Bolivia', *Critique of Anthropology*, vol. 17, no. 3, pp. 293–312.

Giordano, O. and Colina, J. (2000) 'Economía política de las reformas', in H. Sánchez and G. Zuleta (eds.), *La hora de los usuarios. Reflexiones sobre economía política de las reformas de salud* (Washington, DC: Banco Interamericano de Desarrollo, Centro de Estudios Salud y Futuro).

Girault, C. (1991) 'Society and Politics in Haiti: the Divorce between the State and the Nation', in C. Clarke (ed.), *Society and Politics in the Caribbean* (Basingstoke: Macmillan/St Antony's College Oxford), pp. 185–206.

Gledhill, J. (1994) *Power and its Disguises: Anthropological Perspectives on Politics* (London: Pluto Press).

Gledhill, J. (1995) *Neoliberalism, Transnationalisation and Rural Poverty: a Case Study of Michoacán* (Boulder: Westview Press).

Gledhill, J. (1997) 'Liberalism, Socio-Economic Rights and the Politics of Identity: from Moral Economy to Indigenous Rights', in R. Wilson (ed.), *Human Rights, Culture and Context: Anthropological Approaches* (London: Pluto Press), pp. 70–110.

Gledhill, J. (1999) 'Official Masks and Shadow Powers: Towards an Anthropology of the Dark Side of the State', *Urban Anthropology*, vol. 28, nos. 3–4, pp. 199–251.

Gledhill, J. (2000) 'Disappearing the Poor? A Critique of the New Wisdoms of Social Democracy in an Age of Globalisation', paper presented to invited session *Global Capitalism, Neoliberal Policy and Poverty*, Society for the Anthropology of North America, Association for Latina and Latino Anthropologists, 99th Annual Meeting of the American Anthropological Association, San Francisco, 16 Nov.

Glennerster, H. and Hills, J. (eds.) (1998) *The State of Welfare: the Economics of Social Spending* (Oxford: Oxford University Press).

Gobierno de Costa Rica (1998) *Plan de solidaridad: nuestro compromiso con la solidaridad y el desarrollo humano* (San José: Gobierno de Costa Rica).

Golbert, L. and Kessler, G. (2000) 'Cohesión social y violencia urbana. Un estudio exploratorio sobre la Argentina a fines de los 90' (Buenos Aires: CEDES), mimeo.

Goldani, A.M. (1989) *Women's Transitions: the Intersection of Female Life Course, Family and Demographic Transition in Twentieth-Century Brazil*, PhD thesis, University of Austin, Texas.

Gomáriz, E. (1997) *Introducción a los estudios sobre la masculinidad* (San José: Centro Nacional para el Desarrollo de la Mujer y Familia).

Gomes, C. (1997) 'Seguridad social y envejecimiento: la crisis vecina', in C. Rabell (ed.), *Los retos de la población* (México: FLACSO).

Gomes, C. (1998) 'Vida em familia e institucionalização em um contexto de envelhecimento populacional – o caso do Mexico', in *Revista Brasileira de Estudos de População*, vol. 15, no. 1. (Brasilia), pp. 57–78.

Gomes, C. (2000) *Life Course, Households and Institutions – Brazil and Mexico*, XXXVII International CFR-Seminar. Uppsala.

Gómez, J. and Julio, J.M. (2001) 'Transmission Mechanisms and Inflation Targeting: the Case of Colombia´s Disinflation', Banco de la República, *Borradores Semanales de Economía*, no. 168.

Gómez-Dantés, O. (2000) 'Health Reform and Policies for the Poor in México', in P. Lloyd-Sherlock (ed.), *Healthcare Reform and Poverty in Latin America* (London: Institute of Latin American Studies), pp. 128–42.

González, L. (1999) 'The Evolution of Postsecondary Education in Chile', *International Higher Education*, no. 14, pp. 17–18, The Boston College Center for International Higher Education.

González, M.J. (1985) *Plantations, Agriculture and Social Control in Northern Peru, 1875–1930* (Austin: University of Texas Press).

González-Block, M. and Ruiz, A. (1998) 'Institutional Reform of Health Services for the Uninsured Poor in Mexico', mimeo.

González-Block, M.A., Leyva, R., Zapata, O. et al. (1989) 'Health Services Decentralization in Mexico: Formulation, Implementation, and Results of Policy', *Health Policy and Planning*, vol. 4, pp. 301–15.

González de la Rocha, M. (1986) *Los recursos de la pobreza: familias de bajos ingresos de Guadalajara* (Guadalajara, Mexico: CIESAS, El Colegio de Jalisco).

González de la Rocha, M. (1991) 'Economic Crisis, Domestic Reorganisation and Women's Work in Guadalajara, Mexico', *Bulletin of Latin American Research*, vol. VII, no. 2, pp. 207–23.

González de la Rocha, M. (1994) *The Resources of Poverty: Women and Survival in a Mexican City* (Oxford: Blackwell).

González de la Rocha, M. (1995) 'Social Restructuring in Two Mexican Cities: an Analysis of Domestic Groups in Guadalajara and Monterrey', *European Journal of Development Research*, vol.7, no. 2, pp. 389–406.

González de la Rocha, M. (1997) 'Pobreza urbana: carencia de múltiples facetas. Reflexiones sobre los nuevos patrones de migración internacional y la sobrevivencia en Guadalajara México', Paper for Conference on Mexico and the United States in the Context of Global Migration, Riverside, CA, Oct.

González-Rosetti, A. and Bossert, T. (2000) *Enhancing the Political Feasibility of Health Reform: a Comparative Analysis of Chile, Colombia, and Mexico* (Cambridge, Mass.: Harvard School of Public Health).

Goody, J. (1969) *Comparative Studies in Kinship* (London: Allen & Urwin).

Goody, J. (1972) 'Evolution of the Family', in P. Laslett and R. Wall (eds.), *Household and Family in the Past Time* (Cambridge: Cambridge University Press).

Gorenstein, O. (1981) in Assembléia Legislativa do Estado do Rio Grande do Sul, *Seminário Nacional 'A questão da terra'* (Porto Alegre: Comissão de Agricultura e Pecuária, Assembléia Legislativa do Estado do Rio Grande do Sul), pp. 237–9.

Gottieb, S. (2000) 'Drug Firms Use Legal Loopholes to Safeguard Brand Names', *British Medical Journal*, vol. 321, p. 320.

Graham, C. (1994) *Safety Nets, Politics and the Poor: Transitions to Market Economies* (Washington, DC: Brookings Institution).

Graham, C. (1998) *Private Markets for Public Goods: Raising the Stakes in Economic Reform* (Washington, DC: The Brookings Institution).

Graham, C. and Sabot, R. (eds.) (1998) *Beyond Tradeoffs: Market Reform and Equitable Growth in Latin America* (Washington, DC: Inter-American Development Bank).

Graham, C., Grindle, M., Lora, E. and Seddon, J. (1999) *Improving the Odds: Political Strategies for Institutional Reform in Latin America* (Washington, DC: Inter-American Development Bank).

Graham, R. (ed.) (1989) *The Idea of Race in Latin America* (Austin: University of Texas Press).

Granovetter, M. (1973) 'The Strength of Weak Ties', *American Journal of Sociology*, vol. 78 , pp. 1360–80.

Graziano da Silva, J., Balsadi, O.V. and Del Grossi, M.E. (1997) 'O emprego rural e a mercantilização do espaço agrário', *São Paulo em Perspectiva*, vol. 11, no. 2 , pp. 50–64.

Gregory, P. (1986) *The Myth of Market Failure: Employment and the Labor Market in Mexico* (Baltimore: Johns Hopkins Press).

Griffin, C. (1999) 'Empowering Mayors, Hospital Directors, or Patients? The Decentralization of Health Care', in S.J. Burki, G. Perry and W. Dillinger (eds.) *Beyond the Center. Decentralizing the State* (Washington, DC: The World Bank), pp. 75–86.

Griffith-Jones, S. (ed.) (1988) *Managing World Debt* (Brighton: Harvester Wheatsheaf).

Griffith-Jones, S. and Sunkel, O. (1986) *Debt and Development Crises in Latin America: the End of an Illusion* (Oxford: Clarendon).

Griffith-Jones, S. et al. (1996) 'An Evaluation of IDB Lending 1976–92' (Brighton: IDS).

Grimes, O. (1976) *Housing for Low-Income Urban Families: Economics and Policy in the Developing World* (Baltimore: Johns Hopkins University Press).

Grindle, M. (ed.) (1980) *Politics and Policy Implementation in the Third World* (Princeton: Princeton University Press).

Grindle, M. (1991) 'The New Political Economy: Positive Economics and Negative Politics', in G. Meier (ed.), *Politics and Policy Making in Developing Countries: Perspectives on the New Political Economy* (San Francisco: ICS Press).

Grindle, M. (1996) *Challenging the State: Crisis and Innovation in Latin America and Africa* (Cambridge: Cambridge University Press).

Grindle, M. (ed.) (1997) *Getting Good Government: Capacity-Building in the Public Sectors of Developing Countries* (Cambridge, Mass.: Harvard Institute for International Development).

Grindle, M. (1997a) 'Divergent Cultures? When Public Organizations Perform Well in Developing Countries,' *World Development*, vol. 25, no. 4.

Grindle, M. (2000a) *Audacious Reforms: Institutional Invention and Democracy in Latin America* (Baltimore: Johns Hopkins University Press).

Grindle, M. (2000b) 'The Social Agenda and the Politics of Reform in Latin America', in J. Tulchin and A. Garland (eds.), *Social Development in Latin America: the Politics of Reform* (Boulder: Lynne Rienner).

Grindle, M. (2000c) *Surviving across Divides: Education Reform in Bolivia* (Washington, DC: Inter-American Development Bank, INDES).

Grindle, M. and Thomas, J. (1991) *Public Choices and Policy Change: The Political Economy of Reform in Developing Countries* (Baltimore: Johns Hopkins University Press).

Gros, C. (1991) *Colombia indígena: identidad cultural y cambio social* (Bogotá: CEREC).

Gros, C. (1997) *Pour une sociologie des populations indiennes et paysannes de l'Amérique Latine* (Paris: Harmattan).

Gros, C. (1998) 'El movimiento indígena: del nacional populismo al neoliberalismo', in H-J. König (ed.), *El indio como sujeto y objeto de la historia latinoamericana: pasado y presente* (Frankfurt: Vervuert), pp. 183–98.

Grosh, M.E. (1990) 'Social Spending in Latin America: the Story of the 1980s', *World Bank* (d.p. no. 106).

Grundy, E. (1999) 'Co-Residence of Mid Life Children with their Elderly Parents in England and Wales: Changes between 1981 and 1991', Annual Meeting of the Population Association of America, New York.

Grupo Agenda Política de Mujeres Costarricenses (1997) *Agenda política de mujeres costarricenses* (San José: Grupo Agenda Política de Mujeres Costarricenses).

Gudmundson, L. (1986) *Costa Rica Before Coffee: Society and Economy on the Eve of the Export Boom* (Baton Rouge: Louisiana State University Press).

Guedes, T., Lobo, T. and Walker, R. (1997) *Gestión descentralizada de la educación en el Estado de Minas Gerais, Brasil* (Washington: World Bank).

Güendel, L. (1999) Nutrición y derechos de la niñez', in UNICEF–Costa Rica (ed.), *Nuestro derecho a la nutrición y salud en Costa Rica* (San José: UNICEF–Costa Rica), pp. 4–15.

Güendel, L. and González, M. (1998) 'Integration, Human Rights and Social Policy in the Context of Human Poverty', in UNICEF (ed.), *Adolescence, Child Rights and Urban Poverty in Costa Rica* (San José: UNICEF/HABITAT), pp. 17–31.

Guerra, F-X. (1994) 'The Spanish-American Tradition of Representation and its European Roots', *Journal of Latin American Studies*, vol. XXVI, no. 1, pp. 1–35.

Gutelman, M. (1978) *Estructuras y reformas agrarias* (Barcelona: Fontamara).

Gutiérrez de Taliercio, C. (2000) 'Preconditions for Reform in Latin America: Data Analysis' (unpublished paper, Kennedy School of Government).

Gwatkin, D.R. (2001) 'Poverty and Inequalities in Health within Developing Countries: Filling the Information Gap', in D.A. Leon and G. Walt (eds.), *Poverty, Inequality and Health: an International Perspective* (Oxford: Oxford University Press), pp. 217–46.

Gwynne, R. and Kay, C. (1999) *Latin America Transformed* (London: Arnold).

Gwynne, R. and Kay, C. (2000) 'Views from the Periphery: Faces of Neoliberalism in Latin America', *Third World Quarterly*, vol. 21, no. 1, pp. 141–56.

Habermas, J. (1973) *Problemas de legitimación en el capitalismo tardío* (Buenos Aires: Amorrortu Editores).

Habermas, J. (1994) 'Citizenship and National Identity', in B. van Steenbergen (ed.), *The Condition of Citizenship* (London: Sage), pp. 20–35.

Haggard, S. and Kaufman, R. (eds.) (1992) *The Politics of Economic Adjustment* (Princeton: Princeton University Press).

Hale, C.A. (1986) 'Political and Social Ideas in Latin America, 1870-1930', in L. Bethell (ed.), *The Cambridge History of Latin America: Vol. IV: c.1870-1930* (Cambridge: Cambridge University Press), pp. 367–442.

Hall, A. (1986) 'Education, Schooling and Participation', in J. Midgley et al. (eds.), *Community Participation, Social Development and the State* (London: Methuen), pp. 70–86.

Hall, A. (1997) *Sustaining Amazonia: Grassroots Action for Productive Conservation* (Manchester: Manchester University Press).

Hall, A. (ed.) (2000) *Amazonia at the Crossroads: the Challenge of Sustainable Development* (London: Institute of Latin American Studies).

Halperín Donghi, T. (1999) 'Argentines Ponder the Burden of the Past', in J. Adelman (ed.), *Colonial Legacies. The Problem of Persistence in Latin American History* (New York: Routledge), pp. 151–74.

Hamberg, J. (1990) 'Cuban Housing Policy', in S. Halebsky and J. Kirk (eds.), *Transformation and Struggle. Cuba Faces the 1990s* (New York and London: Praeger).

Hamilton, N. (1982) *The Limits of State Autonomy: Post-revolutionary Mexico* (Princeton: Princeton University Press).

Hanchard, M. (ed.) (1999) *Racial Politics in Contemporary Brazil* (Durham, NC: Duke University Press).

Hanson, M. (1974) 'Organizational Bureaucracy in Latin America and the Legacy of Spanish Colonialism', *Journal of Interamerican Studies and World Affairs*, vol. 16, no. 2, pp. 199–219.

Hanson, M. (1997) 'Educational Decentralization: Issues and Challenges', *Occasional Paper Series*, no. 9, CINDE–PREAL (Programme to Promote Educational Reform in Latin America and the Caribbean).

Haramoto, E. (1983) 'Políticas de vivienda social: experiencia chilena en las tres últimas décadas', in J. MacDonald (ed.) *Vivienda social: reflexiones y experiencias* (Santiago: Corporación de Promoción Universitaria), pp. 75–152.

Harberger, A.C. (1993) 'The Other Side of Tax Reform', in R. Dornbusch (ed.), *Policymaking in the Open Economy: Concepts and Case Studies in Economic Performance* (Oxford: Oxford University Press for the World Bank), pp. 149–71.

Harberger, A. (1993a) 'Secrets of Success: a Handful of Heroes', *American Economic Review*, vol. 83 (May).

Hardiman, I. and Midgley, J. (1982) *The Social Dimension of Development: Social Policy and Planning in the Third World* (London: Wiley and Sons).

Hardoy, J.E. and Satterthwaite, D. (1981) *Shelter: Need and Response – Housing, Land and Settlement Policies in Seventeen Third World Nations* (Chichester: Wiley).

Hardoy, J.E. and Satterthwaite, D. (1989) *Squatter Citizen: Life in the Urban Third World* (London: Earthscan).

Hardt, M. and Negri, A. (2000) *Empire* (Cambridge, Mass. and London: Harvard University Press).

Harms, H. (1982) 'Historical Perspectives on the Practice and Purpose of Self-Help Housing', in P.M. Ward (ed.), *Self Help Housing : a Critique* (London : Mansell), pp. 15–55.

Harris, O. (1981) 'Households as Natural Units', in K.Young, C. Wolkowitz and R. McCullagh (eds), *Of Marriage and the Market* (London: CSE Books), pp. 48–67.

Harris, O. (2000) *To Make the Earth Bear Fruit: Ethnographic Essays on Fertility, Work and Gender in Highland Bolivia* (London: Institute of Latin American Studies).

Harris, N. (1995) *The New Untouchables: Immigration and the New World Worker* (London: Penguin).

Harriss, J., Hunter, J. and Lewis, C.M. (eds.) (1997) *The New Institutional Economics and the Third World* (London: Routledge).

Hart, K. (1973) 'Informal Income Opportunities and Urban Employment in Ghana', *Journal of Modern African Studies*, vol. 11, pp. 61–89.

Hart, K. (2000) *The Memory Bank: Money in an Unequal World* (London: Profile Books).

Harvey, N. (ed.) (1993) *Mexico: Dilemmas of Transition* (London: Institute of Latin American Studies, British Academic Press).

Harvey, N. (1998) *The Chiapas Rebellion: The Struggle for Land and Democracy* (Durham, NC and London: Duke University Press).

Heinick, I., Schenkel, E.P. and Vidal, X. (1998) 'Medicamentos de venta libre en Brasil', *Revista Panamericana de Salud Pública*, vol. 3, pp. 385–91.

Held, G. (2000) *Políticas de viviendas de interés social orientadas al mercado: experiencias recientes con subsidios a la demanda en Chile, Costa Rica y Colombia*, CEPAL Serie Financiamiento del desarrollo 96.

Helg, A. (1995) *Our Rightful Share: the Afro-Cuban Struggle for Equality, 1886–1912* (Chapel Hill, NC: University of North Carolina Press).

Hernández, P. et al. (1997) 'Las cuentas nacionales de salud' in J. Frenk (ed.), *Observatorio de la salud. Necesidades, servicios, políticas* (Mexico City: Fundación Méxicana para la Salud).

Hills, J. (1997) *The Future of Welfare: a Guide to the Debate* (York: Joseph Rowntree Foundation).

Hills, J., Ditch, J. and Glennerster, H. (1994) *Beveridge and Social Security: an International Retrospective* (Oxford: Clarendon Press).

Hirschman, A.O. (1963) *Journeys Towards Progress: Studies in Economic Policy-Making in Latin America* (New York: Twentieth Century Fund).

Hirschman, A.O (1981) 'Policymaking and Policy Analysis in Latin America – A Return Journey', in A. Hirschman, *Essays in Trespassing: Economics to Politics and Beyond* (Cambridge: Cambridge University Press).

Hirschman, A.O. (1981) *Essays in Trespassing: Economics to Politics and Beyond* (Cambridge: Cambridge University Press).

Hirschman, A.O. (1984) *Getting Ahead Collectively: Grassroots Experiences in Latin America* (Oxford: Pergamon Press).

Hirschman, A.O. (1992) *Rival Views of Market Society and other Recent Essays* (Cambridge, Mass.: Harvard University Press).

Hirschman, A.O. (1997) *The Passions and the Interests: Political Arguments for Capitalism* (Princeton: Princeton University Press).

Hisamatsu, Y. (1998) 'Urban Bias in Mexico Reexamined', paper presented at the Latin American Studies Association Congress in Chicago.

Hoff, K. et al. (1993) *The Economies of Rural Organisation* (Oxford: Oxford University Press for the World Bank)

Hoffmann, R. (2001) 'Distribuição da renda no Brasil: poucos com muito e muitos com muito pouco, in L. Dowbor and S. Kilsztajn (orgs.), *Economia Social no Brasil* (São Paulo: Editora SENAC), also available at www.eco.unicamp.br/projetos/Hoffmann2.html

Holley, J. (1995) *Estudio de descentralización de la gestión de los servicios de salud. Territorio de capinota, bolivia* (Latin American Health and Nutrition Sustainability Project, Washington, DC: University Research Corporation), Aug.

Holloway, T.H. (1980) *Immigrants on the Land: Coffee and Society in São Paulo, 1886–1934* (Chapel Hill, NC: University of North Carolina Press).

Holloway, T.H. (1993) *Policing Rio de Janeiro: Repression and Resistance in a Nineteenth-Century City* (Stanford: Stanford University Press).

Homedes, N. and Ugalde, A. (1993) 'Patients' Compliance with Medical Treatments in the Third World. What do we Know?', *Health Policy and Planning*, vol. 8, pp. 291–314.

Homedes, N., Paz-Narváez, A., Selva-Sutter, E., Solas, O. and Ugalde, A. (2000) 'Health Reform: Theory and Practice in El Salvador', in P.

Lloyd-Sherlock (ed.), *Healthcare Reform and Poverty in Latin America* (London: Institute of Latin American Studies), pp. 57–77.

Hood, C. (1990) 'A Public Management for All Seasons', *Public Administration*, vol. 69, no. 1, pp. 3–19.

Houtzager, P.P. (1998) 'State and Unions in the Transformation on the Brazilian Countryside, 1964–1979', *Latin American Research Review*, vol. 33, no. 2, pp. 103–42.

Howard, D. (1999) *Colouring the Nation: Race and Ethnicity in the Dominican Republic* (Oxford: Signal).

Huber, E. (1995) *Options for Social Policy in Latin America: Neo-Liberal versus Social Democratic Models*, UNRISD Discussion Paper, no. 66 (Geneva: United Nations Research Institute for Social Development).

Huber, E. (1996) 'Options for Social Policy in Latin America: Neolibeeral versus Social Democratic Models', in G. Esping-Andersen (ed.), *Welfare States in Transition. National Adaptations In Global Economies* (London: Sage/Unrisd).

Huber, E. and Safford, F. (eds.) (1995) *Agrarian Structure and Political Power: Landlord and Peasant in the Making of Latin America* (Pittsburgh: University of Pittsburgh Press).

Huber, E. and Stephens, J. (2000) 'The Political Economy of Pension Reform: Latin America in Comparative Perspective' (paper prepared for the 2000 meeting of the Latin American Studies Association, Miami, March 16–18).

Human Rights Watch World Report (2000) *Events of 1999 (Nov. 1998–Oct.1999)* (New York).

IBGE (Instituto Brasileiro de Geografia e Estatística) (1995) *Pesquisa nacional de amostragem por domicílios* (PNAD) (Rio de Janeiro: IBGE).

IBGE (Instituto Brasileiro de Geografia e Estatística) (1998) *Pesquisa nacional por amostra de domicílios* (PNAD) (Rio de Janeiro: IBGE).

IBGE (Instituto Brasileiro de Geografia e Estatística) (2000) *Indicadores econômicos* (Rio de Janeiro: IBGE).

IDB, see Inter-American Development Bank.

IEA (2000) 'TIMSS 1999. International Mathematics Report', Boston College,

ILANUD (Instituto Latinamericano de Naciones Unidas para la Prevención y Tratamiento del Delincuente) (1999) *Programa Regional de Capacitación contra la Violencia Doméstica* (San José: ILANUD).

IMAS (Instituto Mixto de Ayuda Social) (1998) *Ley no. 7769 Atención a las Mujeres en Condiciones de Pobreza* (San José: IMAS).

IMAS (Instituto Mixto de Ayuda Social)(1999a) *Programa: Atención a las Mujeres en Condiciones de Pobreza* (San José: IMAS).

IMAS (Instituto Mixto de Ayuda Social)(1999b) *Programa Construyendo Oportunidades* (San José: IMAS).

IMAS (Instituto Mixto de Ayuda Social)(1999c) *Plan Anual Operativo 1999* (San José: IMAS).

IMAS (Instituto Mixto de Ayuda Social) (2001) *Area atención integral para el desarrollo de las mujeres. Programas: Creciendo Juntas, Construyendo Oportunidades* (San José: IMAS).

INAMU (Instituto Nacional de las Mujeres) (1998) *Maternidad y paternidad: dos caras del embarazo adolescente* (San José: INAMU).

INAMU (Instituto Nacional de las Mujeres) (2001) *Responsible Paternity Law* (San José: INAMU).

INDEC (Instituto Nacional de Estadística y Censo) (1995) *Situación y evolución social*, Síntesis no. 3 (Buenos Aires: INDEC).

INDEC (Instituto Nacional de Estadística y Censo) (1998) *Statistical Yearbook of the Argentine Republic 1998* (Buenos Aires: INDEC).

INEGI (1977–94) *Encuesta nacional de ingresos y gastos del hogar – Mexico. 1977 y 1994* (Mexico: Instituto Nacional de Estadística Geografíae Informática).

Inter American Development Bank (IDB) (1993) 'Lending for Housing', mimeo.

Inter-American Development Bank (1996) *Economic and Social Progress in Latin America. The 1996 Report* (Washington, DC: Johns Hopkins University Press for the Inter-American Development Bank).

Inter-American Development Bank (IDB) (1998) *Facing up to Inequality in Latin America* (Washington, DC: Inter-American Development Bank).

Inter American Development Bank (1999a) *Facing up to Inequality, Economic and Social Progress in Latin America* (Washington, DC: Inter-American Development Bank Annual Report 1998–9).

Inter-American Development Bank (1999b) *Operational Guidelines in Housing*, Washington, DC.

Inter-American Development Bank (IDB) (2000) *Economic and Social Progress in Latin America, 2000 Report: Development Beyond Economics* (Washington, DC).

International Bank for Reconstruction and Development (see World Bank)

International Bank for Reconstruction and Development (World Bank) (1995) *World Development Report 1995* (Washington DC: OUP).

International Journal of Politics, Culture and Society, col. 14, no. 260.

Iriart, C., Merhy, E.E. and Waitzkin, H. (2001) 'Managed Care in Latin America: the New Common Sense in Health Policy Reform', *Social Science and Medicine*, vol. 52, pp. 1243–53.

Ishan, J. et al. (1999) 'The Forgotten Rationale for Policy Reform: the Productivity of Investments Projects', *Quarterly Journal of Economics*, vol. 114, pp. 149–89.

Israel, A. (1987) *Institutional Development: Incentives and Performance* (Baltimore: Johns Hopkins University Press).

Ivereigh, A. (1995) *Catholicism and Politics in Argentina, 1810-1950* (Basingstoke: Macmillan).

Ivereigh, A. (ed.) (2000) *The Politics of Religion in an Age of Revival: Studies in Nineteenth-Century Europe and Latin America* (London: Institute of Latin American Studies).

Izazola Licea, J. (1997) 'El VIH/SIDA en América Latina y el Caribe: un problema prioritario para la salud y la economía', in J. Frenk (ed.), *Observatorio de la salud. Necesidades, servicios, políticas* (Mexico City: Fundación para la Salud).

Jaramillo, H. (1994) 'Reseña de las reformas de políticas sociales en Colombia in CEPAL', *Proyecto regional de reformas de política pública*, Gobierno de los Países Bajos (UN), Santiago de Chile.

Jaramillo, C.F. (1994a) *Apertura, crisis y recuperación. La agricultura colombiana entre 1990 y 1999* (Bogotá, Colombia: Fonade-Tercer Mundo).

Jaramillo, C.F. (1998) *Liberalization, Crisis and Change in Colombian Agriculture* (Boulder: Westview Press).

Jaramillo, S. (1992) 'Bajo el signo del UPAC. Estructura de producción y política de vivienda en Colombia 1972–1990', in *Cambios estructurales y crecimiento* (Bogotá: Ediciones Uniandes y Tercer Mundo), pp. 183–222.

Jelin, E. (ed.) (1987) *Ciudadanía e identidad: las mujeres en los movimientos sociales latinoamericanos* (Geneva: UNRISD).

Jelin, E. (ed.) (1991) *Family, Household and Gender Relations in Latin America* (London: Kegan Paul).

Jelin, E. (1991a) 'Introduction: Everyday Practices, Family Structures, Social Processes', in E. Jelin (ed.), *Family, Household and Gender Relations in Latin America* (London/Paris: Kegan Paul International/UNESCO), pp. 1–5.

Jelin, E. (1996) 'Citizenship Revisted: Solidarity, Responsibility, and Rights', in E. Jelin and E. Hershberg (eds.), *Constructing Democracy: Human Rights, Citizenship and Society in Latin America* (Boulder: Westview Press), pp. 101–19.

Jelin, E. (1996a) '¿Ciudadanía emergente o exclusión? Movimientos sociales y ONGs en los años noventa', *Sociedad*, vol. 8, pp. 57–81.

Jimenez de la Jara, J. and Bossert, T. (1995) 'Chile's Health Sector Reform: Lessons from Four Reform Periods', in P. Berman (ed.), *Health Sector Reform in Developing Countries* (Cambridge, Mass.: Harvard University Press).

Johnson, P. and Lloyd-Sherlock, P. (eds.) (1996) *Ageing and Social Policy: Global Comparisons* (London: Suntory and Toyota International Centres for Economics and Related Disciplines).

Johnson, P. and Zimmermann, K.F. (eds.) (1993) *Labour Markets in an Ageing Europe* (Cambridge: Cambridge University Press).

Johnson, P., Conrad, C. and Thomson, D. (eds.) (1989) *Workers versus Pensioners: Intergenerational Justice in an Ageing World* (Manchester: Manchester University Press).

Johnson, T.E. Jr. (1987) 'Upward Filtering of Housing Stock: a Study of Upward Filtering of Housing Stock as a Consequence of Informal Sector Upgrading in Developing Countries', *Habitat International*, vol. 11, pp. 173–90.

Jones, G.A. and Ward, P.M. (1998) 'Privatizing the Commons: Reforming the Ejido and Urban Development in Mexico', *International Journal of Urban and Regional Research*, vol. 22, pp. 76–93.

Joseph, G.M. and Nugent, D. (eds.) (1994) *Everyday Forms of State Formation: Revolution and Negotiation of Rule in Modern Mexico* (Durham, NC: Duke University Press).

Joseph, G.M. and Szuchman, M. (eds.) (1996) *I Saw a City Invincible: Urban Portraits of Latin America* (Wilmington, Del.: SR Books).

Julião, F. (1962) *Que são as ligas camponesas?* (Rio de Janeiro: Civilização Brasileira).

Kane, L. (2001) *Popular Education and Social Change in Latin America* (London: Latin American Bureau).

Karst, K.L. (1989) *Belonging to America: Equal Citizenship and the Constitution* (New Haven: Yale University Press).

Kasgaaard, C. (1993) 'Commentary to Cohens: Equality of What? On Welfare Goods and Capabilities', in M. Nussbaum and A. Sen (ed.), *The Quality of Life* (Oxford: OUP).

Katouzian, H. (1980) *Ideology and Method in Economics* (New York: New York University Press).

Katz, F. (ed.) (1988) *Riot, Rebellion and Revolution: Rural Social Conflict in Mexico* (Princeton: Princeton University Press).

Kaufman, M. (1997) 'Community Power, Grassroots Democracy and the Transformation of Social Life', in M. Kaufman and H. Dilla Alfonso (eds.), *Community Power and Grassroots Democracy* (London: Zed), pp. 1–26.

Kay, C. (1989) *Latin American Theories of Development and Underdevelopment* (London: Routledge).

Kay, C. (1995) 'Rural Latin America: Exclusionary and Uneven Agrarian Development', in S. Halebsky and R.L. Harris (eds.), *Capital, Power and Inequality in Latin America* (Boulder: Westview Press), pp. 21–52.

Kay, S. (2001) 'Brazil's Social Security Reform in Comparative Perspective', paper presented at the XXIII Congress of the Latin American Studies Association (LASA), Washington, DC, September 6–8 .

Kaztman, R. (1992) 'Por qué los hombres son tan irresponsables?', *Revista de la CEPAL*, no. 46, pp. 1–9.

Kaztman, R. (ed.) (1999) *Activos y estructuras de oportunidades* (Montevideo: CEPAL/PNUD).

Kaztman, R., Beccaria, L., Filgueira, F., Golbert, L. and Kessler, G. (1999) *Vulnerabilidad, activos y exclusión social en Argentina y Uruguay* (Santiago, Chile: OIT).

Kearney, M. (1996) *Reconceptualizing the Peasantry: Anthropology in Global Perspective* (Boulder and Oxford: Westview Press).

Kearney, M. (2000) 'Transnational Oaxacan Indigenous Identity: The Case of Mixtecs and Zapotecs', *Identities*, vol. 7, no. 2, pp. 173–95.

Kearney, M. and Varese, S. (1995) 'Latin America's Indigenous Peoples: Changing Identities and Forms of Resistance', in S. Halebsky and R.L. Harris (eds.), *Capital, Power and Inequality in Latin America* (Boulder: Westview Press), pp. 207–32.

Kimm, P. (1993) 'Políticas de vivienda, cooperación internacional e integración interamericana: el papel de USAID', in *UNIAPRAVI, anales de la XXXI Conferencia Interamericana para la vivienda* (San José, Costa Rica).

King, E. and Ozler, B. (1998) *What's Decentralization got to do with Learning? The Case of Nicaragua's School Autonomy Reform* (Washington: World Bank), working paper series on impact evaluation of education reforms, no. 9.

Klak, T. (1999) 'Globalisation, Neoliberalism and Economic Change in Central America and the Caribbean', in R. Gwynne and C. Kay (eds), *Latin America Transformed: Globalisation and Modernity* (London: Edward Arnold), pp. 98–126.

Kliksberg, B. (2000) 'Los escenarios sociales en América Latina y el Caribe', *Revista Panamericana de Salud Pública*, vol. 8, pp. 105–11.

Knavery, J.C. (1995) 'La gerencia de la reforma educativa en Venezuela: el caso de las escuelas integrales del Estado Mérida', in R. De la Cruz (ed.), *Ruta a la eficiencia: descentralización de los servicios sociales* (Caracas: IESA), pp. 35–68.

Knight, A. (1986) *The Mexican Revolution: Vol. II: Counter-Revolution and Construction* (Cambridge: Cambridge University Press).

Knight, A. (1990) 'Racism, Revolution and Indigenismo: Mexico, 1910-1940', in R. Graham (ed.), *The Idea of Race in Latin America* (Austin: University of Texas Press), pp. 71–114.

Knight, A. (1991) 'The Political Economy of Revolutionary Mexico, 1900-1910', in C. Abel and C.M. Lewis (eds.), *Latin America, Economic Imperialism and the State* (London: Institute of Latin American Studies/Athlone), pp. 288–317.

Knight, A. (1994) 'Cardenismo: Juggernaut or Jalopy', *Journal of Latin American Studies*, vol. XXVI, no. 1, pp. 73–107.

Kormendi, R.C. and Meguive, P.G. (1985) 'Macroeconomic Determinants of Growth: Cross Country Evidence', *Journal of Monetary Economics*, pp. 141–63.

Korzeniewicz, R.P. and Smith, W.C. (2000) 'Poverty, Inequality, and Growth in Latin America: Searching for the High Road to Globalization', *Latin America Research Review*, vol. 35, pp. 7–44.

Kosacoff, B. (ed.) (2000) *Corporate Strategies under Structural Adjustment in Argentina: Responses by Firms to a New Set of Uncertainties* (Basingstoke: Macmillan).

Kuhn, T. (1962) *The Structure of Scientific Revolutions* (Chicago: University of Chicago Press).

Kuznetsoff, E. (1980) 'Household Compositon and Headship as related to Changes in Modes of Production: São Paulo 1765–1836', *Comparative Studies in Society and History*, vol. 22, no. 1, pp. 78–108.

Kusnetzoff, F. (1987) 'Urban and Housing Policies under Chile's Military Dictatorship 1973–1985', *Latin American Perspectives*, vol. 53, pp. 157–86.

Kusnetzoff, F. (1990) 'The State and Housing in Chile – Regime Types and Policy Choices', in G. Shidlo (ed.), *Housing Policy in Developing Countries* (London: Routledge), pp. 48–66.

Kuznets, S. (1955) 'Economic Growth and Income Distribution', *American Economic Review*, vol. 45.

Labonte R. (1999) 'Brief to the World Trade Organization and Population Health', unpublished paper presented to the International Union for Health Promotion and Education and the Canadian Public Health Association, 8 Nov.

LaForgia, G.M. and Homedes, N. (1992) 'Decentralization of Health Services in Colombia. A Review of Progress and Problems. A Report to the World Bank' (Washington, DC), unpublished report.

Laing, R. (1999) 'Pharmaceutical Management and the Central and Local Levels', in R-L. Kolehmainen-Aitken (ed.) *Myths and Realities about the Decentralization of Health Systems* (Boston: Management Sciences for Health).

Lalama, M. (1999) 'Perfil de consumo de medicamentos en la Ciudad de Quito, Ecuador', *Educación Médica Continua*, vol. 64, pp. 7–9.

Landsberger, H.A. (ed.) (1969) *Latin American Peasant Movements* (Ithaca: Cornell University Press).

Larrañaga, O. (1999) *Eficiencia y equidad en el sistema de salud chileno*, Serie Financiamiento y Desarrollo, Proyecto CEPAL/GTZ Reformas Financieras al Sector Salud en América Latina y el Caribe, Unidad de Financiamiento (Santiago de Chile: Ministerio de Salud/FONASA).

Laurell, A. (1996) *No hay pierde: todos pierden; lo que usted necesita saber sobre la nueva ley del Seguro Social* (MexicoCity: Fundación Friedrich Ebert).

Laurell, A. (1997) *La reforma contra la salud y la seguridad social*, ERA (Fundación Friedrich Ebert), Mexico.

Laurell, A. (2001) 'Health Reform in Mexico: the Promotion of Inequality', *International Journal of Health Services*, vol. 31, p. 2.

Lavalette, M. and Pratt, A. (1997) 'Introduction', in M. Lavalette and A. Pratt (eds.), *Social Policy. A Conceptual and Theoretical Introduction* (London: Sage).

Laws, S. (1996) 'The Single Mothers Debate: a Children's Rights Perspective', in J. Holland and L. Adkins (eds), *Sex, Sensibility and the Gendered Body* (Basingstoke: Macmillan), pp. 60–77.

Lawson, V. (1990) 'Workforce Fragmentation in Latin America and its Empirical Manifestations in Ecuador', *World Development*, vol. 18, no. 5.

Le Grand, J. (1982) *The Strategy of Equality: Redistribution and the Social Services* (London: Allen & Unwin).

Le Grand, J. (1987) *Three Essays on Equity* (London: Suntory Toyota International Centre for Economics and Related Disciplines).

Le Grand, J. (1991) *Equity and Choice: an Essay in Economics and Applied Philosophy* (London: Routledge).

Lechner, N. (2000) 'Desafíos de un desarrollo humano: individualización y capital social', *Instituciones y Desarrollo*, no. 7, Instituto Internacional de Gobernabilidad, Barcelona, Spain.

Lee, K. (1998) 'Globalization and Health Policy. A Review of the Literature and Proposed Research and Policy Agenda', unpublished paper, London School of Hygiene and Tropical Medicine.

Leff, N.H (1982) *Underdevelopment and Development in Brazil*, vols. I and II (London: Allen & Unwin).

Lehmann, D. (ed.) (1974) *Agrarian Reform and Agrarian Reformism* (London: Faber).

Lemer, A.C. (1987) 'The Role of Rental Housing in Developing Countries: A Need for Balance', World Bank Report no. UDD–104.

Lenz, R. and Sánchez, J.M. (c. 1998) 'Equidad en la distribución de recursos en salud. El caso chileno del SNSS: 1977', Seminario de Políticas y Estrategias Innovadoras en Salud, unpublished paper.

León, F. (1999) 'Formación de recursos humanos y empleo en Cuba. Qué hacer después del periodo especial?', paper presented to a symposium on *The Cuban Economy: Problems, Policies, Perspectives*, Carleton University, Ottawa, 28–30 Sept.

Levine, R. and Zervos, S. (1993) 'Looking at the Facts: What we Know about Policy and Growth from Cross-Country Analysis', WPS 1115, (Washington, DC: The World Bank).

Lewis, C. (1993) 'Social Insurance: Ideology and Policy in the Argentine, c.1920–66', in C. Abel and C. Lewis (eds.), *Welfare, Poverty and Development in Latin America* (Basingstoke: Macmillan).

Lewis, C. M. (2000) 'Social Insurance in Brazil and the Argentine: "Reform" and Some Lessons from History', presented in FLACSO-Mexico.

Lewis, C.M. and Lloyd-Sherlock, P. (2001) *Social Security Reform in Brazil and the Argentine since c.1900* (London).

Lewis, C.M. and Torrents, N (eds.) (1994) *Argentina in the Crisis Years (1983-1990): from Alfonsín to Menem* (London: Institute of Latin American Studies).

Lewis, O. (1968) *La Vida: a Puerto Rican Family in the Culture of Poverty* (New York: Vintage Books, Random House).

Lewis, O. (1969) 'Culture and Poverty: Critique and Counter Proposal', *Current Anthropology*, vol. X, nos. 2–3, pp. 1–23.

Lewis, W.A. (1955) *Theory of Economic Growth* (London: Allen & Unwin).

Lexchin, J. (1995) *Deception by Design. Pharmaceutical Promotion in the Third World* (Penang: Consumers International).

Ley numero 100 (1993) Congress of the Colombian Republic (Bogotá).

Lezama, J.L. (1991) 'Ciudad y conflicto: usos del suelo y comercio ambulante en la Ciudad de México', in M. Schteingart (ed.) *Espacio y vivienda en la Ciudad de México* (Mexico City: El Colegio de México), pp. 121–35.

Lievesley, G. (1999) *Democracy in Latin America: Mobilization, Power and the Search for a New Politics* (Manchester: Manchester University Press).

Lijphart, A. and Waisman, C. (eds.) (1996) *Institutional Design in New Democracies: Eastern Europe and Latin America* (Boulder: Westview).

Linz, J.J. and Stepan, A. (eds.) (1996) *Problems of Democratic Transition and Consolidation: Southern Europe, South America and Post-Communist Europe* (Baltimore: Johns Hopkins University Press).

Linz, J. and Valenzuela, A. (eds.) (1994) *The Failure of Presidential Democracy* (Baltimore: Johns Hopkins University Press).

Lipton, M. (1991) 'Market Relaxation and Agricultural Development', in C. Colclough and J. Manor (eds.) *States or Markets? Neo-Liberalism and the Development Policy Debate* (Oxford: Oxford University Press LDS –DSS).

Lipton, M. et al. (1993) 'Including the Poor', *World Bank Regional and Sectoral Series* (Washington).

Lipton, M. and Ravallion, M. (1993) 'Poverty and Policy', *World Bank*, w.p. no. 1130.

Lipton, M. and van der Gaag, J. (1993) 'Poverty: a Research and Policy Framework', in M. Lipton and J. van der Gaag (eds.), *Including the Poor, Proceedings of a Symposium Organised by the World Bank and the International Food Policy Research Institute* (Washington, DC: World Bank), pp. 3–19.

Little, W. and Posada-Carbó, E. (eds.) (1996) *Political Corruption in Europe and Latin America* (London: Macmillan/Institute of Latin American Studies).

Livi-Bacci, M. (1990) *Historia mínima de la población mundial* (Barcelona: Ariel).

Livi-Bacci, M. (1992) *Notas sobre la transición demográfica en Europa y América Latina*, Mexico, mimeo.

Llambi, L. (2000) 'Global-Local Links in Latin America's New Ruralities', in D. Bryceson, C. Kay and J. Mooij (eds.), *Disappearing Peasantries? Rural Labour in Africa, Asia and Latin America* (London: Intermediate Technology), pp. 176–91.

Lloyd-Sherlock, P. (1997) *Old Age and Urban Poverty in the Developing World: the Shanty Towns of Buenos Aires* (Basingstoke: Macmillan).

Lloyd-Sherlock, P. (1997a) 'Healthcare Provision for Elderly People in Argentina: the Crisis of PAMI', *Social Policy and Administration*, vol. 31, no. 4, pp. 371–89.

Lloyd-Sherlock, P. (ed.) (2000) *Healthcare Reform and Poverty in Latin America* (London: Institute of Latin American Studies).

Lloyd-Sherlock, P. (2000a) 'Failing the Needy: Public Social Spending in Latin America', *Journal of International Development*, no. 12.

Lloyd-Sherlock, P. (2000b) 'Healthcare Financing Reform and Equity in Argentina', in P. Lloyd-Sherlock (ed.), *Healthcare Reform and Poverty in Latin America* (London: Institute of Latin American Studies), pp. 143–62.

Lloyd-Sherlock, P. and Novick, D. (2001) '"Voluntary" User Fees in Buenos Aires: Innovation or Imposition?', *International Journal of Health Services*, vol. 31, no. 4.

Lo Vuolo, R. (1996) 'Reformas previsionales en América Latina: una visión crítica en base al caso argentino', *Comercio Exterior*, vol. 46, no. 9, Sept., pp. 692–702 (México), reproduced in *Economia e Sociedade*, no. 6 (June 1996), pp. 153–81 (Instituto de Economia (Unicamp), Brasil); and in *Estudios del Trabajo*, no. 11, Aug.–Dec. 1996, Buenos Aires.

Lo Vuolo, R.M. (1997) 'The Retrenchment of the Welfare State in Latin America: the Case of Argentina', *Social Policy and Administration*, vol. XXXI, no. 4, pp. 390–409.

Lo Vuolo, R. (1998) 'Crisis de integración social y retracción del Estado de Bienestar en Argentina', in *La nueva oscuridad de la política social* (Buenos Aires: Ciepp/Miño y Dávila).

Loáiciga Guillén, M.E. (1994) 'Acerca de la Educación Superior Pública en Guanacaste', *Ciencias Sociales*, no. 66, pp. 7–20.

Lomnitz, L.A. (1977) *Networks and Marginality. Life in a Mexican Shantytown* (New York: Academic Press).

Londoño, J.L. and Székely, M. (1997) *Persistent Poverty and Excess Inequality: Latin America, 1970–1995*, IADB Working Paper series 357.

Long, N. (1989) 'Introduction: the Raison d'Etre for Studying Rural Development Interface', in N. Long (ed.), *Encounters at the Interface* (Wageningen, Holland: PUDOC).

Long, N. and Roberts, B. (1994) 'The Agrarian Structures of Latin America 1930-1990', in L. Bethell (ed.), *The Cambridge History of Latin America: Vol. VI: 1930 to the Present* (Cambridge: Cambridge University Press), pp. 325–92.

López, R. (1995) 'Adjustment and Poverty in Mexican Agriculture: How Farmers' Wealth Affects Supply Responds', *World Bank*, w.p. no. 1494.

López-Linares, R. and Phang Romero, C. (1992) *¿Promoviendo la salud o los negocios?* (Chimbote, Peru: Acción para la Salud).

López Restrepo, I. (1995) *Las etapas de la liberalización de la economía colombiana* (Santiago: CEPAL-UN).

Lordon, F. (2000) *Fonds de pension, piège à cons? Mirage de la démocratie actionnariale* (Paris: Raisons d'Agir Éditions).

Love, J.L. (1994) 'Economic Ideas and Ideologies in Latin America since 1930', in L. Bethell (ed.), *The Cambridge History of Latin America: Vol. VI, Pt. 1: 1930 to the Present* (Cambridge: Cambridge University Press), pp. 393–462.

Love, J.L. and Jacobsen, N. (eds.) (1988) *Guiding the Invisible Hand: Economic Liberalism and the State in Latin American History* (New York: Praeger).

Lowenthal, A.F. (ed.) (1991) *Exporting Democracy: the United States and Latin America* (Baltimore: Johns Hopkins University Press).

Lowenthal, A.F. and Treverton, G.F. (eds.) (1994) *Latin America in a New World* (Boulder: Westview Press).

Loyo, A., Ibarrola, M. and Blanco, A. (2000) 'Estructura del sindicalismo docente en América Latina' (Paper prepared for a seminar on the politics of education reform, Santiago, Chile).

Lozano, R. (1997) 'El peso de la enfermedad en México: avances y desafíos', in J. Frenk (ed.), *Observatorio de la salud. Necesidades, servicios, políticas* (Mexico City: Fundación para la Salud).

Lozano, W. (1997) 'Dominican Republic: Informal Economy, the State and the Urban Poor', in A. Portes, C.F. Dore-Cabral and P. Landolt (eds.), *The Urban Caribbean: Transition to the New Global Economy* (Baltimore: Johns Hopkins University Press), pp. 153–89.

Lozoya Legorreta, X., Velásquez Díaz, G. and Flores Alvarado, A. (1988) *La medicina tradicional en México: experiencia del Programa IMSS-COPLA-MAR 1982–1987* (Mexico City.: Instituto Mexicanos del Seguro Social).

Lustig, N. (ed.) (1995) *Coping with Austerity: Poverty and Inequality in Latin America* (Washington, DC: Brookings Institution).

Lustig, N. (1997) 'Mexico: the Social Costs of Adjustment', in J.A. Lawton (ed.), *Privatization amidst Poverty: Contemporary Challenges in Latin American Political Economy* (Boulder.), pp. 69–110.

MacEwen Scott, A. (1994) *Divisions and Solidarities: Gender, Class and Employment in Latin America* (London: Routledge).

MacEwen Scott, A. (1995) 'Informal Sector or Female Sector? Gender Bias in the Urban Labour Market Models', in D. Elson (ed.), *Male Bias in the Development Process* (Manchester: Manchester University Press), pp. 38–65.

Macpherson, C.B. (1962) *The Political Theory of Possessive Individualism: Hobbes to Locke* (Oxford: Oxford University Press).

Maddison, A. (1991) 'Economic and Social Conditions in Latin America, 1913-1950', in M. Urrutia (ed.), *Long-Term Trends in Latin American Development* (Washington, DC: Inter-American Development Bank), pp. 1–22.

Maddison, A. (1992) *The Political Economy of Poverty, Equity and Growth: Brazil and Mexico* (Oxford: Oxford University Press).

Maddison, A. (1993) *La economía política de la pobreza y el crecimiento: Brasil y Mexico* (Mexico: Fondo de Cultura Eonomica).

Maguire, C. (1995) *Agriculture in Liberalizing Economies: Changing Roles for Governments* (World Bank).

Malaquer de Motes, J. (1992) *Nación e inmigración: los españoles en Cuba (siglos xix y xx)* (Oviedo: Ediciones Júcar).

Mallon, F.E. (1992) 'Indian Communities, Political Cultures and the State in Latin America, 1780-1990', *Journal of Latin American Studies Quincentenary Supplement*, vol. XXIV, pp. 35–53.

Mallon, F.E. (1995) *Peasant and Nation: the Making of Postcolonial Mexico and Peru* (Berkeley: University of California Press).

Malloy, J.A. (1986) *A política de previdência social no Brasil* (Rio de Janeiro: Graal).

Malloy, J.A. and Parodi, C.A. (1993) 'Politics, Equity and Social Security Policy in Brazil: a Case-Study of Statecraft and Citizenship, 1965–85', in C. Abel and C.M. Lewis (eds), *Welfare, Poverty and Development in Latin America* (Basingstoke: Macmillan Press/St. Antony's College), pp. 341–64.

Malloy, J.M. (ed.) (1976) *Authoritarianism and Corporatism in Latin America* (Pittsburgh: University of Pittsburgh Press).

Malloy, J.M. (1979) *The Politics of Social Security in Brazil* (Pittsburgh: University of Pittsburgh Press).

Malloy, J.M. (1986) 'Statecraft, política y crisis de la seguridad social. Una comparación de la América Latina y los Estados Unidos', in C. Mesa-Lago (ed.), *La crisis de la seguridad social y la atención a la Salud* (Mexico: Fondo de Cultura Economica).

Malpezzi, S. and Ball, G. (1991) 'Rent Control in Developing Countries', *World Bank Discussion Papers* 129 (Washington, DC).

Marenco, L., Trejos, A.M., Trejos, J.D. and Vargas, M. (1998) *Del silencio a la palabra: un modelo de trabajo con las mujeres jefas del hogar* (San José: Segunda Vicepresidencia).

Márquez, G. (ed.) (1995) *Reforming the Labour Market in a Liberalized Economy* (Washington, DC: Inter-American Development Bank).

Marshall, T.H. (1950) *Citizenship and Social Class* (Cambridge: Cambridge University Press).

Marshall, T.H. (1981) *The Right to Welfare and Other Essays* (London: Heinemann Educational).

Marshall, T.H. (1985) *Social Policy in the Twentieth Century* (London: Hutchinson).

Martine, G. (1996) 'Brazil's Fertility Decline, 1965–95', *Population and Development Review*, vol. 22, no. 1.

Massey, A. (1997) 'In Search of the State: Markets, Myths and Paradigms', in A. Massey (ed.), *Globalization and Marketization of Government Services: Comparing Contemporary Public Sector Developments* (Basingstoke: Macmillan), pp. 1–15.

Matijascic, M. (2001) *Reformas estruturais e previdência no Brasil: balanço atual e perspectives*, paper presented at the XXIII Congress of the Latin American Studies Association (LASA), Washington, DC, 6–8 Sept.

Mayo, S.K. (1999) 'Subsidies in Housing', *Inter-American Development Bank, Sustainable Development Department Technical Papers Series*.

McCallum, C. (1999) 'Restraining Women: Gender, Sexuality and Modernity in Salvador da Bahia', *Bulletin of Latin American Research*, vol. 18, no. 3, pp. 275–93.

McCallum, J.D. and Benjamin, S. (1985) 'Low-Income Urban Housing in the Third World: Broadening the Economic Perspective', *Urban Studies*, vol. 22, pp. 277–87.

McFarlane, A. (1998) 'Identity, Enlightenment and Political Dissent in Late-Colonial Spanish America', in *Transactions of the Royal Historical Society*, 6th ser., vol. VIII, pp. 309–36.

McFarlane, A. and Posada-Carbó, E. (eds.) (1998) *Independence and Revolution in Spanish America: Perspectives and Problems* (London: Institute of Latin American Studies).

McGinn, N. and Street, S. (1986) 'La descentralización educacional en América Latina: política nacional o lucha de facciones', *La Educación* (Washington), no. 99.

McIntosh, M. (1996) 'Social Anxieties about Lone Motherhood and Ideologies of the Family', in E. Bortolaia Silva (ed.), *Good Enough Mothering? Feminist Perspectives on Lone Motherhood* (London: Routledge), pp. 148–56.

McLaverty, P. and Yip, N.M. (1993) 'The Preference for Owner-Occupation', *Environment and Planning A* 25, pp. 1559–72.

Mead, L. (1986) *Beyond Entitlement: the Social Obligations of Citizenship* (New York:: Free Press).

Medici, A. (2000) 'Las reformas de salud en América Latina y el Caribe', in H. Sánchez and G. Zuleta (eds.), *La hora de los usuarios: reflexiones sobre la economía política de las reformas de salud* (Washington, DC: Banco Interamericano de Desarrollo, Centro de Estudios Salud y Futuro).

Meertens, D. (1997) *Tierra, violencia y género. hombres y mujeres en la historia rural de Colombia 1930–1990* (Bogotá).

MEIC (Ministerio de Economía, Industria y Comercio) (1998) *Encuesta de hogares de propósitos multiples* (San José: Area de Estadísticas y Censos).

Meller, P. (ed.) (1991) *The Latin American Development Debate: Neostructuralism, Neomonetarism and Adjustment Process* (Boulder: Westview Press).

Melo, M. (2002) 'When Institutions Matter: a Comparison of the Politics of Administrative, Social Security, and Tax Reforms in Brazil', in B. Heredia and B.R. Schneider (eds.), *Reinventing Leviathan: The Politics of Administrative Reform in Developing Countries* (Miami: North-South Center Press).

Méndez, J.L. (1997) 'Administrative Modernisation and Political Transition in Developing Countries: the Case of Mexico', paper presented at the Annual Conference of the International Institute of Administrative Sciences (IIAS), Quebec, 14–17 July.

Merino, G.A. (1998) 'Las transferencias federales para la educación en Mexico: una evaluación de sus criterios de equidad y eficiencia', *Gestión y Política Pública* (México), vol. 7, no. 2 , pp. 355–99.

Mesa-Lago, C. (1978) *Social Security in Latin America: Pressure Groups, Stratification and Inequality* (Pittsburgh: University of Pittsburgh Press).

Mesa-Lago, C. (1985) 'Diversas estrategias frente a la crisis de la seguridad social: enfoques socialista, de mercado y mixto', in C. Mesa-Lago (ed.) *La crisis de la seguridad social y la atención a la salud* (Mexico City: Fondo de Cultura Economica).

Mesa-Lago, C. (1986) 'Social Security and Development in Latin America', *CEPAL Review*, vol. 28, pp. 135–150

Mesa-Lago, C. (1989) *Ascent to Bankruptcy: Financing Social Security in Latin America* (Pittsburgh: University of Pittsburgh Press)

Mesa-Lago, C. (1991) *Social Security and Prospects for Equity in Latin America* (Washington, DC: World Bank).

Mesa-Lago, C. (1991a) 'Social Security in Latin America', Inter-American Development Bank (IDB), *Economic and Social Progress in Latin America: 1991 Report* (Washington, DC: IDB).

Mesa-Lago, C. (1992) *Health Care for the Poor in Latin America and the Caribbean* (Washington, DC: PAHO).

Mesa-Lago, C. (ed) (1993) *Cuba after the Cold War* (Pittsburgh and London: University of Pittsburgh Press).

Mesa-Lago, C. (1994) *Changing Social Security in Latin America: Towards Alleviating the Social Cost of Economic Reform* (Boulder: Lynne Rienner).

Mesa-Lago, C. (1998) 'Assessing Economic and Social Performance in the Cuban Transition of the 1990s', *World Development*, vol. 26 no. 5 (May).

Mesa-Lago, C. (1998a) 'La reforma estructural de pensiones en América Latina: tipología, comprobación de presupuestos y enseñanzas', in A. Bonilla García and A.H. Conte-Grand (compiladores), *Pensiones en América Latina. Dos décadas de reforma* (Lima: Oficina Internacional del Trabajo), pp. 77–64.

Mesa-Lago, C. (2000) *Market, Socialist, and Mixed Economies: Comparative Policy and Performance of Chile, Cuba and Costa Rica* (Baltimore and London: The Johns Hopkins University Press).

Mesa-Lago, C. and Córdova MacPas, R. (1998) 'Social Security Reform in El Salvador', in M.A. Cruz-Saco and C. Mesa-Lago (eds.), *Do Options Exist? The Reform of Pension and Health Care Systems in Latin America* (Pittsburgh: University of Pittsburgh Press).

Meuret, D. and Scheerens, J. (1995) 'An International Comparison of Functional and Territorial Decentralisation of Public Educational Systems', paper presented at the Annual Conference of the American Educational Research Association (AERA), San Francisco.

Meyer, C.A. (1999) *The Economics and Politics of NGOs in Latin America* (London: Praeger).

Meyer, L., Segovia, R. and Lajous A. (eds.) (1979) *El conflicto social y los gobiernos del maximato* (Mexico City: Colegio de México).

MFC (Movimiento Familiar Cristiano) (1997) *Reseña histórica del MFC en Costa Rica* (San José: Movimiento Familiar Cristiano).

Middlebrook, K. (1995) *The Paradox of Revolution: Labor, the State and Authoritarianism in Mexico* (Baltimore: The Johns Hopkins University Press).

MIDEPLAN (Ministerio de Planificación Nacional y Política Económica) (1995) *Estadísticas sociodemográficas y económicas desagregadas por sexo, Costa Rica, 1980–1994* (San José: MIDEPLAN).

Midgley, J. (1997) *Social Welfare in Global Context* (London: Sage).

Midgley, J. (1998) *Social Development: the Developmental Perspective in Social Welfare* (London: Sage).

Midgley, J with Hall, A. (eds.) (1986) *Community Participation, Social Development and the State* (London: Methuen).

Midgley, J. and Tracy, M. (1996) *Challenges to Social Security: an International Exploration* (Westport: Auburn House).

Migdal, J.S. (1988) *Strong Societies and Weak States: State-Society Relations and State Capabilities in the Third World* (Princeton: Princeton University Press).

Milanovic, B. (1998) *Income, Inequality and Poverty during the Transition from Planned to Market Economy* (Washington, DC: The World Bank).

Miller, F. (1991) *Latin American Women and the Search for Social Justice* (Hanover: University Press of New England).

Miller, N. (1999) *In the Shadow of the State: Intellectuals and the Quest for National Identity in Twentieth-Century Latin America* (London: Verso).

Miller Klubock, T. (1998) *Contested Communities: Class, Gender, and Politics in Chile's El Teniente Copper Mine, 1904-1951* (Durham, NC: Duke University Press).

Mills, A. (1998) 'The Route to Universal Coverage', in S. Nitayarumphong and A. Mills (eds.), *Achieving Universal Coverage of Health Care*, Ministry of Public Health (Thailand), Bangkok.

Mills, A. et al. (1987) *Decentralization and Health for All Strategy* (Geneva: World Health Organization).

Minrex (1966) *Profile of Cuba* (Havana: Ministry of Foreign Relations).

Miró, C. (1984) 'América Latina: transición demográfica y crisis económica, social y política', in *Memorias del Congreso Latinoamericano de Población y Desarrollo*, vol. I (Mexico City: UNAM, El Colegio de México and PISPAL).

Mizala, A. and Romaguera, P. (1998) 'Desempeño y elección de colegios', *Documento de Trabajo, Serie Economía*, no. 36, Departamento Ingeniera Industrial, Facultad de Ciencias Físicas y Matemáticas, Universidad de Chile.

Moguel Viveiros, R. and Parra Vásquez, M.R. (1998) 'Los ladinos rurales de Huixtán y Oxchuc: un caso de involución social', in M.E. Ramos, R. Moguel Viveros and G. van der Haar (eds.), *Espacios disputados: transformaciones rurales en Chiapas* (Mexico City: Universidad Autónoma Metropolitana and El Colegio de la Frontera Sur), pp. 69–97.

Molina, C.H. (1997) 'La participación popular en el sistema educativa', paper presented at the 2nd International Congress of the Centro Latinoamericano de Administración para el Desarrollo (CLAD), Isla Margarita, Venezuela, 15–18 Oct.

Molyneux, M. (1999) 'The Politics of the Cuban Diaspora in the United States', in V. Bulmer-Thomas and J. Dunkerley (eds.), *The United States and Latin America: the New Agenda* (London: Institute of Latin American Studies/David Rockefeller Center for Latin American Studies, Harvard University), pp. 287–310.

Molyneux, M. (2001) *Women's Movements in International Perspective: Latin American and Beyond* (Basingstoke: Palgrave).

Molyneux, M. (forthcoming) 'Social Capital: A Post-Transition Concept? Questions of Context and Gender from a Latin American Perspective', *Development and Change*

Monreal, Pedro (2000) 'Estrategias de inversión sectorial y reinserción internacional de la economía cubana', paper presented to Latin American Studies Association XXII International Congress, Miami, 16–18 March.

Moore, H. (1994) *Is there a Crisis in the Family?* (Geneva: UNRISD, Occasional Paper 3, World Summit for Social Development).

Moore, H. (1996) 'Mothering and Social Responsibilities in a Cross-Cultural Perspective', in E. Bortolaia Silva (ed.), *Good Enough Mothering? Feminist Perspectives on Lone Motherhood* (London: Routledge), pp. 58–75.

Morales-Gómez, D.A. and Torres, C.A. (eds.) (1992) *Education Policy and Social Change: Experiences from Latin America* (Westport: Praeger).

Morbidity and Mortality Weekly Report (2000) *Public Health Dispatch: Outbreak of Poliomyelitis — Dominican Republic and Haiti*, vol. 49, pp. 1094–104.

Moreno, W. (1994) 'Condiciones de vida y su incidencia en la identidad personal-social de adolescentes nicoyanos', *Ciencias Sociales*, no. 66, pp. 37–44.

Moreno, W. (1997) 'Cambios sociales y rol del adolescente en la estructura familiar', *Ciencias Sociales*, no. 75, pp. 95–101.

Morgan, P. (1995) *Farewell to the Family: Public Policy and Family Breakdown in Britain and the USA* (London: Institute for Economic Affairs).

Morley, S.A. (2000) *La distribución del ingreso en América Latina y el Caribe* (Santiago).

Morley, S. (2001) *The Income Distribution Problem in Latin America* (Santiago: Economic Commission for Latin America and the Caribbean).

Morley, S., Machado, R. and Pettinato, S. (1999) *Indexes of Structural Reform in Latin America*, Serie Reformas Económicas, no. 12 (Santiago de Chile: ECLAC, LC/L.1166, Jan.).

Moser, C.O.N. (1993) 'Market Modernization in Bogotá: Welfare Consequences for Low-Income Market Sellers', in C. Abel and C.M. Lewis (eds.) *Welfare, Poverty and Development in Latin America* (Basingstoke: Macmillan), pp. 317–40.

Moser, C.O.N. (1996) *Confronting Crisis: A Comparative Study of Household Responses to Poverty and Vulnerability in Four Poor Urban Communities* (World Bank).

Moser, C. (1997) *Household Responses to Poverty and Vulnerability* (Washington, DC: The World Bank).

Moser, C. (1998) 'The Asset Vulnerability Framework: Reassessing Urban Poverty Reduction Strategies', in *World Development*, vol. 26, no. 1, pp. 1–19.

Moser, C. and McIlwaine, C. (2000a) *Urban Poor Perceptions of Violence in Colombia* (Washington, DC: World Bank).

Moser, C. and McIlwaine, C. (2000b) *Violence in a Post-Conflict Context: Urban Poor Perceptions from Guatemala* (Washington, DC: World Bank).

Müller, K. (1999) *The Political Economy of Pension Reform in Central-Eastern Europe* (London: Edward Elgar).

Munck, R., Falcón, R. and Galitelli, B. (1987) *Argentina from Anarchism to Peronism, 1895-1955* (London: Zed).

Muñoz, E. (1997) 'Madres adolescentes: una realidad negada', *Otra Mirada*, vol. 1, no. 3, pp. 43–5.

Muñoz, H., De Oliveira, O. and Stern, C. (1983) *Mexico City, Industrialization, Migration, and the Labour Force, 1930–1970* (Paris: UNESCO).

Muñoz G., O. (1977) *Distribución del ingreso en América Latina* (Buenos Aires: El Cid Editor, CLACSO, CIEPLAN).

Murillo, M.V. (1996) 'Latin American Unions and the Reform of Social Service Delivery Systems: Institutional Constraints and Policy Choice' (Washington, DC: Inter-American Development Bank, Office of the Chief Economist).

Murillo, M.V. (1999) 'Recovering Political Dynamics: Teachers' Unions and the Decentralization of Education in Argentina and Mexico', *Journal of Interamerican Studies and World Affairs*, vol. 41, no. 1.

Myers, D. (1978) 'Caracas: the Politics of Intensifying Primacy', *Latin American Urban Research*, vol. 6, pp. 227–58.

Napolitano, V. (1998) 'Between "Traditional" and "New" Catholic Church Religious Discourses in Urban, Western Mexico', *Bulletin of Latin American Research*, vol. 17, no. 3, pp. 323–39.

Narváez Montoya, Ancizar (1996) *El pasado inconcluso: modernidad y postmodernidad* (Pereira: Papiro).

Navarro, J.C., Carnoy, M. and de Moura Castro, C. (1999) 'Education Reform in Latin America: a Review of Issues, Components and Tools', in *Institutional Reforms, Growth and Human Development in Latin America* (Proceedings of a Conference and the Yale Center for International and Area Studies, 16–17 April).

Navarro, J.C., Taylor, K., Bernasconi, A. and Tyler, L. (eds.) (2000) *Perspectivas sobre la reforma educativa: América Central en el contexto de políticas de educación en las Américas* (Washington, DC: HIID, USAID and IDB).

Naya, S. and McCleery, R. (1994) *Relevance of Asian Development Experiences to African Problems* (San Francisco: ICS Press).

Naya, S., Urrutia, M., Mark, S. and Fuentes, A. (eds.) (1989) *Lessons in Development: a Comparative Study of Asia and Latin America* (San Francisco: International Center for Economic Growth).

Needell, J. (1987) 'The *Revolta Contra Vacina* of 1904: the Revolt against

"Modernisation" in *Belle-Époque* Rio de Janeiro', *Hispanic American Historical Review*, vol. LXVII, no. 2, pp. 233–70.

Nelson, J. (ed.) (1990) *Economic Crisis and Policy Choice: the Politics of Adjustment in the Third World* (Princeton: Princeton University Press).

Nelson, J. (1999) *Reforming Health and Education: the World Bank, the IDB, and Complex Institutional Change* (Washington, DC: Overseas Development Council).

Newbrander, W., Collins, D. and Wilson, L. (2000) *Ensuring Equal Access to Health Services. User Fee Systems and the Poor* (Boston: Management Science for Health).

Newland, C. (1996) 'The *Estado Docente* and its Expansion: Spanish-American Elementary Education, 1900-1950', *Journal of Latin American Studies*, vol. XXVI, no. 4, pp. 449–67

Nickson, R.A. (1995) *Local Government in Latin America* (Boulder: Lynne Rienner).

Nickson, R.A. (1997) 'Decentralisation Policy', in P. Lambert and R.A. Nickson (eds.), *The Transition to Democracy in Paraguay* (Basingstoke: Macmillan), pp. 149–64.

Nigenda, G. (1997) 'The Regional Distribution of Doctors in Mexico, 1930–1990: a Policy Assessment', *Health Policy*, vol. 39, no. 2.

Nogueira, M.A. (2000) 'A seguridade possível', *Jornal do Conselho Regional de Serviço Social* (10ª região), no. 57 (Nov.).

Noguera, I. (2000) 'Editorial', *Paginas didacticas*, vol. 5, no. 4, Segundo Semestre, pp. 5–6.

North, D. (1990) *Institutions, Institutional Change and Economic Performance* (Cambridge: Cambridge University Press).

North, D. (1992) *Transaction Costs, Institutions, and Economic Performance* (San Francisco: ICS Press).

Nugent, D. (1997) *Modernity at the Edge of Empire: State, Individual and Nation in the Northern Peruvian Andes, 1885–1935* (Stanford: Stanford University Press).

Nugent, D. (ed.) (1998) *Rural Revolt in Mexico: US Intervention and the Domain of Subaltern Politics* (Durham, NC: Duke University Press).

Nun, J. (1969) 'Sobrepoblación relativa, ejército industrial de reserva y masa marginal', *Revista Latinoamericana de Sociología*, vol. 4, no. 2, pp. 178–237.

Nussbaum, M. and Sen, A. (1993) (ed.) *The Quality of Life* (Oxford: Oxford University Press).

O'Brien, T.F. (1996) *The Revolutionary Mission: American Enterprise in Latin America, 1900-1945* (New York: Cambridge University Press).

O'Donnell, G. (1973) *Modernization and Bureaucratic Authoritarianism: Studies in South American Politics* (Berkeley: Institute of International Studies, University of California).

O'Donnell, G. (1994) 'The State, Democratization, and Some Conceptual Problems (a Latin American View with Glances at Some Post-Communist Countries)', in W.C. Smith, C.H. Acuña and E.A. Gamarra (eds.), *Latin American Political Economy in the Age of Neo-Liberal Reform: Theoretical and Comparative Perspectives for the 1990s* (New Brunswick: Transaction), pp. 157–80.

O'Donnell, G. (1996) 'Delegative Democracy', in L. Diamond and M. Plattner (eds.), *The Global Resurgence of Democracy* (Baltimore: Johns Hopkins University Press), pp. 94–109.

O'Donnell, G. and Wanderley Reis, F. (eds.) (1988) *A democracia no Brasil: dilemmas e perspectives* (São Paulo: Vértice).

O'Donnell, G. et al. (1986) *Transitions from Authoritarian Rule: Latin America* (Washington, DC: John Hopkins University Press).

Ocampo, J.A. (1998) 'Income Distribution, Poverty and Social Expenditure in Latin America', *CEPAL Review*, vol. LXV, pp. 7–14.

OCDE (1989) *The Impact of Development Projects on Poverty* (Paris: OCDE).

OCDE (1995) *Estudios económicos de la OCDE México, 1995* (Paris:OCDE), pp. 104.

OCDE (1997) *Examen de la políticas agrícolas de México* (París), pp. 71–5 .

ODI and Currey, J. (1989) in S. Commander (ed.), *Structural Adjustment in Agriculture* (London: Overseas Development Institute).

OECD (1998) *Human Capital Investment. An International Comparison* (Paris: Center for Educational Research and Innovation).

OECD (2000) '*Literacy in the Information Age: Final Report of the International Adult Survey*', Organization for Co-operation and Development, Statistic Canada, Canada.

OECD (Organisation for Economic Co-operation and Development) (2001) *The Well-being of Nations: The Role of Human and Social Capital* (Paris: OECD).

Oliveira, F.E.B. (1994) *Sistemas de seguridad social en la región – América Latina: problemas y alternativas de solución* (Rio de Janeiro: BID and Instituto de Pesquisas Economicas Aplicadas).

Oliveira, J. and Fleury, S. (1989) *(IM) Previdencia social: 60 anos de historia da previdencia no Brasil* (Rio de Janeiro: ABRASCO and Editora Vozes).

Olof Palme Center (1998) *Health and Nutrition in Cuba: Effects of the U.S. Embargo* (Stockholm: Olof Palme Center).

Olson, M. (1982) *The Rise and Decline of Nations: Economic Growth, Stagflation and Social Rigidities* (New Haven: Yale University Press).

ONE (1998) *Anuario estadístico de Cuba 1996* (Havana: Oficina Nacional de Estadísticas).

ONE (1999) *Anuario demográfico de Cuba 1998* (Havana: Oficina Nacional de Estadísticas).

ONE (1999a) *Anuario estadístico de Cuba 1997* (Havana: Oficina Nacional de Estadísticas).

ONE (2000) *Anuario estadístico de Cuba 1998* (Havana: Oficina Nacional de Estadísticas).

ONE (2000a) *Panorama económico y social. Cuba 2000* (Havana: Oficina Nacional de Estadísticas, 2001).

ONE (2001) *Anuario estadístico de Cuba 1999* (Havana: Oficina Nacional de Estadísticas).

Orléan, A. (1999) *Le pouvoir de la finance* (Paris: Éditions Odile Jacob).

Over, M. (1992) *Economics for Health Sector Analysis: Concepts and Cases* (Washington: World Bank).

Oxfam (2001) *Dare to Lead: Public Health and Company Wealth*, Oxfam Briefing Paper on GlaxoSmithKline (London: Oxfam).

Paalman, M., Bekedam, H., Hawken, L. and Nyheim, D. (1998) 'A Critical Review of Policy Setting in the Health Sector: the Methodology of the 1993 World Development Report', *Health Policy and Planning*, vol. 13, no. 1, pp. 13–31.

Paes de Barros, R. and Mendoça, R. (1997) 'El impacto de tres innovaciones institucionales en la educación brasileña', in W. Savedoff (ed.), *La organización marca la diferencia* (Washington, DC: Banco Interamericano de Desarrollo), pp. 85–145.

Page, M., Marlowe, B. and Molloy, P. (2000) 'The Power of a Poem to Teach Us', *Kappan*, vol. 82, no. 3 (Nov.), pp. 228–9.

PAHO (1998) *Health in the Americas*, vol. 1 (Washington, DC: PAHO).

PAHO (Pan American Health Organization) (1998) *Health in the Americas*, 1998 edition, vol. 1 (Washington, DC: PAHO).

PAHO (1999a) 'Health Ministers Warn of Threats to Health in the Americas', www.paho.org/english/DPI/r199101a.htm, 1 Oct.

PAHO (1999b) 'Statement for the Record by the Pan American Health Organization for the House Committee on International Relations Hearing on Child Survival and Infectious Disease Program', www.paho.org/english/DPI/r1990415.htm 15 April.

PAHO (1999c) 'World Mental Health Day Set', www.paho.org/english/DPI/r1991007.htm ,7 Oct.

Palacinóo, A. (1997) 'Fiesta para las jefas de hogar', *Otra Mirada*, vol. 1, no. 2, pp. 2–4.

Panaritis, E. (2001) 'Do Property Rights Matter? An Urban Case Study from Peru', *Global Outlook: International Urban Research Monitor*, 20–22 April.

Panizza, F. (1993) 'Human Rights: Global Culture and Social Fragmentation', *Bulletin of Latin American Research*, vol. XII, no. 2, pp. 205–14.

Pansters, W. (1996) 'Citizens with Dignity: Opposition and Government in San Luis Potosí, 1938-1993', in R. Aitken (ed.), *Dismantling the Mexican State?* (Basingstoke: Macmillan), pp. 244–66.

Papadópulos, J. (1998) 'The Pension System in Uruguay: a Delayed Reform', in M.A. Cruz-Saco and C. Mesa-Lago (eds.), *Do Options Exist? The Reform of Pension and Health Care Systems in Latin America* (Pittsburgh: Pittsburgh University Press).

Paquette-Vassalli, C. (1998) 'Le logement locatif dans les quartiers populaires de Santiago du Chili: les raisons d'un essor limite', PhD thesis in Urbaism and Management, Ecole Nationale des Ponts et Chausées, Marne-la-Vallée.

Pardo, M. (1998) 'La descentralización educativa en México: aproximaciones para un balance', paper presented at the 3rd International Congress of the Centro Latinoamericano de Administración para el Desarrollo (CLAD), Madrid, 14–17 Oct.

Parry, T.R. (1997) 'Achieving Balance in Decentralization: a Case Study of Education Decentralization in Chile', *World Development*, vol. 25, no.7, pp. 211–25.

Pastor, M. and Zimbalist, A. (1995) 'Waiting for Change: Adjustment and Reform in Cuba', *World Development*, vol. 23, no. 5.

Patrinos, H. and Ariasingam, D. (1997) 'Decentralization of Education, Demand-Side Financing', *Directions in Development* (Washington, DC: The World Bank).

Payne, G. (1989) *Informal Housing and Land Subdivisions in Third World Cities: a Review Of The Literature* (Oxford: CENDEP).

Pazos, F. (1983) 'Cincuenta años de pensamiento económico en la América Latina', *El Trimestre Económico*, vol. L, no. 4, pp. 1915–48.

Pearse, A. (1975) *The Latin American Peasant* (London: Cass).

Pearson, R. (1997) 'Renegotiating the Reproductive Bargain: Gender Analysis of Economic Transition in Cuba in the 1990s', *Development and Change*, vol. 28.

Pécoul, B., Chirac, P., Truiller, P. and Pinel, J. (1999) 'Access to Essential Drugs in Poor Countries. A Lost Battle?', *Journal of the American Medical Association*, vol. 281, pp. 354–60.

Peloso, V.C. and Tenenbaum, B.A. (eds.) (1996) *Liberals, Politics and Power: State Formation in Nineteenth-Century Latin America* (Athens, Ga.: University of Georgia Press).

PEN (Proyecto Estado de la Nación) (1998) *Estado de la nación en desarrollo humano sostenible* (San José: Proyecto Estado de la Nación).

PER (Proyecto Estado de la Región) (1999) *Estado de la región en desarrollo humano sostenible* (San José: Proyecto Estado de la Región).

Pereira García, M.T. (1998) *Orientación educativa* (San José: Editorial Universidad Estatal a Distancia).

Pérez-Iñigo González, A. (1999) *El factor institucional en los resultados y desafíos de la política de vivienda de interés social en Chile*, CEPAL Serie Financiamiento del Desarrollo 78.

Pérez-López, J.F. (1995) *Cuba's Second Economy: from Behind the Scenes to Center Stage* (New Brunswick and London: Transaction Publishers).

Pérez-Stable, M. (1999) *The Cuban Revolution: Origins, Course and Legacy* (New York, Oxford: Oxford University Press).

Perlman, J. (1976) *The Myth of Marginality* (Berkeley: University of California Press).

Persaud, T. (1991) 'Chile's Housing Subsidy Programme: Preliminary Indications of Results', World Bank mimeo.

Persaud, T. (1992) 'Housing Delivery System and the Urban Poor: a Comparison among Six Latin American Countries', *World Bank, Latin America and the Caribbean Technical Department Regional Studies Program Report*, no. 23.

Petras, J. and Morley, M. (1992) *Latin America in the Time of Cholera: Electoral Politics, Market Economics, and Permanent Crisis* (London and New York: Routledge).

Phillips, D. (1990) *Health and Healthcare in the Third World* (London: Longman).

Phoenix, A. (1996) 'Social Constructions of Lone Motherhood: a Case of Competing Discourses', in E. Bortolaia Silva (ed.), *Good Enough Mothering? Feminist Perspectives on Lone Motherhood* (London: Routledge), pp. 175–90.

Pierson, P. (1994) *Dismantling the Welfare State? Reagan, Thatcher and the Politics of Retrenchment* (Cambridge: Cambridge University Press).

Piester, K. (1997) 'Targeting the Poor: the Politics of Social Policy Reforms in Mexico', in D.A. Chalmers et al. (eds.), *The New Politics of Inequality in Latin America: Rethinking, Participation and Representation* (Oxford: Oxford University Press), pp. 469–88.

Pineo, R. and Baer, J. (eds.) (1998) *Cities of Hope: People, Protests and Progress in Urbanising Latin America, 1870–1930* (Boulder: Westview).

Pollitt, C. and Bouckaert, G. (2001) *Public Management Reform: a Comparative Analysis* (Oxford: Oxford University Press).

Porter, D. (1999) 'The History of Public Health: Current Themes and Approaches', *Hygiea Internationalis*, vol. I, no. 1, pp. 9–21.

Portes, A. (1972) 'Rationality in the Slum: an Essay in Interpretive Sociology, *Comparative Studies in Society and History*, vol. 14, pp. 268–86.

Portes, A. (1989) 'Latin American Urbanization in the Years of the Crisis', *Latin American Research Review*, vol. 20, no. 3, pp. 7–49.

Portes, A. (ed.) (1995) *The Economic Sociology of Immigration: Essays on Networks, Ethnicity and Entrepreneurship* (New York: Russell Sage Foundation).

Portes, A. (1998) 'Social Capital: its Origins and Applications in Modern Sociology', *Annual Review of Sociology*, no. 24 .

Portes, A. and Guernizo, L.E. (1991) 'Tropical Capitalists: U.S.-Bound Immigration and Small-Enterprise Development in the Dominican Republic', in S. Díaz-Briquets and S. Weintraub (eds.), *Migration, Remittances and Small Business Development. Mexico and Caribbean Basin Countries* (Boulder: Westview Press), pp. 101–32.

Portes, A. and Itzigsohn, J. (1997) 'Coping with Change: the Politics and Economics of Urban Poverty', in A. Portes, C.F. Dore-Cabral and P. Landolt (eds.), *The Urban Caribbean: Transition to the New Global Economy* (Baltimore: Johns Hopkins University Press), pp. 227–52.

Portes, A. and Landholt, P. (1996) 'The Downside of Social Capital', *The American Prospect*, no. 26.

Portes, A. and Landolt, P. (2000) 'Social Capital: Promise and Pitfalls of its Role in Development', *Journal of Latin American Studies*, vol. XXXII, no. 2, pp. 529–47.

Portes, A. and Schaeffer, R. (1993) 'Competing Perspectives on the Latin American Informal Sector', *Population and Development Review*, vol. XIX, no. 1, pp. 33–60.

Portes, A. and. Stepnick, A. (1993) *City on the Edge. The Transformation of Miami* (Berkeley: University of California Press).

Portes, A., Dore-Cabral, C.F. and Landolt, P. (eds.) (1997) *The Urban Caribbean: Transition to the New Global Economy* (Baltimore: Johns Hopkins University Press).

Portocarrero M., A. (1992) 'Peru: Education for National Identity — Ethnicity and Andean Nationalism', in D.A. Morales-Gómez and C.A. Torres (eds.), *Education, Policy and Social Change: Experiences from Latin America* (Westport: Praeger), pp. 69–82.

Posada-Carbó, E. (ed.) (1995) *Wars, Parties and Nationalism: Essays on the Politics and Society of Nineteenth-Century Latin America* (London: Institute of Latin American Studies).

Posada-Carbó E. (ed.) (1996) *Elections before Democracy: the History Of Elections in Europe and Latin America* (London: Macmillan/Institute of Latin American Studies).

Prawda, J. (1993) 'Educational Decentralization in Latin America: Lessons Learned', *World Development*, vol. 13, no. 3, pp. 253–64.

Prebisch, R. (1950) *The Economic Development of Latin America and its Principal Problems* (New York: United Nations Department of Economic Affairs).

Prebisch, R. (1970) *Change and Development: Latin America's Great Task* (New York: Praeger).

Prebisch, R. (1981) *Capitalismo periférico: crisis y transformación* (Mexico City: Fondo de Cultura Económica).

Price, R. (1964) *Rural Unionization in Brazil* (University of Wisconsin, Madison: Land Tenure Center), Research Paper no. 14.

Prieto, A. (1996) 'Rosario: epidemias, higiene e higienistas en la segunda mitad del Siglo XIX', in M. Zaida Lobato (ed.), *Política, médicos y enfermedades. Lecturas de historia de la salud en la Argentina* (Mar del Plata: Editorial Biblios).

Psacharopoulos, G. and Woodhall, M. (1985) *Education for Development* (Washington, DC: OUP)

Psacharopoulos, G., Morley, S., Fiszbein, A., Lee, H. and Wood, B. (1997) *Poverty and Income Distribution in Latin America: The Story of the 1980s* (Washington, DC: The World Bank).

Putnam, R. (1993) *Making Democracy Work: Civic Traditions in Modern Italy* (Princeton: Princeton University Press).

Putnam, R.D. (2000) *Bowling Alone: the Collapse and Revival of American Community* (New York: Simon & Schuster).

Puyana, A. (1993) 'The Campaign against Absolute Poverty in Colombia: an Evaluation of Liberal Social Policy', in C. Abel and C.M. Lewis (eds.) *Welfare, Poverty and Development in Latin America* (Basingstoke: Macmillan), pp. 387–404.

Puyana, A. (1996) 'Redistributive effects of IDB Lending to Sectors During 1976–92' in S. Griffith-Jones et al., *An Evaluation of IDB Lending 1976–92* (Brighton: IDS).

Puyana, A. and Thorp, R. (2000) *Colombia: la economía política de las expectativas petroleras* (Bogotá: Tercer Mundo- IEPRI-FLACSO).

Puyana, A. (2000) 'Dutch Disease', Macroeconomic Policies, and Rural Poverty in Colombia, *International Journal of Politics, Culture and Society*, Col 14 No. 260.

Puyana, A. (2000) Interview in FLACSO-Mexico.

Quijano, A. (1974) 'The Marginal Pole of the Economy and the Marginalized Labor Force', *Economy and Society*, vol. 3, no. 4, pp. 393–428.

Raczynski, A. (ed.) (1995) *Strategies to Combat Poverty in Latin America* (Washington, DC: Inter-American Development Bank).

Rama, G.W. (1983) 'Education in Latin America: Exclusion or Participation', *CEPAL Review*, vol. 21, pp. 13–38

Ramos, A.R. (1998) *Indigenism: Ethnic Politics in Brazil* (Madison: University of Wisconsin Press).

Randall, L and Anderson, J.B. (eds.) (1999) *Schooling for Success: Preventing Repetition and Dropout in Latin American Primary Schools* (New York: Sharpe).

Rao, M. (ed.) (1999) *Disinvesting in Health. The World Bank's Prescriptions for Health* (New Delhi: Sage Publications).

Ray, T. (1969) *The Politics of the Barrios of Caracas* (University of California Press).

Razzaz, O.M. (1993) 'Examining Property Rights and Investment in Informal Settlements: the Case of Jordon', *Land Economics*, vol. 69, pp. 341–55.

Reid Andrews, G. (1980) *The Afro-Argentines of Buenos Aires, 1800–1900* (Madison: University of Wisconsin Press).

Reid Andrews, G. (1991) *Blacks and Whites in São Paulo, 1888–1988* (Madison: University of Wisconsin Press).

Reimers, F. (1999) 'Education, Poverty, and Inequality in Latin America' (Cambridge, Mass.: Harvard University, Graduate School of Education).

Reimers, F. (ed.) (2000) *Unequal Schools, Unequal Chances: the Challenges of Equal Opportunity in the Americas* (Cambridge, Mass.: Harvard University Press/David Rockefeller Center for Latin American Studies).

Reimers, F. and McGinn, N. (1997) *Informed Dialogue: Using Research to Shape Education Policy around the World* (Westport, CT: Praeger).

Renaud, B. (1988) 'Housing under Economic Structural Adjustment in Chile: an Innovative Approach to Finance and Production', *World Bank Infrastructure and Urban Development Division Working Paper* 88–3.

Reyes Gomez, L. (1999) 'El contexto cultural y economico del envejecimiento. El caso de los zoques de Chiapas', in *Envejecimiento demografico de Mexico: retos y perspectivas* (Mexico: CONAPO y Camara de Diputados).

Reyna, J.L. (1990) 'Hacia la utopia: tenemos que ser menos desiguales', in A. Gurrieri and E. Torres-Rivas (eds.), *Los años noventa. ¿Desarrollo con equidad?* (San José: Facultad Latinoamericana de Ciencias Sociales), pp. 329–54.

Rich, B. (1994) *Mortgaging the Earth: The World Bank, Environmental Impoverishment, and the Crisis of Development* (Boston: Beacon Press).

Richards, B. (1994) 'A Home of One's Own: Housing Policy under Neoliberalism in Chile', unpublished doctoral dissertation, University College London.

Richards, B. (1995) 'Poverty and Housing in Chile: the Development of a Neo-liberal Welfare State', *Habitat International,* vol. 19, pp. 515–27.

Ritter, Archibald (1995) 'The Dual Currency Bifurcation of the Cuban

Economy in the 1990s. Causes, Consequences and Cures', *CEPAL Review*, no. 57.

Rivas, H. (1991) *Políticas de descentralización básica y media en América Latina: estado del arte* (Santiago: UNESCO–OREALC).

Roberts, B. (1973) *Organising Strangers: Poor Families in Guatemala City* (Austin: University of Texas Press).

Roberts, B. (1978) *Cities of Peasants: the Political Economy of Urbanisation in the Third World* (London: Edward Arnold).

Roberts, B. (1994) 'Informal Economy and Family Strategies', *International Journal of Urban and Regional Research*, vol. 18, no. 1, pp. 6–23.

Roberts, B.R. (1995) *The Making of Citizens: Cities of Peasants Revisited* (London: Edward Arnold).

Roberts, B.R. (1996) 'The Social Context of Citizenship in Latin America', *International Journal of Urban and Regional Research*, vol. 20, no. 1, pp. 38–65.

Roberts, P. (1991) 'Anthropological Perspectives on the Household', *IDS Bulletin*, vol. 22, no. 1, pp. 60–64.

Rodrigues, J.A. (1968) *Sindicalismo e desenvolvimento no Brasil* (São Paulo: Difusão Européia do Livro).

Rodríguez, A. and Icaza, A.M. (1993) 'Procesos de expulsión de habitantes de bajos ingresos del centro de Santiago, 1981–1990', *SUR Documentos de Trabajo* 136.

Rodríguez, E. (1999) 'La redefinición de los discursos sobre la familia y el género en Costa Rica (1890–1930)', *Populaçao e Familia* (CEDHAL, Universidade de São Paulo), July–Dec., pp. 147–82.

Rodríguez, E. (2000) *Hijas, novias y esposas: familia, matrimonio y violencia doméstica en el Valle Central de Costa Rica* (1750–1850) (Heredia: Editorial Universidad Nacional).

Rodríguez, E. (forthcoming) 'Construyendo la identidad nacional y redefiniendo el sistema de género: políticas sociales, familia, maternidad y movimiento femenino en Costa Rica (1850–1950)', *Revista de Historia de América*.

Rodríguez, G. and Hobcraft, J. (1990) *Analisis ilustrativo: análisis de los intervalos entre nacimientos con tablas de vida para Colombia* (México City: El Colegio de México).

Rodríguez, J.-L. (1990) *Estrategia del desarrollo económico en Cuba* (Havana: Editorial de Ciencias Sociales).

Rodríguez, J.-L. (2000) 'Informe sobre los resultados económicos del 2000 y el Plan Económico Social para el Año 2001'. *Granma*. 23 Dec.

Rodríguez, J.-L. and Carriazo, G. (1987) *Erradicación de la pobreza en Cuba* (Havana: Editorial de Ciencias Sociales).

Rodríguez, V.E. and Ward, P. (1993) *Policymaking, Politics and Urban Governance in Chihuahua: the Experience of Recent Panista Governments* (Austin: Lyndon B. Johnson School of Public Affairs, University of Texas).

Rodríguez Cháves, B.G. (1999) *Diocésis de Tilarán: análsis del quehacer pastoral con enfasis en la Diocésis de Tilarán* (Tilarán: Diocésis de Tilarán).

Rodrik, D. (1994) 'The Positive Economics of Policy Reform', *American Economic Review*, AEA Papers and Proceedings, vol. 83, no.2, pp. 356–61.

Roemer, J. (1993) 'Distributing Health: the Allocation of Resources by an International Agency', in M. Nussbaum and A. Sen (eds.), *The Quality of Life* (Oxford: Oxford University Press), pp. 339–57.

Rofman, R. (1999) 'El sistema previsional argentino a cuatro años de la reforma: los temas pendientes', *Estudios del Trabajo*, segundo semestre, no. 18.

Rohe, W.M. and Stewart, L.S. (1996) 'Homeownership and Neighbourhood Stability', *Housing Policy Debate*, vol. 7, pp. 37–81.

Rojas, E. (1995) *The Inter-American Development Bank in Low-Cost Housing: the First Three Decades* (Inter-American Development Bank, Operation Policy Division).

Rojas, E. (1999) *The Long Road to Housing Reform* (Inter American Development Bank, Sustainable Development Department).

Rojas, E. and Greene, M. (1995) 'Reaching the Poor: Lessons from the Chilean Housing Experience', *Environment and Urbanization*, vol. 7, pp. 31–50.

Rojas, F. (2000) 'The Political Context of Decentralization in Latin America: Accounting for Particular Demands of Decentralization in the Region', in S.J. Burki and G.E. Perry (eds.), *Annual World Bank Conference on Development in Latin America and the Caribbean 1999: Decentralization and Accountability of the Public Sector* (Washington: World Bank), pp. 9–31.

Rojas, G. (2001) 'Estructura de oportunidades y uso de los activos familiares frente a la pobreza en la Ciudad de México durante los años noventa', paper for Conference on *Activos disponibles, estructura de oportunidades y vulnerabilidad social en América Latina*, Montevideo, Uruguay, 14-15 Aug.

Romero, A. (2000) 'Economía cubana: transformaciones y reinserción internacional a fines del siglo XX', paper presented to Latin America Studies Association XXII International Congress, Miami, 16–18 March.

Romero, J. (1995) 'Gasto público en el sector rural', paper presented at the Conference *Finanzas públicas en México*, El Colegio de México.

Rondinelli, D.E. et al. (1984) *Decentralisation in Developing Countries: a Review of Recent Experience* (Washington: World Bank), Staff Working Paper, no. 581.

Ronfeldt, D. and Martínez, A. (1997) 'A Comment on the Zapatista "Netwar"', in J. Arquilla and D. Ronfeldt (eds.), *In Athena's Camp: Preparing for Conflict in the Information Age* (Santa Monica: The RAND Corporation), available on-line at http://www.rand.org/publications/MR/MR880/

Rosenberg, E. (1982) *Spreading the American Dream: American Economic and Cultural Expansion, 1890–1945* (New York: Hill and Wang).

Rosenberg, E. (1999) *Financial Missionaries to the World: the Politics and Culture of Dollar Diplomacy* (Cambridge, Mass.: Harvard University Press).

Roseneil, S. and Mann, K. (1996) 'Unpalatable Choices and Inadequate Families: Lone Mothers and the Underclass Debate', in E. Bortolaia Silva (ed.), *Good Enough Mothering? Feminist Perspectives on Lone Motherhood* (London: Routledge), pp. 191–210.

Rostow, W.W. (1960) *The Process of Economic Growth*, 2nd edition (Oxford: Clarendon Press).

Rowat, M. (1996) 'Public Sector Reform in the Latin American and Caribbean Region', paper presented at the annual conference of the Commonwealth Association for Public Administration (CAPAM), Malta, 21–24 April.

Roxborough, I. (1989) 'Organized Labour: a Major Victim of the Debt Crisis', in B. Stallings and R. Kaufman (eds.), *Debt and Democracy in Latin America* (Boulder: Westview Press), pp. 91–108.

Roxborough, I. (1994) 'The Urban Working Class and Labour Movement in Latin America since 1930', in L. Bethell (ed.), *Cambridge History of Latin America*, vol. VI, part 2 (Cambridge: Cambridge University Press), pp. 307–78.

Roxborough, I. (1997) 'Citizenship and Social Movements under Neoliberalism', in W.C. Smith and R.P. Korzeniewicz (eds.), *Politics, Social Change and Economic Restructuring in Latin America* (Coral Gables: North-South Center Press), pp. 57–78.

Ruezga Barba, A. (1994) *Estado, seguridad social y marginalidad. Conferencia*

Interamericana de Seguridad Social (CIESS), Serie Estudios, vol. 4, Mexico.

Rugiero Pérez, A.M. (1998) 'Experiencia chilena en vivienda social, 1980–1995', *Boletín INVI*, vol. 13, pp. 3–87.

Ruiz Mier, F. and Giussani, B. (1996) *Descentralización y financiamiento de la provisión de servicios de salud en Bolivia*, Informe de Consultoría a CEPAL, ACDI y ODA, La Paz.

Russell-Wood, A.J.R. (1968) *Fidalgos and Philanthropists* (London: Macmillan).

Sabato, H. (ed.) (1999) *Ciudadanía política y formación de las naciones: perspectivas históricas de América Latina* (Mexico City: Colegio de México).

Safa, H. (1995) *The Myth of the Male Breadwinner: Women and Industrialisation in the Caribbean* (Boulder: Westview).

Safa, H. (1999) *Women Coping With Crisis: Social Consequences of Export-Led Industrialisation in the Dominican Republic* (Miami: University of Miami, North-South Center), North-South Agenda Paper no. 36.

Safford, F. (2000) 'Reflections on the Internal Wars in Nineteenth-Century Latin America', in R. Earle (ed.), *Rumours of Wars: Civil Conflict in Nineteenth-Century Latin America* (London: Institute of Latin American Studies), pp. 6–28.

Safford, F. and Huber, E. (eds.) (1995) *Agrarian Structure and Political Power: Landlord and Peasant in the Making of Latin America* (Pittsburgh: University of Pittsburgh Press).

SAFJP (2000) *Memoria trimestral*, April–June (Buenos Aires: SAFJP).

Sagot, M. (co-ordinator) (1999) *Analysis situacional de los derechos de las niñas y las adolescentes en Costa Rica* (San José: UNICEF/Universidad de Costa Rica, Maestría Regional en Estudios de la Mujer).

Salas, J.M. (1998) 'Algunos apuntes sobre la violencia doméstica desde la perspectiva de los hombres', in E. Rodríguez (ed.), *Violencia doméstica en Costa Rica: Mas allá de los mitos* (San José: FLACSO Sede Costa Rica), Cuaderno de Ciencias Sociales, no. 105, pp. 53–68.

Salazar, M.C. and Alarcón, W. (eds.) (1999) *Child Work and Education: Five Case Studies from Latin America* (Aldershot: Ashgate).

Salvatore, R. and Aguirre, C. (eds.) (1996) *The Birth of the Penitentiary in Latin America: Essays on Criminology, Prison Reform and Social Control* (Austin: University of Texas Press).

Sanderson, S.E. (ed.) (1985) *The Americas and the New International Division of Labor* (New York: Holmes & Meier).

Sandilands, R.J. (1990) *The Life and Political Economy of Lauchlin Currie: New Dealer, Presidential Adviser, and Development Economist* (Pennsylvania: Duke University Press).

Santizo, C. (1997) *Las perspectivas del nuevo federalismo: el sector educativo. Las experiencias de Aguascalientes, Guanajuato y San Luís Potosí* (Mexico City: CIDE).

Sarmiento, L. (1995) *Concentración y pobreza, tres años del salto social* (Bogotá: Consejo Nacional de Planeación).

Saunders, P. (1990) *A Nation of Home Owners* (Hemel Hempstead: Unwin Hyman).

Savedoff, W. (ed.) (1998) *Organization Matters: Agency Problems in Health and Education in Latin America* (Washington, DC: Inter-American Development Bank).

Scarpaci, J.L., Pio-Infante, R. and Gaete, A. (1988) 'Planning Residential Segregation: the Case of Santiago, Chile', *Urban Geography*, vol. 9, pp. 19–36.

Schamis, H. (1999) 'Distributional Coalitions and the Politics of Economic Reform in Latin America', *World Politics*, vol. 5, no 2.

Schiefelbein, E. (1982) *Redes de investigación educativa en América Latina* (Ottawa: IDRC).

Schiefelbein, E. (1991) 'Restructuring Education through Economic Competition', *Journal of Educational Administration*, vol. 29, no. 4, pp. 17–29.

Schiefelbein, E. (1992) *Redefining Basic Education for Latin America. Lessons to be Drawn from the Colombian Escuela Nueva* (Paris: IIEP–Unesco).

Schiefelbein, E. (1996) 'Adventures of a Minister of Education', *International Higher Education*, no. 12, pp. 13–15 (The Boston College Center for International Higher Education).

Schiefelbein, E. (1997) 'Chile: Generating Social Consensus for a Long-Term Reform of Education', *Prospects*, vol. 27, no. 4.

Schiefelbein, E. (1998) *Evaluar los cambios de funciones de la educación pública y privada: un tema pendiente* (UST Chile: CEPAL).

Schiefelbein, E. and Apablaza, V. (1984) *'¿Municipalización o alcaldización?'* (Chile: CPU).

Schiefelbein, E. and Farrell, J. (1982) *Eight Years of their Lives: Through Schooling to Labour Market in Chile* (Ottawa: International Development Research Center – IDRC).

Schiefelbein, E. and Schiefelbein, P. (2000a) 'Three Decentralization Strategies in Two Decades: Chile 1981–2000', *Journal of Educational Administration*, vol. 38, no. 5, pp. 412–23.

Schiefelbein, E. and Schiefelbein, P. (2000b) 'Slow Learning in Development Co-operation to Latin American Education', in J. Carlsson and L. Wohlgemuth (eds.), *Learning in Development Co-operation* (Expert Group on Development Issues – EGDI), pp. 213–27.

Schiefelbein, E. and Schiefelbein, P. (2000c) 'Determinantes de la calidad: ¿qué falta mejorar?', *Perspectivas*, Universidad de Chile, Depto. de Ingeniería Industrial, vol. 4, no. 1, pp. 37– 61.

Schiefelbein, E. and Schiefelbein, P. (2000d) 'Education and Poverty in Chile: Affirmative Action in the 1990s', in F. Reimers (ed), *Unequal Schools, Unequal Chances* (Cambridge, Mass.: The David Rockefeller Center Series on Latin American Studies, Harvard University).

Schiefelbein, E., Wolff, L. and Schiefelbein, P. (1998) *Cost Effectiveness of Education Policies in Latin America: a Survey of Expert Opinion* (Washington, DC: BID)

Schiff, M. and Valdés, A. (1998) *Agriculture and the Macroeoconomy* (Washington, DC: World Bank).

Schifter, J. and Madrigal, J. (1996) *Las gavetas sexuales del Costarricense* (San José: Editorial IMEDIEX).

Schmitt, C.J. (1996) 'A CUT dos colonos: histórias da construção de um novo sindicalismo no campo no Rio Grande do Sul', in Z. Navarro (org.), *Política, protesto e cidadania no campo; as lutas sociais dos colonos e trabalhadores rurais no Rio Grande do Sul* (Porto Alegre: Editora da Universidade/UFRGS), pp. 189–226.

Schmitter, P. (1996) 'Dangers and Dilemmas of Democracy', in L. Diamond and M. Plattner (eds.), *The Global Resurgence of Democracy* (Baltimore: Johns Hopkins University Press), pp. 76–92.

Schteingart, M. and Camas, J. (1998) *Seleccion y analisis de seis conjuntos habitacionales de la zona metropolitana de la Ciudad de Mexico* (México City: CEDDU, El Colegio de México).

Schulthess, W. and Demarco, G. (1993) *Argentina: evolución del sistema nacional de previsión social y propuesta de reforma* (Santiago, Chile: Proyecto Regional de Políticas Financieras para el Desarrollo, CEPAL-PNUD).

Schwarzer, H. (2000) 'Previdência rural e combate à pobreza no Brasil – resultados de um estudo de caso no Pará', *Estudos Sociedade e Agricultura*, no. 14 (April 2000), pp. 72–102.

Schwarzer, H. (2000a) *Impactos socioeconômicos do sistema de aposentadorias rurais no Brasil – evidências empíricas de um estudo de caso no estado do Pará* (Rio de Janeiro, IPEA) (Texto para discussão 729).

Scobie, J.R. (1974) *Buenos Aires: Plaza to Suburb, 1870-1920* (New York: Oxford University Press).

Scobie, J.R. (ed. S. Baily) (1988) *Secondary Cities of Argentina: the Social History of Corrientes, Salta and Mendoza, 1850-1910* (Stanford: Stanford University Press).

Scott, A.M. (1990) 'Patterns of Patriarchy in the Peruvian Working Class', in S. Stichter and J. Parpart (eds), *Women, Employment and the Family in the International Division of Labour* (Basingstoke: Macmillan), pp. 198–220.

Scott, C.D. (1991) 'Transnational Corporations, Comparative Advantage and Food Security in Latin America', in C. Abel and C.M. Lewis (eds.), *Latin America: Economic Imperialism and the State* (London: Institute of Latin American Studies/Athlone), pp. 149–74.

Scott, C.D. (1993) '*Bonos, Beneficios y Bienestar*: a Study of Wages, Work and Welfare on Peruvian Sugar Plantations', in C. Abel and C.M. Lewis (eds.), *Welfare, Poverty and Development in Latin America* (Basingstoke: Macmillan).

Segarra, M. (1997) 'Redefining the Public/Private Mix: NGOs and the Emergency Social Investment Fund in Ecuador', in D.A. Chalmers et al. (eds.), *The New Politics of Inequality in Latin America: Rethinking Participation and Representation* (Oxford: Oxford University Press), pp. 489–514.

Sen, A.K. (1985) *Commodities and Capabilities* (Amsterdam: North-Holland).

Sen, A. (1993) 'Capability and Well-Being', in M. Nussbaum and A. Sen (eds) *The Quality of Life* (Oxford: Clarendon Press).

Sen, A. (1997) *Choice, Welfare, and Measurement* (Cambridge, Mass.: Harvard University Press).

Sen, A. (1998) 'Mortality as an Indicator of Economic Success and Failure', *The Economic Journal*, Jan., pp. 1–25.

Sen, A. (1999) *Development as Freedom* (Oxford: Oxford University Press).

Sen, A. (2001) 'Economic Progress and Health', in D.A. Leon and G. Walt (eds.), *Poverty, Inequality and Health: an International Perspective* (Oxford: Oxford University Press), pp. 333–46.

Sevcenko, N. (1984) *A revolta da vacina: mentes insans em corpos rebeldes* (São Paulo: Brasiliense).

Shanin, T. (ed.) (1971) *Peasants and Peasant Society: Selected Readings* (Harmondsworth: Penguin).

Shanin, T. (1972) *The Awkward Class; Political Sociology of Peasantry in a Developing Society: Russia 1910–1925* (Oxford: Clarendon Press).

Sheahan, J. (1990) *Reducing Poverty in Latin America: Markets, Democracy and Social Change* (Williamstown, Mass.: Williams College Research Series).

Shidlo, G. (1990) *Social Policy in a Non-Democratic Regime: the Case of Public Housing in Brazil* (Boulder: Westview).

Shidlo, G. (1990a) 'Housing Policy in Brazil', in G. Shidlo (ed.), *Housing Policy in Developing Countries* (London: Routledge), pp. 33–47.

Sieder, R. (2000) '"Paz, Progreso, Justicia y Honradez": Law and Citizenship in Alta Verapaz during the Regime of Jorge Ubico', *Bulletin of Latin American Research*, vol. 19, no. 3, pp. 283–302.

Sikkink, K. (1991) *Ideas and Institutions: Developmentalism in Brazil and Argentina* (Ithaca, NY: Cornell University Press).

Silva, A. (ed.) (1994) *Implementing Policy Innovations in Latin America: Politics, Economics and Techniques* (Washington, DC: Inter-American Development Bank).

Silva, E R.A. (2000) 'Efeitos da previdência social rural sobre a questão de gênero', in G. Delgado and J. Celso Cardoso Jr. (orgs.), *A universalização de direitos sociais no Brasil: a previdência rural nos anos 90* (Brasília: IPEA), pp. 101–30.

SIMCE (2000) 'Resultados SIMCE 99. Seminario técnico Mineduc' (Santiago: Mineduc), July.

Skidmore, T.E. (1989) 'Brazil's Slow Road to Democratization, 1974-1985', in A. Stepan (ed.), *Democratizing Brazil: Problems of Transition and Consolidation* (New York: Oxford University Press).

Skinner, R.J., Taylor, J.L. and Wegelin, E.A. (eds.) (1987) *Shelter Upgrading for the Urban Poor: Evaluation of Third World Experience* (Nairobi: UNCHS and the Hague, Institute of Housing Studies).

Sklair, L. (1989) *Assembling for Development. The Maquila Industry in Mexico and the United States* (London: Unwin Hyman).

Slatta, R.W. (1983) *Gauchos and the Vanishing Frontier* (Lincoln, Neb.: University of Nebraska Press).

Smart, C. (1996) 'Deconstructing Motherhood', in E. Bortolaia Silva (ed.), *Good Enough Mothering? Feminist Perspectives on Lone Motherhood*, (London: Routledge), pp. 37–57.

Smith, A. (1986) *The Ethnic Origin of Nations* (Oxford: Basil Blackwell).

Smith, R. (1998) 'Transnational Localities: Community, Technology and the Politics of Membership within the Context of Mexico–U.S. Migration', in M.P. Smith and L. Guarnizo (eds.), *Transnationalism From Below*, Special Issue of *Journal of Comparative Urban and Community Research*, pp. 241–69.

Smith, W.C. and Korzeniewicz, R.P. (eds.) (1997) *Politics, Social Change and Economic Restructuring in Latin America* (Coral Gables: North-South Center Press).

Smith, W.C., Acuña, C.H. and Gamarra, E.A. (eds.) (1994) *Latin American Political Economy in the Age of Neo-Liberal Reform: Theoretical and Comparative Perspectives for the 1990s* (New Brunswick: Transaction).

Smith, W.C., Acuña, C.H. and Gamarra, E.A. (eds.) (1996) *Democracy, Markets, and Structural Reform in Latin America: Argentina, Bolivia, Brazil, Chile, and Mexico* (Miami: North-South Center).

Smolka, M.O. and Sabatini, F. (2000) 'The Land Market Deregulation Debate in Chile', *Landlines*, vol. 12, Jan.

Social Policy and Administration (1997), vol. XXXI, no.4, Special Issue on Latin America.

Sola, L. (1996) 'The State, Structural Reform and Democratization in Brazil', in W.C. Smith, C.H. Acuña and E.A. Gamarra (eds.), *Democracy, Markets, and Structural Reform in Latin America: Argentina, Bolivia, Brazil, Chile, and Mexico* (Miami: North-South Center) , pp. 151–82.

Solari, A. (1977) 'Development and Educational Policy in Latin America', *CEPAL Review*, vol. 3, pp. 59–91.

Solberg, C. (1970) *Immigration and Nationalism: Argentina and Chile, 1880–1914* (Austin: University of Texas Press).

Solberg, C. (1971) 'Agrarian Unrest and Agrarian Policy in Argentina, 1912-30', *Journal of Inter-American Studies*, vol. XIII, no. 1, pp. 15–55.

Soldo, B.J. and Hill, M. (1995) 'Family Structure and Transfer Measures in the Health and Retirement Study. Background and Overview', *The Journal of Human Resources*, vol. XXX, Supplement.

Solimano, A. (1998) 'Growth, Distributive Justice and Social Policy', *CEPAL Review*, vol. LXV, pp. 31–43.

Solimano, A. (ed.) (1998) *Social Inequality: Values, Growth and the State* (Ann Arbor, Mich.: University of Michigan Press).

Solimano, A. (ed.) (2000) *Essays on Peace and Development: the Case of Colombia and International Experience* (Washington, DC: World Bank).

Solimano, A. et al. (eds.) (2000) *Distributive Justice and Economic Development: the Case of Chile and Developing Countries* (Ann Arbor, Mich.: University of Michigan Press).

Solís, L. (1985) *La economía mexicana* (Mexico City: Fondo de Cultura Económica).

Soltow, L. and Stevens, E. (1981) *The Rise of Literacy and the Common School: a Socio-economic Analysis to 1870* (Chicago: Chicago University Press).

Spink, P. (1999) 'Possibilities and Political Imperatives: Seventy Years of Administrative Reform in Latin America', in L.C. Bresser Pereira and P. Spink, *Reforming the State: Managerial Public Administration in Latin America* (Boulder: Lynne Rienner), pp. 91– 114.

Srinavasan, T. (1985) 'Neoclassical Political Economy: the State and Economic Development', *Politics and Society*, vol. 17, no. 2.

Stacey, J. (1997) 'The Neo-Family-Values Campaign', in R. Lancaster and M. di Leonardo (eds.), *The Gender/Sexuality Reader* (New York: Routledge), pp. 432–70.

Stack, C.B. (1974) *All our Kin: Strategies for Survival in a Black Community* (New York: Harper & Row).

Stallings, B. (1987) *Banker to the Third World: U.S. Portfolio Investment in Latin America, 1900–1986* (Berkeley: University of California Press).

Stallings, B. (1992) 'International Influence on Economic Policy: Debt, Stabilization, and Structural Reform', in S. Haggard and R. Kaufman, (eds.), *The Politics of Economic Adjustment* (Princeton: Princeton University Press).

Stallings, B. and Peres, W. (2000) *Crecimiento, empleo y equidad: el impacto de las reformas económicas en América Latina y el Caribe* (Santiago: CEPAL).

Standing, G. (1999) 'Global Feminisation through Flexible Labour: a Theme Revisited', *World Development*, vol. 27, no. 3, pp. 583–602.

Standing, G. and Tokman, V. (eds.) (1991) *Towards Social Adjustment: Labour Market Issues in Structural Adjustment* (Geneva: International Labour Office).

Statistical Abstract of Latin America (SALA) (1969) K. Ruddle and M. Hamour (eds.) (Los Angeles: UCLA Latin American Center Publications).

Statistical Abstract of Latin America (SALA) (1971) K. Ruddle and D.

Oberman (eds.)(Los Angeles: UCLA Latin American Center Publications)

Statistical Abstract of Latin America (SALA) (1981) vol. 21, J.W. Wilkie and S. Haber (eds.) (Los Angeles: UCLA Latin American Center Publications).

Statistical Abstract of Latin America (SALA) (1995) vol. 31, J.W. Wilkie, C.A. Contreras and C. Komisaruk (eds.) (Los Angeles: UCLA Latin American Center Publications).

Stavenhagen, R. (ed.) (1970) *Agrarian Problems and Peasant Movements in Latin America* (New York: Doubleday).

Steinmo, S., Thelen, K. and Longstreth, F. (eds.) (1992) *Structuring Politics: Historical Institutionalism in Comparative Analysis* (Cambridge: Cambridge University Press).

Stepan, A. (ed.) (1989) *Democratizing Brazil: Problems of Transition and Consolidation* (New York: Oxford University Press).

Stepan, A. (ed.) (1992) *Americas: New Interpretive Essays* (Oxford: Oxford University Press).

Stepan, N.L. (1991) *The Hour of Eugenics: Latin America and the Movement for Racial Improvement* (Ithaca, NY: Cornell University Press).

Stephen, L. (1996) 'Relações de gênero: um estudo comparativo sobre as organizações de mulheres rurais no México e no Brasil', in Z. Navarro (org.), *Política, protesto e cidadania no campo; as lutas sociais dos colonos e trabalhadores rurais no Rio Grande do Sul* (Porto Alegre: Editora da Universidade/UFRGS), pp. 29–61.

Stephen, L. (1997) *Women and Social Movements in Latin America; Power from Below* (Texas: University of Texas Press).

Stern, C. and Tuirán, R. (1993) 'Transición demográfica y desigualdad social en México', in IV Conferencia Latinoamericana de Población: *La Transición Demográfica en América Latina y el Caribe* (Mexico City: INEGI – IISUNAM), vol. I.

Stern, R. (2001) 'Consideraciones acerca de los factores relacionados con el acceso a tratamiento de personas con SIDA en América Central', *Boletín Fármacos*, vol. 4, no. 1, www.boletinfarmacos.org.

Stern, S. (ed.) (1987) *Resistance, Rebellion and Consciousness in the Andean Peasant World: Eighteenth to Twentieth Centuries* (Madison: University of Wisconsin Press).

Stewart, F. (1992) *Protecting the Poor during Adjustment in Latin America and the Caribbean in the 80s. How Adequate was the World Bank Response?* (Oxford: Queen Elisabeth House Working Paper).

Stiglitz, J.E. (1991) 'The Invisible Hand and Modern Welfare Economics', *NBER* w.p. no. 3641.

Stillwaggon, E. (1998) *Stunted Lives, Stagnant Economies. Poverty, Disease and Underdevelopment* (New Brunswick: Rutgers University Press).

Stocker, K., Waitzkin, H. and Iriarte, C. (1999) 'The Exportation of Managed Care to Latin America', *The New England Journal of Medicine*, vol. 340, no. 14, pp. 1131–6.

Stolberg, S.G. and Gerth, J. (2000) *New York Times*, 16 Nov.

Stolley, P.D. and Laporte, J.R. (2000) 'The Public Health, the University, and Pharmacoepidemiology', in B.L. Strom (ed.), *Pharmacoepidemiology* (Chichester: John Wiley & Sons, Ltd.), pp. 75–89.

Stoppino, M. (1998) 'Ideología', in N. Bobbio, N. Matteucci and G. Pasquino (eds.), *Diccionario de Política* (Mexico City: Siglo XXI).

Strassman, W.P. (1987) 'Home Based Enterprises in Cities of Developing Countries', *Economic Development and Cultural Change*, pp. 121–44.

Street, B.V. (1995) *Social Literacies: Critical Approaches to Literacy in Development* (London: Longman).

Sugamosto, M. and Doustdar, N.M. (2000) 'Impactos da previdência rural na região Sul: ênfase nas características mesorregionais', in G. Delgado and J. Celso Cardoso Jr. (orgs.), *A universalização de direitos sociais no Brasil: a Previdência Rural nos anos 90* (Brasília: IPEA), pp. 131–64.

Sunkel, O. (ed.) (1993) *Development from Within: Towards a Neostructuralist Approach for Latin America* (Boulder: Lynne Rienner).

Sunkel, O. and Paz, P. (1970) *El subdesarrollo latinoamericano y la teoría del desarrollo* (Mexico City: Siglo Veintiuno Editores).

Sunkel, O. and Zuleta, G. (1990) 'Neostructuralism versus Neoliberalism in the 1990s', *CEPAL Review*, vol. XXXXII.

Supakankunti, S., Janjaroen, W.S., Tangphao, O. et al. (1999) 'Study of the Implications of the WTO TRIPS Agreement for the Pharmaceutical Industry in Thailand' (Bangkok: The Centre for Health Economics, Chulalongkorn University), Oct.

Suzigan, W. and Villela, A.V. (1997) *Industrial Policy in Brazil* (Campinas).

Syrquin, M. and Chenery, H. (1989) *Patterns of Development, 1950–83* (World Bank/Harvard International Institute for Development).

Tamez, S. and Molina, N. (2000) 'Reorganizing the Health Care System in Mexico' in S. Fleury, S. Belmartino and E. Baris (eds.) *Reshaping Health Care in Latin America. A Comparative Analysis of Health Care Reform in Argentina, Brazil And Mexico* (Ottawa: International Development Research Centre).

Tedesco, J.C. (1988) *El rol del estado en la educación* (Santiago: UNESCO – OREALC).

Tedesco, J., Ordonez, V., Hallak, J., Colbert, V., Farrell, J., Schweitzer, J., Prawda, J., Reimers F., Toro, B., Ratinoff, L. and Pelczar, R. (1994) 'Quality, Pertinence and Equity of the Educational Supply, Report of the Interagency Top-Level Mission to Support the Ministry of Education of Chile', *OREALC Bulletin*, no. 33 (Santiago).

Teitel, S. (ed.) (1992) *A New Development Strategy in Latin America: Pathways from Hirschman's Thought* (Baltimore: Johns Hopkins University Press).

Teixeira, Z.A. et al. (1994) *Perspectivas de gênero na produção rural* (Brasília: IPEA), Estudos de Política Agrícola, no. 22.

Tendler, J. (1997) *Good Government in the Tropics* (Baltimore: Johns Hopkins University Press).

Tendler, J. (2000) 'Why Social Policy is Condemned to a Residual Category of Safety Nets, and What to do about it: Thoughts on a Research Agenda for UNRISD', UNRISD Meeting in Stockholm, 23–24 Sept.

Thomas, J.J. (1992) *Informal Economic Activity* (London: Harvester Wheatsheaf).

Thomas, J.J. (1995) *Surviving in the City: the Urban Informal Sector in Latin America* (London: Pluto Press).

Thorp, R. (1991) *Economic Management and Economic Development in Peru and Colombia* (Pittsburgh: University of Pittsburgh Press).

Thorp, R. (1998) *Progress, Poverty and Exclusion: an Economic History of Latin America in the 20th Century* (Washington, DC: IDB).

Thorp, R. (1998a) *Progreso, pobreza y exclusión. Una historia económica de América Latina en el siglo XX* (New York: BID y Unión Europea).

Thorp, R. (ed.) (2000) A*n Economic History of Twentieth-Century Latin America: Vol. 2: Latin America in the 1930s, the Role of the Periphery in World Crisis* (Basingstoke: Macmillan).

Tiffer, C. (1998) 'Status of Adolescents in Conflict with the Criminal Law: The New Model for Juvenile Criminal Justice in Costa Rica', in UNICEF (ed.), *Adolescence, Child Rights and Urban Poverty in Costa Rica* (San José: UNICEF/HABITAT), pp. 115–26.

Timaeus, I., Chackiel, J. and Ruzicka, L. (eds.) (1996) *Adult Mortality in Latin America* (Oxford: Clarendon Press).

Tiramonti, G. (1996) *Los nuevos modelos de gestión educativa y su incidencia sobre la calidad de la educación* (Buenos Aires: FLACSO).

Tiramonti, G. (2000) 'Sindicalismo docente y reforma educativa en América Latina de los '90' (Paper prepared for a seminar on the politics of education reform, Santiago, Chile).

Togores, V. (1996) 'Problemas del empleo en Cuba en los 90. Alternativas de solución', in L. Caramés Viéitez (ed.), *I Foro de Economía: Galicia–América Latina* (Havana).

Togores, V. (1999) 'Cuba: efectos sociales de la crisis y el ajuste económico de los '90', *Balance de la economía cubana a finales de los '90* (Havana: Centro de Estudios de la Economía Cubana, University of Havana).

Tokman, V.E. (ed.) (1992) *Beyond Regulation: the Informal Economy in Latin America* (Boulder: Lynne Rienner).

Tokman, V.E. and O'Donnell, G. (eds.) (1998) *Poverty and Inequality in Latin America: Issues and New Challenges* (Notre Dame, In.: University of Notre Dame Press).

Tomich, T. et al. (1995) *Transforming Agrarian Economies. Opportunities Seized, Opportunities Missed* (Ithaca, NY: Cornell University Press).

Tommasi, M. and Velasco, A. (1996) 'Where Are We in the Political Economy of Reform?' *Policy Reform*, vol. 1.

Topik, S. (co-ord) (1999) *Latin American Perspectives: Special Issue, Creating Markets in Latin America, 1750-1988*, vol. XXVI, no. 1.

Torres, C.A. and Puiggros, A. (eds.) (1999) *Latin American Education: Comparative Perspectives* (Boulder: Westview Press).

Trejos, J.D. and Montiel, N. (1999) *El capital de los pobres en Costa Rica: acceso, utilización y rendimiento* (Washington, DC: Inter American Development Bank).

Trivelli, P. (1987) 'Intra-Urban Socio-economic Settlement Patterns, Public Intervention, and the Determination of the Spatial Structure of the Urban Land Market in Greater Santiago, Chile', unpublished doctoral dissertation, Cornell University.

Trostle, J., Sommerfeld, J. and Simon, J. (1997) 'Strengthening Human Resource Capacity in Developing Countries: Who Are the Actors? What Are their Actions?', in Merilee S. Grindle (ed.), *Getting Good*

Government: Capacity Building in the Public Sectors of Developing Countries (Cambridge, Mass.: Harvard University Press).

Tuirán, R. and Wong, R. (1994) 'Tranferencias familiares en el envejecimiento', in *Seminario sobre Envejecimiento Demografico en Mexico* (Mexico: SOMEDE).

Tulchin, J.S. and Garland, A.M. (eds.) (2000) *Social Development in Latin America: the Politics of Reform* (Boulder: Lynne Rienner Publishers).

Turner, B.S. (1986) *Citizenship and Capitalism: the Debate over Reformism* (London: Allen & Unwin).

Turner, B.S. (ed.) (1993) *Citizenship and Social Theory* (London: SAGE Publications).

Turner, J.F.C. (1967) 'Barriers and Channels for Housing Development in Modernizing Countries', *Journal of the American Institute of Planners*, vol. 33, pp. 167–81.

Turner, J.F.C. (1968a) 'Housing Priorities, Settlement Patterns, and Urban Developing in Modernizing Countries', *Journal of the American Institute of Planners*, vol. 34, pp. 354–63.

Turner, J.F.C. (1968b) 'The Squatter Settlement: an Architecture that Works', *Architectural Design*, vol. 38, pp. 357–60.

Turner, J.F.C. (1976) *Housing By People: Towards Autonomy in Building Environment* (London: Marion Boyars).

Tussie, D. (1995) *The Multilateral Development Banks. Vol. IV: the Inter-American Development Bank* (Boulder.: Lynne Rienner).

Ugalde, A. and Homedes, N. (1988) 'Medicines and Rural Health Services: an Experiment in the Dominican Republic', in S. van der Geest and R. Whyte (eds.), *The Context of Medicines in Developing Countries* (Kluver Academic Publishers), pp. 57–79.

Ugalde, A and Homedes, N. (2001) 'Ventajas y desventajas de la descentralización del sector salud en América Latina', *Situa* (Peru), pp. 6–17.

Ugalde, A. and Jackson, J.T. (1995) 'The World Bank and International Health Policy: a Critical Review', *Journal of International Development*, vol. 7, pp. 525–41.

Ugalde, A. and Zwi, A. (eds.) (1996) *Violencia política y salud en América Latina* (Mexico City: Nueva Imagen).

Umali, D. and Maguire, C. (1995) *Agriculture in Liberalizing Economies: Changing Roles for Governments* (Washington: World Bank).

UN Economic Commission for Latin America (ECLA/CEPAL) (1964) *The Economic Development of Latin America: the Post-War Period* (New York: United Nations).

UN Economic Commission for Latin America (ECLA/CEPAL) (1966) *The Process of Industrialization in Latin America* (New York).

UN Economic Commission for Latin America (ECLA/CEPAL) (1969a) *América Latina: el pensamiento de la CEPAL* (Santiago).

UN Economic Commission for Latin America (ECLA/CEPAL) (1969b) *Development Problems in Latin America* (Austin: University of Texas Press).

UN Economic Commission for Latin America (and the Caribbean) (ECLAC/CEPAL) (1992) *Social Equity and Changing Production Patterns: an Integrated Approach* (Santiago).

UN Economic Commission for Latin America (see also CEPAL).

UNCHS (1989) *Strategies for Low-Income Shelter and Services Development: The Rental-Housing Option* (Nairobi).

UNCHS (1993) *Support Measures to Promote Rental Housing for Low-Income Groups* (Nairobi).

UNCHS (1996) *An Urbanising World: Global Report on Human Settlements 1996* (Oxford: Oxford University Press).

UNDP (United Nations Development Programme) (1995) *Human Development Report 1995* (New York: OUP).

UNDP (United Nations Development Programme) (1996) *Human Development Report 1996* (New York: OUP).

UNDP (United Nations Development Programme) (1997) *Investigación sobre el desarrollo humano en Cuba 1996* (Havana: Editora Caguayo).

UNDP (United Nations Development Programme) (2000) *Human Development Report 2000* (New York: Oxford University Press).

UNECLAC (1996) *Situación de la vivienda en América Latina y el Caribe* (Santiago).

UNESCO (1966) *Statistical Yearbook 1964* (Paris: UNESCO).

UNESCO (1991a) *Education for All: Purpose and Context*, World Conference on Education for All, Monograph I (Paris: UNESCO).

UNESCO (1991b) *Education for All: an Expanded Vision*, World Conference on Education for All, Monograph II (Paris: UNESCO).

UNESCO (1991c) *Education for All: The Requirements*, World Conference on

Education for All, Monograph III (Paris: UNESCO).

UNESCO (1992) *State of Education in Latin America and the Caribbean, 1980–1989* (Santiago, Chile: OREALC).

UNESCO (1995) *World Education Report* (Oxford: UNESCO).

UNESCO (1996) *Education for Development and Peace, Seventh Meeting of Ministers of Education* (Kingston, Jamaica).

UNESCO (1996a) *World Education Report* (Oxford: UNESCO).

UNESCO (2000) *Alfabetismo funcional en siete países de América Latina* (Santiago, Chile: UNESCO, OREALC).

UNESCO (2000a) *World Education Report* (Oxford: UNESCO).

UNESCO/ECLA/UNDP (1981) *Desarollo y educacíon en América Latina y el Caribe*, 4 vols.

UNICEF (United Nations Children's Fund) (1997) *Role of Men in the Lives of Children* (New York: UNICEF).

United Nations (1979) *Review of Rent Control in Developing Countries* (New York).

United Nations (1991) *Socio-Economic Development and Fertility Decline an Application on the Easterlin Synthesis Approach to Data from Fertility Survey. Colombia, Costa Rica, Sri Lanka, Tunisia.*

United Nations (1999) *World Population Prospects. The 1998 Revision* (New York, United Nations).

Uribe, C. (1999) 'Colombia: Teacher and School Incentives', *DRCLAS News* (Cambridge, Mass.: Harvard University).

Uribe, J. (1994) 'Inflación y crecimiento económico en Colombia: 1951–1992', Banco de la República, *Borradores Semanales de Economía*, no. 1.

Urrutia, M. (ed.) (1991) *Long-Term Trends in Latin American Economic Development* (Washington, DC: Inter-American Development Bank).

Urrutia, M. (1991a) 'On the Absence of Economic Populism in Colombia', in R. Dornbusch and S. Edwards (eds.), *The Macroeconomics of Populism in Latin America* (Chicago: University of Chicago Press), pp. 369–92.

Urrutia, M. (1991b) 'Twenty-Five Years of Economic Growth and Social Progress, 1960-85', in M. Urrutia (ed.), *Long-Term Trends in Latin American Economic Development* (Washington, DC: Inter-American Development Bank), pp. 23–80.

Urrutia, M. and Berry, A. (eds.) (1970) *Income Distribution in Colombia* (New Haven: Yale University Press).

Valdés, J.G. (1995) *Pinochet's Economists: The Chicago School in Chile* (Cambridge: Cambridge University Press).

Valdez, A. and Wiens, T. (1996) 'Rural Poverty in Latin America and the Caribbean', Table no. 4, paper presented at the Second Annual WB Conference on Development in LAC, Bogotá, Colombia.

Valença, M.M. (1992) 'The Inevitable Crisis of the Brazilian Housing Finance System', *Urban Studies*, vol. 29, pp. 39–56.

Valladares, L. (1978) 'Working the System: Squatter Response to Resettlement in Rio de Janeiro', *International Journal of Urban and Regional Research*, vol. 2, pp. 12–25.

Van Cott, D.L. (2000) *The Friendly Liquidation of the Past: the Politics of Diversity in Latin America* (Pittsburgh: University of Pittsburgh Press).

Van der Hoeven, R. et al. (ed.) (1994) *Poverty Monitoring: an International Concern* (New York: St. Martin's Press, UNICEF).

Van der Linden, J. (1986) *The Sites And Services Approach Reviewed: Solution or Stop-Gap to the Third World Housing Shortage?* (Aldershot: Gower).

Van Lindert, P. (1991) 'Moving Up or Staying Down? Migrant-Native Differential Mobility in La Paz', *Urban Studies*, vol. 28, pp. 433–63.

Varley, A. (1987) 'The Relationship between Tenure Legislation and Housing Improvement', *Development and Change*, vol. 18, pp. 463–81.

Varley, A. (1993) 'Clientilism or Technocracy? The Politics of Urban Land Regulation in Mexico', in N. Harvey (ed.), *Mexico: the Dilemmas of Transition* (London: Institute of Latin Anerican Studies and British Academic Press), pp. 249–78.

Varley, A. (ed.) (1994) *Disasters, Development and Environment* (Chichester: J. Wiley).

Varley, A. (2000) 'Women and the Home in Mexican Family Law', in E. Dore and M. Molyneux (eds.), *Hidden Histories of Gender and the State in Latin America* (Chapel Hill, NC: Duke University Press), pp. 238–61.

Vaughan, M.K. (1997) *Cultural Politics and Revolution: Teachers, Peasants and Schools in Mexico, 1930-1940* (Tucson: University of Arizona Press).

Vaughan, M.K. (2000) 'Modernizing Patriarchy: State Policies, Rural Households and Women in Mexico, 1930-1940', in E. Dore and M. Molyneux (eds.), *Hidden Histories of Gender and the State in Latin America* (Chapel Hill, NC: Duke University Press), pp. 194–214.

Vega, I. (1987) 'Aportes teóricos de la actualidad en el estudio de la familia', *Revista Costarricense de Psicología*, nos.10–11, pp. 15–23.

Veltmeyer, I., Petras, J. and Vieux, S. (eds.) (1997) *Neoliberalism and Class Conflict in Latin America: a Comparative Perspective on the Political Economy of Structural Adjustment* (Basingstoke: Macmillan).

Vial, G. (2000) 'Los expertos educacionales galopan de nuevo', *Diario La Segunda*, 12 Dec., p. 9.

Vincenzi, A. (1991) *Código Civil y Código de la Familia* (San José: Lehmann Editores).

Vuskovic, P. (1993) *Pobreza y desigualdad en América Latina* (México: Universidad Nacional Autónoma de México).

Wade, P. (1993) *Blackness and Race Mixture: The Dynamics of Racial Identity in Colombia* (Baltimore: Johns Hopkins University Press).

Wade, P. (1995) 'The Cultural Politics of Blackness in Colombia', *American Ethnologist*, vol. XXII, no. 2, pp. 341–51.

Wade, P. (2000) *Music, Race and Nation: Música Tropical in Colombia* (Chicago: University of Chicago Press).

Wade, R. (2001) 'Globalization Inequality. Winners and Losers', *The Economist*, 28 April, pp. 71–4.

Waisman, C.H. (1999) 'Civil Society, State Capacity and the Conflicting Logics of Economic and Political Change', in P. Oxhorn and P.K. Starr (eds.), *Markets and Democracy in Latin America: Conflict and Convergence* (Boulder: Lynne Rienner Publishers), pp. 43–58.

Wallis, J. (1998) 'Understanding the Role of Leadership in Economic Policy Reform', *World Development*, vol. 27, no. 1.

Walsh, K. (1995) *Public Services and Market Mechanisms: Competition, Contracting and the New Public Management* (Basingstoke: Macmillan).

Walter, R.J (1968) *Student Politics in Argentina: the University Reform and its Effects, 1918–1964* (New York: Basic Books).

Walton, J. (1989) 'Debt, Protest and the State', in B. Eckstein (ed.), *Power and Popular Protest: Latin American Social Movements* (Berkeley: University of California Press), pp. 1–60.

Walzer, M. (1989) 'Citizenship', in T. Ball and J. Farr (eds.), *Political Innovation and Conceptual Change* (Cambridge: Cambridge University Press), pp. 201–19.

Ward, P.M. (1986) *Welfare Politics in Mexico: Papering over the Cracks* (London: Allen & Unwin).

Ward, P.M. (1989) 'Land Values and Valorisation Processes in Latin American Cities: a Research Agenda', *Bulletin of Latin American Research*, vol. 8, pp. 45–66.

Ward, P.M. (1997) *Mexico City* (Chichester: John Wiley).

Ward, P.M. (1999) *Colonias and Public Policy in Texas and Mexico: Urbanization by Stealth* (Austin: University of Texas Press).

Warren, K.B. (1998) *Indigenous Movements and their Critics: Pan-Maya Activism in Guatemala* (Princeton: Princeton University Press).

Weaver, F.S. (1980) *Class, State and Industrial Structure: the Historical Process of South American Industrial Growth* (Westport: Greenwood Press).

Weber, M. (1949) *The Methodology of the Social Sciences* (Illinois: The Free Press).

Weffort, F. (1978) *O populismo na política brasileira* (Rio de Janeiro: Paz e Terra).

Weinberg, B. (2000) *Homage to Chiapas* (London and New York: Verso)

Weindling, P. (ed.) (1995) *International Health Organisations and Movements, 1918-1939* (Cambridge: Cambridge University Press).

Weiner, R. (1999) 'Competing Market Discourses in Porfirian Mexico', *Latin American Perspectives*, vol. XXVI, no. 1.

Weingast, B., Shepsle, K. and Johnsen, C. (1981) 'The Political Economy of Benefits and Costs: a Neoclassical Approach to Redistributive Politics', *Journal of Political Economy*, vol. 81.

Weinstein, B. (1996) *For Social Peace: Industrialists and the Remaking of the Working Class in São Paulo, 1920–1964* (Chapel Hill, NC: University of North Carolina Press).

Werlin, H. (1999) 'The Slum Upgrading Myth', *Urban Studies*, vol. 36, pp. 1523–34.

Weschenfelder, C.F. (1981) in Assembléia Legislativa do Estado do Rio Grande do Sul, *Seminário Nacional 'A questão da terra'* (Porto Alegre: Comissão de Agricultura e Pecuária, Assembléia Legislativa do Estado do Rio Grande do Sul), pp. 141–3.

Westwood, S. (1996) '"Feckless Fathers": Masculinities and the British State', in M. Mac an Ghaill (ed.), *Understanding Masculinities: Social Relations and Cultural Arenas* (Buckingham: Open University Press), pp. 21–34.

Weyland, K. (1996) *Democracy without Equity: Failures of Reform in Brazil* (Pittsburgh: University of Pittsburgh Press).

Whitehead, L. (1994) 'State Organisation in Latin America', in L. Bethell (ed.), *The Cambridge History of Latin America: Vol. VI, Part 2: 1930 to the Present* (Cambridge: Cambridge University Press), pp. 3–97.

Whitehead, L. (1996) 'Chronic Fiscal Stress and the Reproduction of Poverty and Inequality in Latin America', in V. Bulmer-Thomas (ed.), *The New Economic Model in Latin America and its Impact on Income Distribution and Poverty* (London: Macmillan/Institute of Latin American Studies), pp. 53–78.

Whitehead, L. (1998) 'Democratic Regimes, Ostracism and Pariahs', in L. Whitehead (ed.), *The International Dimensions of Democratisation: Europe and the Americas* (Oxford: Oxford University Press), pp. 395–412.

Whitehead, N.L. (2000) 'Tribes Make States and States Make Tribes: Warfare and the Creation of Colonial Tribes and States in Northeastern South America', in R.B. Ferguson and N.L. Whitehead (eds.) *War in the Tribal Zone: Expanding States and Indigenous Warfare* (Santa Fe: SAR Press, and Oxford: James Currey), pp. 127–150.

Whitten, N.E. Jr. and Quiroga, D. (1998) '"To Rescue National Dignity" Blackness as a Quality of Nationalist Creativity in Ecuador', in N.E. Whitten and A. Torres (eds.), *Blackness in Latin America and the Caribbean: Social Dynamics and Cultural Transformations*, vol. 1 (Bloomington: Indiana University Press), pp. 75–99.

Wilkinson, R.G. (1996) *Unhealthy Societies: The Afflictions of Inequality* (London: Routledge).

Williamson, J. (ed.) (1985) *Inflation and Indexation* (Washington, DC: Institute for International Economics).

Williamson, J. (1990) *Latin American Adjustment: How Much has Happened?* (Washington, DC: Institute for International Economics).

Williamson, J. (ed.) (1994) *The Political Economy of Policy Reform* (Washington, DC: Institute for International Economics).

Willis, K. (1993) 'Women's Work and Social Network Use in Oaxaca City, Mexico', *Bulletin of Latin American Research*, vol. XII, no. 1, pp. 65–82.

Winkler, D.R. (1989) *Decentralisation in Education: an Economic Perspective* (Washington: World Bank, Population and Human Resource Department).

Winkler, D. (1997) 'Descentralización de la educación: participación en el manejo de las escuelas al nivel local', *Informe*, no. 8 (Chile: Grupo de Desarrollo Humano, Región de América Latina y el Caribe).

Winkler, D. (1999) 'Educating the Poor in Latin America and the Caribbean: Examples of Compensatory Education' (Washington, DC: World Bank).

Winkler, D.R. and Gershberg, A.I. (2000) 'Education Decentralization in Latin America: the Effects on the Quality of Schooling', in S. J. Burki and G. E. Perry (eds.), *Annual World Bank Conference on Development in Latin America and the Caribbean 1999: Decentralization and Accountability of the Public Sector* (Washington: World Bank), pp. 203–225.

Winkler, D. and Rounds, T. (1996) 'Education Reform in Chile; Municipal and Private Sector Response to Decentralization and School Choice', *Economics of Education Review*, vol. 15, no. 4, pp. 365–76.

Wirth, J.D. (1970) *The Politics of Brazilian Development, 1930–1954* (Stanford: Stanford University Press).

Wolf, E.R. (1955) 'Types of Latin American Peasantry: a Preliminary Discussion', *American Anthropologist*, vol. LVII, no. 3, pp. 452–71.

Wolf, E.R. (1957) 'Closed Corporate Peasant Communities in Mesoamerica and Central Java', *Southwestern Journal of Anthropology*, vol. XIII, no. 1, pp. 2–27.

Wolf, E.R. (1966) *Peasants* (Englewood Cliffs, NJ: Prentice-Hall).

Wolf, E.R. and Mintz, S. (1957) 'Haciendas and Plantations in Middle America and the Antilles', *Social and Economic Studies*, vol. VI, no. 3, pp. 180–212.

Wong, R, Soldo, B.J. and Capoferro, C. (2000) 'Generational Social Capital: the Effects on Remittance Streams in Mexico', presented in the Annual Meeting of the Population Association of America, Los Angeles.

Wood, A. (1994) *North-South Trade, Employment and Inequality: Changing Fortunes in a Skills-Driven World* (Oxford: Clarendon Press).

Wood, C.H. and de Carvalho, J.A.M. (1988) *The Demography of Inequality in Brazil* (Cambridge: Cambridge University Press).

World Bank (1992) *The Housing Indicators Program: Volume II Indicator Tables* (Washington, DC).

World Bank (1993) *World Development Report 1993. Investing in Health* (Oxford: Oxford University Press).

World Bank (1993a) *Implementing the World Bank's Strategy to reduce Poverty, Progress and Change* (Washington DC; The World Bank).

World Bank (1993b) *Latin America and the Caribbean, a Decade after the Debt Crisis* (Washington DC, The World Bank).

World Bank (1993c) *Housing: Enabling Markets to Work*, a World Bank Policy Paper.

World Bank (1993d) *Informe sobre el Desarrollo Humano.*

World Bank (International Bank for Reconstruction and Development) (1993e) *Argentina: from Insolvency to Growth* (Washington, DC: World Bank).

World Bank (International Bank for Reconstruction and Development) (1994) *Poverty in Colombia* (Washington, DC: World Bank).

World Bank (1994a) *Averting the Old Age Crisis: Policies to Protect the Old and Promote Growth* (New York: Oxford University Press).

World Bank (1995) *Poverty in Colombia* (Washington: World Bank).

World Bank (1995a) *Priorities and Strategies for Education: A Review* (Washington, DC: World Bank).

World Bank (1996) 'Colombia', *Review of Agricultural and Rural Development Strategy* (Washington: World Bank).

World Bank (1997) *Argentina. Facing the Challenge of Health Insurance Reform* (Washington, DC).

World Bank (1997a) *Policy and Research. Economic Bulletin.*

World Bank (1997b) *The State in a Changing World. World Development Report 1997* (Washington, D.C.: Oxford University Press).

World Bank (1998) *World Development Report 1998/9* (New York: Oxford University Press).

World Bank (2000) *World Development Report 2000/2001: Attacking Poverty* (New York: Oxford University Press).

World Bank (2000a) *Economic Bulletin.*

World Bank (International Bank for Reconstruction and Development) (2000b) *Violence in Colombia: Building Sustainable Peace and Social Capital* (Washington, DC: World Bank).

Wynia, G. (1990) *The Politics of Latin American Development* (Oxford: Oxford University Press).

Yach, D. and Bettcher, D. (1998) 'The Globalization of Public Health', *American Journal of Public Health*, vol. 88, pp. 735–41.

Yepes, F. (2000) 'Health Reform and Equity in Colombia', in P. Lloyd-Sherlock (ed.), *Healthcare Reform and Poverty in Latin America* (London: Institute of Latin American Studies), pp. 163–77.

Yong Kim, J., Shakow, A., Bayona, J., Rhatigan, J. and Rubín de Celis, E.L. (2000) 'Sickness amidst Recovery: Public Debt and Private Suffering in Peru', in J. Yong Kim, J.V. Millen, A. Irwin and J. Gershman (eds.), *Dying for Growth. Global Inequality and the Health of the Poor* (Cambridge, Mass.: Common Courage Press), pp. 127–54.

Youngman, F. (2000) *The Political Economy of Adult Education and Development* (Leicester: NIACE).

Zamora, G. (1990) 'La política laboral del Estado México, 1982–1988', *Revista Mexicana de Sociología*, vol. 52, pp. 111–38.

Zamora, J. (2001) 'Descentralización en el Instituto Salvadoreño del Seguro Social (ISSS)', unpublished paper.

Zavala de Cosío, M.E. (1992) *Cambios de la fecundidad en Mexico y politicas de poblacion* (Mexico: El Colegio de Mexico y Fondo de Cultura Economica).

Zecchini, S. (ed.) (1997) *Lessons from the Economic Transition: Central and Eastern Europe in the 1990s* (OECD. London: Kluwer Academic Publishers).

Zermeño, S. (1997) 'Society and Politics in Contemporary Mexico (Modernization and Modernity in Global Societies)', in W. Pansters (ed.), *Citizens of the Pyramid Essays in Mexican Culture* (Amsterdam: Thela Publishers), pp. 183–208.

Zimbalist, A. and Brundenius, C. (1989) *The Cuban Economy- Measurement and Analysis of Socialist Performance* (Baltimore and London: Johns Hopkins University Press).

Zimmermann, E. (ed.) (1999) *Law, Justice and State Building: Judicial Institutions in Nineteenth-Century Latin America* (London: Institute of Latin American Studies).

Zwi, A. (2001) 'Injuries, Inequalities and Health: from Policy Vacuum to Policy Action', in D.A. Leon and G. Walt (eds.), *Poverty, Inequality and Health: an International Perspective* (Oxford: Oxford University Press), pp. 263–82.

Printed in the United States
21658LVS00002B/82-129